Learning C# 3.0

Other resources from O'Reilly

Learning C# 3.0

Jesse Liberty and Brian MacDonald

O'REILLY®

Beijing · Cambridge · Farnham · Köln · Sebastopol · Taipei · Tokyo

Learning C# 3.0
by Jesse Liberty and Brian MacDonald

Copyright © 2009 Jesse Liberty and Brian MacDonald. All rights reserved.
Printed in the United States of America.

Published by O'Reilly Media, Inc., 1005 Gravenstein Highway North, Sebastopol, CA 95472.

O'Reilly books may be purchased for educational, business, or sales promotional use. Online editions are also available for most titles (*safari.oreilly.com*). For more information, contact our corporate/institutional sales department: (800) 998-9938 or *corporate@oreilly.com*.

Editor: John Osborn
Production Editor: Sumita Mukherji
Copyeditor: Audrey Doyle
Proofreader: Sada Preisch

Indexer: Angela Howard
Interior Designer: David Futato
Cover Illustrator: Karen Montgomery
Illustrator: Jessamyn Read

Printing History:

November 2008:   First Edition.

 This book uses RepKover™, a durable and flexible lay-flat binding.

ISBN: 978-0-596-52106-6
[M]   [10/09]

Table of Contents

Preface

Congratulations! You've decided to learn to program. Maybe you're learning it for a class, maybe you're learning it to get ahead at work, or maybe you're learning it just for fun. Whatever the reason, we've written this book to help you learn C#. You don't need a language reference, or a code analysis book; you want to start from square one and learn to program. In that respect, your desire to learn how to program is more important than which specific language you choose. There are plenty of modern languages out there, and lots of them are quite similar, under the hood.

Why, out of all the languages you could learn, should you pick C#? There are several good reasons:

- C# is the preferred language for use with Microsoft's .NET platform. That means C# was created for writing Windows applications, and as you know, the majority of the world's computers run Windows.

- C# is supported by Visual Studio and its counterpart, Visual C# Express. Visual Studio makes writing code easier and faster in hundreds of different ways. And did we mention C# Express is free?

- C# is designed to be powerful enough to write serious business applications, but simple enough to be easy to learn. C# was influenced by the older, and hugely popular, languages C++ and Java™, but was intended to bring all the good features of those languages without the quirks that they've acquired over the years.

So, although there are plenty of languages you could learn, we think that C# is an excellent choice to start with.

We could tell you about the new features of C# 3.0, or why we enjoy programming in C# after learning C++, but we suspect most of that won't matter to you. We wrote this book for people with no experience with C# or any other programming languages, so the differences between C# 2.0 and C# 3.0 probably don't impress you much. What we can tell you is that C# 3.0 means that the Microsoft .NET team has been refining the language since 2000, and we think the result is a stable, powerful, easy-to-learn language. We commend you on your choice to learn C#, and we'll try to make the experience as smooth as possible.

About This Book

Learning C# 3.0 is an introductory book. We don't assume that you have any prior programming experience, so we start with the very basic fundamentals of the language. We take it slowly and steadily, one concept per chapter, each one building on the last. We don't shy away from the complicated stuff—we introduce object-oriented programming in Chapter 6, and we use object-oriented concepts from there on out. By the latter half of the book, we'll be using intermediate topics like interfaces and delegates, building on what you've already learned. We finish up with two chapters on Windows programming, and two chapters on data, which is the interesting stuff that everybody wants to know about.

The goal of the book is not to get you to write fancy applications without understanding what they do. Our goal is to give you a good grasp of the basics of the language. Once you have that down, you can pick up a more advanced C# book and get the full benefit from it (and of course, we recommend O'Reilly's excellent line of C# books). Even better, once you've learned to *think* in a modern, object-oriented language, it becomes that much easier to learn others. The first programming language is always the hardest to learn; once you've learned C#, learning Visual Basic, or Java, or PHP is mostly just a matter of translating what you already know.

When you're learning a new language, clear, concise explanations are always helpful, and we've got those. Example applications that you can work through yourself are critical, and we have those too. But what really cements the language in your mind is practice, practice, practice, which we'll provide in each chapter. We've spent a lot of time coming up with quiz questions and exercises that underscore what you'll learn in each chapter, and give you the confidence that comes from writing your own code.

Who This Book Is For

We wrote *Learning C# 3.0* for people with no programming experience at all. If you're a student just starting to learn to program, this book is for you. If you have some experience with web design or system administration, and you want to learn about programming, this book is for you. If you're learning on your own because you want to know what this programming thing is all about, good for you! We'll help you get there.

If you already know another programming language, but you haven't run into object-oriented concepts yet, the material in Chapters 1 through 5 will probably be familiar to you in concept, even if you don't recognize the syntax. We recommend that you still read the first five chapters, but Chapter 6 is where it'll get really interesting for you. If you're familiar with C++, you'll find a lot of the syntax in this book familiar, but there's a lot that's new as well (you can say goodbye to pointers, for one thing), so we suggest that you at least skim the early chapters. If have some experience with another language such as Visual Basic, Java, or Ruby, there's a lot here that you'll be familiar with, but with enough syntax differences to trip you up if you're not careful.

If you're proficient in another object-oriented language and you're looking to pick up the changes as you transition to C#, we suggest you look into this book's companion volume, *Programming C# 3.0*, by Jesse Liberty and Donald Xie. That book assumes that you have some programming experience already and ramps up to the complex stuff more quickly.

How This Book Is Organized

Here's a short summary of the chapters in this book and what you'll find inside:

Chapter 1, *C# and .NET Programming*
> Here, we'll introduce you to the C# language and the .NET platform that supports it. That's important background information so that you can see how C# fits into the larger scheme. More important, though, we'll get you started writing real code. You'll create your first working program and see how easy it is to program in C#.

Chapter 2, *Visual Studio 2008 and C# Express 2008*
> When you build something, be it a house, a book, or a program, you have to know your tools. The tools for C# are Visual Studio 2008 and its free counterpart, C# Express. In this chapter, we'll walk you through them so that you're more comfortable with the interface.

Chapter 3, *C# Language Fundamentals*
> Now that you have your feet wet, it's time to begin at the beginning. In this chapter we'll introduce the most basic concepts of C#: statements, types, and variables. We'll also discuss constants and enumerations. And because you want your code to show you something, we'll demonstrate strings and how to write to the screen.

Chapter 4, *Operators*
> After you've learned about variables, you'll want to do something with them, and that's where operators come in. We'll start with the most basic operator, for assignment, and then we'll show you the mathematical operators, and the operators for comparison.

Chapter 5, *Branching*
> Without branching, your program would proceed in a straight line from start to finish. Branching lets your program respond to the values contained in your variables, often using the comparison operators. You'll also learn about the various looping statements that you'll use quite often to carry out an action several times.

Chapter 6, *Object-Oriented Programming*

Object-oriented programming is what makes C# a modern programming language. It's a different way of thinking about programming than you've been learning in the previous five chapters, but it's a natural outgrowth too. In this chapter, we'll put aside the coding for just a bit and talk about what object orientation means, and why it matters to you.

Chapter 7, *Classes and Objects*

Classes, and the objects you get from classes, are the foundation of object-oriented programming. Now that you have the theory down, this chapter lets you get your hands dirty with objects: creating them, using them, and seeing how they work.

Chapter 8, *Inside Methods*

You've been using methods through all the preceding chapters, but after learning about objects, it's time to find out a little more about methods and how they interact with objects. You'll find out about what you put into methods and what comes back out, how to overload methods to make them more versatile, and how properties make writing methods easier.

Chapter 9, *Basic Debugging*

Stuff goes wrong, in life and in code. At this point in the book, you know enough to be dangerous, which means you'll have generated some errors. Fortunately, Visual Studio has a bunch of tools to make errors easier to find and fix. We'll show you how to do that now, to increase your peace of mind for the rest of the book.

Chapter 10, *Arrays*

If objects are good, a bunch of objects, all of the same type, can be better. This chapter shows you a special language feature, called an *array*, that lets you handle lots of objects as a group.

Chapter 11, *Inheritance and Polymorphism*

As you'll learn in Chapter 6, specialization and generalization are two key components of object-oriented programming, and C# implements them with inheritance and polymorphism. You'll see how you can use classes to beget other classes for specialized purposes.

Chapter 12, *Operator Overloading*

When you create your own classes, you'll often need a way to define whether one of your objects is equal to another. You can do that by defining just what "equal" means for your class, and from there, you can define the = operator itself, for your class. You'll see how to redefine other operators as well.

Chapter 13, *Interfaces*

Interfaces build on the concepts of inheritance and polymorphism introduced in Chapter 11. An interface is a contract that states what a class that implements that interface can do, and how to interact with it. That flexibility lets you work with objects without knowing exactly what types they are, as long as you know what interfaces they use.

Chapter 14, *Generics and Collections*

This chapter puts together what you learned in Chapters 10, 11, and 13. Collections are another way of keeping bunches of objects together, but with generics, you don't need to know exactly what type of objects you have in your collection; interfaces make that possible.

Chapter 15, *Strings*

This chapter is all about text, which C# refers to as *strings*. Strings are a bit more complicated than other data types, but you can do some very interesting manipulation with them, as you'll find out.

Chapter 16, *Throwing and Catching Exceptions*

Your code runs in an imperfect world, which means sometimes things will go wrong. Users will enter bad data, network connections will go down, and files will vanish without warning. However, just because something goes wrong doesn't mean your program has to crash. In this chapter you'll learn how to anticipate certain error conditions and allow for them.

Chapter 17, *Delegates and Events*

Up to this point, your methods have called other methods specifically. With *events*, and the delegates that work with them, your object can simply announce that something has happened, and let any other interested objects worry about what to do next. Events are the foundation of how the Windows operating system works.

Chapter 18, *Creating Windows Applications*

With knowledge of events in your hand, it's time to have some fun and write a Windows application or two. The topic of Windows applications could warrant an entire book on its own, but we'll get you started in this chapter.

Chapter 19, *Windows Presentation Foundation*

The Windows Presentation Foundation (WPF) is a new feature that gives you more control over just how your applications look to the user. WPF offers a lot of enhancements over Windows Forms, and we'll show you a few of them in this chapter.

Chapter 20, *ADO.NET and Relational Databases*

All the code you've written in the book so far has used short-lived data that vanishes as soon as the program ends. In the real world, data is stored in databases, and in this chapter, you'll see how to interact with them.

Chapter 21, *LINQ*

Language Integrated Query (LINQ) is a new feature in C# 3.0 that greatly simplifies how your code interacts with data storage. Most interesting of all, you can use it to access data stored elsewhere in the same program. This is another topic that could warrant a book in itself, but we'll introduce you to it here.

Appendix, *Answers to Quizzes and Exercises*

The appendix features the answers to every quiz question and exercise found in the book. We'll provide the complete code for the answers, but more important, we'll explain *why* the answers are what they are.

Conventions Used in This Book

The following font conventions are used in this book:

Italic

Used for pathnames, filenames, Internet addresses (such as domain names and URLs), and new terms where they are defined

Constant width

Used for command lines and options that should be typed verbatim, C# keywords, and code examples

Constant width italic

Used for replaceable items, such as variables or optional elements, within syntax lines or code

Constant width bold

Used for emphasis within program code

Pay special attention to notes set apart from the text with the following icons:

This is a tip. It contains useful supplementary information about the topic at hand.

This is a warning. It helps you solve and avoid annoying problems.

Support: A Note from Jesse Liberty

I provide ongoing support for my books through my website. You can obtain the source code for all of the examples in *Learning C# 3.0* at:

> *http://www.jesseliberty.com*

There, you'll also find access to a book support discussion group that has a section set aside for questions about *Learning C# 3.0*. Before you post a question, however, please check my website to see whether there is a Frequently Asked Questions (FAQ) list or an errata file. If you check these files and still have a question, please go ahead and post it to the discussion center. The most effective way to get help is to ask a precise question or to create a small program that illustrates your area of concern or confusion, and be sure to mention which edition of the book you have.

Using Code Examples

This book is here to help you get your job done. In general, you may use the code in this book in your programs and documentation. You do not need to contact us for permission unless you're reproducing a significant portion of the code. For example, writing a program that uses several chunks of code from this book does not require permission. Selling or distributing a CD-ROM of examples from O'Reilly books *does* require permission. Answering a question by citing this book and quoting example code does not require permission. Incorporating a significant amount of example code from this book into your product's documentation *does* require permission.

We appreciate, but do not require, attribution. An attribution usually includes the title, author, publisher, and ISBN. For example: "*Learning C# 3.0*, by Jesse Liberty and Brian MacDonald. Copyright 2009 Jesse Liberty and Brian MacDonald, 978-0-596-52106-6."

If you feel your use of code examples falls outside fair use or the permission given here, feel free to contact us at *permissions@oreilly.com*.

We'd Like to Hear from You

We have tested and verified the information in this book to the best of our ability, but you may find that features have changed (or even that we have made mistakes!). Please let us know about any errors you find, as well as your suggestions for future editions, by writing to:

O'Reilly Media, Inc.
1005 Gravenstein Highway North
Sebastopol, CA 95472
(800) 998-9938 (in the U.S. or Canada)
(707) 829-0515 (international/local)
(707) 829-0104 (fax)

We have a web page for this book where we list examples and any plans for future editions. You can access this information at:

http://www.oreilly.com/catalog/9780596521066

To comment on the book, send email to:

bookquestions@oreilly.com

For more information about this book and others, as well as additional technical articles and discussion on C# and the .NET Framework, see the O'Reilly website:

http://www.oreilly.com

and the O'Reilly .NET DevCenter:

http://www.ondotnet.com/dotnet/

ONDotnet.com provides independent coverage of fundamental, interoperable, and emerging Microsoft .NET programming and web service technologies.

Safari® Books Online

 When you see a Safari® Books Online icon on the cover of your favorite technology book, that means the book is available online through the O'Reilly Network Safari Bookshelf.

Safari offers a solution that's better than e-books. It's a virtual library that lets you easily search thousands of top tech books, cut and paste code samples, download chapters, and find quick answers when you need the most accurate, current information. Try it for free at *http://safari.oreilly.com*.

Acknowledgments

Jesse Liberty

Thank you to Nicholas Paldino and Glyn Griffiths who helped make this book better than what I'd written, and it must be acknowledged that Brian MacDonald has helped to create an extraordinarily valuable on-ramp to the C# language that is unprecedented in the industry.

Very special thanks to my wife and daughters who have put up with "80-hour days" for far too many months.

I believe that this edition of Learning C# may be the best C# book we've written, in large measure thanks to the work of others, and I'm very grateful. With this, a book on Programming .NET, our books on ASP.NET, and the forthcoming book on Silverlight, we offer a complete course on programming for the Microsoft platform, and that reflects a joyous and wonderful leap of faith from O'Reilly.

Brian MacDonald

Above all, thanks to Jesse for asking me back for another book. I'm also grateful to John Osborn, who first got me involved with O'Reilly, many years ago now. Nick Paldino and Glyn Griffiths provided first-rate technical review, and key insight on both ends of the experience spectrum. Marlowe Shaeffer, Sumita Mukherji, and Rachel Monaghan deserve thanks for their patience and professionalism on the production side, and Audrey Doyle provided an excellent copyedit.

Thanks also to Doug Bellew, a great friend and a great developer, who helped me brainstorm the exercises. Thank you to my son, Alex, for his patience while I locked myself in my office to work on the book. And finally, thanks to my wife, Carole, who always provides both moral and technical support for my books, but who went above and beyond this time.

C# and .NET Programming

Welcome to *Learning C# 3.0*. We're here to teach you the C# language from the ground up. If you've never done any programming before, in any language, start here in Chapter 1, and we'll have you writing real working applications in no time flat—before you reach the end of this chapter. If you have a little programming background in VB 6, PHP 4, or another non-object-oriented language, you'll find a lot in this book that's familiar, but also a lot that's new. You'll probably find the code in the first few chapters to be recognizable, but you may want to read the chapters anyway to get the hang of the syntax. Classes and objects are at the core of how C# works, though, so we'll get to those quickly, once we've covered the basics.

 If you're a programmer migrating from Java or C++, you may find the material in *Programming C# 3.0* by Jesse Liberty and Donald Xie (O'Reilly) a more appropriate fit for your skills.

To start at the very beginning, C# is a modern language created by Microsoft as part of its *.NET platform* of languages. .NET is a layer of software that makes it easier for you to write programs that can communicate with the operating system (in this case, Windows). As the name implies, C# has its roots in C++, but over three versions, it has evolved its own techniques and elements that make it distinct. Most important, C# has the backing of the .NET Framework behind it, which we'll get into shortly. We're not going to assume that you have any C++ experience, so we won't frame our discussions of C# in terms of C++, or any other programming language. What you need to know right now is that you can write applications in C# that will do just about anything you need to do. You can write applications to manage your company's inventory (interacting with a database); you can write applications to analyze documents; you can write games; you can create an entire operating system in C# if you have a mind to. The .NET Framework allows C# to operate seamlessly with Windows, and take advantage of the familiar Windows features that users all over the world already know. You can also create C# applications that you can use on the Web, in much the same way.

To be completely honest, most modern object-oriented languages are rather similar underneath. The choice of one over the other is usually just a matter of personal preference. C# and Visual Basic have the advantage of the .NET Framework, but third-party languages can interact with the framework, too. C#'s similarity to C++ and Java makes it easy to learn for programmers familiar with those languages, but it's also easy to learn as your first language. Once you have the basics of C# down, you'll find it much easier to learn any other language you want to.

Unless we specifically say otherwise, when we refer to C# in this book, we mean *C# 3.0*; when we refer to .NET, we mean the *.NET 3.5 Framework*; and when we refer to Visual Studio, we mean *Visual Studio 2008*. We could spend some time telling you about the cool new features of C# 3.0 over its predecessors—and we're pretty excited about them—but if you're new to the language, it's all new to you, so there's little point in calling attention to specific features.

Finally, when we refer to using Visual Studio 2008, you may be using Visual C# 2008 Express Edition instead. C# Express is the free version of Visual Studio, designed for students and home users, but that doesn't mean it's a toy. In fact, the examples in this book were written and tested using C# Express. C# Express has the same compiler and libraries as Visual Studio, and within the examples in this book, you won't find any significant differences. There are some small differences in look and feel, or in feature names, and any time those come up, we'll mention them.

Installing C# Express

Visual C# 2008 Express Edition has all the features you'll need for the examples in this book, and it has the additional advantage of being completely free from Microsoft. Getting C# Express is very simple—just go here:

> *http://www.microsoft.com/express/download/*

Here, you'll find download links for each of the free Visual Studio 2008 Express Editions. Scroll down to the Visual C# box (it's the green one), select your language, and click the Download link. Save the installer to your hard drive, and then run it. Most of the installation is pretty standard, but there is one step you should pay attention to, shown in Figure 1-1: the installation options.

The MSDN Library contains useful help files, and if you have the space available, you should install it, but it's not strictly necessary for this book. The second option, Microsoft SQL Server 2005 Express Edition, allows you to access databases with your code. You won't need it for a while if you're reading this book straight through, but we do use it in Chapters 20 and 21, so you may want to install it now. (You can install it separately later, if you want.) The Silverlight runtime is an amazing new technology from Microsoft, but we won't be covering it in this book, so you can skip that.

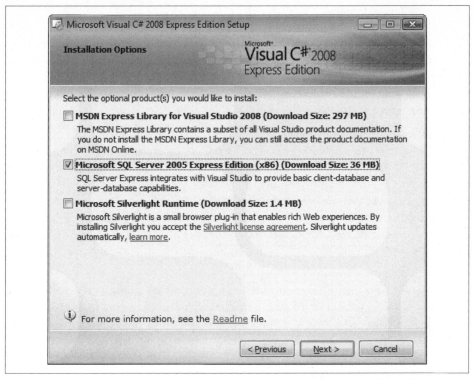

Figure 1-1. During the C# Express installation, select the MSDN Library if you have the space and the SQL Server 2005 Express option if you want to work through the data examples in Chapters 20 and 21.

The rest of the installation is mostly automatic. When you're done, you'll find a link in your Start menu, ready to go.

We'll give you a full tour of Visual Studio and C# Express in the next chapter. For this chapter, we'll tell you exactly what to do and when. Right now, we'll look a little more closely into the .NET platform to get you started, and then it'll be time to write some code.

C# 3.0 and .NET 3.5

In the past, you might have learned a language such as C or Java without much concern about the platform on which you would be programming. These languages had versions available for various operating systems, whether that was a Unix box or a PC running Windows.

C#, however, was created specifically for .NET. Although cross-platform versions of .NET do exist, for now the overwhelming majority of .NET programs will be written to run on a machine running one of the Windows operating systems.

The .NET Platform

When Microsoft announced C# 1.0 in July 2000, its unveiling was part of a much larger event: the announcement of the .NET platform. The .NET platform is a development framework that provides a new way to create Windows applications. However, .NET goes beyond traditional Windows programming to facilitate creating web applications quickly and easily.

Microsoft reportedly devoted 80% of its research and development budget to .NET and its associated technologies. The results of this commitment were very impressive. In 2005, Microsoft rolled out version 2 of the language, the platform, and the tools. Its goal was to radically reduce the amount of boilerplate code you have to write, and to make the creation of web and desktop applications easier by "encapsulating" much of the "plumbing" of a typical application into objects. That means that rather than writing a lot of the code to connect to databases, the Internet, or your filesystem, .NET provides fully tested objects that will do all the heavy lifting for you.

In 2007, .NET version 3.0 brought .NET up-to-date with Microsoft's new Vista and Windows Server 2008 operating systems. The most visible change in this version of the framework was to provide support for the Windows Presentation Foundation (WPF), which opens up new graphics possibilities, such as those you'll find in Windows Vista, as you'll see later in this book. And now, with the release of Visual Studio 2008, .NET version 3.5 supports more new features, including LINQ, a new feature that allows you to query databases with a more natural, object-oriented syntax.

The scope of .NET is huge. The platform consists of three separate product groups:

- A set of languages, including C# and Visual Basic .NET; a set of development tools, including Visual Studio 2008; and powerful tools for building applications, including the *Common Language Runtime* (CLR), a platform for compiling, debugging, and executing .NET applications
- A set of Enterprise Servers, including SQL Server 2008, Exchange, BizTalk, and so on, that provide specialized functionality for relational data storage, email, business-to-business (B2B) commerce, and so forth
- .NET-enabled non-PC devices, from cell phones to game boxes

The .NET Framework

Central to the .NET platform is a development environment known as the *.NET Framework*. The framework provides a lot of features, but for now all you need to know is that the C# language provides you with the elements that allow you to access the framework to make your programs work. You will learn about these elements in the chapters ahead.

The .NET Framework sits on top of any flavor of the Windows operating system. The most important components of the framework are the CLR, which is what allows you to compile and execute applications, and the *Framework Class Library* (FCL), which provides an enormous number of predefined types or classes for you to use in your programs. You will learn how to define your own classes in Chapter 7.

 Detailed coverage of all the FCL classes is beyond the scope of this book. For more information, see *C# 3.0 in a Nutshell* by Joseph Albahari and Ben Albahari (O'Reilly), and the MSDN Library (*http://msdn. microsoft.com/library*).

The C# Language

The C# language is disarmingly simple, which makes it good for beginners, but C# also includes all the support for the structured, component-based, object-oriented programming that one expects of a modern language built on the shoulders of C++ and Java. In other words, it's a fully featured language appropriate for developing large-scale applications, but at the same time it is designed to be easy to learn.

A small team led by two distinguished Microsoft engineers, Anders Hejlsberg and Scott Wiltamuth, developed the original C# language. Hejlsberg is also known for creating Turbo Pascal, a popular language for PC programming, and for leading the team that designed Borland Delphi, one of the first successful integrated development environments (IDEs) for client/server programming.

The goal of C# is to provide a simple, safe, object-oriented, high-performance language for .NET development. C# is simple because there are relatively few *keywords*. Keywords are special words reserved by the language that have a specific meaning within all C# programs, including if, while, and for. You'll learn about these keywords in the coming chapters.

C# is considered safe because the language is *type-safe*, which is an important mechanism to help you find bugs early in the development process, as you'll see later. This makes for code that is easier to maintain and programs that are more reliable.

C# was designed, from the very start, to support object-oriented programming. In this book, we'll explain not only how to write object-oriented programs, but also why object-oriented programming has become so popular. The short answer is this: programs are becoming increasingly complex, and object-oriented programming techniques help you manage that complexity.

C# was designed for .NET, and .NET was designed (in part) for developing web and web-aware programs. The Internet is a primary resource in most .NET applications.

Your First Program: Hello World

At the most fundamental level, a C# application consists of *source code*. Source code is human-readable text written in a text editor. A text editor is like a word processor, but it puts no special characters into the file to support formatting, only the text. You could use any old text editor to write your code, but since you'll be using Visual Studio throughout this book, that's the best choice. Start up C# Express or Visual Studio. The first thing you'll see is the Start Page, which will look similar to Figure 1-2.

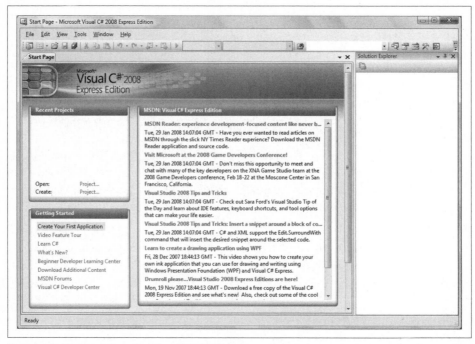

Figure 1-2. The Start Page for Visual C# 2008 Express. It looks pretty empty now, but that won't last long. You'll be using the Create link on the lefthand side.

There's a lot of news in the middle, which you don't need to pay attention to right now. We'll give you a full tour of the Visual Studio interface in Chapter 2, but for now you need the Recent Projects box on the left. If you just installed Visual Studio, that box is empty at the moment, because you haven't created any projects yet. That's about to change. Click Project, next to the Create link. The New Project dialog box opens, as you can see in Figure 1-3.

There are lots of options here that we'll discuss later, but for now we just want to get you started. Select Console Application from the row of templates at the top. When you do that, the content of the Name field at the bottom will change to

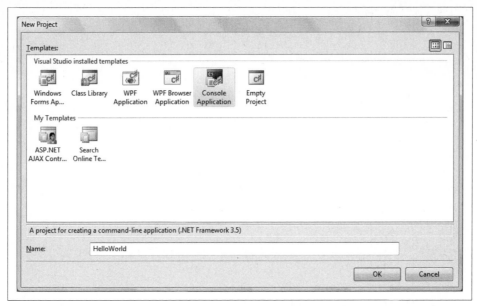

Figure 1-3. This is where you'll create all your Visual Studio projects. There are a lot of template options here, but for now just select Console Application and type HelloWorld in the Name field.

ConsoleApplication1, which is a fine name, but not very descriptive. Change it to HelloWorld (without a space) and then click OK.

Visual Studio creates the project for you, along with the necessary files. Again, you don't need to know about most of this yet, but it's nice that Visual Studio does it for you. It also creates the program where you'll write your code, called *Program.cs*. Finally, Visual Studio opens *Program.cs* in an editing window for you to work on. Visual Studio provides some basic code that's common to all C# console programs, called a *skeleton*, which saves you even more time. Your Visual Studio screen should now look like Figure 1-4.

In this first example, you will create a very simple application that does nothing more than display the words *Hello World* to your monitor. This console application is the traditional first program for learning any new language, and it demonstrates some of the basic elements of a C# program.

After you write your Hello World program and compile it, we'll provide a line-by-line analysis of the source code. This analysis will give you a brief preview of the language; we'll describe the fundamentals much more fully in Chapter 3.

As we mentioned, the skeleton of the program is already there for you, but you still need to write a little code. The editing window you're looking at now works much like any word processing program you're familiar with, or even like Windows Notepad. However, you'll find that Visual Studio has a lot of helpful features for writing

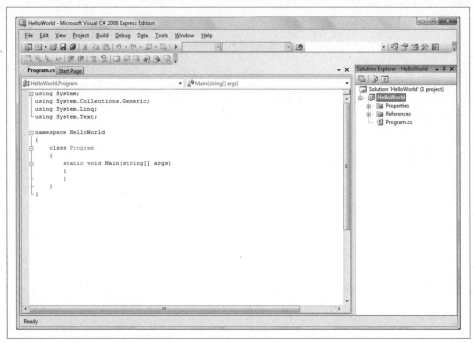

Figure 1-4. Visual Studio does all the work of setting up your application automatically, which saves a lot of time. It even creates this program skeleton for you, ready for you to add your own code.

code that those other applications lack. Right now, click after the open brace ({) underneath static void Main. Press Enter once to open up some space (notice that Visual Studio indents for you automatically—this is a good thing), and then type the following:

```
// every console app starts with Main
System.Console.WriteLine("Hello World!");
```

As you type, you'll notice that Visual Studio automatically colors your code, and that it'll open small windows (called *IntelliSense* windows) suggesting code that you might want to include. Don't worry about any of that for now; just type the code as shown here.

Example 1-1 shows the code that you should see in your editing window right now. The lines that you added are shown here in bold. Be sure to pay attention to the capitalization, especially capitals where you wouldn't normally expect them, as in WriteLine. C# is case-sensitive, and if you lowercase the *L* here, you'll get an error message (and not necessarily a helpful error message).

Example 1-1. A simple source code file; this application doesn't look like much, but it's a fully functional application that you'll run in just a moment

```
using System;
using System.Collections.Generic;
using System.Linq;
using System.Text;

namespace HelloWorld
{
   class Program
   {
      static void Main(string[] args)
      {
         // every console app starts with Main
         System.Console.WriteLine("Hello World!");
      }
   }
}
```

You should save your code before you go any further. Click the Save All button ( ) on the toolbar. You'll see a dialog box asking you where you want to save your work; the *My Documents/Visual Studio 2008/Projects* folder is the default, but you can save your work wherever you like. Each project you create will have its own subfolder.

We'll explain this program detail in a bit. For now, just look at the language—the program is readable; it is in normal text. The words may be strange and the layout unusual, but there are no special characters—just the normal text produced by your keyboard.

The source code makes up a set of instructions for the application to follow. The *syntax* for these instructions is strictly defined by the language. In C#, source code consists of a series of statements. A *statement* is an instruction to the compiler. Each instruction must be formed correctly, and one task you'll face when learning C# will be to learn the correct syntax of the language. For example, in C#, every statement ends with a semicolon.

Each instruction has a *semantic* meaning that expresses what you are trying to accomplish. Although you must follow the rules of C# syntax, the semantics of the language are far more important in developing effective object-oriented programs. This book will provide insight into both the syntax and the semantics of good C# programs.

We know you'll want to run your new program right away, but bear with us for just a moment while we explain just what Visual Studio has to do to make that happen.

The Compiler

After you write your program in an editor and save it to disk, you must *compile* it. Compiling is the process of turning the code that *you* can read into code that the *machine* can read. For that, you need a compiler. Then, once you've compiled the program, you need to run and test it.

The job of the compiler is to turn your source code into a working program. It turns out to be just slightly more complicated than that because .NET uses an intermediate language called Microsoft Intermediate Language (MSIL, sometimes abbreviated as IL). The compiler reads your source code and produces MSIL. When you run the program, the .NET Just In Time (JIT) compiler reads your MSIL code and produces an executable application in memory. You won't see any of this happen, but it's a good idea to know what's going on behind the scenes.

 The MSIL code is actually stored in an *.exe* file, but this file does not contain executable code. It contains the information needed by the JIT to execute the code when you run it.

Visual Studio provides a built-in compiler that you'll use pretty much all the time. To compile and run Hello World, select Debug → Start Without Debugging, and your program executes, as shown in Figure 1-5. You can also press Ctrl-F5 to do the same thing. You may notice a button on the toolbar (▶) that will also compile and run your program, but you don't want to use that this time. If you do (and feel free to try this), your program will still execute, but the console window will close immediately, before you have a chance to see what you've done. Start Without Debugging opens the window, but adds the line "Press any key to continue…" after your program's output. Go ahead and press a key now to dismiss the window and end the program.

Presto! You are a C# programmer. That's it, close the book, you've done it. OK, don't close the book—there are details to examine, but take a moment to congratulate yourself. Have a cookie.

Granted, the program you created is one of the simplest C# programs imaginable, but it is a complete C# program, and it can be used to examine many of the elements common to C# programs.

If your program didn't run as anticipated, don't panic. If something is wrong in the code, Visual Studio will pop up a dialog box saying "There were build errors. Would you like to continue and run the last successful build?" In a program this simple, you most likely made what's called a *syntax error*, which is a term programmers use because they don't want to admit they made a typo, which is usually what happened. Select No in this dialog and Visual Studio will open an error window at the bottom of the interface with a message that may or may not be helpful, depending on exactly what's wrong.

Figure 1-5. These are the results you'll see in the command window after you've compiled and run Hello World.

Go back and check your code very carefully, and make sure it matches the code in Example 1-1 exactly. Make sure there's a semicolon at the end of the line containing the WriteLine, and that you've capitalized correctly. Make sure you have open and close quotation marks around "Hello World" and make sure you have open and close parentheses around the quotes. Make sure the first line you added starts with two forward slashes (//); the entire line should appear in green, if you've done it correctly. Make any necessary fixes, and then try to build and run the program again.

Examining Your First Program

The single greatest challenge when learning to program is that you must learn everything before you can learn anything. Even this simple Hello World program uses many features of the language that we will discuss in coming chapters, including classes, namespaces, statements, static methods, objects, strings, blocks, and libraries.

It's as though you were learning to drive a car. You must learn to steer, accelerate, brake, and understand the flow of traffic. Right now, we're going to get you out on the highway and just let you steer for a while. Over time, you'll learn how to speed up and slow down. Along the way, you'll learn to set the radio and adjust the heat so that you'll be more comfortable. In no time you'll be driving, and then won't your parents begin to worry.

Hang on tight; we're going to zip through this quickly and come back to the details in subsequent chapters.

The first four lines in the program are called using statements:

```
using System;
using System.Collections.Generic;
using System.Linq;
using System.Text;
```

Visual Studio inserted these for you automatically. These using statements provide a shorthand way to access various parts of the .NET Framework that you might want to use in your program. In fact, you used only the first one this time around, but it doesn't hurt anything to have the others there. We'll discuss the System part in just a minute.

The next line in the program defines a *namespace*:

```
namespace HelloWorld
{
```

You will create many names when programming in C#. Every object and every type of object must be named. It is possible for the names you assign to conflict with the names assigned by Microsoft or other vendors. A namespace is a way of distinguishing your names from anybody else's.

In this program, you've created a namespace called HelloWorld. Visual Studio assigned this namespace for you automatically because that was the name you gave your project. The items defined in your namespace must be enclosed in braces ({}). Thus, the second line of the Hello World program is an open brace to mark the beginning of the HelloWorld namespace. The open brace is matched by a closing brace at the end of the program. Get used to seeing these braces—you'll use them a lot in C#, usually with braces nested inside braces. Forgetting to include a closing brace is a common syntax mistake. Some programmers like to type the closing brace immediately after the opening one, but on a new line, and then go back and fill in the code between the braces.

Within the braces of the namespace, you write other programming constructs. For instance, you might define a class. *Classes* define a category, or *type*, of object. The .NET Framework provides thousands of classes, and you can define new ones of your own as well. Classes are used to define the attributes and behavior of Windows controls (buttons, listboxes, and so on), as well as constructs that mimic the important attributes or behavior of things in the world, such as employees, students, telephones, and so on.

Classes are the core of C# and object-oriented programming. You'll learn about classes in detail in Chapters 6 and 7.

Every class named within the namespace braces is implicitly prefixed with the name HelloWorld. The dot operator (.) separates the namespace from the name of the class within the namespace. Thus, if you were to create the class MyClass within the namespace HelloWorld, the real name of that class would be HelloWorld.MyClass.

You can read this as either "HelloWorld dot MyClass" or "HelloWorld MyClass." Like the braces, you use the dot operator quite a lot; you'll see various other uses as we proceed.

The third line in our Hello World program creates a class named `Program`. Again, this is the default name for the class, which Visual Studio provided for you. Like a namespace, a class is defined within braces. The following code represents the opening of the `Program` class definition:

```
class Program
{
```

A *method* is a relatively small block of code that performs an action. Methods are always contained within classes. The `Main( )` method is a special method in C#—it's the "entry point" for every C# application; it is where your program begins. The next few lines in Hello World mark the beginning of the `Main( )` method:

```
static void Main(string[] args)
{
```

We cover methods in detail in Chapter 8, but we mention them in virtually every chapter in this book.

A *comment* (shown here in bold) appears just after the start of the `Main( )` method:

```
static void Main(string[] args)
{
    // every console app starts with Main
```

A comment is just a note to yourself. You insert comments to make the code more readable to yourself and other programmers. You'll be surprised how helpful those comments are six months later when you have no idea what a line of code you wrote actually does.

You can place comments anywhere in your program that you think the explanation will be helpful; they have no effect on the running program. The compiler knows to ignore them.

C# recognizes three styles of comments. The comment in Hello World begins with two slashes (//). The slashes indicate that everything to the right on the same line is a comment.

The second style is to begin your comment with a forward slash followed by an asterisk (/*) and to end your comment with the opposite pattern (*/). These pairs of characters are called the opening C-style comment and the closing C-style comment, respectively.

These comment symbols were inherited from the C language—thus the names used to identify them. They are also used in C++ and Java.

Everything between these comment symbols is a comment. C-style comments can span more than one line, as in the following:

```
/* This begins a comment
This line is still within the comment
Here comes the end of the comment */
```

The third and final style of comments uses three forward slashes (///). This is an XML-style comment and is used for advanced documentation techniques, so we won't discuss it in this book.

 You will note that we don't use many comments in the examples in this book. Most of that is for space reasons; we'd rather explain what the code does in the text than clutter the pages with comments.

Notice that the Main( ) method is defined with the keywords static and void:

```
static void Main(string[] args)
```

The static keyword indicates that you can access this method without having an object of your class available. Whereas a class defines a type, each instance of that type is an *object* (much as *Car* defines a type of vehicle and your aging rust-bucket or shiny roadster is an individual instance of *Car*). Thus, whereas Button defines a type of control for a Windows program, any individual program will have many Button objects, each with its own label (such as OK, Cancel, or Retry).

Normally, methods can be called only if you have an object, but static methods are special and are called without an object. (We'll cover the use of static methods, other than Main( ), in Chapter 7.)

The second keyword in the statement defining the Main( ) method is void:

```
static void Main(string[] args)
```

Typically, one method *calls*, or invokes, another method. The called method will do the work, and it can return a value to the method that called it. (You'll see how methods call one another and return values in Chapter 8.) If a method does not return a value, it is declared void. The keyword void is a signal to the compiler that your method will not return a value to the calling method.

The operating system calls Main( ) when the program is invoked. It is possible for Main( ) to return a value (typically an error code) that might be used by the operating system. In this case, though, you've declared that Main( ) will not return a value.

Every method name is followed by parentheses:

```
static void Main(string[] args)
```

When you create your own method, you may want it to use data from elsewhere in your application. To do that, you *pass* values into your method so that the method can manipulate or use those values. These values are called *parameters* or *arguments*. (We cover method parameters in Chapter 8.) When you pass in values, those values are contained inside the parentheses. In this case, Main( ) has a single parameter: string[ ] args. Don't worry about that for now; that's another bit of code Visual Studio inserted for you, but it doesn't make a difference in this program. You can delete that parameter, and your program will still run the same. Don't delete the parentheses, though; all method calls must be followed by the parentheses, even if the parentheses are empty.

The *body* of the method is always enclosed within braces. Within the braces for Main( ) is a single line of code:

```
System.Console.WriteLine("Hello World!");
```

The Console is an object that represents the window on your screen. The Console class is defined within the System namespace, and so its full identification is System.Console.

The Console class has a static method, WriteLine( ), which you access not with an instance of Console, but through the Console class itself. Because you access the method with the dot operator, you write System.Console.WriteLine.

The WriteLine( ) method declares a single parameter: the text you want to display. In C#, a set of characters is referred to as a *string*. You'll learn a lot more about strings in Chapter 15, but for now, just know that a string is a block of text in quotes. When you pass a string in to the method, the string is an *argument*. The argument ("Hello World") corresponds to the parameter the method expects, and the string is displayed. The complete call to the method is:

```
System.Console.WriteLine("Hello World!");
```

If you will use many objects from the System namespace (and you will), you can save typing by telling the compiler that many of the objects you'll refer to are in that namespace. That's what the using directive is for at the beginning of your program:

```
using System;
```

With this line in place, you can use the Console class name without explicitly identifying that it is in the System namespace. With the using declaration, you can rewrite the contents of Main( ) as follows:

```
Console.WriteLine("Hello World!");
```

The final series of lines close the various nested opening braces. The first closes the brace for Main( ), the second closes the brace for the class, and the third closes the brace for the namespace. Each opening brace must be matched by a closing brace.

The class is defined within the namespace declaration, and thus you do not close the namespace until after you've closed the class. Similarly, the method Main( ) is declared within the class, so you do not close the class until after you've closed the method.

Whew! That was a lot to take in all at once! Don't panic; in coming chapters, we'll explain in detail all the concepts we introduced here.

The Integrated Development Environment

Although you *can* perform all of these writing and compiling tasks using Notepad and various command-line tools, your programming life will be much easier if you use the integrated development environment (IDE) called Visual Studio 2008. Visual Studio 2008 was designed with .NET development in mind, and it greatly simplifies the writing of C# program code. This book assumes you are using Visual C# 2008 Express or Visual Studio 2008, both of which provide the Visual Studio 2008 development environment.

 The overwhelming majority of C# programmers will be building Windows and web applications for the .NET platform using Visual Studio 2008 or Visual C# 2008 Express, and we've tested all the examples for this book in that environment.

Excellent open source C# compilers are available, such as those from the Mono project (*http://www.mono-project.com*) and #develop (*http://www.icsharpcode.net/OpenSource/SD/*). Everything in this book should work with those compilers, but we have not tested with them and cannot guarantee 100% compatibility.

The Visual Studio 2008 IDE provides enormous advantages to the C# programmer. This book tacitly assumes that you'll use Visual Studio 2008 or Visual C# 2008 Express for your work. However, the discussion focuses more on the language and the platform than on the tools.

Nonetheless, Chapter 2 provides an introduction to the IDE in some detail. Chapter 9 returns to the IDE to examine the debugger, which will help you find and correct problems in your code.

You can use the C# language to develop four types of applications:

Console applications
> A console application runs in a console window, as you saw with Hello World. A console window (or DOS box) provides simple text-based output. Console applications are very helpful when you're learning a language because they strip away the distraction of the Windows graphical user interface (GUI). Rather than spending your time creating complex windowing applications, you can focus on the details of the language constructs, such as how you create classes and methods, how you branch based on runtime conditions, and how you loop. We will cover all of these topics in detail in later chapters.

Windows applications

A Windows application runs on a PC's desktop. You are already familiar with Windows applications such as Microsoft Word and Excel. Windows applications are much more complex than console applications and can take advantage of the full suite of menus, controls, and other widgets you've come to expect in a modern desktop application. In this book, you'll learn how to create Windows Forms applications in Chapter 18, and the fancier WPF applications in Chapter 19.

ASP.NET applications

An ASP.NET application runs on a web server and delivers its functionality through a browser such as Internet Explorer or Firefox, typically over the Web. ASP.NET technology facilitates developing web applications quickly and easily. You'll learn more about ASP.NET applications in Chapter 18.

 For an introduction to ASP.NET, see *Learning ASP.NET 3.5* by Jesse Liberty et al. (O'Reilly).

Web services

Web services are complex applications that can be accessed using standard Internet protocols, and that can provide services such as current stock quotes, ISBN-to-title conversions, and so forth that other applications can use. Web services are an advanced topic, and we won't cover them in this book.

This book will focus primarily on the basics of the C# language, using simple console applications for most of the examples, to illustrate language fundamentals.

Summary

- C# was initially created specifically for use with the .NET platform.
- C# is used with the .NET Framework, which allows you access to a number of libraries that are specifically intended for use with Windows.
- The Common Language Runtime (CLR) is the component of the .NET Framework that allows you to compile and execute applications written in either C# or Visual Basic .NET.
- C# is designed to be simple, type-safe, object-oriented, and high-performance.
- C# applications consist of human-readable source code, written in a text editor. The source code is compiled into Microsoft Intermediate Language (MSIL) which, at runtime, is compiled into machine code.
- A namespace is a way of grouping the names that you assign to elements in your application so that they don't conflict with other names, either yours or those assigned by Microsoft or other developers.

- Classes are the core building blocks of C# and object-oriented programming because they allow you to create new types that model types in the "problem domain"—that is, that model things in the area you are concerned with.

- A method is a named block of code that performs an action and that may return a value.

- A comment is a note for the programmer and does not affect the running of the application.

- A string is a set of text characters enclosed in quotes.

- You can use C# to develop console applications, Windows applications, web applications, and web services.

This chapter wasn't that long and yet you've come a very long way. You got a crash-course introduction to the C# language, and you saw a little of what went into creating it and what goes on underneath. Most important, though, you wrote, compiled, and ran a real working application. You can already call yourself a C# programmer. Granted, creating an application with Notepad and the command-line compiler is a bit painful, and there's no reason why you should be fumbling around with a unicycle when you've got a fully loaded Ferrari just waiting for you to slip behind the wheel. So, we're going to take just a quick break in the next chapter to show you around the Visual Studio IDE, and then we'll come right back to the fundamentals of the language.

Test Your Knowledge: Quiz

Question 1-1. What is the CLR?

Question 1-2. What is the .NET Framework?

Question 1-3. What does it mean to say that C# is a "safe" language?

Question 1-4. What is a keyword?

Question 1-5. What does the compiler do?

Question 1-6. What is MSIL?

Question 1-7. What is the JIT?

Question 1-8. What is a namespace?

Question 1-9. What is a string?

Question 1-10. What are the four types of applications you can build in Visual Studio 2008?

Test Your Knowledge: Exercise

Exercise 1-1. Write an application that emits the words "What a great book!" to the console window.

Hint: open Visual Studio, create a console application, and, if you get stuck, consider copying or modifying the code shown in the chapter. Remember, these exercises are for your own edification, no one is grading them, and making mistakes is an opportunity to explore and learn more—this is true in just about everything except nuclear physics.

So, *Don't Panic!*

CHAPTER 2

Visual Studio 2008 and C# Express 2008

In Chapter 1, you learned that you *can* create your C# applications using Notepad. In this chapter, you'll learn why you never *will*. Microsoft developed Visual Studio 2008 to facilitate the creation of Windows and web applications. You will find that this integrated development environment (IDE) is a *very* powerful tool that will greatly simplify your work.

Visual Studio 2008 offers many advantages to the .NET developer, among them:

- A modern interface, using a tabbed document metaphor for code and layout screens, and dockable toolbars and information windows.

- Convenient access to multiple design and code windows (this will make more sense when you are creating web applications, as shown in Chapter 20).

- WYSIWYG (What You See Is What You Get) visual design of Windows and Web Forms.

- Code completion, which allows you to enter code with fewer errors and less typing.

- IntelliSense, which displays tips for every method, providing the return type and the types of all the parameters.

- Dynamic, context-sensitive help, which allows you to view topics and samples relevant to the code you are writing at the moment. You can also search the complete SDK library from within the IDE.

- Immediate flagging of syntax errors, which allows you to fix problems as they are entered.

- A Start Page, which provides easy access to new and existing projects.

- The same code editor for all .NET languages, which shortens the learning curve. Each language can have specialized aspects, but all languages benefit from shared features, such as incremental search, code outlining, collapsing text, line numbering, and color-coded keywords.

- An HTML editor, which provides both Design and HTML views that update each other in real time.

- A Solution Explorer, which displays all the files that make up your solution in outline form.

- An integrated debugger, which allows you to step through code, observe program runtime behavior, and set breakpoints, even across multiple languages and multiple processes.

- Customization capability, which allows you to set user preferences for IDE appearance and behavior.

- Integrated support for source control software.

- A built-in task list.

- The ability to modify your controls' properties, either declaratively or through the Properties window.

- The ability to integrate custom controls that you create or purchase from a third party.

- Rapid and easy deployment, including the ability to copy an entire website development project from one machine to another.

- The ability to integrate third-party tools into Visual Studio.

- The ability to program extensions to Visual Studio.

- The ability to rename methods, properties, and so forth and have them renamed automatically throughout the program.

- A Server Explorer, which allows you to log on to servers that you have network access to, access the data and services on those servers, drag-and-drop data sources onto controls, and perform a variety of other chores.

- Integrated build and compile support.

- The ability to drag-and-drop controls onto your web page, either in Design mode or in HTML mode.

Visual Studio 2008 and Visual C# 2008 Express are highly useful tools that can save you hours of repetitive tasks. They are also large and complex programs, so it is impossible for us to explore every nook and cranny in this chapter. Instead, we'll take you on a quick tour of the interface and lay the foundation for understanding and using C# Express, which is our IDE of choice for this book, as well as point out some of the nastier traps you might run into along the way.

 Just about every feature we describe in this chapter can also be found in Visual Studio 2008. If there are any significant differences, we'll point them out specifically, but for the most part, you can treat the two IDEs as identical.

Before You Read Further

This chapter has a lot of information in it, and you won't need all of it all at once. In fact, much of the information will not even apply to console applications, but will be valuable when you are ready to create Windows or web applications.

Many readers like to skim this chapter the first time through, and then come back for the details later. But it is your book, you paid for it (you *did* pay for it, didn't you?), and so you are free to read the entire chapter, take notes as you go, skip it entirely, or otherwise use it to your best advantage.

Whether or not you read this chapter, we do strongly recommend that you spend time (lots and lots of time) exploring C# Express in detail. You will forever be surprised at how much is in there and how much you can set it up to behave as you want; it is your principal development tool. Ignoring C# Express would be like a race car driver never looking under the hood. In time, you not only want to know how to change the oil, but also want to understand how the valves work and why the linkage sticks.

The Start Page

The Start Page is the first thing you see when you open C# Express (unless you configure it otherwise). From here, you can create new projects or open a project you worked on in a previous session. You can also find out what is new in .NET, access .NET newsgroups and websites, search for help online, download useful code, or adjust C# Express to your personal requirements. Figure 2-1 shows a typical Start Page, which you already saw briefly in Chapter 1.

The Start Page has a window on the left that includes a list of your recent projects; you can click on any one to open it. Below those links, you'll find the Open link, which lets you open any existing project on your computer. Under that is the Create link, which lets you create a new project. The Getting Started box on the lower left provides links to features and helpful sites. Most of the real estate on the Start Page is taken up by the large box in the middle, which contains useful articles from MSDN online, if you have an active Internet connection.

Projects and Solutions

A C# program is built from *source files*, which are text files containing the code you write. Source code files are named with the *.cs* extension. The *Program.cs* file you created in Chapter 1 is an example.

A typical C# Express 2008 application can have a number of other files (such as assembly information files, references, icons, data connections, and more). C# Express 2008 organizes these files into a container called a *project*.

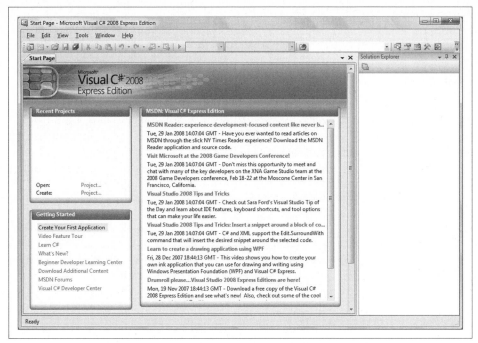

Figure 2-1. The C# Express Start Page is the first thing you'll see when you start C# Express. From here, there are many different links to get you started.

C# Express 2008 provides two types of containers for your source code, folders, files, and related material: the *project* and the *solution*. A *project* is a set of files that work together to create an executable program (*.exe*) or a dynamic link library (*.dll*). Large, complex projects may contain multiple *.dll* files.

A *solution* is a set of related projects, although it may also have just one project—which is what you'll do most often in this book. Each time you create a new project, C# Express 2008 either adds it to an existing solution or creates a new solution.

Solutions are defined within a file named for the solution, and they have the extension *.sln*. The *.sln* file contains metadata, which is basically information about the data. The metadata describes the projects that compose the solution and information about building the solution. You won't have to worry about these for the most part.

 Visual Studio 2008 also creates a file with the same base name as the *.sln* file, but with the filename extension *.sou* (such as *mySolution.sln* and *mySolution.sou*). The *.sou* file contains metadata used to customize the IDE for the specific user.

There are a number of ways to open an existing solution. The simplest way is to select Open Project from the Start menu (which opens a project and its enclosing solution). Alternatively, you can open a solution in C# Express 2008 just by double-clicking the *.sln* file in Windows Explorer.

Typically, the build process results in the contents of a project being compiled into an executable (*.exe*) file or a dynamic link library (*.dll*) file. This book focuses on creating executable files.

 The metadata describing the project is contained in a separate file named after the project with the extension *.csproj*. The project file contains version information, build settings, and references to other source files to include as part of the project.

Project Types

You can create many types of projects in the full version of Visual Studio 2008, including:

- Console Application projects
- Windows Application projects
- Windows Service projects
- WPF Application projects
- WPF Browser Application projects
- Windows Control Library projects
- Web Control Library projects
- Class Library projects
- Smart device templates
- Crystal Reports Windows Application projects
- SQL Server projects
- Word and Excel Document and Template projects

Note that web applications are missing from this list. Web applications do not use projects, just solutions.

Visual C# Express, being a "light" version of the Visual Studio product, can't produce nearly as many types of projects. C# Express is limited to console applications, Windows Forms applications, WPF applications, WPF browser applications, and class libraries.

A typical .NET application comprises many items: source files (such as *.cs* files), assemblies (such as *.exe* and *.dll* files) and assembly information files, data sources (such as .*mdb* files), references, and icons, as well as miscellaneous other files and folders. Visual Studio 2008 makes all of this easier for you by organizing these items into a folder that represents the project. The project folder is housed in a solution. When you create a new project, Visual Studio 2008 automatically creates the solution.

Templates

When you create a new project with C# Express, you'll see the New Project dialog box, shown in Figure 2-2.

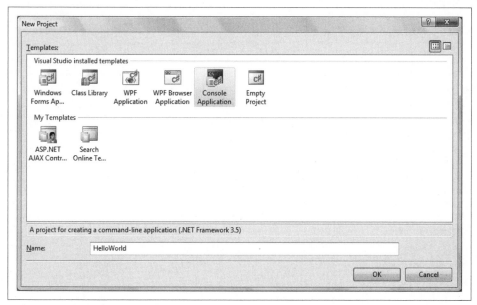

Figure 2-2. The New Project dialog is where every new C# application starts.

In the New Project dialog, if you're using Visual C# Express, you'll see only the templates you can choose from for your project. If you're using Visual Studio 2008, this dialog box will look different, with two panes. You select the project type (in the left-hand pane) and the template (in the right). There are a variety of templates for each project type. A *template* is a file that C# Express 2008 uses to set up the initial state of your project.

If you're using Visual Studio 2008, for the examples in this book you'll always choose Visual C# for the project type, and in most cases you'll choose Console Application as the template. Specify the name of the directory in which your project will be stored in the Location box and name your project in the Name box. C# Express doesn't give you the option of choosing the file location; the files are stored in your local *My Documents* folder, in a subfolder called *Visual Studio 2008*.

Project names can contain any standard characters, except leading or trailing spaces, Windows or DOS keywords, and any of the following special characters: # % & * | \ : " < > ? /.

Inside the Integrated Development Environment

The C# Express IDE is centered on its editor. An editor is much like a word processor, except that it produces simple text (that is, text with no formatting, such as bold and italics). All source code files are simple text files. The color that you saw applied to some of the text in the Hello World project in Chapter 1 isn't just formatting; it's a form of highlighting that Visual Studio applies to help you differentiate between keywords, comments, and other kinds of code elements.

The C# Express IDE also provides support for building graphical user interfaces (GUIs), which are integral to Windows and web projects. The following pages introduce some of the key features of the IDE.

The IDE is a Multiple Document Interface (MDI) application, much like other Windows applications you may be used to, such as Word and Excel. There is a main window, and within the main window are a number of smaller windows. The central window is the text editing window. Figure 2-3 shows the basic layout.

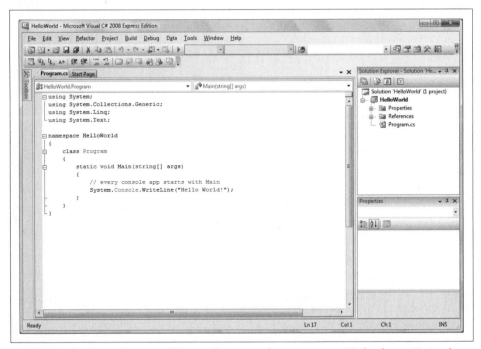

Figure 2-3. The IDE is where you'll be spending most of your time as a C# developer. Notice that the interface contains multiple windows.

To the left of the editing window are a number of tabbed windows that contain tools you may need when creating Windows and web applications. To the right of the editing window are both stacked and tabbed windows. Shown on top is the Solution Explorer, which allows you to examine and manipulate the files in the solution. Below the Solution Explorer is the Properties window. The Properties window is used extensively when you're creating web and Windows desktop applications, but you won't see it when you create console applications.

In Visual Studio 2008, at the bottom of the IDE are five tabbed windows—Error List, Task List, Output, Find Results, and Find Symbol Results—but they don't appear in C# Express.

All of these windows, plus the Toolbox, are resizable and dockable. You can resize any of them by placing the mouse cursor over the edge you want to move. The cursor will change to a double-arrow resizing cursor, at which point you can drag the window edge one way or the other, just like most other windows in the Windows interface.

Right-clicking on the title bar of a dockable window pops up a menu with five mutually exclusive check items:

Floating
> The window will not dock when dragged against the edge of the C# Express 2008 window. The floating window can be placed anywhere on the desktop, even outside the C# Express 2008 window.

Dockable
> The window can be dragged and docked along any side of the C# Express 2008 window, as you'll see later in this chapter.

Tabbed Document
> The window occupies the work surface, with a set of tabs for navigation.

Auto Hide
> The window will disappear, indicated only by a tab, when the cursor is not over the window. It will reappear when the cursor is over the tab. A pushpin in the upper-right corner of the window will be pointing down when Auto Hide is turned off and pointing sideways when it is turned on.

Hide
> The window disappears. To see the window again (to unhide it), use the View main menu item.

If you click the title bar of a window and drag it, it floats free. You can now place it where you want. C# Express 2008 provides guides to help you with locating the window. To see this at work, grab the Properties window and pull it free of its current position. As you move about, the IDE positioning indicators appear, as shown in Figure 2-4.

As you click on each positioning indicator, a shadow appears to show you where the window would go if you release the mouse. Notice in the center of the editing window that there is a cluster of five indicators. If you choose the center square, the window will be tabbed with the current window. To put the Properties window back where it belongs, hover over the Solution Explorer window; a five-part indicator will appear, and you can select the lower indicator to place the Properties window below the tabbed set of the Solution Explorer.

You can also double-click on either the title bar or the tab to dock and undock the window. Double-clicking on the title while docked undocks the entire group. Double-clicking on the tab undocks just the one window, leaving the rest of the group docked.

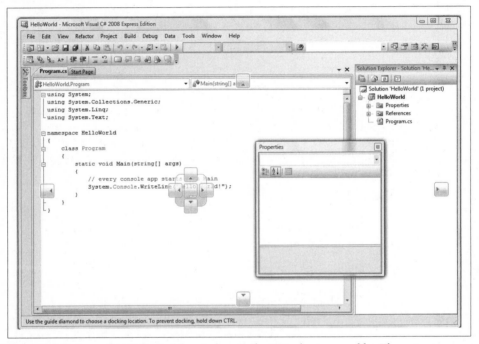

Figure 2-4. You can reposition all of the windows in the IDE wherever you like. The arrow icons are a help when you're positioning windows.

Building and Running Applications

You can run your application at any time by selecting either Start or Start Without Debugging from the Debug menu, or you can accomplish the same results by pressing either F5 or Ctrl-F5, respectively. You can also start the program by clicking the Start icon (▶) on the Standard toolbar.

For console applications, as we mentioned in Chapter 1, the advantage of running the program with Ctrl-F5 is that C# Express 2008 will open your application in a console window, display its results, and then add a line to press a key when you are ready. This keeps the window open until you've seen the results and pressed a key, at which point the window will close. If you choose Start (with debugging) on a console application, if the application doesn't require any user input (as Hello World doesn't), the console window may appear and disappear too quickly for you to see what it did.

You can *build* the program (that is, generate the *.exe* and *.dll* files) by selecting a command under the Build menu. You have the option of building the entire solution or only the currently selected project.

Menus

The menus provide access to many of the commands and capabilities of C# Express 2008. The more commonly used menu commands are duplicated with toolbar buttons for ease of use.

The menus and toolbars are context-sensitive, meaning that the available selection depends on what part of the IDE is currently selected, and what activities are expected or allowed. For example, if the current active window is a code-editing window for a console application such as Hello World, the top-level menu commands are File, Edit, View, Refactor, Project, Build, Debug, Data, Tools, Test (only in the full Visual Studio), Window, and Help.

Many of the menu items have keyboard shortcuts, listed adjacent to the menu item itself. These are composed of one or more keys (referred to as a *chord*), pressed simultaneously. Shortcut keys can be a huge productivity boost because you can use them to perform common tasks quickly, without removing your hands from the keyboard, but it's really a matter of personal preference.

The following sections describe some of the more important menu items and their submenus, focusing on those aspects that are interesting and different from common Windows commands.

The File Menu

The File menu provides access to a number of file-, project-, and solution-related commands. Many of these commands are context-sensitive.

As in most Windows applications, the New menu item creates new items to work on, the Open item opens existing items, and the Save item saves your work. One item you may not have seen before is Save All, which will save all the open files in an open solution. This can be very useful when you're working with a large solution.

The Edit Menu

The Edit menu contains the text editing and searching commands that one would expect, but also includes commands useful in editing code. The most useful are discussed next.

The Clipboard Ring

The Clipboard Ring is like copy-and-paste on steroids. You can copy a number of different selections to the Windows clipboard, using the Edit → Cut (Ctrl-X) or Edit → Copy (Ctrl-C) command. Then use Ctrl-Shift-V to cycle through all the selections, and paste the correct one when it comes around.

> You can change C# Express hot keys systematically or individually; the ones we refer to here and throughout this book are the "standard keys" used when programming in C#. Your mileage may vary.

This submenu item is context-sensitive and is visible only when editing a code window.

Find and Replace

C# Express 2008 includes a number of advanced Find and Replace options that you'll use frequently. The most common ones are discussed in this section.

Quick Find and Quick Replace. These are just slightly jazzed names for slightly jazzed versions of the typical Find and Replace. You can access Quick Find with Ctrl-F and Quick Replace with Ctrl-H. Both commands bring up essentially the same dialog boxes, switchable by a tab at the top of the dialog box, as shown in Figure 2-5.

The search string defaults to the text currently selected in the code window, or, if nothing is selected, to the text immediately after the current cursor location.

The "Look in" drop-down offers a choice of Current Document, All Open Documents, Current Project, Entire Solution, or Current Method.

You can expand or collapse the search options by clicking on the plus/minus button next to the "Find options" item. By default, "Search hidden text" is checked, which allows the search to include code sections currently collapsed in the code window. The Use checkbox allows the use of either regular expressions or wildcards.

> *Regular expressions* are a language unto themselves, expressly designed for incredibly powerful and sophisticated searches. A full explanation of regular expressions is beyond the scope of this book, and isn't really necessary for the sorts of searches you normally conduct when writing code. For a complete discussion of regular expressions, see the SDK documentation, or *Mastering Regular Expressions*, Third Edition, by Jeffrey E. F. Friedl (O'Reilly).

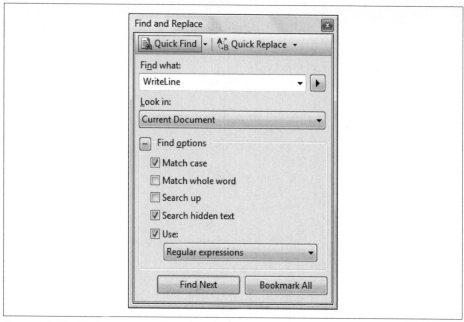

Figure 2-5. The Find and Replace features work mostly like they do in any Windows application, although in C# Express, you have the option of searching single files or the whole solution, and other advanced features such as regular expressions.

If the Use checkbox is checked, the Expression Builder button to the right of the "Find what" text box becomes enabled, providing a very handy way to insert valid regular expression or wildcard characters.

Once you've entered a search string in the "Find what" text box, the Find Next button becomes enabled. In Quick Find mode, there is also a Bookmark All button, which finds all occurrences of the search string and places a bookmark (described shortly) next to the code.

In Quick Replace mode, there is also a "Replace with" text box, and buttons for replacing either a single occurrence or all occurrences of the search string.

Find in Files. Find in Files (Ctrl-Shift-F) is a very powerful search utility that finds text strings anywhere in a directory or in subdirectories (subfolders). It presents the dialog box shown in Figure 2-6. Checkboxes present several self-explanatory options, including the ability to search using either wildcards or regular expressions. Depending on how many files you have in your solution, you may want to use this kind of search as your default first choice.

Find Symbol. Clicking the Find Symbol command (Alt-F12) will bring up the Find Symbol dialog box, which allows you to search for symbols (such as namespaces, classes, and interfaces) and their members (such as properties, methods, events, and

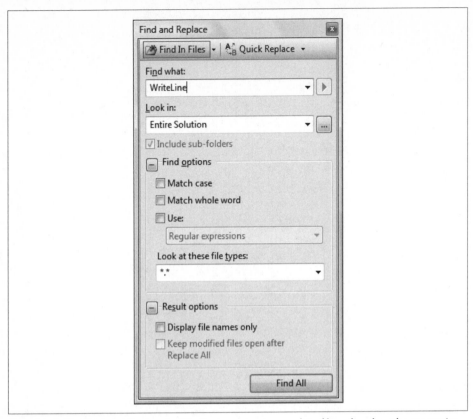

Figure 2-6. The Find and Replace in Files feature lets you search in files other than the one you're working with right now.

variables). It also allows you to search in external components for which the source code is not available.

The search results will be displayed in a window labeled Find Symbol Results. From there, you can move to each location in the code by double-clicking on each result.

Go To

The Go To command brings up the Go To Line dialog box, which allows you to enter a line number and immediately go to that line. It is context-sensitive and is visible only when editing a text window.

Insert File As Text

The Insert File As Text command allows you to insert the contents of any file into your source code, as though you had typed it in. It is context-sensitive and is visible only when editing a text window.

You'll see a standard file-browsing dialog box to search for the file you want to insert. The default file extension will correspond to the project language, but you can search for any file with any extension.

Advanced

The Advanced command is context-sensitive and is visible only when editing a code window. It has many submenu items. These include commands for:

- Viewing whitespace (making tabs and space characters visible on the screen)
- Toggling word wrap
- Commenting and uncommenting blocks of text
- Increasing and decreasing line indenting
- Incremental searching (see "Incremental search")

The following three options are available only in Visual Studio, not C# Express:

- Creating or removing tabs in a selection (converting spaces to tabs and vice versa)
- Forcing selected text to uppercase or lowercase
- Deleting horizontal whitespace

Incremental search

Incremental search allows you to search an editing window by entering the search string character by character. As you enter each character the cursor moves to the first occurrence of matching text.

To use incremental search in a window, select the command on the Advanced submenu, or press Ctrl-I. The cursor icon will change to a pair of binoculars with an arrow indicating the direction of the search. Begin typing the text string to search for.

The case sensitivity of an incremental search will come from the previous Find, Replace, Find in Files, or Replace in Files search (described earlier).

The search will proceed downward and from left to right from the current location. To search backward, use Ctrl-Shift-I.

The key combinations listed in Table 2-1 apply to incremental searching.

Table 2-1. Incremental searching

Key combination	Description
Esc	Stop the search.
Backspace	Remove a character from the search text.
Ctrl-Shift-I	Change the direction of the search.
Ctrl-I	Move to the next occurrence in the file for the current search text.

Bookmarks

Bookmarks are useful for marking spots in your code and easily navigating from marked spot to marked spot. There are several context-sensitive commands on the Bookmarks submenu (listed in Table 2-2). Note that, unless you add the item to the task list, bookmarks are lost when you close the file, although they are saved when you close the solution (as long as the file was still open).

Table 2-2. Bookmark commands

Command	Description
Toggle Bookmark	Places or removes a bookmark at the current line. When a bookmark is set, a blue rectangular icon will appear in the column along the left edge of the code window.
Enable/Disable	Enables or disables the checkboxes for all bookmarks in the Bookmarks window (does not remove bookmarks).
Previous Bookmark	Moves to the previous bookmark.
Next Bookmark	Moves to the next bookmark.
Clear	Removes the bookmark.
Previous Bookmark in Folder (Visual Studio only)	Moves to the previous bookmark in the folder.
Next Bookmark in Folder (Visual Studio only)	Moves to the next bookmark in the folder.
Previous Bookmark in Document	Moves to the previous bookmark in the current document.
Next Bookmark in Document	Moves to the next bookmark in the current document.
Add Task List Shortcut	Adds an entry to the task list (described in "The View Menu" later in this chapter) for the current line. When a task list entry is set, a curved arrow icon appears in the column along the left edge of the code window.

This menu item appears only when the current window is a code window.

Outlining

C# Express 2008 allows you to *outline*, or collapse and expand, sections of your code to make it easier to view the overall structure. When a section is collapsed, it appears with a plus sign in a box along the left edge of the code window. Clicking on the plus sign expands the region.

You can nest the outlined regions so that one section can contain one or more other collapsed sections. Several commands are available to facilitate outlining (shown in Table 2-3).

Table 2-3. Outlining commands

Command	Description
Toggle Outlining Expansion	Reverses the current outlining state of the innermost section in which the cursor lies.
Toggle All Outlining	Sets all sections to the same outlining state. If some sections are expanded and some are collapsed, all will become collapsed.

Table 2-3. Outlining commands (continued)

Command	Description
Stop Outlining	Expands all sections and removes the outlining symbols from view.
Collapse to Definitions	Automatically creates sections for each procedure in the code window and collapses them all.

You can set the default behavior of outlining using the Tools → Options menu item. Go to Text Editor, and then the specific language for which you want to set the options.

IntelliSense

Microsoft IntelliSense technology makes your life much easier. It has real-time, context-sensitive help available, which appears right under your cursor. Code completion automatically completes your thoughts for you, drastically reducing your typing (and therefore, your typing errors). Drop-down lists provide all methods and properties possible in the current context, available at a keystroke or mouse click.

You can configure the default IntelliSense features by going to Tools → Options and then the language-specific pages under Text Editor.

Most of the IntelliSense features appear as you type inside a code window or allow the mouse to hover over a portion of the code. In addition, the Edit → IntelliSense menu item offers numerous commands, the most important of which are shown in Table 2-4.

Table 2-4. IntelliSense commands

Command	Description
List Members	Displays a list of all possible members available for the current context. Keystrokes incrementally search the list. Press any key to insert the highlighted selection into your code; that key becomes the next character after the inserted name. Use the Tab key to select without entering any additional characters.
	This can also be accessed by right-clicking and selecting List Member from the context-sensitive menu.
Parameter Info	Displays a list of numbers, names, and types of parameters required for a method, sub, function, or attribute.
Quick Info	Displays the complete declaration for any identifier (such as a variable name or class name) in your code. This is also enabled by hovering the mouse cursor over any identifier.
Complete Word	Automatically completes the typing of any identifier once you type in enough characters to uniquely identify it. This works only if the identifier is being entered in a valid location in the code.
Insert Snippet	Displays a selection of code snippets to insert, such as the complete syntax for a `switch` case block or an `if` block.
Surround With	Displays a selection of code snippets to surround a block of code, such as a class declaration.

The member list presents itself when you type a dot operator following any class or member name.

Every member of the class is listed, and each member's type is indicated by an icon. There are icons for methods, fields, properties, events, and so forth. In addition, each icon may have a second icon overlaid to indicate the accessibility of the member: public, private, protected, and so on. If there is no accessibility icon, the member is public.

 If the member list does not appear, make sure you have added all the necessary using statements.

Two of the subcommands under the IntelliSense menu item, Insert Snippet and Surround With, tap into a great feature to reduce typing and minimize errors: *code snippets*. A code snippet is a chunk of code that replaces an alias. A short alias is replaced with a much longer code snippet. For example, the alias switch would be replaced with:

```
switch ( switch_on )
{
    default:
}
```

with the expression switch_on highlighted in yellow and the cursor in place, ready to type in your own expression. In fact, all the editable fields will be highlighted, and you can use the Tab key to navigate through them, or Shift-Tab to go backward. Any changes made to the editable field are immediately propagated to all the instances of that field in the code snippet. Press Enter or Esc to end the field editing and return to normal editing.

To do a straight alias replacement, either select Insert Snippet from the menu, or more easily, press Ctrl-K, Ctrl-X. Or, just type an alias in the code window and an IntelliSense menu will pop up with a list of aliases, with the current one highlighted. Press Tab to insert the snippet.

Alternatively, a code snippet can surround highlighted lines of code—say, with a for construct. To surround lines of code with a code snippet construct, highlight the code and then either select Surround With from the menu or press Ctrl-K, Ctrl-S.

The View Menu

The View menu is a context-sensitive menu that provides access to the myriad windows available in the C# Express 2008 IDE. You will probably keep many of these windows open all the time; others you will use rarely, if at all.

The View menu is context-sensitive. For example, with an ASP.NET content file on the work surface, the first three menu items will be Code, Designer, and Markup; the Code and Designer menu items will be omitted if you're looking at a code-behind file. You don't need to worry about what these terms mean for now; you'll see them in the closing chapters of the book.

When the application is running, a number of other windows, primarily used for debugging, become visible or available. You access these windows via the Debug → Windows menu item, not from the View menu item.

C# Express 2008 can store several different window layouts. In particular, it remembers a completely different set of open windows during debug sessions than it does during normal editing. These layouts are stored per-user, not per-project or per-solution.

Class View

The Class View window (Ctrl-Shift-C) shows all the classes in the solution in a hierarchical manner. A typical Class View window, somewhat expanded, is shown in Figure 2-7.

As with the Solution Explorer, you can right-click any item in the Class View window, which exposes a pop-up menu with a number of context-sensitive menu items. This can provide a convenient way to sort the display of classes in a project or solution, or to add a method, property, or field to a class.

Code Definition

The Code Definition window (Ctrl-W, D) is used in developing web pages, but is available only in the full version of Visual Studio.

Error List

The Error List window (Ctrl-W, Ctrl-E), which is available in all editor views, displays errors, warnings, and messages generated as you edit and compile your project. Syntax errors flagged by IntelliSense are displayed here, as well as deployment errors. Double-clicking on an error in this list will open the offending file and move the cursor to the error location.

Output

The Output window (Ctrl-Alt-O) displays status messages from the IDE, such as build progress. You can set the Output window to display by default when a build starts by going to Tools → Options → Projects and Solutions → General and checking "Show Output window when build starts".

This window is available in all editor views.

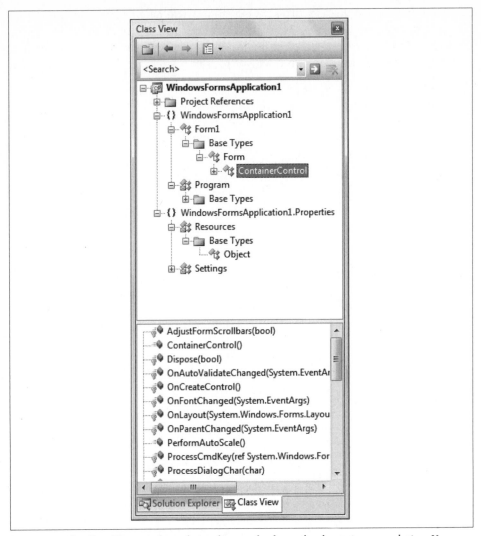

Figure 2-7. The Class View window, obviously enough, shows the classes in your solution. You won't have many of these at first, but Windows applications will have plenty.

Properties

The Properties window (F4) displays all the properties for the currently selected item. Some of the properties (such as Font) may have subproperties, indicated by a plus sign next to their entries in the window. The property values on the right side of the window are editable.

One thing that can be confusing is that certain items have more than one set of properties. For example, a Form content file can show two different sets of properties, depending on whether you select the source file in the Solution Explorer or the form as shown in the Design view.

A typical Properties window is shown in Figure 2-8.

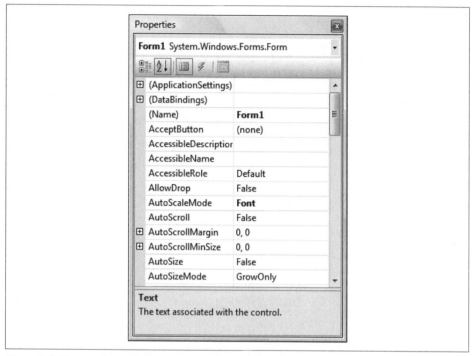

Figure 2-8. You won't use the Properties window much with console applications, but when you design Windows Forms, you'll use it a lot.

The name and type of the current object are displayed in the field at the top of the window. In Figure 2-8, it is an object named Form1, of type Form, contained in the System.Windows.Forms namespace.

You can edit most properties in place in the Properties window. The Font property has subproperties that you can set directly in the window by clicking on the plus sign to expand its subproperties, and then editing the subproperties in place.

The Properties window has several buttons just below the name and type of the object. The first two buttons on the left toggle the list by category or alphabetically. The next two buttons from the left toggle between displaying properties for the selected item and displaying events for the selected item. The rightmost button displays property pages for the object, if there are any.

Some objects have both a Properties window and property pages. The property pages display additional properties not shown in the Properties window.

The box below the list of properties displays a brief description of the selected property.

Task List

In large applications, keeping a to-do list can be quite helpful. C# Express 2008 provides this functionality with the Task List window.

Toolbox

The Toolbox command (Ctrl-Alt-X) displays the Toolbox if it is not currently displayed. If it is currently displayed, nothing happens—it does not toggle the display. To hide the Toolbox, click on the X in the Toolbox title bar.

Other Windows

Several other windows have been relegated to a submenu called Other Windows. These include:

The Command window (Ctrl-Alt-A)
> You use this window to enter commands directly.

The Object Test Bench window
> This window lets you conduct tests on your classes as you write them, but only in Visual Studio.

The Property Manager window
> You use this window only for C++ projects; it isn't available in C# Express.

The Resource View window (Ctrl-Shift-E)
> This window displays the resource files included in the project. Resources are nonexecutable data deployed with an application, such as icons and graphics, culture-specific text messages, and persisted data objects.

The Macro Explorer window (Alt-F8)
> Visual Studio 2008 offers the ability to automate repetitive chores with macros. A *macro* is a set of instructions written in VB.NET, either created manually or recorded by the IDE, saved in a file. The Macro Explorer is the one of the main tools for viewing, managing, and executing macros. It provides access into the Macro IDE.

The Start Page
> This item simply reopens the Start Page, if you closed it.

The Web Browser
> This item opens a web browser within the Visual Studio window.

The Refactor Menu

Refactoring is the process of taking code duplicated in various parts of your program and extracting it out to a callable method. This is an advanced procedure, so you won't see any refactoring in this book.

 For details on refactoring, we highly recommend the book *Refactoring: Improving the Design of Existing Code*, by Martin Fowler et al. (Addison-Wesley Professional).

The Refactor menu item is available when you're looking at a code window for a web page, user control, or language source code file. It is also available from context menus when you right-click on an identifier in a Class View, Object Browser, or Solution Explorer window.

The refactoring menu items will modify your code—for example, extracting common code to a method and then calling that method in the place from which it was extracted.

The Project Menu

The Project menu provides functionality related to project management. It is visible only when the solution is selected in the Solution Explorer. All of the functionality exposed by the Project menu is also available in the Solution Explorer, by right-clicking on the solution.

The Build Menu

The Build menu offers menu items for building the current project (highlighted in the Solution Explorer) or the solution. It also exposes the Configuration Manager for configuring the build process.

The Debug Menu

The Debug menu allows you to start an application with or without debugging, set breakpoints in the code, and control the debugging session.

The Data Menu

The context-sensitive Data menu is visible only when in Design mode when creating, for example, web applications.

The Format Menu

The Format menu is visible only in Design mode when creating, for example, web applications; further, the commands under it are context-sensitive to the control(s) currently selected.

The Tools Menu

The Tools menu presents commands accessing a wide variety of functionality, ranging from connecting to databases to accessing external tools to setting IDE options. Some of the more useful commands are described in the following sections.

Connect to Device

The Connect to Device command (available only in Visual Studio) brings up a dialog box that allows you to connect to either a physical mobile device or an emulator.

Device Emulator Manager

The Device Emulator Manager command (also available only in Visual Studio) helps you keep track of the various settings for devices and their emulators for which you may be developing.

Connect to Database

The Connect to Database command brings up the dialog box that allows you to select a server, log in to that server, and connect to the database on the server. Microsoft SQL Server is the default database (surprise!), but the Change button allows you to connect to any number of other databases, including any for which there are Oracle or ODBC providers.

Connect to Server

The Connect to Server command (available only in Visual Studio) brings up a dialog box that lets you enter a remote server to connect to, either by name or by IP address.

Code Snippets Manager

The Code Snippets Manager command (Ctrl-K, Ctrl-B) brings up the Code Snippets Manager dialog box, which allows you to maintain the code snippets (described in "IntelliSense" earlier in this chapter). This dialog box allows you to add or remove code snippets for any of the supported languages. You can also import code snippets and search online for code snippets.

Choose Toolbox Items

The Choose Toolbox Items command brings up the Choose Toolbox dialog box, allowing you to add COM components and custom controls. The details of doing so are beyond the scope of this book, but they are covered in full in *Programming ASP.NET 3. 5* by Jesse Liberty et al. (O'Reilly).

External Tools

Depending on the options selected at the time C# Express 2008 was installed on your machine, you may have one or more external tools available on the Tools menu. These might include tools such as Create GUID and Dotfuscator Community Edition. (Use of these tools is beyond the scope of this book.)

The Tools → External Tools command allows you to add additional external tools to the Tools menu. When you select this command, you are presented with the External Tools dialog box. This dialog box has fields for the tool title, the command to execute the tool, any arguments and the initial directory, as well as several checkboxes for different behaviors.

Import and Export Settings

The Import and Export Settings command brings up the Import and Export Settings dialog box, which is a wizard for importing and exporting IDE settings. With this wizard, you can transfer your carefully wrought IDE settings from one machine to the next.

Options

The Options command also brings up the Options dialog box that allows you to set a wide variety of options, ranging from the number of items to display in lists of recently used items to HTML Designer options.

The Window Menu

The Window menu is the same as the Window menu you'll find in most standard Windows applications. It displays a list of all the currently open windows, allowing you to bring any window to the foreground by clicking on it. Note that all the file windows currently displayed in the IDE also have tabs along the top edge of the work surface, below the toolbars (unless you have selected MDI mode in Tools → Options → Environment → General), and you can select windows by clicking on a tab.

The Help Menu

The Help menu provides access to a number of submenus.

If you are developing on a machine with enough horsepower, Dynamic Help is a wonderful thing. Otherwise, it can diminish the responsiveness of the IDE.

Summary

- Visual Studio 2008 is a powerful tool with many features to make writing programs easier.
- The Start Page provides an overview of your programming environment and a list of recent projects.
- A solution is a set of related projects, and a project is a set of related code files and associated resources, such as images and so on.
- Visual Studio 2008 has a number of templates that allow you to create particular types of projects, such as windows or web applications.
- Among other things, C# Express 2008 provides WYSIWYG support for building, testing, and debugging graphical user interfaces (GUIs).
- Every window in C# Express 2008 can be resized and moved.
- To run your application, select Start or Start Without Debugging, or press F5 or Ctrl-F5.
- The Clipboard Ring can hold a number of different selections that you can cycle through.
- The Find and Replace feature lets you locate text strings in the current file or other files, using normal text or regular expressions.
- Bookmarks enable you to mark spots in your code so that you can easily find them later.
- IntelliSense saves you keystrokes and can help you discover methods and required arguments by (for example) listing possible completions to what you're typing.
- The Properties window displays properties for the currently selected item.

There's your whirlwind tour of the C# Express interface. If you're new to programming, the IDE probably looks quite intimidating—it has a lot more features and windows than your average Windows application. As with any Windows application, though, you'll quickly find that you use some of the features quite often, and those will become second nature, allowing you to ignore the rest until you need them. We don't expect you to be an expert on the IDE after just reading this chapter, but we do hope you're a bit more comfortable with it. Now, enough poking about in the Toolbox—let's hammer some nails! It's time to start learning the basics of the C# language, starting with types, variables, and constants, and that's what's ahead in Chapter 3.

Test Your Knowledge: Quiz

Question 2-1. What is the difference between a project and a solution?

Question 2-2. How do you move windows in the IDE?

Question 2-3. What does the pushpin do on a window?

Question 2-4. What is the difference between pressing F5 and pressing Ctrl-F5 from within C# Express 2008?

Question 2-5. What is the Clipboard Ring?

Question 2-6. How do you retrieve items from the Clipboard Ring?

Question 2-7. What is Find Symbol for?

Question 2-8. What are bookmarks?

Question 2-9. What is IntelliSense?

Question 2-10. What is a code snippet?

Test Your Knowledge: Exercises

Exercise 2-1. Insert a bookmark before the `Console.Writeline()` statement in Hello World. Navigate away from it and then use the Bookmarks menu item to return to it.

Exercise 2-2. Undock the Solution Explorer window from the right side of the IDE and move it to the left. Leave it there if you like, or move it back.

Exercise 2-3. Insert a code snippet for a `for` loop from the Edit → IntelliSense menu into your Hello World program after the `WriteLine()` statement. (It won't do anything for now; you'll learn about for loops in Chapter 5.)

CHAPTER 3

C# Language Fundamentals

Chapter 1 demonstrates a very simple C# program that prints the text string "Hello World!" to the console screen and provides a line-by-line analysis of that program. However, even that simple program was complex enough that we had to skip some of the details. In this chapter, we'll begin an in-depth exploration of the syntax and structure of the C# language. The *syntax* of a language is the order of the keywords, where you put semicolons, and so forth. The *semantics* are what you are expressing in the code, and how your code fits together. Syntax is trivial and unimportant, but because compilers are absolute sticklers for correct syntax, novice programmers pay a lot of attention to syntax until they are comfortable. Fortunately, Visual Studio 2008 makes managing syntax much easier so that you can focus on semantics, which are far more important.

In this chapter, we'll introduce statements and expressions, the building blocks of any program. You'll learn about variables and constants, which let you store values for use in your program. We'll also begin an explanation of types, and we'll take a look at strings, which you saw briefly in the Hello World program. This is all very basic stuff, but it's the foundation you need to start getting fancy. Without variables, your applications can't actually process any data. All variables need types, and variables are used in expressions. You'll see how neatly this all fits together.

Statements

In C#, a complete program instruction is called a *statement* and each statement ends with a semicolon (;). Forgetting a semicolon is a very common mistake for novice programmers, but Visual Studio will catch you if you do it. Programs consist of sequences of statements, such as the following:

```
int myVariable;                     // a statement
myVariable = 23;                    // another statement
int anotherVariable = myVariable;   // yet another statement
```

The compiler starts at the beginning of a source code file and reads downward, executing each statement in the order in which the compiler encounters it. This would be entirely straightforward, and terribly limiting, were it not for branching. Branching allows you to change the order in which statements are evaluated, and even take different paths depending on the value of your variables, but let's not get ahead of ourselves. We'll get to branching in Chapter 5.

Types

C# is a *strongly typed* language. That means that every object you create or use in a C# program must have a specific *type*. In other words, you must declare the object to be an integer or a string or a Dog or a Button. Essentially, the type indicates the characteristics of the object and what it can do.

Types come in two flavors: those that are built into the language (*intrinsic* types) and those you create yourself (classes and interfaces, discussed in Chapters 7 and 13). C# offers a number of intrinsic types, shown in Table 3-1.

Table 3-1. The intrinsic types built into C#

C# type	Size (in bytes)	.NET type	Description
byte	1	Byte	Unsigned (values between 0 and 255).
char	2	Char	Unicode characters (a modern way of storing most characters, including international language characters).
bool	1	Boolean	True or false.
sbyte	1	SByte	Signed (values between −128 and 127).
short	2	Int16	Signed (short) (values between −32,768 and 32,767).
ushort	2	UInt16	Unsigned (short) (values between 0 and 65,535).
int	4	Int32	Signed integer values between −2,147,483,648 and 2,147,483,647.
uint	4	UInt32	Unsigned integer values between 0 and 4,294,967,295.
float	4	Single	Floating-point number. Holds the values from approximately +/−1.5 × 10^{-45} to approximately +/−3.4 × 10^{38} with seven significant figures.
double	8	Double	Double-precision floating-point. Holds the values from approximately +/−5.0 × 10^{-324} to approximately +/−1.8 × 10^{308} with 15 to 16 significant figures.
decimal	12	Decimal	Fixed-precision up to 28 digits and the position of the decimal point. This type is typically used in financial calculations. Requires the suffix "m" or "M" when you declare a constant.
long	8	Int64	Signed integers ranging from −9,223,372,036,854,775,808 to 9,223,372,036,854,775,807.
ulong	8	UInt64	Unsigned integers ranging from 0 to approximately 1.85 × 10^{19}.

Each type has a name (such as int) and a size (such as 4 bytes). The size tells you how many bytes each object of this type occupies in memory. Programmers generally don't like to waste memory if they can avoid it, but with the cost of memory these days, you don't need to be particular about the memory cost of types. Most of the time, if you're using whole numbers you'll use an int, even if a short would be fine. Likewise, double is the commonly used type for decimal numbers, even though float is just fine in most cases. The Description column in Table 3-1 lists the minimum and maximum values you can hold in objects of each type.

> Each C# type corresponds to an underlying .NET type. Thus, what C# calls an int, .NET calls an Int32. This is interesting only if you care about sharing objects across languages.

Intrinsic types aren't very flexible, although you'll use them a lot. You can use them to add two numbers together, and they can display their values as strings. User-defined types can do a lot more; their abilities are determined by the methods you create, which we'll get to in Chapter 8.

Objects of an intrinsic type are called *variables*, and we'll talk about those later in this chapter.

Numeric Types

Most of the intrinsic types are used for working with numeric values (byte, sbyte, short, ushort, int, uint, float, double, decimal, long, and ulong).

You can divide the numeric types into two sets: unsigned and signed. An unsigned value (byte, ushort, uint, ulong) can hold only positive values. A signed value (sbyte, short, int, long) can hold positive or negative values, but in a different range of values. For example, short and ushort are both 16-bit values, which means they can hold one of 65,536 possible values (2^{16}). The ushort holds only positive (unsigned) numbers, so the range is from 0 to 65,535 (not 65,536, because you need one spot for zero). A short is signed, and can hold values from –32,768 to 32,767 (again, not 32,768, because you need one spot for zero).

You also can categorize types into those used for integer values (whole numbers) and those used for floating-point values (fractional or rational numbers). The byte, sbyte, ushort, uint, ulong, short, int, and long types all hold whole number values.

> The byte and sbyte types are not used very often, and we won't describe them in this book.

The double and float types hold fractional values. Although double is larger than float, and you would think that float would suffice most of the time, the compiler assumes that any number with a decimal point in it is a double unless you follow the number with the letter f. That is, 4.7 is assumed to be double, but 4.7f is a float. The decimal value type was added to the language to support scientific and financial applications; to use it, you append an m to the end, just as you do with the f for a float. The float and double types have a very slight amount of imprecision to them if the values are very large or very small—not something you'll need to worry about in this book, certainly, but it might cause problems if you were trying to do very precise scientific or financial calculations, which is why decimal is there.

Typically, you decide which size integer to use (short, int, or long) based on the magnitude of the value you want to store. For example, a ushort can only hold values from 0 through 65,535, whereas a uint can hold values from 0 through 4,294,967,295.

That being said, in real life most of the time you'll simply declare your numeric variables to be of type int, unless there is a good reason to do otherwise. (Most programmers choose signed types unless they have a good reason to use an unsigned value. This is, in part, just a matter of tradition.)

Suppose you need to keep track of inventory for a book warehouse. You expect to house up to 40,000 or even 50,000 copies of each book. A signed short can only hold up to 32,767 values. You might be tempted to use an unsigned short (which can hold up to 65,535 values), but it is easier and preferable to just use a signed int (with a maximum value of 2,147,483,647). That way, if you have a runaway bestseller, your program won't break (if you anticipate selling more than 2 billion copies of your book, perhaps you'll want to use a long!).

 Throughout this book, we will use int wherever it works, even if short or byte might be usable alternatives. Memory is cheap these days, and programmer time is expensive. There are circumstances where the difference in memory usage would be significant (for example, if you are going to hold 1 billion values in memory), but we'll keep things simple by using the int type whenever possible.

Nonnumeric Types: char and bool

In addition to the numeric types, the C# language offers two other types: char and bool.

The char type is used from time to time when you need to hold a single character. The char type can represent a simple character (A), a Unicode character (\u0041), or an escape sequence ('\n'). We won't discuss Unicode characters in this book, and you'll see escape sequences later, where we'll explain them in context. When you refer to a char in your code, you need to surround it with single quotes, like this: 'A'.

The one remaining important type is bool, which holds a Boolean value. A Boolean value is one that is either true or false. Boolean values are used frequently in C# programming, as you'll see throughout this book. Virtually every comparison (is myDog bigger than yourDog?) results in a Boolean value.

The bool type was named after George Boole (1815–1864), an English mathematician who published *An Investigation into the Laws of Thought, on Which Are Founded the Mathematical Theories of Logic and Probabilities*, and thus created the science of Boolean algebra.

Types and Compiler Errors

The compiler will help you by complaining if you try to use a type improperly. The compiler complains in one of two ways: it issues a warning or it issues an error.

You are well advised to treat warnings as errors. Stop what you are doing, figure out why there is a warning, and fix the problem. Never ignore a compiler warning unless you are certain that you know exactly why the warning was issued and that you know something the compiler does not.

To have Visual Studio enforce this for you, follow these steps:

1. Right-click on a project in the Solution Explorer, and select Properties from the pop-up menu.

2. Click on the Build tab in the Properties window.

3. In the "Treat all warnings as errors" section of the page, select the All radio button.

Programmers talk about design time, compile time, and runtime. Design time is when you are designing the program, compile time is when you compile the program, and runtime is (surprise!) when you run the program.

The earlier in your development process that you unearth a bug, the better. It is easier to fix a bug in your logic at design time than to fix the bug once it has been written into code. Likewise, it is better (and cheaper) to find bugs in your program at compile time than at runtime. Not only is it better, it is more reliable. A compile-time bug will fail every time you run the compiler, but a runtime bug can hide. Runtime bugs can slip under a crack in your logic and lurk there (sometimes for months), biding their time, waiting to come out when it will be most expensive (or most embarrassing) to you.

It will be a constant theme of this book that you *want* the compiler to find bugs. The compiler is your friend (though we admit, at times it feels like your nemesis). The more bugs the compiler finds, the fewer bugs your users will find.

A strongly typed language such as C# helps the compiler find bugs in your code. Here's how: suppose you tell the compiler that milo is of type Dog. Sometime later you try to use `milo` to display text (calling the `ShowText` method). Oops, `Dogs` don't display text. Your compiler will stop with an error:

```
Dog does not contain a definition for 'ShowText'
```

Very nice. Now you can go figure out whether you used the wrong object or you called the wrong method.

Visual Studio .NET actually finds the error even before the compiler does. When you try to add a method, as soon as you type the dot character, IntelliSense pops up a list of valid methods to help you, as shown in Figure 3-1.

Figure 3-1. IntelliSense is your friend. When you start to type in a method, IntelliSense helpfully provides a list of possible methods, to ensure that you pick a valid one.

When you try to add a method that does not exist, it won't be in the list. That is a pretty good clue that you are not using the object properly.

WriteLine( ) and Output

The .NET Framework provides a useful method for displaying output on the screen in console applications: `System.Console.WriteLine( )`. How you use this method will become clearer as you progress through the book, but the fundamentals are straight-forward. You call the method, and in the parentheses you pass in a string that you want printed to the console (the screen), as in the Hello World application in Chapter 1.

That's useful; a string is fixed text, and you might want to output a value that can change, depending on the content of your program. For that, you can also pass in substitution parameters. A *substitution parameter* is just a placeholder for a value you want to display. For example, you might pass in the substitution parameter {0} as part of the string, and then when you run the program, you'll substitute the value held in the variable `myInt` so that its value is displayed where the parameter {0} appears in the `WriteLine( )` statement.

Here's how it works. Each substitution parameter is a number between braces, starting with 0 for the first parameter, 1 for the next, and so on. So, if you're using just one substitution parameter, it might look like this:

```
System.Console.WriteLine("Age of student: {0}", myInt);
```

Notice that you follow the quoted string with a comma and then a variable name. The value of the variable will be substituted into the parameter. If myInt has the value 15, the statement shown previously causes the following to display:

```
Age of student: 15
```

If you have more than one parameter, the variable values will be substituted in the order they appear in the method, as in the following:

```
System.Console.WriteLine("Age of first student: {0},
    age of second student: {1}", myInt, myOtherInt);
```

If myInt has the value 15 and myOtherInt has the value 20, this will cause the following to display:

```
Age of first student: 15, and age of second student: 20.
```

There are other special characters that you can use to format the output, like this:

```
System.Console.WriteLine("Student ages:\nFirst student:\t{0}\n
                 Second student:\t{1}", myInt, myOtherInt);
```

This produces output that looks like this:

```
Student ages:
First student:    15
Second student:   20
```

The characters that begin with a slash character (\) are called *escaped characters*. The slash is a signal to the compiler that what follows is an escaped character. The code and the slash together are considered a single character. The escaped character \t indicates a tab, and the character \n indicates a newline (a line feed, or a carriage return). The string here will print the characters Student ages: followed by a newline (\n), then the text First student: followed by a tab (\t), then the value of the first parameter ({0}), and a newline character (\n), then the text Second student: followed by a tab (\t), and finally the value of the second parameter ({1}).

You'll see a great deal more about WriteLine( ) in later chapters.

Variables and Assignment

A C# variable is roughly the same as the variables you remember from your ninth grade algebra class: it's a placeholder for a value. To put it more technically, a variable is an instance of an intrinsic type (such as int) that can hold a value:

```
int myVariable = 15;
```

You *initialize* a variable by writing its type (int in this case), its *identifier*, and then assigning a value to that variable. The equals sign (=) is the *operator* for assignment. You're not defining an equation in a mathematical sense; you're telling the compiler to set the contents of the variable on the left of the operator to the value of whatever is on the right of the operator. In this specific case, you're saying "myVariable is an int, and it's assigned the value of 15." There are other operators, and we'll cover them in Chapter 4, but you need to know about assignment now because variables aren't much good without it.

An *identifier* is just an arbitrary name you assign to a variable, method, class, or other element. In this case, the variable's identifier is myVariable.

You can define variables without initializing them; just leave off the assignment and the value:

```
int myVariable;
```

You can then assign a value to myVariable later in your program:

```
int myVariable;
// some other code here
myVariable = 15; // assign 15 to myVariable
```

You can also change the value of a variable later in the program. That is why they're called variables; their values can vary, and that's what makes them useful.

```
int myVariable;
// some other code here
myVariable = 15; // assign 15 to myVariable
// some other code here
myVariable = 12; // now it is 12
```

Technically, a variable is a named storage location (that is, stored in memory) with a type. After the final line of code in the previous example, the value 12 is stored in the named location myVariable.

Example 3-1 illustrates the use of variables. To test this program, open Visual Studio .NET and create a console application, just as you did with Hello World in Chapter 1. Type in the code shown in bold in Example 3-1.

Example 3-1. You initialize a variable by declaring its type and assigning it a value; later, you can assign it a different value

```
using System;
using System.Collections.Generic;
using System.Linq;
using System.Text;

namespace Example_3_1____Using_variables
{
    class Values
    {
        static void Main( )
```

Example 3-1. You initialize a variable by declaring its type and assigning it a value; later, you can assign it a different value (continued)

```
        {
            int myInt = 7;
            System.Console.WriteLine("Initialized, myInt: {0}", myInt);
            myInt = 5;
            System.Console.WriteLine("After assignment, myInt: {0}", myInt);
        }
    }
}
```

Press Ctrl-F5, or select Debug → Start Without Debugging to build and run this application. As we mentioned in Chapter 1, if you press F5, the console window will disappear almost immediately; using Ctrl-F5 allows the window to stick around so that you can read it. The output looks like this:

```
Initialized, myInt: 7
After assignment, myInt: 5
```

Example 3-1 initializes the variable myInt to the value 7, displays that value, reassigns the variable with the value 5, and displays it again.

Definite Assignment

C# requires *definite assignment*; you have to initialize a variable, or assign a value to it, before you can "use" it—that is, before you can output it or manipulate it in any way. To test this rule, change the line that initializes myInt in Example 3-1 to:

```
    int myInt;
```

Save the revised program shown in Example 3-2.

Example 3-2. You have to initialize variables before you can use them; this code won't compile

```
using System;
using System.Collections.Generic;
using System.Linq;
using System.Text;

namespace Example_3_2____Definite_Assignment
{
    class Values
    {
        static void Main()
        {
            int myInt;
            System.Console.WriteLine("Initialized, myInt: {0}", myInt);
            myInt = 5;
            System.Console.WriteLine("After assignment, myInt: {0}", myInt);
        }
    }
}
```

When you try to compile Example 3-2, the C# compiler will open the Error List window in the IDE, and will display the following error message:

```
Use of unassigned local variable 'myInt'
```

You can't use an uninitialized variable in C#; doing so violates the rule of definite assignment. In this case, "using" the variable `myInt` means passing it to `WriteLine( )`.

So, does this mean you must initialize every variable? No, but if you don't initialize your variable, you must assign a value to it before you attempt to use it. Example 3-3 illustrates a corrected program.

Example 3-3. This code fixes Example 3-2; you don't have to initialize the variable when you create it, but you do have to assign some value to it before you use it

```csharp
using System;
using System.Collections.Generic;
using System.Linq;
using System.Text;

namespace Example_3_3____Definite_assignment
{
    class Values
    {
        static void Main( )
        {
            int myInt;
            //other code here...
            myInt = 7; // assign to it
            System.Console.WriteLine("Assigned, myInt: {0}", myInt);
            myInt = 5;
            System.Console.WriteLine("Reassigned, myInt: {0}", myInt);
        }
    }
}
```

You can even assign the same value to multiple variables, like this:

```csharp
int a, b, c, d;
a = b = c = d = 5;
```

In this case, a, b, c, and d would all have the value 5. This works because the C# compiler performs the rightmost assignment first; that is, d = 5. That assignment itself returns a value, the value 5. The compiler then assigns that returned value to c. That second assignment also returns a value, and so on, until all the variables have been assigned.

Implicitly Typed Variables

There's one additional type of variable we can discuss, now that you understand assignment: the *implicitly typed variable*. The C# compiler can determine the type of a variable by analyzing the type of the value that you assign to it. For example, look at these assignment statements:

```
var firstVariable = 6;
var secondVariable = 3.5;
var thirdVariable = "I'm a string!";
```

The compiler assigns firstVariable as type int, secondVariable as type double, and thirdVariable as type string. You don't have to explicitly assign the type.

Be very clear, though: these variables *are* typed, and if you later try to assign an object of the wrong type to them you will generate a compiler error. And once the implicit type is set, it cannot be changed, not even explicitly. If you try to do something like this, you'll get an error:

```
firstVariable = secondVariable;
```

Just as if you had explicitly declared firstVariable to be of type int, once it is implicitly typed, you cannot assign the value of a variable of type double to it, because you would lose part of the value, as you'll see in Chapter 4.

You may be wondering: if the compiler can determine the types of the variables for you, why not just use var all the time, instead of bothering with explicitly declaring types? A key reason is that implicit types make your code harder to read, and thus harder to maintain. This is more than enough reason to avoid using var except where needed. A second reason is that the compiler may guess incorrectly, and thus introduce small but nasty errors into your code. If you were writing a math program, and you used var with your assignments like this:

```
var a = 12;
var b = 7;
```

the compiler will decide that both a and b should be of type int. But if you were thinking they should be of type double, and later try something like this:

```
a = 7.4;
b = 5.5;
```

you'll get an error, because the compiler can't read your mind.

Casting

You can cause the compiler to ignore its rules of type safety and treat an object of one type as though it were an object of another type, if the types are compatible. This is called *casting*. Casting can be either implicit or explicit.

An *implicit conversion* happens automatically; the compiler takes care of it for you. If you have a short, and you assign it to a variable of type int, the compiler automatically (and silently) casts it for you. You don't have to take any action. This is safe, because an int variable can hold any value that might have been in a short variable.

```
short myShort = 5;
// other code here...
int myint = myShort; // implicit conversion
```

Programmers often talk about this as though the short were being turned into an int. What is actually happening is that the compiler is accepting a short where it expects to find an int, because that is a safe thing to do.

Implicit conversion works only when there is no possibility of loss of data, though. Take a look at this:

```
int myInt;
double myDouble = 4.7;
myInt = myDouble;
```

If you try that assignment, the compiler gives you an error message because you can't squeeze a decimal number into an integer space. You would lose the fractional part (.7). In fact, even if you wrote:

```
int myInt;
double myDouble = 4
myInt = myDouble;
```

the compiler would still generate an error. Although there is no fractional part to lose in this case (the double is holding a whole number), the compiler can't take the chance that something might happen that could change the conditions, so it simply rejects all assignments of a double to an int.

This is where *explicit conversions* come in—when there is danger of losing data. For example, although the compiler will let you convert an int to a double implicitly (there's no chance you can lose data), it will not let you implicitly convert a double to an int, as you've seen.

If you happen to know that it is perfectly safe in your particular situation to make the assignment—if you know what you are doing—you can force the compiler to accept the assignment with an explicit cast.

Again, some programmers talk about "casting the double into an integer," but you're not really changing either variable at all; you're just instructing the compiler to ignore its type-safety rules for this moment and accept the assignment of the value held by the double variable to the integer variable. The compiler will comply, and it will in fact throw away any fractional part.

You specify an explicit conversion by placing the type you want to assign to in parentheses, immediately in front of the variable with the risky value:

```
int myDouble = 4.7;
// other code here...
int myInt = (int) myDouble; // explicit conversion
```

The keyword (int) is necessary to make the explicit conversion; without it the compiler will generate an error. Notice, though, that in this case, you're slicing off the fractional value of the double; and myInt will have only the integral part (4), which is why we say you should know what you're doing.

Sometimes you need an explicit conversion (though not often), but it is usually when you are taking an object out of a collection and you need to convert it to its "real" type, all of which we'll discuss in a later chapter. Even then, you test to make sure the object you have is what you think it is. With this sort of explicit conversion, you are almost guaranteed to lose value sooner or later.

Constants

Variables are a powerful tool, but sometimes you want to use a defined value, one whose value you want to ensure remains constant. A *constant* is like a variable in that it can store a value. However, unlike a variable, you cannot change the value of a constant while the program runs.

For example, you might need to work with the Fahrenheit freezing and boiling points of water in a program simulating a chemistry experiment. Your program will be clearer if you name the variables that store these values `FreezingPoint` and `BoilingPoint`, but you do not want to permit their values to be changed while the program is executing. The solution is to use a constant. Constants come in three flavors: *literals*, *symbolic* constants, and *enumerations*.

Literal Constants

A literal constant is just a value. For example, 32 is a literal constant. It does not have a name; it is just a literal value. And you can't make the value 32 represent any other value. The value of 32 is always 32. You can't assign a new value to 32, and you can't make 32 represent the value 99 no matter how hard you might try. You'll use literal constants a lot, but you probably won't think of them as such.

Symbolic Constants

Symbolic constants assign a name to a constant value. You declare a symbolic constant using the following syntax:

```
const type identifier = value;
```

The const keyword is followed by a type, an identifier, the assignment operator (=), and the value to assign to the constant.

This is similar to declaring a variable except that you start with the keyword const and symbolic constants *must* be initialized. Once initialized, a symbolic constant cannot be altered. For example, in the following declaration, 32 is a literal constant and `FreezingPoint` is a symbolic constant of type int:

```
const int FreezingPoint = 32;
```

Example 3-4 illustrates the use of symbolic constants.

Example 3-4. This program defines two symbolic constants and outputs their values; it won't compile, though, because of the attempt to assign a new value to a constant

```
using System;
using System.Collections.Generic;
using System.Linq;
using System.Text;

namespace Example_3_4____Symbolic_Constants
{
    class Values
    {
        static void Main()
        {
            const int FreezingPoint = 32; // degrees Fahrenheit
            const int BoilingPoint = 212;

            System.Console.WriteLine("Freezing point of water: {0}",
                                     FreezingPoint);
            System.Console.WriteLine("Boiling point of water: {0}",
                                     BoilingPoint);

            BoilingPoint = 21;
        }
    }
}
```

Example 3-4 creates two symbolic integer constants: FreezingPoint and BoilingPoint. (See the "Naming Conventions" sidebar for a discussion of how to name symbolic constants.)

These constants serve the same purpose as using the literal values 32 and 212 for the freezing and boiling points of water, respectively, in expressions that require them. However, because the constants have names, they convey far more meaning. It might seem easier to just use the literal values 32 and 212 instead of going to the trouble of declaring the constants, but if you decide to switch this program to Celsius, you can reinitialize these constants at compile time to 0 and 100, respectively, and all the rest of the code should continue to work.

If you try to run the program shown in Example 3-4, you'll receive the following error:

```
The left-hand side of an assignment must be a variable, property or indexer
```

That's because the assignment in this line is illegal:

```
BoilingPoint = 21;
```

You can't assign a new value to a constant, so the compiler complains. To fix this problem, simply comment out the offending line by adding two slashes in front of it, like this:

```
// BoilingPoint = 21;
```

Now the program runs as expected, without an error.

Enumerations

Enumerations provide a powerful alternative to literal or simple symbolic constants. An *enumeration* is a distinct value type, consisting of a set of named constants (called the enumerator list).

In Example 3-4, you created two related constants:

```
const int FreezingPoint = 32;
const int BoilingPoint = 212;
```

You might want to add a number of other useful constants to this list as well, such as:

```
const int LightJacketWeather = 60;
const int SwimmingWeather = 72;
const int WickedCold = 0;
```

Notice, however, that this process is somewhat cumbersome; also, this syntax doesn't show any logical connection among these various constants—they're just a set of unrelated values. *You* know that these constants all refer to temperature, but the compiler has no way of knowing that. C# provides an alternative construct, the *enumeration*, which allows you to group logically related constants, as in the following:

```
enum Temperatures
{
    WickedCold = 0,
    FreezingPoint = 32,
    LightJacketWeather = 60,
    SwimmingWeather = 72,
    BoilingPoint = 212,
}
```

The entries in the enumeration are separated by commas. Many programmers like to leave a comma after the last entry in an enumeration as a convenience for adding more values later. Other programmers find this, at best, sloppy. The code will compile either way.

The syntax for specifying an enumeration uses the enum keyword, as follows:

enum *identifier* [*:base-type*] {*enumerator-list*};

 In a specification statement such as the preceding example, the square brackets indicate an optional element. Thus, you can declare an enum with no base type, simply by leaving it out (leave out the square brackets as well).

There are also optional attributes and modifiers you can use, but you don't need them right now. An enumeration begins with the keyword enum, which is generally followed by an identifier; in this case, Temperatures:

```
enum Temperatures
```

The base type is the underlying type for the enumeration. You might specify that you are declaring constant ints, constant longs, or something else. If you leave out this optional value (and often you will), it defaults to int, but you are free to use any of the integral types (ushort, long) except for char. For example, the following fragment declares an enumeration with unsigned integers (uint) as the base type:

```
enum ServingSizes : uint
{
    Small = 1,
    Regular = 2,
    Large = 3
}
```

Notice that an enum declaration ends with the enumerator list, which contains the constant assignments for the enumeration, each separated by a comma. Example 3-5 rewrites Example 3-4 to use an enumeration.

Example 3-5. An enumeration represents a set of values that you don't want to change while your program is running

```
using System;
using System.Collections.Generic;
using System.Linq;
using System.Text;

namespace Example_3_5____Enumerations
{
    class Values
    {
        // declare the enumeration
```

Example 3-5. An enumeration represents a set of values that you don't want to change while your program is running (continued)

```
enum Temperatures
{
    WickedCold = 0,
    FreezingPoint = 32,
    LightJacketWeather = 60,
    SwimmingWeather = 72,
    BoilingPoint = 212,
}

static void Main( )
{
    System.Console.WriteLine("Freezing point of water: {0}",
                            (int)Temperatures.FreezingPoint);
    System.Console.WriteLine("Boiling point of water: {0}",
                            (int)Temperatures.BoilingPoint);
}
}
}
```

In Example 3-5, you declare an enumerated constant called Temperatures. When you want to use any of the values in an enumeration in a program, the values of the enumeration must be qualified by the enumeration name. That is, you can't just refer to FreezingPoint; instead, you use the enumeration identifier (Temperature) followed by the dot operator and then the enumerated constant (FreezingPoint). This is called *qualifying* the identifier FreezingPoint. Thus, to refer to the FreezingPoint, you use the full identifier Temperature.FreezingPoint.

You might want to display the value of an enumerated constant to the console, as in the following:

```
Console.WriteLine("The freezing point of water is {0}",
                  (int) Temperature.FreezingPoint);
```

To make this work properly, you must cast the constant to its underlying type (int). In this case, you are saying, "Treat this enumerated constant as an int." Because you know the underlying type is int, this is safe to do. (See "Casting" earlier in this chapter.)

In Example 3-5, the values in the two enumerated constants FreezingPoint and BoilingPoint are both cast to type int; then that integer value is passed to WriteLine( ) and displayed.

Each constant in an enumeration corresponds to a numerical value. In Example 3-5, each enumerated value is an integer. If you don't specifically set it otherwise, the enumeration begins at 0 and each subsequent value counts up from the previous. Thus, if you create the following enumeration:

```
enum SomeValues
{
```

```
    First,
    Second,
    Third = 20,
    Fourth
}
```

the value of First will be 0, Second will be 1, Third will be 20, and Fourth will be 21.

Strings

It is nearly impossible to write a C# program without creating strings, and we wouldn't want to deprive you of them here. Strings are actually complex classes that we'll cover much more thoroughly in Chapter 15. For now, though, all you need to know is that a string object holds a series of characters.

You declare a string variable using the string keyword much as you would create an instance of any type:

```
string myString;
```

You specify a *string literal* by enclosing it in double quotes:

```
"Hello World"
```

You already used a string literal back in Chapter 1, in the Hello World example.

You'll frequently initialize a string variable by assigning it a string literal:

```
string myString = "Hello World";
```

Whitespace

In the C# language, spaces, tabs, and newlines are considered to be *whitespace* (so named because you see only the white of the underlying "page"). Extra whitespace is generally ignored in C# statements. Thus, you can write:

```
myVariable = 5;
```

or:

```
myVariable         =             5    ;
```

and the compiler will treat the two statements as identical. The key is to use whitespace to make the program more readable to the programmer; the compiler is indifferent.

The exception to this rule is that whitespace within a string is treated as literal; it is not ignored. If you write:

```
Console.WriteLine("Hello World")
```

each space between "Hello" and "World" is treated as another character in the string. (In this case, there is only one space character.)

Problems arise only when you do not leave space between logical program elements that require it. For instance, the expression:

```
int             myVariable    =               5          ;
```

is the same as:

```
int myVariable=5;
```

but it is *not* the same as:

```
intmyVariable =5;
```

The compiler knows that the whitespace on either side of the assignment operator is extra, but at least some whitespace between the type declaration int and the variable name myVariable is *not* extra; it is required.

This is not surprising; the whitespace allows the compiler to *parse* the keyword int rather than some unknown term intmyVariable. You are free to add as much or as little whitespace between int and myVariable as you care to, but there must be at least one whitespace character (typically a space or tab).

 Visual Basic programmers take note: in C#, the end-of-line has no special significance. Statements are ended with semicolons, not newline characters. There is no line continuation character because none is needed.

Summary

- A complete program instruction is called a statement. Each statement ends with a semicolon (;).
- All objects, variables, and constants must have a specific type.
- Most of the intrinsic types are used for working with numeric values. You will commonly use int for whole numbers and double or float for fractional values.
- The char type is used for holding a single character.
- The bool type can hold only the value true or false.
- A variable is an instance of a type. You initialize a variable by creating it with an assigned value.
- You can use the var keyword to create a variable without a type, but only if you assign it immediately. The complier will determine the type of the variable from the value assigned.
- You can cast a value from one type to another as long as the compiler knows how to turn the original type into the cast-to type. If no information can be lost, you may cast from one type to another implicitly. If information may be lost, you must cast explicitly. You accomplish the cast by prefacing the variable with the name of the type you want to cast to, in parentheses.

- A constant is similar to a variable, but the value cannot be changed while the program is running. Literal constants are simply values used on their own. Symbolic constants, indicated with the const keyword, are values with assigned names, which you use like variables, but the values cannot change.

- An enumeration is a value type that consists of a set of named constants.

- A string object holds a series of characters (such as a word or sentence). A string literal is simply text enclosed by double quotes. You can assign a string to a string variable, just as you would make any other assignment.

- Extra whitespace (spaces, tabs, and newline characters) is ignored by the compiler, unless it appears within a string.

We promised you fundamentals in this chapter, and that's what you got. Just about every programming language you want to learn starts with data types, variables, and assignment. Without variables to hold your data, there isn't much to program with. So, now you know how to hold onto data within the bounds of your program. But what can you do with it? At the moment, you know how to print it out to the screen, and that's about it. That will change in Chapter 4. There, we'll show you how to manipulate the data with some basic operators, just like you remember from math class. We'll also show you how to compare variables too, which may not sound like much, but it's critically important, as you'll see in Chapter 5.

Test Your Knowledge: Quiz

Question 3-1. What defines a statement in C#?

Question 3-2. What values can a bool type have?

Question 3-3. What are the two kinds of *types* in C#, and what's the difference between them?

Question 3-4. What is the difference between a float and a double?

Question 3-5. What's the definition of a variable?

Question 3-6. What does definite assignment mean?

Question 3-7. Which of the following code statements will compile?

```
int myInt = 25;
long myLong = myInt;
int newInt = myLong;
```

Question 3-8. For each of the following pieces of data, which variable type would you use, and which should be represented with constants?

- Your age in years
- The speed of light in meters per second
- The number of widgets in your warehouse
- The amount of money in your bank account
- The text of the U.S. Declaration of Independence

Question 3-9. Given the following declaration, how would you refer to the constant for Green and what would its value be?

```
enum WavelengthsOfLight
{
  Red = 7000,
  Orange = 6200,
  Yellow = 5800,
  Green = 5300,
  Blue = 4700,
  Violet = 4200
}
```

Question 3-10. How do you indicate a string literal?

Test Your Knowledge: Exercises

Exercise 3-1. We'll start easy for this project. Write a short program that creates five variables, one of each of the following types: int, float, double, char, and string. Name the variables whatever you like. Initialize the variables with the following values:

- int: 42
- float: 98.6
- double: 12345.6789
- char: Z
- string: The quick brown fox jumped over the lazy dogs.

Then, output the values to the console.

Exercise 3-2. As you gain more experience with programming, you'll frequently find yourself adapting some code that you wrote before, instead of writing a new program from scratch—and there's no time like the present to start. Modify the program in Exercise 3-1 so that after you've output the values of the variables the first time, you change them to the following:

- `int`: 25
- `float`: 100.3
- `double`: 98765.4321
- `char`: M
- `string`: A quick movement of the enemy will jeopardize six gun boats.

Then output the values to the console a second time.

Exercise 3-3. Write a new program to declare a constant `double`. Call the constant `Pi`, set its value to 3.14159, and output its value to the screen. Then change the value of `Pi` to 3.1 and output its value again. What happens when you try to compile this program?

Exercise 3-4. Write a new program and create a constant enumeration with constants for each month of the year. Give each month the value equal to its numeric place in the calendar, so January is 1, February is 2, and so on. Then output the value for June, with an appropriate message.

CHAPTER 4

Operators

An *operator* is a symbol (such as =, +, or >) that causes C# to take an action. That action might be an assignment of a value to a variable, the addition of two values, a comparison of two values, and so forth. In that respect, most C# operators aren't much different from the ones you remember from math class, and they're intended to be just that intuitive. There are some special operators whose meanings aren't obvious, and we'll cover those, too.

In the preceding chapter, you were introduced to the assignment operator. The single equals sign (=) is used to assign a value to a variable; in this case, the value 15 to the variable myVariable:

```
myVariable = 15;
```

C# has many different operators that you'll learn about in this chapter. There's a full set of mathematical operators, and a related set of operators just for incrementing and decrementing in integral values by one, which actually are quite useful for controlling loops, as you'll learn in Chapter 5. Operators are also available for comparing two values that are used in the branching statements, as we'll also demonstrate in Chapter 5.

Expressions

Any statement that returns a value is an *expression*. You've already seen the assignment expression, which we'll discuss in more detail in a moment, and we've mentioned that the assignment expression returns the value that's assigned. In this chapter, you'll see a number of mathematical expressions, which return a computed value, and also comparison expressions, which return the Boolean value true or false.

The Assignment Operator (=)

As you saw in Chapter 3, the assignment operator causes the operand on the left side of the operator to have its value changed to whatever is on the right side of the operator. The following expression assigns the value 15 to myVariable:

```
myVariable = 15;
```

The operand on the right doesn't have to be a constant; it can be another variable. For example, if myVariable is set to 15, you can then write this:

```
myOtherVariable = myVariable;
```

This means that myOtherVariable is now equal to the value in myVariable, which is 15. Remember that in assignment, it's the variable on the left that gets the assigned value.

The assignment operator also allows you to *chain* assignments, assigning the same value to multiple variables, as follows:

```
myOtherVariable = myVariable = 15;
```

The preceding statement assigns 15 to myVariable, and then also assigns the value (15) to myOtherVariable. This works because the statement:

```
myVariable = 15;
```

is an expression; it evaluates to the value assigned. That is, the expression:

```
myVariable = 15;
```

itself evaluates to 15, and it is this value (15) that is then assigned to myOtherVariable.

 It is important not to confuse the assignment operator (=) with the equality, or equals, operator (==), which has two equals signs and is described later in the chapter. The assignment operator does not test for equality; it assigns a value.

Mathematical Operators

C# uses five mathematical operators: four for standard calculations and one to return the remainder when dividing integers. The following sections consider the use of these operators.

Simple Arithmetic Operators (+, –, *, /)

C# offers four operators for simple arithmetic: the addition (+), subtraction (–), multiplication (*), and division (/) operators. The + and – operators are obvious, and work as you might expect. The * operator for multiplication may look a bit odd if you're not used to it, but there's nothing else special about it. Division, however, is slightly unusual, depending on the types you're dividing.

When you divide two integers, C# divides like a child in the third grade: it throws away any fractional remainder. Thus, dividing 17 by 4 returns a value of 4 (C# discards the remainder of 1).

This limitation is specific to *integer* division. If you do not want the fractional part thrown away, you can use one of the types that support decimal values, such as float or double. Division between two floats (using the / operator) returns a decimal answer. Integer and floating-point division is illustrated in Example 4-1.

Example 4-1. Integer division is different from float division; in integer division, C# discards the remainder

```
using System;
using System.Collections.Generic;
using System.Linq;
using System.Text;

namespace Example_4_1____Integer_and_Float_Division
{
    class Program
    {
        public static void Main( )
        {
            int smallInt = 5;
            int largeInt = 12;
            int intQuotient;
            intQuotient = largeInt / smallInt;
            Console.WriteLine("Dividing integers. {0} / {1} = {2}",
                            largeInt, smallInt, intQuotient);

            float smallFloat = 5;
            float largeFloat = 12;
            float FloatQuotient;
            FloatQuotient = largeFloat / smallFloat;
            Console.WriteLine("Dividing floats. {0} / {1} = {2}",
                              largeFloat, smallFloat, FloatQuotient);

        }
    }
}
```

The output looks like this:

```
Dividing integers. 12 / 5 = 2
Dividing floats. 12 / 5 = 2.4
```

The Modulus Operator (%)

Of course, you might want to calculate the remainder from an integer division, not throw it away. For that, C# provides a special operator, modulus (%), to retrieve the remainder. For example, the statement 17%4 returns 1 (the remainder after integer division).

You read that statement as "Seventeen modulo four equals one" or, for short, "Seventeen mod four."

Example 4-2 demonstrates the effect of division on integers, floats, doubles, and decimals. Notice the escaped characters used in the output, which we discussed in "WriteLine( ) and Output" in Chapter 3.

Example 4-2. The modulus operator (%) is what you use to get the remainder from an integer division operation

```
using System;
using System.Collections.Generic;
using System.Linq;
using System.Text;

namespace Example_4_2____Modulus_operator
{
    class ValuesProgram
    {
        static void Main( )
        {
            int firstInt, secondInt;
            float firstFloat, secondFloat;
            double firstDouble, secondDouble;
            decimal firstDecimal, secondDecimal;

            firstInt = 17;
            secondInt = 4;
            firstFloat = 17;
            secondFloat = 4;
            firstDouble = 17;
            secondDouble = 4;
            firstDecimal = 17;
            secondDecimal = 4;
            Console.WriteLine("Integer:\t{0}\nfloat:\t\t{1}",
                    firstInt / secondInt, firstFloat / secondFloat);
            Console.WriteLine("double:\t\t{0}\ndecimal:\t{1}",
                    firstDouble / secondDouble, firstDecimal / secondDecimal);
```

Example 4-2. The modulus operator (%) is what you use to get the remainder from an integer division operation (continued)

```
Console.WriteLine("\nRemainder (modulus) from integer division:\t{0}",
                    firstInt % secondInt);


        }
    }
}
```

The output looks like this:

```
Integer:            4
float:              4.25
double:             4.25
decimal:            4.25
Remainder(modulus) from integer division:         1
```

The modulus operator is more than a curiosity; it greatly simplifies finding every *n*th value, as you'll see in Chapter 5.

Increment and Decrement Operators

You'll often find yourself needing to manipulate the value in a variable, and then store that result back in the original variable. Suppose, for example, that you have a variable inventory, which you use to keep track of the quantity of widgets you have in your warehouse. You wouldn't want to have to create new variables every time inventory increases or decreases; you want the current value to always be available in inventory. C# provides several operators for just these kinds of calculations.

The Calculate and Reassign Operators

Suppose you want to increase the mySalary variable by 5,000 (congratulations on your raise!). You can do this by writing:

```
mySalary = mySalary + 5000;
```

In simple arithmetic, this would make no sense, but that's because it's not an equation, it's a C# assignment expression. In C#, this line means "add 5,000 to the value in mySalary, and assign the sum back to mySalary." Thus, after this operation completes, mySalary will have been incremented by 5,000. You can perform this kind of assignment with any mathematical operator:

```
mySalary = mySalary * 5000;
mySalary = mySalary - 5000;
```

and so forth.

The need to perform this kind of manipulation is so common that C# includes special operators for self-assignment. These operators are +=, -=, *=, /=, and %=, which, respectively, combine addition, subtraction, multiplication, division, and modulus with self-assignment. Thus, you can write the previous three examples as:

```
mySalary += 5000;
mySalary *= 5000;
mySalary -= 5000;
```

These three instructions, respectively, increment mySalary by 5,000, multiply mySalary by 5,000, and subtract 5,000 from the mySalary variable.

Increment or Decrement by 1

You may have noticed from the preceding section that C# developers like to save keystrokes. Another mathematical operation you'll use a lot is incrementing and decrementing by exactly 1. You'll find that you need counters of all sorts, starting with loop controllers in Chapter 5. C# provides two additional special operators for these purposes: increment (++) and decrement (--).

So, if you want to increment the variable myAge by 1, you can write:

```
myAge++;
```

This is equivalent to writing either of the following:

```
myAge = myAge + 1;
myAge += 1;
```

The Prefix and Postfix Operators

To complicate matters further, you might want to increment a variable and assign the results to a second variable:

```
resultingValue = originalValue++;
```

That raises a question: do you want to assign before you increment the value, or after? In other words, if originalValue starts out with the value 10, do you want to end with both resultingValue and originalValue equal to 11, or do you want resultingValue to be equal to 10 (the original value) and originalValue to be equal to 11?

C# offers two specialized ways to use the increment and decrement operators: *prefix* and *postfix*. The way you use the ++ operator determines the order in which the increment/decrement and assignment take place.

To use the prefix operator to increment, place the ++ symbol before the variable name; to use the postfix operator to increment, place the ++ symbol after the variable name:

```
result = ++original; // prefix
result = original++; // postfix
```

It is important to understand the different effects of prefix and postfix, as illustrated in Example 4-3. Note the output.

Example 4-3. The prefix and postfix operators behave slightly differently; the prefix operator increments before you assign; the postfix operator assigns, then increments

```
using System;
using System.Collections.Generic;
using System.Linq;
using System.Text;

namespace Example_4_3____Prefix_and_Postfix
{
    class Program
    {
        static void Main( )
        {
            int original = 10;
            int result;

            // increment then assign
            result = ++original;
            Console.WriteLine("After prefix: {0}, {1}", original, result);

            // assign then increment
            result = original++;
            Console.WriteLine("After postfix: {0}, {1}", original, result);
        }
    }
}
```

The output looks like this:

```
After prefix: 11, 11
After postfix: 12, 11
```

Look at the prefix increment from Example 4-3 again:

```
result = ++original;
```

The semantics of the prefix increment operator are "increment the value of `original` and then assign the incremented value to `result`." So, `original` starts with a value of 10, you increment that to 11, and assign it to `result`. In the end, both variables have the value of 11.

Now look at the postfix increment:

```
result = original++;
```

The semantics here are "assign the value of `original` to `result`, and then increment `original`." The value of `original` is 11 at this point, which gets assigned to `result`, and then `original` is incremented.

The prefix and postfix operators work the same way with the decrement operators, for the same reasons, as shown in Example 4-4. Again, note the output.

Example 4-4. Decrementing with the prefix and postfix operators works the same as incrementing

```
using System;
using System.Collections.Generic;
using System.Linq;
using System.Text;

namespace Example_4_4____Decrement_Operators
{
    using System;
    class Program
    {
        static void Main()
        {
            int original = 10;
            int result;

            // increment then assign
            result = --original;
            Console.WriteLine("After prefix: {0}, {1}", original, result);

            // assign then increment
            result = original--;
            Console.WriteLine("After postfix: {0}, {1}", original, result);
        }
    }
}
```

The output looks like this:

```
After prefix: 9, 9
After postfix: 8, 9
```

The increment operators are meant to be a convenient shortcut to save you keystrokes, and as you go through this book, you'll see them used in various common ways, such as controlling loops. Remember, though, that one of the goals of good programming is readability. If you overuse the prefix and postfix operators in an attempt to be efficient with your typing, but six months from now you're trying to puzzle out what your code does and how, you haven't really saved any time. If you think that using these operators will make your code confusing, go ahead and write out the expression the long way. You may thank yourself later.

Relational Operators

Relational operators compare two values and then return a Boolean value (true or false, as described in Chapter 3). The *greater than* operator (>), for example, returns true if the value on the left of the operator is greater than the value on the right. Thus, 5>2 returns the value true, whereas 2>5 returns the value false.

The relational operators for C# are shown in Table 4-1. This table assumes two variables: `bigValue` and `smallValue`, in which `bigValue` has been assigned the value 100, and `smallValue` the value 50.

Table 4-1. C# relational operators (assumes bigValue = 100 and smallValue = 50)

Name	Operator	Given this statement	The expression evaluates to
Equals	==	`bigValue == 100` `bigValue == 80`	True False
Not equals	!=	`bigValue != 100` `bigValue != 80`	False True
Greater than	>	`bigValue >` `smallValue`	True

Greater than or equal to	>=	`bigValue >=`
		`smallValue`
		`smallValue >=`
		`bigValue`
			True
			
			False

Less than	<	`bigValue <` `smallValue`	False

Less than or equal to	<=	`smallValue <=`
		`bigValue`
		`bigValue <=`
		`smallValue`
			True
			
			False

Each of these relational operators acts as you might expect. Notice that most of these operators are composed of two characters. For example, the "greater than or equal to" operator (>=) is made up of the greater-than symbol (>) and the equals sign (=). The symbols must appear in that order for the operator to be valid; =< isn't a valid operator, and => is a different operator altogether, but one you won't see until much later in the book.

Notice also that the equals operator is made up of two equals signs (==) because the single equals sign alone (=) is reserved for the assignment operator.

A very common beginner mistake is to confuse the assignment operator (=) with the equals operator (==). Even experienced programmers do this from time to time. Just remember that the latter has two equals signs, and the former only one.

The C# equals operator (==) tests for equality between the objects on either side of the operator. This operator evaluates to a Boolean value (`true` or `false`). Thus, the statement:

```
myX == 5;
```

evaluates to `true` if and only if the `myX` variable has a value of 5.

Logical Operators and Conditionals

As you program, you'll often want to test whether a condition is true; for example, using the if statement, which you'll see in the next chapter. C# provides a set of logical operators for this: and, or, and not. These operators work with the Boolean variables introduced in Chapter 3. Remember that a bool variable can hold only one of two values: true or false. Boolean expressions can be a bit confusing if you're not used to them, but they're critical to controlling the flow of your program, as you'll learn in Chapter 5. Let's take this slowly, with some examples. Start with three bool variables:

```
bool p = true;
bool q = false;
book r = true;
```

The variable p, by itself, evaluates to true, as does r, and q by itself evaluates to false. Easy enough. The and operator, which uses the symbol &&, evaluates to true only if *both* variables are true:

```
p && q   // evaluates false
p && r   // evaluates true
```

The or operator, which uses the symbol ||, evaluates to true if *either* variable is true:

```
p || q   // evaluates true
```

The only way for an or expression to evaluate to false is if *both* variables are false. Of course, if both variables are true, the expression still evaluates to true.

The not operator is slightly different; it operates on only a single variable, and evaluates to the *opposite* of the value of the variable:

```
!p   // evaluates false
!q   // evaluates true
```

 You may have noticed that the and and or operators use doubled symbols (&& and ||) instead of single ones (& and |). The single symbols are for *logical* or *bitwise* operations, which you don't need to bother with in this chapter.

Let's make things a bit more complicated. Often you will want to test whether two conditions are true, whether only one is true, or whether neither is true. An individual expression is enclosed in parentheses, and that expression is evaluated before anything else. Table 4-2 shows some more examples. The examples in this table assume two variables, x and y, in which x has the value 5 and y has the value 7.

Table 4-2. Logical operators

Name	Operator	Given this statement	The expression evaluates to	Logic
And	&&	(x == 3) && (y == 7)	False	Both must be true.
Or	||	(x == 3) || (y == 7)	True	Either or both must be true.
Not	!	!(x == 3)	True	Expression must be false.

The first line in Table 4-2 uses the and operator:

```
(x == 3) && (y == 7)
```

The entire expression evaluates false because one side (x == 3) is false. (Remember that x has the value 5 and y has the value 7.)

With the or operator, only one side must be true; the expression is false only if both sides are false. So, in the case of the example in Table 4-2:

```
(x == 3) || (y == 7)
```

the entire expression evaluates true because one side (y == 7) is true.

With a not operator, the statement is true if the expression is false, and vice versa. So, in the accompanying example:

```
!(x == 3)
```

the entire expression is true because the tested expression (x == 3) is false. (The logic is: "it is true that it is not true that *x* is equal to 3.")

Boolean logic takes a little time and practice to get used to before you can "read" these expressions naturally, but with a little experience it becomes second nature. You'll be seeing them a lot, starting in the next chapter. Conditional operators are what allow your program to take actions in response to certain data values. Without them, your program could run in only a straight line, from start to finish.

The Conditional Operator

Although most operators are unary (they require one term, such as myValue++) or binary (they require two terms, such as a+b), there is one *ternary* operator, which requires three terms, named the conditional operator (? :):

```
cond-expr ? expression1 : expression2
```

This operator evaluates a *conditional* expression (an expression that returns a value of type bool) and then invokes either *expression1* if the value returned from the conditional expression is true, or *expression2* if the value returned is false. The logic is: "if this is true, do the first; otherwise, do the second." Example 4-5 illustrates this concept.

Example 4-5. The ternary operator is a simple kind of control flow statement; depending on the value of the expression, it can take one of two stated actions

```
using System;
using System.Collections.Generic;
using System.Linq;
using System.Text;

namespace Example_4_5____Ternary_Operator
{
    class ValuesProgram
    {
        static void Main()
        {
            int valueOne = 10;
            int valueTwo = 20;

            int maxValue = valueOne > valueTwo ? valueOne : valueTwo;

            Console.WriteLine("ValueOne: {0}, valueTwo: {1}, maxValue: {2}",
              valueOne, valueTwo, maxValue);

        }
    }
}
```

The output looks like this:

```
ValueOne: 10, valueTwo: 20, maxValue: 20
```

In Example 4-5, the ternary operator is being used to test whether valueOne is greater than valueTwo. If so, the value of valueOne is assigned to the integer variable maxValue; otherwise, the value of valueTwo is assigned to maxValue.

As with the increment operator, although the conditional operator can save you some keystrokes, you can achieve the same effect with an if statement, which we'll discuss in Chapter 5. If you think there may be some confusion as a result of using the conditional operator, you're probably better off writing it out.

Operator Precedence

The compiler must know the order in which to evaluate a series of operators. For example, if you write:

```
myVariable = 5 + 7 * 3;
```

there are three operators for the compiler to evaluate (=, +, and *). It could, for example, operate left to right, which would assign the value 5 to myVariable, then add 7 to the 5 (12) and multiply by 3 (36)—but of course, then it would throw that 36 away. This is clearly not what is intended.

The rules of precedence tell the compiler which operators to evaluate first. As is the case in algebra, multiplication has higher precedence than addition, so 5+7×3 is equal to 26 rather than 36. Both multiplication and addition have higher precedence than assignment, so the compiler will do the math and then assign the result (26) to myVariable only after the math is completed.

In C#, you can also use parentheses to change the order of precedence much as you would in algebra. Thus, you can change the result by writing:

```
myVariable = (5+7) * 3;
```

Grouping the elements of the assignment in this way causes the compiler to add 5+7, multiply the result by 3, and then assign that value (36) to myVariable.

Table 4-3 summarizes operator precedence in C#, using x and y as possible terms to be operated upon.[*]

Table 4-3. Operator precedence

Category	Operators
Primary	`(x) x.y x->y f(x) a[x] x++ x-- new typeof sizeof checked unchecked stackalloc`
Unary	`+ - ! ~ ++x --x (T)x *x &x`
Multiplicative	`* / %`
Additive	`+ -`
Shift	`<< >>`
Relational	`< > <= >= is as`
Equality	`== !=`
Logical (bitwise) AND	`&`
Logical (bitwise) XOR	`^`
Logical (bitwise) OR	`|`
Conditional AND	`&&`
Conditional OR	`||`
Conditional	`?:`
Assignment	`= *= /= %= += -= <<= >>= &= ^= |=`

The operators are listed in precedence order according to the category in which they fit. That is, the primary operators (such as x++) are evaluated before the unary operators (such as !). Multiplication is evaluated before addition.

There are a lot of operators in this table, and you don't need to memorize their order of precedence. It never hurts to use parentheses if you're not sure of the exact order.

---

[*] This table includes operators that are beyond the scope of this book. For a fuller explanation of each, please see *Programming C#*, Fifth Edition, by Jesse Liberty and Donald Xie (O'Reilly).

The compiler doesn't mind if you use them where they're not needed, and it may help to make the operation clearer to readers of your code.

In some complex equations, you might need to nest parentheses to ensure the proper order of operations. For example, say you want to know how many seconds a hypothetical family wastes each morning. The adults spend 20 minutes over coffee each morning and 10 minutes reading the newspaper. The children waste 30 minutes dawdling and 10 minutes arguing.

Here's the algorithm:

```
(((minDrinkingCoffee + minReadingNewspaper )* numAdults ) +
((minDawdling + minArguing) * numChildren)) * secondsPerMinute;
```

 An *algorithm* is a well-defined series of steps to accomplish a task.

Although this works, it is hard to read and hard to get right. It's much easier to use interim variables:

```
wastedByEachAdult = minDrinkingCoffee + minReadingNewspaper;
wastedByAllAdults = wastedByEachAdult * numAdults;
wastedByEachKid = minDawdling + minArguing;
wastedByAllKids = wastedByEachKid * numChildren;
wastedByFamily = wastedByAllAdults + wastedByAllKids;
totalSeconds = wastedByFamily * 60;
```

The latter example uses many more interim variables, but it is far easier to read, understand, and (most importantly) debug. As you step through this program in your debugger, you can see the interim values and make sure they are correct. See Chapter 9 for more information.

Summary

- An operator is a symbol that causes C# to take an action.
- The assignment operator (=) assigns a value to an object or variable.
- C# includes four simple arithmetic operators, +, -, *, and /, and numerous variations such as +=, which increments a variable on the left side of the operator by the value on the right side.
- When you divide integers, C# discards any fractional remainder.
- The modulus operator (%) returns just the remainder from integer division.
- C# includes numerous special operators, such as the self-increment (++) and self-decrement (--) operators.

- To increment a value before assigning it, you use the prefix operator (++x); to increment the value after assigning it, use the postfix operator (x++). The same rule applies to the decrement operator.

- The relational operators compare two values and return a Boolean. These operators are often used in conditional statements.

- The conditional operator (? :) is the only ternary operator found in C#. The test condition is found to the left of the question mark; it invokes the expression to the left of the colon if the tested condition evaluates true and the expression to the right of the colon if the tested condition evaluates false.

- The compiler evaluates operators according to a series of precedence rules, and parentheses have the "highest" precedence.

- It is good programming practice to use parentheses to make your order of precedence explicit if there may be any ambiguity.

You saw a lot of math in this chapter, which is certainly useful, because your programs will often perform mathematical operations. We also mentioned several times that these operators will be useful in Chapter 5. Chapter 5 deals with branching, the technique by which you enable your program to take different actions depending on the values contained in the variables. Chapter 5 is going to tie together what you've learned so far, and enable you to take the next step with your programming skills.

Test Your Knowledge: Quiz

Question 4-1. What is the difference between the = and == operators?

Question 4-2. Suppose I have four different variables, a, b, c, and d. What's the shortest way to assign them all the value 36?

Question 4-3. What's the difference between dividing two ints and dividing two doubles?

Question 4-4. What is the purpose of the % operator?

Question 4-5. What is the output of these operations?

- 4 * 8
- (4 + 8) / (4 − 2)
- 4 + 8 / 4 − 2

Question 4-6. Let `myInt = 25` to start. What is the value of `myInt` at each stage of the following code?

```
myInt += 5;
myInt -= 15;
myInt *= 4;
myInt /= 3;
```

Question 4-7. Describe the difference between the prefix and postfix operators.

Question 4-8. Let x = 25 and y = 5. What do these expressions evaluate to?

```
(x >= y)
(x >= y * 5)
(x == y)
(x = y)
```

Question 4-9. Let x = 25 and y = 5. What do these expressions evaluate to?

```
(x >= y) && (y <= x)
!(x > y)
!(x < y) && (x > y)
((x > y) || !(x < y)) && (x > y)
((x > y) && ((y < x) || (x > y))) && (x == y)
```

Question 4-10. Arrange these operators in order of precedence:

```
%
!=
?:
&&
++
```

Test Your Knowledge: Exercises

Exercise 4-1. Write a program that assigns the value 25 to variable x, and 5 to variable y. Output the sum, difference, product, quotient, and modulus of x and y.

Exercise 4-2. What will be the output of the following method? Why?

```
static void Main()
{
    int varA = 5;
    int varB = ++varA;
    int varC = varB++;
    Console.WriteLine( "A: {0}, B: {1}, C: {2}", varA, varB, varC );
}
```

Exercise 4-3. Imagine an amusement park ride that holds two passengers. Because of safety restrictions, the combined weight of the two passengers must be more than 100 pounds, but no more than 300 pounds. Now imagine a family of four who want to ride this ride. Abby weighs 135 pounds, Bob weighs 175 pounds, their son Charlie weighs 55 pounds, and their daughter Dawn weighs 45 pounds.

Write a program that calculates whether the weight of the two combined passengers falls within the accepted range. Use constants for the maximum and minimum weights, and for the weight of each family member. The output should look something like this, for Abby and Dawn:

```
Abby and Dawn can ride? True
```

Calculate three separate cases: whether the two parents can ride together, just Bob and Charlie, and just the kids.

Exercise 4-4. Now it's time for a little high school math. Take a sphere of radius 5. Calculate and output the surface area, and the volume of the sphere. Then use the ternary operator to indicate which of the two is greater. Make Pi a constant float, and use a value of 3.14159 for precision. You should probably also make the radius a constant.

CHAPTER 5

Branching

All the statements in your program execute in order. Unfortunately, that's not very useful, unless you want your program to do exactly the same thing every time you run it. In fact, often you won't want to execute all the code, but rather you'll want the program to do one thing if a variable has a certain value and something different if the variable has another value. That means you need to be able to cause your program to pick and choose which statements to execute based on conditions that change as the program runs. This process is called *branching*, and there are two ways to accomplish it: unconditionally and conditionally.

As the name implies, unconditional branching happens every time the branch point is reached. An unconditional branch happens, for example, whenever the compiler encounters a new method call. We introduced you to methods in Chapter 1, and you've been using the Main( ) and WriteLine( ) methods extensively in the past three chapters. When the compiler reaches the WriteLine( ) call, the compiler stops execution in the Main( ) method and branches to the WriteLine( ) method, which exists elsewhere in the .NET Framework. When the WriteLine( ) method completes its execution—or *returns*—execution picks up in the original method on the line just below the branch point (the line where the WriteLine( ) method was called).

Conditional branching is more complicated. Methods can branch based on the evaluation of certain conditions that occur at runtime. For instance, you might create a branch that will calculate an employee's federal withholding tax only when his earnings are greater than the minimum taxable by law. C# provides a number of statements that support conditional branching, such as if, else, and switch. We'll show you how to use each of these statements later in this chapter.

A second way that methods break out of their mindless step-by-step processing of instructions is by looping. A loop causes the method to repeat a set of steps until some condition is met (for example, "Keep asking for input until the user tells you to stop or until you receive 10 values"). C# provides many statements for looping, including for, while, and do...while, which are also discussed in this chapter.

Unconditional Branching Statements

The simplest example of an unconditional branch is a method call. You've caused a method branch with the WriteLine( ) methods you've used so far, but any method, whether a built-in part of the language or a method you create yourself (as you'll see in Chapter 8), causes program execution to branch. When a method call is reached, the program doesn't test to evaluate the state of any variable; the program execution branches immediately (and unconditionally) to the start of the new method.

You call a method by writing its name; for example:

```
UpdateSalary( ); // invokes the method UpdateSalary
```

As we explained, when the compiler encounters a method call, it stops execution of the current method and branches to the new method. When that new method completes its execution, the compiler picks up where it left off in the original method. You can see how this works in Figure 5-1.

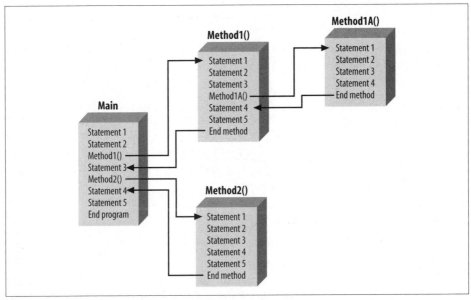

Figure 5-1. Branching allows the execution to move around to different parts of your program, instead of simply proceeding in a straight line.

As Figure 5-1 shows, called methods can call other methods in turn, and you'll often see unconditional branching several methods deep. In Figure 5-1, execution begins in a method called Main( ). Statement1 and Statement2 execute; then the compiler sees a call to Method1( ). The program execution branches unconditionally to the first line of Method1( ), where the first three statements are executed. At the call to Method1A( ), the execution branches again, this time to the start of Method1A( ).

The four statements in Method1A( ) are executed, and Method1A( ) returns. Execution resumes on the first statement after the method call in Method1( ), which is Statement4. Execution continues until Method1( ) ends, at which time execution resumes back in Main( ) at Statement3. At the call to Method2( ), execution branches again; all the statements in Method2( ) execute, and then Main( ) resumes at Statement4. When Main( ) ends, the program itself ends. As you can see, branching takes straight-line program execution and breaks it up quite a bit—and this is just a simple example. However, the program always retains a strict order of execution; nothing is skipped.

You can see the effect of method calls in Example 5-1. Execution begins in Main( ), but branches to a method named SomeMethod( ). The WriteLine( ) statements in each method assist you in seeing where you are in the code as the program executes.

Example 5-1. Executing a method is the most common form of unconditional branching; when a method is called, execution jumps to the method code; when the method is complete, execution picks up where it left off in the calling method

```
using System;
using System.Collections.Generic;
using System.Linq;
using System.Text;

namespace Example_5_1____Branching_to_a_Method
{
    class Program
    {
        static void Main()
        {
            Console.WriteLine("In Main! Calling SomeMethod()...");
            SomeMethod();
            Console.WriteLine("Back in Main().");
        }
        static void SomeMethod()
        {
            Console.WriteLine("Greetings from SomeMethod!");
        }
    }
}
```

The output looks like this:

```
In Main! Calling SomeMethod()...
Greetings from SomeMethod!
Back in Main().
```

Each method in this example outputs a handy message to indicate where the execution is. The program flow begins in Main( ) and proceeds until SomeMethod( ) is invoked. (Invoking a method is often referred to as *calling* the method.) At that point, program flow branches to the method. When the method completes, program flow resumes at the next line after the call to that method.

You can also create an unconditional branch by using one of the unconditional branch keywords: goto, break, continue, return, or throw. The first three of these are discussed later in this chapter, the return statement is discussed in Chapter 7, and the final statement, throw, is discussed in Chapter 16.

Conditional Branching Statements

Although methods branch unconditionally, often you will want to branch within a method depending on a condition that you evaluate while the program is running. This is known as *conditional branching*. Conditional branching statements allow you to write logic such as "If you are over 25 years old, then you may rent a car." This is where the comparison operators you learned about in Chapter 4 become really useful.

C# provides a number of constructs that allow you to write conditional branches into your programs, including the if, else, and switch statements.

if Statements

The simplest branching statement is if. An if statement says, "If a particular condition is true, then execute the following statement; otherwise, skip it." The condition is a Boolean expression. As you learned in Chapters 3 and 4, a Boolean expression evaluates to either true or false, which makes it a perfect fit for the if statement.

The formal description of an if statement is:

```
if (expression)
    Statement1
```

This is the kind of description of the if statement you are likely to find in your compiler documentation. It shows you that the if statement takes an expression (a statement that returns a value) in parentheses, and executes Statement1 if the expression evaluates true. Statement1 doesn't have to be just one statement—it can actually be a block of statements within braces. As long as you include the braces, the compiler treats your code as just one statement. Example 5-2 shows how this works.

Example 5-2. The if statement evaluates an expression, and executes a statement if the expression is true, or skips it if the expression is false

```
using System;
using System.Collections.Generic;
using System.Linq;
using System.Text;

namespace Example_5_2____The_if_Statement
{
    class Program
    {
```

Example 5-2. The if statement evaluates an expression, and executes a statement if the expression is true, or skips it if the expression is false (continued)

```
static void Main( )
{
    int valueOne = 10;
    int valueTwo = 20;
    int valueThree = 30;

    Console.WriteLine("Testing valueOne against valueTwo...");
    if (valueOne > valueTwo)
    {
        Console.WriteLine("ValueOne: {0} larger than ValueTwo: {1}",
                          valueOne, valueTwo);
    }

    Console.WriteLine("Testing valueThree against valueTwo...");
    if (valueThree > valueTwo)
    {
        Console.WriteLine("ValueThree: {0} larger than ValueTwo: {1}",
                          valueThree, valueTwo);
    }
}
}
```

 Just about anywhere in C# that you are expected to provide a statement, you can instead provide a block of statements within braces. (See the "Brace Styles" sidebar in this chapter.)

In this simple program, you declare three variables, valueOne, valueTwo, and valueThree, with the values 10, 20, and 30, respectively. In the first if statement, you test whether valueOne is greater than valueTwo:

```
if ( valueOne > valueTwo )
{
    Console.WriteLine("ValueOne: {0} larger than ValueTwo: {1}",
                      valueOne, valueTwo);
}
```

Because valueOne (10) is less than valueTwo (20) this if statement fails (the condition returns false). Therefore, the body of the if statement (the statements within the braces) doesn't execute, and the WriteLine never executes.

You then test whether valueThree is greater than valueTwo:

```
if ( valueThree > valueTwo )
{
    Console.WriteLine("ValueThree: {0} larger than ValueTwo: {1}",
                      valueThree, valueTwo );
} // end if
```

Because valueThree (30) *is* greater than valueTwo (20), the test returns true, and thus the statement executes. The statement in this case is the block in which you call the WriteLine( ) method, shown in bold. The output reflects that the first if fails but the second succeeds:

```
Testing valueOne against valueTwo...
Testing valueThree against valueTwo...
ValueThree: 30 larger than ValueTwo: 20
```

Single-Statement if Blocks

Notice that the if statement blocks shown in Example 5-2 each contain only a single statement, one call to WriteLine( ). In such cases, you can leave out the braces enclosing the if block. Thus, you might rewrite Example 5-2 as shown in Example 5-3.

Example 5-3. When your if statement block contains only a single statement, you can leave out the braces

```
using System;
using System.Collections.Generic;
using System.Linq;
using System.Text;

namespace Example_5_3____if_Block_without_Braces
{
    class Program
    {
        static void Main()
        {
            int valueOne = 10;
            int valueTwo = 20;
            int valueThree = 30;

            Console.WriteLine("Testing valueOne against valueTwo...");
            if (valueOne > valueTwo)
                Console.WriteLine("ValueOne: {0} larger than ValueTwo: {1}",
                                valueOne, valueTwo);

            Console.WriteLine("Testing valueThree against valueTwo...");
            if (valueThree > valueTwo)
                Console.WriteLine("ValueThree: {0} larger than ValueTwo: {1}",
                                valueThree, valueTwo);
        }
    }
}
```

It is generally a good idea, however, to use the braces even when your if block has only a single statement. There are two reasons for this advice. First, the code is somewhat easier to read and understand with the braces. Code that is easier to read is easier to maintain.

When programmers talk about *maintaining* code, they mean either adding to the code as requirements change or fixing the code as bugs are discovered. You may find yourself maintaining code that you wrote months or years ago, or maintaining code somebody else wrote. In those cases, clear, readable code is a lifesaver.

The second reason for using braces is to avoid a common error: adding a second statement to the `if` and forgetting to add the braces. Consider the code shown in Example 5-4. The programmer has changed the value of `valueThree` to 10 and added a second statement to the second `if` block, as shown in bold.

Example 5-4. When you add a second statement to an if block, be sure to enclose it in the braces, or you may get unexpected results

```
using System;
using System.Collections.Generic;
using System.Linq;
using System.Text;

namespace Example_5_4____Adding_to_an_if_Block
{
    class Program
    {
        static void Main()
        {
            int valueOne = 10;
            int valueTwo = 20;
            int valueThree = 10;

            Console.WriteLine("Testing valueOne against valueTwo...");
            if (valueOne > valueTwo)
                Console.WriteLine("ValueOne: {0} larger than ValueTwo: {1}",
                                   valueOne, valueTwo);

            Console.WriteLine("Testing valueThree against valueTwo...");
            if (valueThree > valueTwo)
                Console.WriteLine("ValueThree: {0} larger than ValueTwo: {1}",
                                   valueThree, valueTwo);
                Console.WriteLine("Good thing you tested again!");
        }
    }
}
```

Now, before reading any further, review the code and decide what the output should be. Don't cheat by looking past this paragraph. Then, when you think you know what the output will be, take a look at this:

```
Testing valueOne against valueTwo...
Testing valueThree against valueTwo...
Good thing you tested again!
```

Were you surprised?

The programmer was fooled by the lack of braces and the indentation. Indentation is whitespace, and as we mentioned in Chapter 3, whitespace is ignored by the compiler. From the perspective of the programmer, the second statement ("Good thing...") looks to be part of the if block:

```
if ( valueThree > valueTwo )
    Console.WriteLine("ValueThree: {0} larger than ValueTwo: {1}",
                        valueThree, valueTwo);
    Console.WriteLine("Good thing you tested again!");
```

The compiler, however, considers only the first statement after the if test to be part of the if statement. The second statement is not part of the if statement. To the compiler, the if statement looks like this:

```
if ( valueThree > valueTwo )
    Console.WriteLine("ValueThree: {0} larger than ValueTwo: {1}",
                        valueThree, valueTwo);

    Console.WriteLine("Good thing you tested again!");
```

If you want the second statement to be part of the if statement, you must use braces, as in the following:

```
if ( valueThree > valueTwo )
{
    Console.WriteLine("ValueThree: {0} larger than ValueTwo: {1}",
                        valueThree, valueTwo);
    Console.WriteLine("Good thing you tested again!");
}
```

Because of this potential for confusion, many C# programmers use braces with every if statement, even if the statement is only one line.

Short-Circuit Evaluation

Consider the following code snippet:

```
int x = 8;
int y = 15;
if ((x == 8) || (y == 12))
```

The if statement here is a bit complicated. The entire if statement is in parentheses, as are all if statements in C#. Thus, everything within the outer set of parentheses must evaluate true for the if statement to be true.

Within the outer parentheses are two expressions, (x == 8) and (y == 12), which are separated by an or operator (||). Because x is 8, the first term (x == 8) evaluates true. There is no need to evaluate the second term (y == 12). It doesn't matter whether y is 12; the entire expression will be true, because the first part is true. (Remember, for

Brace Styles

There are many ways you can form braces around an if statement (and around other blocks of code), but most C# programmers will use one of three styles:

```
if (condition)
{
    // statement
}

if (condition)
    {
    // statement
    }

if (condition){
    // statement
}
```

The first style, used throughout this book, is to put the braces under the keyword if and to indent the contents of the if block. The second style, which is not very popular anymore, is to indent the braces with the contents of the if block. The third style is to put the opening brace on the same line as the if statement and the closing brace under the if statement.

The third style is called K&R style, after Brian W. Kernighan and Dennis M. Ritchie, the authors of the seminal book *The C Programming Language* (Prentice Hall). Their book was so influential that many programmers feel a strong commitment to this style of braces. Although it does save room in a book, we consider the K&R style to be a bit less clear, and so this book will use the first style.

Of course, most software departments have standards or guidelines of their own, which usually include rules about indentation and braces. You should always follow your company's official guidelines, but know that all three of these styles work.

an or statement to evaluate true, just one of the expressions has to be true.) Similarly, consider this snippet:

```
int x = 8;
int y = 12;
if ((x == 5) && (y == 12))
```

Again, there is no need to evaluate the second term. Because the first term is false, the and must fail. (Remember, for an and statement to evaluate true, both tested expressions must evaluate true.)

In cases such as these, the C# compiler will short-circuit the evaluation; the second test will never be performed. This allows you to create if statements in which you first check a value before you take action on it, avoiding the possibility of an exception. Here's a short example:

```
public bool QuotientOverTwenty(float dividend, float divisor)
{
   if ( ( divisor != 0 ) && ( dividend / divisor > 20 ) )
   {
      return true;
   }
   return false;
}
```

In this code, you want to determine whether the quotient is greater than 20, but you must first make sure you are not dividing by zero (division by zero causes the system to throw an exception). With short-circuiting, the second part of the `if` statement (the division) will never occur if the first part is false (that is, if the divisor is zero).

if...else Statements

Often, you will find that you want to take one set of actions when the condition tests true, and a different set of actions when the condition tests false. This allows you to write logic such as "If you are over 25 years old, then you may rent a car; *otherwise*, you must take the train."

The *otherwise* portion of the logic follows the `else` statement. For example, you can modify Example 5-2 to print an appropriate message whether or not `valueOne` is greater than `valueTwo`, as shown in Example 5-5.

Example 5-5. Adding an else statement to your if statement lets you take an action if the condition in the if statement is false—it's the "or" to the if's "either"

```
using System;
using System.Collections.Generic;
using System.Linq;
using System.Text;

namespace Example_5_5____The_else_Statement
{
    class Program
    {
        static void Main( )
        {
            int valueOne = 10;
            int valueTwo = 20;

            Console.WriteLine("Testing valueOne against valueTwo...");
            if (valueOne > valueTwo)
            {
                Console.WriteLine("ValueOne: {0} larger than ValueTwo: {1}",
                                valueOne, valueTwo);
            }
            else
```

Example 5-5. Adding an else statement to your if statement lets you take an action if the condition in the if statement is false—it's the "or" to the if's "either" (continued)

```
            {
                Console.WriteLine("Nope, ValueOne: {0} is NOT larger than ValueTwo:
                                {1}", valueOne, valueTwo);
            }
        }
    }
}
```

The output looks like this:

```
Testing valueOne against valueTwo...
Nope, ValueOne: 10 is NOT larger than ValueTwo: 20
```

Because the test in the if statement fails (valueOne is *not* larger than valueTwo), the body of the if statement is skipped and the body of the else statement is executed. Had the test succeeded, the if statement body would execute and the else statement would be skipped.

Nested if Statements

You've seen how to make your if statement take action for two possible options, but what if there are more than two choices? In that case, you can *nest* if statements— that is, contain one if inside another—to handle complex conditions. For example, suppose you need to write a program to evaluate the temperature and specifically to return the following types of information:

- If the temperature is 32 degrees or lower, the program should warn you about ice on the road.

- If the temperature is exactly 32 degrees, the program should tell you that there may be water on the road.

- If the temperature is higher than 32 degrees, the program should assure you that there is no ice.

There are many good ways to write this program. Example 5-6 illustrates one approach using nested if statements.

Example 5-6. You can nest if statements safely, one inside the other

```
using System;
using System.Collections.Generic;
using System.Linq;
using System.Text;

namespace Example_5_6____Nested_if_Statements
{
    class Program
    {
        static void Main()
```

Example 5-6. You can nest if statements safely, one inside the other (continued)

```
        {
            int temp = 32;

            if (temp <= 32)
            {
                Console.WriteLine("Warning! Ice on road!");
                if (temp == 32)
                {
                    Console.WriteLine("Temp exactly freezing, beware of water.");
                }
                else
                {
                    Console.WriteLine("Watch for black ice! Temp: {0}", temp);
                }
            }
            else
            {
                Console.WriteLine("No ice; drive with confidence.");
            }
        }
    }
}
```

The logic of Example 5-6 is that it tests whether the temperature is less than or equal to 32. If so, it prints a warning:

```
if (temp <= 32)
{
    Console.WriteLine("Warning! Ice on road!");
```

The program then checks whether the temperature is equal to 32 degrees. If so, it prints one message; if not, the temperature must be less than 32, and the program prints the next message. Notice that this second if statement is nested within the first if, so the logic of the else statement is: "because it has been established that the temperature is less than or equal to 32, and it isn't equal to 32, it must be less than 32."

Another way you can chain together more than one possibility with if statements is to use the else if idiom. The program tests the condition in the first if statement. If that first statement is false, control passes to the else statement, which is immediately followed by another if that tests a different condition. For example, you could rewrite Example 5-6 to test whether the temperature is greater than, less than, or exactly equal to freezing with three tests, as shown in Example 5-7.

Example 5-7. The else if construct is another way of chaining together if statements without nesting

```
using System;
using System.Collections.Generic;
using System.Linq;
```

Example 5-7. The else if construct is another way of chaining together if statements without nesting (continued)

```csharp
using System.Text;

namespace Example_5_7____else_if
{
    class Program
    {
        static void Main( )
        {
            int temp = 32;

            if (temp < 32)
            {
                Console.WriteLine("Warning! Ice on road!");
            }
            else if (temp == 32)
            {
                Console.WriteLine("Temp exactly freezing, beware of water.");
            }
            else
            {
                Console.WriteLine("No ice; drive with confidence.");
            }
        }
    }
}
```

In this case, the condition in the first if statement tests whether temp is less than 32, not less than or equal to 32. Because temp is hardwired to exactly 32, the first expression is false, and control passes to the else if statement. The second statement is true, so the third case, the else statement, never executes. Please note, however, that this code is *identical* (as far as the compiler is concerned) to the following:

```csharp
static void Main( )
{
    int temp = 32;
    if ( temp < 32 )
    {
        Console.WriteLine( "Warning! Ice on road!" );
    }
    else
    {
        if ( temp == 32 )
        {
            Console.WriteLine("Temp exactly freezing, beware of water.");
        }
        else
        {
            Console.WriteLine("No ice; drive with confidence.");
        }
    }
}
```

In any case, if you do use the else if idiom, be sure to use an else (not an else if) as your final test, making it the default case that will execute when nothing else does.

switch Statements

Nested if statements are hard to read, hard to get right, and hard to debug. When you have a complex set of choices to make, the switch statement is a more powerful alternative. The logic of a switch statement is this: "pick a matching value and act accordingly."

```
switch (expression)
{
    case constant-expression:
        statement
        jump-statement
    [default:
        statement]
}
```

The expression you are testing (or "switching on") is put in parentheses in the head of the switch statement. Each case statement compares a constant value with the expression. The constant expression can be a literal, symbolic, or enumerated constant.

The compiler starts with the first case statement and works its way down the list, looking for a value that matches the expression. If a case is matched, the statement (or block of statements) associated with that case is executed.

The case block must end with a jump statement. Typically, the jump statement is break, which abruptly ends the entire switch statement. When you execute a break in a switch statement, execution continues after the closing brace of the switch statement. (We'll consider the use of the optional default keyword later in this section.)

In the next, somewhat whimsical listing (Example 5-8), the user is asked to choose her political affiliation among Democrat, Republican, or Progressive. To keep the code simple, we'll hard-wire the choice to be Democrat.

Example 5-8. Use a switch statement to compare a value to a set of constants, and take action accordingly; a switch statement is easier to use and more readable than nested if statements

```
using System;
using System.Collections.Generic;
using System.Linq;
using System.Text;

namespace Example_5_8____The_switch_Statement
{
    class Program
    {
        enum Party
        {
            Democrat,
```

Example 5-8. Use a switch statement to compare a value to a set of constants, and take action accordingly; a switch statement is easier to use and more readable than nested if statements

```
        Republican,
        Progressive
    }
    static void Main( )
    {
        // hardwire to Democratic
        Party myChoice = Party.Democrat;

        // switch on the value of myChoice
        switch (myChoice)
        {
            case Party.Democrat:
                Console.WriteLine("You voted Democratic.");
                break;
            case Party.Republican:
                Console.WriteLine("You voted Republican.");
                break;
            case Party.Progressive:
                Console.WriteLine("You voted Progressive.");
                break;
        }
        Console.WriteLine("Thank you for voting.");
    }
}
}
```

The output looks like this:

```
You voted Democratic.
Thank you for voting.
```

Rather than using a complicated if statement, Example 5-8 uses a switch statement. The user's choice is evaluated in the head of the switch statement, and the block of statements that gets executed depends on whatever case matches (in this instance, Democrat).

The statements between the case statement and the break are executed in series. You can have more than one statement here without braces; in effect, the case statement and the closing break statement act as the braces.

We hardwired the choice here, but if you're accepting user input instead, it is possible that the user will not make a choice among Democrat, Republican, and Progressive. You may want to provide a default case that will be executed whenever no valid choice has been made. You can do that with the default keyword, as shown in Example 5-9. This example already has some built-in safety, because you can't hardwire a choice that's not a member of the enum, and the switch statement has a block for each possible member of the enum. We've commented out the Democrat choice, making it invalid, so that you can see the default statement at work.

Example 5-9. The default statement gives you a backup that will always be executed, if the user doesn't make a valid choice

```
using System;
using System.Collections.Generic;
using System.Linq;
using System.Text;

namespace Example_5_9____The_default_statement
{
    class Program
    {
        enum Party
        {
            Democrat,
            Republican,
            Progressive
        }
        static void Main( )
        {
            // hardwire to Democratic
            Party myChoice = Party.Democrat;

            // switch on the value of myChoice
            switch (myChoice)
            {
                /* case Party.Democrat:
                    Console.WriteLine("You voted Democratic.");
                    break; */
                case Party.Republican:
                    Console.WriteLine("You voted Republican.");
                    break;
                case Party.Progressive:
                    Console.WriteLine("You voted Progressive.");
                    break;
                default:
                    Console.WriteLine("You did not make a valid choice.");
                    break;
            }
            Console.WriteLine("Thank you for voting.");
        }
    }
}
```

The output looks like this:

```
You did not make a valid choice.
Thank you for voting.
```

If the user does not choose one of the values that correspond to a case statement, the default statement will execute. In this case, a message is simply printed telling the user she did not make a valid choice; in production code, you would put all this in a while loop, re-prompting the user until a valid choice is made (or the user elects to quit).

Fall-Through and Jump-to Cases

If two cases will execute the same code, you can create what's known as a "fall-through" case, grouping the case statements together with the same code, as shown here:

```
case CompassionateRepublican:
case Republican:
    Console.WriteLine("You voted Republican.\n");
    Console.WriteLine("Don't you feel compassionate?");
    break;
```

In this example, if the user chooses either CompassionateRepublican or Republican, the same set of statements will be executed.

Note that you can fall through only if the first case executes no code. In this example, the first case, CompassionateRepublican, meets that criterion. Thus, you can fall through to the second case.

If, however, you want to execute a statement with one case and then fall through to the next, you must use the goto keyword to jump to the next case you want to execute.

 The goto keyword is an unconditional branch. When the compiler sees this word, it immediately transfers the flow (jumps) to wherever the goto points. Thus, even within this conditional branching statement, you've inserted an unconditional branch.

For example, if you create a NewLeft party, you might want the NewLeft voting choice to print a message and then fall through to Democrat (that is, to continue on with the statements in the Democrat case). You might (incorrectly) try writing the following:

```
case NewLeft:
    Console.WriteLine("The NewLeft members are voting Democratic.");
case Democrat:
    Console.WriteLine("You voted Democratic.\n");
    break;
```

This code will not compile; it will fail with the error:

```
Control cannot fall through from one case label (case '4:') to another
```

This is a potentially misleading error message. Control *can* fall through from one case label to another, but only if there is no code in the first case label.

 Notice that the error displays the name of the case with its numeric value (4) rather than its symbolic value (NewLeft). Remember that NewLeft is just the name of the constant. Behind the scenes of your enum, the values look like this:

```
const int Democrat = 0;
const int CompassionateRepublican = 1;
const int Republican = 2;
const int Progressive = 3;
const int NewLeft = 4;
```

Because the `NewLeft` case has a statement, the `WriteLine( )` method, you must use a goto statement to fall through:

```
case NewLeft:
    Console.WriteLine("The NewLeft members are voting Democratic.");
    goto case Democrat;
case Democrat:
    Console.WriteLine("You voted Democratic.\n");
    break;
```

This code will compile and execute as you expect.

 The goto can jump over labels; you do not need to put `NewLeft` just above `Democrat`. In fact, you can put `NewLeft` last in the list (just before `default`), and it will continue to work properly.

Switch on string Statements

In the previous example, the `switch` value was an integral constant. C# also offers the ability to switch on a `string`. Thus, you can rewrite Example 5-9 to switch on the string "NewLeft", as in Example 5-10.

Example 5-10. You can switch on a string, as well as on an integral constant

```
using System;
using System.Collections.Generic;
using System.Linq;
using System.Text;

namespace Example_5_10____Switching_on_a_String
{
    class Program
    {
        static void Main( )
        {
            String myChoice = "NewLeft";

            // switch on the string value of myChoice
            switch (myChoice)
            {
                case "NewLeft":
                    Console.WriteLine(
                    "The NewLeft members are voting Democratic.");
                    goto case "Democrat";
                case "Democrat":
                    Console.WriteLine("You voted Democratic.\n");
                    break;
                case "CompassionateRepublican": // fall through
                case "Republican":
                    Console.WriteLine("You voted Republican.\n");
                    Console.WriteLine("Don't you feel compassionate?");
                    break;
```

Example 5-10. You can switch on a string, as well as on an integral constant (continued)

```
                case "Progressive":
                    Console.WriteLine("You voted Progressive.\n");
                    break;
                default:
                    Console.WriteLine("You did not make a valid choice.");
                    break;
            }
            Console.WriteLine("Thank you for voting.");
        }
    }
}
```

ReadLine( ) and Input

In Chapter 3, you learned how to use WriteLine( ) to output messages to the console. Up until now, though, we haven't shown you how to get any input from your users. The looping statements that we'll introduce in the next section often go well with user input, so we'll cover that now. C# has a ReadLine( ) statement that corresponds to WriteLine( ), and as you might guess, it reads in a string from the console into a string variable. The use of ReadLine( ) is rather simple. To take input from the console and assign it to the string inputString, you'd do this:

```
string inputString;
inputString = Console.ReadLine( );
```

Whatever the user types at the console, until he presses Enter—in other words, one line—is assigned to inputString.

It usually helps to give the user a prompt to let him know what he should be entering at a ReadLine( ), so it makes sense to start with a WriteLine( ):

```
Console.WriteLine("Enter your input string.")
inputString = Console.ReadLine( );
```

Often, though, you'll want the user to enter his input on the same line, immediately after the prompt. In that case, you can use Write( ) instead of WriteLine( ). Write( ) outputs text to the console, the same as WriteLine( ), but it doesn't send a newline character. In other words, if you follow a Write( ) with a ReadLine( ), the cursor waits at the end of the output for the user's input:

```
Console.Write("Enter your name here: ");
string userName = Console.ReadLine( );
```

You'll notice that ReadLine( ) accepts only a string, which can be a problem if you want your user to enter a number that you want to calculate with. C# will happily accept the number, but as a *string*, and you'll quickly find that C# doesn't implicitly convert from string to int, for example. So, this won't work:

```
Console.Write("Enter your age: ");
string myInt = Console.ReadLine( );
```

```
if (myInt >= 18)
    Console.WriteLine("You may buy a ticket.");
```

Fortunately, this is an easy problem to fix. You just need to convert the string to an int32 type, and for that, C# offers the Convert class. You can fix the error in the code we just showed you like this:

```
Console.Write("Enter your age: ");
string inputAge = Console.ReadLine();
int myInt = Convert.ToInt32(inputAge);
if (myInt >= 18)
    Console.WriteLine("You may buy a ticket.");
```

You can even combine the input and conversion into a single step, like this:

```
int myInt = Convert.ToInt32(Console.ReadLine());
```

The Convert class can convert to a number of classes, including ToInt32 (and various other types of int), ToDouble, ToBoolean, ToChar, and ToString. However, there are some limitations, most of which are easy to predict. You can convert a char to a string easily (you get a string with just one character), but you can't convert a string to a char if it's more than one character long. You can't convert a char to a double, no matter what you do, because the two types are incompatible. This means that if your code requires a conversion, you should include some error-checking code to ensure that your program doesn't crash if the user enters bad data—for example, if the user enters "Q" in the age-checking code we just showed you. We'll get to that in Chapter 16; for the time being, we'll assume that you have perfect users who always do just what they're told, and never enter bad data. (When you're done with them, can you send them over our way? We'd love to meet them.)

Iteration (Looping) Statements

There are many situations in which you will want to do the same thing again and again, perhaps slightly changing a value each time you repeat the action. This is called *iteration*, or looping. Typically, you'll iterate (or loop) over a set of items, taking the same action on each item in the collection. This is the programming equivalent of an assembly line. On an assembly line, you might take 100 car bodies and put a windshield on each one as it comes by. In an iterative program, you might work your way through a collection of text boxes on a form, retrieving the value from each in turn and using those values to update a database.

C# provides an extensive suite of iteration statements, including for and while, and also do...while and foreach loops. You can also create a loop by using the goto statement. In the remainder of this chapter, we'll consider the use of goto, for, while, and do...while. However, we'll postpone coverage of foreach until Chapter 10, until after we've introduced you to arrays.

Creating Loops with goto

We used the goto statement earlier in this chapter as an unconditional branch in a switch statement. The more common use of goto, however, is to create a loop. In fact, the goto statement is the seed from which all other looping statements have been germinated. Unfortunately, it is a semolina seed, producer of "spaghetti code" (see the "Spaghetti Code" sidebar) and endless confusion.

Spaghetti Code

goto can cause your method to loop back and forth in ways that are difficult to follow. If you were to try to draw the flow of control in a program that makes extensive use of goto statements, the resulting morass of intersecting and overlapping lines might look like a plate of spaghetti—hence the term *spaghetti code*.

Spaghetti code is a contemptuous epithet; no one *wants* to write spaghetti code, and so most experienced programmers avoid using goto to create loops.

Because of the problems created by the goto statement, it is rarely used in C# outside of switch statements, but in the interest of completeness, here's how you create goto loops:

1. Create a label.
2. goto that label.

The *label* is an identifier followed by a colon. You place the label in your code, and then you use the goto keyword to jump to that label. The goto command is typically tied to an if statement, as illustrated in Example 5-11.

Example 5-11. You can use the goto statement to create a loop, but there are much better ways to do it

```
using System;
using System.Collections.Generic;
using System.Linq;
using System.Text;

namespace Example_5_11____The_goto_Statement
{
    class Program
    {

        public static void Main()
        {
            int counterVariable = 0;

        repeat: // the label
```

Example 5-11. You can use the goto statement to create a loop, but there are much better ways to do it (continued)

```
            Console.WriteLine("counterVariable: {0}", counterVariable);

            // increment the counter
            counterVariable++;

            if (counterVariable < 10)
            {
                goto repeat; // the dastardly deed
            }
        }
    }
}
```

The output looks like this:

```
counterVariable: 0
counterVariable: 1
counterVariable: 2
counterVariable: 3
counterVariable: 4
counterVariable: 5
counterVariable: 6
counterVariable: 7
counterVariable: 8
counterVariable: 9
```

This code is not terribly complex; you've used only a single goto statement. However, with multiple such statements and labels scattered through your code, tracing the flow of execution becomes very difficult.

Back in the days before compilers, goto was the only option for branching, but it resulted in some unsightly code. It was the phenomenon of spaghetti code that led to the creation of alternatives, such as the while loop.

The while Loop

The semantics of the while loop are "While this condition is true, do this work." The syntax is:

```
while (Boolean expression) statement
```

As usual, the Boolean expression is any expression that evaluates to true or false. The statement executed within the while statement can of course be a block of statements within braces. Example 5-12 illustrates the use of the while loop.

Example 5-12. The while loop accomplishes the same result as the goto loop in the previous example, but it's clearer and easier to maintain

```
using System;
using System.Collections.Generic;
using System.Linq;
using System.Text;

namespace Example_5_12____The_while_Loop
{
    class Program
    {
        public static void Main()
        {
            int counterVariable = 0;

            // while the counter variable is less than 10
            // print out its value
            while (counterVariable < 10)
            {
                Console.WriteLine("counterVariable: {0}", counterVariable);
                counterVariable++;
            }
        }
    }
}
```

The output looks like this:

```
counterVariable: 0
counterVariable: 1
counterVariable: 2
counterVariable: 3
counterVariable: 4
counterVariable: 5
counterVariable: 6
counterVariable: 7
counterVariable: 8
counterVariable: 9
```

The code in Example 5-12 produces results identical to the code in Example 5-11, but the logic is a bit clearer. The while statement is nicely self-contained, and it reads like an English sentence: "while counterVariable is less than 10, print this message and increment counterVariable."

Notice that the while loop tests the value of counterVariable before entering the loop. This ensures that the loop will not run if the condition tested is false. Thus, if counterVariable is initialized to 11, the loop will never run.

The do...while Loop

There are times when a while loop might not serve your purpose. In certain situations, you might want to reverse the semantics from "Run while this is true" to the subtly different "Do this, and repeat while this condition remains true." In other words, take the action, and then, after the action is completed, check the condition. Such a loop will *always* run at least once.

To ensure that the action is taken before the condition is tested, use a do...while loop:

```
do statement while (boolean-expression);
```

The syntax is to write the keyword do, followed by your statement (or block), the while keyword, and the condition to test in parentheses. The statement must end with a semicolon, unlike the plain while loop.

Example 5-13 rewrites Example 5-12 to use a do...while loop.

Example 5-13. The do...while loop is similar to the while loop, but the condition is tested at the end, meaning that the loop is always guaranteed to run at least once

```
using System;
using System.Collections.Generic;
using System.Linq;
using System.Text;

namespace Example_5_13____The_do._._.while_Loop
{
    class Program
    {
        public static void Main( )
        {
            int counterVariable = 11;

            // display the message and then test that the value is
            // less than 10
            do
            {
                Console.WriteLine("counterVariable: {0}", counterVariable);
                counterVariable++;
            } while (counterVariable < 10);
        }
    }
}
```

The output looks like this:

```
counterVariable: 11
```

In Example 5-13, counterVariable is initialized to 11 and the while test fails, but only after the body of the loop has run once.

The for Loop

A careful examination of the while loop in Example 5-12 reveals a pattern often seen in iterative statements: initialize a variable (counterVariable=0), test the variable (counterVariable<10), execute a series of statements, and increment the variable (counterVariable++). The for loop allows you to combine all these steps in a single statement. You write a for loop with the keyword for, followed by the for header, inside the parentheses, using the syntax:

```
for ([initializers]; [expression]; [iterators]) statement
```

The first part of the header is the *initializer*, in which you initialize a variable. The second part is the Boolean expression to test. The third part is the *iterator*, in which you update the value of the counter variable. These three parts correspond to the three parts of the while loop we mentioned earlier. All of this is enclosed in parentheses.

A simple for loop is shown in Example 5-14.

Example 5-14. A for loop combines several features of the while loop into a single expression, simplifying your code

```csharp
using System;
using System.Collections.Generic;
using System.Linq;
using System.Text;

namespace Example_5_14____The_for_Loop
{
    class Program
    {

        public static void Main()
        {
            for (int counter = 0; counter < 10; counter++)
            {
                Console.WriteLine("counter: {0} ", counter);
            }
        }
    }
}
```

The output looks like this:

```
counter: 0
counter: 1
counter: 2
counter: 3
counter: 4
counter: 5
counter: 6
counter: 7
counter: 8
counter: 9
```

The counter variable is initialized to zero in the initializer:

```
for (int counter=0; counter<10; counter++)
```

The value of counter is tested in the expression part of the header:

```
for (int counter=0; counter<10; counter++)
```

Finally, the value of counter is incremented in the iterator part of the header:

```
for (int counter=0; counter<10; counter++)
```

The initialization part runs only once, when the for loop begins. The integer value counter is created and initialized to zero, and the test is then executed. Because counter is less than 10, the body of the for loop runs and the value is displayed.

After the loop completes, the iterator part of the header runs and counter is incremented. The value of the counter is tested, and, if the test evaluates true, the body of the for statement is executed again.

 Your iterator doesn't just have to be ++. You can use --, or any other expression that changes the value of the counter variable, as the needs of your program dictate. Also, for the purposes of a for loop, counter++ and ++counter will have the same result.

The logic of the for loop is as though you said, "For every value of counter, which I initialize to zero, take this action if the test returns true, and after the action, update the value of counter."

Controlling a for loop with the modulus operator

Remember the modulus operator, which we introduced in Chapter 4 and which we said would be useful later? Well, it really comes into its own in controlling for loops. When you perform modulus n on a number that is a multiple of n, the result is zero. Thus, 80%10=0 because 80 is an even multiple of 10. This fact allows you to set up loops in which you take an action every nth time through the loop by testing a counter to see whether %n is equal to zero, as illustrated in Example 5-15.

Example 5-15. The modulus operator is perfect for controlling a for loop; here, you use it to find the 10th iteration

```
using System;
using System.Collections.Generic;
using System.Linq;
using System.Text;

namespace Example_5_15____The_Modulus_Operator
{
    class Program
    {
```

Example 5-15. The modulus operator is perfect for controlling a for loop; here, you use it to find the 10th iteration (continued)

```csharp
public static void Main( )
{
    for (int counter = 1; counter <= 100; counter++)
    {
        Console.Write("{0} ", counter);

        if (counter % 10 == 0)
        {
            Console.WriteLine("\t{0}", counter);
        }
    }
}
}
```

The output looks like this:

```
1 2 3 4 5 6 7 8 9 10        10
11 12 13 14 15 16 17 18 19 20    20
21 22 23 24 25 26 27 28 29 30    30
31 32 33 34 35 36 37 38 39 40    40
41 42 43 44 45 46 47 48 49 50    50
51 52 53 54 55 56 57 58 59 60    60
61 62 63 64 65 66 67 68 69 70    70
71 72 73 74 75 76 77 78 79 80    80
81 82 83 84 85 86 87 88 89 90    90
91 92 93 94 95 96 97 98 99 100   100
```

In Example 5-15, the value of the counter variable is incremented each time through the loop. Within the loop, the value of counter is compared with the result of modulus 10 (counter % 10). When this evaluates to zero, the value of counter is evenly divisible by 10, and the value is printed in the righthand column.

Breaking out of a for loop

It is possible to exit from a for loop even before the test condition has been fulfilled. To end a for loop prematurely, use the unconditional branching statement break.

The break statement halts the for loop, and execution resumes after the for loop statement (or closing brace), as in Example 5-16.

Example 5-16. You can use the break statement to exit a for loop prematurely

```csharp
using System;
using System.Collections.Generic;
using System.Linq;
using System.Text;

namespace Example_5_16____The_break_Statement
```

Example 5-16. You can use the break statement to exit a for loop prematurely (continued)

```
{
    class Program
    {
        public static void Main( )
        {
            for (int counter = 0; counter < 10; counter++)
            {
                Console.WriteLine("counter: {0} ", counter);

                // if condition is met, break out.
                if (counter == 5)
                {
                    {
                        Console.WriteLine("Breaking out of the loop");
                        break;
                    }
                }

            }
            Console.WriteLine("For loop ended");
        }
    }
}
```

The output looks like this:

```
counter: 0
counter: 1
counter: 2
counter: 3
counter: 4
counter: 5
Breaking out of the loop
For loop ended
```

In this for loop, you test whether the value counter is equal to 5. If that value is found (and in this case, it always will be), you break out of the loop.

The continue statement

Rather than breaking out of a loop, you may at times want to say, "Don't execute any more statements in this loop, but start the loop again from the top of the next iteration." To accomplish this, use the unconditional branching statement continue.

 break and continue generate multiple exit points and make for hard-to-understand, and thus hard-to-maintain, code. Use them with care.

Example 5-17 illustrates the mechanics of both continue and break. This code, suggested by one of our technical reviewers, Donald Xie, is intended to create a traffic signal processing system.

Example 5-17. The break and continue statements allow you to exit a loop or to skip to the next iteration of the loop, but having multiple ways out of a loop is bad practice

```
using System;
using System.Collections.Generic;
using System.Linq;
using System.Text;

namespace Example_5_17____The_break_and_continue_Statements
{
    class Program
    {
        public static int Main( )
        {
            string signal = "0"; // initialize to neutral
            while (signal != "X") // X indicates stop
            {
                Console.Write("Enter a signal. 0 for normal conditions,
                             X to stop, A to Abort: ");
                signal = Console.ReadLine( );

                // do some work here, no matter what signal you
                // receive
                Console.WriteLine("Received: {0}", signal);

                if (signal == "A")
                {
                    // faulty - abort signal processing
                    // Log the problem and abort.
                    Console.WriteLine("Fault! Abort\n");
                    break;
                }

                if (signal == "0")
                {
                    // normal traffic condition
                    // log and continue on
                    Console.WriteLine("All is well.\n");
                    continue;
                }

                // Problem. Take action and then log the problem
                // and then continue on
                Console.WriteLine("{0} -- raise alarm!\n", signal);
            }
            return 0;
        }
    }
}
```

The signals are simulated by entering numerals and uppercase characters from the keyboard, using the `Console.ReadLine( )` method, which reads a line of text from the keyboard. `ReadLine( )` reads a line of text into a string variable. The program ends when you press the A key.

The algorithm is simple: receipt of a "0" (zero) means normal conditions, and no further action is required except to log the event. (In this case, the program simply writes a message to the console; a real application might enter a timestamped record in a database.)

On receipt of an Abort signal (simulated with an uppercase A), the problem is logged and the process is ended. Finally, for any other event, an alarm is raised, perhaps notifying the police. (Note that this sample does not actually notify the police, though it does print out a harrowing message to the console.) If the signal is X, the alarm is raised but the `while` loop is also terminated.

Here's one sample output:

```
Enter a signal. X = stop. A = Abort: 0
Received: 0
All is well.
Enter a signal. X = stop. A = Abort: 1
Received: 1
1 -- raise alarm!
Enter a signal. X = stop. A = Abort: X
Received: X
X -- raise alarm!
```

Here's a second sample output:

```
Enter a signal. X = stop. A = Abort: A
Received: A
Fault! Abort
```

The point of this exercise is that when the A signal is received, the action in the `if` statement is taken and then the program breaks out of the loop, without raising the alarm. When the signal is 0, it is also undesirable to raise the alarm, so the program continues from the top of the loop.

 Be sure to use uppercase when entering X or A. To keep the code simple, there is no code to check for lowercase letters or other inappropriate input.

Optional for loop header elements

You will remember that the `for` loop header has three parts—initialization, expression, and iteration—and the syntax is as follows:

```
for ([initializers]; [expression]; [iterators]) statement
```

Each part of the for loop header is optional. You can, for example, initialize the value outside the for loop, as shown in Example 5-18.

Example 5-18. You can use a for loop without initializing the control variable, but you'll need to be sure to initialize it somewhere else in your code

```csharp
using System;
using System.Collections.Generic;
using System.Linq;
using System.Text;

namespace Example_5_18____for_Loop_Without_Initialization
{
    class Program
    {

        public static void Main( )
        {
            int counter = 0;
            // some work here
            counter = 3;
            // more work here

            for (; counter < 10; counter++)
            {
                Console.WriteLine("counter: {0} ", counter);
            }
        }
    }
}
```

The output looks like this:

```
counter: 3
counter: 4
counter: 5
counter: 6
counter: 7
counter: 8
counter: 9
```

In this example, the counter variable was initialized and modified before the for loop began. Notice that a semicolon is used to hold the place of the missing initialization statement.

You can also leave out the iteration step if you have reason to increment the counter variable inside the loop, as shown in Example 5-19. Skipping the increment step undermines the purpose of using a for loop, and isn't recommended. If you do happen to use it, you must be certain that the counter will increment every time through the loop, no matter what the rest of the code in the loop does. If you somehow skip the increment step, your loop may never end.

Example 5-19. You can also use a for loop without the iterator step, but you'll have to increment the variable inside the loop somewhere

```csharp
using System;
using System.Collections.Generic;
using System.Linq;
using System.Text;

namespace Example_5_19____for_Loop_Without_Iterator
{
    class Program
    {

        public static void Main( )
        {

            for (int counter = 0; counter < 10; ) // no increment
            {
                Console.WriteLine("counter: {0} ", counter);

                // do more work here

                counter++; // increment counter
            }
        }
    }
}
```

You can mix and match which statements you leave out of a for loop.

If you create a for loop with no initializer or incrementer, like this:
```csharp
for  ( ; counter < 10 ; )
```
you have a while loop in for loop's clothing; and of course that construct is silly, and thus not used very often.

It is even possible to leave *all* the statements out, creating what is known as a *forever* loop:
```csharp
for ( ;; )
```

You can also create a forever loop with a while(true) loop:
```csharp
while ( true )
```

You break out of a forever (or while(true)) loop with a break statement. A forever loop is shown in Example 5-20.

Example 5-20. A forever loop runs without ever ending

```
using System;
using System.Collections.Generic;
using System.Linq;
using System.Text;

namespace Example_5_20____A_Forever_Loop
{
    class Program
    {
        public static void Main( )
        {
            int counterVariable = 0; // initialization

            for (; ; )  // forever
            {
                Console.WriteLine("counter: {0} ", counterVariable++); // increment

                if (counterVariable > 10) // test
                {
                    break;
                }
            }
        }
    }
}
```

The output looks like this:

```
counter: 0
counter: 1
counter: 2
counter: 3
counter: 4
counter: 5
counter: 6
counter: 7
counter: 8
counter: 9
counter: 10
```

Use a forever loop to indicate that the "normal" case is to continue the loop indefinitely; for example, if your program is waiting for an event to occur somewhere in the system. The conditions for breaking out of the loop would then be exceptional and managed inside the body of the loop.

Although it is possible to use a forever loop to good effect, Example 5-20 is a degenerate case. The initialization, increment, and test would be done more cleanly in the header of the for loop, and the program would then be easier to understand. It is shown here to illustrate that a forever loop is possible.

Summary

- Branching causes your program to depart from a top-down statement-by-statement execution.

- A method call is the most common form of *unconditional* branching. When the method completes, execution returns to the point where it left off.

- Conditional branching enables your program to branch based on runtime conditions, typically based on the value or relative value of one or more objects or variables.

- The if construct executes a statement if a condition is true and skips it otherwise.

- When the condition in an if statement is actually two conditions joined by an or operator, if the first condition evaluates to true, the second condition will not be evaluated at all. This is called short-circuiting.

- The if...else construct lets you take one set of actions if the condition tested evaluates true, and a different set of actions if the condition tested evaluates false.

- if statements can be nested to evaluate more complex conditions.

- The switch statement lets you compare the value of an expression with several constant values (integers, enumerated constants, or strings), and take action depending on which value matches.

- It is good programming practice for switch statements to include a default statement that executes if no other matches are found.

- Iteration, or looping, allows you to take the same action several times consecutively. Iterations are typically controlled by a conditional expression.

- The goto statement is used to redirect execution to another point in the program, but its use is typically discouraged.

- The while loop executes a block of code while the tested condition evaluates true. The condition is tested before each iteration.

- The do...while loop is similar to the while loop, but the condition is evaluated at the end of the iteration so that the iterated statement is guaranteed to execute at least once.

- The for loop is used to execute a statement a specific number of times. The header of the for loop can be used to initialize one or more variables, test a logical condition, and modify the variables. The typical use of a for loop is to initialize a counter once, test that a condition is using that counter before each iteration, and modify the counter after each iteration.

Now you've seen how you can control the flow of your programs, and combined with user input, we hope you can see how your programs are now a lot more powerful. The ability to react to changes in data is what most applications are all about.

That completes our tour of the fundamentals of programming, and now you're ready to take the next step. Everything you've done so far is what's called *procedural programming*, but in Chapter 6, that's going to change. There's nothing wrong with procedural programming; in fact, most modern languages have their roots in procedural programming, and you'll probably find that you now can understand the fundamentals of other languages with procedural roots, such as Visual Basic and JavaScript.

The basic data types you have to work with right now, though, form a somewhat short list—you can do plenty of math, determine true or false, and work with text in the form of strings. That's a good start, but what if you want to model a somewhat more complex object with your code—a dog, for example, or an employee, or a book? You need a data type that's much more advanced, one that you define yourself. That's *object-oriented* programming, and that's the subject of the next chapter.

Test Your Knowledge: Quiz

Question 5-1. What statements are generally used for conditional branching?

Question 5-2. True or false: an if statement's condition must evaluate to an expression.

Question 5-3. Why should you use braces when there is only one statement following the if?

Question 5-4. What kind of expression can be placed in a switch statement?

Question 5-5. True or false: you can never fall through in a switch statement.

Question 5-6. Name two uses of goto.

Question 5-7. What is the difference between while and do...while?

Question 5-8. What are the three parts of a for loop header?

Question 5-9. What does the keyword continue do?

Question 5-10. What are two ways to create a loop that never ends until you hit a break statement?

Test Your Knowledge: Exercises

Exercise 5-1. Create a program that counts from 1 to 10 three times, using the while, do...while, and for statements, and outputs the results to the screen.

Exercise 5-2. Create a program that prompts a user for input, accepts an integer, then evaluates whether that input is zero, odd or even, a multiple of 10, or too large (more than 100) by using multiple levels of if statements.

Exercise 5-3. Rewrite the program from Exercise 5-2 to do the same work with a switch statement.

Exercise 5-4. Create a program that initializes a variable i at 0 and counts up, and initializes a second variable j at 25 and counts down. Use a single for loop to increment i and decrement j simultaneously, and output the values of i and j at each iteration of the loop. When i is greater than j, end the loop and print out the message "Crossed over!"

CHAPTER 6

Object-Oriented Programming

Windows and web programs are enormously complex programs that present information to users in graphically rich ways, offering complicated user interfaces, complete with drop-down and pop-up menus, buttons, listboxes, and so forth. Behind these interfaces, programs model complex business relationships, such as those among customers, products, orders, and inventory. Users can interact with such a program in hundreds, if not thousands, of different ways, and the program must respond appropriately every time.

To manage this complexity, programmers have developed a technique called *object-oriented programming*. It is based on a very simple premise: you manage complexity by modeling its essential aspects. The closer your program models the problem you are trying to solve, the easier it is to understand (and thus to write and to maintain) that program.

Programmers refer to the problem you are trying to solve and all the information you know that relates to your problem as the *problem domain*. For example, if you are writing a program to manage the inventory and sales of a company, the problem domain would include everything you know about how the company acquires and manages inventory, makes sales, handles the income from sales, tracks sales figures, and so forth. The sales manager and the stock room manager would be problem-domain experts who can help you understand the situation better.

A well-designed object-oriented program is filled with *objects* (things) from the problem domain. For example, if the problem domain is an ATM for banking, the *things* (objects) in your domain might include *customers*, *accounts*, *monthly statements*, and so forth.

At the first level of design, you'll think about how these objects interact and what their state, capabilities, and responsibilities are:

State

   A programmer refers to the current conditions and values of an object as that object's state. For example, you might have an object representing a customer.

The customer's state includes the customer's address, phone number, and email, as well as the customer's credit rating, recent purchase history, and so forth. A different customer would have different state.

Capabilities

The customer has many capabilities, but a developer cares about modeling only those that are relevant to the problem domain. Thus, a customer object might be able to make a deposit, transfer funds, withdraw cash, and so forth.

Responsibilities

Along with capabilities come responsibilities. The customer object is responsible for managing its own address. In a well-designed program, no other object needs to know the details of the customer's address. The address might be stored as data within the customer object, or it might be stored in a database, but it is up to the customer object to know how to retrieve and update her own address. (The *monthly-statement* object should not know the customer's address, though it might ask the *customer* object for the customer address. This way, when the customer moves, the responsibility for knowing the new address is located in a single object: the *customer*.) This ability for an object to own responsibility for its own internal state and actions is known as *encapsulation*.

Of course, all of the objects in your program are just *metaphors* for the objects in your problem domain.

Metaphors

Many of the concepts used throughout this book, and any book on programming, are actually metaphors. We get so used to the metaphors that we forget they *are* metaphors. You are used to talking about a window in your program, but of course there is no such thing; there is just a rectangle with text and images in it. It looks like a window into your document, so we call it a window. Of course, you don't actually have a document either, just bits in memory. No folders, no buttons—these are all just metaphors.

There are many levels to these metaphors. When you see a window on the screen, the window metaphor is enhanced by an image drawn on your monitor. That image is created by lighting tiny dots, called *pixels*. These pixels are lit in response to instructions written in your C# program. Each C# instruction is itself a metaphor; there is just a series of 1s and 0s. Of course, the 1s and 0s are just metaphors for electricity in wires. Of course, electricity is a metaphor, as are electrons, as is quantum physics. You get the idea.

Good metaphors can be very powerful. The art of object-oriented programming is really the art of conceiving good metaphors to simplify solving complex problems.

Creating Models

Humans are model-builders. We create models of the world to manage complexity and to help us understand problems we're trying to solve. You see models all the time. Street maps are models of roadways. Globes are models of the Earth. Atomic models are models of the interaction of subatomic particles.

Models are simplifications. There is little point to a model that is as complex as the object in the problem domain. If you had a map of the United States that had every rock, blade of grass, and bit of dirt in the entire country, the map would have to be as big as the country itself. Your road atlas of the United States eschews all sorts of irrelevant detail, focusing only on those aspects of the problem domain (such as the country's roads) that are important to solving the problem (getting from place to place). If you want to drive from Boston to New York City, you don't care where the trees are; you care where the exits and interchanges are located. Therefore, the network of roads is what appears in the atlas.

Albert Einstein once said: "Things should be made as simple as possible, but not any simpler." A model must be faithful to those aspects of the problem domain that are relevant. For example, a road map must provide accurate relative distances. The distance from Boston to New York must be proportional to the actual driving distance. If 1 inch represents 25 miles at the start of the trip, it must represent 25 miles throughout the trip, or the map will be unusable. (Although not every map has to include a strict scale, depending on what you're using it for, but a road map needs to.)

A good object-oriented design is an accurate model of the problem you are trying to solve. Your design choices influence not only how you solve the problem, but also how you think about the problem. A good design, like a good model, allows you to examine the relevant details of the problem without confusion or distraction.

Classes and Objects

We perceive the world to be composed of things. Look at your computer. You do not see various bits of plastic and glass amorphously merging with the surrounding environment. You naturally and inevitably see distinct things: a computer, a keyboard, a monitor, speakers, pens, paper. Things.

More importantly, even before you decide to do it, you've categorized these things. You immediately classify the computer on your desk as a specific instance of a type of thing: this computer is one of type computer. This particular pen in your pocket is an instance of a more general type of thing, pens. It is so natural you can't avoid it, and yet the process is so subtle, it's difficult to articulate. When I see my dog Milo, I can't help also seeing him *as a dog*, not just as an individual entity.

The theory behind object-oriented programming is that for computer programs to accurately model the world, the programs should reflect this human tendency to think about individual things and types of things. In C#, you do that by creating a class to define a type and creating an object to model a thing.

A *class* defines a new type of thing. The class defines the common characteristics of every object of that new type. For example, you might define a class Car. Every car will share certain characteristics (wheels, brake, accelerator, and so on). Your car and my car both belong to the class of Cars; they are of type Car.

An *object* is an individual instance of a class. Each individual car (your particular car, my particular car) is an instance of the class Car, and thus is an object. An object is just a thing.

Defining a Class

When you define a class, you describe the characteristics and behavior of objects of that type. In C#, you describe characteristics with *member fields*:

```
class Dog
{
    private int weight; // member field
    private string name; // member field
}
```

Member fields are used to hold each object's state. For example, the state of the Dog is defined by its current weight and name. The state of an Employee might be defined by (among other things) her current salary, management level, and performance rating. Classes can have instances of other classes as member fields; a Car class might include an Engine class with its own members. Chapter 7 includes a full discussion of member fields.

You define the behavior of your new type with *methods*. Methods contain code to perform an action:

```
class Dog
{
    private int weight;
    private string name;

    public void Bark()      // member method
    {
    // code here to bark
    }
}
```

The keywords public and private are known as *access modifiers*, which are used to specify what methods of which classes can access particular members. For instance, public members can be called from methods in any class, whereas private members are visible only to the methods of the class defining the member. Thus, objects of any class can call Bark on an instance of Dog, but only methods of the Dog class have access to the weight and name of a Dog. We discuss access modifiers in Chapter 7.

A class typically defines a number of methods to do the work of that class. A Dog class might contain methods for barking, eating, napping, and so forth. An Employee class might contain methods for adjusting salary, submitting annual reviews, and evaluating performance objectives.

Methods can manipulate the state of the object by changing the values in member fields, or a method could interact with other objects of its own type or with objects of other types. This interaction among objects is crucial to object-oriented programming.

For example, a method in Dog might change the state of the Dog (for example, a Feed method might change the Dog's weight), interact with other Dogs (Bark and Sniff), or interact with People (BegForFood). A Product object might interact with a Customer object, and a Video object might interact with an EditingWindow object.

Designing a good C# program is not unlike forming a good team; you look for players (or objects, in the case of a program) who have different skills and to whom you can delegate the various tasks you must accomplish. Those players cooperate with one another to get the job done.

In a good object-oriented program, you will design objects that represent things in your problem domain. You will then divide the work of the program among your objects, assigning responsibility to objects based on their ability.

Class Relationships

The heart of object-oriented design is establishing relationships among the classes. Classes interact and relate to one another in various ways.

The simplest interaction is when a method in one class is used to call a method in a second class. For example, the Manager class might have a method that calls the UpdateSalary method on an object of type Employee. We then say that the Manager class and the Employee class are *associated*. Association among classes simply means they interact.

Some complicated types are *composed* of other types. For example, an automobile might be composed of wheels, engine, transmission, and so forth. You might model this by creating a Wheel class, an Engine class, and a Transmission class. You could then create an Automobile class, and each automobile object would have four instances of the Wheel class and one instance each of the Engine and Transmission classes. This is commonly called the *has-a* relationship. Another way to view this relationship is to say that the Automobile class *aggregates* the Wheel, Engine, and Transmission classes, or that the Automobile class is *composed of* Wheel, Engine, and Transmission objects.

 Some programming languages (such as C++) distinguish between the *is-composed-of* (composition) and the *has-a* (aggregation) relationships, but this distinction does not apply in C#, and they are treated as equivalent.

This process of aggregation (or composition) allows you to build very complex classes by assembling and combining relatively simple classes. The .NET Framework provides a String class to handle text strings. You might create your own Address class out of five text strings (address line 1, address line 2, city, state, and zip code). You might then create a second class, Employee, which has as one of its members an instance of Address.

The Three Pillars of Object-Oriented Programming

Object-oriented programming is built on three pillars: *encapsulation*, *specialization*, and *polymorphism*.

Each class should be fully encapsulated; that is, it should fully define the state and responsibilities of that type. Specialization allows you to establish hierarchical relationships among your classes. Polymorphism allows you to treat a group of hierarchically related objects in a similar way and have the objects sort out how to implement the programming instructions.

Encapsulation

The first pillar of object-oriented programming is encapsulation. The idea behind encapsulation is that you want to keep each type or class discrete and self-contained so that you can change the implementation of one class without affecting any other class.

A class that provides a method that other classes can use is called a *server*. A class that uses that method is called a *client*. Encapsulation allows you to change the details of how a server does its work without breaking anything in the implementation of the client.

This is accomplished by drawing a bright and shining line between the *public* interface of a class and its *private implementation*. The public interface is a contract issued by your class that consists of two parts. The first part says, "I promise to be able to do this work." Specifically, you'll see that a public interface says, "Call this method, with these parameters, and I'll do this work, and return this value." The second part says, "You are allowed to access these values (and no others)." C# implements this second part of the interface through *properties* (discussed in Chapter 8).

A client can rely on a public interface not to change. If the public interface does change, the client must be recompiled and perhaps redesigned.

On the other hand, the private implementation is, as its name implies, private to the server. The designer of the server class is free to change *how* it does the work promised in the public interface, as long as it continues to fulfill the terms of its implicit contract: it must take the given parameters, do the promised work, and return the promised value and allow access to the public properties.

For example, you might have a public method NetPresentValue( ) that promises as follows: "Give me a dollar amount and a number of years, and I'll return the net present value." How you compute that amount is your business; as long as you return the net present value given a dollar amount and number of years, the client doesn't care whether you look it up in a table, compute the value, or ask your friend who is really good at math.

You might implement your Net Present Value interface initially by keeping a table of values. Sometime later, you might change your program to compute the net present value using the appropriate algebra. That is encapsulated within your class, and it does not affect the client. As long as you don't change the public interface (that is, as long as you don't change the number or type of parameters expected, or change the type of the return value), your clients will not break when you change the implementation.

Specialization

The second pillar of object-oriented programming, specialization, is implemented in C# through inheritance; specifically, by declaring that a new class derives from an existing class. The specialized class *inherits* the characteristics of the more general class. The specialized class is called a *derived* class, and the more general class is known as a *base* class.

The specialization relationship is referred to as the *is-a* relationship. A dog *is a* mammal; a car *is a* vehicle. (Dog would be derived from the base class Mammal and Car from the base class Vehicle.)

For example, a Manager is a special type of Employee. The Manager adds new capabilities (hiring, firing, rewarding, praising) and a new state (annual objectives, management level, and so on). The Manager, however, also inherits the characteristics and capabilities common to all Employees. Thus, a Manager has an address, a name, and an employee ID, and Managers can be given raises, can be laid off, and so forth.

Specialization allows you to create a family of objects. In Windows, a button is a control. A listbox is a control. Controls have certain characteristics (color, size, location) and certain abilities (can be drawn, can be selected). These characteristics and abilities are inherited by all of their derived types, which allows for a very powerful form of reuse. Rather than cutting and pasting code from one type to another, the derived type inherits the shared fields and methods. If you change how a shared ability is implemented in the base class, you do not have to update code in every derived type; they inherit the changes.

You'll see specialization at work in Chapter 11.

Polymorphism

Polymorphism, the third pillar of object-oriented programming, is closely related to inheritance. The prefix *poly* means "many"; *morph* means "form." Thus, polymorphism refers to the ability of a single type or class to take many forms.

About the Examples in This Book

Object-oriented programming is designed to help you manage complex programs. Unfortunately, it is very difficult to show complex problems and their solutions in a primer on C#. The complexity of these problems gets in the way of what you're trying to learn about. Because of necessity, the examples in this book will be simple. The simplicity may hide some of the motivation for the technique, but it makes the technique clearer. You'll have to take it on faith, for now, that these techniques scale up well to very complex problems.

Most of the chapters of this book focus on the syntax of C#. You need the syntax of the language to be able to write a program at all, but it's important to keep in mind that the syntax of any language is less important than its semantics. The meaning of what you are writing and why you're writing it is the real focus of object-oriented programming, and thus of this book.

Don't let concern with syntax get in the way of understanding the semantics. The compiler can help you get the syntax right (if only by complaining when you get it wrong), and the documentation can remind you of the syntax, but understanding the semantics—the meaning of the construct—is the hard part. Throughout this book, we work hard to explain not only *how* you do something, but also *why* and *when* you do it.

Sometimes you will know you have a collection of a general type—for example, a collection of controls—but you do not know (or care) about the specific subtype of each control (one may be a button, another a listbox). The important thing is that you know they all inherit shared abilities (such as the `Draw` method) and that you can treat them all as controls. If you write a programming instruction that tells each control to draw itself, the `Draw( )` method is implemented properly on a per-control basis (buttons draw as buttons, listboxes draw as listboxes). You do not need to know how each subtype accomplishes this; you only need to know that each type is defined to be able to draw.

Polymorphism allows you to treat a collection of disparate derived types (buttons, listboxes) as a group. You treat the general group of controls the same way, and each individual control does the right thing according to its specific type. Chapter 11 provides details and examples.

Object-Oriented Analysis and Design

Before you program anything, other than a trivial demonstration program, you need to take two steps: analysis and design. Analysis is the process of understanding and detailing the problem you are trying to solve. Design is the actual planning of your solution.

With trivial problems (such as computing the Fibonacci series), you may not need an extensive analysis period, but with complex business problems the analysis process can take weeks, or even months. One powerful analysis technique is to create what are called *use-case scenarios*, in which you describe in some detail how the system will be used. Among the other considerations in the analysis period are determining your success factors (how do you know whether your program works?) and writing a specification of your program's requirements.

Once you've analyzed the problem, you design the solution. Imagining the classes you will use and their interrelationships is key to the design process. You might design a simple program on the fly, without this careful planning; but in any serious business application, you will want to take some time to think through the issues.

There are many powerful design techniques you might use. How much time you put into design* before you begin coding will depend on the philosophy of the organization you work for; the size of your team; and your background, experience, and training.†

---

* See *The Unified Modeling Language User Guide*, Second Edition, by Grady Booch et al. (Addison-Wesley).
† See *Agile Software Development Principles, Patterns, and Practices* by Robert C. Martin (Prentice Hall).

Jesse says: My approach to managing complexity is to keep team size very small. I have worked on large development teams, and over the years I've come to agree with one of the best developers I've ever met, Ed Belove, that the ideal size for a team of developers is three. Three highly skilled programmers can be incredibly productive, and with three, you don't need a manager. Three people can have only one conversation at a time. Three people can never be evenly split on a decision. One day I'll write a book on programming in teams of three, but this isn't it, so we'll stay focused on C# programming, rather than on design debates.

Summary

- Object-oriented programming helps programmers manage complexity by modeling essential aspects of the real-world problem.
- A class defines a new type in your program and is typically used as a representation for a type of thing in the problem domain.
- An object is an instance of a class.
- State is the current condition of an object.
- Many classes define member fields, which are typically private variables visible to every method of the class, but not outside the class.
- The behavior of the class is defined with methods, which contain code to perform an action. Methods can manipulate the state of the object and interact with other objects.
- The three pillars of object-oriented programming are encapsulation, specialization, and polymorphism.
- Encapsulation requires that each class should be discrete and self-contained. Each class should "know" or "do" one discrete thing or set of things.
- Specialization is implemented by deriving more specific classes from generalized (base) classes through inheritance.
- Polymorphism allows you to treat a collection of objects of types, all derived from a common base, as though each was an instance of that base type.
- Analysis is the process of detailing the problem you're trying to solve.
- Design is the planning of the solution to the problem.

This chapter was a bit of a departure from what we've been teaching you so far. We got away from the hands-on code to talk in broader terms about object-oriented programming and the theory behind it. That's an indication of how important these object-oriented concepts are to C#—this is the only time in this book we'll devote a chapter purely to theory without letting you put your hands on the code. But now that we've taken a timeout to teach you the theory, it's time to get back in the game. Chapter 7 shows you how to create and use classes and objects, and then Chapter 8 goes into more detail about methods.

Test Your Knowledge: Quiz

Question 6-1. How do you create a user-defined type in C#?

Question 6-2. What is the difference between a class and an object?

Question 6-3. Why should member fields be private?

Question 6-4. What is encapsulation?

Question 6-5. What is specialization and how is it implemented in C#?

Question 6-6. What is polymorphism?

Question 6-7. What is the difference between the *is-a* and the *has-a* relationship?

Question 6-8. What are access modifiers?

Question 6-9. Describe the differences between state, capabilities, and responsibilities.

Question 6-10. What is a use-case scenario?

Test Your Knowledge: Exercises

Exercise 6-1. A visual representation of a class, its member fields and methods, and its place in the hierarchy is called a *class diagram*. There are several accepted methods for drawing a class diagram, but we won't hold you to any of those right now. For this exercise, simply draw a class diagram for a class named vehicle, listing some member fields and methods that you think that class should have. Then add to your diagram the derived classes car, boat, and plane, and list their fields and methods (remember that all derived classes inherit the fields and methods of their parent class).

Exercise 6-2. You've defined a class as a diagram; now try defining one in code. Define a class Book, in which a book has a title, author, and ISBN, and the book can be read or shelved. You don't need to fill in the code for any methods you include; simply include a comment in the body, like we did for the Dog class earlier in the chapter.

CHAPTER 7

Classes and Objects

In Chapter 3, we introduced you to the intrinsic types built into the C# language. Those simple types allow you to hold and manipulate numeric values and strings. The true power of C#, however, lies in its capacity to let the programmer define new types to suit particular problems. That ability to create new types is what characterizes an object-oriented language. You specify new types in C# by declaring and defining *classes*.

Particular instances of a class are called *objects*. The difference between a class and an object is the same as the difference between the concept of a Dog and the particular dog who is sitting at your feet as you read this. You can't play fetch with the definition of a Dog, only with an instance.

A Dog class describes what dogs are like; they have weight, height, eye color, hair color, disposition, and so forth. They also have actions they can take, such as eat, walk, bark, and sleep. A particular dog (such as Jesse's dog, Milo) will have a specific weight (62 pounds), height (22 inches), eye color (black), hair color (yellow), disposition (angelic), and so forth. He is capable of all the actions—*methods*, in programming parlance—of any dog (though if you knew him, you might imagine that eating is the only method he implements).

The huge advantage of classes in object-oriented programming is that classes encapsulate the characteristics and capabilities of a type in a single, self-contained unit.

Suppose, for example, that you want to sort the contents of an instance of a Windows listbox control. The listbox control is defined as a class. One of the properties of that class is that it knows how to sort itself. Sorting is *encapsulated* within the class, and the details of how the listbox sorts itself are not made visible to other classes. If you want a listbox sorted, you just tell the listbox to sort itself and it takes care of the details.

So, you simply write a method that tells the listbox to sort itself—and that's what happens. How it sorts is of no concern; that it does so is all you need to know.

As we noted in Chapter 6, this is called encapsulation, which, along with polymorphism and specialization, is one of three cardinal principles of object-oriented programming. Chapter 11 discusses polymorphism and inheritance.

An old programming joke asks: how many object-oriented programmers does it take to change a lightbulb? Answer: none, you just tell the lightbulb to change itself. This chapter explains the C# language features that are used to specify new classes. The elements of a class—its behaviors and its state—are known collectively as its *class members*.

Class behavior is created by writing methods (sometimes called member functions). A method is a routine that every object of the class can execute. For example, a Dog class might have a Bark method, and a listbox class might have a Sort method.

Class state is maintained by *fields* (sometimes called member variables). Fields may be primitive types (an int to hold the age of the dog or a set of strings to hold the contents of the listbox), or fields may be objects of other classes (for example, an Employee class may have a field of type Address).

Finally, classes may also have *properties*, which act like methods to the creator of the class, but look like fields to clients of the class. A *client* is any object that interacts with instances of the class.

Defining Classes

When you define a new class, you define the characteristics of all objects of that class, as well as their behaviors. For example, if you create your own windowing operating system, you might want to create screen widgets (known as *controls* in Windows). One control of interest might be a listbox, a control that is very useful for presenting a list of choices to the user and enabling the user to select from the list.

Listboxes have a variety of characteristics: height, width, location, and text color, for example. Programmers have also come to expect certain behaviors of listboxes—they can be opened, closed, sorted, and so on.

Object-oriented programming allows you to create a new type, ListBox, which encapsulates these characteristics and capabilities.

To define a new type or class, you first declare it and then define its methods and fields. You declare a class using the class keyword. The complete syntax is:

```
[attributes] [access-modifiers] class identifier [:base-class]
{class-body}
```

Attributes are used to provide special metadata about a class (that is, information about the structure or use of the class). You won't need to use attributes in this book, but you may run into them if you venture into more advanced topics.

Access modifiers are discussed later in this chapter. (Typically, your classes will use the keyword public as an access modifier.)

The *identifier* is the name of the class that you provide. Typically, C# classes are named with nouns (Dog, Employee, ListBox). The naming convention (not required, but strongly encouraged) is to use Pascal notation. In Pascal notation, you don't use under-bars or hyphens, but if the name has two words (Golden Retriever), you push the two words together, each word beginning with an uppercase letter (GoldenRetriever).

As we mentioned earlier, inheritance is one of the pillars of object-oriented programming. The optional *base class* is key to inheritance, as we'll explain in Chapter 11.

The member definitions that make up the *class body* are enclosed by open and closed curly braces ({}):

```
class Dog
{
    int age; // the dog's age
    int weight; // the dog's weight
    Bark() { //... }
    Eat() { // ... }
}
```

Methods within the class definition of Dog define all the things a dog can do. The fields (member variables) such as age and weight describe all of the dog's attributes or state.

Instantiating Objects

To make an actual instance, or *object*, of the Dog class, you must declare the object and allocate memory for the object. These two steps combined are necessary to create, or *instantiate*, the object. Here's how you do it.

First, you declare the object by writing the name of the class (Dog) followed by an identifier (name) for the object or instance of that class:

```
Dog milo; // declare milo to be an instance of Dog
```

This is not unlike the way you create a local variable; you declare the type (in this case, Dog), followed by the identifier (milo). Notice also that by convention, the identifier for the object is written in Camel notation. Camel notation is just like Pascal notation except that the very first letter is lowercase. Thus, a variable or object name might be myDog, designatedDriver, or plantManager.

The declaration alone doesn't actually create an instance, however. To create an instance of a class, you must also allocate memory for the object using the keyword new:

```
milo = new Dog( ); // allocate memory for milo
```

You can combine the declaration of the `Dog` type with the memory allocation into a single line:

```
Dog milo = new Dog( );
```

This code declares `milo` to be an object of type `Dog` and also creates a new instance of `Dog`. You'll see what the parentheses are for in "Constructors" later in this chapter.

In C#, *everything* happens within a class. No methods can run outside a class, not even `Main( )`. The `Main( )` method is the entry point for your program; it is called by the operating system, and it is where execution of your program begins. Typically, you'll create a small class to house `Main( )`, because like every method, `Main( )` must live within a class. Some of the examples in this book use a class named `Tester` to house `Main( )`:

```
public class Tester
{
    public static void Main( )
    {
        //...
    }
}
```

Even though `Tester` was created to house the `Main( )` method, you've not yet instantiated any objects of type `Tester`. To do so, you would write:

```
Tester myTester = new Tester( ); // instantiate an object of type Tester
```

As you'll see later in this chapter, creating an instance of the `Tester` class allows you to call other methods on the object you've created (`myTester`).

Classes Versus Objects

One way to understand the difference between a class and an instance (object) is to consider the distinction between the type `int` and a variable of type `int`.

You can't assign a value to a type:

```
int = 5; // error
```

Instead, you assign a value to an object of that type (in this case, a variable of type `int`):

```
int myInteger;
myInteger = 5; // ok
```

Similarly, you can't assign values to fields in a class; you must assign values to fields in an object. Thus, you can't write:

```
Dog.weight = 5;
```

This is not meaningful. It isn't true that every dog's weight is 5 pounds. You must instead write:

```
milo.weight = 5;
```

This says that a particular dog's weight (Milo's weight) is 5 pounds.

Creating a Box Class

We'll start out with a very simple class—a three-dimensional box. The internal state of the box should keep track of the length, width, and height of the box. You probably also want some way to show the box to the user. In a graphical environment, you would probably draw the box, but because we're working with console applications, we'll compromise and just output the dimensions.

You might implement such a class by defining a single method and three variables, as shown in Example 7-1.

Example 7-1. The Box class is a very simple class with just three member fields and one method

```
using System;
using System.Collections.Generic;
using System.Linq;
using System.Text;

namespace Example_7_1____The_Box_Class
{
    public class Box
    {
        // private variables
        private int length;
        private int width;
        private int height;

        // public methods
        public void DisplayBox()
        {
            Console.WriteLine("Stub for displaying the box.");
        }
    }

    public class Tester
    {
        static void Main()
        {
            Box boxObject = new Box();
            boxObject.DisplayBox();
        }
    }
}
```

This code creates a new user-defined type: Box. The Box class definition begins with the declaration of a number of member variables: Length, Width, and Height.

The keyword private indicates that these values can be accessed only by methods of this class. The private keyword is an access modifier, explained later in this chapter.

Many C# programmers prefer to put all of the member fields together, either at the very top or at the very bottom of the class declaration, though that is not required by the language.

The only method declared within the Box class is the method DisplayBox( ). The DisplayBox( ) method is defined to return void; that is, it will not return a value to the method that invokes it. For now, the body of this method has been "stubbed out."

Stubbing out a method is a temporary measure you might use when you first write a program to allow you to think about the overall structure without filling in every detail when you create a class. When you stub out a method body, you leave out the internal logic and just mark the method, perhaps with a message to the console:

```csharp
public void DisplayBox( )
{
    Console.WriteLine("Stub for displaying the box.");
}
```

After the closing brace, a second class, Tester, is defined. Tester contains our now familiar Main( ) method. In Main( ), an instance of Box is created, named boxObject:

```csharp
Box boxObject = new Box( );
```

 Technically, an unnamed instance of Box is created in an area of memory called the *heap*, and a reference to that object is returned and used to initialize the Box reference named boxObject. Because that is cumbersome, we'll simply say that a Box instance named boxObject was created.

Because boxObject is an instance of Box, Main( ) can make use of the DisplayBox( ) method defined for objects of that type and can call it to display the dimensions of the box:

```csharp
boxObject.DisplayBox( );
```

You invoke a method on an object by writing the name of the object (boxObject) followed by the dot operator (.), the method name (DisplayBox), and the parameter list in parentheses (in this case, the list is empty). You'll see how to pass in values to initialize the member variables in "Constructors" later in this chapter.

Access Modifiers

An access modifier determines which class methods—including methods of other classes—can see and use a member variable or method within a class. Table 7-1 summarizes the C# access modifiers.

Table 7-1. Access modifiers

Access modifier	Restrictions
public	No restrictions. Members that are marked public are visible to any method of any class.
private	The members in class A that are marked private are accessible only to methods of class A.
protected	The members in class A that are marked protected are accessible to methods of class A and also to methods of classes derived from class A. The protected access modifier is used with derived classes, as explained in Chapter 11.
internal	The members in class A that are marked internal are accessible to methods of any class in A's assembly. An *assembly* is a collection of files that appear to the programmer as a single executable or DLL.
protected internal	The members in class A that are marked protected internal are accessible to methods of class A, to methods of classes derived from class A, and also to any class in A's assembly. This is effectively protected *or* internal; there is no concept of protected *and* internal.

Public methods are part of the class's public interface: they define how this class behaves. Private methods are "helper methods" used by the public methods to accomplish the work of the class. Because the internal workings of the class are private, helper methods need not (and should not) be exposed to other classes.

The Box class and its method DisplayBox( ) are both declared public so that any other class can make use of them. If DisplayBox( ) had been private, you wouldn't be able to invoke DisplayBox( ) from any method of any class other than methods of Box itself. In Example 7-1, DisplayBox( ) was invoked from a method of Tester (not Box), and this was legal because both the class (Box) and the method (DisplayBox) were marked public.

It is good programming practice to explicitly set the accessibility of all methods and members of your class. Although you can rely on the fact that class members are declared private by default, making their access explicit indicates a conscious decision and is self-documenting.

Method Arguments

The behavior of a class is defined by the methods of that class. To make your methods as flexible as possible, you can define *parameters*: information passed into the method when the method is invoked. Thus, rather than having to write one method when you want to sort your listbox from *A* to *Z*, and a second method when you want to sort it from *Z* to *A*, you define a more general Sort( ) method and pass in a parameter specifying the order of the sort.

Methods can take any number of parameters. The parameter list follows the method name and is enclosed in parentheses. Inside the parentheses, you provide the type of the parameter and the name that the method will use to refer to that parameter.

The terms *argument* and *parameter* are often used interchangeably, though some programmers insist on differentiating between the parameter declaration and the arguments passed in when the method is invoked.

For example, the following declaration defines a method named MyMethod( ) that returns void (that is, it returns no value at all) and takes two parameters (an int and a Button):

```
void MyMethod (int firstParam, Button secondParam)
{
   // ...
}
```

Within the body of the method, the parameters act as local variables, as though you had declared them in the body of the method and initialized them with the values passed in. Example 7-2 illustrates how you pass values into a method; in this case, values of type int and float.

Example 7-2. To pass parameters into a method, you include them in parentheses after the method name

```
using System;
using System.Collections.Generic;
using System.Linq;
using System.Text;

public class MyClass
{
   public void SomeMethod( int firstParam, float secondParam )
   {
      Console.WriteLine("Here are the parameters received: {0}, {1}",
                     firstParam, secondParam );
   }
}

public class Tester
{
   static void Main( )
   {
      int howManyPeople = 5;
      float pi = 3.14f;
      MyClass mc = new MyClass( );
      mc.SomeMethod( howManyPeople, pi );
   }
}
```

Here is the output:

```
Here are the parameters received: 5, 3.14
```

When you instantiate a float with a decimal part (3.14), you must append the letter f (as in 3.14f) to signal to the compiler that the value is a float and not a double.

The method SomeMethod( ) takes two parameters, firstParam and secondParam, and displays them using Console.WriteLine( ). firstParam is an int, and secondParam is a float. These parameters are treated as *local variables* within SomeMethod( ). Local variables are used only within the method. You can manipulate these values within the method, but they go *out of scope* and are discarded after the method ends. When you pass value-type parameters to a method, you aren't passing the variables themselves; you're creating local variables with the same type and value as the parameters you pass in. In this case, you can't manipulate the values of howManyPeople or pi within SomeMethod( ), because SomeMethod( ) has access only to firstParam and secondParam. (Notice that the names used inside the method don't need to be the same as the names used for the same values outside the method.) Sometimes you'll want the method to change the value of the parameter, not the local variable, and you can do that with *reference parameters*, which we'll discuss in Chapter 8.

The *scope* of a variable refers to the parts of the program where you can use that variable. The scope of a local variable is the method where it's used. You can't refer to firstParam in Main( ), for example, because Main( ) is outside the scope of firstParam.

In the calling method (Main), two local variables (howManyPeople and pi) are created and initialized. These variables are passed as the parameters to SomeMethod( ). The compiler maps howManyPeople to firstParam and pi to secondParam, based on their relative positions in the parameter list.

Return Types

You've seen in several places so far in this book that methods can return a type, or they can return nothing at all if the return type is void. You've mostly used void methods up until now, specifically Main( ), although WriteLine( ) is a void method as well. The constructors you've worked with *do* return a value—they return an instance of the class.

What you may not know is that you can use a method call in place of an object, if the method returns the appropriate type. For example, suppose you have a class Multiplier, such as this:

```
public class Multiplier
{
    public int Multiply(int firstOperand, int secondOperand)
    {
        return firstOperand * secondOperand;
    }
}
```

You can call that `Multiply( )` method anyplace you'd expect an `int`, like this:

```
int x = 4;
int y = 10;
Multiplier myMultiplier = new Multiplier( );
int result = myMultiplier.Multiply(x, y);
```

Here, you're assigning the return value of the `Multiply( )` method to an `int`, which works fine, because the return type of the `Multiply( )` method is `int`. You can do the same with any of the intrinsic types, or with classes you create.

Constructors

In Example 7-1, notice that the statement that creates the Box object looks as though it is invoking a `Box( )` method, because of the parentheses:

```
Box boxObject = new Box( );
```

In fact, a member method *is* invoked whenever you instantiate an object. This method is called a *constructor*. Each time you define a class, you are free to define your own constructor, but if you don't, the compiler will provide one for you invisibly and automatically.

The job of a constructor is to create an instance of the object specified by a class and to put it into a valid state. Before the constructor runs, the object is just a blob of memory; after the constructor completes, the memory holds a valid instance of the class.

The Box class of Example 7-1 does not define a constructor, so the compiler implicitly provides one. The constructor provided by the compiler creates the object but takes no other action.

 Any constructor that takes no arguments is called a *default constructor*. The constructor provided by the compiler takes no arguments, and hence is a default constructor. This terminology has caused a great deal of confusion. You can create your own default constructor, and if you do not create a constructor at all, the compiler will create a default constructor for you, by default.

If you do not explicitly initialize your member variables, they are initialized to innocuous values (integers to 0, strings to an empty string, and so on). Table 7-2 lists the default values assigned to some of the common types.

Table 7-2. Primitive types and their default values

Type	Default value
Numeric (`int`, `long`, and so on)	0
`Bool`	False
`Char`	The null character (`'\0'`)

Table 7-2. Primitive types and their default values (continued)

Type	Default value
Enum	0
Reference	null

Typically, you'll want to define your own constructor and provide it with arguments so that the constructor can set the initial state for your object. In Example 7-3, you'll pass in some initial values for Box so that the object is created with meaningful data.

You declare a constructor like you do any other member method, except:

- The name of the constructor must be the same as the name of the class.
- Constructors have no return type (not even void).

If there are arguments to be passed, you define an argument list just as you would for any other method. Example 7-3 declares a constructor for the Box class that accepts three arguments, one each for the length, width, and height for the new Box object you are creating.

Example 7-3. To create a constructor, you create a method with the same name as the class that initializes the internal variables

```
using System;
using System.Collections.Generic;
using System.Linq;
using System.Text;

namespace Example_7_3____Constructor
{
    public class Box
    {
        // private variables
        private int length;
        private int width;
        private int height;

        // public methods
        public void DisplayBox()
        {
            Console.WriteLine("Length: {0}, Width: {1}, Height: {2}",
                            length, width, height);
        }

        // constructor
        public Box(int theLength, int theWidth, int theHeight)
        {
            length = theLength;
            width = theWidth;
            height = theHeight;
        }
    }
```

```
public class Tester
{
    static void Main( )
    {
        Box boxObject = new Box(4, 8, 3);
        boxObject.DisplayBox( );
    }
}
}
```

The output looks like this:

```
Length: 4, Width: 8, Height: 3
```

In this example, the constructor takes a series of integer values and initializes all the member variables based on these parameters.

When the constructor finishes, the Box object exists and the values have been initialized. When DisplayBox( ) is called in Main( ), the values are displayed.

Try commenting out one of the assignments and running the program again. You'll find that each member variable that isn't assigned to by you is initialized by the compiler to zero. Integer member variables are set to zero if you don't otherwise assign them. Remember that value types (such as integers) must be initialized; if you don't tell the constructor what to do, it sets innocuous values.

Initializers

If you know that certain member variables should always have the same value when the object is created, you can initialize the values of these member variables in an *initializer*, instead of having to do so in the constructor. You create an initializer by assigning an initial value to a class member:

```
private int Second = 30; // initializer
```

Suppose that, for whatever reason, the boxes you're creating in your program are always 6 inches high. You might rewrite your Box class to use an initializer so that the value of height is always initialized, as shown in bold in Example 7-4.

Example 7-4. You use an initializer to set the value of a member variable within the class itself, so you don't need to do it in the constructor

```
using System;
using System.Collections.Generic;
using System.Linq;
using System.Text;
```

Example 7-4. You use an initializer to set the value of a member variable within the class itself, so you don't need to do it in the constructor (continued)

```
namespace Example_7_4____Initializer
{
    public class Box
    {
        // private variables
        private int length;
        private int width;
        private int height = 6;

        // public methods
        public void DisplayBox()
        {
            Console.WriteLine("Length: {0}, Width: {1}, Height: {2}",
                             length, width, height);
        }

        // constructor
        public Box(int theLength, int theWidth)
        {
            length = theLength;
            width = theWidth;
        }
    }

    public class Tester
    {
        static void Main()
        {
            Box boxObject = new Box(4, 8);
            boxObject.DisplayBox();
        }
    }
}
```

The output looks like this:

```
Length: 4, Width: 8, Height: 6
```

If you do not provide a specific initializer, the constructor initializes each integer member variable to zero (0). In the case shown, however, the height member is initialized to 6:

```
private int height = 6;
```

Later in this chapter, you will see that you can have more than one constructor. If you assign 6 to height in more than one of these, you can avoid the problem of having to keep all the constructors consistent with one another by initializing the height member, rather than assigning 6 in each of the constructors.

Object Initializers

Although you normally set the properties of your object with a constructor, that's not the only way to do it. C# also offers *object initializers*, which let you set any accessible members of your object when you create it. Notice that we said *accessible*, which means you can set public members, but not private ones. Suppose you have this Dog class, with member fields that are public:

```
public class Dog
{
    public string name;
    public int weight;

    // constructor
    public Dog(string myName)
    {
        name = myName;
    }
}
```

Notice here that the constructor takes a string to set the dog's name, but it doesn't take a weight. That's fine, because weight is public, so you could easily set it later, like this:

```
Dog milo = new Dog("Milo");
Milo.weight = 5;
```

With an object initializer, though, you can set the public weight immediately after you create the object, like this:

```
Dog milo = new Dog("Milo") { weight = 5 };
```

There's not a whole lot of reason to do this; you could just rewrite the constructor to accept the weight. In fact, it's generally a bad idea to have your member fields be public, as we've said. However, this technique has some advantages with *anonymous types*.

Anonymous Types

From time to time you find yourself creating a class only so that you can create a single instance of it, never to use that class again. C# allows you to dispense with all that and combine object initializers and implicitly typed variables, which you learned about back in Chapter 3, to create a class with no name at all: an *anonymous type*.

You create an instance of an anonymous type with the keyword new, just as you would if you were instantiating an object of a declared class. Instead of passing parameters to a constructor, though, you use braces and define the member fields that you want your anonymous class to contain, like this:

```
new { Color = "Blue", Size = 13 }
```

The compiler creates a new class with two member fields. Notice that we've capitalized the names of the fields in this declaration, which is contrary to the naming scheme we've been using. That's because these aren't fields, but properties, which we'll explain more fully in the next chapter. In brief, properties look like fields to the users of your class, and look like methods to the creator of your class.

This new class contains two properties, Color and Size. Just as with implicitly typed variables, the compiler can determine that Color is a String and Size is an int, and it types them accordingly. And as with implicitly typed variables, you can't declare the property without assigning it a value, because the compiler needs that value to determine the property's type.

Of course, the compiler *does* assign your class a name for its own internal purposes; it just doesn't tell *you* what that name is. So how do you use an anonymous class? You can use the var keyword to assign an instance of that class to a variable:

```
var myShoe = new { Color = "Blue", Size = 13 };
```

You can now access each of the properties using dot notation:

```
Stirng whatColor = myShoe.Color;
int howBig = myShoe.Size;
```

These fields are read-only, however. If you try to assign a new value to one of them, you'll get an error:

```
myShoe.Size = 12; // error
```

This technique is only really useful when your class contains only read-only data, and no methods. That might seem like a rather limited use, but it's very handy with LINQ, so you'll see anonymous methods again in Chapter 21, but not before then.

The this Keyword

The keyword this refers to the current instance of an object. The this reference is a hidden parameter in every nonstatic method of a class (we'll discuss static methods shortly). There are three ways in which the this reference is typically used. The first way is to qualify instance members that have the same name as parameters, as in the following:

```
public void SomeMethod (int length)
{
    this.length = length;
}
```

In this example, SomeMethod( ) takes a parameter (length) with the same name as a member variable of the class. The this reference is used to resolve the ambiguity. Whereas this.length refers to the member variable, length refers to the parameter.

You can, for example, use the this reference to make assigning to a field more explicit:

```
public void SetBox(int length, int newWidth, int newHeight)
{
    this.length = length;      // use of "this" required
    this.width = newWidth;     // use of "this" optional
    height = newHeight;        // use of "this" not needed
}
```

If the name of the parameter is the same as the name of the member variable, you *must* use the this reference to distinguish between the two, but if the names are different (such as newWidth and newHeight), the use of the this reference is optional.

> The argument in favor of naming the argument to a method that is the same as the name of the member is that the relationship between the two is made explicit. The counterargument is that using the same name for both the parameter and the member variable can cause confusion as to which one you are referring to at any given moment.

The second use of the this reference is to pass the current object as a parameter to another method, as in the following code:

```
class SomeClass
{
    public void FirstMethod(OtherClass otherObject)
    {
        otherObject.SecondMethod(this);
    }
    // ...
}
```

This code snippet establishes two classes, SomeClass and OtherClass (the definition of OtherClass isn't shown here). SomeClass has a method named FirstMethod( ), and OtherClass has a method named SecondMethod( ).

Inside FirstMethod( ), we'd like to invoke SecondMethod( ), passing in the current object (an instance of SomeClass) for further processing. To do so, you pass in the this reference, which refers to the current instance of SomeClass.

The third use of this is with indexers, which we cover in Chapter 14.

Static and Instance Members

The fields, properties, and methods of a class can be either *instance members* or *static members*. Instance members are associated with instances of a type, whereas static members are associated with the class itself, and not with any particular instance. All methods are instance methods unless you explicitly mark them with the keyword static.

The vast majority of methods will be instance methods. The semantics of an instance method are that you are taking an action on a specific object. From time to time, however, it is convenient to be able to invoke a method without having an instance of the class, and for that, you will use a static method.

You access a static member through the name of the class in which it is declared. For example, suppose you have a class named Button and have instantiated objects of that class named btnUpdate and btnDelete.

Suppose that the Button class has an instance method Draw( ) and a static method GetButtonCount( ). The job of Draw( ) is to draw the current button, and the job of GetButtonCount( ) is to return the number of buttons currently visible on the form. Since GetButtonCount( ) applies to more than just the one button, it wouldn't make sense to call it on a specific instance of Button; therefore, it's static.

You access an instance method through an instance of the class—that is, through an object:

```
btnUpdate.SomeMethod( );
```

You access a static method through the class name, not through an instance:

```
Button.GetButtonCount( );
```

Invoking Static Methods

Static methods are said to operate on the class, rather than on an instance of the class. They do not have a this reference, as there is no instance to point to.

Static methods cannot directly access nonstatic members. You will remember that Main( ) is marked static. For Main( ) to call a nonstatic method of any class, including its own class, it must instantiate an object. In addition, static methods can access only static member fields of the same class.

For the next example, use Visual Studio to create a new console application named StaticTester. Visual Studio creates a namespace, StaticTester, and a class named Program. Rename Program to Tester. Delete the args parameter to Main( ). When you are done, your source code should look like this:

```
using System;
namespace StaticTester
{
    class Tester
    {
        static void Main( )
        {
        }
    }
}
```

That is a good starting point. Until now, you've always done all the work of the program right in the Main( ) method, but now you'll create an instance method, Run( ). The work of the program will now be done in the Run( ) method, rather than in the Main( ) method.

Within the class, but not within the Main( ) method (that is, just before Main( )), declare a new instance method named Run( ).

When you declare a method, you write the accessor (public), followed by the return type, the identifier, and then parentheses:

```
public void Run( )
```

The parentheses can hold parameters, but Run( ) won't have any parameters, so you can just leave the parentheses empty. Create braces for the method, and within the braces, add a statement to print "Hello World" to the console:

```
public void Run( )
{
    Console.WriteLine("Hello World");
}
```

Run( ) is an instance method. Main( ) is a static method and so it cannot invoke Run( ) directly. Therefore, to call Run( ) from inside Main( ), you need to create an instance of the Tester class and call Run( ) on that instance. Add this line inside Main( ):

```
Tester t = new Tester( );
```

When you type the keyword new, IntelliSense tries to help you with the class name. You'll find that Tester is in the list; it is a legitimate class like any other. On the next line, invoke Run( ) on your Tester object t:

```
t.Run( );
```

When you type t followed by the dot operator, IntelliSense presents all the public methods of the Tester class, as shown in Figure 7-1.

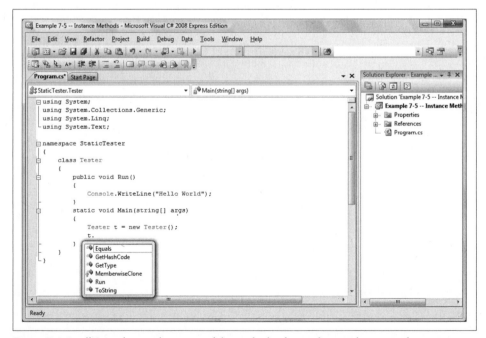

Figure 7-1. IntelliSense knows the names of the methods of your class, and presents them to you when you type the dot operator.

Notice that the Tester class has a number of methods you did not create (Equals, GetHashCode, and others). Every class in C# derives from the Object class, and these methods are part of the Object class. We cover this in Chapter 11.

When your program is complete, it looks like Example 7-5.

Example 7-5. You use an instance method to invoke a method from within a static method, such as Main()

```
using System;
using System.Collections.Generic;
using System.Linq;
using System.Text;

namespace Example_7_5____Instance_Methods
{
    // create the class
    class Tester
    {
        // Run is an instance method
        public void Run()
        {
            Console.WriteLine( "Hello World" );
        }

        // Main is static
        static void Main()
        {
            // create an instance
            Tester t = new Tester();

            // invoke the instance method
            t.Run();
        }
    }
}
```

The output looks like this:

```
Hello World
```

This is the model you'll use from now on in most console applications. The Main() method will be limited to instantiating an object and then invoking the Run() method.

Using Static Fields

A common use of static member variables, or fields, is to keep track of the number of instances/objects that currently exist for your class. In the next example, you'll create a Cat class. The Cat class might be used in a pet-store simulation.

For this example, the Cat class has been stripped to its absolute essentials. The complete listing is shown in Example 7-6. An analysis follows the example.

Example 7-6. Use static fields to keep track of data that applies to the class, not to a specific instance of the class, such as a counter that tracks the number of objects created of that class

```
using System;
using System.Collections.Generic;
using System.Linq;
using System.Text;

namespace Example_7_6____Static_Fields
{
    // declare a Cat class, stripped down
    public class Cat
    {
        // a private static member to keep track of how many Cat objects
        // have been created
        private static int instances = 0;
        private int weight;
        private String name;

        // cat constructor, increments the count of Cats
        public Cat( String name, int weight )
        {
            instances++;
            this.name = name;
            this.weight = weight;
        }

        // Static method to retrieve the current number of Cats
        public static void HowManyCats( )
        {
            Console.WriteLine( "{0} cats adopted", instances );
        }
        public void TellWeight( )
        {
            Console.WriteLine( "{0} is {1} pounds", name, weight );
        }
    }

    class Tester
    {
        public void Run( )
        {
            Cat.HowManyCats( );
            Cat frisky = new Cat( "Frisky", 5 );
            frisky.TellWeight( );
            Cat.HowManyCats( );
            Cat whiskers = new Cat( "Whiskers", 7 );
```

```
        whiskers.TellWeight( );
        Cat.HowManyCats( );
    }

    static void Main( )
    {
        Tester t = new Tester( );
        t.Run( );
    }
  }
}
```

Here is the output:

```
0 cats adopted
Frisky is 5 pounds
1 cats adopted
Whiskers is 7 pounds
2 cats adopted
```

The Cat class begins by defining a static member variable, instances, that is initialized to zero. When you initialize a static variable, the initialization always takes place before any reference is made to that variable. This static member field will keep track of the number of Cat objects created. Each time the constructor runs (creating a new object), the instances field is incremented.

The Cat class also defines two instance fields: name and weight. These track the name and weight of each individual Cat object.

The Cat class defines two methods: HowManyCats( ) and TellWeight( ). HowManyCats( ) is static. The number of Cats is not an attribute of any given Cat; it is an attribute of the entire class. That is, there's only *one* instance of the instances variable for *all* Cat objects. TellWeight( ) is an instance method. The name and weight of each cat is unique for each instance—each Cat has its own instance of the name and weight variables.

The Main( ) method accesses the static HowManyCats( ) method directly, through the class name:

```
Cat.HowManyCats( );
```

Main( ) then creates an instance of Cat and accesses the instance method, TellWeight( ), through the instance of Cat:

```
Cat frisky = new Cat( )
frisky.TellWeight( );
```

Each time a new Cat is created, HowManyCats( ) reports the increase.

Finalizing Objects

Unlike many other programming languages (C, C++, Pascal, and so on), C# provides *garbage collection*. Your objects are destroyed after you are done with them—although not immediately after; they're destroyed when the garbage collection process runs, which is determined by the system. You do not need to worry about cleaning up after your objects unless you use unmanaged or scarce resources. An unmanaged resource is an operating-system feature outside the .NET Framework, such as a connection to a database. A scarce resource is a resource that you have in limited quantity, perhaps because of licensing limitations or limited bandwidth. Graphics resources, such as fonts and brushes, are considered scarce because of the way the operating system works.

If you do control an unmanaged resource, you need to explicitly free that resource when you are done with it. Typically, you'll manage this by implementing the IDisposable interface. (You will learn more about interfaces in Chapter 13.)

The IDisposable interface requires you to create a method named Dispose( ), which will be called by your clients.

If you provide a Dispose( ) method, you should stop the garbage collector from calling your object's destructor. To stop the garbage collector, call the static method GC.SuppressFinalize( ), passing in the this reference for your object. Your finalizer can then call your Dispose( ) method. Thus, you might write:

```
using System;
class Testing : IDisposable
{
   bool is_disposed = false;
   protected virtual void Dispose( bool disposing )
   {
      if ( !is_disposed ) // only dispose once!
      {
         if ( disposing )
         {
            // OK to reference other objects
         }
         // perform cleanup for this object
         Console.WriteLine( "Disposing..." );
      }
      this.is_disposed = true;
   }
    public void Dispose( )
   {
      Dispose( true );
      GC.SuppressFinalize( this );
   }
}
```

For some objects, you'd rather have your clients call a Close( ) method because that is the keyword they use historically (such as File.Close( )).You can implement this by creating a private Dispose( ) method and a public Close( ) method and having your Close( ) method invoke Dispose( ).

Because you cannot be certain that your user will call Dispose( ) reliably, and because finalization is nondeterministic (that is, you can't control when the garbage collector will run), C# provides a using statement to ensure that Dispose( ) is called at the earliest possible time. The idiom is to declare which objects you are using and then to create a scope for these objects with curly braces. When the close brace is reached, the Dispose( ) method will be called on the object automatically, as illustrated here:

```
using System.Drawing;
class Tester
{
 public static void Main( )
 {
    using (Font theFont = new Font("Arial", 10.0f))
    {
    // use the font
    }
 }
}
```

The keyword using is *overdetermined*—that is, it is used in two ways in C#. The first way is to indicate that you are using a namespace, as you see in the preceding code snippet:

```
using System.Drawing
```

The second way is in the using statement that creates a scope to ensure finalization, as you see in this line:

```
using (Font theFont = new Font("Arial",10.0f))
```

Because Windows lets you have only a small number of Font objects, we want to dispose of it at the earliest opportunity. In this code snippet, the Font object is created within the using statement. When the using statement ends, Dispose( ) is guaranteed to be called on the Font object.

Memory Allocation: The Stack Versus the Heap

Objects created within methods are called *local* variables, as we discussed earlier. They are local to the method, as opposed to belonging to the whole object, as member variables are. The object is created within the method, used within the method, and then destroyed sometime after the method ends. Local objects are not part of the object's state—they are temporary value holders, useful only within the particular method.

Local variables of intrinsic types such as int are created on a portion of memory known as *the stack*. The stack is allocated and de-allocated as methods are invoked. When you start a method, all its local variables are created on the stack. When the method ends, local variables are destroyed.

These variables are referred to as local because they exist (and are visible) only during the lifetime of the method. They are said to have *local scope*. When the method ends, the variable goes *out of scope* and is destroyed.

C# divides the world of types into value types and reference types. *Value types* are created on the stack. All the intrinsic types (int, long) are value types (as are structs, discussed later in this chapter), and thus are created on the stack.

Objects, on the other hand, are *reference types*. Reference types are created on an undifferentiated block of memory known as *the heap*. When you declare an instance of a reference type, what you are actually declaring is a *reference*, which is a variable that refers to another object. The reference acts like an alias for the object.

That is, when you write:

```
Dog milo = new Dog( );
```

the new operator creates a Dog object on the heap and returns a reference to it. That reference is assigned to milo. Thus, milo is a reference object that refers to a Dog object on the heap. It is common to say that milo is a reference to a Dog, or even that milo is a "Dog object," but technically that is incorrect. milo is actually a reference that refers to an (unnamed) Dog object on the heap.

The reference milo acts as an alias for that unnamed object. For all practical purposes, however, you can treat milo as though it were the Dog object itself. In other words, it's fine to go on referring to milo as a Dog object. He won't mind.

The implication of using references is that you can have more than one reference to the same object. To see this difference between creating value types and reference types, examine Example 7-7. A complete analysis follows the output.

Example 7-7. Value types are created on the stack, and reference types are created on the heap

```
using System;
using System.Collections.Generic;
using System.Linq;
using System.Text;

namespace Example_7_7____Value_and_Reference_Types
{
    public class Dog
    {
        public int weight;
    }
```

```
class Tester
{
    public void Run( )
    {
        // create an integer
        int firstInt = 5;

        // create a second integer
        int secondInt = firstInt;

        // display the two integers
        Console.WriteLine( "firstInt: {0} secondInt: {1}",
                           firstInt, secondInt );

        // modify the second integer
        secondInt = 7;

        // display the two integers
        Console.WriteLine( "firstInt: {0} secondInt: {1}",
                           firstInt, secondInt );

        // create a dog
        Dog milo = new Dog( );

        // assign a value to weight
        milo.weight = 5;

        // create a second reference to the dog
        Dog fido = milo;

        // display their values
        Console.WriteLine( "milo: {0}, fido: {1}",
                           milo.weight, fido.weight );

        // assign a new weight to the second reference
        fido.weight = 7;

        // display the two values
        Console.WriteLine( "milo: {0}, fido: {1}",
                           milo.weight, fido.weight );
    }

    static void Main( )
    {
        Tester t = new Tester( );
        t.Run( );
    }
}
}
```

The output looks like this:

```
firstInt: 5 secondInt: 5
firstInt: 5 secondInt: 7
Milo: 5, fido: 5
Milo: 7, fido: 7
```

The program begins by creating an integer, firstInt, and initializing it with the value 5. The second integer, secondInt, is then created and initialized with the value in firstInt. Their values are displayed as output:

```
firstInt: 5 secondInt: 5
```

These values are identical. Because int is a value type, a copy of the firstInt value is made and assigned to secondInt; secondInt is an independent second variable, as illustrated in Figure 7-2.

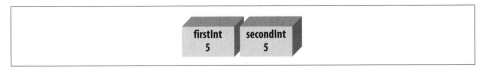

Figure 7-2. secondInt is a copy of firstInt.

Then the program assigns a new value to secondInt:

```
secondInt = 7;
```

Because these variables are value types, independent of one another, the first variable is unaffected. Only the copy is changed, as illustrated in Figure 7-3.

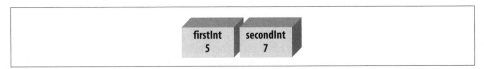

Figure 7-3. Only the copy is changed.

When the values are displayed, they are different:

```
firstInt: 5 secondInt: 7
```

Your next step is to create a simple Dog class with only one member variable, called weight. Note that this field is given an access modifier of public, which specifies that any method of any class can access this field. (Generally, you will not make member variables public. The weight field was made public to simplify this example.)

You instantiate a Dog object and save a reference to that dog in the reference milo:

```
Dog milo = new Dog();
```

You assign the value 5 to milo's weight field:

```
milo.weight = 5;
```

You commonly say that you've set `milo`'s weight to 5, but actually you've set the `weight` field of the unnamed object on the heap to which `milo` refers, as shown in Figure 7-4.

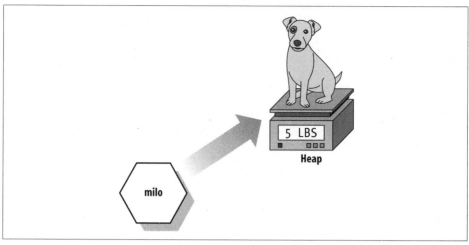

Figure 7-4. milo is a reference to an unnamed Dog object.

Next, you create a second reference to `Dog` and initialize it by setting it equal to `milo`. This creates a new reference to the same object on the heap.

```
Dog fido = milo;
```

Notice that this is syntactically similar to creating a second `int` variable and initializing it with an existing `int`, as you did before:

```
int secondInt = firstInt;
Dog fido = milo;
```

The difference is that `Dog` is a reference type, so `fido` is not a copy of `milo`—it is a second reference to the same object to which `milo` refers. That is, you now have an object on the heap with two references to it, as illustrated in Figure 7-5.

When you change the weight of that object through the `fido` reference:

```
fido.weight = 7;
```

you change the weight of the same object to which `milo` refers. The output reflects this:

```
Milo: 7, fido: 7
```

It isn't that `fido` is changing `milo`; it is that by changing the (unnamed) object on the heap to which `fido` refers you simultaneously change the value of `milo` because they refer to the same unnamed object.

If you had used the keyword new when creating fido, you'd have created a new instance of Dog on the heap, and fido and milo would not point to the same Dog object.

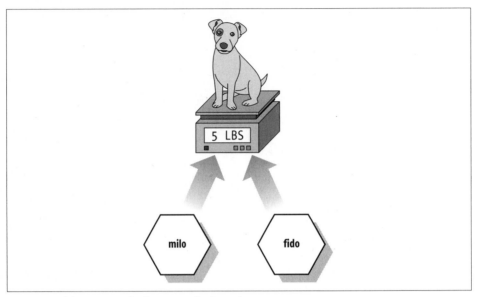

Figure 7-5. fido is a second reference to the Dog object.

Structs

Structs are value types, but they are similar to classes in that they can contain constructors, properties, methods, and fields, all explained in this chapter. Structs can also support operators and indexers (see Chapter 14).

On the other hand, structs don't support inheritance or destructors (see Chapter 11) or field initialization. You define a struct almost exactly like you define a class:

```
[attributes] [access-modifiers] struct identifier [:interface-list]
{ struct-members }
```

Structs implicitly derive from Object (as do all types in C#, including the built-in types) but cannot inherit from any other class or struct (as classes can). Structs are also implicitly *sealed* (that is, no class or struct can derive from a struct; see Chapter 11); this is not true for classes.

The goal of structs is to be "lightweight"—requiring little memory overhead—but their use is so constrained, and the savings are so minimal, that most programmers make little use of them.

C++ programmers *beware*: structs in C++ are identical to classes (except for visibility)— that is not true in C#.

If you need a class that acts as a value object, you can create a *struct* (see the "Structs" sidebar). The use of structs is so unusual that we do not cover them (beyond the sidebar) for the rest of this book. You should know what they are, but you'll probably never need to use one.

Summary

- When you define a new class, you declare its name with the class keyword, and then define its methods, fields, and properties.

- To instantiate an object, you declare the name of the class, followed by an identifier for the object, much as you would a local variable. You then need to allocate memory for the actual (unnamed) object that will be created on the heap; you do so with the keyword new.

- You invoke a method on an object by writing the name of the object, followed by the dot operator, and the method name followed by parentheses. Parameters, if any, are placed within the parentheses.

- Access modifiers dictate which methods of external classes can see and use a variable or method within a class. All members of the class are visible to all methods of its own class.

- Members marked public have no restrictions, and are visible to methods of any class.

- Members marked private are visible only to methods within the same class.

- Members marked protected are visible to methods within the same class, and methods in derived classes.

- If you know the return type of a method, you can use a method call anyplace you would use an instance of that type.

- A constructor is a special method invoked when a new object is created. If you do not define any constructors at all for your class, the compiler will provide a default constructor that does nothing. A default constructor is a constructor that takes no parameters. You are free to create your own default constructor for your class.

- You can initialize the values of your member variables when you define them in your class.

- Object initializers allow you to set the public fields of an object immediately after you create the object.

- Anonymous types allow you to create a class with no name, and initialize its fields immediately. The compiler will implicitly assign types to those fields. You can use the var keyword to create an instance of the anonymous object.

- The this keyword is used to refer to the current instance of an object.

- Every nonstatic method of a class has an implicit this variable passed into the method.

- Static members are associated with the class itself, not with a particular instance. Static members are declared with the keyword static, and are invoked through the class name. Static methods do not have a this parameter because there is no instance to refer to.

- C# does not specifically require a finalizer method in your classes because the framework will destroy any object that is not in use.

- You should provide a Dispose( ) method if your class uses unmanaged resources.

- Local value type variables are created on the stack. When the method ends, these variables go out of scope and are destroyed.

- Objects are reference types, and are created on the heap. When you declare an instance of a reference type, you are actually creating a reference to that object's location in memory. If you declare a reference to an object on the heap within a method, when the method ends that reference is destroyed. If there are no remaining references to the object on the heap, the object itself is destroyed by the garbage collector at some later time.

- You can define a reference to an existing object by declaring the class and an identifier and then assigning to that identifier an existing object; the two identifiers now both refer to the same (unnamed) object on the heap.

You spent the preceding chapter learning the theory, and now you've seen some of the practice behind the most powerful concept in C#. Hopefully by this point, you've seen how you can model just about anything with carefully defined classes and methods. You may have noticed a few limitations of the methods we've shown you so far, though. For example, methods can return only a single value—what if you want to manipulate and return two or more values? Or what if you're not quite sure how many parameters you'll have when you call the method? Maybe you'll create a Dog object with a name and a weight, but perhaps sometimes you just have the name, and you'll need to add the weight later. C# methods are flexible enough to handle all of these cases, and in the next chapter, you'll spend time looking at them more closely.

Test Your Knowledge: Quiz

Question 7-1. What is the difference between a class and an object?

Question 7-2. What does the keyword private do?

Question 7-3. What does the keyword public do?

Question 7-4. What method is called when you create an object?

Question 7-5. What is a default constructor?

Question 7-6. What types can a constructor return?

Question 7-7. How do you initialize the value of a member variable in a class?

Question 7-8. What does the keyword this refer to?

Question 7-9. What is the difference between a static method and an instance method?

Question 7-10. Where are reference types created? Where are value types created?

Test Your Knowledge: Exercises

Exercise 7-1. Write a program with a Math class that has four methods: Add, Subtract, Multiply, and Divide, each of which takes two parameters. Call each method from Main( ) and provide an appropriate output statement to demonstrate that each method works. You don't need to have the user provide input; just provide the two integers to the methods within Main( ).

Exercise 7-2. Modify the program from Exercise 7-1 so that you do not have to create an instance of Math to call the four methods. Call the four methods again from Main( ) to demonstrate that they work.

Exercise 7-3. Create a class Book that you could use to keep track of book objects. Each Book object should have a title, author, publisher, and ISBN (which should be a string, rather than a numeric type, so that the ISBN can start with a 0 or include an X). The class should have a DisplayBook( ) method to output that information to the console. In Main( ), create three Book objects with this data.

Programming C# 3.0	Jesse Liberty and Donald Xie	O'Reilly	9780596527433
C# 3.0 In a Nutshell	Joseph Albahari and Ben Albahari	O'Reilly	9780596527570
C# 3.0 Cookbook	Jay Hilyard and Stephen Teilhet	O'Reilly	9780596516109

Because all three books have the same publisher, you should initialize that field in your class.

Exercise 7-4. You might think it isn't possible to draw geometric shapes using the console output, and you'd be mostly right. We can simulate drawing shapes, though, by imagining a graph and displaying, say, the coordinates of the four corners of a square. Start with a class called Point. This is a simple enough class; it should have members for an *x* coordinate and a *y* coordinate, a constructor, and a method for displaying the coordinates in the form (x,y). For now, make the x and y members public, to keep things simple.

Now create a class Square. Internally, the class should keep track of all four points of the square, but in the constructor, you should accept just a single Point and a length (make it an integer, to keep it simple). You should also have a method to output the coordinates of all four points. In Main( ), create the initial Point, then create a Square and output its corners.

CHAPTER 8

Inside Methods

In Chapter 7, you saw that classes consist of fields and methods. Fields hold the state of the object, and methods define the object's behavior.

In this chapter, you'll explore how methods work in more detail. You've already seen how to create methods, and in this chapter you'll learn about method *overloading*, a technique that allows you to create more than one method with the same name. This enables your clients to invoke the method with different parameter types.

This chapter also introduces *properties*. To clients of your class, properties look like member variables, but properties are implemented as methods. This allows you to keep your data members safe from outside interference, which is called *data hiding*, while providing your clients with convenient access to the state of your class.

Chapter 7 described the difference between value types (such as int and long) and reference types. The most common value types are the "built-in" or "primitive" types, and the most common reference types are the user-defined types. This chapter explores the implications of passing value types to methods and shows how you can pass value types *by reference*, allowing the called method to act on the original object in the calling method.

Overloading Methods

Often, you'll want to have more than one method with the same name. The most common example of this is to have more than one constructor with the same name, which allows you to create the object with different types of parameters, or a different number of parameters. For example, if you were creating a Box object, you might have circumstances where you want to create the Box object by passing in the length, width, and height. Other times, you might want to create a Box object by passing in an existing Box object. Still other times, you might want to pass in just a length, without width and height. Overloading the constructor allows you to provide these various options.

Chapter 7 explained that your constructor is automatically invoked when your object is created. Let's return to the Box class created in that chapter. The constructor in that chapter took three integers for length, width, and height. That works fine for most boxes, but suppose you have a situation where some of the boxes might need a color. That's an entirely different parameter, and with a different data type, as well (a string, in this case). Some boxes might need a color; others might not. You can provide separate constructors for the colored and noncolored boxes.

To overload your constructor, you must make sure that each constructor has a unique *signature*. The signature of a method is composed of its name and its parameter list, but not its return type. Two methods differ in their signatures if they have different names or different parameter lists, which means having different numbers or types of parameters. The following four lines of code show how you might distinguish methods by signature:

```
void MyMethod(int p1);
void MyMethod(int p1, int p2);    // different number
void MyMethod(int p1, string s1); // different types
void SomeMethod(int p1);          // different name
```

You can overload any method, not just constructors. The first three methods are all overloads of the MyMethod( ) method. The first method differs from the second and third in the number of parameters. The second method closely resembles the third version, but the second parameter in each is a different type. In the second method, the second parameter (p2) is an integer; in the third method, the second parameter (s1) is a string. These changes to the number or type of parameters are sufficient changes in the signature to allow the compiler to distinguish the methods.

The fourth method differs from the other three methods by having a different name. This is not method overloading, just different methods, but it illustrates that two methods can have the same number and type of parameters if they have different names. Thus, the fourth method and the first have the same parameter list, but their names are different.

A class can have any number of methods, as long as each one's signature differs from that of all the others. Example 8-1 illustrates a new version of the Box class with two constructors: one that takes three integers and one that takes three integers and a string for the color.

Example 8-1. Overloading a method is a way to provide flexibility in the parameters that clients provide to your class methods

```
using System;
using System.Collections.Generic;
using System.Linq;
using System.Text;

namespace Example_8_1____Overloading
{
```

Example 8-1. Overloading a method is a way to provide flexibility in the parameters that clients provide to your class methods (continued)

```
public class Box
{
    // private variables
    private int length;
    private int width;
    private int height;
    private string color;

    // public methods
    public void DisplayBox()
    {
        Console.WriteLine("Length: {0}, Width: {1}, Height: {2}
                    Color: {3}", length, width, height, color);
    }

    // constructor
    public Box(int theLength, int theWidth, int theHeight)
    {
        length = theLength;
        width = theWidth;
        height = theHeight;
        color = "brown";
    }

    public Box(int theLength, int theWidth, int theHeight,
                string theColor)
    {
        length = theLength;
        width = theWidth;
        height = theHeight;
        color = theColor;
    }
}

public class Tester
{
    static void Main()
    {
        Box box1 = new Box(4, 8, 3);
        box1.DisplayBox();
        Box blueBox = new Box(3, 5, 7, "blue");
        blueBox.DisplayBox();
    }
}
```

The output looks like this:

```
Length: 4, Width: 8, Height: 3 Color: brown
Length: 3, Width: 5, Height: 7 Color: blue
```

If a function's signature consisted only of the function name, the compiler would not know which constructors to call when constructing the new Box objects, box1 and blueBox. However, because the signature includes the parameters and their types, the compiler is able to match the constructor call for blueBox with the constructor whose signature requires a string object:

```
Box blueBox = new Box(3, 5, 7, "blue");
```

```
public Box(int theLength, int theWidth, int theHeight, string theColor)
```

Likewise, the compiler is able to associate the box1 constructor call with the constructor whose signature specifies just three integer arguments:

```
Box box1 = new Box(4, 8, 3);
```

```
public Box(int theLength, int theWidth, int theHeight)
```

Notice that the constructor that doesn't take a color automatically assigns a color of "brown" to all boxes created with that constructor. We changed the DisplayBox( ) method to output the color of the box, so you see that box1 is brown in the output.

 When you overload a method, you must change the signature (the name, number, or type of the parameters). You are free, as well, to change the return type, but this is optional. Changing only the return type does not overload the method, and creating two methods with the same signature but differing return types generates a compile error.

Encapsulating Data with Properties

Most of the time, you'll want to designate the member variables of a class as private. This means that only member methods of that class can access their value. When you prevent methods outside the class from directly accessing member variables, you're enforcing *data hiding*, which is an aspect of the encapsulation of a class, as we discussed in Chapter 6.

That's fine, but if the members are private, how do your other classes access that data? The answer for C# programmers is *properties*. Properties allow other methods (called *clients*) to access the state of your class as though they were accessing member fields directly, although you're actually implementing that access through a class method.

This solution is ideal. The client wants direct access to the state of the object. As the class designer, though, you want to hide the internal state of the class in class fields and provide indirect access through a method. For example, you might want external classes to be able to read a value, but not change it; or you might want to write some code so that the internal field can accept only values in a certain range. If you grant external classes free access to your member fields, you can't control any of that.

The property provides both the illusion of direct access for the client and the reality of indirect access for the class developer.

By separating the class state from the method that accesses that state (a process called *decoupling*), you're free to change the internal state of the object whenever you need to. When the Box class is first created, the length value might be stored as a member variable. Later on, you might redesign the class so that the length value is computed or maybe retrieved from a database. If the client had direct access to the original length member variable, changing how that value is resolved would break the client. By decoupling and forcing the client to go through a property, the Box class can change how it manages its internal state without breaking client code.

In short, properties provide the data hiding required by good object-oriented design. Example 8-2 creates a property called length, which is then discussed in the paragraphs that follow.

Example 8-2. Properties provide data hiding by supplying the client with a method that looks like the client is accessing the member variable directly

```csharp
using System;
using System.Collections.Generic;
using System.Linq;
using System.Text;

namespace Example_8_2____Properties
{
    public class Box
    {
        // private variables
        private int length;
        private int width;
        private int height;

        // property
        public int Length
        {
            get
            {
                return length;
            }
            set
            {
                length = value;
            }
        }

        // public methods
        public void DisplayBox()
        {
            Console.WriteLine("Length: {0}, Width: {1}, Height:
                        {2}", length, width, height);
        }
```

Example 8-2. Properties provide data hiding by supplying the client with a method that looks like the client is accessing the member variable directly (continued)

```
        // constructor
        public Box(int theLength, int theWidth, int theHeight)
        {
            length = theLength;
            width = theWidth;
            height = theHeight;
        }

    }

    public class Tester
    {
        public void Run()
        {
            // create a box for testing and display it
            Box testBox = new Box(3, 5, 7);
            testBox.DisplayBox();

            // access the length, store it in a local variable
            int testLength = testBox.Length;
            Console.WriteLine("Length of box is: {0}", testLength);

            // increment the length
            testLength++;

            // assign the new value to the member variable
            testBox.Length = testLength;

            // display the box again to test the new value
            testBox.DisplayBox();
        }

        static void Main()
        {
            Tester t = new Tester();
            t.Run();
        }
    }
}
```

The output should look something like this:

```
Length: 3, Width: 5, Height: 7
Length of box is: 3
Length: 4, Width: 5, Height: 7
```

You create a property by writing the property type and name followed by a pair of braces. Within the braces, you can declare the get and set accessors. These accessors are very similar to methods, but they are actually part of the property itself.

The purpose of these accessors is to provide the client with simple ways to retrieve and change the value of the private member length, as you'll see.

Neither of these accessors has explicit parameters, though the set accessor has an *implicit* parameter called value, which is used to set the value of the member variable.

 By convention, property names are written in Pascal notation (initial uppercase), and member fields have initial lowercase. This isn't mandatory, but it makes it easier to distinguish between the field and the property.

In Example 8-2, the declaration of the length property creates both get and set accessors:

```
// property
public int Length
{
    get
    {
        return length;
    }
    set
    {
        length = value;
    }
}
```

Each accessor has an *accessor body*, which does the work of retrieving or setting the property value. The property value might be stored in a database (in which case, the accessor would do whatever work is needed to interact with the database), or it might just be stored in a private member variable (in this case, length):

```
private int length;
```

The get Accessor

The body of the get accessor (sometimes called a "getter") is similar to a class method that returns an object of the type of the property. In Example 8-2, the accessor for the Length property is similar to a method that returns an int. It returns the value of the private member variable length in which the value of the property has been stored:

```
get
{
    return length;
}
```

In this example, the value of a private int member variable is returned, but you could just as easily retrieve an integer value from a database or compute it on the fly.

Remember, this description is from the perspective of the author of the Box class. To the client (user) of the Box class, Length is a property, and how the Box class returns its length is encapsulated within the Box class—the client doesn't know or care.

Whenever you need to retrieve the value (other than to assign to it), the get accessor is invoked. For example, in the following code, the value of the Box object's Length property is assigned to a local variable. You use the dot operator to call the accessor, exactly as you would if you were accessing a public property.

To the client, the local variable testLength is assigned the value of the Length property of testBox (the Box object). To the creator of the Box object, however, the get accessor is called, which in this case returns the value of the length member variable:

```
Box testBox = new Box(3, 5, 7);
int testLength = testBox.Length;
```

The set Accessor

The set accessor (sometimes called a "setter") sets the value of a property. When you define a set accessor, you must use the value keyword to represent the argument whose value is assigned to the property:

```
set
{
    length = value;
}
```

Here, again, a private member variable is used to store the value of the property, but the set accessor could write to a database or update other member variables as needed.

When external code assigns a value to the property, the set accessor is automatically invoked, and the implicit parameter value is set to the value you assign:

```
testLength++;
testBox.Length = testLength;
```

The first line increments a local variable named testLength. As far as the client is concerned, that new value is assigned to the Length property of the local Box object testBox. Again, this looks the same as though you were assigning to a public variable. To the author of the Box class, however, the local variable testLength is passed in to the set accessor as the implicit parameter value and assigned (in this case) to the local member variable length.

The advantage of this approach is that the client can interact with the properties directly, without sacrificing the data hiding and encapsulation sacrosanct in good object-oriented design.

You can create a read-only property by not implementing the set part of the property. Similarly, you can create a write-only property by not implementing the get part.

Automatic Properties

Although we mentioned that the accessors may calculate values on the fly, or access a database to obtain a value, most of the time you'll just use them to retrieve or set an internal member directly, like you saw with the Length property:

```
public int Length
{
    get
    {
        return length;
    }
    set
    {
        length = value;
    }
}
```

As you can imagine, if you have a lot of private member fields in your class, creating accessors for all of them is both repetitive and mindless. Therefore, if all you're doing is retrieving or setting a private member, you can use a shortcut syntax called *automatic properties*. That syntax works like this:

```
public int Length { get; set; }
```

Simple, isn't it? This syntax will save you a lot of typing in complicated classes. Remember, though, that if you want to do anything other than simply retrieve or assign the value, you'll need to create the accessor by hand. It's also worth mentioning that if you use the automatic properties, you shouldn't also create the private members; the compiler will do that for you behind the scenes.

Returning Multiple Values

Methods can return only a single value, but this isn't always convenient. Suppose you have a class called Doubler, which contains a method we'll call DoubleInt( ) that takes two integers and doubles them. Simple enough, right?

The problem is that although DoubleInt( ) can accept two integers, and can process them both, it can return only one of them. Example 8-3 shows a way that you might try to write DoubleInt( ).

Example 8-3. This is our first attempt at retrieving multiple values

```
using System;
using System.Collections.Generic;
using System.Linq;
using System.Text;

namespace Example_8_3____Returning_multiple_values
{
    class Doubler
    {
        public void DoubleInt(int firstNum, int secondNum)
        {
            firstNum = firstNum * 2;
            secondNum = secondNum * 2;
        }
    }
    class Tester
    {
        public void Run()
        {
            int first = 5;
            int second = 10;
            Console.WriteLine("Before doubling:");
            Console.WriteLine("First number: {0}, Second number: {1}",
                            first, second);

            Doubler d = new Doubler();
            d.DoubleInt(first, second);
            Console.WriteLine("After doubling:");
            Console.WriteLine("First number: {0}, Second number: {1}",
                            first, second);
        }

        static void Main(string[] args)
        {
            Tester t = new Tester();
            t.Run();
        }
    }
}
```

The output will look something like this:

```
Before doubling:
First number: 5, Second number: 10
After doubling:
First number: 5, Second number: 10
```

Obviously, that's not the desired result. The problem is with the parameters. You pass in two integer parameters to DoubleInt( ), and you modify those two parameters in DoubleInt( ), but when the values are accessed back in Run( ) they are unchanged. This is because integers are value types.

Passing Value Types by Reference

As we discussed in Chapter 7, C# divides the world of types into value types and reference types. All intrinsic types (such as int and long) are value types. Instances of classes (objects) are reference types.

When you pass a value type (such as an int) into a method, a copy is made. When you make changes to the parameter, you're actually making changes to the copy. Back in the Run( ) method, the original integer variables—first and second—are unaffected by the changes made in DoubleInt( ).

What you need is a way to pass in the integer parameters by reference so that changes made in the method are made to the original object in the calling method. When you pass an object by reference, the parameter refers to the same object. Thus, when you make changes in DoubleInt( ), the changes are made to the original variables in Run( ). You do this by prefacing the parameters with the keyword ref.

Technically, when you pass a reference type, the reference itself is passed by value; but the copy that is made is a copy of a reference, and thus that copy points to the same (unnamed) object on the heap as did the original reference object. That is how you achieve the semantics of "pass by reference" in C# using pass by value. However, that's all behind-the-scenes stuff, and it's acceptable to say that you're passing objects by reference.

This requires two small modifications to the code in Example 8-3. First, change the parameters of the DoubleInt( ) method to indicate that the parameters are ref (reference) parameters:

```
public void DoubleInt(ref int firstNum, ref int secondNum)
```

Second, modify the call to DoubleInt( ) to pass the arguments as references:

```
d.DoubleInt(ref first, ref second);
```

If you leave out the second step of marking the arguments with the keyword ref, the compiler will complain that the argument cannot be converted from an int to a ref int.

These changes are shown in Example 8-4.

Example 8-4. You can use the ref keyword to pass by reference

```
using System;
using System.Collections.Generic;
using System.Linq;
using System.Text;

namespace Example_8_4____Passing_by_Reference
```

Example 8-4. You can use the ref keyword to pass by reference (continued)

```
{
    class Doubler
    {
        public void DoubleInt(ref int firstNum, ref int secondNum)
        {
            firstNum = firstNum * 2;
            secondNum = secondNum * 2;
        }
    }
    class Tester
    {
        public void Run()
        {
            int first = 5;
            int second = 10;
            Console.WriteLine("Before doubling:");
            Console.WriteLine("First number: {0}, Second number: {1}",
                            first, second);

            Doubler d = new Doubler();
            d.DoubleInt(ref first, ref second);
            Console.WriteLine("After doubling:");
            Console.WriteLine("First number: {0}, Second number: {1}",
                            first, second);
        }

        static void Main(string[] args)
        {
            Tester t = new Tester();
            t.Run();
        }
    }
}
```

This time, the output looks like this:

```
Before doubling:
First number: 5, Second number: 10
After doubling:
First number: 10, Second number: 20
```

These results are more like what you'd expect.

By declaring these parameters to be ref parameters, you instruct the compiler to pass them by reference. Instead of a copy being made, the parameters in DoubleInt() are references to the corresponding variables (first and second) that were created in Run(). When you change these values in DoubleInt(), the change is reflected in Run().

Keep in mind that ref parameters are references to the actual original value—it is as though you said, "Here, work on this one." Conversely, value parameters are copies—it is as though you said, "Here, work on one *just like* this."

out Parameters and Definite Assignment

As we noted in Chapter 4, C# imposes *definite assignment*, which requires that all variables be assigned a value before they are used. Suppose you have a method for returning all three parameters from a Box object. You'd call the method something like this:

```
myBox.GetDimensions( ref myLength, ref myWidth, ref myHeight);
```

Because of definite assignment, though, you'd have to initialize those three variables before you can pass them to your method:

```
int myLength = 0;
int myWidth = 0;
int myHeight = 0;
myBox.GetDimensions( ref myLength, ref myWidth, ref myHeight);
```

It seems silly to initialize these values, because you immediately pass them by reference into GetDimensions( ) where they'll be changed; but if you don't initialize them, the compiler will raise an error for each of the variables.

C# provides the out modifier for situations such as this, in which initializing a parameter is only a formality. The out modifier removes the requirement that a reference parameter be initialized. The parameters to GetDimension( ), for example, provide no information to the method; they are simply a mechanism for getting information out of it. Thus, by marking all three as out parameters using the out keyword, you eliminate the need to initialize them outside the method.

Within the called method, the out parameters must be assigned a value before the method returns. Here are the altered parameter declarations for GetDimensions( ):

```
public void GetDimensions( out int theLength, out int theWidth
                           out int theHeight )
{
    theLength = length;
    theWidth = width;
    theHeight = height;
}
```

Here is the new invocation of the method in Run( ):

```
int myLength;
int myWidth;
int myHeight;
myBox.GetDimensions( out myLength, out myWidth, out myHeight);
```

The keyword out implies the same semantics as the keyword ref, except that it also allows you to use the variable without first initializing it in the calling method.

Summary

- Overloading is the act of creating two or more methods with the same name, but that differ in the number, type of parameters, or both.

- Properties appear to clients to be members, but appear to the designer of the class to be methods. This allows the designer to modify how the property retrieves its value without breaking the semantics of the client program.

- Properties include get and set accessors that are used to retrieve and modify a member field, respectively. The set accessor has an implicit parameter named value that represents the value to be assigned through the property.

- Automatic properties provide a shorthand way of creating properties, if all you want to do is set or retrieve a value, as opposed to doing any other processing in the accessor.

- When you "pass by reference," the called method affects the object referred to in the calling method. When you pass by value, the changes in the called method are not reflected in the calling method. You can pass value types by reference by using either the ref or the out keyword.

- The out parameter eliminates the requirement to initialize a variable before passing it to a method.

Now you have an idea of how methods work, and just how essential they are to your classes. Classes with no methods can still be very useful for holding data, but they won't be able to do much on their own. You'll be seeing methods extensively throughout the rest of this book, to the point where you probably won't even think much about them anymore. You may have noticed that method calls make the flow of your program much more complicated than the straight line it was in the early chapters. That's entirely appropriate, but one side-effect of complicating the flow is that it can become harder to find bugs. If your program has methods that call other methods that call still more methods, and it crashes, where should you start to look for the bug? Fortunately, Visual Studio can help you out; it has a whole set of tools designed to help you find and diagnose bugs. We'll take a quick break from the C# theory to examine those tools in Chapter 9. We think you'll thank us for it in later chapters.

Test Your Knowledge: Quiz

Question 8-1. What is the purpose of method overloading?

Question 8-2. How must overloaded methods differ from each other?

Question 8-3. What is the signature of a method?

Question 8-4. What are properties?

Question 8-5. What object-oriented programming principle do properties enforce?

Question 8-6. How do you create a read-only property?

Question 8-7. What is the purpose of automatic properties?

Question 8-8. How do you retrieve more than one return value from a method?

Question 8-9. Where must you use the keyword ref?

Question 8-10. What is the keyword out used for?

Test Your Knowledge: Exercises

Exercise 8-1. Write a program with an overloaded method for tripling the value of the argument. You don't need to create a separate class for this; just use static methods right in Tester. One version of the method should triple an int value, and the other version should triple a float value. Call both methods to demonstrate that they work.

Exercise 8-2. Create a Dog class, where the Dog objects have both a weight and a color, hidden from the client. Create a Dog object, then retrieve its color and display it to the user. Ask the user for a weight, and use that input to set the Dog's weight.

Exercise 8-3. Write a program with just one method that takes an int value, supplied by the user, and returns both double and triple that value. You don't need a separate class; just put the method in Tester. In Run( ), output the results to the console to make sure it worked.

Exercise 8-4. Modify the program from Exercise 8-3 so that you don't need to initialize the variables that will hold the doubled and tripled values before calling the method.

CHAPTER 9
Basic Debugging

Mistakes happen. It's a simple fact of life, and it's true in programming, too. Even the most experienced programmers make mistakes, sometimes the same mistakes over and over. You've probably made a few as you've gone through the exercises in this book. Mistakes are normal, and they are easy to make, especially in a programming language such as C#; we even have a special word for programming mistakes: *bugs*. You've probably noticed that the compiler (that's Visual Studio or C# Express) catches a lot of your bugs, and tells you what's wrong. It's even right a lot of the time, although it's certainly not perfect. The more you learn, and the more you have the basics of the language down, the more complicated your mistakes become. Staring at the code and puzzling it out isn't an effective way to find bugs anymore. For that, you need a *debugger*. Fortunately, Visual Studio (including C# Express) comes with a great debugger built right in.

The debugger is your friend. There is simply no tool more powerful than a debugger for learning C# and for writing quality C# programs. Put simply, the debugger is a tool that helps you understand what is really going on when your program is running. It is the X-ray of software development, allowing you to see inside programs and diagnose potential problems.

Without a debugger, you are guessing; with a debugger, you are seeing. It is as simple as that. Whatever time you invest in learning to use your debugger is time well spent.

The debugger is also a powerful tool for understanding code written by others. By putting someone else's code into the debugger and stepping through it, you can see exactly how the methods work and what data they manipulate.

The Visual Studio debugger provides a number of windows for watching and interacting with your program while it executes. Getting comfortable with the debugger can mean the difference between finding bugs quickly and struggling for hours or days. Now that you're programming with classes, and execution that jumps around to different methods, it's an appropriate time to take a break from learning the specifics of the language and to learn some debugging techniques that will help reduce your frustration later on.

 Debugging is one of the very few areas where Visual Studio 2008 and C# Express differ dramatically. The full Visual Studio offers several windows and options that just aren't available in C# Express. Most of the basic functionality is in both versions, but Visual Studio makes it easier to get to, and has some extra bells and whistles. We'll tell you whenever there's a difference between the products.

Setting a Breakpoint

To get started with the debugger, return to Example 8-1 in Chapter 8. You'll be putting a *breakpoint* on the first line of Main( ) to see how this code actually works. A breakpoint is an instruction to the debugger to stop running. You set a breakpoint, run the program, and the debugger runs the program up until the breakpoint. Then you have the opportunity to examine the value of your variables at this point in the execution. Examining your program as it runs can help you untangle otherwise impenetrable problems. You'll often set multiple breakpoints, which allows you to skip through your program, examining the state of your object at selected locations.

You can set a breakpoint in many different ways. The easiest is to click in the left margin of the code window. This causes a red dot to appear in the margin next to the relevant line of code, which is also highlighted in red, as shown in Figure 9-1 (although you can't see the color in the book). Open Example 8-1 from Chapter 8, if you haven't already, and click in the gray margin next to the first line of Main( ) (Tester t = new Tester( )). Notice that as you hover over the breakpoint, a tool tip tells you the line on which the breakpoint appears.

You are now ready to run the program to the breakpoint. To do so, you must be sure to run in debug mode, which you can do by clicking the Start button (▶) or by choosing the Start Debugging item from the Debug menu. In any case, the program starts and runs to the breakpoint, as shown in Figure 9-2.

 Up until now, we've encouraged you to select Start Without Debugging so that your console window won't vanish on you. If you want to use the debugger, though, you'll need to "start with debugging," obviously. Any breakpoint you set will keep your console window from vanishing.

The first thing to notice is that the program has stopped execution just *before* executing the statement with the breakpoint. In this case, that means the Tester object t hasn't yet been created. Your console window is open, but blank, because your program hasn't done anything yet. You'll also notice that the red breakpoint symbol

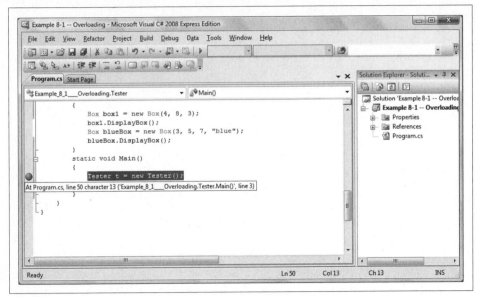

Figure 9-1. Setting a breakpoint is easy; just click in the left margin. A red dot appears to show where the breakpoint is set.

now has a yellow arrow in it. If you had more than one breakpoint in your program, the arrow would show you which one you're stopped at now. The statement that's about to be executed is highlighted in yellow to help you find it. Also, a number of helpful windows are open, and we'll get to those in a moment.

The most useful feature of the debugger is the ability to *step into* the code, or execute the program one line at a time, watching the changes that happen with each line. To step into the code, press the F11 function key twice. With the first key press, the Tester object is created. The second key press moves you to the next line in the code, which calls the Run( ) method. Press the key once more to *step inside* the code for the Run( ) method where the program creates a new Box object, box1.

F11 and F10 are the step command keys. The difference is that F10 steps over method calls, whereas F11 steps into them. With F10, the methods are executed, but you don't see each step within the method in the debugger; the highlighting jumps to the next statement after the method call. When you step into the method call with F11, on the other hand, the highlighting will move to the first line of the called method.

If you use F11 to step into a method you actually meant to step over, Shift-F11 will step you out. The method you stepped into will run to completion, and you'll break on the first line back in the calling method.

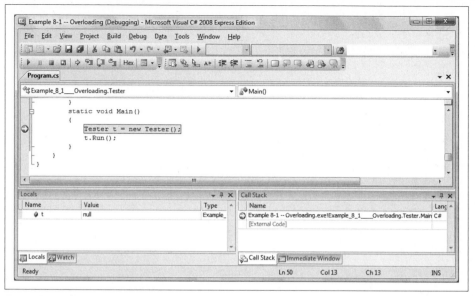

Figure 9-2. When execution stops at the breakpoint, the red breakpoint icon sprouts a yellow arrow.

Using the Debug Menu to Set Your Breakpoint

In Visual Studio, but not C# Express, instead of clicking in the margin to set your breakpoint, you can use Debug → New Breakpoint → Break at Function (or use the keyboard shortcut for the menu item, Ctrl-D, N). This brings up the New Breakpoint dialog box, as shown in Figure 9-3. In this dialog box, you can specify the name of the method where you want to break, and even the line and character within the method, if you know them.

You can also examine and manipulate all the breakpoints together in the Breakpoints window, as shown in Figure 9-4. You can access this window in Visual Studio by selecting Debug → Windows → Breakpoints, or by pressing Ctrl-Alt-B. Unfortunately, this window is completely unavailable in C# Express, which is probably the greatest deficiency in its debugging suite.

Setting Conditions and Hit Counts

The default behavior is for the breakpoint to cause the program to break every time you pass that line of code. Sometimes you only want to break (for example) every 20th time it passes that line of code, or only if the value of some variable is greater than, for example, 0. You can set conditions on the breakpoint by right-clicking on it in the Editor window or in the Breakpoints window, as shown in Figure 9-5.

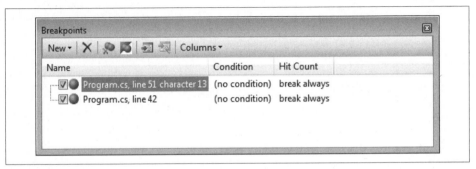

Figure 9-3. *The New Breakpoint dialog lets you set a breakpoint down to the character, if you want to be that precise.*

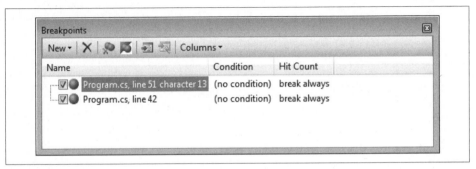

Figure 9-4. *The Breakpoints window lets you manage your breakpoints, but only if you're using Visual Studio.*

In C# Express, you'll see only the first two options on this menu: Delete Breakpoint and Disable Breakpoint. In Visual Studio, you can choose either Hit Count or Condition. If you choose Hit Count, you are offered variations such as "break when the hit count is a multiple of", as shown in Figure 9-6.

If you choose Condition, an open-ended condition text box is provided. In Figure 9-7, we have typed in theValue > 20 as an example.

Examining Values: The Autos and Locals Windows

Look at the tabs below the code window—if you're using Visual Studio, you'll find a Locals window and an Autos window, possibly as tabs in a single window along with some others. If you're using C# Express, the Autos window won't be there, but Locals will be. Both of these display your local variables. The difference is that the Autos window shows variables used in the current statement and the previous statement. (The current statement is the statement at the current execution location,

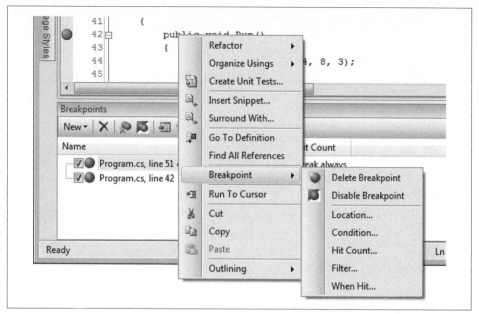

Figure 9-5. In Visual Studio, the Breakpoint menu allows you to select various options for your breakpoint settings.

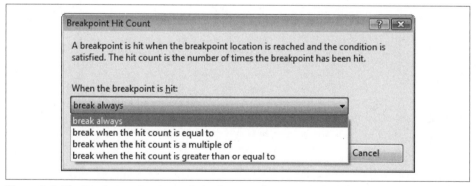

Figure 9-6. The Breakpoint Hit Count dialog lets you choose how often you want this point to be reached before breaking.

which is highlighted *automatically* in the debugger—thus, the window's name.) The Locals window displays all the variables in the current method, including parameters, as shown in Figure 9-8, along with each variable's current value and type.

> The debugger stacks the Autos and Locals windows together with other tabs, as shown in Figure 9-8. You are free to separate these windows or to move them to be tabbed with other windows. You can simply drag-and-drop the windows where you want them. When you drop one window onto another, the two windows are tabbed together.

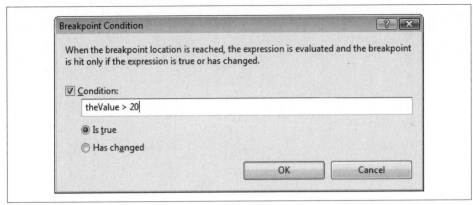

Figure 9-7. *The Breakpoint Condition dialog is more open-ended, offering greater flexibility in your breakpoints.*

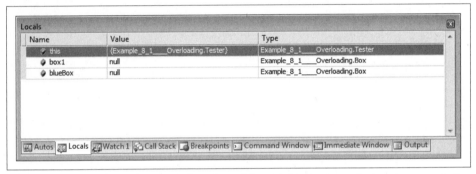

Figure 9-8. *The Locals window shows the values of the variables in the method you're currently in.*

To see how this works, put a breakpoint on the first line of the Run( ) method and run the program. When the program stops, press F10 to step over the creation of the new Box object. The Autos window shows you that the new Box has been created, as shown in Figure 9-9.

Because box1 has just been created, it is shown in red. Notice the plus sign (+) next to box1. box1 is a member of the Box class, as you know, and that class has several members. Clicking the plus sign reveals the internal state of this object, as shown in Figure 9-10.

Press F11 a few more times, and you'll see that the Autos window changes to show you the new values, appropriate to the current line of code.

As mentioned earlier, the Locals window lets you look at all the variables in the current method simultaneously. If you look at the Locals window while the execution is in the Box constructor, you'll see the local variables theLength, theWidth, and theHeight (the parameters to the constructor) and this (the current object).

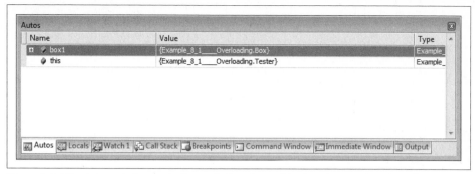

Figure 9-9. The Autos window is similar to the Locals window, but shows values from the current statement.

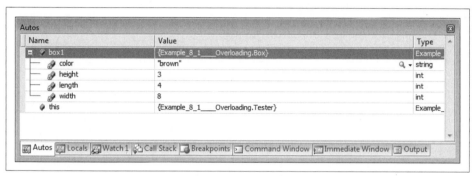

Figure 9-10. Expanding the variable gives you a look at the state of the object.

Expand the this variable, and you'll see the Box object, with its members uninitialized. Press F11 to progress through the assignment of values to the member variables of the Box class. As you press the F11 key, the update is reflected in the Locals window, as shown in Figure 9-11.

Name	Value	Type
⊟ this	{Example_8_1___Overloading.Box}	Example_8_1___Overloading.Box
color	null	string
height	3	int
length	4	int
width	8	int
theLength	4	int
theWidth	8	int
theHeight	3	int

Autos Locals Watch 1 Call Stack Breakpoints Command Window Immediate Window Output

Figure 9-11. If you watch the Locals window as you step through the application, you can see the assignment of the object's member fields.

Explore the Locals and Autos windows as you step through the program. When you want to stop, choose the Stop Debugging item from the Debug menu to stop processing and return to the editor.

Setting Your Watch

When you're debugging a program with many local variables, you usually don't want to watch all of them; you need to keep track of only a few. You can track specific variables and objects in the Watch window. You can have up to four Watch windows at a time in Visual Studio, but just the one in C# Express. Watch windows are like by-invitation versions of the Locals window; they list the objects you ask the debugger to keep an eye on, and you can see their values change as you step through the program, as illustrated in Figure 9-12.

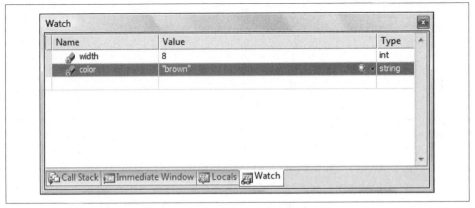

Figure 9-12. A Watch window lets you keep an eye on just the variables you want to track.

The Watch windows are usually tabbed with the Locals window. You can add a watch by right-clicking on a variable and choosing Add Watch or you can just drag the variable to the Watch window. The variable will be added to your Watch window. To remove a variable that you've added to your Watch window, you can right-click on it in the Watch list and select Delete Watch.

In Visual Studio only, if you just need to peek at a variable, and perhaps to experiment with manipulating its value, you can right-click on it and choose QuickWatch, which opens a dialog box with watch information about a single object, as shown in Figure 9-13.

You can enter any expression into the Expression field and evaluate it from within the QuickWatch window. For example, suppose you had a QuickWatch on the length variable, which is set to 4.

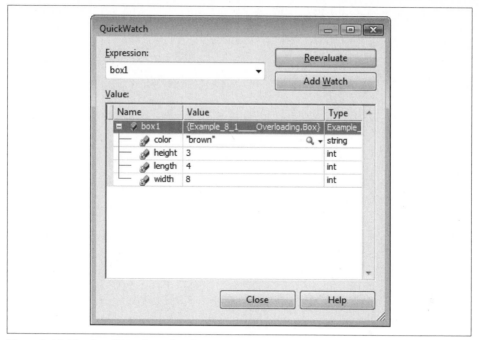

Figure 9-13. The QuickWatch window lets you examine the properties of a specific variable.

If you want to know the impact of multiplying length by width (set to 8), enter:

```
length * width
```

into the Expression window and click Reevaluate. The value is shown in the Value window, as in Figure 9-14.

If you decide that you want to add the variable to a Watch window after all, click the Add Watch button.

The Call Stack

As you step in and out of methods, the Call Stack window keeps track of the order and hierarchy of method calls. Figure 9-15 shows a close-up picture of the Call Stack window. You can see that the Box constructor was called by the Run( ) method, while the Run( ) method was in turn called by Main( ).

In this case, if you double-click on the second line in the Call Stack window, the debugger shows you the line in Run( ) that called the Box constructor, as shown in Figure 9-16. Notice that the debugger puts a green curved arrow on the line in the call stack you've double-clicked on, and a matching arrow in the editor to the line that corresponds to that call. This way, if you're debugging a method and you think the data causing the problem came from outside the method, you can quickly find where the method call came from and check the values at that point.

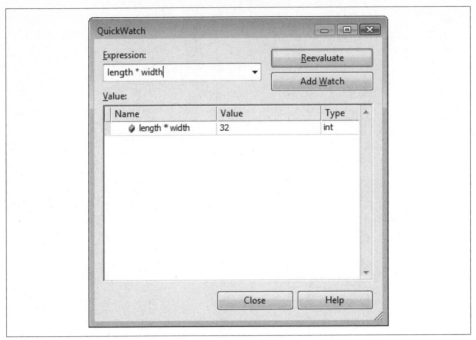

Figure 9-14. The QuickWatch recalculation feature lets you test out various adjustments to a variable without rewriting your code.

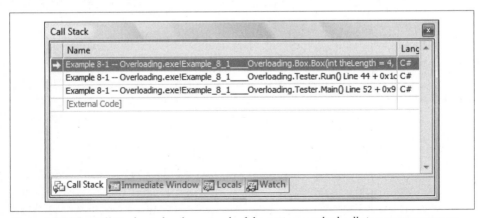

Figure 9-15. The Call Stack window keeps track of the various method calls in your program, no matter how deep you nest them.

Stopping Debugging

Sometimes, as you're debugging, you'll realize that something has gone wrong enough that there's no point in running the program to its end, or maybe you just want to fix the problem right now, before running any further. When that happens, you want to just end the program where it is, stop the debugging, and go back to

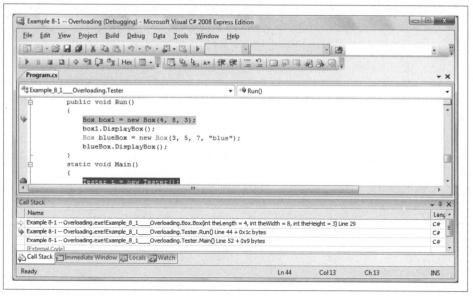

Figure 9-16. If you click on a method in the Call Stack window, Visual Studio will take you to that line.

your editing window. Fortunately, that's pretty easy. To stop debugging and end the program, just click Debug → Stop Debugging, or click the Stop button (■) on the Debugging toolbar.

Summary

- Visual Studio includes a powerful debugger that lets you step through your program and examine the value of variables and objects as methods execute.

- You can set breakpoints in your code, which causes execution to stop when it reaches that point. Breakpoints can be set to stop every time, every *n*th time, or when a particular condition is true.

- Press F11 to step into called methods, and F10 to skip over method calls.

- The Autos window displays the values of the variables used in the current statement and the previous statement. The Locals window shows the values of all the variables in the current method.

- The Watch window allows you to keep an eye on variables or objects as your method executes, not only revealing their value, but in the case of complex objects, allowing you to "drill down" into their internal state.

- The QuickWatch window displays information about a single object, and allows you to manipulate that object without changing the value of the object in the running program.

- The Call Stack window shows you the method that called your currently executing method, and the method that invoked *that* method, and so forth, so that you can see how you arrived at the currently executing method.

We hope that at this point, you're comfortable enough with Visual Studio's various debugging tools that you'll have an increased sense of confidence as you approach the rest of the chapters in this book. The tools won't prevent you from making mistakes, because that is normal and is nothing to worry about. They will help you find those mistakes more quickly, and get you back on your way.

Before we get back into the intensively object-oriented content, there's one more piece of the puzzle that you should know about. Up to this point, you've written programs that dealt with just one object at a time. That's about to change. The next chapter deals with arrays, which are a way to handle a group of similar objects as though they were one object.

Test Your Knowledge: Quiz

Question 9-1. What is the easiest way to set a breakpoint?

Question 9-2. What does the breakpoint icon look like when the execution stops?

Question 9-3. How do you step over or into a method?

Question 9-4. How can you disable breakpoints, and set conditions on breakpoints?

Question 9-5. What is the difference between the Locals window and the Autos window?

Question 9-6. How can you see the internal state of an object in the Locals window?

Question 9-7. What is the easiest way to set a watch on a variable?

Question 9-8. How do you open a QuickWatch window?

Question 9-9. What does the call stack show and why is it useful?

Question 9-10. How can you find a particular method call in your code from the Call Stack window?

Test Your Knowledge: Exercises

Exercise 9-1. You'll use the following program for this exercise. Either type it into Visual Studio, or copy it from this book's website. Note that this is spaghetti code—you'd never write method calls like this, but that's why this is the debugging chapter.

```
using System;
using System.Collections.Generic;
using System.Linq;
using System.Text;

namespace Exercise_9_1
{
    class Tester
    {
        public void Run()
        {
            int myInt = 42;
            float myFloat = 9.685f;
            Console.WriteLine("Before starting: \n value of myInt:
                    {0} \n value of myFloat: {1}", myInt, myFloat);
            // pass the variables by reference
            Multiply( ref myInt, ref myFloat );
            Console.WriteLine("After finishing: \n value of myInt:
                    {0} \n value of myFloat: {1}", myInt, myFloat);
        }
        private static void Multiply (ref int theInt,
                                        ref float theFloat)
        {
            theInt = theInt * 2;
            theFloat = theFloat *2;
            Divide( ref theInt, ref theFloat);
        }
        private static void Divide (ref int theInt,
                                        ref float theFloat)
        {
            theInt = theInt / 3;
            theFloat = theFloat / 3;
            Add(ref theInt, ref theFloat);
        }
        public static void Add(ref int theInt,
                                ref float theFloat)
        {
            theInt = theInt + theInt;
            theFloat = theFloat + theFloat;
        }
        static void Main()
        {
            Tester t = new Tester();
            t.Run();
        }
    }
}
```

1. Place a breakpoint in Run( ) on the following line, and then run the program:

```
Console.WriteLine("Before starting: \n value of myInt:
              {0} \n value of myFloat: {1}", myInt, myFloat);
```

What are the values of myInt and myFloat at the breakpoint?

2. Step into the Multiply( ) method, up to the call to Divide( ). What are the values of theInt and theFloat at this point?

3. Stop debugging, run the program again, and when it reaches the breakpoint in Run( ), set a watch on myInt. Step through the methods. When does the value of myInt change?

4. Set another breakpoint in Add( ) at this line:

```
theInt = theInt + theInt;
```

Run the program. How many calls are in the call stack when the program reaches this breakpoint?

Exercise 9-2. The program in this exercise is similar to the first, but it has a logic error. Type this program into Visual Studio, or download it from this book's website:

```
using System;
using System.Collections.Generic;
using System.Linq;
using System.Text;

namespace Exercise_9_2
{
    class Tester
    {
        public void Run()
        {
            int myInt = 42;
            float myFloat = 9.685f;
            Console.WriteLine("Before starting: \n value of myInt:
                      {0} \n value of myFloat: {1}", myInt, myFloat);
            // pass the variables by reference
            Multiply( ref myInt, ref myFloat );
            Console.WriteLine("After finishing: \n value of myInt:
                      {0} \n value of myFloat: {1}", myInt, myFloat);
        }
        private static void Multiply (ref int theInt,
                                        ref float theFloat)
        {
            theInt = theInt * 2;
            theFloat = theFloat *2;
            Divide( ref theInt, ref theFloat);
        }
        private static void Divide (ref int theInt,
                                      ref float theFloat)
```

```
    {
        theInt = theInt * 3;
        theFloat = theFloat * 3;
        Add(ref theInt, ref theFloat);
    }
    public static void Add(ref int theInt,
                                ref float theFloat)
    {
        theInt = theInt - theInt;
        theFloat = theFloat - theFloat;
    }
    static void Main( )
    {
        Tester t = new Tester( );
        t.Run( );
    }
    }
}
```

If you run this program, you will not get the same results as you did in the preceding exercise. Use the debugging tools you just learned about to find the error. Correct the error, and then run the program again to see whether the results are correct.

Exercise 9-3. Type the following program into Visual Studio, or download it from the book's website:

```
using System;
using System.Collections.Generic;
using System.Linq;
using System.Text;

namespace Exercise_9_3
{
    class Program
    {
        public static int Factorial(int myInt)
        {
            int result = 1;
            for (int i = 1; i < myInt; i++)
            {
                result = result * i;
            }
            return result;
        }

        static void Main( )
        {
            int input = 5;
            Console.WriteLine("{0} factorial is {1}",
                                input, Factorial(input) );
        }
    }
}
```

This program is supposed to take the factorial of the value of input, except it's not working properly. (The factorial of *n* is the product of all the positive integers less than or equal to *n*. So, the factorial of 5 is $5 \times 4 \times 3 \times 2 \times 1 = 120$.) Find the error and resolve it.

CHAPTER 10

Arrays

Almost all of the examples in previous chapters have dealt with one object at a time. In many applications, however, you want to work with a *collection* of objects all at the same time. The simplest collection in C# is the *array*, and it's the only collection type for which C# provides built-in support. The other collection types, such as stack and queue, are not part of the language; they are part of the Framework Class Library, and we'll cover those in detail in Chapter 14. The cool thing about arrays is that you can pass them around as though they were a single object, yet they contain several objects of the same type. Arrays really come into their own in combination with loops, which you learned about back in Chapter 5. In this chapter, you will learn to work with three types of arrays: one-dimensional arrays, multidimensional rectangular arrays, and jagged arrays.

Using Arrays

An *array* is a collection of objects, all of the same type (all ints, all strings, and so on). Arrays are also *indexed*, meaning that the language provides a way for you to say "Get me the third item in the array." Indexing also means that the items in the array are stored in a specific order, which further means that you can loop through the contents of the array in order. That process is called iteration, and we'll show you how to do it in a minute. Arrays are a standard feature of almost all modern languages, and C# provides built-in syntax for declaring and using arrays.

Arrays are a bit tricky to visualize at first—a bunch of objects occupying the space of a single object. To picture a basic array (also called a *one-dimensional* array—you'll see why it's called that shortly), imagine a series of mailboxes, all lined up one after the other, as shown in Figure 10-1. Each mailbox can hold exactly one object in C#. Each mailbox also has a number (an address in the real world; an *index* in C#), so you can identify which item is in which box. Unlike real-world mailboxes, though, all the mailboxes must hold the same kind of object; you declare the type of object that the mailboxes will hold when you declare the array.

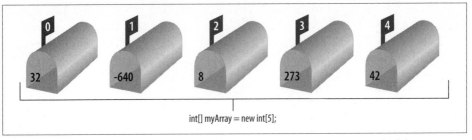

int[] myArray = new int[5];

Figure 10-1. An array of five integers. Each "mailbox" is one item in the array, which has its own address (the index), and can hold exactly one object.

The important thing about arrays is that you can treat the entire array (the set of mailboxes) as a single entity, with a single name. As you'll see, using loops, you can easily perform an operation on each element within an array in turn.

Declaring Arrays

The syntax for arrays uses the square bracket characters [ ]. For starters, you declare a C# array with the following syntax:

```
type[] array name;
```

For example:

```
int[] myIntArray;
```

 As usual, you are not actually declaring an array. Technically, you are declaring a variable (myIntArray) that will hold a reference to an array of integers. As always, we'll use the shorthand and refer to myIntArray as the array, knowing that we really mean it is a variable that holds a reference to an (unnamed) array.

The square brackets tell the C# compiler that you are declaring an array, and the type specifies the type of the elements it will contain. In the previous example, myIntArray is an array of integers.

To instantiate a new array, you use the new keyword. Inside the square brackets, you specify how many elements you want to be in the array. For example:

```
myIntArray = new int[5];
```

This statement creates and initializes an array of five integers, all of which are initialized to the value zero.

It is important to distinguish between the array (which is a collection) and the elements held in the array (which can be of any type, as long as all the elements in the array are the same type). myIntArray is the array; its elements are the five integers it holds.

C# arrays are reference types, created on the heap. Thus, the array to which the variable myIntArray refers is allocated on the heap. The *elements* of an array are allocated based on their own type. Because integers are value types, the elements in myIntArray will be value types, and thus all the elements will be created inside the block of memory allocated for the array. Because an array is a reference type, it will always be passed by reference, even if the elements in the array are value types.

Understanding Default Values

When you create an array of value types, each element initially contains the default value for the type stored in the array (see Table 3-1 in Chapter 3). The statement you saw earlier:

```
myIntArray = new int[5];
```

creates an array of five integers, with the value of each set to 0, which is the default value for integer types.

If you create an array of reference types (anything other than the primitive types), those objects are not initialized to their default value. Instead, the references held in the array are initialized to null. If you attempt to access an element in an array of reference types before you have specifically initialized the elements, you will generate an exception.

Suppose you have created a Button class. You'd declare an array of Button objects with the following statement:

```
Button[] myButtonArray;
```

and instantiate the actual array like this:

```
myButtonArray = new Button[3];
```

You can shorten this to:

```
Button[] myButtonArray = new Button[3];
```

This statement does *not* create an array with references to three Button objects. Instead, this creates the array myButtonArray with three null references. To use this array, you must first create and assign the Button objects for each reference in the array, using the Button class's constructor as usual. You can construct the objects in a loop that adds them one by one to the array, as you'll see later in this chapter.

Accessing Array Elements

You can access a single element of an array using square brackets ([]), which are called the *index operator*. Each element of the array has an index, and you can access the element at a particular index by placing the index number of the element you want inside the brackets. For example, if you have an array of ints, and you want to assign the element with index 3 to another variable, you'd do it like this:

```
int myInt = myIntArray[3];
```

There are two things to remember here. The first is that myIntArray[3] isn't an array; it's just an int, like any other int. It just happens to be an int that's an element of an array. The second thing is that myIntArray[3] isn't the third element in the array—it's actually the fourth element. Arrays in C# are *zero-based*, which means that the index of the first element is always zero—in this case, myIntArray[0]. This also means that if you declared myIntArray[] to have five elements, the highest index is 4, not 5. If you try to access myIntArray[5], you'll get an error. We know this is counterintuitive, but you'll get used to it quickly enough.

Arrays also have a property called Length, which tells you how many objects the array holds—this is useful, because you won't always know this when you write your code. Because the indexes start at 0, that means the highest index in an array is always equal to Length - 1. Or to put it another way, arrays are indexed from 0 to Length - 1.

Arrays and Loops

We mentioned earlier that arrays really come into their own when you combine them with loops. Suppose you want to have an array of the first 10 even integers. You need to start with an array of size 10:

```
int[] myIntArray = new int[10];
```

Easy enough. Then you need to populate the array with even integers. You can do that with a for loop like this:

```
for (int i = 0; i < myIntArray.Length; i++)
{
    myIntArray[i] = 2 * (i + 1);
}
```

Take a closer look at the for loop. The loop control variable i starts at 0, which is also the first element in the array. You want the loop to fill each element in the array, so the condition for ending the loop is i < myIntArray.Length. Remember that myIntArray.Length is going to be 10 in this case, but you want the loop to stop when i is equal to 9. Since i starts at 0, that means the loop will run 10 times. Therefore, it's important to use <, not <=, in the condition.

Inside the loop, you use myIntArray[i] to *iterate* through the loop. That is, the first time through, you'll be setting myIntArray[0]; the next time, myIntArray[1]; and so on. 2 * (i + 1) simply calculates the next even number, and assigns it to the current element of the array. (We used 2 * (i + 1) instead of 2 * i so that the first element in the array would be 2, rather than 0.)

To output the contents of the array to the console, you use a similar loop:

```
for (int i = 0; i < myIntArray.Length; i++)
{
    Console.WriteLine("Value in index {0} is {1}.", i, myIntArray[i]);
}
```

Notice that the header of the for loop is exactly the same as the previous one. This is how you iterate through the array and take an action on each element. You also don't need to know how many elements are in the array when you write the for loop; you stop the loop when i reaches myIntArray.Length.

Example 10-1 shows the whole program, brief as it is.

Example 10-1. for loops are the most common way to work with arrays

```
using System;
using System.Collections.Generic;
using System.Linq;
using System.Text;

namespace Example_10_1____Using_arrays
{
    class Tester
    {
        public void Run()
        {
            int[] myIntArray = new int[10];

            //populate the array
            for (int i = 0; i < myIntArray.Length; i++)
            {
                myIntArray[i] = 2 * (i + 1);
            }

            //output the array
            for (int i = 0; i < myIntArray.Length; i++)
            {
                Console.WriteLine("Value in index {0} is {1}.",
                            i, myIntArray[i]);
            }

        }
        static void Main(string[] args)
        {
            Tester t = new Tester();
            t.Run();
        }
    }
}
```

The output should look like this:

```
Value in index 0 is 2.
Value in index 1 is 4.
Value in index 2 is 6.
Value in index 3 is 8.
Value in index 4 is 10.
Value in index 5 is 12.
Value in index 6 is 14.
Value in index 7 is 16.
```

```
Value in index 8 is 18.
Value in index 9 is 20.
```

Go ahead and change the < in the first loop to <=, and run the program again. You'll get yourself a nice crash. That's because when the loop runs the final time (when i equals 10), the body of the loop tries to assign a value to myIntArray[10], which doesn't exist. You're trying to write into an area of memory that's not there, and the compiler doesn't like that.

You can use arrays with user-defined classes as well, of course, but you have to do a bit of extra work because the objects won't be initialized automatically. Example 10-2 shows a simple Employee class being used with an array. Notice that the class includes an automatic property for the Employee ID, as introduced in Chapter 8.

Example 10-2. You can use objects with arrays almost as easily as primitive types

```
using System;
using System.Collections.Generic;
using System.Linq;
using System.Text;

namespace Example_10_2____Arrays_and_Objects
{
    // a simple class to store in the array
    public class Employee
    {
        public int EmpID { get; set; }

        public Employee(int empID)
        {
            EmpID = empID;
        }
    }
    public class Tester
    {
        static void Main()
        {
            Employee[] empArray;
            empArray = new Employee[3];

            // populate the arrays
            for (int i = 0; i < empArray.Length; i++)
            {
                empArray[i] = new Employee(i + 1005);
            }

            // output array values
            Console.WriteLine("\nemployee IDs:");
            for (int i = 0; i < empArray.Length; i++)
            {
```

Example 10-2. You can use objects with arrays almost as easily as primitive types (continued)

```
            Console.WriteLine(empArray[i].EmpID);
        }
    }
  }
}
```

The output looks like this:

```
employee IDs:
1005
1006
1007
```

In this example, the Employee IDs start at 1005 and proceed from there. You see that you need to create each `Employee` object with the `new` keyword in the `for` loop. To access the `EmpID` member of each `Employee` object, you use the dot notation: `empArray[i].EmpID`. Notice that the dot comes after the square brackets. Remember that `empArray` represents the entire array, but `empArray[i]` represents a single `Employee`, so you can access the member fields and methods of each individual object.

The foreach Statement

The `foreach` statement allows you to iterate through all the items in an array or other collection, examining each item in turn. The syntax for the `foreach` statement is:

```
foreach (type identifier in expression) statement
```

You can update Example 10-1 to replace the second `for` statement (the one that iterates over the contents of the populated array) with a `foreach` statement, as shown in Example 10-3.

Example 10-3. You can use the foreach statement to iterate through an array instead of using a for loop

```
foreach (int i in myIntArray)
{
    Console.WriteLine("The value is {0}.", i);
}
```

The output will be nearly the same. Note that in this case, though, `i` doesn't represent the index of the array element; it represents the array element itself. In Example 10-1, we used `i` to output the index as well as the value. Here, that's not an option. If you specifically want to output the index as well as the value, you're better off using the `for` loop.

Initializing Array Elements

You can initialize the contents of an array at the time you create it by providing a list of values delimited by curly braces ({}). C# provides a longer and a shorter syntax:

```
int[] myIntArray = new int[5] { 2, 4, 6, 8, 10 };
int[] myIntArray = { 2, 4, 6, 8, 10 };
```

In the shorter syntax, C# automatically creates an array of the proper size for the number of elements in the braces. There is no practical difference between these two statements, and most programmers will use the shorter syntax.

The params Keyword

One of the more unusual uses of arrays is the params keyword. If you have a method that accepts an array, the params keyword allows you to pass that method a variable number of parameters, instead of explicitly declaring the array. Of course, the parameters must all be of the same type. Because of the params keyword, the method will receive an array of that type.

In the next example, you create a method, DisplayVals( ), that takes a variable number of integer arguments:

```
public void DisplayVals(params int[] intVals)
```

Inside the method, you can iterate over the array as you would over any other array of integers:

```
foreach (int i in intVals)
{
    Console.WriteLine("DisplayVals {0}",i);
}
```

The calling method, however, need not explicitly create an array: it can simply pass in integers, and the compiler will assemble the parameters into an array for the DisplayVals( ) method:

```
t.DisplayVals(5,6,7,8);
```

You are also free to pass in an array if you prefer:

```
int [] explicitArray = new int[5] {1,2,3,4,5};
t.DisplayVals(explicitArray);
```

 You can use only one params argument for each method you create, and the params argument must be the last argument in the method's signature.

Example 10-4 illustrates using the params keyword.

Example 10-4. You can use the params keyword to pass a variable number of parameters to a method that accepts an array

```csharp
using System;
using System.Collections.Generic;
using System.Linq;
using System.Text;

namespace Example_10_4____params_keyword
{
    public class Tester
    {
        static void Main()
        {
            Tester t = new Tester();
            t.DisplayVals(5, 6, 7, 8);
            int[] explicitArray = new int[] { 1, 2, 3, 4, 5 };
            t.DisplayVals(explicitArray);
        }

        public void DisplayVals(params int[] intVals)
        {
            foreach (int i in intVals)
            {
                Console.WriteLine("DisplayVals {0}", i);
            }
        }
    }
}
```

The output looks like this:

```
DisplayVals 5
DisplayVals 6
DisplayVals 7
DisplayVals 8
DisplayVals 1
DisplayVals 2
DisplayVals 3
DisplayVals 4
DisplayVals 5
```

Multidimensional Arrays

If we simplify the mailbox analogy from earlier in the chapter, you can think of an array as a long row of slots into which you can place values. This single row of slots is called a *one-dimensional array*. Now imagine 10 rows of slots, stacked on top of each other. What you're picturing is a classic *two-dimensional array* of rows and columns. The rows run across the array and the columns run up and down the array, as shown in Figure 10-2.

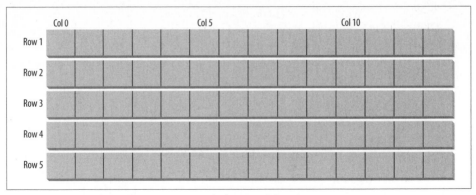

Figure 10-2. Rows and columns create a multidimensional array.

Two-dimensional arrays aren't too hard to picture, but a third dimension is a bit harder to imagine, but still not too hard, if you remember your high school geometry. OK, now imagine four dimensions. Now imagine 10.

Those of you who are not string-theory physicists have probably given up, as have we. Maybe we can't picture what 10-dimensional arrays look like, but that doesn't matter to C#. Multidimensional arrays can be useful, even if you can't quite picture them.

C# supports two types of multidimensional arrays: rectangular and jagged. In a rectangular array, every row is the same length. A jagged array, however, is an array of arrays, each of which can be a different length.

Rectangular Arrays

A *rectangular array* is an array of two (or more) dimensions. In the classic two-dimensional array, the first dimension is the number of rows and the second dimension is the number of columns.

To declare a two-dimensional array, use the following syntax:

```
type [,] array name
```

For example, to declare and instantiate a two-dimensional rectangular array named myRectangularArray that contains two rows and three columns of integers, you would write:

```
int [,] myRectangularArray = new int[2,3];
```

To retrieve the value of the element in the second row and the first column, you'd do something like this:

```
int myInt = myRectangularArray[1,0];
```

Remember that the indexes start at 0 for multidimensional arrays, too.

Two-dimensional arrays also work well with for loops, but to iterate over both dimensions, you need two for loops, one nested inside the other. For example, if you have a 4×3 array, you might populate it like this:

```
const int rows = 4;
const int columns = 3;

for ( int i = 0; i < rows; i++ )
{
    for ( int j = 0; j < columns; j++ )
    {
        rectangularArray[i, j] = i + j;
    }
}
```

Each time through the outer for loop, the inner loop iterates completely from j = 0 to j < columns, which fills one row of the two-dimensional array. Then i is incremented, j is reset to 0, and it starts over again.

Example 10-5 declares, instantiates, initializes, and prints the contents of a two-dimensional array. In this example, a for loop is used to initialize the elements of the array.

Example 10-5. A rectangular array is a two-dimensional array (consisting of rows and columns) where each row is the same length

```
using System;
using System.Collections.Generic;
using System.Linq;
using System.Text;

namespace Example_10_5____Rectangular_array
{
    public class Tester
    {
        static void Main( )
        {
            const int rows = 4;
            const int columns = 3;

            // declare a 4x3 integer array
            int[,] rectangularArray = new int[rows, columns];

            // populate the array
            for (int i = 0; i < rows; i++)
            {
                for (int j = 0; j < columns; j++)
                {
                    rectangularArray[i, j] = i + j;
                }
            }

            // report the contents of the array
```

Example 10-5. A rectangular array is a two-dimensional array (consisting of rows and columns) where each row is the same length (continued)

```
for (int i = 0; i < rows; i++)
{
    for (int j = 0; j < columns; j++)
    {
        Console.WriteLine("rectangularArray[{0},{1}] = {2}",
                          i, j, rectangularArray[i, j]);
    }
}
}
}
```

The output looks like this:

```
rectangularArray[0,0] = 0
rectangularArray[0,1] = 1
rectangularArray[0,2] = 2
rectangularArray[1,0] = 1
rectangularArray[1,1] = 2
rectangularArray[1,2] = 3
rectangularArray[2,0] = 2
rectangularArray[2,1] = 3
rectangularArray[2,2] = 4
rectangularArray[3,0] = 3
rectangularArray[3,1] = 4
rectangularArray[3,2] = 5
```

The brackets in the int[,] declaration indicate that the type is an array of integers, and the comma indicates the array has two dimensions (two commas would indicate three dimensions, and so on). The actual instantiation of rectangularArray with new int[rows, columns] sets the size of each dimension. Here, the declaration and instantiation have been combined:

```
int[,] rectangularArray = new int[rows, columns];
```

The program fills the rectangle with a pair of nested for loops, iterating through each column in each row. Thus, the first element filled is rectangularArray[0,0], followed by rectangularArray[0,1] and rectangularArray[0,2]. Once this is done, the program moves on to the next rows: rectangularArray[1,0], rectangularArray[1,1], rectangularArray[1,2], and so forth, until all the columns in all the rows are filled.

Just as you can initialize a one-dimensional array using bracketed lists of values, you can initialize a two-dimensional array using similar syntax. Example 10-6 declares a two-dimensional array (rectangularArray), initializes its elements using bracketed lists of values, and then prints out the contents.

Example 10-6. You can initialize a multidimensional array just as you would a one-dimensional array

```
using System;
using System.Collections.Generic;
using System.Linq;
using System.Text;

namespace Example_10_6____Initializing_multidimensional_arrays
{
    public class Tester
    {
        static void Main()
        {
            const int rows = 4;
            const int columns = 3;

            // imply a 4x3 array
            int[,] rectangularArray =
            {
                {0,1,2}, {3,4,5}, {6,7,8}, {9,10,11}
            };

            for (int i = 0; i < rows; i++)
            {
                for (int j = 0; j < columns; j++)
                {
                    Console.WriteLine("rectangularArray[{0},{1}] =
                            {2}", i, j, rectangularArray[i, j]);
                }
            }
        }
    }
}
```

The output looks like this:

```
rectangularArray[0,0] = 0
rectangularArray[0,1] = 1
rectangularArray[0,2] = 2
rectangularArray[1,0] = 3
rectangularArray[1,1] = 4
rectangularArray[1,2] = 5
rectangularArray[2,0] = 6
rectangularArray[2,1] = 7
rectangularArray[2,2] = 8
rectangularArray[3,0] = 9
rectangularArray[3,1] = 10
rectangularArray[3,2] = 11
```

The preceding example is very similar to Example 10-5, but this time you *imply* the exact dimensions of the array by how you initialize it:

```
int[,] rectangularArray =
{
```

```
    {0,1,2}, {3,4,5}, {6,7,8}, {9,10,11}
};
```

Assigning values in four bracketed lists, each consisting of three elements, implies a 4 (rows) × 3 (columns) array.

If you had written this as:

```
int[,] rectangularArray =
{
    {0,1,2,3}, {4,5,6,7}, {8,9,10,11}
};
```

you would instead have implied a 3 × 4 array.

You can see that the C# compiler understands the implications of the way you grouped the input values, because it is able to access the objects with the appropriate offsets, as illustrated in the output.

C# arrays are "smart" and they keep track of their bounds. When you imply a 4 × 3 array, you must treat it as such, and not as a 3 × 4 array, or just an array of 12 integers (as you can with some other C-family languages).

Jagged Arrays

The easiest way to think of a *jagged array* is as an array of arrays—that is, imagine an array where each element is also an array itself. It is called "jagged" because each row need not be the same size as all the others, and thus a graphical representation of the array would not be square.

When you create a jagged array, you declare the number of rows in your array. Each row will hold an array, which can be of any length. These arrays must each be declared. You can then fill in the values for the elements in these "inner" arrays.

In a jagged array, each dimension is a one-dimensional array. To declare a jagged array, use the following syntax, where the number of brackets indicates the number of dimensions of the array:

```
type [] []...
```

For example, you would declare a two-dimensional jagged array of integers named myJaggedArray, as follows:

```
int [] [] myJaggedArray;
```

You would access the fifth element of the third array by writing myJaggedArray[2][4].

Example 10-7 creates a jagged array named myJaggedArray, initializes its elements, and then prints their content. To save writing code, the program takes advantage of the fact that integer array elements are automatically initialized to zero, and it initializes the values of only the nonzero elements.

Example 10-7. A jagged array is an "array of arrays"; each row can have a variable number of elements

```
using System;
using System.Collections.Generic;
using System.Linq;
using System.Text;

namespace Example_10_7____Jagged_arrays
{
    class Program
    {
        public class Tester
        {
            static void Main( )
            {
                const int rows = 4;

                // declare the jagged array as 4 rows high
                int[][] jaggedArray = new int[rows][];

                // the first row has 5 elements
                jaggedArray[0] = new int[5];

                // a row with 2 elements
                jaggedArray[1] = new int[2];

                // a row with 3 elements
                jaggedArray[2] = new int[3];

                // the last row has 5 elements
                jaggedArray[3] = new int[5];

                // Fill some (but not all) elements of the rows
                jaggedArray[0][3] = 15;
                jaggedArray[1][1] = 12;
                jaggedArray[2][1] = 9;
                jaggedArray[2][2] = 99;
                jaggedArray[3][0] = 10;
                jaggedArray[3][1] = 11;
                jaggedArray[3][2] = 12;
                jaggedArray[3][3] = 13;
                jaggedArray[3][4] = 14;

                for (int i = 0; i < 5; i++)
                {
                    Console.WriteLine("jaggedArray[0][{0}] = {1}",
                                      i, jaggedArray[0][i]);
                }

                for (int i = 0; i < 2; i++)
                {
                    Console.WriteLine("jaggedArray[1][{0}] = {1}",
                                      i, jaggedArray[1][i]);
```

Example 10-7. A jagged array is an "array of arrays"; each row can have a variable number of elements (continued)

```
            }

            for (int i = 0; i < 3; i++)
            {
                Console.WriteLine("jaggedArray[2][{0}] = {1}",
                                  i, jaggedArray[2][i]);
            }
            for (int i = 0;.i < 5; i++)
            {
                Console.WriteLine("jaggedArray[3][{0}] = {1}",
                                  i, jaggedArray[3][i]);
            }
        }
    }
}
```

The output looks like this:

```
jaggedArray[0][0] = 0
jaggedArray[0][1] = 0
jaggedArray[0][2] = 0
jaggedArray[0][3] = 15
jaggedArray[0][4] = 0
jaggedArray[1][0] = 0
jaggedArray[1][1] = 12
jaggedArray[2][0] = 0
jaggedArray[2][1] = 9
jaggedArray[2][2] = 99
jaggedArray[3][0] = 10
jaggedArray[3][1] = 11
jaggedArray[3][2] = 12
jaggedArray[3][3] = 13
jaggedArray[3][4] = 14
```

In this example, a jagged array is created with four rows:

```
int[][] jaggedArray = new int[rows][];
```

Notice that the second dimension is not specified. This value is set by creating a new array for each row. Each of these arrays can have a different size:

```
// the first row has 5 elements
jaggedArray[0] = new int[5];
// a row with 2 elements
jaggedArray[1] = new int[2];
// a row with 3 elements
jaggedArray[2] = new int[3];
// the last row has 5 elements
jaggedArray[3] = new int[5];
```

Once an array is specified for each row, you only need to populate the various members of each array and then print out their contents to ensure that all went as expected.

Another way of outputting the values would be to use two nested for loops, and use the Length property of the array to control the loop:

```
for (int i = 0; i < jaggedArray.Length; i++ )
{
    for (int j = 0; j < jaggedArray[i].Length; j++)
    {
        Console.WriteLine("jaggedArray[{0}][{1}] = {2}",
        i, j, jaggedArray[i][j]);
    }
}
```

In this case, the "outer" for loop iterates over the rows in the array. The "inner" loop outputs each column in the given row. Because you're using Length to control how many times the loop runs, it doesn't matter that each row is a different length. If you didn't use Length, and simply tried to use the maximum dimensions, you'd get an error the first time the program tried to access a null element in a short row.

Notice that when you access the members of the rectangular array, you put the indexes all within one set of square brackets:

```
rectangularArrayrectangularArray[i,j]
```

whereas with a jagged array, you need a pair of brackets:

```
jaggedArray[i][j]
```

You can keep this straight by thinking of the first as a single array of more than one dimension and the jagged array as an *array of arrays*.

Array Methods

Although you've been using arrays as built-in types throughout this chapter, an array is actually an object of type System.Array. Arrays in C# thus provide you with the best of both worlds: easy-to-use syntax underpinned with an actual class definition so that instances of an array have access to the methods and properties of System.Array. You've seen the Length property of arrays used several times already. Some of the other important methods and properties appear in Table 10-1.

Table 10-1. System.Array methods and properties

Method or property	Purpose
BinarySearch( )	Overloaded public static method that searches a one-dimensional sorted array
Clear( )	Public static method that sets a range of elements in the array either to zero or to a null reference, depending on the element type
Copy( )	Overloaded public static method that copies a section of one array to another array

Table 10-1. System.Array methods and properties (continued)

Method or property	Purpose
CreateInstance( )	Overloaded public static method that instantiates a new instance of an array
IndexOf( )	Overloaded public static method that returns the index (offset) of the first instance of a value in a one-dimensional array
LastIndexOf( )	Overloaded public static method that returns the index of the last instance of a value in a one-dimensional array
Reverse( )	Overloaded public static method that reverses the order of the elements in a one-dimensional array
Sort( )	Overloaded public static method that sorts the values in a one-dimensional array
Length	Public property that returns the length of the array

Sorting Arrays

Two useful static methods from Table 10-1 that deserve a closer look are Sort( ) and Reverse( ). These methods do what you think they would: Reverse( ) reverses the order of elements in the array, and Sort( ) sorts the elements in order. These two methods are fully supported for arrays of the built-in C# types, such as string, so sorting an array of strings puts the elements in alphabetical order, and sorting an array of ints puts them in numeric order. Making the Sort( ) method work with your own classes is a bit trickier, because you must implement the IComparable interface (see Chapter 13 for more on interfaces). Example 10-8 demonstrates the use of these two methods to manipulate String objects.

Example 10-8. Array.Sort and Array.Reverse are static methods that let you sort and reverse the contents of an array

```
using System;
using System.Collections.Generic;
using System.Linq;
using System.Text;

namespace Example_10_8____Sorting_and_Reversing_Arrays
{
    public class Tester
    {
        public static void PrintMyArray(string[] theArray)
        {

            foreach (string str in theArray)
            {
                Console.WriteLine("Value: {0}", str);
            }
            Console.WriteLine("\n");
        }

        static void Main()
```

Example 10-8. Array.Sort and Array.Reverse are static methods that let you sort and reverse the contents of an array (continued)

```
    {
        String[] myArray =
        {
            "Proust", "Faulkner", "Mann", "Hugo"
        };

        PrintMyArray(myArray);
        Array.Reverse(myArray);
        PrintMyArray(myArray);

        String[] myOtherArray =
        {
            "We", "Hold", "These", "Truths",
            "To", "Be", "Self", "Evident",
        };

        PrintMyArray(myOtherArray);
        Array.Sort(myOtherArray);
        PrintMyArray(myOtherArray);

    }
  }
}
```

The output looks like this:

```
Value: Proust
Value: Faulkner
Value: Mann
Value: Hugo

Value: Hugo
Value: Mann
Value: Faulkner
Value: Proust

Value: We
Value: Hold
Value: These
Value: Truths
Value: To
Value: Be
Value: Self
Value: Evident

Value: Be
Value: Evident
Value: Hold
Value: Self
Value: These
Value: To
```

```
Value: Truths
Value: We
```

The example begins by creating `myArray`, an array of strings with the words:

```
"Proust", "Faulkner", "Mann", "Hugo"
```

This array is printed, and then passed to the `Array.Reverse()` method, where it is printed again to see that the array itself has been reversed:

```
Value: Hugo
Value: Mann
Value: Faulkner
Value: Proust
```

Similarly, the example creates a second array, `myOtherArray`, containing the words:

```
"We", "Hold", "These", "Truths",
"To", "Be", "Self", "Evident",
```

This is passed to the `Array.Sort()` method. Then `Array.Sort()` happily sorts them alphabetically:

```
Value: Be
Value: Evident
Value: Hold
Value: Self
Value: These
Value: To
Value: Truths
Value: We
```

 `Array.Sort()` and `Array.Reverse()` are static methods, meaning you call them on the class, not the object, as we discussed in Chapter 7. That means you don't call `myArray.Reverse()` to reverse the elements; instead, you call the static method and pass in the array as an argument, like this:

```
Array.Reverse(myArray);
```

Summary

- An array is an indexed collection of objects, all of the same type.
- You declare an array by giving the type of objects the array contains, followed by the square bracket operator ([]), followed by the name of the array. You then instantiate the array with the `new` keyword and the number of elements the array will contain.
- The index of the first element in the array is always zero, and the index of the last element in the array is always `Length-1`.
- You can use a `for` loop to iterate through the array, by using the loop's counter as the index to the array.

- The foreach statement allows you to iterate through the items in the array (or any other collection) without the need for a counter.
- The elements of an array can be initialized when the array is created by providing the values of the members in curly braces ({}).
- The params keyword lets you pass an arbitrary number of parameters of the same type into a method; the method will treat the parameters as a single array.
- Arrays can contain more than one dimension. A two-dimensional array has two indexes, which you can think of as rows and columns.
- A rectangular array is a two-dimensional array in which all the rows have the same number of columns.
- A jagged array is an array of arrays—the rows do not need to be all the same length.
- The Length property of an array returns the total number of elements in the array.
- The array class contains a number of methods for searching, sorting, and manipulating the elements.

Although arrays may seem like a simple topic more suited to discussing with the fundamentals of C#, they work equally well with objects, so we delayed showing them to you until after we'd discussed classes and methods. Arrays, along with the other collection types, are some of the easiest ways to pass a bunch of similar objects to a method. It's time to get back into the serious object-oriented stuff, though. Back in Chapter 6, we told you that the three pillars of object-oriented programming are encapsulation, specialization, and polymorphism. You saw how encapsulation works in Chapters 7 and 8. Now the next chapter deals with both specialization and polymorphism, in the form of inheritance.

Test Your Knowledge: Quiz

Question 10-1. What is the index of the seventh member of an array?

Question 10-2. Can an array hold objects of varying types?

Question 10-3. How do you specify the number of elements in an array?

Question 10-4. Are arrays reference types or value types? Where are the elements of the array created?

Question 10-5. How do you specify the highest index in any array?

Question 10-6. What are the two ways to initialize an array of three values?

Question 10-7. What are two ways to iterate through the items in an array?

Question 10-8. What does the params keyword do?

Question 10-9. What are the two types of multidimensional arrays and what is the difference between them?

Question 10-10. If you have a random array of float values, and you need them to be in order, with the largest value first, what methods should you use?

Test Your Knowledge: Exercises

Exercise 10-1. Declare a Dog class with two private members: weight (an int) and name (a string). Be sure to add properties to access the members. Then create an array that holds three Dog objects (Milo, 26 pounds; Frisky, 10 pounds; and Laika, 50 pounds). Output each dog's name and weight.

Exercise 10-2. Create an array of 10 integers. Populate the array by having the user enter integers at the console (use Console.Readline). Don't worry about error checking for this exercise. Output the integers sorted from greatest to least.

Exercise 10-3. Extend Exercise 10-1 by creating a two-dimensional array that represents a collection of strings that indicate the awards each dog has won at dog shows. Each dog may have a different number of awards won. Output the contents of the array to check its validity.

Exercise 10-4. Create a two-dimensional array that represents a chessboard (an 8×8 array). Each element in the array should contain the string "black" or the string "white", depending on where it is on the board. Create a method that initializes the array with the strings. Then create a method that asks the reader to enter two integers for the coordinates of a square, and returns whether that square is black or white.

CHAPTER 11

Inheritance and Polymorphism

In Chapter 6, we explained how classes derive from one another and described how classes can *inherit* properties and methods from their parent classes. In Chapter 7, you learned how to create your own classes and use objects of those classes, but you didn't see how the inheritance aspect works in practice. That's about to change.

We mentioned in Chapter 6 that the three key principles of object-oriented programming are encapsulation (discussed in Chapter 7), specialization, and polymorphism. This chapter focuses on *specialization*, which is implemented in C# through *inheritance*. You'll see how to create your own class hierarchy, and how to enforce that child classes implement the methods of their parent classes. You'll even see how to create completely abstract classes, and why you'd want to. You can't create an instance of an abstract class; you can only inherit from it. This chapter also explains how instances of a child class can be treated as though they were instances of one of the child class's ancestor classes, a process known as *polymorphism*. This chapter ends with a consideration of *sealed classes*, which cannot be specialized, and a discussion of the root of all classes, the Object class.

Specialization and Generalization

Before we can start to show you the syntax of inheritance, we first have to give you a little more object-oriented background, so you can see why inheritance works the way it does. Classes and their instances (objects) do not exist in a vacuum, but rather in a network of interdependencies and relationships, just as we, as social animals, live in a world of relationships and categories.

One of the most important relationships among objects in the real world is specialization, which can be described as the *is-a* relationship. When we say that a dog *is a* mammal, we mean that the dog is a specialized kind of mammal. It has all the characteristics of any mammal (it bears live young, nurses with milk, has hair), but it specializes these characteristics to the familiar characteristics of *Canis domesticus*. A cat is also a mammal. As such, we expect it to share certain characteristics with the dog that are generalized in Mammal, but to differ in those characteristics that are specialized in cats.

The specialization and generalization relationships are both reciprocal and hierarchical. Specialization is just generalization in the opposite direction: Mammal generalizes what is common among dogs and cats, and dogs and cats specialize mammals to their own specific subtypes.

These relationships are *hierarchical* because they create a relationship tree, with specialized types branching off from more generalized types. As you move "up" the hierarchy, you achieve greater generalization. You move up toward Mammal to generalize that dogs, cats, and horses all bear live young. As you move "down" the hierarchy, you specialize. Thus, the cat specializes Mammal in having claws (a characteristic) and purring (a behavior).

To use a more programming-specific example, every widget that you see in a standard Windows interface is called a *control*. So, when you say that ListBox and Button *are* Controls, you indicate that there are characteristics and behaviors of Controls that you expect to find in both of these types. In other words, Control generalizes the shared characteristics of both ListBox and Button, while each specializes its own particular characteristics and behaviors.

To put it another way, all Controls, which includes ListBoxes and Buttons, have certain common behaviors—they're all drawn on the screen, for one thing. But a Button can be clicked, which a ListBox can't. A ListBox has contents, which can be sorted. A Button can't do that.

The Unified Modeling Language (UML) is a standardized language for describing an object-oriented system. UML has many different visual representations, but in this case, all you need to know is that classes are represented as boxes. The name of the class appears at the top of the box, and (optionally) methods and members can be listed in the sections within the box.

You can use UML to model specialization relationships, as shown in Figure 11-1. Note that the arrow points from the more specialized class up to the more general class. In the figure, the more specialized Button and ListBox classes point up to the more general Control class.

When you start out designing classes from scratch, you'll often find that you have several classes that do the same thing. When this occurs, you can *factor out* these commonalities into a shared base class, which is more general than the specialized classes. This factoring is beneficial to you, because it allows you to reuse common code, and anytime you can reuse code instead of copying it to a new class is a good thing. That gives you code that is easier to maintain, because the changes are located in a single class rather than scattered among numerous classes.

For example, suppose you started out creating a series of objects, as illustrated in Figure 11-2. After working with RadioButtons, CheckBoxes, and Command buttons for a while, you realize that they share certain characteristics and behaviors that are more specialized than Control, but more general than any of the three. You might factor these common traits and behaviors into a common base class, Button, and rearrange your inheritance hierarchy, as shown in Figure 11-3. This is how you'd use generalization in object-oriented development.

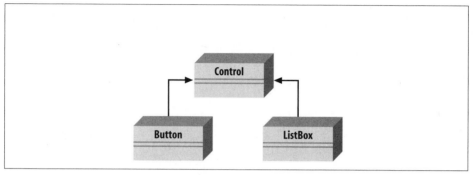

Figure 11-1. An is-a relationship between ListBox, Button, and Control. Both ListBoxes and Buttons are specialized versions of Controls.

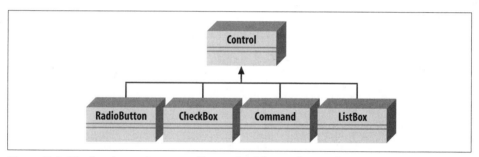

Figure 11-2. The four lower classes are all specialized forms of Control.

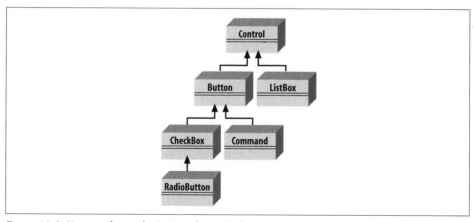

Figure 11-3. You can factor the Button class to isolate common traits.

The UML diagram in Figure 11-3 depicts the relationship among the factored classes and shows that both ListBox and Button derive from Control, and that Button is specialized into CheckBox and Command. Finally, RadioButton derives from CheckBox. You can thus say that RadioButton is a CheckBox, which in turn is a Button, and that Buttons are Controls.

This is not the only, or even necessarily the best, organization for these objects. Whenever you design your own classes, you'll probably come up with several different ways to organize them. It's a reasonable starting point for understanding how these types (classes) relate to one another, though.

Inheritance

Now that you have the background of specialization down, and a starting-point example to work with, you can see how to use this idea in your code. In C#, the specialization relationship is implemented using a principle called *inheritance*. This is not the only way to implement specialization, but it is the most common and most natural way.

Saying that ListBox inherits from (or derives from) Control indicates that it specializes Control. Control is referred to as the *base* class, and ListBox is referred to as the *derived* class. That is, ListBox derives its characteristics and behaviors from Control and then specializes to its own particular needs.

 You'll often see the immediate base class referred to as the *parent* class and the derived class referred to as the *child* class, whereas the topmost class, Object, is called the *root* class.

Implementing Inheritance

In C#, you create a derived class by adding a colon after the name of the derived class, followed by the name of the base class:

```
public class ListBox : Control
```

This code declares a new class, ListBox, which derives from Control. You can read the colon as "derives from."

The derived class inherits all the members of the base class (both member variables and methods). In other words, suppose Control has member fields called top and left, to indicate where on the screen the upper-left corner of the Control will be drawn. If ListBox derives from Control, ListBox also has the member fields top and left. The same is true of methods: if Control has a method called DrawControl(), ListBox does too.

Methods of the derived class have access to all the public and protected members of the base class. That means that if the drawControl() method in Control is marked as protected, the ListBox class can call that method, whereas a class that doesn't derive from Control wouldn't be able to.

The derived class is free to implement its own version of a base class method—that is, ListBox can have its own drawControl( ) method. This is called *hiding* the base class method and is accomplished by marking the method with the keyword new. (Many C# programmers advise never hiding base class methods as it is unreliable, hard to maintain, and confusing.) The new keyword indicates that the derived class has intentionally hidden and replaced the base class method. (We also discuss the new keyword in "Versioning with new and override" later in this chapter.)

 This is a different use of the keyword new than you saw earlier in this book. In Chapter 7, we used new to create an object on the heap; here, we're using new to replace the base class method. Programmers say the keyword new is *overloaded*, which means that the word has more than one meaning or use.

Example 11-1 shows the ListBox class inheriting from Control, and demonstrates all the features we just talked about. Note that although Control and ListBox are the names of legitimate Windows classes, that's not what we're showing you here. These are custom classes with familiar names to help you understand the inheritance relationship.

Example 11-1. You can derive a new class ListBox from its parent, Control

```
using System;
using System.Collections.Generic;
using System.Linq;
using System.Text;

namespace Example_11_1____Inheritance
{
    public class Control
    {
        // these members are private and thus invisible
        // to derived class methods

        private int top;
        private int left;

        // constructor takes two integers to
        // fix location on the console
        public Control(int top, int left)
        {
            this.top = top;
            this.left = left;
        }

        // simulates drawing the control
        public void DrawControl()
        {
```

Example 11-1. You can derive a new class ListBox from its parent, Control (continued)

```
        Console.WriteLine("Drawing Control at {0}, {1}", top, left);
    }

}

// ListBox derives from Control
public class ListBox : Control
{
    private string mListBoxContents; // new member variable


    // constructor adds a parameter
    public ListBox(int top, int left, string theContent)
                    : base(top, left) // call base constructor
    {
        mListBoxContents = theContent;
    }

    // a new version (note the keyword) because in the
    // derived method we change the behavior
    public new void DrawControl()
    {
        base.DrawControl(); // invoke the base method
        Console.WriteLine("Writing string to the ListBox: {0}",
                          mListBoxContents);
    }
}

public class Tester
{
    public static void Main()
    {
        // create a base instance
        Control myControl = new Control(5, 10);
        myControl.DrawControl();

        // create a derived instance
        ListBox lb = new ListBox(20, 30, "Hello world");
        lb.DrawControl();
    }
}
}
```

The output looks like this:

```
Drawing Control at 5, 10
Drawing Control at 20, 30
Writing string to the ListBox: Hello world
```

Example 11-1 starts with the declaration of the base class Control. This class implements a constructor and a simple DrawControl() method. There are two private member variables, top and left. That's the basic part; after that, it gets interesting. We'll analyze the rest of the program in detail in the following sections.

Calling the Base Class Constructor

In Example 11-1, the new class ListBox derives from Control:

```
public class ListBox : Control
```

ListBox has its own constructor, which takes three parameters, as opposed to two for Control. This is often the case with derived classes: the constructor does what the parent's constructor does, plus a bit more. In cases such as these, it saves code for the derived class simply to call the parent class's constructor, and then do whatever special setup the derived class needs.

In this case, the ListBox constructor invokes the constructor of its parent by placing a colon (:) after the parameter list and then invoking the base class constructor with the keyword base:

```
public ListBox(int top, int left, string theContent)
            : base(top, left) // call base constructor
```

Because classes cannot inherit constructors, a derived class must implement its own constructor and can only make use of the constructor of its base class by calling it explicitly.

If the base class has an accessible default constructor, the derived constructor is not required to invoke the base constructor explicitly; instead, the default constructor is called implicitly as the object is constructed. However, if the base class does *not* have a default constructor, every derived constructor *must* explicitly invoke one of the base class constructors using the base keyword. The keyword base identifies the base class for the current object.

 As we discussed in Chapter 7, if you do not declare a constructor of any kind, the compiler creates a default constructor for you. Whether you write it yourself or you use the one provided by the compiler, a default constructor is one that takes no parameters. Note, however, that once you do create a constructor of any kind (with or without parameters), the compiler does *not* create a default constructor for you.

Hiding the Base Class Method

As we mentioned, Control has a simple method called DrawControl(), which simulates drawing the control on the screen. The ListBox inherits the DrawControl() method, but the ListBox also needs to simulate writing text to the ListBox. Therefore, the ListBox implements its own DrawControl() method, using the new keyword to indicate that this method hides the parent method:

```
public new void DrawControl()
{
    base.DrawControl(); // invoke the base method
    Console.WriteLine("Writing string to the ListBox: {0}",
                  mListBoxContents);
}
```

As we mentioned, hiding the parent class's method is frowned upon. A better way to implement the ListBox control's new method is with a virtual method, which we'll discuss in a moment.

Controlling Access

You can restrict the visibility of a class and its members through the use of access modifiers, such as public, private, and protected. (See Chapter 8 for a discussion of access modifiers.)

As you've seen, public allows a member to be accessed by the member methods of other classes, whereas private indicates that the member is visible only to member methods of its own class. The protected keyword extends visibility to methods of derived classes.

Classes, as well as their members, can be designated with any of these accessibility levels. If a class member has a different access designation than the class, the more restricted access applies. In other words, if you define a class, MyClass, as follows:

```
public class MyClass
{
    // ...
    protected int myValue;
}
```

the accessibility for myValue is protected, even though the class itself is public. A public class is one that is visible to any other class that wishes to interact with it. If you create a new class, MyOtherClass, which derives from MyClass, like this:

```
public class MyClass : MyOtherClass
{
    Console.WriteLine("myValue: {0}", myValue);
}
```

MyOtherClass can access myValue, because MyOtherClass derives from MyClass, and myValue is protected. Any class that doesn't derive from MyClass would not be able to access myValue.

It is more common to make properties and methods protected than it is to make member variables protected. Member variables are almost always private.

Polymorphism

There are two powerful aspects to inheritance. One is code reuse. When you create a ListBox class, you're able to reuse some of the logic in the base (Control) class.

What is arguably more powerful, however, is the second aspect of inheritance: *polymorphism*. *Poly* means many and *morph* means form. Thus, polymorphism refers to being able to use many forms of a type without regard to the details.

When the phone company sends your phone a ring signal, it does not know what type of phone is on the other end of the line. You might have an old-fashioned Western Electric phone that energizes a motor to ring a bell, or you might have an electronic phone that plays digital music.

As far as the phone company is concerned, it knows only about the "base type" *phone* and expects that any "derived" instance of this type knows how to ring. When the phone company tells your phone to ring, it, effectively, calls your phone's ring method, and old-fashioned phones ring, digital phones trill, and cutting-edge phones announce your name. The phone company doesn't know or care what your individual phone does; it treats your telephone polymorphically.

Creating Polymorphic Types

Because a ListBox *is a* Control and a Button *is a* Control, you expect to be able to use either of these types in situations that call for a Control. For example, a form might want to keep a collection of all the derived instances of Control it manages (buttons, lists, and so on) so that when the form is opened, it can tell each of its Controls to draw itself. For this operation, the form does not want to know which elements are ListBoxes and which are Buttons; it just wants to tick through its collection and tell each one to "draw." In short, the form wants to treat all its Control objects polymorphically.

You implement polymorphism in two steps:

1. Create a base class with virtual methods.
2. Create derived classes that override the behavior of the base class's virtual methods.

To create a method in a base class that supports polymorphism, you mark the method as virtual. For example, to indicate that the method DrawControl( ) of class Control in Example 11-1 is polymorphic, add the keyword virtual to its declaration, as follows:

```
public virtual void DrawControl( )
```

Each derived class is free to inherit and use the base class's DrawControl( ) method as is, or to implement its own version of DrawControl( ). If a derived class does override the DrawControl( ) method, that overridden version will be invoked for each instance of the derived class. You override the base class virtual method by using the keyword override in the derived class method definition, and then add the modified code for that overridden method.

Example 11-2 shows how to override virtual methods. The Control and ListBox classes are back, and they've brought along a Button class, which also derives from Control.

Example 11-2. Virtual methods allow derived classes to implement their own version of the method

```
using System;
using System.Collections.Generic;
using System.Linq;
using System.Text;

namespace Example_11_2____Polymorphism
{
    public class Control
    {
        // these members are protected and thus visible
        // to derived class methods.
        protected int top;
        protected int left;

        // constructor takes two integers to
        // fix location on the console
        public Control (int top, int left)
        {
            this.top = top;
            this.left = left;
        }

        // simulates drawing the control
        public virtual void DrawControl( )
        {
            Console.WriteLine("Control: drawing Control at {0}, {1}",
                            top, left);
        }

    }

    // ListBox derives from Control
    public class ListBox : Control
    {
        private string listBoxContents; // new member variable

        // constructor adds a parameter
        // and calls the base constructor
        public ListBox( int top, int left, string contents)
                    : base(top, left)
        {
            listBoxContents = contents;
        }
```

Example 11-2. Virtual methods allow derived classes to implement their own version of the method (continued)

```
        // an overridden version (note keyword) because in the
        // derived method we change the behavior
        public override void DrawControl( )
        {
            base.DrawControl( ); // invoke the base method
            Console.WriteLine("Writing string to the ListBox: {0}",
                              listBoxContents);
        }

    } // end ListBox

    // Button also derives from Control
    public class Button : Control
    {
        // constructor has no body because it simply calls
        // the base class constructor
        public Button( int top, int left) : base(top, left)
        { }

        // an overridden version (note keyword) because in the
        // derived method we change the behavior
        public override void DrawControl( )
        {
            Console.WriteLine("Drawing a button at {0}, {1}\n",
                              top, left);
        }
    } // end Button

    public class Tester
    {
        static void Main( )
        {
            Control myControl = new Control(1, 2);
            ListBox myListBox = new ListBox(3, 4,
                                    "Standalone listbox");
            Button myButton = new Button(5, 6);
            myControl.DrawControl( );
            myListBox.DrawControl( );
            myButton.DrawControl( );

            Control[] controlArray = new Control[3];
            controlArray[0] = new Control(1, 2);
            controlArray[1] = new ListBox(3, 4,
                                "Listbox in array");
            controlArray[2] = new Button(5, 6);

            for (int i = 0; i < controlArray.Length; i++)
            {
                controlArray[i].DrawControl( );
            } // end for
        } // end Main
```

Example 11-2. Virtual methods allow derived classes to implement their own version of the method (continued)

```
    }        // end Tester
}
```

The output looks like this:

```
Control: drawing Control at 1, 2
Control: drawing Control at 3, 4
Writing string to the ListBox: Standalone listbox
Drawing a button at 5, 6

Control: drawing Control at 1, 2
Control: drawing Control at 3, 4
Writing string to the ListBox: Listbox in array
Drawing a button at 5, 6
```

Overriding Virtual Methods

In Example 11-2, ListBox derives from Control and implements its own version of DrawControl( ), using the override keyword:

```
public override void DrawWindow( )
{
    base.DrawWindow( ); // invoke the base method
    Console.WriteLine ("Writing string to the listbox: {0}",
    listBoxContents);
}
```

The keyword override tells the compiler that this class has intentionally overridden how DrawControl( ) works. Similarly, you override DrawControl( ) in another class that derives from Control: the Button class.

The only reason this override works is because in the base class (Control), the DrawControl( ) method is marked as virtual:

```
public virtual void DrawControl( )
{
    Console.WriteLine("Control: drawing Control at {0}, {1}",
                    top, left);
}
```

If DrawControl( ) weren't marked as virtual, the derived classes wouldn't be able to override it.

Using Objects Polymorphically

The really interesting part of this example, from a polymorphic point of view, happens in the body of the example. You create three objects: a Control, a ListBox, and a Button. Then you call DrawControl( ) on each:

```
Control myControl = new Control(1, 2);
ListBox myListBox = new ListBox(3, 4, "Standalone listbox");
Button myButton = new Button(5, 6);
myControl.DrawControl();
myListBox.DrawControl();
myButton.DrawControl();
```

This works much as you might expect. The correct DrawControl() method is called for each. So far, *nothing polymorphic has been done*, because each of the three classes has its own version of DrawControl(), which is what you're calling here. The real magic starts when you create an array of Control objects. As you learned in Chapter 10, an array can contain only objects of the same type. On the face of it, then, you wouldn't expect that you could store a Control, a ListBox, and a Button all in the same array.

But because a ListBox *is* a Control, you are free to place a ListBox into an array of Controls. Similarly, you can add a Button to a collection of Controls, because a Button *is a* Control.

```
Control[] controlArray = new Control[3];
controlArray[0] = new Control(1, 2);
controlArray[1] = new ListBox(3, 4, "Listbox in array");
controlArray[2] = new Button(5, 6);
```

The first line of the preceding code declares an array named controlArray that will hold three Control objects. The next three lines add new Control objects to the array. The first adds an object of type Control. The second adds an object of type ListBox (which is a Control because ListBox derives from Control), and the third adds an object of type Button, which is also a type of Control.

What happens when you call DrawControl() on each of these objects?

```
for (int i = 0; i < 3; i++)
{
    controlArray[i].DrawControl();
}
```

This code calls DrawControl() on each element in the array in turn. All the compiler knows is that it has three Control objects and that you've called DrawControl() on each. If you had not marked DrawControl() as virtual, Control's original DrawControl() method would be called three times.

However, because you did mark DrawControl() as virtual, and because the derived classes override that method, when you call DrawControl() on the array the right thing happens for each object in the array. Specifically, the compiler determines the *runtime type* of the actual objects (a Control, a ListBox, and a Button) and calls the right method on each. This is the essence of polymorphism—that the for loop, and the code within it, have no idea what kinds of objects are going to be in the array, except that they all derive from Control, and therefore have valid DrawControl() methods. The for loop doesn't need to know any more than that.

The runtime type of an object is the actual (derived) type. At compile time, you do not have to decide what kinds of objects will be added to your collection, as long as they all derive from the declared type (in this case, Control). At runtime, the actual type is discovered and the right method is called. This allows you to pick the actual type of objects to add to the collection while the program is running.

The compiler now knows to use the overridden method when treating these objects polymorphically. The compiler is responsible for tracking the real type of the object and for handling the late binding so that ListBox.DrawControl( ) is called when the Control reference really points to a ListBox object.

Versioning with new and override

In C#, the programmer's decision to override a virtual method is made explicit with the override keyword. This helps you release new versions of your code; changes to the base class will not break existing code in the derived classes. The requirement to use the override keyword helps to prevent that problem.

Here's how: assume for a moment that Company A wrote the Control base class you saw previously in Example 11-2. Suppose also that the ListBox and RadioButton classes were written by programmers from Company B, using a purchased copy of Company A's Control class as a base. The programmers in Company B have little or no control over the design of the Control class, including future changes that Company A might choose to make.

Now suppose that one of the programmers for Company B decides to add a Sort( ) method to ListBox:

```
public class ListBox : Control
{
    public virtual void Sort() {...}
}
```

This presents no problems until Company A, the author of Control, releases version 2 of its Control class, and the programmers in Company A also add a Sort( ) method to their public class Control:

```
public class Control
{
    // ...
    public virtual void Sort() {...}
}
```

In other object-oriented languages (such as C++), the new virtual Sort( ) method in Control would now act as a base virtual method for the Sort( ) method in ListBox, which is not what the developer of ListBox intended.

C# prevents this confusion. In C#, a virtual function is always considered to be the *root of virtual dispatch*; that is, once C# finds a virtual method, it looks no further up the inheritance hierarchy.

If a new virtual Sort() function is introduced into Control, the runtime behavior of ListBox is unchanged.

When ListBox is compiled again, however, the compiler generates a *warning*:

```
...\class1.cs(54,24): warning CS0114: 'ListBox.Sort()' hides
inherited member 'Control.Sort()'.
To make the current member override that implementation,
add the override keyword. Otherwise add the new keyword.
```

Never ignore a warning. Treat it as an error, until you are satisfied that you understand it and that not only is it innocuous, but also there is nothing you can do to eliminate it. Your goal, (almost) always, is to compile warning-free code.

To remove the warning, the programmer must indicate what he intends. He can mark the ListBox Sort() method as new to indicate that it is *not* an override of the virtual method in Control:

```
public class ListBox : Control
{
    public new virtual void Sort() {...}
```

This action removes the warning. If, on the other hand, the programmer does want to override the method in Control, he need only use the override keyword to make that intention explicit:

```
public class ListBox : Control
{
    public override void Sort() {...}
```

To avoid this warning, it might be tempting to add the new keyword to all your virtual methods. This is a *bad* idea. When new appears in the code, it ought to document the versioning of the code. It points a potential client to the base class to see what you are intentionally not overriding. Using new scattershot undermines this documentation and reduces the utility of a warning that exists to help identify a real issue.

If the programmer now creates any new classes that derive from ListBox, those derived classes will inherit the Sort() method from ListBox, not from the base Control class.

Abstract Classes

Each type of `Control` has a different shape and appearance. Drop-down `ListBoxes` look very different from `Buttons`. Clearly, every subclass of `Control` *should* implement its own `DrawControl()` method—but so far, nothing in the `Control` class enforces that they must do so. To require subclasses to implement a method of their base, you need to designate that method as *abstract*, rather than virtual.

An abstract method has no implementation. It creates a method name and signature that must be implemented in all derived classes. Furthermore, making at least one method of any class abstract has the side effect of making the entire class abstract.

Abstract classes establish a base for derived classes, but it is not legal to instantiate an object of an abstract class. Once you declare a method to be abstract, you prohibit the creation of any instances of that class.

Thus, if you were to designate `DrawControl()` as an abstract method in the `Control` class, the `Control` class itself would become abstract. Then you could derive from `Control`, but you could not create any `Control` instances. That makes sense, because the `Control` class is an abstraction—there is no such thing as a simple `Control` object, only objects derived from `Control`.

Making `Control.DrawControl()` abstract means that each class derived from `Control` would have to implement its own `DrawControl()` method. If the derived class failed to implement the abstract method, that derived class would also be abstract, and again no instances would be possible.

The Idea Behind Abstraction

Abstract classes should not just be an implementation trick; they should represent the idea of an abstraction that establishes a "contract" for all derived classes. In other words, abstract classes mandate the public methods of the classes that will implement the abstraction.

The idea of an abstract `Control` class ought to lay out the common characteristics and behaviors of all `Controls`, even though you never intend to instantiate the abstraction `Control` itself.

The idea of an abstract class is implied in the word *abstract*. It serves to implement the abstraction "Control" that will be manifest in the various concrete instances of `Control`, such as button, listbox, drop-down, and so forth. The abstract class establishes what a `Control` is, even though you never intend to create a plain "Control" by itself. An alternative to using abstract is to define an interface, as we describe in Chapter 13.

You designate a method as abstract simply by placing the abstract keyword at the beginning of the method definition:

```
abstract public void DrawControl();
```

(Because the method can have no implementation, there are no braces, only a semicolon.)

If one or more methods are abstract, the class definition must also be marked abstract, as in the following:

```
public abstract class Control
```

Example 11-3 illustrates the creation of an abstract Control class and an abstract DrawControl() method.

Example 11-3. Abstract methods form a contract so that all derived classes must implement their own versions of the method

```
using System;
using System.Collections.Generic;
using System.Linq;
using System.Text;

namespace Example_11_3____Abstract_Methods
{
    public abstract class Control
    {
        protected int top;
        protected int left;

        // constructor takes two integers to
        // fix location on the console
        public Control(int top, int left)
        {
            this.top = top;
            this.left = left;
        }

        // simulates drawing the control
        // notice: no implementation
        public abstract void DrawControl();

    }      // end class Control

    // ListBox derives from Control
    public class ListBox : Control
    {
        private string listBoxContents; // new member variable

        // constructor adds a parameter
        public ListBox( int top, int left, string contents)
                        : base(top, left) // call base constructor
        {
```

Example 11-3. Abstract methods form a contract so that all derived classes must implement their own versions of the method (continued)

```
        listBoxContents = contents;
    }


    // an overridden version implementing the
    // abstract method
    public override void DrawControl( )
    {
        Console.WriteLine("Writing string to the listbox: {0}",
                        listBoxContents);
    }
}     // end class ListBox

public class Button : Control
{
    public Button( int top, int left) : base(top, left) { }

    // override the abstract method
    public override void DrawControl( )
    {
        Console.WriteLine("Drawing a button at {0}, {1}\n",
                        top, left);
    }
}         // end class Button

public class Tester
{
    static void Main( )
    {
        Control[] controlArray = new Control[3];
        controlArray[0] = new ListBox(1, 2, "First ListBox");
        controlArray[1] = new ListBox(3, 4, "Second ListBox");
        controlArray[2] = new Button(5, 6);

        for (int i = 0; i < 3; i++)
        {
            controlArray[i].DrawControl( );
        }     // end for loop
    }         // end main
}             // end class Tester
}
```

The output looks like this:

```
Writing string to the listbox: First ListBox
Writing string to the listbox: Second ListBox
Drawing a button at 5, 6
```

In Example 11-3, the Control class has been declared abstract and therefore cannot be instantiated. If you replace the first array member:

```
controlArray[0] = new ListBox(1,2,"First ListBox");
```

with this code:

```
controlArray[0] = new Control(1,2);
```

the program generates the following error at compile time:

```
Cannot create an instance of the abstract class or interface 'Control'
```

You can instantiate the ListBox and Button objects because these classes override the abstract method, thus making the classes *concrete* (that is, not abstract).

Often, an abstract class will include nonabstract methods. Typically, these will be marked virtual, providing the programmer who derives from your abstract class the choice of using the implementation provided in the abstract class, or overriding it. Once again, however, all abstract methods must, eventually, be overridden to make an instance of the (derived) class.

Sealed Classes

The opposite side of the design coin from abstract is *sealed*. In contrast to an abstract class, which is intended to be derived from and to provide a template for its subclasses to follow, a sealed class does not allow classes to derive from it at all. The sealed keyword placed before the class declaration prevents any classes from deriving from it. Classes are most often marked sealed to prevent accidental (or intentional) inheritance.

If you change the declaration of Control in Example 11-3 from abstract to sealed (eliminating the abstract keyword from the DrawControl( ) declaration as well), the program fails to compile. If you try to build this project, the compiler returns the following error message:

```
'ListBox' cannot inherit from sealed type 'Class'
```

among many other complaints (such as that you cannot create a new protected member in a sealed class).

Microsoft recommends using sealed when you know that you won't need to create derived classes, and also when your class consists of nothing but static methods and properties.

The Root of All Classes: Object

All C# classes, of any type, ultimately derive from a single class: Object. Object is the base class for all other classes.

A base class is the immediate "parent" of a derived class. A derived class can be the base to further derived classes, creating an inheritance *tree* or hierarchy. A *root* class is the topmost class in an inheritance hierarchy. In C#, the root class is Object. The nomenclature is a bit confusing until you imagine an upside-down tree, with the root on top and the derived classes below. Thus, the base class is considered to be "above" the derived class.

Object provides a number of methods that subclasses can override. These include Equals( ), which determines whether two objects are the same, and ToString( ), which returns a string to represent the current object. Specifically, ToString( ) returns a string with the name of the class to which the object belongs. Table 11-1 summarizes the methods of Object.

Table 11-1. The Object class

Method	What it does
Equals( )	Evaluates whether two objects are equivalent
GetHashCode( )	Allows objects to provide their own hash function for use in collections (see Chapter 14)
GetType( )	Provides access to the type of the object
ToString( )	Provides a string representation of the object
Finalize( )	Cleans up nonmemory resources; implemented by a finalizer

In Example 11-4, the Dog class overrides the ToString( ) method inherited from Object, to return the weight of the Dog. You wouldn't expect to be able to convert a Dog object to a string, but if you override the ToString( ) method, that's essentially what you're doing.

Example 11-4. Overriding the ToString( ) method of Object allows a user-defined class to return a string

```
using System;

public class Dog
{
    private int weight;

    // constructor
    public Dog( int weight )
    {
        this.weight = weight;
    }

    // override Object.ToString
    public override string ToString( )
    {
        return weight.ToString( );
    }
}

public class Tester
{
    static void Main( )
    {
```

Example 11-4. Overriding the ToString( ) method of Object allows a user-defined class to return a string (continued)

```
    int i = 5;
    Console.WriteLine( "The value of i is: {0}", i.ToString() );

    Dog milo = new Dog( 62 );
    Console.WriteLine( "My dog Milo weighs {0} pounds", milo);
  }
}
```

The output looks like this:

```
The value of i is: 5
My dog Milo weighs 62 pounds
```

Some classes (such as Console) have methods that expect a string (such as WriteLine( )). These methods will call the ToString( ) method on your class if you've overridden the inherited ToString( ) method from Object. This lets you pass a Dog to Console. WriteLine, and the correct information will display.

This example also takes advantage of the startling fact that intrinsic types (int, long, and so forth) can also be treated as though they derive from Object, and thus you can call ToString( ) on an int variable! Calling ToString( ) on an intrinsic type returns a string representation of the variable's value.

The documentation for Object.ToString( ) reveals its signature:

```
public virtual string ToString( );
```

It is a public virtual method that returns a string and takes no parameters. All the built-in types, such as int, derive from Object and so can invoke Object's methods.

 The Console class's Write( ) and WriteLine( ) methods call ToString( ) for you on objects that you pass in for display. Thus, by overriding ToString( ) in the Dog class, you did not have to pass in milo.ToString( ), but rather could just pass in milo!

If you comment out the overridden function, the base method will be invoked. The base class default behavior is to return a string with the name of the class itself. Thus, the output would be changed to the meaningless:

```
My dog Milo weighs Dog pounds
```

 Classes do not need to declare explicitly that they derive from Object; the inheritance is implicit.

Summary

- Specialization is described as the *is-a* relationship; the reverse of specialization is generalization.

- Specialization and generalization are reciprocal and hierarchical—that is, specialization is reciprocal to generalization, and each class can have any number of specialized derived classes but only one parent class that it specializes: thus creating a branching hierarchy.

- C# implements specialization through inheritance.

- The inherited class derives the public and protected characteristics and behaviors of the base class, and is free to add or modify its own characteristics and behaviors.

- You implement inheritance by adding a colon after the name of the derived class, followed by the name of its base class.

- A derived class can invoke the constructor of its base class by placing a colon after the parameter list and invoking the base class constructor with the keyword base.

- Classes, like members, can also use the access modifiers public, private, and protected, though the vast majority of nonnested classes will be public.

- A method marked as virtual in the base class can be overridden by derived classes if the derived classes use the keyword override in their method definition. This is the key to polymorphism: when you call the virtual method on a derived object, the overridden behavior is invoked.

- A derived class can break the polymorphism of a derived method but must signal that intent with the keyword new. This is unusual and complex, and can be confusing, but it is provided to allow for versioning of derived classes. Typically, you will use the keyword override (rather than new) to indicate that you are modifying the behavior of the base class's method.

- A method marked as abstract has no implementation—instead, it provides a virtual method name and signature that all derived classes *must* override. Any class with an abstract method is an abstract class, and cannot be instantiated.

- Any class marked as sealed cannot be derived from.

- In C#, all classes (and built-in types) are ultimately derived from the Object class implicitly, and thus inherit a number of useful methods, such as ToString.

The topics in this chapter were a bit more complex than anything we've discussed up to this point, but they allow you to see the power and scope of C# in particular and object-oriented languages in general. We think it's pretty impressive that every object built into C# derives from just one class (Object), and once you grasp that, you can see how you might harness that power to create your own derived classes.

You also saw a lot of overloading in this chapter, and you can see how derived classes can build in their parents' method implementations to create new and different methods. In the next chapter, you'll take that to the extreme, and see that you can even override simple operators, such as + and -, in almost the same way as you did with methods.

Test Your Knowlege: Quiz

Question 11-1. What is the relationship between specialization and generalization?

Question 11-2. How is specialization implemented in C#?

Question 11-3. What is the syntax for inheritance in C#?

Question 11-4. How do you implement polymorphism?

Question 11-5. What are the two meanings of the keyword new?

Question 11-6. How do you call a base class constructor from a derived class?

Question 11-7. What is an abstract method?

Question 11-8. What is a sealed class?

Question 11-9. What is the base class of Int32?

Question 11-10. What is the base class of any class you create if you do not otherwise indicate a base class?

Test Your Knowledge: Exercises

Exercise 11-1. Create a base class, Telephone, and derive a class ElectronicPhone from it. In Telephone, create a protected string member phonetype and a public method Ring( ) which outputs a text message such as this: "Ringing the <phonetype>." In ElectronicPhone, the constructor should set the phonetype to "Digital." In the Run( ) method, call Ring( ) on the ElectronicPhone to test the inheritance.

Exercise 11-2. Extend Exercise 11-1 to illustrate a polymorphic method. Have the derived class override the Ring( ) method to display a different message.

Exercise 11-3. Change the Telephone class to abstract, and make Ring( ) an abstract method. Derive two new classes from Telephone: DigitalPhone and TalkingPhone. Each derived class should set the phonetype, and override the Ring( ) method.

Exercise 11-4. Phones these days do a lot more than ring, as you know. Add a method to DigitalPhone called VoiceMail( ) that outputs the message "You have a message. Press Play to retrieve." Now add a new class, DigitalCellPhone, that derives from DigitalPhone and implements a version of VoiceMail( ) that outputs the message "You have a message. Call to retrieve."

CHAPTER 12

Operator Overloading

Back in Chapters 3 and 4, you learned about the C# built-in types, such as integer (int) and Boolean (bool), and the various operators that let you work with those types, from the simple mathematical operators (such as + and %) to the comparison operators (== and <=) to the logical operators (&& and ||). Using most of these operators with the basic types is simple and intuitive. If you try to use those operators with classes you've created in the past few chapters, though, you'll get an error. Back in Chapter 8, you saw how to *overload* the methods of your class, giving them additional functions, depending on the parameters. C# lets you extend that overloading ability to operators—arithmetic ones, comparison ones, and even the operator for casting one type to another—which is what we'll show you in this chapter. Although being able to overload the arithmetic operators is great, it's the equality operators that are really useful to overload, as you'll see.

Designing the Fraction Class

For example, suppose you define a type to represent fractional numbers; you might reasonably name it Fraction. The following constructors establish two Fraction objects, the first representing 1/2 and the second representing 3/4:

```
Fraction firstFraction = new Fraction(1,2); // create 1/2
Fraction secondFraction = new Fraction(3,4); // create 3/4
```

It's reasonable to create this class so that the first parameter will represent the numerator and the second parameter will represent the denominator. In general, when you create your classes, you should stick to an obvious and intuitive interpretation whenever you can.

If you want your Fraction class to have all the functionality of the built-in types, you'll need to be able to perform arithmetic on instances of your fractions (add two fractions, multiply them, and so on). You should also be able to convert fractions to and from built-in types, such as int.

Hypothetically, you could implement methods for each of these operations. For example, for your Fraction type, you might create an Add( ) method, which you would invoke like this:

```
// add 1/2 and 3/4
Fraction theSum = firstFraction.Add(secondFraction);
```

This works just fine, but it's not very obvious. It's hard to read, and it's not how the user would automatically expect addition to work. It also doesn't look like addition of the built-in types, such as int. It would be much better to be able to write:

```
// add 1/2 and 3/4 using + operator
Fraction theSum = firstFraction + secondFraction;
```

Statements that use operators (in this case, the plus sign) are intuitive and easy to use. Equally important, this use of operators is consistent with how built-in types are added, multiplied, and so forth.

The C# syntax for overloading an operator is to write the keyword operator followed by the operator to overload. The next section demonstrates how you might do this for the Fraction class.

Using the operator Keyword

In C#, operators are static methods. The return value of an operator represents the result of an operation. The operator's parameters are the operands.

You can define an addition operator for a Fraction class as you would any other class method, but with a bit of a difference. Instead of a method name, you use the C# syntax of combining the operator keyword with the plus sign (+) operator, combined with the keyword static. For example, the overloaded addition operator (the operator+ method) takes two Fraction objects (the fractions you want to add) as parameters and returns a reference to another Fraction object representing the sum of the two parameters. Here is its signature:

```
public static Fraction operator+(Fraction lhs, Fraction rhs)
```

And here's what you can do with it. Assume, for instance, that you've defined two fractions representing the portion of a pie you've eaten for breakfast and lunch, respectively. (You love pie.)

```
Fraction pieIAteForBreakfast = new Fraction(1,2); // 1/2 of a pie
Fraction pieIAteForLunch = new Fraction(1,3);     // 1/3 of a pie
```

The overloaded operator+ allows you to figure out how much pie you've eaten in total. (And there's still 1/6 of the pie leftover for dinner!) You would write:

```
Fraction totalPigOut = pieIAteForBreakfast + pieIAteForLunch;
```

The compiler takes the first operand (pieIAteForBreakfast) and passes it to operator+ as the parameter lhs; it passes the second operand (pieIAteForLunch) as rhs. These two Fractions are then added, and the result is returned and assigned to the Fraction object named totalPigOut.

 It is our convention to name the parameters to a binary operator lhs and rhs. A binary operator is an operator that takes two operands. The parameter name lhs stands for "lefthand side" and reminds us that the first parameter represents the lefthand side of the operation. Similarly, rhs stands for "righthand side."

To see how this works, you'll create a Fraction class, as described previously. We'll show you the complete listing first, in Example 12-1, and then we'll take it apart and explain what it does.

Example 12-1. Implementing operator+ for Fraction isn't difficult; you define it as you would any method of the class, but using the keyword operator

```
using System;
using System.Collections.Generic;
using System.Linq;
using System.Text;

namespace Example_12_1____Overloading_Addition
{
    public class Fraction
    {
        private int numerator;
        private int denominator;

        // create a fraction by passing in the numerator
        // and denominator
        public Fraction(int numerator, int denominator)
        {
            this.numerator = numerator;
            this.denominator = denominator;
        }

        // overloaded operator + takes two fractions
        // and returns their sum
        public static Fraction operator+ (Fraction lhs, Fraction rhs)
        {
            // like fractions (shared denominator) can be added
            // by adding their numerators
            if (lhs.denominator == rhs.denominator)
            {
                return new Fraction(lhs.numerator + rhs.numerator,
                                lhs.denominator);
            }

            // simplistic solution for unlike fractions
            // 1/2 + 3/4 == (1*4) + (3*2) / (2*4) == 10/8
            // this method does not reduce.
```

```
            int firstProduct = lhs.numerator * rhs.denominator;
            int secondProduct = rhs.numerator * lhs.denominator;
            return new Fraction( firstProduct + secondProduct,
                                 lhs.denominator * rhs.denominator );
        }

        // return a string representation of the fraction
        public override string ToString( )
        {
            String s = numerator.ToString( ) + "/" + denominator.ToString( );
            return s;
        }
    }


    public class Tester
    {
        public void Run( )
        {
            Fraction firstFraction = new Fraction(3, 4);
            Console.WriteLine("firstFraction: {0}", firstFraction.ToString( ));

            Fraction secondFraction = new Fraction(2, 4);
            Console.WriteLine("secondFraction: {0}", secondFraction.ToString( ));

            Fraction sumOfTwoFractions = firstFraction + secondFraction;
            Console.WriteLine( "firstFraction + secondFraction =
                        sumOfTwoFractions: {0}", sumOfTwoFractions.ToString( ));

        }
        static void Main( )
        {
            Tester t = new Tester( );
            t.Run( );
        }
    }
}
```

The output looks like this:

```
firstFraction: 3/4
secondFraction: 2/4
firstFraction + secondFraction = sumOfTwoFractions: 5/4
```

Let's take this one step at a time, so you can see how this class works. In Example 12-1, you start by creating a Fraction class. The private member data is the numerator and denominator, stored as integers:

```
public class Fraction
{
    private int numerator;
    private int denominator;
```

The constructor just initializes these values; that's simple enough.

The overloaded addition operator takes two Fraction objects, returns a Fraction, and is marked static:

```
public static Fraction operator+ (Fraction lhs, Fraction rhs)
{
```

As you'd expect for adding fractions, if the denominators for the fractions are the same, you add the numerators and return a new Fraction object created by passing in the sum of the numerators as the new numerator and the shared denominator as the new denominator:

```
if (lhs.denominator == rhs.denominator)
{
    return new Fraction(lhs.numerator + rhs.numerator,
                        lhs.denominator);
}
```

The Fraction object's firstFraction and secondFraction are passed in to the overloaded addition operator as lhs and rhs, respectively. The new Fraction is returned to the calling method, Run( ), where it is assigned to sumOfTwoFractions:

```
Fraction sumOfTwoFractions = firstFraction + secondFraction;
Console.WriteLine( "firstFraction + secondFraction = sumOfTwoFractions: {0}",
                    sumOfTwoFractions.ToString() );
```

Back in the implementation of the operator, if the denominators are different, you cross-multiply before adding, which is the standard method for adding unlike fractions:

```
int firstProduct = lhs.numerator * rhs.denominator;
int secondProduct = rhs.numerator * lhs.denominator;
return new Fraction( firstProduct + secondProduct,
                     lhs.denominator * rhs.denominator );
```

The two local variables, firstProduct and secondProduct, are temporary; they are destroyed when the method returns. The new Fraction created, however, is not temporary; it returned to Run( ) as in the case where the denominators are equal.

A good Fraction class would, no doubt, implement all the arithmetic operators (addition, subtraction, multiplication, division). To overload the multiplication operator, you would write operator*; to overload the division operator, you would write operator/.

The Fraction class also overrides the ToString( ) method (inherited from Object, as discussed in Chapter 11) to allow you to display the fractions by passing them to Console.WriteLine( ):

```
public override string ToString()
{
    String s = numerator.ToString() + "/" + denominator.ToString();
    return s;
}
```

When you run this application, you can see that the ToString( ) method works as planned, and the overloaded operator allows you to add firstFraction and secondFraction as intuitively as though they were ints.

Creating Useful Operators

Operator overloading can make your code more intuitive and enable you to use instances of your classes as though they were built-in types. However, when you overload an operator for your class, the way you're using it has to make sense. If you start to give your operators values that don't naturally follow from their traditional meanings, you'll just confuse anyone else who tries to use your class, possibly including yourself.

For example, although it might be tempting to overload the increment operator (++) on an employee class to invoke a method incrementing the employee's pay level, this can create tremendous confusion. The increment operator normally means "increase this scalar value by one." Giving it the new meaning of "increase this employee's pay level" may be obvious when you implement the operator, but confusing to other programmers who have to maintain the code. It is best to use operator overloading sparingly, and only when its meaning is clear and consistent with how the built-in classes operate. You'll find that there aren't very many situations where it makes sense to overload the traditional arithmetic operators.

The Equals Operator

Although we've just warned you away from wildly implementing overloaded arithmetic operators, the comparison operators, especially ==, are another story. It's very common to overload the == operator to determine whether two objects are equal. What "equal" means is up to you, although your criteria should be reasonable. You might decide that two Employee objects are equal if they have the same name, or you may decide that simply having the same employee ID is sufficient.

Overloading the == operator works the same as overloading any other operator. Simply use the keyword operator with the == symbol, and place your code inside the method. The == operator always returns a Boolean (true or false), so you'll need to declare the operator as a public static bool. For example, for the Fraction class, your operator might look like this:

```
public static bool operator== ( Fraction lhs, Fraction rhs )
{
    if ( lhs.denominator == rhs.denominator &&
        lhs.numerator == rhs.numerator )
    {
        return true;
    }
    // code here to handle unlike fractions
```

```
        return false;
    }
```

Notice that there's no else clause here. If the numerator and denominator are equal, the operator returns true, and exits. If they're not equal, the return statement after the if is executed, so there's no need for an else.

C# insists that if you overload the equals operator, you must also overload the not-equals operator (!=). It's good programming practice to have the inequality operator delegate its work to the equality operator, like this:

```
public static bool operator !=(Fraction lhs, Fraction rhs)
{
    return !(lhs==rhs);
}
```

As you can see, the != operator will return the opposite of the value of the == operator, which is exactly what you want. This way, if you change your definition of equality, you can change the code in the == operator overload, and the != operator will still return the opposite.

Similarly, the less than (<) and greater than (>) operators must be paired, as must the less than or equal to (<=) and greater than or equal to (>=) operators.

The Object class (which is the root of every class in C#) offers a virtual method called Equals( ). (We discuss virtual methods in Chapter 11.) If you overload the equals operator (==), it is recommended that you also override the Equals( ) method.

Overriding the Equals( ) method allows your class to be compatible with other .NET languages that do not overload operators (but do support method overloading). That way, even if you can't use the == operator, you can still use the Equals( ) method to do the same thing.

The Object class implements the Equals( ) method with this signature:

```
public virtual bool Equals(object o)
```

From this signature, you can see that your override of this method will take an object as a parameter, and return a bool (true if the two objects are equal, where "equality" is however you define it).

By overriding this method, you allow your Fraction class to act polymorphically with all other objects. For example, anywhere you can call Equals( ) on two Objects, you can call Equals( ) on two Fractions.

Inside the body of Equals( ), you need to ensure that you are comparing one Fraction object with another Fraction object. If the other object is not a fraction, they cannot be equal, and you'll return false:

```
public override bool Equals(object o)
{

    if ( ! (o is Fraction) )
```

```
    {
        return false;
    }
    return this == (Fraction) o;
}
```

The is operator is used to check the runtime type of an object (in this case, Fraction). Therefore, o is Fraction evaluates true if o is, in fact, a Fraction or a type derived from Fraction.

Once you know that you are comparing two Fractions, you can delegate the decision as to their equality to the overloaded operator (operator==) that you've already written, just as you did with the != operator. This allows you to avoid duplicate code. Notice, though, that before you can compare this to o, you need to cast o to a Fraction. We discussed casting with intrinsic types back in Chapter 3.

In this way, the Equals( ) method determines only that you do in fact have two fractions. If so, it delegates deciding whether the two fractions are truly equal to the already implemented operator ==.

The complete modification of the Fraction class is shown in Example 12-2, followed by the analysis.

Example 12-2. Implementing the == operator is similar to implementing the addition operator before. However, you also have to implement != and Equals( )

```
using System;
using System.Collections.Generic;
using System.Linq;
using System.Text;

namespace Example_12_2____Overloading_Equality
{
    public class Fraction
    {
        private int numerator;
        private int denominator;

        // create a fraction by passing in the numerator
        // and denominator
        public Fraction(int numerator, int denominator)
        {
            this.numerator = numerator;
            this.denominator = denominator;
        }

        // overloaded operator+ takes two fractions
        // and returns their sum
        public static Fraction operator+ (Fraction lhs, Fraction rhs)
        {
            // like fractions (shared denominator) can be added
            // by adding their numerators
            if (lhs.denominator == rhs.denominator)
```

Example 12-2. Implementing the == operator is similar to implementing the addition operator before. However, you also have to implement != and Equals() (continued)

```
        {
            return new Fraction(lhs.numerator + rhs.numerator,
                                lhs.denominator);
        }

        // simplistic solution for unlike fractions
        // 1/2 + 3/4 == (1*4) + (3*2) / (2*4) == 10/8
        // this method does not reduce.
        int firstProduct = lhs.numerator * rhs.denominator;
        int secondProduct = rhs.numerator * lhs.denominator;
        return new Fraction( firstProduct + secondProduct,
                             lhs.denominator * rhs.denominator );
    }

    // test whether two Fractions are equal
    public static bool operator== (Fraction lhs, Fraction rhs)
    {
        if (lhs.denominator == rhs.denominator &&
            lhs.numerator == rhs.numerator)
        {
            return true;
        }
        // code here to handle unlike fractions
        return false;
    }

    // delegates to operator ==
    public static bool operator !=(Fraction lhs, Fraction rhs)
    {
        return !(lhs == rhs);
    }

    // tests for same types, then delegates
    public override bool Equals(object o)
    {
        if (!(o is Fraction))
        {
            return false;
        }
        return this == (Fraction)o;
    }

    // return a string representation of the fraction
    public override string ToString()
    {
        String s = numerator.ToString() + "/"
                    + denominator.ToString();
        return s;
    }
}
```

Example 12-2. Implementing the == operator is similar to implementing the addition operator before. However, you also have to implement != and Equals() (continued)

```
public class Tester
{
    public void Run()
    {
        Fraction f1 = new Fraction(3, 4);
        Console.WriteLine("f1: {0}", f1.ToString());

        Fraction f2 = new Fraction(2, 4);
        Console.WriteLine("f2: {0}", f2.ToString());

        Fraction f3 = f1 + f2;
        Console.WriteLine("f1 + f2 = f3: {0}", f3.ToString());

        Fraction f4 = new Fraction(5, 4);

        if (f4 == f3)
        {
            Console.WriteLine("f4: {0} == F3: {1}",
                            f4.ToString(), f3.ToString());
        }

        if (f4 != f2)
        {
            Console.WriteLine("f4: {0} != F2: {1}",
                            f4.ToString(), f2.ToString());
        }

        if (f4.Equals(f3))
        {
            Console.WriteLine("{0}.Equals({1})",
                            f4.ToString(), f3.ToString());
        }

    }
    static void Main()
    {
        Tester t = new Tester();
        t.Run();
    }
}
}
```

The output looks like this:

```
f1: 3/4
f2: 2/4
f1 + f2 = f3: 5/4
f4: 5/4 == F3: 5/4
f4: 5/4 != F2: 2/4
5/4.Equals(5/4)
```

Example 12-2 implements the overloaded equals operator, operator==. If the fractions have the same denominator, you test whether the numerators are equal. If they are, you return true; otherwise, you return false.

```
public static bool operator== (Fraction lhs, Fraction rhs)
{
    if (lhs.denominator == rhs.denominator &&
        lhs.numerator == rhs.numerator)
    {
        return true;
    }
    // code here to handle unlike fractions
    return false;
}
```

 We've simplified the math here to keep the example readable. Testing for true equality (such as 3/4 = 6/8) is an interesting challenge you might want to try.

This method is invoked in the Run( ) method when you write:

```
if (f4 == f3)
```

The if statement expects a Boolean value, which is what operator== returns. The next thing the class does is implement the != operator, which as we discussed simply returns the opposite of the == operator.

In addition to implementing the == and != operators, you implement the Equals( ) method, for the reasons explained previously:

```
public override bool Equals( object o )
{
    if ( !( o is Fraction ) )
    {
        return false;
    }
    return this == (Fraction)o;
}
```

If the two objects are not both Fractions, you return false; otherwise, you delegate to the == operator, casting o to a Fraction type. Put a breakpoint on the return line, and you'll find that you step back into operator==. The value returned by operator== is the value returned by the Equals( ) method if both objects are fractions.

Conversion Operators

As you learned back in Chapter 3, C# will convert (for example) an int to a long *implicitly* but will only allow you to convert a long to an int *explicitly*. The conversion from int to long is implicit because you know that any int will fit into a long without losing any information. The reverse operation, from long to int, must be explicit (using a cast) because it is possible to lose information in the conversion:

```
int myInt = 5;
long myLong;
myLong = myInt;        // implicit
myInt = (int) myLong;  // explicit
```

It would certainly be useful to convert your `Fraction` objects to intrinsic types (such as `int`) and back. Given an `int`, you can support an implicit conversion to a fraction because any whole value is equal to that value over 1 (15 == 15/1).

Given a fraction, you might want to provide an explicit conversion back to an integer, understanding that some information might be lost. Thus, you might convert 9/4 to the integer value 2 (truncating to the nearest whole number).

 A more sophisticated `Fraction` class might not truncate, but rather round to the nearest whole number. Again, we're trying to keep this example simple, but feel free to implement a more sophisticated method.

To implement the conversion operator, you still use the keyword `operator`, but instead of the symbol you're overriding, you use the type that you're converting to. For example, to convert your `Fraction` to an `int`, you'd do this:

```
public static implicit operator Fraction( int theInt )
```

You use the keyword `implicit` when the conversion is guaranteed to succeed and no information will be lost; otherwise, you use `explicit`. `implicit` and `explicit` are actually operators, often called cast or casting operators because their job is to cast from one type to another (`int` to `Fraction` or `Fraction` to `int`).

Example 12-3 illustrates how you might implement implicit and explicit conversions in your `Fraction` class. We've omitted the overloaded addition and equality operators from the example code in the book, because those haven't changed, but they're still there. We'll explain how it works afterward.

Example 12-3. Overriding the conversion operators allows both implicit and explicit conversion between types

```
using System;
using System.Collections.Generic;
using System.Linq;
using System.Text;

namespace Example_12_3____Conversion_Operators
{
    public class Fraction
    {
        private int numerator;
        private int denominator;

        // create a fraction by passing in the numerator
        // and denominator
```

```
        public Fraction(int numerator, int denominator)
        {
            this.numerator = numerator;
            this.denominator = denominator;
        }

        // overload the constructor to create a
        // fraction from a whole number
        public Fraction(int wholeNumber)
        {
            Console.WriteLine("In constructor taking a whole number");
            numerator = wholeNumber;
            denominator = 1;
        }

        // convert ints to Fractions implicitly
        public static implicit operator Fraction(int theInt)
        {
            Console.WriteLine("Implicitly converting int to Fraction");
            return new Fraction(theInt);
        }

        // convert Fractions to ints explicitly
        public static explicit operator int(Fraction theFraction)
        {
            Console.WriteLine("Explicitly converting Fraction to int");
            return theFraction.numerator / theFraction.denominator;
        }

        // operator + goes here
        // equality operators go here

        // return a string representation of the fraction
        public override string ToString()
        {
            String s = numerator.ToString() + "/" + denominator.ToString();
            return s;
        }
    }

    public class Tester
    {
        public void Run()
        {
            Fraction f1 = new Fraction(3, 4);
            Fraction f2 = new Fraction(2, 4);
            Fraction f3 = f1 + f2;

            Console.WriteLine("adding f3 + 5...");
            Fraction f4 = f3 + 5;
            Console.WriteLine("f3 + 5 = f4: {0}", f4.ToString());
```

```
            Console.WriteLine("\nAssigning f4 to an int...");
            int truncated = (int)f4;
            Console.WriteLine("When you truncate f4 you get {0}",
            truncated);
        }
        static void Main()
        {
            Tester t = new Tester();
            t.Run();
        }
    }
}
```

The output looks like this:

```
adding f3 + 5...
Implicitly converting int to Fraction
In constructor taking a whole number
f3 + 5 = f4: 25/4

Assigning f4 to an int...
Explicitly converting Fraction to int
When you truncate f4 you get 6
```

In Example 12-3, you add a second constructor that takes a whole number and creates a Fraction:

```
public Fraction(int wholeNumber)
{
    Console.WriteLine("In constructor taking a whole number");
    numerator = wholeNumber;
    denominator = 1;
}
```

> Notice that in this and the following code samples, you add WriteLine() statements to indicate when you've entered the method. This is an alternative to stepping through in a debugger. Although using the debugger is usually more effective, this kind of output can help you trace the execution of your program for review at a later time.

You want to be able to convert Fractions to and from ints. To do so, you create the conversion operators. As discussed previously, converting from a Fraction to an int requires truncating the value, and so must be explicit:

```
public static explicit operator int(Fraction theFraction)
{
    Console.WriteLine("Explicitly converting Fraction to int");
    return theFraction.numerator / theFraction.denominator;
}
```

Note the use of the explicit keyword, indicating that this requires an explicit cast from a Fraction to an int. The method itself simply divides the numerator by the denominator. Since you're returning an int, this is integer division, which means that any remainder will be discarded.

You see the cast in the Run( ) method:

```
int truncated = (int) f4;
```

The cast from an int to a Fraction, on the other hand, is perfectly safe, so it can be implicit. This is what it looks like in the Run( ) method:

```
Fraction f4 = f3 + 5;
```

Notice that there is no explicit cast in this statement. When you add the int to the Fraction, the int is implicitly cast to a Fraction. The implementation of this is to create a new Fraction object and to return it:

```
public static implicit operator Fraction(int theInt)
{
    Console.WriteLine("Implicitly converting int to Fraction");
    return new Fraction(theInt);
}
```

Using the implicit cast operator causes the constructor to be invoked:

```
public Fraction(int wholeNumber)
{
    Console.WriteLine("In constructor taking a whole number");
    numerator = wholeNumber;
    denominator = 1;
}
```

You see this sequence of events represented in the output:

```
Implicitly converting int to Fraction
In constructor taking a whole number
```

Summary

- You can overload operators in much the same way that you would overload methods.
- To overload an operator, use the static keyword with the operator keyword, and the name of the operator you're overloading.
- It is good programming practice to use operator overloading sparingly and to be sure that the meaning of the overload is obvious and intuitive.
- When you overload the equals (==) operator, you should also override the Equals( ) method for compatibility with other .NET languages.
- If you overload the == operator, you must also overload the != operator. Similarly, the < and > operators are paired, as are the <= and >= operators.

- You can also overload conversion operators to allow one type to be implicitly or explicitly cast to another type. When doing so, you must use the keyword `implicit` when the conversion is guaranteed to succeed without loss of information, and `explicit` when there is a risk that information might be lost.

Now you know how to overload constructors, regular class methods, and even operators. That's a lot of overloading going on, but it's all with good reason—to make your user-defined classes flexible and extensible. In the next chapter, we'll look at yet another method of extension: interfaces. Interfaces let you dictate the methods that a class will have, without using inheritance. It's complicated, but powerful, as you'll see.

Test Your Knowledge: Quiz

Question 12-1. What is operator overloading?

Question 12-2. Are operators implemented as properties, static methods, or instance methods?

Question 12-3. What keyword do you use to overload an operator?

Question 12-4. How does the compiler translate:

```
Fraction f3 = f2 + f1;
```

assuming that f2 and f1 are Fraction objects and you have overloaded the + operator for the Fraction class?

Question 12-5. Which of the following overloads are reasonable?

1. Overloading the == operator for a Dog class such that two Dog objects with the same name are equal
2. Overloading the - operator of a Box class such that subtracting one Box object from another produces a new Box object with a volume equal to the difference between the other two Box objects
3. Overloading the -- operator of an Employee class so that the employee's hours are reduced
4. Overloading the + operator of a BankAccount class to merge the balance of two accounts

Question 12-6. Which of the comparison operators are paired?

Question 12-7. What should you also do if you overload the == operator?

Question 12-8. What is the purpose of the Equals( ) method?

Question 12-9. What keyword(s) do you use to overload the conversion operators?

Question 12-10. When should you use implicit conversion, and when should you use explicit conversion?

Test Your Knowledge: Exercises

Exercise 12-1. Create a class Invoice, which has a string member vendor and a double member amount, as well as a method to output the two properties of the invoice. Overload the addition operator so that if the vendor properties match, the amount properties of the two invoices are added together in a new invoice. If the vendor properties do not match, the new invoice is blank. Include some test code to test the addition operator.

Exercise 12-2. Modify the Invoice class so that two invoices are considered equal if the vendor and amount properties match. Test your methods.

Exercise 12-3. Modify the Invoice class once more so that you can determine whether one invoice is greater than or less than another. Test your methods.

Exercise 12-4. Create a class Foot and a class Meter. Each should have a single parameter that stores the length of the object, and a simple method to output that length. Create a casting operator for each class: one that converts a Foot object to a Meter object, and one that converts a Meter object to a Foot object. Test these operators to make sure they work.

CHAPTER 13

Interfaces

Back in Chapter 11, you saw how inheritance and abstract methods can dictate the methods that a class has to implement. However, it isn't always necessary to create a new parent class, even an abstract one, to guarantee the behaviors of your class. For example, you might want to dictate that your class must be *storable* (capable of being written to disk) or *printable*. "Storable" isn't a good candidate for a class, because it doesn't model an object; instead, it describes a set of behaviors that you want your class to have. Such a description is called an *interface*. The interface defines the methods that a class must implement, but it doesn't dictate *how* the class implements these required methods. This provides a lot of flexibility on the part of the class designer, yet it allows client classes to use those methods with confidence, because the interface methods are guaranteed to be implemented. There are a lot of interesting things you can do with interfaces, including implementing multiple interfaces, combining them, inheriting them, and casting to them. All of it can be tricky to understand at first, so we'll describe them all thoroughly in this chapter.

What Interfaces Are

An interface is a contract. When you design an interface, you're saying, "If you want to provide this capability, you must implement these methods, provide these properties and indexers, and support these events." The *implementer* of the interface agrees to the contract and implements the required elements.

 You saw methods and properties in Chapter 8. We'll discuss indexers in Chapter 14 and events in Chapter 17. We promise you don't need to know about them for this chapter.

When you specify interfaces, it is easy to get confused about who is responsible for what. There are three concepts to keep clear:

The interface

This is the contract. By convention, interface names begin with a capital *I*, so your interface might have a name such as IPrintable. The IPrintable interface might require, among other things, a Print( ) method. This states that any class that wants to implement IPrintable must implement a Print( ) method, but it does *not* specify how that method works internally. That is up to the designer of the implementing class.

The implementing class

This is the class that agrees to the contract described by the interface. For example, Document might be a class that implements IPrintable and thus implements the Print( ) method in whatever way the designer of the Document class thinks is appropriate.

The client class

The client calls methods on the implementing class. For example, you might have an Editor class that has an array of IPrintable objects (every object in the class is an instance of a type that implements IPrintable, even if they aren't all the same type). The client can expect to be able to call Print( ) on each object, and although each individual object may implement the method differently, each will do so appropriately and without complaint.

Interfaces Versus Abstract Base Classes

Programmers learning C# often ask about the difference between an interface and an abstract base class. The key difference is that an abstract base class serves as the base class for a family of derived classes, and an interface is meant to be mixed in with other inheritance chains. That is, a class can inherit from only a single parent class, but it can implement multiple interfaces.

In addition, when you derive from an abstract class, you must override all the abstract methods in the abstract base class, but you don't have to override any nonabstract methods. You can simply use the implementation that the base class provides. This is called *partial implementation*, and it's very common with abstract classes. Interfaces don't have any implementation, so you must implement every method defined in the interface. You can't partially implement an interface.

Inheriting from an abstract class implements the *is-a* relationship, introduced in Chapter 6. Implementing an interface defines a different relationship, one you've not seen until now: the *implements* relationship. These two relationships are subtly different. A car *is a* vehicle, but it might *implement* the CanBeBoughtWithABigLoan capability (as can a house, for example).

One critical thing to remember about interfaces is that an interface is *not* a class, and you can't instantiate an instance of an interface. For example, this won't work:

```
IPrintable myPrintable = new IPrintable( );
```

Interfaces aren't classes, so they don't have constructors, and you can't have an instance of an interface. However—and this is where it gets a bit confusing—if you have a class that implements the interface, you can create a reference to an object of that class, of the type of the interface. Confused? Look at an example. Suppose you have a Document class that you know implements IPrintable. Although you can't create an IPrintable object, you can do this:

```
IPrintable myPrintable = new Document( );
```

myPrintable is called a *reference*, which in this case refers to some (unnamed) Document object. All your code needs to know about myPrintable is that it refers to some object that implements the IPrintable interface—it could be a Document, it could be a Memo, it could be a GreatAmericanNovel. Doesn't matter. This lets you treat interface references *polymorphically*, just like you can use inheritance to treat objects polymorphically (see Chapter 11 for a refresher, if you need it). You'll see how this works a little later in the chapter.

Interfaces are a critical addition to any framework, and they are used extensively throughout .NET. For example, the collection classes (stacks, queues, and dictionaries, which we'll cover in detail in Chapter 14) are defined, in large measure, by the interfaces they implement.

Implementing an Interface

The syntax for defining an interface is very similar to the syntax for defining a class:

```
[attributes] [access-modifier] interface interface-name [:base-list]
{interface-body}
```

 The optional *attributes* are beyond the scope of this book. In short, every .NET application contains code, data, and metadata. Attributes are objects that are embedded in your program (invisible at runtime) and contain metadata—that is, data about your classes and your program. You don't need to worry about them for our purposes here.

Access modifiers (public, private, and so forth) work just as they do with classes. (See Chapter 7 for more about access modifiers.) The interface keyword is followed by an identifier (the interface name). It is recommended (but not required) to begin the name of your interface with a capital *I* (IStorable, ICloneable, IGetNoKickFromChampagne, and so on). We will discuss the optional base list later in this chapter.

Now, suppose you are the author of a Document class, which specifies that Document objects can be stored in a database. You decide to have Document implement the IStorable interface. It isn't required that you do so, but by implementing the IStorable interface, you signal to potential clients that the Document class can be used just like any other IStorable object. This will, for example, allow your clients to add your Document objects to an array of IStorable references:

```
IStorable[] myStorableArray = new IStorable[3];
```

As we discussed earlier, the array doesn't specifically need to know that it holds a Document object, just that it holds objects that implement IStorable.

To implement the IStorable interface, use the same syntax as though the new Document class were inheriting from IStorable—a colon (:) followed by the interface name:

```
public class Document : IStorable
```

You can read this as "define a public class named Document that implements the IStorable interface." The compiler distinguishes whether the colon indicates inheritance or implementation of an interface by checking to see whether IStorable is defined, and whether it is an interface or base class.

If you derive from a base class and you also implement one or more interfaces, you use a single colon and separate the base class and the interfaces by commas. The base class must be listed first; the interfaces may be listed in any order.

```
public MyBigClass : TheBaseClass, IPrintable, IStorable, IClaudius, IAndThou
```

In this declaration, the new class MyBigClass derives from TheBaseClass and implements four interfaces.

Suppose that the definition of IStorable requires a void Read( ) method, and a void Write( ) method that takes an object. In that case, your definition of the Document class that implements the IStorable interface might look like this:

```
public class Document : IStorable
{
    public void Read( ) {...}
    public void Write(object obj) {...}
    // ...
}
```

It is now your responsibility, as the author of the Document class, to provide a meaningful implementation of the IStorable methods. Having designated Document as implementing IStorable, you must implement all the IStorable methods, or you will generate an error when you compile. Example 13-1 illustrates defining and implementing the IStorable interface. Have a look at it first, and we'll take it apart afterward.

Example 13-1. Implementing an interface simply requires implementing all of its properties and methods, in whatever way is best for your class

```csharp
using System;
using System.Collections.Generic;
using System.Linq;
using System.Text;

namespace Example_13_1____Implementing_Interface
{
    interface IStorable
    {
        void Read();
        void Write( object obj );
        int Status { get; set; }
    }


    public class Document : IStorable
    {

        public Document( string s )
        {
            Console.WriteLine( "Creating document with: {0}", s );
        }

#region IStorable

        public void Read()
        {
            Console.WriteLine( "Executing Document's Read
                              Method for IStorable" );
        }

        public void Write( object o )
        {
            Console.WriteLine( "Executing Document's Write
                              Method for IStorable" );
        }

        // property required by IStorable
        public int Status { get; set;}

#endregion

    }

    class Tester
    {
        public void Run()
        {
            Document doc = new Document( "Test Document" );
            doc.Status = -1;
            doc.Read();
```

Example 13-1. Implementing an interface simply requires implementing all of its properties and methods, in whatever way is best for your class (continued)

```
            Console.WriteLine( "Document Status: {0}", doc.Status );
        }

        static void Main( )
        {
            Tester t = new Tester( );
            t.Run( );
        }
    }
}
```

The output looks like this:

```
Creating document with: Test Document
Executing Document's Read Method for IStorable
Document Status: -1
```

Defining the Interface

In Example 13-1, the first few lines define an interface, IStorable, which has two methods (Read( ) and Write( )) and a property (Status) of type int:

```
interface IStorable
{
    void Read( );
    void Write(object obj);
    int Status { get; set; }
}
```

Notice that the IStorable method declarations for Read( ) and Write( ) do not include access modifiers (public, protected, internal, private). In fact, providing an access modifier generates a compile error. Interface methods are implicitly public because an interface is a contract meant to be used by other classes. In addition, you must declare these methods to be public, and not static, when you implement the interface.

In the interface declaration, the methods are otherwise defined just like methods in a class: you indicate the return type (void), followed by the identifier (Write), followed by the parameter list (object obj), and, of course, you end all statements with a semicolon. The methods in the interface declaration have no body, however.

An interface can also require that the implementing class provide a property (see Chapter 8 for a discussion of properties). Notice that the declaration of the Status property does not provide an implementation for get( ) and set( ), but simply designates that there *must be* a get( ) and a set( ):

```
int Status { get; set; }
```

You can't define member variables in an interface, but defining properties like this has the same practical effect.

Implementing the Interface on the Client

Once you've defined the IStorable interface, you can define classes that implement your interface. Keep in mind that you cannot create an instance of an interface; instead, you instantiate a class that implements the interface.

The class implementing the interface must fulfill the contract exactly and completely. Thus, your Document class must provide both a Read( ) and a Write( ) method and the Status property:

```
public class Document : IStorable
{
```

This statement defines Document as a class that defines IStorable. We also like to separate the implementation of an interface in a *region*—this is a Visual Studio convenience that allows you to collapse and expand the code within the region to make the code easier to read:

```
#region IStorable
  //...
#endregion
```

Within the region, you place the code that implements the two required methods and the required property. In this case, we're not really reading or writing anything. To keep things simple in the example, we're just announcing to the console that we've invoked the appropriate method; you'll have to use your imagination a bit:

```
public void Read( )
{
    Console.WriteLine( "Executing Document's Read
                        Method for IStorable" );
}

public void Write( object o )
{
    Console.WriteLine( "Executing Document's Write
                        Method for IStorable" );
}
```

Notice that the Write( ) method takes an instance of class object as a parameter, even though the method never uses it. Perhaps your specific implementation would do something with an object, but it doesn't have to. Exactly how your Document class fulfills the requirements of the interface is entirely up to you.

Although IStorable dictates that Document must have a Status property, it does not know or care whether Document stores the actual status as a member variable or looks it up in a database. Example 13-1 implements the Status property with an automatic property (introduced in Chapter 8). Another class that implements IStorable could provide the Status property in an entirely different manner (such as by looking it up in a database).

Implementing More Than One Interface

Classes can derive from only one class (and if it doesn't explicitly derive from a class, it implicitly derives from Object).

 Some languages, such as C++, support inheritance from multiple base classes. C# allows inheritance from only a single class, but interfaces don't have that limitation.

When you design your class, you can choose not to implement any interfaces, you can implement a single interface, or you can implement more than one. For example, in addition to IStorable, you might have a second interface, ICompressible, for files that can be compressed to save disk space. This new interface might have methods of Compress( ) and Decompress( ), for example. If your Document class can be stored and compressed, you might choose to have Document implement both the IStorable and ICompressible interfaces.

 Both IStorable and ICompressible are interfaces created for this book and are not part of the standard .NET Framework.

Example 13-2 shows the complete listing of the new ICompressible interface and demonstrates how you modify the Document class to implement the two interfaces.

Example 13-2. Implementing multiple interfaces isn't much more difficult than implementing a single one; you just have to implement the required methods for both interfaces

```
using System;
using System.Collections.Generic;
using System.Linq;
using System.Text;

namespace Example_13_2____Multiple_Interfaces
{
    interface IStorable
    {
        void Read( );
        void Write(object obj);
        int Status { get; set; }
    }

    // here's the new interface
    interface ICompressible
    {
        void Compress( );
        void Decompress( );
    }
```

```csharp
public class Document : IStorable, ICompressible
{
    public Document(string s)
    {
        Console.WriteLine("Creating document with: {0}", s);
    }

    #region IStorable

    public void Read()
    {
        Console.WriteLine("Executing Document's Read Method
                        for IStorable");
    }

    public void Write(object o)
    {
        Console.WriteLine("Executing Document's Write Method
                        for IStorable");
    }

    public int Status{ get; set;}

    #endregion     // IStorable

    #region ICompressible

    public void Compress()
    {
        Console.WriteLine("Executing Document's Compress Method
                        for ICompressible");
    }
    public void Decompress()
    {
        Console.WriteLine("Executing Document's Decompress Method
                        for ICompressible");
    }
    #endregion  // ICompressible

}

class Tester
{
    public void Run()
    {
        Document doc = new Document("Test Document");
        doc.Status = -1;
        doc.Read();          // invoke method from IStorable
        doc.Compress();      // invoke method from ICompressible
        Console.WriteLine("Document Status: {0}", doc.Status);
    }
```

```
        static void Main( )
        {
            Tester t = new Tester( );
            t.Run( );
        }
    }
}
```

The output looks like this:

```
Creating document with: Test Document
Executing Document's Read Method for IStorable
Executing Document's Compress Method for ICompressible
Document Status: -1
```

As Example 13-2 shows, you declare the fact that your Document class will implement two interfaces by adding the second interface to the declaration (in the base list), separating the two interfaces with commas:

```
public class Document : IStorable, ICompressible
```

Once you've done this, the Document class must also implement the methods specified by the ICompressible interface. ICompressible has only two methods, Compress( ) and Decompress( ), which are specified as:

```
interface ICompressible
{
    void Compress( );
    void Decompress( );
}
```

In this simplified example, Document implements these two methods as follows, printing notification messages to the console:

```
public void Compress( )
{
    Console.WriteLine("Executing Document's Compress
                    Method for ICompressible");
}
public void Decompress( )
{
    Console.WriteLine("Executing Document's Decompress
                    Method for ICompressible");
}
```

Once again, these methods don't really do anything other than output a message announcing their intentions; that's deliberate, to keep the example short.

As you can see, implementing multiple interfaces isn't hard at all; each interface mandates additional methods that your class has to provide. You could implement several interfaces in this way.

Casting to an Interface

You can access the members of an interface through an object of any class that implements the interface. For example, because Document implements IStorable, you can access the IStorable methods and property through any Document instance:

```
Document doc = new Document("Test Document");
doc.Status = -1;
doc.Read();
```

At times, though, you won't know that you have a Document object; you'll only know that you have objects that implement IStorable, for example, if you have an array of IStorable objects, as we mentioned earlier. You can create a reference of type IStorable, and assign that to each member in the array, accessing the IStorable methods and property. You cannot, however, access the Document-specific methods because all the compiler knows is that you have an IStorable, not a Document.

As we mentioned before, you cannot instantiate an interface directly; that is, you cannot write:

```
IStorable isDoc = new IStorable;
```

You can, however, create an instance of the implementing class and then assign that object to a reference to any of the interfaces it implements:

```
Document myDoc = new Document(...);
IStorable myStorable = myDoc;
```

You can read this line as "assign the IStorable-implementing object myDoc to the IStorable reference myStorable."

You are now free to use the IStorable reference to access the IStorable methods and properties of the document:

```
myStorable.Status = 0;
myStorable.Read();
```

Notice that the IStorable reference myStorable has access to the IStorable automatic property Status. However, myStorable would *not* have access to the Document's private member variables, if it had any. The IStorable reference knows only about the IStorable interface, not about the Document's internal members.

Thus far, you have assigned the Document object (myDoc) to an IStorable reference.

The is and as Operators

Sometimes, however, you may not know at compile time whether an object supports a particular interface. For instance, if you have an array of IStorable objects, you might not know whether any given object in the collection also implements ICompressible (some do, some do not). Let's set aside the question of whether this is a good design, and move on to how we solve the problem.

Anytime you see casting, you can question the design of the program. It is common for casting to be the result of poor or lazy design. That being said, sometimes casting is unavoidable, especially when dealing with collections that you did not create. This is one of those situations where experience over time will help you tell good designs from bad.

You could try casting each member blindly to ICompressible. If the object in question doesn't implement ICompressible, an error will be raised. You could then handle that error, using techniques we'll explain in Chapter 16. That's a sloppy and ineffective way to do it, though. The is and as operators provide a much better way.

The is operator lets you query whether an object implements an interface (or derives from a base class). The form of the is operator is:

```
if ( expression is type )
```

The is operator evaluates true if the *expression* (which must be a reference type, such as an instance of a class) can be safely cast to *type* without throwing an exception.

The as operator is similar to is, but it goes a step further. The as operator tries to cast the object to the type, and if an exception would be thrown, it instead returns null:

```
ICompressible myCompressible = myObject as ICompressible
if ( myCompressible != null )
```

The is operator is slightly less efficient than using as, so the as operator is slightly preferred over the is operator, except when you want to do the test but not actually do the cast (a rare situation).

Example 13-3 illustrates the use of both the is and the as operators by creating two classes. The Note class implements IStorable. The Document class derives from Note (and thus inherits the implementation of IStorable) and adds a property (ID) along with an implementation of ICompressible.

In this example, you'll create an array of Note objects (which could be either Notes or Documents) and then, if you want to access either ICompressible or the ID, you'll need to test the Note to see whether it is of the correct type. Both the is and the as operators are demonstrated. The entire program is documented fully immediately after the source code.

Example 13-3. The is and as operators allow you to determine whether an object can be cast to an interface

```
using System;
using System.Collections.Generic;
using System.Linq;
using System.Text;
```

Example 13-3. The is and as operators allow you to determine whether an object can be cast to an interface (continued)

```
namespace Example_13_3____is_and_as
{
    interface IStorable
    {
        void Read( );
        void Write(object obj);
        int Status { get; set; }
    }

    interface ICompressible
    {
        void Compress( );
        void Decompress( );
    }

    public class Note : IStorable
    {
        private string myString;

        public Note(string theString)
        {
            myString = theString;
        }

        public override string ToString( )
        {
            return myString;
        }

        #region IStorable

        public void Read( )
        {
            Console.WriteLine("Executing Note's Read Method
                            for IStorable");
        }

        public void Write(object o)
        {
            Console.WriteLine("Executing Note's Write Method
                            for IStorable");
        }

        public int Status { get; set; }

        #endregion // IStorable

    }

    public class Document : Note, ICompressible
    {
```

```
        private int documentID;
        public int ID
        {
            get { return this.documentID; }
        }

        public Document(string docString, int documentID)
                        : base(docString)
        {
            this.documentID = documentID;
        }

        #region ICompressible

        public void Compress()
        {
            Console.WriteLine("Executing Document's Compress Method
                            for ICompressible");
        }
        public void Decompress()
        {
            Console.WriteLine("Executing Document's Decompress Method
                            for ICompressible");
        }
        #endregion   // ICompressible

    }  // end Document class

    class Tester
    {
        public void Run()
        {
            string testString = "String ";
            Note[] myNoteArray = new Note[3];

            for (int i = 0; i < 3; i++)
            {
                string docText = testString + i.ToString();
                if (i % 2 == 0)
                {
                    Document myDocument = new Document(
                                docText, (i + 5) * 10);
                    myNoteArray[i] = myDocument;
                }
                else
                {
                    Note myNote = new Note(docText);
                    myNoteArray[i] = myNote;
                }
            }
```

Example 13-3. The is and as operators allow you to determine whether an object can be cast to an interface (continued)

```
foreach (Note theNote in myNoteArray)
{
    Console.WriteLine("\nTesting {0} with IS", theNote);

    theNote.Read( );     // all notes can do this
    if (theNote is ICompressible)
    {
        ICompressible myCompressible =
                    theNote as ICompressible;
        myCompressible.Compress( );
    }
    else
    {
        Console.WriteLine("This storable object is
                            not compressible.");
    }

    if (theNote is Document)
    {
        Document myDoc = theNote as Document;

        // clean cast
        myDoc = theNote as Document;
        Console.WriteLine("my documentID is {0}", myDoc.ID);
    }
}

foreach (Note theNote in myNoteArray)
{
    Console.WriteLine("\nTesting {0} with AS", theNote);
    ICompressible myCompressible = theNote as ICompressible;
    if (myCompressible != null)
    {
        myCompressible.Compress( );
    }
    else
    {
        Console.WriteLine("This storable object is
                            not compressible.");
    }     // end else

    Document theDoc = theNote as Document;
    if (theDoc != null)
    {
        Console.WriteLine("My documentID is {0}",
            ((Document)theNote).ID);
    }
    else
    {
        Console.WriteLine("Not a document.");
    }
```

Example 13-3. The is and as operators allow you to determine whether an object can be cast to an interface (continued)

```
            }
        }

        static void Main( )
        {
            Tester t = new Tester( );
            t.Run( );
        }
    }           // end class Tester
}
```

The output looks like this:

```
Testing String 0 with IS
Executing Note's Read Method for IStorable
Executing Document's Compress Method for ICompressible
my documentID is 50

Testing String 1 with IS
Executing Note's Read Method for IStorable
This storable object is not compressible.

Testing String 2 with IS
Executing Note's Read Method for IStorable
Executing Document's Compress Method for ICompressible
my documentID is 70

Testing String 0 with AS
Executing Document's Compress Method for ICompressible
My documentID is 50

Testing String 1 with AS
This storable object is not compressible.
Not a document.

Testing String 2 with AS
Executing Document's Compress Method for ICompressible
My documentID is 70
```

The best way to understand this program is to take it apart piece by piece.

Within the namespace, you declare two interfaces, IStorable and ICompressible, and then two classes: Note, which implements IStorable; and Document, which derives from Note (and thus inherits the implementation of IStorable) and which also implements ICompressible. Finally, you add the class Tester to test the program.

Within the Run( ) method of the Tester class, you create an array of Note objects, and you add to that array two Document instances and one Note instance. You use the counter i of the for loop as a control—if i is even, you create a Document object; if it's odd, you create a Note.

You then iterate through the array, extracting each Note in turn, and use the is operator to test first whether the Note can safely be assigned to an ICompressible reference:

```
if (theNote is ICompressible)
{
    ICompressible myCompressible = theNote as ICompressible;
    myCompressible.Compress( );
}
else
{
    Console.WriteLine("This storable object is not compressible.");
}
```

If it can, you cast theNote to ICompressible, and call the Compress( ) method.

Then you check whether the Note can safely be cast to a Document:

```
if (theNote is Document)
{
    Document myDoc = theNote as Document;

    // clean cast
    myDoc = theNote as Document;
    Console.WriteLine("my documentID is {0}", myDoc.ID);
}
```

In the case shown, these tests amount to the same thing, but you can imagine that you could have a collection with many types derived from Note, some of which implement ICompressible and some of which do not.

You can use the interim variable as we've done here:

```
myDoc = theNote as Document;
Console.WriteLine( "my documentID is {0}", myDoc.ID );
```

Or, you can cast and access the property all in one ugly but effective line, as you do in the second loop:

```
Console.WriteLine( "My documentID is {0}",
    ( ( Document ) theNote ).ID );
```

The extra parentheses are required to ensure that the cast is done before the attempt at accessing the property.

The second foreach loop uses the as operator to accomplish the same work, and the results are identical. (The second foreach loop actually generates less intermediate language code, and thus is slightly more efficient.)

Extending Interfaces

You can extend an existing interface to add new methods or members. For example, you might extend ICompressible with a new interface, ILoggedCompressible, which extends the original interface with methods to keep track of the bytes saved.

One such method might be called LogSavedBytes( ). The following code creates a new interface named ILoggedCompressible that is identical to ICompressible except that it adds the method LogSavedBytes:

```
interface ILoggedCompressible : ICompressible
{
    void LogSavedBytes( );
}
```

Classes are now free to implement either ICompressible or ILoggedCompressible, depending on whether they need the additional functionality. If a class does implement ILoggedCompressible, it must implement all the methods of both ILoggedCompressible and ICompressible. Objects of that type can be cast either to ILoggedCompressible or to ICompressible.

Example 13-4 extends ICompressible to create ILoggedCompressible, and then casts the Document first to be of type IStorable and then to be of type ILoggedCompressible. Finally, the example casts the Document object to ICompressible. This last cast is safe because any object that implements ILoggedCompressible must also have implemented ICompressible (the former is a superset of the latter). This is the same logic that says you can cast any object of a derived type to an object of a base type (that is, if Student derives from Human, then all Students are Human, even though not all Humans are Students).

Example 13-4. You can extend an interface to create a new interface with additional methods or members

```
using System;
using System.Collections.Generic;
using System.Linq;
using System.Text;

namespace Example_13_4____Extending_Interfaces
{
    interface ICompressible
    {
        void Compress( );
        void Decompress( );
    }

    // extend ICompressible to log the bytes saved
    interface ILoggedCompressible : ICompressible
    {
        void LogSavedBytes( );
    }

    public class Document : ILoggedCompressible
    {

        public Document(string s)
        {
```

```
                Console.WriteLine("Creating document with: {0}", s);
        }

        #region

        public void Compress()
        {
            Console.WriteLine("Executing Compress");
        }

        public void Decompress()
        {
            Console.WriteLine("Executing Decompress");
        }

        public void LogSavedBytes()
        {
            Console.WriteLine("Executing LogSavedBytes");
        }

        #endregion //ILoggedCompressible

    }

    class Tester
    {
        public void Run()
        {
            Document doc = new Document("Test Document");

            ILoggedCompressible myLoggedCompressible =
                            doc as ILoggedCompressible;
            if (myLoggedCompressible != null)
            {
                Console.Write("\nCalling both ICompressible and ");
                Console.WriteLine("ILoggedCompressible methods...");
                myLoggedCompressible.Compress();
                myLoggedCompressible.LogSavedBytes();
            }
            else
            {
                Console.WriteLine("Something went wrong!
                            Not ILoggedCompressible");
            }
        }

        static void Main()
        {
            Tester t = new Tester();
            t.Run();
        }
```

Example 13-4. You can extend an interface to create a new interface with additional methods or members (continued)

```
    }
}
```

The output looks like this:

```
Creating document with: Test Document

Calling both ICompressible and ILoggedCompressible methods...
Executing Compress
Executing LogSavedBytes
```

Example 13-4 starts by creating the `ILoggedCompressible` interface, which extends the `ICompressible` interface:

```
// extend ICompressible to log the bytes saved
interface ILoggedCompressible : ICompressible
{
    void LogSavedBytes( );
}
```

Notice that the syntax for extending an interface is the same as that for deriving from a class. This extended interface defines only one new method (`LogSavedBytes( )`), but any class implementing this interface must also implement the base interface (`ICompressible`) and all its members. (In this sense, it is reasonable to say that an `ILoggedCompressible` object *is an* `ICompressible` object.)

Combining Interfaces

You can also create new interfaces by combining existing interfaces and optionally adding new methods or properties. For example, you might decide to combine the definitions of `IStorable` and `ICompressible` into a new interface called `IStorableCompressible`. This interface would combine the methods of each of the other two interfaces, but would also add a new method, `LogOriginalSize( )`, to store the original size of the precompressed item:

```
interface IStorableCompressible : IStorable, ILoggedCompressible
{
    void LogOriginalSize( );
}
```

Having created this interface, you can now modify `Document` to implement `IStorableCompressible`:

```
public class Document : IStorableCompressible
```

You now can cast the `Document` object to any of the four interfaces you've created so far:

```
IStorable storableDoc = doc as IStorable;
ILoggedCompressible logCompressDoc = doc as ILoggedCompressible;
```

```
ICompressible compressDoc = doc as ICompressible;
IStorableCompressible storCompressDoc = doc as IStorableCompressible;
```

When you cast to the new combined interface, you can invoke any of the methods of any of the interfaces it extends or combines. The following code invokes four methods on iscDoc (the IStorableCompressible object). Only one of these methods is defined in IStorableCompressible, but all four are methods defined by interfaces that IStorableCompressible extends or combines.

```
if (iscDoc != null)
{
    storCompressDoc.Read();  // Read() from IStorable
    storCompressDoc.Compress();  // Compress() from ICompressible
    storCompressDoc.LogSavedBytes();      // LogSavedBytes() from
                                          // ILoggedCompressible
    storCompressDoc.LogOriginalSize(); // LogOriginalSize() from
                                          // IStorableCompressible
}
```

Overriding Interface Methods

When you create an implementing class, you're free to mark any or all of the methods from the interface as virtual. Derived classes can then override or provide new implementations, just as they might with any other virtual instance method.

For example, a Document class might implement the IStorable interface and mark its Read() and Write() methods as virtual. In an earlier example, we created a base class Note and a derived class Document. While the Note class implements Read() and Write() to save to a file, the Document class might implement Read() and Write() to read from and write to a database.

Example 13-5 uses the Note and Document classes, but we've taken out the extra complexity we added in the last few examples, to focus on overriding an interface implementation. Note implements the IStorable-required Read() method as a virtual method, and Document overrides that implementation.

 Notice that Note does not mark Write() as virtual. You'll see the implications of this decision in the analysis that follows Example 13-5.

The complete listing is shown in Example 13-5.

Example 13-5. You can override an interface implementation in the same way that you would override any virtual method of a parent class

```
using System;
using System.Collections.Generic;
using System.Linq;
using System.Text;
```

Example 13-5. You can override an interface implementation in the same way that you would override any virtual method of a parent class (continued)

```csharp
namespace Example_13_5____Overriding_Interface_Implementation
{
    interface IStorable
    {
        void Read( );
        void Write( );
    }

    public class Note : IStorable
    {
        public Note(string s)
        {
            Console.WriteLine("Creating Note with: {0}", s);
        }

        // Note's version of Read( ) is virtual.
        public virtual void Read( )
        {
            Console.WriteLine("Note Read Method for IStorable");
        }

        // Note's version of Write( ) is NOT virtual!
        public void Write( )
        {
            Console.WriteLine("Note Write Method for IStorable");
        }
    }

    public class Document : Note
    {
        public Document(string s) : base(s)
        {
            Console.WriteLine("Creating Document with: {0}", s);
        }

        // override the Read method
        public override void Read( )
        {
            Console.WriteLine("Overriding the Read method
                        for Document!");
        }

        // implement my own Write method
        public new void Write( )
        {
            Console.WriteLine("Implementing a new Write method
                        for Document!");
        }
    }

    class Tester
```

Example 13-5. You can override an interface implementation in the same way that you would override any virtual method of a parent class (continued)

```csharp
    {
        public void Run( )
        {
            Note theNote = new Document("Test Document");

            theNote.Read( );
            theNote.Write( );

            Console.WriteLine("\n");

            IStorable isStorable = theNote as IStorable;
            if (isStorable != null)
            {
                isStorable.Read( );
                isStorable.Write( );
            }
            Console.WriteLine("\n");

            // This time create a reference to the derived type
            Document theDoc = new Document("Second Test");

            theDoc.Read( );
            theDoc.Write( );
            Console.WriteLine("\n");

            IStorable isStorable2 = theDoc as IStorable;
            if (isStorable != null)
            {
                isStorable2.Read( );
                isStorable2.Write( );
            }
        }

        static void Main( )
        {
            Tester t = new Tester( );
            t.Run( );
        }
    }
}
```

The output looks like this:

```
Creating Note with: Test Document
Creating Document with: Test Document
Overriding the Read method for Document!
Note Write Method for IStorable

Overriding the Read method for Document!
Note Write Method for IStorable
```

```
Creating Note with: Second Test
Creating Document with: Second Test
Overriding the Read method for Document!
Implementing a new Write method for Document!

Overriding the Read method for Document!
Note Write Method for IStorable
```

In Example 13-5, the IStorable interface is simplified for clarity's sake:

```
interface IStorable
{
    void Read( );
    void Write( );
}
```

The Note class implements the IStorable interface:

```
public class Note : IStorable
```

The designer of Note has opted to make the Read(...) method virtual but not to make the Write(...) method virtual:

```
public virtual void Read( )
public void Write( )
```

 In a real-world application, you would almost certainly mark both methods as virtual, but we've differentiated them to demonstrate that the developer is free to pick and choose which methods are made virtual.

The new class, Document, derives from Note:

```
public class Document : Note
```

It is not necessary for Document to override Read( ), but it is free to do so and has done so here:

```
public override void Read( )
```

To illustrate the implications of marking an implementing method as virtual, the Run( ) method calls the Read( ) and Write( ) methods in four ways:

- Through the Note class reference to a Document object
- Through an interface reference created from the Note class reference to the Document object
- Through a Document object
- Through an interface reference created from the Document object

Virtual implementations of interface methods are polymorphic, just like the virtual methods of classes.

When you call the nonpolymorphic Write( ) method on the IStorable interface cast from the derived Document, you actually get the Note's Write method, because Write( ) is implemented in the base class and is nonvirtual.

To see polymorphism at work with interfaces, you'll create a reference to the Note class and initialize it with a new instance of the derived Document class:

```
Note theDocument = new Document("Test Document");
```

Invoke the Read and Write methods:

```
theDocument.Read();
theDocument.Write();
```

The output reveals that the (virtual) Read( ) method is called polymorphically—that is, the Document class overrides the Note class's Read( ), and the nonvirtual Write( ) method of the Note class is invoked because the Write( ) method was not made virtual.

```
Overriding the Read method for Document!
Note Write Method for IStorable
```

The overridden method of Read( ) is called because you've created a new Document object:

```
Note theDocument = new Document("Test Document");
```

The nonvirtual Write method of Note is called because you've assigned theDocument to a reference to a Note:

```
Note theDocument = new Document("Test Document");
```

To illustrate calling the methods through an interface that is created from the Note class reference to the Document object, create an interface reference named isDocument. Use the as operator to cast the Note (theDocument) to the IStorable reference:

```
IStorable isDocument = theDocument as IStorable;
```

Then invoke the Read( ) and Write( ) methods for theDocument through that interface:

```
if (isDocument != null)
{
    isDocument.Read();
    isDocument.Write();
}
```

The output is the same: once again, the virtual Read( ) method is polymorphic, and the nonvirtual Write( ) method is not:

```
Overriding the Read method for Document
Note Write Method for IStorable
```

Next, create a second Document object, this time assigning its address to a reference to a Document, rather than a reference to a Note. This will be used to illustrate the final cases (a call through a Document object and a call through an interface created from the Document object):

```
Document theDoc = new Document("Second Test");
```

Call the methods on the Document object:

```
theDoc.Read( );
theDoc.Write( );
```

Again, the virtual Read( ) method is polymorphic and the nonvirtual Write( ) method is not, but this time you get the Write( ) method for Document because you are calling the method on a Document object:

```
Overriding the Read method for Document!
Implementing a new Write method for Document!
```

Finally, cast the Document object to an IStorable reference and call Read( ) and Write( ):

```
IStorable isDocument2 = theDoc as IStorable;
if (isDocument != null)
{
    isDocument2.Read( );
    isDocument2.Write( );
}
```

The Read( ) method is called polymorphically, but the Write( ) method for Note is called because Note implements IStorable, and Write( ) is not polymorphic:

```
Overriding the Read method for Document!
Note Write Method for IStorable
```

Explicit Interface Implementation

In the implementation shown so far, the class that implements the interface (Document) creates a member method with the same signature and return type as the method detailed in the interface. It is not necessary to explicitly state that Document is implementing IStorable, for example; the compiler understands this implicitly.

What happens, however, if the class implements two interfaces, each of which has a method with the same signature? This might happen if the class implements interfaces defined by two different organizations or even two different programmers. The next example creates two interfaces: IStorable and ITalk. ITalk implements a Read( ) method that reads a book aloud. Unfortunately, this conflicts with the Read( ) method in IStorable.

Because both IStorable and ITalk have a Read( ) method, the implementing Document class must use *explicit implementation* for at least one of the methods. With explicit implementation, the implementing class (Document) explicitly identifies the interface for the method:

```
void ITalk.Read( )
```

Marking the Read( ) method as a member of the ITalk interface resolves the conflict between the identical Read( ) methods. There are some additional aspects you should keep in mind.

First, the explicit implementation method cannot have an access modifier:

```
void ITalk.Read( )
```

This method is implicitly public. In fact, a method declared through explicit implementation cannot be declared with the abstract, virtual, override, or new keyword, either.

Most importantly, you cannot access the explicitly implemented method through the object itself. When you write:

```
theDoc.Read( );
```

the compiler assumes you mean the implicitly implemented interface for IStorable. The only way to access an explicitly implemented interface is through a cast to the interface:

```
ITalk itDoc = theDoc as ITalk;
if (itDoc != null)
{
  itDoc.Read( );
}
```

Explicit implementation is demonstrated in Example 13-6. Note that there is no need to use explicit implementation with the other method of ITalk:

```
public void Talk( )
```

Because there is no conflict, this can be declared as usual.

Example 13-6. Explicit implementation allows you to avoid conflicts when two interfaces have methods with the same name

```
using System;
using System.Collections.Generic;
using System.Linq;
using System.Text;

namespace Example_13_6_____Explicit_Interfaces
{
    interface IStorable
    {
        void Read( );
        void Write( );
    }

    interface ITalk
    {
        void Talk( );
        void Read( );
    }

    // Modify Document to also implement ITalk
    public class Document : IStorable, ITalk
    {
```

```
        // the document constructor
        public Document(string s)
        {
            Console.WriteLine("Creating document with: {0}", s);
        }

        // Implicit implementation
        public virtual void Read( )
        {
            Console.WriteLine("Document Read Method for IStorable");
        }

        public void Write( )
        {
            Console.WriteLine("Document Write Method for IStorable");
        }

        // Explicit implementation
        void ITalk.Read( )
        {
            Console.WriteLine("Implementing ITalk.Read");
        }

        public void Talk( )
        {
            Console.WriteLine("Implementing ITalk.Talk");
        }
    }

    class Tester
    {
        public void Run( )
        {
            // Create a Document object
            Document theDoc = new Document("Test Document");
            IStorable isDoc = theDoc as IStorable;
            if (isDoc != null)
            {
                isDoc.Read( );
            }

            // Cast to an ITalk interface
            ITalk itDoc = theDoc as ITalk;
            if (itDoc != null)
            {
                itDoc.Read( );
            }

            theDoc.Read( );
            theDoc.Talk( );
        }
```

Example 13-6. Explicit implementation allows you to avoid conflicts when two interfaces have methods with the same name (continued)

```
    static void Main( )
    {
        Tester t = new Tester( );
        t.Run( );
    }
}
}
```

The output looks like this:

```
Creating document with: Test Document
Document Read Method for IStorable
Implementing ITalk.Read
Document Read Method for IStorable
Implementing ITalk.Talk
```

The first thing the program does is create an IStorable reference to a Document. Then it invokes the Read( ) method of IStorable:

```
IStorable isDoc = theDoc as IStorable;
if (isDoc != null)
{
    isDoc.Read( );
}
```

Then you cast the document to an ITalk interface, and invoke the Read( ) method of ITalk:

```
ITalk itDoc = theDoc as ITalk;
if (itDoc != null)
{
    itDoc.Read( );
}
```

The output shows that both of these calls work as expected.

The next thing you do is to call the Read( ) and Talk( ) methods directly on the Document:

```
theDoc.Read( );
theDoc.Talk( );
```

As you can see in the output, the Read( ) method defaults to the version from IStorable, because that version is implicit. The Talk( ) method is the version from ITalk, because that's the only interface here with a Talk( ) method.

Summary

• An interface is a contract through which a class guarantees that it will implement certain methods, provide certain properties and indexers, and support certain events, all of which are specified in the interface definition.

- You cannot create an instance of an interface. To access the interface methods, you need to create an instance of a class that implements that interface.
- You declare an interface much like you would a class, but using the keyword `interface`. You can apply access modifiers to the interface, as you would with a class.
- In the interface definition, the method declarations cannot have access modifiers.
- To implement an interface on a class, you use the colon operator, followed by the name of the interface, similar to the syntax for inheritance.
- Classes can derive from no more than one class, but can implement any number of interfaces. If a class has a base class and one or more interfaces, the base class must be listed first (after the colon). Separate the base class and interface names by commas.
- When you define a class that implements an interface, you must then implement all the required members of that interface.
- In situations where you don't know what type of object you have, and you know only that the object implements a specific interface, you can create a reference to the interface and assign the object to that reference, providing you with access to the implemented interface methods.
- You can use the `is` operator to determine whether an object derives from a base class or implements an interface. The `is` operator returns a Boolean value indicating whether the cast is valid, but it does not perform the cast.
- The as operator attempts to cast a reference to a base type or an interface, and returns null if the cast is not valid.
- You can extend an interface to add new methods or members. In the new interface definition, use the colon operator followed by the name of the original interface. This is very similar to derivation in classes.
- The extended interface subsumes the original interface, so any class that implements the extended interface must also implement the original interface as well.
- A class that implements an interface may mark any of the interface methods as `virtual`. These methods may then be overridden by derived classes.
- When a class implements two or more interfaces with methods that have the same name, you resolve the conflict by prefixing the method name with the name of the interface and the dot operator (for example, `IStorable.Write()`). If you do this, you cannot specify an access modifier, as the method is implicitly public.

You saw in this chapter how interfaces encourage polymorphism, allowing you to dictate the methods your classes implement, while still providing flexibility in your designs. They're admittedly somewhat tricky to understand at first, but as you get more practice with them, you'll get more comfortable with them. In this chapter, you used arrays to demonstrate the polymorphic features of interfaces, and that's a pretty common use. However, the array isn't the only collection class in C#. In fact, although arrays are simplest to understand, which is why we introduced them first, in many ways they're the most limited of the collection classes. In the next chapter, you'll learn about the other collection classes, and how you can use them with generics to get even more flexibility.

Test Your Knowledge: Quiz

Question 13-1. What is the difference between an interface and a class that implements an interface?

Question 13-2. What is the difference between an interface and an abstract base class?

Question 13-3. How do you create an instance of an interface?

Question 13-4. How do you indicate that class `MyClass` derives from class `MyBase` and implements the interfaces `ISuppose` and `IDo`?

Question 13-5. What two operators can tell you whether an object's class implements an interface?

Question 13-6. What is the difference between the `is` and `as` operators?

Question 13-7. What does it mean to "extend" an interface?

Question 13-8. What is the syntax for extending an interface?

Question 13-9. What does it mean to override an interface implementation?

Question 13-10. What is explicit interface implementation and why would you use it?

Test Your Knowledge: Exercises

Exercise 13-1. Define an interface `IConvertible` that indicates that the class can convert a block of code to C# or VB. The interface should have two methods: `ConvertToCSharp` and `ConvertToVB`. Each method should take a string and return a string.

Exercise 13-2. Implement that interface and test it by creating a class `ProgramHelper` that implements `IConvertible`. You don't have to write methods to convert the string; just use simple string messages to simulate the conversion. Test your new class with a string of fake code to make sure it works.

Exercise 13-3. Extend the `IConvertible` interface by creating a new interface, `ICodeChecker`. The new interface should implement one new method, `CodeCheckSyntax`, which takes two strings: the string to check and the language to use. The method should return a `bool`. Revise the `ProgramHelper` class from Exercise 13-2 to use the new interface.

Exercise 13-4. Demonstrate the use of `is` and `as`. Create a new class, `ProgramConverter`, which implements `IConvertible`. `ProgramConverter` should implement the `ConvertToCSharp()` and `ConvertToVB()` methods. Revise `ProgramHelper` so that it derives from `ProgramConverter` and implements `ICodeChecker`. Test your class by creating an array of `ProgramConverter` objects, some of which are `ProgramConverters` and some of which are `ProgramHelpers`. Then call the conversion methods and the code check methods on each item in the array to test which ones implement `ICodeChecker` and which ones do not.

CHAPTER 14

Generics and Collections

You saw in Chapter 10 that arrays are useful for when you have a group of objects of the same type, and you need to treat them as a group—as a *collection*. Arrays are the simplest collection in C#, and they're the one that you learn when you're starting out, to get you accustomed to thinking about collections. However, arrays are probably the least flexible of the standard collections used in C#, because you have to define the size of an array when you create it. C# actually has a bunch of collection classes, but the five most commonly used are:

- Array
- List
- Stack
- Queue
- Dictionary

This chapter will introduce each of the latter four collections, and will show how the C# feature called *generics* is used to make these collections type-safe—and why type safety is important.

You can also create classes that *act like* collections, and you can provide support for your collection classes so that they support some or all of the behavior expected of collections, such as the ability to be used in a foreach loop or to access their members using an indexer:

```
Employee joe = MyCompany[EmployeeID]
```

Generics

Before generics, all the collection classes (then just ArrayList, Stack, and Queue) were defined to hold objects of type Object (the root class). Thus, you could add integers and strings to the same collection, and when you took items out of the collection, you had to cast them to their "real" type. This was ugly, and it was error-prone (the compiler could not tell whether you had a collection of integers and added a string).

With generics, the designer of the class (the person who creates the Stack class) can say, "This class will hold only one type, and that type will be defined by the developer who makes an instance of this class."

The user of the generic Stack class (that's you) defines an instance of the Stack and the type it will hold. The compiler can now enforce that only objects of the designated type are stored in the collection—that's type safety. That's important because, as you've seen, you'll often want to use a collection polymorphically, and if there's a string lurking in what you think is a collection of ints, you may be surprised when you try to divide each of them by 2.

The designer adds a type placeholder (technically called a *type parameter*), which is usually represented by the letter *T* in angle brackets:

```
class Stack<T>
```

The user of the Stack class puts in the actual type when instantiating the class, like this:

```
Stack<Employee> = new Stack<Employee>
```

 You can create your own generic classes, but that's an advanced topic we won't get into here.

Collection Interfaces

The .NET Framework provides a number of interfaces, such as IEnumerable and ICollection, which the designer of a collection must implement to provide full collection semantics. For example, ICollection allows your collection to be enumerated in a foreach loop. You'll see how these work in a little bit, when we explain the C# collection types. First, though, we're going to show you how to make your own collections, so you can understand how they work.

Creating Your Own Collections

The goal in creating your own collections is to make them as similar to the standard .NET collections as possible. This reduces confusion, and makes for easier-to-use classes and easier-to-maintain code.

Creating Indexers

One feature you should provide is to allow users of your collection to add to or extract from the collection with an indexer, just as you would do with an array.

For example, suppose you create a ListBox control named myListBox that contains a list of strings stored in a one-dimensional array, a private member variable named myStrings. A ListBox control contains member properties and methods in addition to its array of strings, so the ListBox itself is not an array. However, it would be convenient to be able to access the ListBox array with an index, just as though the ListBox itself were an array.[*] For example, such a property would let you do things like this:

```
string theFirstString = myListBox[0];
string theLastString = myListBox[Length-1];
```

An *indexer* is a C# construct that allows you to treat a class as though it were an array. In the preceding example, you are treating the ListBox as though it were an array of strings, even though it is more than that. An indexer is a special kind of property, but like all properties, it includes get and set accessors to specify its behavior.

You declare an indexer property within a class using the following syntax:

```
type  this [type argument]{get; set;}
```

For example:

```
public string this[int index]
{
    get {...};
    set {...};
}
```

The return type determines the type of object that will be returned by the indexer, and the type argument specifies what kind of argument will be used to index into the collection that contains the target objects. Although it is common to use integers as index values, you can index a collection on other types as well, including strings. You can even provide an indexer with multiple parameters to create a multidimensional array.

The this keyword is a reference to the object in which the indexer appears. As with a normal property, you also must define get and set accessors, which determine how the requested object is retrieved from or assigned to its collection.

Example 14-1 declares a ListBox control (ListBoxTest) that contains a simple array (myStrings) and a simple indexer for accessing its contents.

Example 14-1. Creating a simple indexer is very similar to creating a property

```
using System;
using System.Collections.Generic;
using System.Linq;
using System.Text;

namespace Example_14_1____Simple_Indexer
{
    // a simplified ListBox control
```

---

[*] The actual ListBox control provided by both Windows Forms and ASP.NET has a collection called Items that is a collection, and it is the Items collection that implements the indexer.

```
public class ListBoxTest
{
    private string[] strings;
    private int ctr = 0;

    // initialize the ListBox with strings
    public ListBoxTest( params string[] initialStrings )
    {
        // allocate space for the strings
        strings = new String[256];

        // copy the strings passed in to the constructor
        foreach ( string s in initialStrings )
        {
            strings[ctr++] = s;
        }
    }

    // add a single string to the end of the ListBox
    public void Add( string theString )
    {
        if ( ctr >= strings.Length )
        {
            // handle bad index
        }
        else
            strings[ctr++] = theString;
    }

    // allow array-like access

    public string this[int index]
    {
        get
        {
            if ( index < 0 || index >= strings.Length )
            {
                // handle bad index
            }
            return strings[index];
        }
        set
        {
            // add new items only through the Add method
            if ( index >= ctr )
            {
                // handle error
            }
            else
            {
                strings[index] = value;
            }
```

```
        }
    }

    // publish how many strings you hold
    public int GetNumEntries()
    {
        return ctr;
    }
}

public class Tester
{
    static void Main()
    {
        // create a new ListBox and initialize
        ListBoxTest lbt =
            new ListBoxTest( "Hello", "World" );

        // add a few strings
        lbt.Add( "Proust" );
        lbt.Add( "Faulkner" );
        lbt.Add( "Mann" );
        lbt.Add( "Hugo" );

        // test the access
        string subst = "Universe";
        lbt[1] = subst;

        // access all the strings
        for ( int i = 0; i < lbt.GetNumEntries(); i++ )
        {
            Console.WriteLine( "lbt[{0}]: {1}", i, lbt[i] );
        }
    }
}
```

The output looks like this:

```
lbt[0]: Hello
lbt[1]: Universe
lbt[2]: Proust
lbt[3]: Faulkner
lbt[4]: Mann
lbt[5]: Hugo
```

To keep Example 14-1 simple, we've stripped the ListBox control down to the few features we care about. The listing ignores everything else a ListBox can do, and focuses only on the list of strings the ListBox maintains, and methods for manipulating them. In a real application, of course, these are a small fraction of the total methods of a ListBox, whose principal job is to display the strings and enable user choice.

The first things to notice in this example are the two private members:

```
private string[] strings;
private int ctr = 0;
```

The ListBox maintains a simple array of strings, cleverly named strings. The member variable ctr will keep track of how many strings have been added to this array. Initialize the array in the constructor with the statement:

```
strings = new string[256];
```

The Add( ) method of ListBoxTest does nothing more than append a new string to its internal array (strings), though a more complex object might write the strings to a database or other more complex data structure. The Add( ) method also increments the counter, so the class has a reliable count of how many strings it holds.

The key item in ListBoxTest is the indexer. An indexer uses the this keyword:

```
public string this[int index]
```

The syntax of the indexer is very similar to that for properties. There is either a get accessor, a set accessor, or both. In the case shown, the get accessor endeavors to implement rudimentary bounds checking, and assuming the index requested is acceptable, it returns the value requested:

```
get
{
    if (index < 0 || index >= strings.Length)
    {
        // handle bad index
    }
    return strings[index];
}
```

How you handle a bad index is up to you. For the purposes of this example, we'll assume there aren't any. However, you'll see how to deal with these sorts of errors in Chapter 16.

The set accessor checks to make sure that the index you are setting already has a value in the ListBox. If not, it treats the set as an error. The way this class is set up, you can add new elements only with the Add( ) method, so it's illegal to try to add one with set. The set accessor takes advantage of the implicit parameter value that represents whatever is assigned using the index operator:

```
set
{
    if (index >= ctr )
    {
        // handle error
    }
    else
    {
        strings[index] = value;
    }
}
```

Thus, if you write:

```
lbt[5] = "Hello World"
```

the compiler will call the indexer set accessor on your object and pass in the string Hello World as an implicit parameter named value.

Indexers and Assignment

In Example 14-1, you cannot assign to an index that does not have a value. Thus, if you write:

```
lbt[10] = "wow!";
```

you will trigger the error handler in the set accessor, which will note that the index you've passed in (10) is larger than the counter (6).

This code is kept simple, and so we don't handle any errors, as we mentioned. There are any number of other checks you'd want to make on the value passed in (for example, checking that you were not passed a negative index and that it does not exceed the size of the underlying strings[] array).

In Main( ), you create an instance of the ListBoxTest class named lbt and pass in two strings as parameters:

```
ListBoxTest lbt = new ListBoxTest("Hello", "World");
```

Then, call Add( ) to add four more strings:

```
// add a few strings
lbt.Add( "Proust" );
lbt.Add( "Faulkner" );
lbt.Add( "Mann" );
lbt.Add( "Hugo" );
```

Before examining the values, you modify the second value (at index 1):

```
string subst = "Universe";
lbt[1] = subst;
```

Finally, you display each value with a loop:

```
for (int i = 0;i<lbt.GetNumEntries( );i++)
{
    Console.WriteLine("lbt[{0}]: {1}",i,lbt[i]);
}
```

Indexing on Other Values

C# does not require that you always use an integer value as the index to a collection. Using integers is simply the most common method, because that makes it easier to iterate over the collection with a for loop. When you create a custom collection class and create your indexer, you are free to create indexers that index on strings and other types. In fact, you can overload the index value so that a given collection can be indexed, for example, by an integer value and also by a string value, depending on the needs of the client.

Example 14-2 illustrates a string index. The indexer calls FindString( ), which is a helper method that returns a record based on the value of the string provided. Notice that the overloaded indexer and the indexer from Example 14-1 are able to coexist.

Example 14-2. Overloading an index allows you the flexibility of indexing with an integer, or some other type

```
using System;
using System.Collections.Generic;
using System.Linq;
using System.Text;

namespace Example_14_2____Overloaded_Indexer
{
    // a simplified ListBox control
    public class ListBoxTest
    {
        private string[] strings;
        private int ctr = 0;

        // initialize the ListBox with strings
        public ListBoxTest(params string[] initialStrings)
        {
            // allocate space for the strings
            strings = new String[256];

            // copy the strings passed in to the constructor
            foreach (string s in initialStrings)
            {
                strings[ctr++] = s;
            }
        }

        // add a single string to the end of the ListBox
        public void Add(string theString)
        {
            if (ctr >= strings.Length)
            {
                // handle bad index
            }
            else
            {
                strings[ctr++] = theString;
            }
        }


        // allow array-like access
        public string this[int index]
        {
```

Example 14-2. Overloading an index allows you the flexibility of indexing with an integer, or some other type (continued)

```csharp
        get
        {
            if (index < 0 || index >= strings.Length)
            {
                // handle bad index
            }
            return strings[index];
        }
        set
        {
            // add only through the add method
            if (index >= ctr)
            {
                // handle error
            }
            else
            {
                strings[index] = value;
            }
        }
    }

    private int FindString(string searchString)
    {
        for (int i = 0; i < strings.Length; i++)
        {
            if (strings[i].StartsWith(searchString))
            {
                return i;
            }
        }
        return -1;
    }

    // index on string
    public string this[string index]
    {
        get
        {
            if (index.Length == 0)
            {
                // handle bad index
            }
            return this[FindString(index)];
        }
        set
        {
            // no need to check the index here because
            // find string will handle a bad index value
            strings[FindString(index)] = value;
        }
    }
```

Example 14-2. Overloading an index allows you the flexibility of indexing with an integer, or some other type (continued)

```
        // publish how many strings you hold
        public int GetNumEntries( )
        {
            return ctr;
        }
    }

    public class Tester
    {
        static void Main( )
        {
            // create a new ListBox and initialize
            ListBoxTest lbt =
                new ListBoxTest("Hello", "World");

            // add a few strings
            lbt.Add("Proust");
            lbt.Add("Faulkner");
            lbt.Add("Mann");
            lbt.Add("Hugo");

            // test the access
            string subst = "Universe";
            lbt[1] = subst;
            lbt["Hel"] = "GoodBye";
            // lbt["xyz"] = "oops";

            // access all the strings
            for (int i = 0; i < lbt.GetNumEntries( ); i++)
            {
                Console.WriteLine("lbt[{0}]: {1}", i, lbt[i]);
            }
        }
    }
}
```

The output looks like this:

```
lbt[0]: GoodBye
lbt[1]: Universe
lbt[2]: Proust
lbt[3]: Faulkner
lbt[4]: Mann
lbt[5]: Hugo
```

Example 14-2 is identical to Example 14-1 except for the addition of an overloaded indexer, which can match a string, and the method FindString, created to support that index.

The FindString method simply iterates through the strings held in myStrings until it finds a string that starts with the target string used in the index. We're using a method of the string class called StartsWith( ), which, as you might imagine, indicates whether a string starts with a specified substring. You'll learn more about the string methods in Chapter 15. If found, the FindString method returns the index of that string; otherwise, it returns the value -1. If more than one entry meets the criterion, FindString returns the matching entry with the lowest numerical index; that is, the one that comes first.

You can see in Main( ) that the user passes in a string segment to the index, just as with an integer:

```
lbt["Hel"] = "GoodBye";
```

This calls the overloaded index, which does some rudimentary error-checking (in this case, making sure the string passed in has at least one letter) and then passes the value (Hel) to FindString. It gets back a numerical index and uses that index to index into myStrings:

```
return this[FindString(index)];
```

The set value works in the same way:

```
myStrings[FindString(index)] = value;
```

> The careful reader will note that if the string does not match, a value of -1 is returned, which is then used as an index into myStrings. This action then generates an exception (System.NullReferenceException), as you can see by uncommenting the following line in Main( ):
>
> ```
> lbt["xyz"] = "oops";
> ```
>
> Again, this is an issue that you would handle in real-world code. We haven't explained exception handling yet (that's in Chapter 16), so for the moment you don't need to worry about it.

Generic Collection Interfaces

The .NET Framework provides standard interfaces for enumerating and comparing collections. These standard interfaces are type-safe, but the type is *generic*; that is, you can declare an ICollection of any type by substituting the actual type (int, string, or Employee) for the generic type in the interface declaration (<T>).

For example, if you were creating an interface called IStorable, but you didn't know what kinds of objects would be stored, you'd declare the interface like this:

```
interface IStorable<T>
{
    // method declarations here
}
```

Later on, if you wanted to create a class Document that implemented IStorable to store strings, you'd do it like this:

```
public class Document : IStorable<String>
```

replacing T with the type you want to apply the interface to (in this case, string).

Shockingly, perhaps, that is all there is to generics. The creator of the class says, in essence, "This applies to some type <T> to be named later (when the interface or class is used) and the programmer using the interface or collection type replaces <T> with the actual type (for example, int, string, Employee, and so on)."

The key generic collection interfaces are listed in Table 14-1. C# also provides non-generic interfaces (ICollection, IEnumerator—without the <T> after them), but we will focus on the generic collections, which should be preferred whenever possible as they are type-safe.

Table 14-1. Generic collection interfaces

Interface	Purpose
ICollection<T>	Base interface for generic collections
IEnumerator<T> IEnumerable<T>	Required for collections that will be enumerated with foreach
IComparer<T> IComparable<T>	Required for collections that will be sorted
IList<T>	Used by indexable collections (see "Generic Lists: List<T>" later in this chapter)
IDictionary<K,V>	Used for key/value-based collections (see "Dictionaries" later in this chapter)

The IEnumerable<T> Interface

You can support the foreach statement in ListBoxTest by implementing the IEnumerable<T> interface.

You read this as "IEnumerable of <T>" or "the generic interface IEnumerable."

IEnumerable has only one method, GetEnumerator( ), whose job is to return an implementation of IEnumerator<T>. The C# language provides special help in creating the enumerator, using the new keyword yield, as demonstrated in Example 14-3 and explained shortly.

Example 14-3. Making a ListBox an enumerable class requires implementing the IEnumerable<T> interface

```
using System;
using System.Collections.Generic;
using System.Linq;
using System.Text;

namespace Example_14_3____Enumerable_Class
{
```

```
public class ListBoxTest : IEnumerable<String>
{
    private string[] strings;
    private int ctr = 0;

    // Enumerable classes return an enumerator
    public IEnumerator<string> GetEnumerator( )
    {
        foreach (string s in strings)
        {
            yield return s;
        }
    }
    // required to fulfill IEnumerable
    System.Collections.IEnumerator
        System.Collections.IEnumerable.GetEnumerator( )
    {
        throw new NotImplementedException( );
    }

    // initialize the ListBox with strings
    public ListBoxTest(params string[] initialStrings)
    {
        // allocate space for the strings
        strings = new String[256];

        // copy the strings passed in to the constructor
        foreach (string s in initialStrings)
        {
            strings[ctr++] = s;
        }
    }

    // add a single string to the end of the ListBox
    public void Add(string theString)
    {
        strings[ctr] = theString;
        ctr++;
    }

    // allow array-like access
    public string this[int index]
    {
        get
        {
            if (index < 0 || index >= strings.Length)
            {
                // handle bad index
            }
            return strings[index];
        }
```

```
            set
            {
                strings[index] = value;
            }
        }

        // publish how many strings you hold
        public int GetNumEntries()
        {
            return ctr;
        }

    }

    public class Tester
    {
        static void Main()
        {
            // create a new ListBox and initialize
            ListBoxTest lbt =
                new ListBoxTest("Hello", "World");

            // add a few strings
            lbt.Add("Proust");
            lbt.Add("Faulkner");
            lbt.Add("Mann");
            lbt.Add("Hugo");

            // test the access
            string subst = "Universe";
            lbt[1] = subst;

            // access all the strings
            foreach (string s in lbt)
            {
                if (s == null)
                {
                    break;
                }

                Console.WriteLine("Value: {0}", s);
            }
        }
    }
}
```

The output looks like this:

```
Value: Hello
Value: Universe
Value: Proust
```

```
Value: Faulkner
Value: Mann
Value: Hugo
```

The program begins in Main( ), creating a new ListBoxTest object and passing two strings to the constructor. When the object is created, an array of Strings is created with enough room for 256 strings. Four more strings are added using the Add method, and the second string is updated, just as in the previous example.

The big change in this version of the program is that a foreach loop is called, retrieving each string in the ListBox. The foreach loop looks very simple, and it's supposed to, but it's actually much more complicated behind the scenes. For a foreach loop to work properly, it needs a reference to an IEnumerator<T> (which is, remember, not an object itself, but an object that implements IEnumerator<T>). However, you don't need to worry about how to create an enumerator, because of the IEnumerable<T> interface. IEnumerable<T> has just one method, GetEnumerator( ), which returns a reference to an IEnumerator<T>. (Remember that IEnumerable and IEnumerator are not the same things.)

The foreach loop *automatically* uses the IEnumerable<T> interface, invoking GetEnumerator( ).

The GetEnumerator method near the top of the class is declared to return an IEnumerator of type string:

```
public IEnumerator<string> GetEnumerator( )
```

The implementation iterates through the array of strings, yielding each in turn:

```
foreach ( string s in strings )
{
    yield return s;
}
```

It doesn't look like this method returns an IEnumerator, but it does, and that's because of yield. The keyword yield is used here explicitly to return a value to the enumerator object. By using the yield keyword, all the bookkeeping for keeping track of which element is next, resetting the iterator, and so forth is provided for you by the framework, so you don't need to worry about it.

The method we just showed you is for the generic IEnumerator<T> interface. Note that our implementation also includes an implementation of the nongeneric GetEnumerator( ) method. This is required by the definition of the generic IEnumerable<T>. Even though it's required to be there, you won't use it, and so it's typically defined to just throw an exception, since you don't expect to call it:

```
// required to fulfill IEnumerable
System.Collections.IEnumerator System.Collections.IEnumerable.GetEnumerator( )
{
    throw new NotImplementedException( );
}
```

Again, we'll explain exceptions in Chapter 16, but this is basically just a way of saying, "Don't use this method. If you *do* use this method, something has gone wrong."

The difference between Examples 14-3 and 14-2 is just the foreach loop, but that small difference means that your ListBoxTest class in Example 14-3 needs to implement IEnumerable<T>, which means it has to implement both the generic and the nongeneric versions of GetEnumerator( ).

As you can see, you need a lot of "plumbing" to make foreach work, and it may not seem like it's worth it. The framework collections, though, all do support foreach, and all that plumbing is hidden from you, making it appear like a very simple loop. If you want your collection to work like the framework collections (and you do, right?), you'll need to support foreach as well. Fortunately, the IEnumerable<T> interface and the yield keyword do a lot of the work for you, and you can use them without knowing exactly what they do. (If you want to find out, though, you can check out the Microsoft Developer Network at *http://msdn2.microsoft.com* for more detail than you ever wanted.)

Framework Generic Collections

We spent time explaining what generic collections are and how they work so that you'd have an appreciation for how they're created and what they can do. Most of the time, you won't need to create your own collection, because the .NET Framework provides four very useful generic collections, as we discussed earlier (List, Stack, Queue, and Dictionary). We describe each in turn in the next few sections.

Generic Lists: List<T>

The classic problem with the Array type is its fixed size. If you do not know in advance how many objects an array will hold, you run the risk of declaring either too small an array (and running out of room) or too large an array (and wasting memory).

The generic List class is, essentially, an array whose size is dynamically increased as required. Lists provide a number of useful methods and properties for their manipulation. Some of the most important are shown in Table 14-2.

Table 14-2. List properties and methods

Method or property	Purpose
Capacity	Property to get or set the number of elements the List can contain; this value is increased automatically if count exceeds capacity; you might set this value to reduce the number of reallocations, and you may call Trim( ) to reduce this value to the actual Count
Count	Property to get the number of elements currently in the list
Item	Property that .NET requires for the List class as an indexer; you'll never see this in C#; you can use the standard [ ] syntax instead

Table 14-2. List properties and methods (continued)

Method or property	Purpose
Add( )	Public method to add an object to the List
AddRange( )	Public method that adds the elements of an ICollection to the end of the List
BinarySearch( )	Overloaded public method that uses a binary search to locate a specific element in a sorted List
Clear( )	Removes all elements from the List
Contains( )	Determines whether an element is in the List
CopyTo( )	Overloaded public method that copies a List to a one-dimensional array; commonly used to convert a List to an array for methods that accept only arrays, not collections
Exists( )	Determines whether the List contains elements that meet the specified criteria
Find( )	Returns the first List element that meets specified criteria
FindAll( )	Returns all List elements that meet specified criteria
GetEnumerator( )	Overloaded public method that returns an enumerator to iterate through a List
GetRange( )	Copies a range of elements to a new List
IndexOf( )	Overloaded public method that returns the index of the first occurrence of a value
Insert( )	Inserts an element into a List
InsertRange( )	Inserts the elements of a collection into the List
LastIndexOf( )	Overloaded public method that returns the index of the last occurrence of a List element that meets specified criteria
Remove( )	Removes the first occurrence of a specific object
RemoveAt( )	Removes the element at the specified index
RemoveRange( )	Removes a range of elements
Reverse( )	Reverses the order of elements in the List
Sort( )	Sorts the List
ToArray( )	Copies the elements of the List to a new array; commonly used to convert a List to an array for methods that accept only arrays, not collections
TrimExcess( )	Sets the capacity to the actual number of elements in the List

When you create a List, you do not define how many objects it will contain. You add to the List using the Add( ) method, and the List takes care of its own internal bookkeeping, as illustrated in Example 14-4.

Example 14-4. A List offers all the functionality of an array, but without the need to know how many elements it will hold when it's created

```
using System;
using System.Collections.Generic;
using System.Linq;
using System.Text;

namespace Example_14_4____List
{
```

```csharp
// a simple class to store in the List
public class Employee
{
    private int empID;

    public Employee(int empID) //constructor
    {
        this.empID = empID;
    }
    public override string ToString( )
    {
        return empID.ToString( );
    }
}

public class Tester
{
    static void Main( )
    {

        List<Employee> empList = new List<Employee>( );
        List<int> intList = new List<int>( );

        // populate the Lists
        for (int i = 0; i < 5; i++)
        {
            intList.Add(i * 5);
            empList.Add(new Employee(i + 100));
        }

        // print the contents of the int List
        for (int i = 0; i < intList.Count; i++)
        {
            Console.Write("{0} ", intList[i].ToString( ));
        }

        Console.WriteLine("\n");

        // print the contents of the Employee List
        for (int i = 0; i < empList.Count; i++)
        {
            Console.Write("{0} ", empList[i].ToString( ));
        }

        Console.WriteLine("\n");
        Console.WriteLine("empList.Capacity: {0}", empList.Capacity);
    }
}
```

The output looks like this:

```
0 5 10 15 20
100 101 102 103 104
empList.Capacity: 8
```

The `List` class has a property, `Capacity`, which is the number of elements the `List` is capable of storing; however, this capacity is automatically increased each time you reach the limit.

The `Add( )` method takes care of a lot of things behind the scenes here—it increases the capacity of the `List` (if necessary), inserts the new item at the end of the list, and provides it with an appropriate index. You can't do that with an array.

Sorting objects with the generic list

The `List` implements the `Sort( )` method. You can sort any `List` that contains objects that implement `IComparable`. All the built-in types do implement this interface, so you can sort a `List<integer>` or a `List<string>`.

On the other hand, if you want to sort a `List<Employee>`, you must change the `Employee` class to implement `IComparable`:

```
public class Employee : IComparable<Employee>
```

As part of the `IComparable` interface contract, the `Employee` object must provide a `CompareTo( )` method:

```
public int CompareTo(Employee rhs)
{
    return this.empID.CompareTo(rhs.empID);
}
```

The `CompareTo( )` method takes an `Employee` as a parameter. You know this is correct because the interface is generic, which means that the `List` was specified with the `Employee` class when you created it, so you can assume type safety. The `Employee` object must compare itself to the second `Employee` object that was passed in (called rhs) and return -1 if it is smaller than the second `Employee`, 1 if it is greater, and 0 if the two `Employee` objects are equal to each other.

It is up to the designer of the `Employee` class to determine what *smaller than*, *greater than*, and *equal to* mean for an employee. In this example, you'll compare the `Employee` objects based on the value of their empId members. The empId member is an int, and since int is a built-in type, it already has its own default `CompareTo( )` method, which will do an integer comparison of the two values. So, the `CompareTo( )` method for `Employee` just calls the `CompareTo( )` method of EmpID, which returns an int property. You let the int `CompareTo( )` do the work of the comparison, and then return the result.

To see whether the sort is working, you'll add integers and `Employee` instances to their respective lists with random values. (See the sidebar about the `Random` class.)

The Random Class

To create random values you instantiate an object of class Random. That's pretty simple to do:

```
Random r = new Random( );
```

To cause your Random instance to generate random values, you call its Next( ) method. One version of the Next( ) method allows you to specify the largest random number you want. For example, to generate a random number between 0 and 99, you pass in the value 100, like this:

```
Random r = new Random( );
r.Next(100);
```

Random number generators do not, technically, create true random numbers; they create what computer scientists call *pseudorandom numbers*. They're not completely random because a mathematical process is used to create them, but they're more than random enough for this example.

Example 14-5 creates an integer list and an Employee list, populates them both with random numbers, and prints their values. It then sorts both lists and prints the new values.

Example 14-5. The List class includes methods that make sorting easy

```csharp
using System;
using System.Collections.Generic;
using System.Linq;
using System.Text;

namespace Example_14_5____Sorting_a_List
{
    // a simple class to store in the list
    public class Employee : IComparable<Employee>
    {
        private int empID;

        public Employee(int empID)
        {
            this.empID = empID;
        }

        public override string ToString( )
        {
            return empID.ToString( );
        }


        public bool Equals(Employee other)
        {
```

Example 14-5. The List class includes methods that make sorting easy (continued)

```
        if (this.empID == other.empID)
        {
            return true;
        }
        else
        {
            return false;
        }
    }

    // Comparer delegates back to Employee
    // Employee uses the integer's default
    // CompareTo method

    public int CompareTo(Employee rhs)
    {
        return this.empID.CompareTo(rhs.empID);
    }

}
public class Tester
{
    static void Main( )
    {

        List<Employee> empList = new List<Employee>( );
        List<Int32> intList = new List<Int32>( );

        // generate random numbers for both the
        // integers and the employee IDs
        Random r = new Random( );

        // populate the list
        for (int i = 0; i < 5; i++)
        {
            // add a random employee id
            empList.Add(new Employee(r.Next(10) + 100));

            // add a random integer
            intList.Add(r.Next(10));
        }


        // display all the contents of the int list
        Console.WriteLine("List<int> before sorting:");
        for (int i = 0; i < intList.Count; i++)
        {
            Console.Write("{0} ", intList[i].ToString( ));
        }
        Console.WriteLine("\n");

        // display all the contents of the Employee list
```

Example 14-5. The List class includes methods that make sorting easy (continued)

```
            Console.WriteLine("List<Employee> before sorting:");
            for (int i = 0; i < empList.Count; i++)
            {
                Console.Write("{0} ", empList[i].ToString());
            }
            Console.WriteLine("\n");

            // sort and display the int list
            Console.WriteLine("List<int>after sorting:");
            intList.Sort();
            for (int i = 0; i < intList.Count; i++)
            {
                Console.Write("{0} ", intList[i].ToString());
            }
            Console.WriteLine("\n");

            // sort and display the Employee list
            Console.WriteLine("List<Employee>after sorting:");

            //Employee.EmployeeComparer c = Employee.GetComparer();
            //empList.Sort(c);

            empList.Sort();

            // display all the contents of the Employee list
            for (int i = 0; i < empList.Count; i++)
            {
                Console.Write("{0} ", empList[i].ToString());
            }
            Console.WriteLine("\n");

        }
    }
}
```

The output looks something like this:

```
List<int> before sorting:
6 9 8 3 6
List<Employee> before sorting:
108 103 107 102 109
List<int>after sorting:
3 6 6 8 9
List<Employee>after sorting:
102 103 107 108 109
```

The output shows that the lists of integers and Employees were generated with random numbers—which means the numbers will be different each time you run the program. When sorted, the display shows that the values have been ordered properly.

Controlling sorting by implementing IComparer<T>

When you call Sort( ) on the List in Example 14-5, the default implementation of IComparer is called behind the scenes, which uses an algorithm called "Quick Sort" to call the IComparable implementation of CompareTo( ) on each element in the List.

You are free, however, to create your own implementation of IComparer, which you might want to do if you need control over how the sort ordering is defined. In the next example, you will add a second field to Employee: yearsOfSvc. You want to be able to sort the Employee objects in the List either by ID or by years of service, and you want to make that decision at runtime.

To accomplish this, you will create a custom implementation of IComparer, which you will pass to the Sort( ) method of List. You'll implement a new class, EmployeeComparer, which will implement IComparer and will know how to sort Employees.

To simplify the programmer's ability to choose how a given set of Employees are sorted, you'll add a property, WhichComparison, of type Employee.EmployeeComparer. ComparisonType (an enumeration):

```
public
Employee.EmployeeComparer.ComparisonType  WhichComparison
{
    get { return whichComparison; }
    set { whichComparison = value; }
}
```

The point to this is that when you create an EmployeeComparer, you can pass it WhichComparison, which will be of type ComparisonType. ComparisonType is an enumeration with one of two values, empID or yearsOfSvc (indicating that you want to sort by employee ID or years of service, respectively):

```
public enum ComparisonType
{
    EmpID,
    YearsOfService
};
```

It may seem convoluted, but later on, if you decide to add another property to the Employee class—lastName, for example—and you want to sort by the new lastName property, you can very easily add LastName to the enumeration (note the capitalization), making the comparison much easier.

Before invoking Sort( ), you will create an instance of EmployeeComparer and set its ComparisonType property:

```
Employee.EmployeeComparer c = Employee.GetComparer( );
c.WhichComparison=Employee.EmployeeComparer.ComparisonType.EmpID;
empList.Sort(c);
```

The `EmployeeComparer` class must provide a `Compare()` method. When you invoke `Sort()`, the `List` will call that `Compare()` method on the `EmployeeComparer`, which in turn will delegate the comparison to the `Employee.CompareTo()` method, passing in its `WhichComparison` property:

```
public int Compare( Employee lhs, Employee rhs )
{
    return lhs.CompareTo( rhs, WhichComparison );
}
```

Your `Employee` object must implement a custom version of `CompareTo()`. This custom method needs to accept the `Employee` object to compare to (which we've been calling `rhs`), and a member of the `ComparisonType` enum you defined earlier. Depending on the value of `ComparisonType`, you'll need code to compare the value of either `empID` or `yearsOfSvc`. Both `empID` and `yearsOfSvc` are ints, so once again you can just delegate to the `CompareTo()` method of int in both cases. If you added a `LastName` member to the enum, you'd need to add another case statement that would call the string class's `CompareTo()` method:

```
public int CompareTo
    (
    Employee rhs,
    Employee.EmployeeComparer.ComparisonType whichComparison
    )
{
    switch (whichComparison)
    {
        case Employee.EmployeeComparer.ComparisonType.EmpID:
            return this.empID.CompareTo(rhs.empID);
        case Employee.EmployeeComparer.ComparisonType.Yrs:
            return this.yearsOfSvc.CompareTo(rhs.yearsOfSvc);
    }
    return 0;
}
```

The complete source for this example is shown in Example 14-6. We've removed the integer list to simplify the example, and we've enhanced the output of the employee's `ToString()` method so that you can see the effects of the sort.

Example 14-6. You can sort a List by differing properties of your class, if you implement your own IComparer

```
using System;
using System.Collections.Generic;
using System.Linq;
using System.Text;

namespace Example_14_6____Custom_IComparer
{
    public class Employee : IComparable<Employee>
    {
        private int empID;
```

```
    private int yearsOfSvc = 1;

    public Employee(int empID)
    {
        this.empID = empID;
    }

    public Employee(int empID, int yearsOfSvc)
    {
        this.empID = empID;
        this.yearsOfSvc = yearsOfSvc;
    }

    public override string ToString()
    {
        return "ID: " + empID.ToString() + ". Years of Svc: "
                    + yearsOfSvc.ToString();
    }

    public bool Equals(Employee other)
    {
        if (this.empID == other.empID)
        {
            return true;
        }
        else
        {
            return false;
        }
    }

    // static method to get a Comparer object
    public static EmployeeComparer GetComparer()
    {
        return new Employee.EmployeeComparer();
    }

    // Comparer delegates back to Employee
    // Employee uses the integer's default
    // CompareTo method
    public int CompareTo(Employee rhs)
    {
        return this.empID.CompareTo(rhs.empID);
    }

    // Special implementation to be called by custom comparer
    public int CompareTo(Employee rhs,
                Employee.EmployeeComparer.ComparisonType which)
    {
        switch (which)
        {
```

```
        case Employee.EmployeeComparer.ComparisonType.EmpID:
            return this.empID.CompareTo(rhs.empID);
        case Employee.EmployeeComparer.ComparisonType.
                    YearsOfService:
            return this.yearsOfSvc.CompareTo(rhs.yearsOfSvc);
    }
    return 0;
}


// nested class which implements IComparer
public class EmployeeComparer : IComparer<Employee>
{
    // private state variable
    private Employee.EmployeeComparer.ComparisonType
                whichComparison;
    // enumeration of comparison types
    public enum ComparisonType
    {
        EmpID,
        YearsOfService
    };

    public bool Equals(Employee lhs, Employee rhs)
    {
        return this.Compare(lhs, rhs) == 0;
    }

    // Tell the Employee objects to compare themselves
    public int Compare(Employee lhs, Employee rhs)
    {
        return lhs.CompareTo(rhs, WhichComparison);
    }

    public Employee.EmployeeComparer.ComparisonType
                WhichComparison
    {
        get { return whichComparison; }
        set { whichComparison = value; }
    }
}
}

public class Tester
{
    static void Main( )
    {
        List<Employee> empList = new List<Employee>( );

        // generate random numbers for
        // both the integers and the
```

Example 14-6. You can sort a List by differing properties of your class, if you implement your own IComparer (continued)

```
        // employee IDs
        Random r = new Random( );

        // populate the list
        for (int i = 0; i < 5; i++)
        {
            // add a random employee ID
            empList.Add(new Employee(r.Next(10) + 100,
                                r.Next(20)));
        }

        // display all the contents of the Employee list
        for (int i = 0; i < empList.Count; i++)
        {
            Console.Write("\n{0} ", empList[i].ToString( ));
        }
        Console.WriteLine("\n");

        // sort and display the employee list
        Employee.EmployeeComparer c = Employee.GetComparer( );
        c.WhichComparison =
                Employee.EmployeeComparer.ComparisonType.EmpID;
        empList.Sort(c);

        // display all the contents of the Employee list
        for (int i = 0; i < empList.Count; i++)
        {
            Console.Write("\n{0} ", empList[i].ToString( ));
        }
        Console.WriteLine("\n");

        c.WhichComparison =
            Employee.EmployeeComparer.ComparisonType.YearsOfService;
        empList.Sort(c);

        for (int i = 0; i < empList.Count; i++)
        {
            Console.Write("\n{0} ", empList[i].ToString( ));
        }
        Console.WriteLine("\n");
    }
  }
}
```

The output looks like this for one run of the program:

```
ID: 103. Years of Svc: 11
ID: 108. Years of Svc: 15
ID: 107. Years of Svc: 14
ID: 108. Years of Svc: 5
ID: 102. Years of Svc: 0
```

```
ID: 102. Years of Svc: 0
ID: 103. Years of Svc: 11
ID: 107. Years of Svc: 14
ID: 108. Years of Svc: 15
ID: 108. Years of Svc: 5

ID: 102. Years of Svc: 0
ID: 108. Years of Svc: 5
ID: 103. Years of Svc: 11
ID: 107. Years of Svc: 14
ID: 108. Years of Svc: 15
```

The first block of output shows the Employee objects as they are added to the List. The employee ID values and the years of service are in random order. The second block shows the results of sorting by the employee ID, and the third block shows the results of sorting by years of service.

As you can see, the List is a lot like an array, but more programmable and versatile. There are plenty of situations where a simple array is all you need, and they're easiest to learn, so you shouldn't abandon them altogether. But when you need to go beyond the basics, a List can be useful. The other collection classes are more specific in their uses, as you'll see.

Generic Queues

A *queue* is what you'll hear referred to as a first-in, first-out (FIFO) collection. This is just a fancy way of saying that you add items to the queue one at a time, and you remove items one at a time, such that items are removed in the same order in which you added them. The classic analogy is to a line (or queue, if you are British) at a ticket window. The first person in line ought to be the first person to come off the line to buy a ticket.

A queue is a good collection to use when you are managing a limited resource. For example, you might want your clients to send messages to a resource that can handle only one message at a time. You would then create a message queue so that you can say to your clients: "Your message is important to us. Messages are handled in the order in which they are received."

The Queue class has a number of member methods and properties, the most important of which are shown in Table 14-3.

Table 14-3. Queue methods and properties

Method or property	Purpose
Count	Public property that returns the number of elements in the Queue
Clear( )	Removes all objects from the Queue
Contains( )	Determines whether an element is in the Queue
CopyTo( )	Copies the Queue elements to an existing one-dimensional array

Table 14-3. Queue methods and properties (continued)

Method or property	Purpose
Dequeue( )	Removes and returns the object at the beginning of the Queue
Enqueue( )	Adds an object to the end of the Queue
GetEnumerator( )	Returns an enumerator for the Queue
Peek( )	Returns a reference to the object at the beginning of the Queue without removing it
ToArray( )	Copies the elements to a new array

Add elements to your queue with the Enqueue( ) method and take them off the queue with Dequeue( ), or by using an enumerator, as shown in Example 14-7.

Example 14-7. A queue always returns items in the same order in which they were added

```
using System;
using System.Collections.Generic;
using System.Linq;
using System.Text;

namespace Example_14_7____Queues
{
    public class Tester
    {

        static void Main( )
        {
            Queue<Int32> intQueue = new Queue<Int32>( );

            // populate the Queue.
            for (int i = 0; i < 5; i++)
            {
                intQueue.Enqueue(i * 5);
            }

            // Display the Queue.
            Console.Write("intQueue values:\t");
            PrintValues(intQueue);

            // Remove an element from the Queue.
            Console.WriteLine("\n(Dequeue)\t{0}", intQueue.Dequeue( ));

            // Display the Queue.
            Console.Write("intQueue values:\t");
            PrintValues(intQueue);

            // Remove another element from the Queue.
            Console.WriteLine("\n(Dequeue)\t{0}", intQueue.Dequeue( ));

            // Display the Queue.
            Console.Write("intQueue values:\t");
            PrintValues(intQueue);
```

```
        // View the first element in the
        // Queue but do not remove.
        Console.WriteLine("\n(Peek)  \t{0}", intQueue.Peek());

        // Display the Queue.
        Console.Write("intQueue values:\t");
        PrintValues(intQueue);
    }

    public static void PrintValues(IEnumerable<Int32> myCollection)
    {
        IEnumerator<Int32> myEnumerator = myCollection.GetEnumerator();
        while (myEnumerator.MoveNext())
        {
            Console.Write("{0} ", myEnumerator.Current);
        }
        Console.WriteLine();
    }

    }
}
```

The output looks like this:

```
intQueue values:      0 5 10 15 20

(Dequeue)      0
intQueue values:      5 10 15 20

(Dequeue)      5
intQueue values:      10 15 20

(Peek)       10
intQueue values:      10 15 20
```

We've dispensed with the Employee class to save room, but of course you can enqueue user-defined objects as well. The output shows that queuing an object adds it to the Queue, and Dequeue( ) returns the object as well as removes it from the Queue. The Queue class also provides a Peek( ) method that allows you to see, but not remove, the next element.

Take a closer look at the PrintValues( ) method:

```
public static void PrintValues(IEnumerable<Int32> myCollection)
{
    IEnumerator<Int32> myEnumerator = myCollection.GetEnumerator();
    while (myEnumerator.MoveNext())
    {
        Console.Write("{0} ", myEnumerator.Current);
    }
```

Because the Queue class is enumerable, you can pass it to the PrintValues( ) method, which takes an IEnumerable interface. The conversion is implicit. In the PrintValues method, you call GetEnumerator, which is the single method required by all IEnumerable classes, as we mentioned earlier in the chapter. GetEnumerator( ) returns an IEnumerator, which you then use to enumerate all the objects in the collection. MoveNext( ) is a method of IEnumerator, so no matter what collection type you're using, you can always call MoveNext( ) to retrieve the next value. Current is the property of IEnumerator that represents the current value, so you can output the current value in the queue by outputting myEnumerator.Current. When there are no more values in the collection, MoveNext( ) returns false, which ends the while loop.

Note that we're using a while loop here to demonstrate how IEnumerator works; in practice, you'd probably use a foreach loop instead.

Generic Stacks

The Stack is the natural partner of the Queue. A *stack* is a last-in, first-out (LIFO) collection, so the items are removed in the *opposite* of the order in which they were added. Think of a stack as a stack of dishes at a buffet table, or a stack of coins on your desk. You add a dish on top, and that's the first dish you take off the stack. You've already seen a form of stack in Chapter 9, when we described the call stack. Each time you call a method, it's added to the top of the call stack. When a method returns, it's removed from the top of the stack.

The principal methods for adding to and removing from a stack are Push( ) and Pop( ); these method names are nonintuitive, but they're traditional with stacks. Push( ) adds an item to the stack, and Pop( ) removes it. Stack also offers a Peek( ) method, very much like Queue. The significant methods and properties for Stack are shown in Table 14-4.

Table 14-4. Stack methods and properties

Method or property	Purpose
Count	Public property that gets the number of elements in the Stack
Clear( )	Removes all objects from the Stack
Contains( )	Determines whether an element is in the Stack
CopyTo( )	Copies the Stack elements to an existing one-dimensional array
GetEnumerator( )	Returns an enumerator for the Stack
Peek( )	Returns the object at the top of the Stack without removing it
Pop( )	Removes and returns the object at the top of the Stack
Push( )	Inserts an object at the top of the Stack
ToArray( )	Copies the elements to a new array

The List, Queue, and Stack types contain multiple versions of the CopyTo( ) and ToArray( ) methods for copying their elements to an array. In the case of a Stack, the CopyTo( ) method will copy its elements to an existing one-dimensional array, over-writing the contents of the array, beginning at the index you specify. The ToArray( ) method returns a new array with the contents of the Stack's elements.

Example 14-8 illustrates several of the Stack methods.

Example 14-8. Stacks are similar to Queues, but items are removed in the reverse of the order in which they were added

```
using System;
using System.Collections.Generic;
using System.Linq;
using System.Text;

namespace Example_14_8____Stacks
{
    public class Tester
    {
        static void Main( )
        {
            Stack<Int32> intStack = new Stack<Int32>( );

            // populate the Stack

            for (int i = 0; i < 8; i++)
            {
                intStack.Push(i * 5);
            }

            // Display the Stack.
            Console.Write("intStack values:\t");
            PrintValues(intStack);

            // Remove an element from the Stack.
            Console.WriteLine("\n(Pop)\t{0}", intStack.Pop( ));

            // Display the Stack.
            Console.Write("intStack values:\t");
            PrintValues(intStack);

            // Remove another element from the Stack.
            Console.WriteLine("\n(Pop)\t{0}", intStack.Pop( ));

            // Display the Stack.
            Console.Write("intStack values:\t");
            PrintValues(intStack);

            // View the first element in the
            // Stack but do not remove.
            Console.WriteLine("\n(Peek)   \t{0}", intStack.Peek( ));
```

```
                // Display the Stack.
                Console.Write("intStack values:\t");
                PrintValues(intStack);

                // Declare an array object which will
                // hold 12 integers
                int[] targetArray = new int[12];

                for (int i = 0; i < targetArray.Length; i++)
                {
                    targetArray[i] = i * 100 + 100;
                }

                // Display the values of the target Array instance.
                Console.WriteLine("\nTarget array:  ");
                PrintValues(targetArray);

                // Copy the entire source Stack to the
                // target Array instance, starting at index 6.
                intStack.CopyTo(targetArray, 6);

                // Display the values of the target Array instance.
                Console.WriteLine("\nTarget array after copy:  ");
                PrintValues(targetArray);
            }

        public static void PrintValues(IEnumerable<Int32> myCollection)
        {
            IEnumerator<Int32> enumerator = myCollection.GetEnumerator();
            while (enumerator.MoveNext())
            {
                Console.Write("{0}  ", enumerator.Current);
            }
            Console.WriteLine();
        }
    }
}
```

The output looks like this:

```
    intStack values:       35  30  25  20  15  10  5  0

    (Pop)   35
    intStack values:       30  25  20  15  10  5  0

    (Pop)   30
    intStack values:       25  20  15  10  5  0
```

```
(Peek)           25
intStack values:        25  20  15  10  5  0

Target array:
100   200   300   400   500   600   700   800   900   1000   1100   1200

Target array after copy:
100   200   300   400   500   600   25   20   15   10   5   0
```

The output reflects that the items pushed onto the Stack were popped in reverse order.

We can see the effect of CopyTo( ) by examining the target array before and after calling CopyTo( ). The array elements are overwritten beginning with the index specified (6).

Dictionaries

A *dictionary* is a collection that associates a *key* with a *value*. That is, it uses a non-numeric index. A language dictionary, such as *Webster's*, associates a word (the key) with its definition (the value).

To see the value of dictionaries, start by imagining that you want to keep a list of the state capitals. One approach might be to put them in an array:

```
string[] stateCapitals = new string[50];
```

The stateCapitals array will hold 50 state capitals. Each capital is accessed by an index into the array. For example, to access the capital for Arkansas, you need to know that Arkansas is the fourth state in alphabetical order:

```
string capitalOfArkansas = stateCapitals[3];
```

It is inconvenient, however, to access state capitals using array notation. After all, if you need the capital for Massachusetts, there is no easy way to determine that Massachusetts is the 21st state alphabetically.

It would be far more convenient to store the capital with the state name. A dictionary allows you to store a value (in this case, the capital) with a key (in this case, the name of the state).

A .NET Framework dictionary can associate any kind of key (string, integer, or object) with any kind of value (string, integer, or object). Typically, the key is fairly short and the value fairly complex, though in this case, we'll use short strings for both.

The most important attributes of a good dictionary are that it is easy to add values and it is quick to retrieve values. Table 14-5 lists some of the more important methods and properties of Dictionary.

Table 14-5. Dictionary methods and properties

Method or property	Purpose
Count	Public property that gets the number of elements in the Dictionary
Item	The indexer for the Dictionary
Keys	Public property that gets a collection containing the keys in the Dictionary
Values	Public property that gets a collection containing the values in the Dictionary
Add( )	Adds an entry with a specified Key and Value
Clear( )	Removes all objects from the Dictionary
ContainsKey( )	Determines whether the Dictionary has a specified key
ContainsValue( )	Determines whether the Dictionary has a specified value
GetEnumerator( )	Returns an enumerator for the Dictionary
Remove( )	Removes the entry with the specified Key

The key in a Dictionary can be a primitive type, or it can be an instance of a user-defined type (an object).

Objects used as keys for a Dictionary must implement the method GetHashCode( ) as well as Equals. This is how the Dictionary works behind the scenes—there is actually a numeric index assigned to the value, but that index is associated with the key, so you never need to know what it is. GetHashCode( ) is so fundamental that it's actually implemented in Object, the root base class. In most cases, you don't need to worry about writing the GetHashCode( ) method; you can simply use the inherited implementation from Object.

Dictionaries implement the IDictionary<TKey,TValue> interface (where TKey is the key type and TValue is the value type). IDictionary provides a public property, Item. The Item property retrieves a value with the specified key.

The Item property is implemented with the index operator ([]). Thus, you access items in any Dictionary object using the same syntax as you would with an array. If you had a dictionary called addresses, which holds the addresses of various businesses, with the company name as the key, you'd access the address for O'Reilly like this:

```
addresses["O'Reilly"]
```

Note the quotation marks around "O'Reilly"—you need them because you're using a string as your indexer.

Example 14-9 demonstrates adding items to a Dictionary and then retrieving them with the indexer (which implicitly uses the Dictionary's Item property).

Example 14-9. The Dictionary collection uses nonnumeric indexers

```
using System;
using System.Collections.Generic;
using System.Linq;
using System.Text;
```

Example 14-9. The Dictionary collection uses nonnumeric indexers (continued)

```
namespace Example_14_9____Dictionaries
{
    public class Tester
    {
        static void Main( )
        {
            // Create and initialize a new Dictionary.
            Dictionary<string, string> dict =
                        new Dictionary<string, string>( );

            dict.Add("Alabama", "Montgomery");
            dict.Add("Alaska", "Juneau");
            dict.Add("Arizona", "Phoenix");
            dict.Add("Arkansas", "Little Rock");
            dict.Add("California", "Sacramento");
            dict.Add("Colorado", "Denver");
            dict.Add("Connecticut", "Hartford");
            dict.Add("Delaware", "Dover");
            dict.Add("Florida", "Tallahassee");
            dict.Add("Georgia", "Atlanta");
            dict.Add("Hawaii", "Honolulu");
            dict.Add("Idaho", "Boise");
            dict.Add("Illinois", "Springfield");
            dict.Add("Indiana", "Indianapolis");
            dict.Add("Iowa", "Des Moines");
            dict.Add("Kansas", "Topeka");
            dict.Add("Kentucky", "Frankfort");
            dict.Add("Louisiana", "Baton Rouge");
            dict.Add("Maine", "Augusta");
            dict.Add("Maryland", "Annapolis");
            dict.Add("Massachusetts", "Boston");
            dict.Add("Michigan", "Lansing");
            dict.Add("Minnesota", "St. Paul");
            dict.Add("Mississippi", "Jackson");
            dict.Add("Missouri", "Jefferson City");
            dict.Add("Montana", "Helena");
            dict.Add("Nebraska", "Lincoln");
            dict.Add("Nevada", "Carson City");
            dict.Add("New Hampshire", "Concord");
            dict.Add("New Jersey", "Trenton");
            dict.Add("New Mexico", "Santa Fe");
            dict.Add("New York", "Albany");
            dict.Add("North Carolina", "Raleigh");
            dict.Add("North Dakota", "Bismarck");
            dict.Add("Ohio", "Columbus");
            dict.Add("Oklahoma", "Oklahoma City");
            dict.Add("Oregon", "Salem");
            dict.Add("Pennsylvania", "Harrisburg");
            dict.Add("Rhode Island", "Providence");
            dict.Add("South Carolina", "Columbia");
            dict.Add("South Dakota", "Pierre");
            dict.Add("Tennessee", "Nashville");
            dict.Add("Texas", "Austin");
```

```
            dict.Add("Utah", "Salt Lake City");
            dict.Add("Vermont", "Montpelier");
            dict.Add("Virginia", "Richmond");
            dict.Add("Washington", "Olympia");
            dict.Add("West Virginia", "Charleston");
            dict.Add("Wisconsin", "Madison");
            dict.Add("Wyoming", "Cheyenne");

            // access a state

            Console.WriteLine("The capital of Massachusetts is {0}",
                            dict["Massachusetts"]);

        }
    }
}
```

The output looks like this:

```
The capital of Massachusetts is Boston
```

Example 14-9 begins by instantiating a new `Dictionary` object with the type of the key and of the value declared to be a string.

We then added 50 key/value pairs. In this example, the state name is the key and the capital is the value (though in a typical dictionary, the value is almost always larger than the key).

 You must not change the value of the key object once you use it in a dictionary.

Summary

- The .NET Framework provides a number of type-safe generic collections, including the `List<T>`, `Stack<T>`, `Queue<T>`, and `Dictionary<Tkey><Tvalue>`.

- Generics allow the collection designer to create a single collection without regard for the type of object it will hold, but to allow the collection *user* to define, at compile time, which type the object will hold. This enlists the compiler in finding bugs; if you add an object of the wrong type to a collection, it will be found at compile time, not at runtime.

- You are free to create your own generic collection types as well.

- The .NET Framework provides a number of interfaces that collections must implement if they wish to act like the built-in collections (such as being iterated by a `foreach` loop).

- An indexer allows you to access or assign objects to and from a collection just as you do with an array (for example, `myCollection[5] = "hello"`).

- Indexers need not be restricted to integers. It is common to create indexers that take a string to assign or retrieve a value.
- All framework collections implement the Sort( ) method. If you want to be able to sort a collection of objects of a user-defined type, however, the defining class must implement the IComparable interface.
- The generic list collection, List<T>, works like an array whose size is increased dynamically as you add elements.
- The Queue<T> class is a first-in, first-out collection.
- The Stack<T> class is a last-in, first-out collection.
- A Dictionary<k,v> is a collection that associates a key with a value. Typically, the key is short and the value is large.

You saw a handful of strings used in various places in this chapter, and you may wonder why we haven't discussed strings directly yet. That's because although strings can be used almost like any other primitive data type in their most basic form, the string class has a number of methods to it, so we deferred discussing them for a while. That's about to change, though; Chapter 15 is all about strings, and how to make them do what you want.

Test Your Knowledge: Quiz

Question 14-1. What is the convention for naming an indexer?

Question 14-2. What types can be used in an indexer to index a collection?

Question 14-3. What are the preconditions for calling Sort( ) on a collection?

Question 14-4. What is the purpose of generics?

Question 14-5. What is the purpose of the IEnumerable<T> interface?

Question 14-6. What do you use the yield keyword for?

Question 14-7. What is the principal difference between a List<T> and an array?

Question 14-8. What is the Capacity property of the List used for?

Question 14-9. What is the difference between a Stack and a Queue?

Question 14-10. In a Dictionary, what is the meaning of the key and the value?

Test Your Knowledge: Exercises

Exercise 14-1. Create an abstract `Animal` class that has private members `weight` and `name`, and abstract methods `Speak( )`, `Move( )`, and `ToString( )`. Derive from `Animal` a `Cat` class and a `Dog` class that override the methods appropriately. Create an `Animal` array, populate it with `Dog`s and `Cat`s, and then call each member's overridden virtual methods.

Exercise 14-2. Replace the array in Exercise 14-1 with a `List`. Sort the animals by size. You can simplify by just calling `ToString( )` before and after the sort. Remember that you'll need to implement `IComparable`.

Exercise 14-3. Replace the list from Exercise 14-2 with both a `Stack` and a `Queue`. Remove the sort function. Output the contents of each collection and see the difference in the order in which the animals are returned.

Exercise 14-4. Rewrite Exercise 14-2 to allow `Animals` to be sorted either by weight or alphabetically by name.

CHAPTER 15

Strings

There was a time when people thought of computers as manipulating numeric values exclusively. Among the first uses of computers was to calculate missile trajectories during World War II, and for a very long time programming was taught in the math department of major universities.

Today, most programs are concerned more with manipulating and displaying strings of characters in addition to strings of numbers. Typically, these strings are used for word processing, document manipulation, and the creation of web pages.

C# provides built-in support for a fully functional string type. More importantly, C# treats strings as objects that encapsulate all the manipulation, sorting, and searching methods normally applied to strings of characters.

 The .NET Framework provides a String class (uppercase *S*). The C# language offers an alias to the String class as the string class (lowercase *s*). These class names are interchangeable, and you are free to use either upper- or lowercase.

Complex string manipulation and pattern matching is aided by the use of *regular expressions*. Regular expressions are a powerful technology for describing and manipulating text. Underlying regular expressions is a technique called *pattern matching*, which involves comparing one string to another, or comparing a series of wildcards that represent a type of string to a literal string. A regular expression is *applied* to a string—that is, to a set of characters. Often, that string is an entire text document. We'll explain regular expressions in more detail later in this chapter.

In this chapter, you will learn to work with the C# string type and the .NET Framework System.String class that it aliases. You will see how to extract substrings, manipulate and concatenate strings, and build new strings with the StringBuilder class. In addition, you will find a short introduction to the Regex class used to match strings based on regular expressions.

Creating Strings

C# treats strings as though they were built-in types (much as it does with arrays). C# strings are flexible, powerful, and easy to use.

In .NET, each string object is an *immutable* sequence of Unicode characters. In other words, methods that appear to change the string actually return a modified copy; the original string remains intact.

The declaration of the System.String class is (in part):

```
public sealed class String :
   IComparable, ICloneable, IConvertible, IEnumerable
```

This declaration reveals that the class is sealed, meaning that it is not possible to derive from the String class. The class also implements four system interfaces—IComparable, ICloneable, IConvertible, and IEnumerable—which dictate functionality that System.String shares with other classes in the .NET Framework: the ability to be sorted, copied, converted to other types, and enumerated in foreach loops, respectively.

String Literals

The most common way to create a string is to assign a quoted string of characters, known as a *string literal*, to a user-defined variable of type string. The following code declares a string called newString that contains the phrase "This book teaches C#":

```
string newString = "This book teaches C#";
```

To be precise, newString is a string object that is initialized with the string literal "This book teaches C#". If you pass newString to the WriteLine method of the Console object, the string "This book teaches C#" will be displayed.

Escape Characters

Quoted strings can include *escape characters* (often referred to as "escape sequences"). Escape characters are a way to signal that the letters or characters that follow have a special meaning (for example, the two characters \n do not mean print a slash and then an *n*, but rather print a newline). You indicate escape characters by preceding a letter or punctuation mark with a backslash (\). The two most common escape characters are \n, which is used to create a newline, and \t, which is used to insert a tab into a string. If you need to include a quotation mark (") within a string, you indicate that the quote mark is part of the string (rather than ending the string) by escaping it:

```
Console.Writeline("This \"string\" has quotes around it");
```

This will produce the output: This "string" has quotes around it.

If you want to display the backslash character itself, you must escape it with (you guessed it) another backslash. Thus, if you were writing the string c:\myDirectory, you'd write:

```
"c:\\myDirectory"
```

Verbatim Strings

Strings can also be created using *verbatim string literals*, which start with the "at" (@) symbol. This tells the String constructor that the string should be used *as is* (verbatim), even if it spans multiple lines or includes escape characters. In a verbatim string literal, backslashes and the characters that follow them are simply considered additional characters of the string. Thus, the following two definitions are equivalent:

```
string s1 = "My \'favorite\' book is in the directory \\books";
string s2 = @"My 'favorite' book is in the directory \books";
```

In s1, a nonverbatim string literal is used, and so the quote and backslash characters must be *escaped* (preceded by a backslash character). The verbatim string s2 does not require the escape characters.

The following example illustrates two ways to specify multiline verbatim strings. The first definition uses a nonverbatim string with a newline escape character (\n) to signal the line break. The second definition uses a verbatim string literal:

```
string s3 = "Line One\nLine Two";
string s4 = @"Line One
Line Two";
```

If you want to use quotation marks in a verbatim string literal, you use two quotation marks, like this:

```
string s5 = @"This string has ""quotation marks"" in it.";
```

Again, these declarations are interchangeable. Which one you use is a matter of convenience and personal style.

The ToString( ) Method

Another common way to create a string is to call the ToString( ) method on an object and assign the result to a string variable. All the built-in types override this method to simplify the task of converting a value (often a numeric value) to a string representation of that value. In the following example, the ToString( ) method of an integer type is called to store its value in a string:

```
int myInteger = 5;
string integerString = myInteger.ToString( );
```

The call to myInteger.ToString( ) returns a string object that is then assigned to the string variable, integerString.

Manipulating Strings

The String class provides a host of methods for comparing, searching, and manipulating strings, the most important of which are shown in Table 15-1.

Table 15-1. String class properties and methods

Method or property	Explanation
Chars	Property that returns the string indexer
Compare( )	Overloaded public static method that compares two strings
Copy( )	Public static method that creates a new string by copying another
Equals( )	Overloaded public static and instance methods that determine whether two strings have the same value
Format( )	Overloaded public static method that formats a string using a format specification
Length	Property that returns the number of characters in the instance
PadLeft( )	Right-aligns the characters in the string, padding to the left with spaces or a specified character
PadRight( )	Left-aligns the characters in the string, padding to the right with spaces or a specified character
Remove( )	Deletes the specified number of characters
Split( )	Divides a string, returning the substrings delimited by the specified characters
StartsWith( )	Indicates whether the string starts with the specified characters
Substring( )	Retrieves a substring
ToCharArray( )	Copies the characters from the string to a character array
ToLower( )	Returns a copy of the string in lowercase
ToUpper( )	Returns a copy of the string in uppercase
Trim( )	Removes all occurrences of a set of specified characters from the beginning and end of the string
TrimEnd( )	Behaves like Trim( ), but only at the end of the string
TrimStart( )	Behaves like Trim( ), but only at the start of the string

Comparing Strings

The Compare( ) method of String is overloaded. The first version takes two strings and returns a negative number if the first string is alphabetically before the second, a positive number if the first string is alphabetically after the second, and zero if they are equal. The second version works just like the first but is case-insensitive. Example 15-1 illustrates the use of Compare( ).

Example 15-1. The Compare() method for the String class has two versions, one case-sensitive and the other not

```
using System;
using System.Collections.Generic;
using System.Linq;
using System.Text;
```

Example 15-1. The Compare() method for the String class has two versions, one case-sensitive and the other not (continued)

```
namespace Example_15_1____Comparing_Strings
{
    class Tester
    {
        public void Run()
        {
            // create some strings to work with
            string s1 = "abcd";
            string s2 = "ABCD";
            int result; // hold the results of comparisons

            // compare two strings, case-sensitive
            result = string.Compare(s1, s2);
            Console.WriteLine("Compare s1: {0}, s2: {1},
                            result: {2}\n", s1, s2, result);

            // overloaded compare, takes Boolean "ignore case"
            //(true = ignore case)
            result = string.Compare(s1, s2, true);
            Console.WriteLine("Compare insensitive.
                            result: {0}\n", result);
        }

        static void Main()
        {
            Tester t = new Tester();
            t.Run();
        }
    }
}
```

The output looks like this:

```
Compare s1: abcd, s2: ABCD, result: -1
Compare insensitive. result: 0
```

Example 15-1 begins by declaring two strings, s1 and s2, and initializing them with string literals:

```
string s1 = "abcd";
string s2 = "ABCD";
```

Compare() is used with many types. A negative return value indicates that the first parameter is less than the second; a positive result indicates that the first parameter is greater than the second; and a zero indicates that they are equal. In Unicode (as in ASCII), a lowercase letter has a smaller value than an uppercase letter; with strings that are identical except for case, lowercase comes first alphabetically. Thus, the output properly indicates that s1 (abcd) is "less than" s2 (ABCD):

```
compare s1: abcd, s2: ABCD, result: -1
```

The second comparison uses an overloaded version of Compare( ), which takes a third Boolean parameter, the value of which determines whether case should be ignored in the comparison. If the value of this "ignore case" parameter is true, the comparison is made without regard to case. This time the result is 0, indicating that the two strings are identical:

```
Compare insensitive. result: 0
```

Concatenating Strings

There are a couple of ways to concatenate strings in C#. You can use the Concat( ) method, which is a static public method of the String class:

```
string s3 = string.Concat(s1,s2);
```

Or you can simply use the overloaded concatenation (+) operator:

```
string s4 = s1 + s2;
```

Example 15-2 demonstrates both of these methods.

Example 15-2. Concatenating strings is amazingly easy—just use the overloaded + operator

```
using System;
using System.Collections.Generic;
using System.Linq;
using System.Text;

namespace Example_15_2____Concatenating_Strings
{
    class Tester
    {
        public void Run( )
        {
            string s1 = "abcd";
            string s2 = "ABCD";

            // concatenation method
            string s3 = string.Concat(s1, s2);
            Console.WriteLine("s3 concatenated from
                            s1 and s2: {0}", s3);

            // use the overloaded operator
            string s4 = s1 + s2;
            Console.WriteLine("s4 concatenated from
                            s1 + s2: {0}", s4);
        }

        static void Main( )
        {
            Tester t = new Tester( );
            t.Run( );
        }
```

*Example 15-2. Concatenating strings is amazingly easy—just use the overloaded
+ operator (continued)*

```
        }
}
```

The output looks like this:

```
s3 concatenated from s1 and s2: abcdABCD
s4 concatenated from s1 + s2: abcdABCD
```

In Example 15-2, the new string s3 is created by calling the static Concat( ) method
and passing in s1 and s2, and the string s4 is created by using the overloaded concatenation operator (+) that concatenates two strings and returns a string as a result.

Copying Strings

There are two ways to copy strings; 99.9% of the time you will just write:

```
oneString = theOtherString;
```

and not worry about what is going on in memory.

There is a second, somewhat awkward way to copy strings:

```
myString = String.Copy(yourString);
```

and this actually does something subtly different. The difference is somewhat
advanced, but here it is in a nutshell.

When you use the assignment operator (=) you create a second reference to the same
object in memory, but when you use Copy you create a new string that is initialized
with the value of the first string, and then create a reference to that new string.

"Huh?" we hear you cry. Example 15-3 will make it clear.

*Example 15-3. You'll usually copy strings with the assignment operator, but the String.Copy()
method has a subtle difference*

```
using System;
using System.Collections.Generic;
using System.Linq;
using System.Text;

namespace Example_15_3____Copying_Strings
{
    class Tester
    {
        public void Run( )
        {
            string s1 = "abcd";

            Console.WriteLine("string s1: {0}", s1);
            Console.WriteLine("string s2 = s1; ");
```

Example 15-3. You'll usually copy strings with the assignment operator, but the String.Copy()
method has a subtle difference (continued)

```
        string s2 = s1;
        Console.WriteLine("s1: {0} s2: {1}", s1, s2);
        Console.WriteLine("s1 == s2? {0}", s1 == s2);
        Console.WriteLine("ReferenceEquals(s1,s2): {0}",
                            ReferenceEquals(s1, s2));
        Console.WriteLine(" \nstring s2 = string.Copy( s1 ); ");

        string s3 = string.Copy(s1);
        Console.WriteLine("s1: {0} s3: {1}", s1, s3);
        Console.WriteLine("s1 == s3? {0}", s1 == s3);
        Console.WriteLine("ReferenceEquals(s1,s3): {0}",
                            ReferenceEquals(s1, s3));
        Console.WriteLine(" \ns2 = \"Hello\"; ");

        s1 = "Hello";
        Console.WriteLine("s1: {0} s2: {1}", s1, s2);
        Console.WriteLine("s1 == s2? {0}", s1 == s2);
        Console.WriteLine("ReferenceEquals(s1,s2): {0}",
                            ReferenceEquals(s1, s2));
    }

    static void Main()
    {
        Tester t = new Tester();
        t.Run();
    }
  }
}
```

The output looks like this:

```
string s1: abcd
string s2 = s1;
s1: abcd s2: abcd
s1 == s2? True
ReferenceEquals(s1,s2): True

string s2 = string.Copy( s1 );
s1: abcd s3: abcd
s1 == s3? True
ReferenceEquals(s1,s3): False

s1 = "Hello";
s1: Hello s2: abcd
s1 == s2? False
ReferenceEquals(s1,s2): False
```

In Example 15-3, you start by initializing one string:

```
string s1 = "abcd";
```

You then assign the value of s1 to s2 using the assignment operator:

```
s2 = s1;
```

You print their values, as shown in the first section of results, and find that not only do the two string references have the same value, as indicated by using the equality operator (==), but also that ReferenceEquals returns true as well. ReferenceEquals is a static method that returns true when the two objects passed in are the same instance. Therefore, the two references refer to the same object.

On the other hand, if you create s3 and assign its value using String.Copy(s1), although the two values are equal (as shown by using the equality operator) they refer to different objects in memory (as shown by the fact that ReferenceEquals returns false).

Now, returning to s1 and s2, which refer to the same object, if you change either one, for example, when you write:

```
s1 = "Hello";
```

s3 goes on referring to the original string, but s1 now refers to a brand-new string.

If you later write:

```
S3 = "Goodbye";
```

(not shown in the example), the original string referred to by s1 will no longer have any references to it, and it will be mercifully and painlessly destroyed by the garbage collector.

Testing for Equality

The .NET String class provides three ways to test for the equality of two strings. First, you can use the overloaded Equals() method and ask one string (say, s6) directly whether another string (s5) is of equal value:

```
Console.WriteLine( "\nDoes s6.Equals(s5)?: {0}", s6.Equals(s5));
```

You can also pass both strings to String's static method, Equals():

```
Console.WriteLine( "Does Equals(s6,s5)?: {0}" string.Equals(s6,s5));
```

Or you can use the String class's overloaded equality operator (==):

```
Console.WriteLine( "Does s6==s5?: {0}", s6 == s5);
```

In each of these cases, the returned result is a Boolean value (true for equal and false for unequal). Example 15-4 demonstrates these techniques.

Example 15-4. You can test strings for equality using the Equals() method, or the overloaded == operator

```
using System;
using System.Collections.Generic;
using System.Linq;
```

Example 15-4. You can test strings for equality using the Equals() method, or the overloaded ==
operator (continued)

```
using System.Text;

namespace Example_15_4____String_Equality
{
    class Tester
    {
        public void Run( )
        {
            string s1 = "abcd";
            string s2 = "ABCD";

            // the string copy method
            string s5 = string.Copy(s2);
            Console.WriteLine("s5 copied from s2: {0}", s5);
            string s6 = s5;
            Console.WriteLine("s6 = s5: {0}", s6);

            // member method
            Console.WriteLine("\nDoes s6.Equals(s5)?: {0}",
            s6.Equals(s5));

            // static method
            Console.WriteLine("Does Equals(s6,s5)?: {0}",
            string.Equals(s6, s5));

            // overloaded operator
            Console.WriteLine("Does s6==s5?: {0}", s6 == s5);
        }

        static void Main( )
        {
            Tester t = new Tester( );
            t.Run( );
        }
    }
}
```

The output looks like this:

```
s5 copied from s2: ABCD
s6 = s5: ABCD
 Does s6.Equals(s5)?: True
Does Equals(s6,s5)?: True
Does s6==s5?: True
```

The equality operator is the most natural of the three methods to use when you have
two string objects.

Other Useful String Methods

The String class includes a number of useful methods and properties for finding specific characters or substrings within a string, as well as for manipulating the contents of the string. Example 15-5 demonstrates a few methods, such as locating substrings, finding the index of a substring, and inserting text from one string into another. Following the output is a complete analysis.

Example 15-5. The String class has several useful methods, including Length, EndsWith(), and Index

```
using System;
using System.Collections.Generic;
using System.Linq;
using System.Text;

namespace Example_15_5____String_Methods
{
    class Tester
    {
        public void Run()
        {
            string s1 = "abcd";
            string s2 = "ABCD";
            string s3 = @"Liberty Associates, Inc.
 provides custom .NET development,
 on-site Training and Consulting";

            // the string copy method
            string s5 = string.Copy(s2);
            Console.WriteLine("s5 copied from s2: {0}", s5);

            // Two useful properties: the index and the length
            Console.WriteLine("\nString s3 is {0} characters long. ", s3.Length);
            Console.WriteLine("The 5th character is {0}\n", s3[4]);

            // test whether a string ends with a set of characters
            Console.WriteLine("s3:{0}\nEnds with Training?: {1}\n", s3,
                        s3.EndsWith("Training"));
            Console.WriteLine("Ends with Consulting?: {0}",
                        s3.EndsWith("Consulting"));

            // return the index of the substring
            Console.WriteLine("\nThe first occurrence of Training ");
            Console.WriteLine("in s3 is {0}\n", s3.IndexOf("Training"));

            // insert the word "excellent" before "training"
            string s10 = s3.Insert(71, "excellent ");
            Console.WriteLine("s10: {0}\n", s10);
```

```
            // you can combine the two as follows:
            string s11 = s3.Insert(s3.IndexOf("Training"), "excellent ");
            Console.WriteLine("s11: {0}\n", s11);
        }
        static void Main()
        {
            Tester t = new Tester();
            t.Run();
        }
    }
}
```

The output looks like this:

```
s5 copied from s2: ABCD

String s3 is 94 characters long.
The 5th character is r

s3:Liberty Associates, Inc.
 provides custom .NET development,
 on-site Training and Consulting
Ends with Training?: False

Ends with Consulting?: True

The first occurrence of Training
in s3 is 71

s10: Liberty Associates, Inc.
 provides custom .NET development,
 on-site excellent Training and Consulting

s11: Liberty Associates, Inc.
 provides custom .NET development,
 on-site excellent Training and Consulting
```

The Length property returns the length of the entire string, and the index operator ([]) is used to access a particular character within a string. Just like arrays, the index numbering in a string starts at zero.

```
Console.WriteLine(
"\nString s3 is {0} characters long. ",
s5.Length);
Console.WriteLine(
"The 5th character is {0}\n", s3[4]);
```

Here's the output:

```
String s3 is 4 characters long.
The 5th character is r
```

The EndsWith( ) method asks a string whether a substring is found at the end of the string. Thus, you might first ask whether s3 ends with the word *Training* (which it does not), and then whether it ends with the word *Consulting* (which it does):

```
Console.WriteLine("s3:{0}\nEnds with Training?: {1}\n",
 s3,
 s3.EndsWith("Training") );
Console.WriteLine(
 "Ends with Consulting?: {0}",
 s3.EndsWith("Consulting"));
```

The output reflects that the first test fails and the second succeeds:

```
Ends with Training?: False
Ends with Consulting?: True
```

The IndexOf( ) method locates a substring within a string, and the Insert( ) method inserts a new substring into a copy of the original string. The following code locates the first occurrence of *Training* in s3:

```
Console.WriteLine("\nThe first occurrence of Training ");
Console.WriteLine ("in s3 is {0}\n",
 s3.IndexOf("Training"));
```

The output indicates that the offset is 71:

```
The first occurrence of Training
in s3 is 71
```

Then use that value to insert the word *excellent*, followed by a space, into that string.

Actually, the insertion is into a copy of the string returned by the Insert( ) method and assigned to s10:

```
string s10 = s3.Insert(71,"excellent ");
Console.WriteLine("s10: {0}\n",s10);
```

Here's the output:

```
s10: Liberty Associates, Inc.
 provides custom .NET development,
 on-site excellent Training and Consulting
```

Finally, you can combine these operations to make a more efficient insertion statement:

```
string s11 = s3.Insert(s3.IndexOf("Training"),"excellent ");
Console.WriteLine("s11: {0}\n",s11);
```

with the identical result:

```
s11: Liberty Associates, Inc.
 provides custom .NET development,
 on-site excellent Training and Consulting
```

Finding Substrings

The String class has methods for finding and extracting substrings. For example, the IndexOf( ) method returns the index of the *first* occurrence of a string (or of any character in an array of characters) within a target string. For example, given the definition of the string s1 as:

```
string s1 = "One Two Three Four";
```

you can find the first instance of the characters *hre* by writing:

```
int index = s1.IndexOf("hre");
```

This code sets the int variable index to 9, which is the offset of the letters *hre* in the string s1.

Similarly, the LastIndexOf( ) method returns the index of the *last* occurrence of a string or substring.

Though the following code:

```
s1.IndexOf("o");
```

returns the value 6 (the first occurrence of the lowercase letter *o* is at the end of the word *Two*), the method call:

```
s1.LastIndexOf("o");
```

returns the value 15 (the last occurrence of *o* is in the word *Four*).

The Substring( ) method returns a contiguous series of characters. You can ask it for all the characters starting at a particular offset and ending either with the end of the string or with an offset that you (optionally) provide. Example 15-6 illustrates the Substring( ) method.

Example 15-6. You use the Substring() method to pull substrings out of a string by index

```
using System;
using System.Collections.Generic;
using System.Linq;
using System.Text;

namespace Example_15_6____Finding_Substrings
{
    class Tester
    {
        public void Run()
        {
            // create some strings to work with
            string s1 = "One Two Three Four";

            int index;

            // get the index of the last space
            index = s1.LastIndexOf(" ");
```

```
            // get the last word.
            string s2 = s1.Substring(index + 1);

            // set s1 to the substring starting at 0
            // and ending at index (the start of the last word)
            // thus s1 has "one two three"
            s1 = s1.Substring(0, index);

            // find the last space in s1 (after two)
            index = s1.LastIndexOf(" ");

            // set s3 to the substring starting at
            // index, the space after "two" plus one more
            // thus s3 = "three"
            string s3 = s1.Substring(index + 1);
            // reset s1 to the substring starting at 0
            // and ending at index, thus the string "one two"
            s1 = s1.Substring(0, index);

            // reset index to the space between
            // "one" and "two"
            index = s1.LastIndexOf(" ");

            // set s4 to the substring starting one
            // space after index, thus the substring "two"
            string s4 = s1.Substring(index + 1);

            // reset s1 to the substring starting at 0
            // and ending at index, thus "one"
            s1 = s1.Substring(0, index);

            // set index to the last space, but there is
            // none so index now = -1
            index = s1.LastIndexOf(" ");

            // set s5 to the substring at one past
            // the last space. there was no last space
            // so this sets s5 to the substring starting
            // at zero
            string s5 = s1.Substring(index + 1);

            Console.WriteLine("s2: {0}\ns3: {1}", s2, s3);
            Console.WriteLine("s4: {0}\ns5: {1}\n", s4, s5);
            Console.WriteLine("s1: {0}\n", s1);
        }

        static void Main( )
        {
            Tester t = new Tester( );
            t.Run( );
        }
    }
}
```

The output looks like this:

```
s2: Four
s3: Three
s4: Two
s5: One

s1: One
```

Example 15-6 is not the most elegant solution possible to the problem of extracting words from a string, but it is a good first approximation, and it illustrates a useful technique. The example begins by creating a string, s1:

```
string s1 = "One Two Three Four";
```

The local variable index is assigned the value of the last literal space in the string (which comes before the word *Four*):

```
index=s1.LastIndexOf(" ");
```

The substring that begins one position later is assigned to the new string, s2:

```
string s2 = s1.Substring(index+1);
```

This extracts the characters from index+1 to the end of the line (the string "Four") and assigns the value "Four" to s2.

The next step is to remove the word *Four* from s1; assign to s1 the substring of s1 that begins at 0 and ends at the index:

```
s1 = s1.Substring(0,index);
```

 After this line executes, the variable s1 will point to a new string object that will contain the appropriate substring of the string that s1 used to point to. That original string will eventually be destroyed by the garbage collector because no variable now references it.

You reassign index to the last (remaining) space, which points you to the beginning of the word *Three*. You then extract the word *Three* into string s3. Continue like this until you've populated s4 and s5. Finally, display the results:

```
s2: Four
s3: Three
s4: Two
s5: One
s1: One
```

Splitting Strings

A more effective solution to the problem illustrated in Example 15-6 would be to use the String class's Split() method, which parses a string into substrings. To use Split(), pass in an array of *delimiters* (characters that indicate where to divide the words). The method returns an array of substrings (which Example 15-7 illustrates). The complete analysis follows the code.

Example 15-7. The Split() method returns an array of substrings, based on delimiters that you define

```csharp
using System;
using System.Collections.Generic;
using System.Linq;
using System.Text;

namespace Example_15_7____Splitting_Strings
{
    class Tester
    {
        public void Run()
        {
            // create some strings to work with
            string s1 = "One,Two,Three Liberty Associates, Inc.";
            // constants for the space and comma characters
            const char Space = ' ';
            const char Comma = ',';

            // array of delimiters to split the sentence with
            char[] delimiters = new char[]
            {
                Space,
                Comma
            };

            int ctr = 1;

            // split the string and then iterate over the
            // resulting array of strings

            String[] resultArray = s1.Split(delimiters);

            foreach (String subString in resultArray)
            {
                Console.WriteLine(ctr++ + ":" + subString);
            }
        }

        static void Main()
        {
            Tester t = new Tester();
            t.Run();
        }
    }
}
```

The output looks like this:

```
1: One
2: Two
3: Three
4: Liberty
5: Associates
```

```
6:
7: Inc.
```

Example 15-7 starts by creating a string to parse:

```
string s1 = "One,Two,Three Liberty Associates, Inc.";
```

The delimiters are set to the space and comma characters. Then call Split( ) on the string, passing in the delimiters:

```
String[] resultArray = s1.Split(delimiters);
```

Split( ) returns an array of the substrings that you can then iterate over using the foreach loop, as explained in Chapter 10:

```
foreach (String subString in resultArray)
```

 You can, of course, combine the call to split with the iteration, as in the following:

```
foreach (string subString in s1.Split(delimiters))
```

C# programmers are fond of combining statements like this. The advantage of splitting the statement into two, however, and of using an interim variable like resultArray is that you can examine the contents of resultArray in the debugger.

Start the foreach loop by initializing output to an empty string, and then create each line of the output in three steps. Start with the incremented value ctr. Then use the += operator to add the colon, then the substring returned by Split( ):

```
Console.WriteLine(ctr++ + ":" + subString);
```

With each concatenation, a new copy of the string is made, and all three steps are repeated for each substring found by Split( ).

This repeated copying of the string is terribly inefficient. The problem is that the string type is not designed for this kind of operation. What you want is to create a new string by appending a formatted string each time through the loop. The class you need is StringBuilder.

The StringBuilder Class

You can use the System.Text.StringBuilder class for creating and modifying strings. Table 15-2 summarizes the important members of StringBuilder.

Table 15-2. StringBuilder members

Method or property	Explanation
Append( )	Overloaded public method that appends a typed object to the end of the current StringBuilder
AppendFormat( )	Overloaded public method that replaces format specifiers with the formatted value of an object

Table 15-2. StringBuilder members (continued)

Method or property	Explanation
EnsureCapacity( )	Ensures that the current StringBuilder has a capacity at least as large as the specified value
Capacity	Property that retrieves or assigns the number of characters the StringBuilder is capable of holding
Insert( )	Overloaded public method that inserts an object at the specified position
Length	Property that retrieves or assigns the length of the StringBuilder
MaxCapacity	Property that retrieves the maximum capacity of the StringBuilder
Remove( )	Removes the specified range of characters
Replace( )	Overloaded public method that replaces all instances of the specified characters with new characters

Unlike String, StringBuilder is mutable; when you modify an instance of the StringBuilder class, you modify the actual string, not a copy.

Example 15-8 replaces the String object in Example 15-7 with a StringBuilder object.

Example 15-8. Unlike the String class, the StringBuilder class can be modified instead of copied, which is more efficient

```
using System;
using System.Collections.Generic;
using System.Linq;
using System.Text;

namespace Example_15_8____StringBuilder
{
    class Tester
    {
        public void Run( )
        {
            // create some strings to work with
            string s1 = "One,Two,Three Liberty Associates, Inc.";

            // constants for the space and comma characters
            const char Space = ' ';
            const char Comma = ',';

            // array of delimiters to split the sentence with
            char[] delimiters = new char[]
            {
                Space,
                Comma
            };

            // use a StringBuilder class to build the
            // output string
```

```
        StringBuilder output = new StringBuilder( );
        int ctr = 1;

        // split the string and then iterate over the
        // resulting array of strings
        foreach (string subString in s1.Split(delimiters))
        {
            // AppendFormat appends a formatted string
            output.AppendFormat("{0}: {1}\n", ctr++, subString);
        }
        Console.WriteLine(output);

    }
    static void Main( )
    {
        Tester t = new Tester( );
        t.Run( );
    }
  }
}
```

Only the last part of the program is modified. Rather than using the concatenation operator to modify the string, use the `AppendFormat( )` method of `StringBuilder` to append new formatted strings as you create them. This is much easier and far more efficient. The output is identical:

```
1: One
2: Two
3: Three
4: Liberty
5: Associates
6:
7: Inc.
```

Because you passed in delimiters of both comma and space, the space after the comma between *Associates* and *Inc.* is returned as a word, numbered 6 in the preceding code. That is not what you want. To eliminate this, you need to tell `Split( )` to match a comma (as between *One*, *Two*, and *Three*), a space (as between *Liberty* and *Associates*), or a comma followed by a space. It is that last bit that is tricky and requires that you use a regular expression.

Regular Expressions

As noted earlier, regular expressions provide a very powerful way to describe and manipulate text through pattern matching.

The result of applying a regular expression to a string is either to return a substring or to return a new string representing a modification of some part of the original string. (Remember that string objects are immutable and so cannot be changed by the regular expression.)

By applying a properly constructed regular expression to the following string:

```
One,Two,Three Liberty Associates, Inc.
```

you can return any or all of its substrings (such as "Liberty" or "One") or modified versions of its substrings (such as "LIBeRtY" or "OnE"). What the regular expression does is determined by the syntax of the regular expression itself.

A regular expression consists of two types of characters: *literals* and *metacharacters*. A literal is a character you want to match in the target string. A metacharacter is a special symbol that acts as a command to the regular expression parser. The parser is the engine responsible for understanding the regular expression. For example, if you create a regular expression:

```
^(From|To|Subject|Date):
```

this will match any of the following substrings: *From*, *To*, *Subject*, or *Date*, as long as the substring starts a new line (^) and ends with a colon (:).

The caret (^) indicates to the regular expression parser that the string you're searching for must begin a new line. The substrings *From* and *To* are literals, and the metacharacters left and right parentheses ((,)) and vertical bar (|) are all used to group sets of literals and indicate that any of the choices should match. Thus, you would read the following line as "match any string that begins a new line, followed by any of the four literal strings From, To, Subject, or Date, and followed by a colon":

```
^(From|To|Subject|Date):
```

 A full explanation of regular expressions is beyond the scope of this book, but we will explain all the regular expressions that we use in the examples. For a complete understanding of regular expressions, we recommend *Mastering Regular Expressions*, Third Edition, by Jeffrey E. F. Friedl (O'Reilly).

The Regex Class

The .NET Framework provides an object-oriented approach to regular expression pattern matching and replacement.

The Framework Class Library (FCL) namespace System.Text.RegularExpressions is the home to all the .NET Framework objects associated with regular expressions. The central class for regular expression support is Regex, which provides methods and properties for working with regular expressions, the most important of which are shown in Table 15-3.

Table 15-3. Regex members

Method or property	Explanation
Regex constructor	Overloaded; creates an instance of Regex
Options	Property that returns the options passed in to the constructor
IsMatch	Method that indicates whether a match is found in the input string
Match	Searches an input string and returns a match for a regular expression
Matches	Searches an input string and returns all successful matches for a regular expression
Replace	Replaces all occurrences of a pattern with a replacement string
Split	Splits an input string into an array of substrings based on a regular expression

Example 15-9 rewrites Example 15-8 to use regular expressions and thus to solve the problem of searching for more than one type of delimiter.

Example 15-9. Regular expressions are indispensable for matching patterns in text

```
using System;
using System.Collections.Generic;
using System.Linq;
using System.Text;
using System.Text.RegularExpressions;

namespace Example_15_9____Regular_Expressions
{
    class Tester
    {
        public void Run()
        {
            string s1 =
            "One,Two,Three Liberty Associates, Inc.";
            Regex theRegex = new Regex(" |, |,");
            StringBuilder sBuilder = new StringBuilder();
            int id = 1;

            foreach (string subString in theRegex.Split(s1))
            {
                sBuilder.AppendFormat("{0}: {1}\n", id++, subString);
            }
            Console.WriteLine("{0}", sBuilder);
        }

        static void Main()
        {
            Tester t = new Tester();
            t.Run();
        }
    }
}
```

The output looks like this:

```
1: One
2: Two
3: Three
4: Liberty
5: Associates
6: Inc.
```

Example 15-9 begins by creating a string, s1, identical to the string used in Example 15-8:

```
string s1 = "One,Two,Three Liberty Associates, Inc.";
```

and a regular expression that is used to search the string:

```
Regex theRegex = new Regex(" |,|, ");
```

One of the overloaded constructors for Regex takes a regular expression string as its parameter.

 This can be a bit confusing. In the context of a C# program, which is the regular expression—the text passed in to the constructor or the Regex object itself? It is true that the text string passed to the constructor is a regular expression in the traditional sense of the term. From a C# (that is, object-oriented) point of view, however, the argument to the constructor is just a string of characters; it is the object called theRegex that is the regular expression object.

The rest of the program proceeds like Example 15-8, except that rather than calling the Split( ) method of String on string s1, the Split( ) method of Regex is called. theRegex.Split( ) acts in much the same way as String.Split( ), returning an array of strings as a result of matching the regular expression pattern within theRegex. Because it matches a regular expression, rather than using a set of delimiters, you have much greater control over how the string is split.

Summary

- C# strings can be sorted, searched, and otherwise manipulated.
- The String class is sealed, meaning it cannot be derived from. It implements the IComparable, ICloneable, IConvertible, and IEnumerable interfaces, indicating that you can compare two strings (to sort them), clone a string (to create a duplicate), convert a string to another type (for example, converting the string "15" to the integer 15), and enumerate over a string using a foreach statement, respectively.
- A string literal is a quoted string of characters assigned to a variable of type string. This is the most common use of strings.
- Escape characters allow you to add special characters to strings that you would otherwise not be able to represent.

- A verbatim string literal starts with an @ symbol and indicates that the string should be used exactly as is. Verbatim strings do not require escape characters.

- You can concatenate strings with the Concat( ) method or the + operator.

- You can copy strings with the Copy( ) method or the = operator.

- You can test for equality of two strings with the Equals( ) method or the == operator.

- The String class also includes methods for finding and extracting substrings, such as IndexOf( ), LastIndexOf( ), and Substring( ).

- You can use the Split( ) method with an array of delimiters to divide a string into substrings.

- Strings are immutable. Every time you appear to modify a string, a copy is made with the modification and the original string is released to the garbage collector.

- The StringBuilder class allows you to assemble the contents of a string with greater efficiency and then to call its ToString( ) method to generate the string you need once it is fully assembled.

- Regular expressions provide pattern-matching abilities that enable you to search and manipulate text.

Although you've seen and used strings throughout this book, this chapter should give you an indication of just how powerful and flexible the String class is. However, now that you have the ability to let users enter strings instead of just integers or single characters, you open yourself up to the possibility that your users could provide some input that you can't handle. The more you interact with users, the greater the odds that they'll do something you didn't expect, and that could break your code. Fortunately, that doesn't have to be a disaster. C# provides an Exception class that allows you to anticipate certain types of errors, and take the appropriate action when they occur.

Test Your Knowledge: Quiz

Question 15-1. What is the difference between string and String (lower- and uppercase)?

Question 15-2. Some of the interfaces implemented by the string are IComparable, ICloneable, IConvertible, and IEnumerable. What do these guarantee to you as a client of the String class?

Question 15-3. What is a string literal?

Question 15-4. What is the purpose of escape characters? Give two examples.

Question 15-5. What are verbatim strings?

Question 15-6. What does it mean that strings are immutable?

Question 15-7. What are the two ways to concatenate strings?

Question 15-8. What does Split( ) do?

Question 15-9. Why would you use the StringBuilder class instead of a string, and how do you create a string with one?

Question 15-10. What are regular expressions?

Test Your Knowledge: Exercises

Exercise 15-1. Create the following six strings:

- String 1: "Hello "
- String 2: "World"
- String 3 (a verbatim string): "Come visit us at *http://www.LibertyAssociates.com*"
- String 4: a concatenation of strings 1 and 2
- String 5: "world"
- String 6: a copy of string 3

Once you have the strings created, do the following:

1. Output the length of each string.
2. Output the third character in each string.
3. Output whether the character *H* appears in each string.
4. Output which strings are the same as string 2.
5. Output which strings are the same as string 2, ignoring case.

Exercise 15-2. Take the following famous string:

To be, or not to be: That is the question: Whether 'tis nobler in the mind to suffer the slings and arrows of outrageous fortune, or to take arms against a sea of troubles, and by opposing end them?

Reverse the order of the words in the string, and output the reversed string to the console.

Exercise 15-3. Take the following famous string:

> We choose to go to the moon. We choose to go to the moon in this decade and do the other things, not because they are easy, but because they are hard, because that goal will serve to organize and measure the best of our energies and skills, because that challenge is one that we are willing to accept, one we are unwilling to postpone, and one which we intend to win, and the others, too.

Write a program to determine and output to the screen the number of times the word *the* occurs in the string.

Exercise 15-4. Take the following string:

> We hold these truths to be self-evident, that all men are created equal, that they are endowed by their Creator with certain unalienable Rights, that among these are Life, Liberty and the pursuit of Happiness.

and use a regular expression to split the string into words. Then create a new string that lists each word, one to a line, each prefaced with a line number.

CHAPTER 16

Throwing and Catching Exceptions

Things go wrong. Programmers always need to plan for the inevitable problems that arise while their program is running: networks go down, disks fail, computers exhaust their memory, and so forth.

In C#, you address these problems with *exceptions*. An exception is an object that contains information about an unusual program occurrence. When an exceptional circumstance arises, an exception is "thrown." (You'll also hear that an exception is *raised*.) You might throw an exception in your own methods (for example, if you realize that an invalid parameter has been provided), or an exception might be thrown in a class provided by the Framework Class Library, or FCL (for example, if you try to write to a read-only file). Many exceptions are thrown by the .NET runtime when the program can no longer continue due to an operating system problem (such as a security violation).

Your job as programmer is to *try* potentially dangerous code—that is, to mark out code that might throw an exception. If an exception is thrown, you *catch* the exception by writing appropriate code in your "catch block." Both try and catch are keywords in C#. Catching an exception is sometimes referred to as *handling* the exception, and the catch block is often called an *exception handler*.

Ideally, you can provide some code in the catch block so that when the exception is caught, the program can fix the problem and continue. Even if your program can't continue, by catching the exception you have an opportunity to print a meaningful error message and terminate gracefully—that is, your program ends and tells the user what happened and why, instead of simply crashing.

This chapter describes how to write your programs to catch and handle exceptions. This chapter also shows you how to use the properties of the Exception class to provide information to the user about what went wrong, and it shows you how to create and use your own custom exception types.

Bugs, Errors, and Exceptions

It is important to distinguish exceptions from *bugs* and *errors*. A bug is a programmer mistake that should be fixed before the code is made available to users. An exception is usually not the result of a programmer mistake (though such mistakes can also raise exceptions). Rather, exceptions are raised as a result of problems that you can predict, but can't prevent, because they depend on factors outside your program. A network connection dropping suddenly, or running out of disk space, are both examples of exceptions that you can handle.

An error is caused by user action. For example, the user might enter a number where a letter is expected. Once again, an error might cause an exception, but you can prevent that by implementing code to validate user input. Whenever possible, you should anticipate user errors and write code to prevent them, instead of relying on exceptions.

Even if you remove all bugs and anticipate all user errors, you will still run into predictable but unpreventable problems, such as running out of memory or attempting to open a file that no longer exists. These are exceptions. You cannot prevent exceptions, but you can handle them so that they do not bring down your program.

Throwing Exceptions

As you'll see shortly, exceptions are objects provided by the .NET Framework. All exceptions are of type `System.Exception` or of types derived from `System.Exception`.

C# includes a number of predefined exception types that you can use in your own programs. (These are actually defined in the Base Class Library's `System` namespace, and are therefore available to all .NET languages, not just C#.) These exception types include `ArgumentNullException`, `InvalidCastException`, and `OverflowException`, as well as many others. Most of them have obvious purposes, based on their name. For example, `ArgumentNullException` is thrown when an argument to a method is null when that is not an expected (or acceptable) value.

Most of the time, the predefined exceptions will be all you need for your program, but you can define custom exceptions if you need them. Microsoft suggests that all the exceptions you use in your program derive from `System.Exception`.

Searching for an Exception Handler

When your program encounters an exceptional circumstance, such as running out of memory, it throws an exception, as we mentioned. Exceptions must be *handled* before the program can continue. As we discussed, the exception handler is a `catch` block located somewhere in your code. It can be located in the current method, or it can be somewhere else higher up the call stack (which we defined in Chapter 9).

Where the exception handler is located dictates what the program does after the exception is handled.

If the currently running method does not handle the exception, the current function terminates. Control returns to the calling function, which then gets a chance to handle the exception. If that calling function does not have an exception handler, the function that called that one gets a chance. This process is called *unwinding the stack*. If none of the calling functions handles the exception, including Main(), program control passes to the Common Language Runtime (CLR), which abruptly terminates your program—this is generally considered bad.

In other words, if method A calls method B, and method B calls method C, these method calls are all placed on the stack. When a programmer talks about "unwinding the stack," she means that you back up from C to B to A, as illustrated in Figure 16-1.

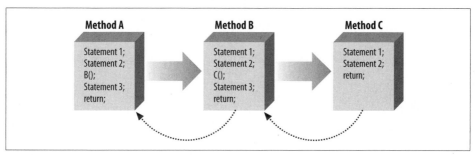

Figure 16-1. *You've seen the call stack in action in previous chapters. When an exception is thrown in method C, the program will unwind the stack until it finds an exception handler.*

The point to remember here is that if you must unwind the stack from C to B to A to handle the exception, when you are done, program control is in method A. You don't automatically return to C, and any code in C that wasn't executed may never be reached now. That's why it's a good idea to place your exception handlers as close as you can to the point where an exception is likely to be thrown, keeping in mind that you want to handle the exception at a point where you can take useful corrective action.

The throw Statement

Most of the time, the system generates exceptions for you. However, you can also generate your own exceptions, and that's useful for the purposes of demonstration in this chapter, so we'll show you how to do that first. To signal an abnormal condition in a C# program, you throw an exception by using the throw keyword. The following line of code creates a new instance of System.Exception and then throws it:

```
throw new System.Exception();
```

Remember that exceptions are objects in C#, not simply messages, so the throw statement here actually creates a new Exception object, which is why it looks like it's calling a constructor. Example 16-1 illustrates what happens if you throw an exception and there is no exception handler to catch and handle the exception. In this example, you'll throw an exception even though nothing has actually gone wrong, just to illustrate how an exception can bring your program to a halt.

Example 16-1. The unhandled exception in this example will crash your program, which is what you're trying to avoid

```
using System;
using System.Collections.Generic;
using System.Linq;
using System.Text;

namespace Example_16_1____Unhandled_Exception
{
    class Tester
    {
        public void Run( )
        {
            Console.WriteLine("Entering Run...");
            Method1( );
            Console.WriteLine("Exiting Run...");
        }

        public void Method1( )
        {
            Console.WriteLine("Entering Method1...");
            Method2( );
            Console.WriteLine("Exiting Method1...");
        }

        public void Method2( )
        {
            Console.WriteLine("Entering Method2...");
            throw new System.Exception( );
            // this next line can never execute
            Console.WriteLine("Exiting Method2...");
        }
        static void Main( )
        {
            Console.WriteLine("Entering Main...");
            Tester t = new Tester( );
            t.Run( );
            Console.WriteLine("Exiting Main...");
        }
    }
}
```

The output looks like this:

```
Entering Main...
Entering Run...
Entering Method1...
Entering Method2...

Unhandled Exception: System.Exception: Exception of type
'System.Exception' was thrown.
    at Example_16_1____Unhandled_Exception.Tester.Method2()
    in C:\Documents\Visual Studio 2008\Projects\Chapter 16\
    Example 16-1 -- Unhandled Exception\Example 16-1 -- Unhandled
    Exception\Program.cs:line 27
    at Example_16_1____Unhandled_Exception.Tester.Main()
    in C:Documents\Visual Studio 2008\Projects\Chapter 16\Example 16-1
    -- Unhandled Exception\Example 16-1 -- Unhandled Exception\
    Program.cs:line 35
```

If you're trying this example in Windows Vista, you won't see this output immediately. Instead, you'll see a dialog box telling you that the program has stopped working and that Windows is searching for a solution to the problem. It won't find one, so go ahead and click Cancel, and you'll see the error message.

When you run this code, you'll also receive a warning that the following line is unreachable:

```
Console.WriteLine( "Exiting Method2..." );
```

That's because the compiler can tell that there's no way this line will ever be reached. In this example, you can ignore the warning, but as noted earlier, you should usually try to write warning-free code.

This simple example writes to the console as it enters and exits each method. Main() calls Run(), which in turn calls Method1(). After printing out the "Entering Method1" message, Method1() immediately calls Method2(). Method2() prints out the first message and throws an object of type System.Exception.

Execution immediately stops, and the CLR looks to see whether there is a handler in Method2(). There is not, and so the runtime unwinds the stack (never printing the "exiting" statement) to Method1(). Again, there is no handler, and the runtime unwinds the stack back to Main(). With no exception handler there, the default handler is called, which prints the error message and terminates the program. Obviously, this isn't what you want your users to see.

The try and catch Statements

As you saw, the exception in your previous example stopped your program dead. That's usually not the desired behavior. What you need is a way to tell the compiler, "If any exceptions are thrown in this section of code, take this action." That way, your program can continue on from the error or at least end gracefully. This process is called *handling* the exception. To handle exceptions, take the following steps:

1. Execute any code that you suspect might throw an exception (such as code that opens a file or allocates memory) within a try block.

2. Catch any exceptions that are thrown in a catch block.

A try block is created using the keyword try and is enclosed in braces. You don't need any extra code to create the try block; it just indicates the area of code where you want to watch for exceptions. A catch block holds the code where you take action based on the type of exception thrown. It is created using the keyword catch and is also enclosed in braces. In the abstract, the try/catch block looks like this:

```
try
{
    // Potentially hazardous code goes here.
}
catch
{
    // Exception handler code goes here.
}
```

Example 16-2 illustrates these constructs. Note that Example 16-2 is identical to Example 16-1 except that now the program includes a try/catch block.

Example 16-2. The try and catch blocks in this example let you avoid the crash of the previous example

```
using System;
using System.Collections.Generic;
using System.Linq;
using System.Text;

namespace Example_16_2____try_and_catch_blocks
{
    class Tester
    {
        public void Run()
        {
            Console.WriteLine("Entering Run...");
            Method1();
            Console.WriteLine("Exiting Run...");
        }

        public void Method1()
        {
            Console.WriteLine("Entering Method1...");
            Method2();
            Console.WriteLine("Exiting Method1...");
        }

        public void Method2()
```

```
    {
        Console.WriteLine("Entering Method2...");
        try
        {
            Console.WriteLine("Entering try block...");
            throw new System.Exception();
            // this next line can never execute
            Console.WriteLine("Exiting try block...");
        }
        catch
        {
            Console.WriteLine("Exception caught and handled!");
        }
        Console.WriteLine("Exiting Method2...");

    }
    static void Main()
    {
        Console.WriteLine("Entering Main...");
        Tester t = new Tester();
        t.Run();
        Console.WriteLine("Exiting Main...");
    }
}
}
```

The output looks like this:

```
Entering Main...
Entering Run...
Entering Method1...
Entering Method2...
Entering try block...
Exception caught and handled!
Exiting Method2...
Exiting Method1...
Exiting Run...
Exiting Main...
```

Following the try block is the catch block. In a real catch statement, you would try to include code to fix the problem—if you can fix it without interrupting the user, so much the better. For example, if the exception is raised because a database connection is down, you might retry the connection, assuming it's safe to do so. You might also interact with the user to solve the problem, such as offering the user the opportunity to close other applications and free up memory. In Example 16-2, the catch block simply reports that the exception has been caught and handled.

Notice that all the exit statements are now written. With the exception handled, execution resumes immediately after the catch block.

How the Call Stack Works

Examine the output of Example 16-2 carefully. You see the code enter Main( ), Method1( ), Method2( ), and the try block. You never see it exit the try block, though it does exit Method2( ), Method1( ), and Main( ). What happened?

When the exception is thrown, execution halts immediately and is handed to the catch block. It *never* returns to the original code path. It never gets to the line that prints the exit statement for the try block. The catch block handles the error, and then execution falls through to the code following the catch block.

If there is no exception handler at all, as we discussed, the stack is unwound, returning to the calling method in search of an exception handler. This unwinding continues until the Main( ) method is reached, and if no exception handler is found, the default (ugly) exception handler is invoked and the program terminates.

In this example, because there *is* a catch block, the stack does not need to unwind. The exception is handled, and the program can continue execution. Unwinding the stack becomes a bit clearer if you move the try/catch blocks up to Method1( ), as Example 16-3 shows.

Example 16-3. The catch block has now moved from Method2 to Method1, so the program needs to unwind the stack by one level before finding the handler

```
using System;
using System.Collections.Generic;
using System.Linq;
using System.Text;

namespace Example_16_3____Unwinding_the_Stack
{
    class Tester
    {
        public void Run()
        {
            Console.WriteLine("Entering Run...");
            Method1();
            Console.WriteLine("Exiting Run...");
        }

        public void Method1()
        {
            Console.WriteLine("Entering Method1...");
            try
            {
                Console.WriteLine("Entering try block...");
                Method2();
                Console.WriteLine("Exiting try block...");
            }
            catch
            {
```

Example 16-3. The catch block has now moved from Method2 to Method1, so the program needs to unwind the stack by one level before finding the handler (continued)

```
                Console.WriteLine("Exception caught and handled!");
            }
            Console.WriteLine("Exiting Method1...");

        }

        public void Method2( )
        {
            Console.WriteLine("Entering Method2...");
            throw new System.Exception( );
            Console.WriteLine("Exiting Method2...");
        }
        static void Main( )
        {
            Console.WriteLine("Entering Main...");
            Tester t = new Tester( );
            t.Run( );
            Console.WriteLine("Exiting Main...");
        }
    }
}
```

Now the output looks like this:

```
Entering Main...
Entering Run...
Entering Method1...
Entering try block...
Entering Method2...
Exception caught and handled!
Exiting Method1...
Exiting Run...
Exiting Main...
```

This time the exception is not handled in Method2( ); it is handled in Method1( ). When Method2( ) is called, it uses Console.WriteLine( ) to display its first milestone:

```
Entering Method2...
```

Then Method2( ) throws an exception and execution halts. The runtime looks for a handler in Method2( ), but there isn't one. Then the stack begins to unwind, and the runtime looks for a handler in the calling function: Method1( ). There is a catch block in Method1( ), so its code is executed. Execution then resumes immediately following the catch statement, printing the exit statement for Method1( ) and then for Main( ).

Notice that even though the exception is handled, you are now in Method1, and there is no automatic way to return to where you were in Method2.

If you're not entirely sure why the Exiting try block statement and the Exiting Method2 statement are not printed, try putting the code into a debugger and then stepping through it.

Creating Dedicated catch Statements

So far, you've been working with generic catch statements only. You can create dedicated catch statements that handle only some exceptions and not others, based on the type of exception thrown. Example 16-4 illustrates how to specify which exception you'd like to handle. This example performs some simple division. As you'd expect, dividing by zero is illegal, and C# has a specific exception just for that. For the purposes of demonstration, we'll say that the dividend in the operation also cannot be zero. Mathematically, that's perfectly legal, but we'll assume that a result of zero would cause problems elsewhere in the program. Obviously, C# doesn't have an exception type for that, so we'll use a more general exception for that case.

Example 16-4. Each of these three dedicated catch statements is intended for a different type of exception

```csharp
using System;
using System.Collections.Generic;
using System.Linq;
using System.Text;

namespace Example_16_4____Dedicated_catch_Statements
{
    class Tester
    {

        public void Run()
        {
            try
            {
                double a = 5;
                double b = 7;
                Console.WriteLine("Dividing {0} by {1}...", a, b);
                Console.WriteLine("{0} / {1} = {2}", a, b,
                                DoDivide(a, b));
            }

            // most specific exception type first
            catch (DivideByZeroException)
            {
                Console.WriteLine("DivideByZeroException caught!");
            }

            catch (ArithmeticException)
            {
                Console.WriteLine("ArithmeticException caught!");
            }

            // generic exception type last
            catch
            {
                Console.WriteLine("Unknown exception caught");
```

Example 16-4. Each of these three dedicated catch statements is intended for a different type of exception (continued)

```
        }
    }

    // do the division if legal
    public double DoDivide(double a, double b)
    {
        if (b == 0)
        {
            throw new DivideByZeroException();
        }
        if (a == 0)
        {
            throw new ArithmeticException();
        }
        return a / b;
    }

    static void Main()
    {
        Console.WriteLine("Enter Main...");
        Tester t = new Tester();
        t.Run();
        Console.WriteLine("Exit Main...");
    }
  }
}
```

In Example 16-4, the `DoDivide()` method does not let you divide zero by another number, nor does it let you divide a number by zero. If you try to divide by zero, it throws an instance of `DivideByZeroException`. As we mentioned, we'll also assume you don't want to allow division of zero by any number; in that case, you will throw an `ArithmeticException`.

When the exception is thrown, the runtime examines each exception handler in the order in which it appears in the code and matches the first one it can. If you were to run this program with a=5 and b=7, the output would be:

```
5 / 7 = 0.7142857142857143
```

As you'd expect, no exception is thrown. However, when you change the value of a to 0, the output is:

```
ArithmeticException caught!
```

The exception is thrown, and the runtime examines the first exception: `DivideByZeroException`. Because this does not match, it goes on to the next handler, `ArithmeticException`, which does match.

In a final pass through, suppose you change a to 7 and b to 0. This throws the `DivideByZeroException`.

You have to be particularly careful with the order of the catch statements in this case because the DivideByZeroException is derived from ArithmeticException. If you reverse the catch statements, the DivideByZeroException matches the ArithmeticException handler and the exception never gets to the DivideByZeroException handler. In fact, if their order is reversed, it is impossible for *any* exception to reach the DivideByZeroException handler. Then the compiler recognizes that the DivideByZeroException handler cannot be reached and reports a compile error!

Typically, a method catches every exception it can anticipate for the code it is running. However, it is possible to distribute your try/catch statements, catching some specific exceptions in one function and more generic exceptions in higher calling functions. Your design goals should dictate exactly where you put each try and catch statement.

Assume you have a method A that calls another method B, which in turn calls method C, which calls method D, which then calls method E. Method E is deep in your code, and methods B and A are higher up. If you anticipate that method E might throw an exception, you should create a try/catch block deep in your code to catch that exception as close as possible to the place where the problem arises—but only if there's sensible action to take at the level of method E. Many programmers will put an exception handler at the top of their program (or at the top of each module) to handle unanticipated exceptions that would otherwise "slip by" and trigger the built-in exception handler. This at least allows your program to fail gracefully (and for some programs, to log an error, or notify someone by email). It often turns out that these "last chance" exception handlers in early versions of the application lead to the addition of one or two more specific exception handlers in future versions.

The finally Statement

In some instances, throwing an exception and unwinding the stack can create a problem. For example, if you opened a file, connected to a database, or otherwise committed a resource, you might need an opportunity to close the file or database connection. As you saw in the previous examples, when an exception is thrown, it can leave behind code in the method that never gets executed. If that orphaned code is where you closed the file, your program could end without cleaning up after itself.

If there is some action you *must* take regardless of whether an exception is thrown, such as closing a file, you have two strategies to choose from. One approach is to enclose the dangerous action in a try block and then to perform the necessary action (close the file) in both the catch and try blocks. However, this is an ugly duplication of code, and it's error-prone. C# provides a better alternative in the finally block.

You create a finally block with the keyword finally, and you enclose the block in braces. The code in the finally block is guaranteed to be executed regardless of whether an exception is thrown. The TestFunc( ) method in Example 16-5 simulates opening a file as its first action. The method then undertakes some mathematical operations, and then the file is closed.

 A finally block can be created with or without catch blocks, but a finally block requires a try block to execute. It is an error to exit a finally block with break, continue, return, or goto.

It is possible that sometime between opening and closing the file, an exception will be thrown. If this happens, the file could remain open. No matter what happens, at the end of this method, the file should be closed, so the file close function call is moved to a finally block, where it is executed regardless of whether an exception is thrown. Example 16-5 uses a finally block.

Example 16-5. If you have code that must run at the end of a method, no matter what exceptions are thrown, using a finally block will guarantee that the code will run

```
using System;
using System.Collections.Generic;
using System.Linq;
using System.Text;

namespace Example_16_5____finally_Block
{
    class Tester
    {
        public void Run()
        {
            try
            {
                Console.WriteLine("Open file here.");
                double a = 5;
                double b = 0;
                Console.WriteLine("{0} / {1} = {2}", a, b,
                                DoDivide(a, b));
                Console.WriteLine("This line may or may not print");
            }

            // most derived exception type first
            catch (DivideByZeroException)
            {
                Console.WriteLine("DivideByZeroException caught!");
            }
            catch
            {
                Console.WriteLine("Unknown exception caught");
            }
            finally
            {
                Console.WriteLine("Close file here.");
            }
        }
```

```
    // do the division if legal
    public double DoDivide(double a, double b)
    {
        if (b == 0)
        {
            throw new DivideByZeroException();
        }
        if (a == 0)
        {
            throw new ArithmeticException();
        }
        return a / b;
    }

    static void Main()
    {
        Console.WriteLine("Enter Main...");
        Tester t = new Tester();
        t.Run();
        Console.WriteLine("Exit Main...");
    }
  }
}
```

The output looks like this:

```
Enter Main...
Open file here.
DivideByZeroException caught!
Close file here.
Exit Main...
```

In Example 16-5, we've removed one of the catch blocks from Example 16-4 to save space, and added a finally block. Whether or not an exception is thrown, the finally block is executed; thus, in both examples, the following message is output:

```
Close file here.
```

Of course, in a real application, you would actually open the file in the try block, and you'd actually close the file in the finally block. We're leaving out the details of file manipulation to keep the example simple.

Exception Class Methods and Properties

So far you've been using the exception as a *sentinel*—that is, the presence of the exception signals the errors—but you haven't touched or examined the Exception object itself. The System.Exception class provides a number of useful methods and properties.

The Message property provides information about the exception, such as why it was thrown. The Message property is read-only; the code throwing the exception can pass in the message as an argument to the exception constructor, but the Message property cannot be modified by any method once set in the constructor.

The HelpLink property provides a link to a help file associated with the exception. This property is read/write. In Example 16-6, the Exception.HelpLink property is set and retrieved to provide information to the user about the DivideByZeroException. It is generally a good idea to provide a help file link for any exceptions you create so that the user can learn how to correct the exceptional circumstance.

The read-only StackTrace property is set by the CLR. This property is used to provide a *stack trace* for the error statement. A stack trace is used to display the call stack: the series of method calls that lead to the method in which the exception was thrown.

 Keep in mind that although a stack trace is useful to a developer tracking down an error it's probably not useful to an end user. When you're using a stack trace, consider who's going to see it.

Example 16-6. The Exception class has properties to provide a message, a link to a help file, or a stack trace

```
using System;
using System.Collections.Generic;
using System.Linq;
using System.Text;

namespace Example_16_6____Exception_Class_Properties
{
    class Tester
    {
        public void Run( )
        {
            try
            {
                Console.WriteLine("Open file here");
                double a = 12;
                double b = 0;
                Console.WriteLine("{0} / {1} = {2}", a, b,
                                DoDivide(a, b));
                Console.WriteLine("This line may or may not print");
            }

            // most derived exception type first
            catch (DivideByZeroException e)
            {
                Console.WriteLine("\nDivideByZeroException! Msg: {0}",
                                e.Message);
                Console.WriteLine("\nHelpLink: {0}", e.HelpLink);
                Console.WriteLine("\nHere's a stack trace: {0}\n",
```

```
                            e.StackTrace);
            }
            catch
            {
                Console.WriteLine("Unknown exception caught");
            }
            finally
            {
                Console.WriteLine("Close file here.");
            }

        }

        // do the division if legal
        public double DoDivide(double a, double b)
        {
            if (b == 0)
            {
                DivideByZeroException e = new DivideByZeroException( );
                e.HelpLink = "http://www.libertyassociates.com";
                throw e;
            }
            if (a == 0)
            {
                throw new ArithmeticException( );
            }
            return a / b;
        }

        static void Main( )
        {
            Console.WriteLine("Enter Main...");
            Tester t = new Tester( );
            t.Run( );
            Console.WriteLine("Exit Main...");
        }
    }
}
```

The output looks like this:

```
Enter Main...
Open file here

DivideByZeroException! Msg: Attempted to divide by zero.

HelpLink: http://www.libertyassociates.com

Here's a stack trace:    at Example_16_6____Exception_Class_
  Properties.Tester.DoDivide(Double a, Double b) in C:\AppData\
  Local\Temporary Projects\Example 16-6 -- Exception Class
```

```
Properties\Program.cs:line 46
   at Example_16_6____Exception_Class_Properties.Tester.Run( )
   in C:AppData\Local\Temporary Projects\Example 16-6 --
   Exception Class Properties\Program.cs:line 17

Close file here.
Exit Main...
```

In the output of Example 16-6, the stack trace lists the methods in the reverse order in which they were called; by reviewing this order, you can infer that the exception was thrown in DoDivide( ), which was called by Run( ). When methods are deeply nested, the stack trace can help you understand the order of method calls and thus track down the point at which the exception occurred, and how you got there, if your method is called from several different points in the application.

In this example, rather than simply throwing a DivideByZeroException, you create a new instance of the exception object:

```
DivideByZeroException e = new DivideByZeroException( );
```

This works just like instantiating any other object; you used the new keyword and called the constructor. You can then use the instance, e, to set the properties of the object as you would any other object with public properties. You do not pass in a custom message, and so the default message is printed:

```
DivideByZeroException! Msg: Attempted to divide by zero.
```

> The designer of each Exception class has the option to provide a default message for that exception type. All the standard exceptions provide a default message, and it is a good idea to add a default message to your custom exceptions as well (see "Custom Exceptions" later in this chapter).

If you want, you can modify this line of code to pass in a custom message:

```
new DivideByZeroException(
  "You tried to divide by zero which is not meaningful");
```

In this case, the output message reflects the custom message:

```
DivideByZeroException! Msg:
You tried to divide by zero which is not meaningful
```

Before throwing the exception, set the HelpLink property:

```
e.HelpLink = "http://www.libertyassociates.com";
```

When this exception is caught, Console.WriteLine prints both the Message and the HelpLink:

```
catch (DivideByZeroException e)
{
   Console.WriteLine("\nDivideByZeroException! Msg: {0}",
   e.Message);
   Console.WriteLine("\nHelpLink: {0}", e.HelpLink);
```

The Message and HelpLink properties allow you to provide useful information to the user. The exception handler also prints the StackTrace by getting the StackTrace property of the Exception object:

```
Console.WriteLine("\nHere's a stack trace: {0}\n",
  e.StackTrace);
```

The output of this call reflects a full StackTrace leading to the moment the exception was thrown. In this case, only two methods were executed before the exception, DoDivide( ) and Run( ):

```
Here's a stack trace:    at Example_16_6____Exception_Class_
   Properties.Tester.DoDivide(Double a, Double b) in Program.cs:line 46
   at Example_16_6____Exception_Class_Properties.Tester.Run( )
   in:line 17
```

Note that we've shortened the pathnames, so your printout might look a little different.

Custom Exceptions

The intrinsic exception types C# provides, coupled with the custom messages shown in the previous example, will often be all you need to provide extensive information to a catch block when an exception is thrown.

Sometimes, however, you will want to provide more extensive information or need special capabilities in your exception. It is a trivial matter to create your own *custom exception* class. Even though you'll rarely need to do it, Example 16-7 illustrates the creation of a custom exception.

Example 16-7. Although C# provides a range of exceptions that you'll use most of the time, you can define a custom exception if you need it

```
using System;
using System.Collections.Generic;
using System.Linq;
using System.Text;

namespace Example_16_7____Custom_Exception
{
    // custom exception class
    public class MyCustomException : System.Exception
    {
        public MyCustomException(string message) :
            base(message) // pass the message up to the base class
        {
        }
    }

    class Tester
    {
```

Example 16-7. Although C# provides a range of exceptions that you'll use most of the time, you can define a custom exception if you need it (continued)

```csharp
public void Run( )
{
    try
    {
        Console.WriteLine("Open file here");
        double a = 0;
        double b = 5;
        Console.WriteLine("{0} / {1} = {2}", a, b,
                            DoDivide(a, b));
        Console.WriteLine("This line may or may not print");
    }

    // most derived exception type first
    catch (System.DivideByZeroException e)
    {
        Console.WriteLine("\nDivideByZeroException! Msg: {0}",
                            e.Message);
        Console.WriteLine("\nHelpLink: {0}\n", e.HelpLink);
    }
    // catch custom exception
    catch (MyCustomException e)
    {
        Console.WriteLine("\nMyCustomException! Msg: {0}",
                            e.Message);
        Console.WriteLine("\nHelpLink: {0}\n", e.HelpLink);
    }
    catch // catch any uncaught exceptions
    {
        Console.WriteLine("Unknown exception caught");
    }
    finally
    {
        Console.WriteLine("Close file here.");
    }
}

// do the division if legal
public double DoDivide(double a, double b)
{
    if (b == 0)
    {
        DivideByZeroException e = new DivideByZeroException( );
        e.HelpLink = "http://www.libertyassociates.com";
        throw e;
    }
    if (a == 0)
    {
        // create a custom exception instance
        MyCustomException e = new MyCustomException("Can't
                            have zero dividend");
```

```
                e.HelpLink =
                  "http://www.libertyassociates.com/NoZeroDividend.htm";
                throw e;
            }
            return a / b;
        }

        static void Main()
        {
            Console.WriteLine("Enter Main...");
            Tester t = new Tester();
            t.Run();
            Console.WriteLine("Exit Main...");
        }
    }
}
```

The output looks like this:

```
Enter Main...
Open file here

MyCustomException! Msg: Can't have zero dividend

HelpLink: http://www.libertyassociates.com/NoZeroDividend.htm

Close file here.
Exit Main...
```

MyCustomException is derived from System.Exception and consists of nothing more than a constructor that takes a string message that it passes to its base class. There's no code inside the constructor at all.

The advantage of creating this custom exception class is that it better reflects the particular design of the Tester class. That is, you've decided that, for whatever reason, it's not legal to have a zero dividend in this class.

Using the ArithmeticException rather than a custom exception would work as well, but it might confuse other programmers because a zero dividend wouldn't normally be considered an arithmetic error. Using a custom exception indicates that the exception was raised because of a violation of rules that are particular to your class.

You are free, of course, to add methods and properties to your custom exception classes as needed.

Summary

- Throwing (or raising) an exception halts execution of your program at that point, and execution proceeds in the most immediately available catch block (exception handler).

- A bug is a programming mistake that should be fixed before the program is released. An exception, however, is the result of a predictable but unpreventable problem that arises during runtime (for example, running out of disk space).

- When a program encounters a problem that it cannot solve or work around, it may throw an exception to halt execution and allow the exception handler to fix or work around the problem.

- All exceptions used in C# derive from System.Exception, and all exceptions in your program should derive from System.Exception.

- You can throw an exception yourself using the throw keyword.

- It is good programming practice to enclose code that has a high risk of throwing an exception within a try block and to provide an exception handler (a catch block) and perhaps a finally block.

- The catch block follows the try block and contains the code used to handle the exception.

- If an exception was not raised within a try block, or there is no catch block, the stack is unwound until a catch block is found. If no catch block is ever found, the built-in exception handler is invoked, which terminates your program with an error message.

- You can create dedicated catch statements to catch specific types of exceptions taking advantage of the inheritance hierarchy of exceptions.

- Any action that must be taken whether or not an exception is raised (such as closing a file) should be enclosed in a finally block.

- An exception object can contain information about the circumstances that cause the exception to be raised. Typically, exception objects contain at least a text message explaining the exception, in the Message property.

- You can define your own exception class, derived from System.Exception, if you need to provide more specific information about your exception.

With this chapter, you've taken a step toward the real world of development—you've discarded the idea that the world is populated by perfect users who never enter bad data, and perfect systems that never drop your connection when you need it. Although no code is ever bulletproof, yours is no longer made of tinfoil. Now that you can let your programs out of their isolated corner of your system, it's time to let them interact with other things going on in your environment, things called *events*. In the next chapter, you'll see how to let your code play well with others.

Test Your Knowledge: Quiz

Question 16-1. What is an exception, in C# terms?

Question 16-2. What's the difference between a bug and an exception?

Question 16-3. What's the syntax for generating an exception?

Question 16-4. What's the syntax for handling an exception?

Question 16-5. What does the framework do if no exception handler is found in the method that throws an event?

Question 16-6. When an exception handler is used, where does the program execution resume, after the handler code is run?

Question 16-7. What is the syntax for throwing a new `ArgumentNull` exception?

Question 16-8. How do you write code to handle various exceptions differently?

Question 16-9. What is the `finally` statement?

Question 16-10. Why would you want to create a custom exception?

Test Your Knowledge: Exercises

Exercise 16-1. Create a simple array of three integers. Ask the user which array element she wants to see. Output the integer that the user asked for (remember that the user probably won't ask for a zero-based index). Provide a way for the user to indicate whether she wants another integer, or to end the program. Provide a handler that deals with invalid input.

Exercise 16-2. Modify the example in Exercise 16-1 to handle two specific errors: the `IndexOutOfRangeException`, which is used when the user enters a number that's not valid for the array, and the `FormatException`, which is used when the entered value doesn't match the expected format—in this case, if the user enters something that isn't a number. Leave the existing handler as a default.

Exercise 16-3. Create a Cat class with one int property: Age. Write a program that creates a List of Cat objects in a try block. Create multiple catch statements to handle an ArgumentOutOfRangeException and an unknown exception, and a finally block to simulate deallocating the Cat objects. Write test code to throw an exception that you will catch and handle.

Exercise 16-4. Modify the test code you wrote in Exercise 16-3 so that it does not throw an error. Create a custom error type CustomCatError that derives from System. ApplicationException, and create a handler for it. Add a method to CatManager that checks the cat's age and throws a new error of type CustomCatError if the age is less than or equal to 0, with an appropriate message. Write some test code to test your new exception.

CHAPTER 17

Delegates and Events

When a head of state dies, the president of the United States sometimes does not have time to attend the funeral personally. Instead, he dispatches a delegate. Often this delegate is the vice president, but sometimes the VP is unavailable and the president must send someone else, such as the secretary of state or even the first lady. He does not want to "hardwire" his delegated authority to a single person; he might delegate this responsibility to anyone who is able to execute the correct international protocol.

The president defines in advance what responsibility will be delegated (attend the funeral), what items will be passed (condolences, kind words), and what value he hopes to get back (good will). He then assigns a particular person to that delegated responsibility at "runtime" as the course of his presidency progresses.

In programming, you are often faced with situations where you need to execute a particular action, but you don't know in advance which method, or even which object, you'll want to call upon to execute it. For example, you might want to tell an object to play a media file during runtime, but you might not know what object will be playing the file, or whether it's a video, a sound file, an animation, or something else. Rather than hardcoding a particular media player object, you would create a *delegate*, and then resolve that delegate to a particular method when the program executes.

In the early, dark, and primitive days of computing, a program would begin execution and then proceed through its steps until it completed. If the user was involved, the interaction was strictly controlled and limited to filling in fields. That's the model you've followed in all the console applications in this book so far, but it's not how you're used to interacting with applications these days.

Today's graphical user interface (GUI) programming model uses a different approach, known as *event-driven programming*. A modern program presents the user interface and waits for the user to take an action. The user might take many different actions, such as choosing among menu selections, pushing buttons, updating text fields, clicking icons, and so forth. Each action causes an event to be raised.

Other events can be raised without direct user action, such as events that correspond to timer ticks of the internal clock, email being received, file-copy operations completing, and so forth.

An *event* is the encapsulation of the idea that "something happened" to which the program must respond. Events and delegates are tightly coupled concepts because flexible event handling requires that the response to the event be dispatched to the appropriate event handler. An event handler is typically implemented in C# via a delegate. Visual Studio does a lot of work for you in creating event handlers, but you should know how they work first, and then we'll show you Windows application programming in the next chapter.

Delegates

A delegate is a reference type, like the other reference types you've seen in this book, but instead of referring to an object, a delegate refers to a *method*. This is called *encapsulating* the method. When you create the delegate, you specify a method signature and return type; you can encapsulate any matching method with that delegate.

You create a delegate with the delegate keyword, followed by a return type and the signature of the methods that can be delegated to it, as in the following:

```
public delegate int FindResult(object obj1, object obj2);
```

This declaration defines a delegate named FindResult, which will encapsulate any method that takes two objects as parameters and that returns an int.

Once the delegate is defined, you can encapsulate a member method with that delegate by creating an instance of the delegate, passing in a method that matches the return type and signature. Notice that the delegate has no method body; that's because you're not defining the method here. You're simply saying that this delegate can encapsulate any method with the appropriate signature; you don't care what it does or how it does it, as long as it has the right parameters and returns the correct type.

As an alternative, you can use anonymous methods or lambda expressions, as described later in this chapter. In either case, you can use the delegate to invoke that encapsulated method.

Delegates *decouple* the class that declares the delegate from the class that uses the delegate. That's part of the principle of encapsulation that we talked about back in Chapter 6. The class that declares the delegate FindResult doesn't need to know how the result is found, or what class uses the delegate; all it needs to do is get an int back.

For example, suppose you have a class called MediaStorage that you use to store and manage various media files—audio files, video files, animation files; the type of file doesn't matter to the class. Suppose further that you want this class to be able to play the files to make sure they can be played successfully, and report on whether they played properly or not (as a way of testing whether the file is valid). The MediaStorage class doesn't need to know how to play the files; it just needs to receive a code indicating whether the file played successfully or not.

You could fulfill this requirement with interfaces, although it may not be worth it to you to define an entirely new interface and create an instance of it when you could use a delegate instead. In this case, we'll be testing only two types of media files, so we'll use delegates. If there were a wider range of media file types, you might want to define an appropriate interface.

The delegate declaration in MediaStorage is rather simple:

```
public delegate int PlayMedia();
```

This delegate takes no parameters, but expects an int as a return value, to indicate whether the file played successfully. A value of 0 indicates success; anything else indicates failure. Note again that the method has no body.

The only other method in MediaStorage is ReportResult(), which outputs to the console the result from the media test:

```
public void ReportResult(PlayMedia playerDelegate)
{
    if (playerDelegate() == 0)
    {
        Console.WriteLine("Media played successfully.");
    }
    else
    {
        Console.WriteLine("Media did not play successfully.");
    }
}
```

This looks like a normal method, except for the parameter it takes: playerDelegate, which is not an int, as you might expect, but rather a delegate, of type PlayMedia, which you declared earlier. It's not easy to think of a method in the same terms that you might normally think of an object, but that's how delegates work.

In the body of the method, you can't declare playerDelegate directly as an integer, because playerDelegate is a reference to a method. Instead, you evaluate the method that the delegate points to, and compare the result. That's why you're testing playerDelegate() == 0. From there, you just output an appropriate message.

Take a look now at one of the media player classes:

```
public class AudioPlayer
{
    private int audioPlayerStatus;

    public int PlayAudioFile()
```

```
        {
            Console.WriteLine("Simulating playing an audio file here.");
            audioPlayerStatus = 0;
            return audioPlayerStatus;
        }
    }
```

This class has one private internal member, and a simple public method that simulates playing an audio file and returning a status code in the form of an int. This method, PlayAudioFile( ), has the signature the delegate requires, so this method can be used with the delegate. (Of course, a real media player would have many more methods than just this one, but we're keeping things simple for testing purposes.)

The other media player class is VideoPlayer, with a similar PlayVideoFile( ) method.

Within the body of the program, you first need to instantiate the MediaStorage class, and then one of each of the players:

```
MediaStorage myMediaStorage = new MediaStorage( );

AudioPlayer myAudioPlayer = new AudioPlayer( );
VideoPlayer myVideoPlayer = new VideoPlayer( );
```

That's easy enough. The next thing you need to do is instantiate the delegates. The delegates are of the type MediaStorage.PlayMedia (note that you're using the MediaStorage class here, not the object of that class you created a minute ago). You still use the keyword new to instantiate the delegate, but you pass the method PlayAudioFile as a parameter to the delegate when it's created. The result is that audioPlayerDelegate is a delegate of type PlayMedia, which you can now work with as a reference to that method:

```
// instantiate the delegates
MediaStorage.PlayMedia audioPlayerDelegate = new
                MediaStorage.PlayMedia(myAudioPlayer.PlayAudioFile);
MediaStorage.PlayMedia videoPlayerDelegate = new
                MediaStorage.PlayMedia(myVideoPlayer.PlayVideoFile);
```

Now that you have the two delegate instances, you use the delegates with the ReportResult( ) method to see whether the media files were valid. Notice here that what you're passing to the ReportResult( ) method is a reference to a method in a different class altogether:

```
myMediaStorage.ReportResult(audioPlayerDelegate);
myMediaStorage.ReportResult(videoPlayerDelegate);
```

The outcome of this is the first line causes ReportResult( ) to call the PlayAudioFile( ) method, but the second line causes it to call the PlayVideoFile( ) method. At compile time, ReportResult( ) doesn't know which method it is going to call—it finds out only when it is invoked at runtime. All it needs to know is that any method it will be asked to call will match the signature defined by the PlayMedia delegate.

The full program is shown in Example 17-1, followed by the outcome.

Example 17-1. Working with delegates seems complicated at first, but you just need to remember that you're passing a reference to a method

```
using System;
using System.Collections.Generic;
using System.Linq;
using System.Text;

namespace Example_17_1____Using_Delegates
{
    public class MediaStorage
    {
        public delegate int PlayMedia( );

        public void ReportResult(PlayMedia playerDelegate)
        {
            if (playerDelegate( ) == 0)
            {
                Console.WriteLine("Media played successfully.");
            }
            else
            {
                Console.WriteLine("Media did not play successfully.");
            }
        }

    }

    public class AudioPlayer
    {
        private int audioPlayerStatus;

        public int PlayAudioFile( )
        {
            Console.WriteLine("Simulating playing an audio file here.");
            audioPlayerStatus = 0;
            return audioPlayerStatus;
        }
    }

    public class VideoPlayer
    {
        private int videoPlayerStatus;

        public int PlayVideoFile( )
        {
            Console.WriteLine("Simulating a failed video file here.");
            videoPlayerStatus = -1;
            return videoPlayerStatus;
        }
    }
```

```
public class Tester
{
    public void Run( )
    {
        MediaStorage myMediaStorage = new MediaStorage( );

        // instantiate the two media players
        AudioPlayer myAudioPlayer = new AudioPlayer( );
        VideoPlayer myVideoPlayer = new VideoPlayer( );

        // instantiate the delegates
        MediaStorage.PlayMedia audioPlayerDelegate = new
                MediaStorage.PlayMedia(myAudioPlayer.PlayAudioFile);
        MediaStorage.PlayMedia videoPlayerDelegate = new
                MediaStorage.PlayMedia(myVideoPlayer.PlayVideoFile);

        // call the delegates
        myMediaStorage.ReportResult(audioPlayerDelegate);
        myMediaStorage.ReportResult(videoPlayerDelegate);

    }
}

class Program
{
    static void Main(string[] args)
    {
        Tester t = new Tester( );
        t.Run( );
    }
}
}
```

Just for variety, the video player class returns an error code. Of course, you'd probably want your MediaStorage class to take more action than simply reporting that the file didn't play, but we won't go into that here. This is what the output looks like:

```
Simulating playing an audio file here.
Media played successfully.
Simulating a failed video file here.
Media did not play successfully.
```

Events

GUIs, such as Microsoft Windows and web browsers, require that programs respond to *events*. An event might be a button click, a menu selection, the completion of a file transfer, and so forth. In short, something happens and you must respond to it. You cannot predict the order in which events will arise. The system is quiescent until the event, and then springs into action to handle it.

In a GUI environment, any number of controls can *raise* an event. For example, when you click a button, it might raise the Click event. When you add to a drop-down list, it might raise a ListChanged event.

Other classes will be interested in responding to these events. How they respond is not of interest to the class raising the event. The button says, "I was clicked," and the responding classes react appropriately.

Publishing and Subscribing

In C#, any object can *publish* a set of events to which other classes can *subscribe*. When the publishing class raises an event, all the subscribed classes are notified. With this mechanism, your object can say, "Here are things I can notify you about," and other classes might sign up, saying, "Yes, let me know when that happens." For example, a button might notify any number of interested observers when it is clicked. The button is called the *publisher* because the button publishes the Click event and the other classes are the *subscribers* because they subscribe to the Click event. Note that the publishing class does not know or care who (if anyone) subscribes; it just raises the event. Who responds to that event, and how they respond, is not the concern of the publishing class.

 This design implements the Publish/Subscribe (Observer) Pattern described in the seminal work *Design Patterns* by Erich Gamma et al. (Addison-Wesley).

As a second example, a Clock might notify interested classes whenever the time changes by one second. The Clock class could itself be responsible for the user interface representation of the time, rather than raising an event, so why bother with the indirection of using delegates? The advantage of the publish/subscribe idiom is that the Clock class doesn't need to know how its information will be used; this way, the monitoring of the time is *decoupled* from the representation of that information, just as in the previous example the request to play the media was decoupled from the details of the player itself. In addition, any number of classes can be notified when an event is raised. The subscribing classes do not need to know how the Clock works, and the Clock does not need to know what they are going to do in response to the event. The subscribing classes don't need to know about each other, either.

The publisher and the subscribers are decoupled by the delegate. This is highly desirable; it makes for more flexible and robust code. The Clock can change how it detects time without breaking any of the subscribing classes. The subscribing classes can change how they respond to time changes without breaking the Clock. Publishers and subscribers operate independently of one another, and that makes for code that is easier to maintain.

Events and Delegates

Events in C# are implemented with delegates. The publishing class defines a delegate. The subscribing class does two things: first, it creates a method that matches the signature of the delegate, and then it creates an instance of that delegate type encapsulating that method. When the event is raised, the subscribing class's methods are invoked through the delegate.

A method that handles an event is called an *event handler*. You can declare your event handlers as you would any other delegate.

By convention, event handlers in the .NET Framework always return void and take two parameters. The first parameter is the "source" of the event (that is, the publishing object). The second parameter is an object derived from EventArgs. Your event handlers will need to follow this design pattern.

EventArgs is the base class for all event data. Other than its constructor, the EventArgs class inherits all its methods from Object, though it does add a public static field named Empty, which represents an event with no state (to allow for the efficient use of events with no state). In other words, the EventArgs class is an empty bucket that you can use to supply any information you want about the event, or no information at all. What the subscribing class does with that information is the subscriber's business; it doesn't matter to the publisher. In this way, the subscribing class can easily match the required delegate signature, by simply taking a parameter of type EventArgs. The subscriber might use all, some, or none of the information passed in EventArgs; it doesn't matter.

Suppose you want to create a Clock class that uses delegates to notify potential subscribers whenever the local time changes its value by one second. Call this delegate SecondChangeHandler.

The declaration for the SecondChangeHandler delegate is:

```
public delegate void SecondChangeHandler(
    object clock, TimeInfoEventArgs timeInformation);
```

This delegate will encapsulate any method that returns void and that takes two parameters. The first parameter is an object that represents the Clock (the object raising the event), and the second parameter is an object of type TimeInfoEventArgs, derived from EventArgs, that will contain useful information for anyone interested in this event. TimeInfoEventArgs is defined as follows:

```
public class TimeInfoEventArgs : EventArgs
{
    public int hour;
    public int minute;
    public int second;

    public TimeInfoEventArgs(int hour, int minute, int second)
    {
```

```
            this.hour = hour;
            this.minute = minute;
            this.second = second;
        }
    }
```

The `TimeInfoEventArgs` object will have information about the current hour, minute, and second. It defines a constructor and three public integer variables.

In addition to its delegate, the `Clock` class has three member variables—hour, minute, and second—as well as a single method, `Run( )`:

```
public void Run( )
{
    for (; ; )
    {
        // sleep 100 milliseconds
        Thread.Sleep(100);

        // get the current time
        System.DateTime dt = System.DateTime.Now;
        // if the second has changed
        // notify the subscribers
        if (dt.Second != second)
        {
            // create the TimeInfoEventArgs object
            // to pass to the subscriber
            TimeInfoEventArgs timeInformation =
                new TimeInfoEventArgs(dt.Hour, dt.Minute, dt.Second);

            // if anyone has subscribed, notify them
            if (SecondChanged != null)
            {
                SecondChanged(this, timeInformation);
            }
        }

        // update the state
        this.second = dt.Second;
        this.minute = dt.Minute;
        this.hour = dt.Hour;
    }
}
```

`Run( )` creates an infinite for loop that periodically checks the system time. If the time has changed from the `Clock` object's current time, it notifies all of its subscribers and then updates its own state.

The first step is to sleep for 10 milliseconds:

```
Thread.Sleep(100);
```

This line uses a method you haven't seen yet, a static method of the `Thread` class from the `System.Threading` namespace. The `Thread` class is an advanced topic we won't cover in this book, but in this case, `Thread.Sleep( )` simply serves the function of making your program check the clock every 100 milliseconds. Without the call to `Sleep( )`, your program would check the system clock so often that your processor couldn't do anything else. You also need to add `using System.Threading;` to your `using` statements for `Sleep( )` to work.

After sleeping for 100 milliseconds, the method checks the current time:

```
System.DateTime dt = System.DateTime.Now;
```

About every 10 times it checks, the second will have incremented. The method notices that change and notifies its subscribers. To do so, it first creates a new `TimeInfoEventArgs` object:

```
if (dt.Second != second)
{
    // create the TimeInfoEventArgs object
    // to pass to the subscriber
    TimeInfoEventArgs timeInformation =
        new TimeInfoEventArgs(dt.Hour, dt.Minute, dt.Second);
```

It then notifies the subscribers by firing the `SecondChanged` event. `SecondChanged` is the instance of the delegate type `SecondChangeHandler` that was declared earlier in the class:

```
// if anyone has subscribed, notify them
if (SecondChanged != null)
{
    SecondChanged(this, timeInformation);
}
```

If an event has no subscribers registered, it will evaluate to `null`. The preceding test checks that the value is not `null`, ensuring that there are subscribers before calling `SecondChanged`.

Like all events, `SecondChanged` takes two arguments: the source of the event and the object derived from `EventArgs`. In the snippet, you see that the clock's `this` reference is passed because the clock is the source of the event. The second parameter is the `TimeInfoEventArgs` object, `timeInformation`, created in the preceding snippet.

Raising the event will invoke whatever methods have been registered with the `Clock` class through the delegate. We'll examine this in a moment.

Once the event is raised, you update the state of the `Clock` class:

```
this.second = dt.Second;
this.minute = dt.Minute;
this.hour = dt.Hour;
```

All that is left is to create classes that can subscribe to this event. You'll create two. First will be the `DisplayClock` class. The job of `DisplayClock` is not to keep track of time, but rather to display the current time to the console.

The example simplifies this class down to two methods. The first is a helper method named Subscribe( ) that is used to subscribe to the clock's SecondChanged delegate. The second method is the event handler TimeHasChanged( ):

```
public class DisplayClock
{
    public void Subscribe(Clock theClock)
    {
        theClock.SecondChanged +=
            new Clock.SecondChangeHandler(TimeHasChanged);
    }

    public void TimeHasChanged(object theClock, TimeInfoEventArgs ti)
    {
        Console.WriteLine("Current Time: {0}:{1}:{2}",
          ti.hour.ToString( ), ti.minute.ToString( ), ti.second.ToString( ));
    }
}
```

When the first method, Subscribe( ), is invoked, it creates a new SecondChangeHandler delegate, passing in its event handler method, TimeHasChanged( ). It then registers that delegate with the SecondChanged event of Clock. The += operator is the mechanism by which classes can register their event handlers with the event. As you'll see, using the += operator allows multiple classes to register handlers for a single event. Delegates with multiple subscribers are called *multicast* delegates.

You will create a second class that will also respond to this event, LogCurrentTime. This class would normally log the event to a file, but for our demonstration purposes, it will log to the standard console:

```
public class LogCurrentTime
{
    public void Subscribe(Clock theClock)
    {
        theClock.SecondChanged +=
            new Clock.SecondChangeHandler(WriteLogEntry);
    }

    public void WriteLogEntry(object theClock, TimeInfoEventArgs ti)
    {
        Console.WriteLine("Logging to file: {0}:{1}:{2}",
          ti.hour.ToString( ), ti.minute.ToString( ), ti.second.ToString( ));
    }
}
```

Although in this example these two classes are very similar, in a production program any number of disparate classes might subscribe to an event.

All that remains is to create a Clock class, create the DisplayClock class, and tell it to subscribe to the event. You then will create a LogCurrentTime class and tell it to subscribe as well. Finally, you'll tell the Clock to run. All of this is shown in Example 17-2 (you'll need to press Ctrl-C to terminate this application).

Example 17-2. You can implement events with delegates by setting up a publishing class with a delegate and subscribing classes that handle the event

```csharp
using System;
using System.Collections.Generic;
using System.Linq;
using System.Text;
using System.Threading;

namespace Example_17_2____Delegates_and_Events
{
    // a class to hold the information about the event
    // in this case it will hold only information
    // available in the clock class, but could hold
    // additional state information
    public class TimeInfoEventArgs : EventArgs
    {
        public int hour;
        public int minute;
        public int second;

        public TimeInfoEventArgs(int hour, int minute, int second)
        {
            this.hour = hour;
            this.minute = minute;
            this.second = second;
        }
    }

    // The publisher: the class that other classes
    // will observe. This class publishes one delegate:
    // SecondChangeHandler.
    public class Clock
    {
        private int hour;
        private int minute;
        private int second;

        // the delegate the subscribers must implement
        public delegate void SecondChangeHandler(object clock,
                            TimeInfoEventArgs timeInformation);

        // an instance of the delegate
        public SecondChangeHandler SecondChanged;

        // set the clock running
        // it will raise an event for each new second
        public void Run()
        {
            for (; ; )
            {
                // sleep 100 milliseconds
                Thread.Sleep(100);
```

```
                // get the current time
                System.DateTime dt = System.DateTime.Now;
                // if the second has changed
                // notify the subscribers
                if (dt.Second != second)
                {
                    // create the TimeInfoEventArgs object
                    // to pass to the subscriber
                    TimeInfoEventArgs timeInformation =
                        new TimeInfoEventArgs(dt.Hour, dt.Minute, dt.Second);

                    // if anyone has subscribed, notify them
                    if (SecondChanged != null)
                    {
                        SecondChanged(this, timeInformation);
                    }
                }

                // update the state
                this.second = dt.Second;
                this.minute = dt.Minute;
                this.hour = dt.Hour;
            }
        }
    }

    // A subscriber: DisplayClock subscribes to the
    // clock's events. The job of DisplayClock is
    // to display the current time
    public class DisplayClock
    {
        // given a clock, subscribe to
        // its SecondChangeHandler event
        public void Subscribe(Clock theClock)
        {
            theClock.SecondChanged +=
                new Clock.SecondChangeHandler(TimeHasChanged);
        }

        // the method that implements the
        // delegated functionality
        public void TimeHasChanged(object theClock, TimeInfoEventArgs ti)
        {
            Console.WriteLine("Current Time: {0}:{1}:{2}",
                ti.hour.ToString(), ti.minute.ToString(), ti.second.ToString());
        }
    }
    // a second subscriber whose job is to write to a file
    public class LogCurrentTime
    {
        public void Subscribe(Clock theClock)
```

Example 17-2. You can implement events with delegates by setting up a publishing class with a delegate and subscribing classes that handle the event (continued)

```
        {
            theClock.SecondChanged +=
                new Clock.SecondChangeHandler(WriteLogEntry);
        }

        // this method should write to a file
        // we write to the console to see the effect
        // this object keeps no state
        public void WriteLogEntry(object theClock, TimeInfoEventArgs ti)
        {
            Console.WriteLine("Logging to file: {0}:{1}:{2}",
                ti.hour.ToString( ), ti.minute.ToString( ), ti.second.ToString( ));
        }
    }

    public class Tester
    {
        public void Run( )
        {
            // create a new clock
            Clock theClock = new Clock( );

            // create the display and tell it to
            // subscribe to the clock just created
            DisplayClock dc = new DisplayClock( );
            dc.Subscribe(theClock);

            // create a Log object and tell it
            // to subscribe to the clock
            LogCurrentTime lct = new LogCurrentTime( );
            lct.Subscribe(theClock);

            // Get the clock started
            theClock.Run( );
        }
    }

    public class Program
    {
        public static void Main( )
        {
            Tester t = new Tester( );
            t.Run( );
        }
    }
}
```

The output will look something like this, depending on what time it is when you run the program:

```
Current Time: 14:53:56
Logging to file: 14:53:56
```

```
Current Time: 14:53:57
Logging to file: 14:53:57
Current Time: 14:53:58
Logging to file: 14:53:58
Current Time: 14:53:59
Logging to file: 14:53:59
Current Time: 14:54:0
Logging to file: 14:54:0
```

The net effect of this code is to create two classes, `DisplayClock` and `LogCurrentTime`, both of which subscribe to a third class's event (`Clock.SecondChanged`).

`SecondChanged` is a multicast delegate field, initially referring to nothing. In time, it refers to a single delegate, and then later to multiple delegates. When the observer classes wish to be notified, they create an instance of the delegate and then add these delegates to `SecondChanged`. For example, in `DisplayClock.Subscribe( )`, you see this line of code:

```
theClock.SecondChanged +=
    new Clock.SecondChangeHandler(TimeHasChanged);
```

It turns out that the `LogCurrentTime` class also wants to be notified. In its `Subscribe( )` method is very similar code:

```
public void Subscribe(Clock theClock)
{
    theClock.SecondChanged +=
        new Clock.SecondChangeHandler(WriteLogEntry);
}
```

Solving Delegate Problems with Events

There is a potential problem with Example 17-2, however. What if the `LogCurrentTime` class was not so considerate, and it used the assignment operator (=) rather than the subscribe operator (+=), as in the following?

```
public void Subscribe(Clock theClock)
{
    theClock.SecondChanged =
        new Clock.SecondChangeHandler(WriteLogEntry);
}
```

If you make that one tiny change to the example, you'll find that the `WriteLogEntry( )` method is called, but the `TimeHasChanged( )` method is *not* called. The assignment operator *replaced* the delegate held in the `SecondChanged` multicast delegate. This is not good.

A second problem is that other methods can call `SecondChangeHandler` directly. For example, you might add the following code to the `Run( )` method of your `Tester` class:

```
Console.WriteLine("Calling the method directly!");
System.DateTime dt = System.DateTime.Now.AddHours(2);
```

```
TimeInfoEventArgs timeInformation =
    new TimeInfoEventArgs( dt.Hour,dt.Minute,dt.Second);
theClock.SecondChanged(theClock, timeInformation);
```

Here, Main( ) has created its own TimeInfoEventArgs object and invoked SecondChanged directly. This runs fine, even though it is not what the designer of the Clock class intended. Here is the output:

```
Calling the method directly!
Current Time: 18:36:27
Logging to file: 18:36:27
Current Time: 16:36:27
Logging to file: 16:36:27
```

The problem is that the designer of the Clock class intended the methods encapsulated by the delegate to be invoked only when the event is fired. Here, Main( ) has gone around through the back door and invoked those methods itself. What is more, it has passed in bogus data (passing in a time construct set to two hours into the future!).

How can you, as the designer of the Clock class, ensure that no one calls the delegated method directly? You can make the delegate private, but then it won't be possible for clients to register with your delegate at all. What's needed is a way to say, "This delegate is designed for event handling: you may subscribe and unsubscribe, but you may not invoke it directly."

The event Keyword

The solution to this dilemma is to use the event keyword. The event keyword indicates to the compiler that the delegate can be invoked only by the defining class, and that other classes can subscribe to and unsubscribe from the delegate using only the appropriate += and -= operators, respectively.

To fix your program, change your definition of SecondChanged from:

```
public SecondChangeHandler SecondChanged;
```

to the following:

```
public event SecondChangeHandler SecondChanged;
```

Adding the event keyword fixes both problems. Classes can no longer attempt to subscribe to the event using the assignment operator (=), as they could previously, nor can they invoke the event directly, as was done in the preceding example. Either of these attempts will now generate a compile error:

```
The event 'Example_17_3__Delegates_and_events.Clock.SecondChanged'
can only appear on the left-hand side of += or -= (except when used
from within the type 'Example_17_3__Delegates_and_events.Clock')
```

There are two ways of looking at SecondChanged now that you've modified it. In one sense, it is simply a delegate instance to which you've restricted access using the keyword event. In another, more important sense, SecondChanged *is* an event, implemented by a delegate of type SecondChangeHandler. These two statements mean the same thing, but the latter is a more object-oriented way of looking at it, and better reflects the intent of this keyword: to create an event that your object can raise, and to which other objects can respond.

The complete source, modified to use the event rather than the unrestricted delegate, is shown in Example 17-3.

Example 17-3. Using the event keyword turns your delegate into an event, and restricts other classes' ability to interact with it to subscribing or unsubscribing

```
using System;
using System.Collections.Generic;
using System.Linq;
using System.Text;
using System.Threading;

namespace Example_17_3____Delegates_and_Events
{
    // a class to hold the information about the event
    // in this case it will hold only information
    // available in the clock class, but could hold
    // additional state information
    public class TimeInfoEventArgs : EventArgs
    {
        public int hour;
        public int minute;
        public int second;

        public TimeInfoEventArgs(int hour, int minute, int second)
        {
            this.hour = hour;
            this.minute = minute;
            this.second = second;
        }
    }

    // The publisher: the class that other classes
    // will observe. This class publishes one delegate:
    // SecondChanged.
    public class Clock
    {
        private int hour;
        private int minute;
        private int second;

        // the delegate the subscribers must implement
        public delegate void SecondChangeHandler(object clock,
                    TimeInfoEventArgs timeInformation);
```

```
        // an instance of the delegate with event keyword added
        public event SecondChangeHandler SecondChanged;
        // set the clock running
        // it will raise an event for each new second
        public void Run( )
        {
            for (; ; )
            {
                // sleep 10 milliseconds
                Thread.Sleep(100);

                // get the current time
                System.DateTime dt = System.DateTime.Now;
                // if the second has changed
                // notify the subscribers
                if (dt.Second != second)
                {
                    // create the TimeInfoEventArgs object
                    // to pass to the subscriber
                    TimeInfoEventArgs timeInformation =
                        new TimeInfoEventArgs(dt.Hour, dt.Minute, dt.Second);

                    // if anyone has subscribed, notify them
                    if (SecondChanged != null)
                    {
                        SecondChanged(this, timeInformation);
                    }
                }

                // update the state
                this.second = dt.Second;
                this.minute = dt.Minute;
                this.hour = dt.Hour;
            }
        }
    }

    // A subscriber: DisplayClock subscribes to the
    // clock's events. The job of DisplayClock is
    // to display the current time
    public class DisplayClock
    {
        // given a clock, subscribe to
        // its SecondChangeHandler event
        public void Subscribe(Clock theClock)
        {
            theClock.SecondChanged +=
                    new Clock.SecondChangeHandler(TimeHasChanged);
        }

        // the method that implements the
```

```csharp
        // delegated functionality
        public void TimeHasChanged(object theClock, TimeInfoEventArgs ti)
        {
            Console.WriteLine("Current Time: {0}:{1}:{2}",
              ti.hour.ToString( ), ti.minute.ToString( ), ti.second.ToString( ));
        }
    }
    // a second subscriber whose job is to write to a file
    public class LogCurrentTime
    {
        public void Subscribe(Clock theClock)
        {
            theClock.SecondChanged +=
                    new Clock.SecondChangeHandler(WriteLogEntry);
        }

        // this method should write to a file
        // we write to the console to see the effect
        // this object keeps no state
        public void WriteLogEntry(object theClock, TimeInfoEventArgs ti)
        {
            Console.WriteLine("Logging to file: {0}:{1}:{2}",
              ti.hour.ToString( ), ti.minute.ToString( ), ti.second.ToString( ));
        }
    }

    public class Tester
    {
        public void Run( )
        {
            // create a new clock
            Clock theClock = new Clock( );

            // create the display and tell it to
            // subscribe to the clock just created
            DisplayClock dc = new DisplayClock( );
            dc.Subscribe(theClock);

            // create a Log object and tell it
            // to subscribe to the clock
            LogCurrentTime lct = new LogCurrentTime( );
            lct.Subscribe(theClock);

            // Get the clock started
            theClock.Run( );
        }
    }
```

```
public class Program
{
    public static void Main()
    {
        Tester t = new Tester();
        t.Run();
    }
}
}
```

Using Anonymous Methods

In the previous example, you subscribed to the event by invoking a new instance of
the delegate, passing in the name of a method that implements the event:

```
theClock.SecondChanged +=
        new Clock.SecondChangeHandler(TimeHasChanged);
```

You can also assign this delegate by writing the shortened version:

```
theClock.SecondChanged += TimeHasChanged;
```

Later in the code, you must define TimeHasChanged as a method that matches the signature of the SecondChangeHandler delegate:

```
public void TimeHasChanged(object theClock, TimeInfoEventArgs ti)
{
    Console.WriteLine("Current Time: {0}:{1}:{2}",
        ti.hour.ToString(), ti.minute.ToString(), ti.second.ToString());
}
```

Anonymous methods allow you to pass a code block rather than the name of the
method. This can make for code that is more efficient and easier to maintain, and the
anonymous method has access to the variables in the scope in which they are
defined.

```
clock.SecondChanged += delegate( object theClock, TimeInfoEventArgs ti )
{
    Console.WriteLine( "Current Time: {0}:{1}:{2}",
        ti.hour.ToString(), ti.minute.ToString(), ti.second.ToString() );
};
```

Notice that rather than registering an instance of a delegate, you use the keyword
delegate, followed by the parameters that would be passed to your method, followed by the body of your method encased in braces and terminated by a semicolon.

This method has no name; hence, it is *anonymous*. You cannot invoke the method
except through the delegate; but that is exactly what you want.

Lambda Expressions

C# 3.0 extends the concept of anonymous methods and introduces *lambda expressions*, which are more powerful and flexible than anonymous methods.

 Lambda expressions get their name from *lambda calculus*, which is a complicated topic, but in a nutshell, it's a mathematical notation for describing functions. That's pretty much what's going on here; lambda expressions describe methods without naming them.

You define a lambda expression using this syntax:

```
(input parameters) => {expression or statement block};
```

The lambda operator => is newly introduced in C# 3.0 and is read as "goes to". The left operand is a list of zero or more input parameters, and the right operand is the body of the lambda expression. Notice that => is an operator, which means that the preceding line of code is an expression. Just as x + x is an expression that returns a value—if x is 2, the expression returns the int value 4—a lambda expression is an expression that returns a method. It's not a method by itself. It's tricky to think of expressions as returning a method instead of a value, but at the beginning of this chapter, you wouldn't have thought of passing a method as a parameter, either.

You can thus rewrite the delegate definition as follows:

```
theClock.OnSecondChange +=
    (aClock, ti) =>
    {
        Console.WriteLine("Current Time: {0}:{1}:{2}",
                        ti.hour.ToString(),
                        ti.minute.ToString(),
                        ti.second.ToString());
    };
```

You read this as "theClock's OnSecondChange delegate adds an anonymous delegate defined by this lambda expression." The two parameters, aClock and ti, go to the WriteLine expression that writes out the hour and minute and second from ti.

The two input parameters, aClock and ti, are of type Clock and TimeInfoEventArgs, respectively. You don't need to specify their types, because the C# compiler infers their type from the OnSecondChange delegate definition. If the compiler is unable to infer the type of your operands, you may specify them explicitly, like this:

```
(Clock aClock, TimeInfoEventArgs ti) => {...};
```

You might also want to specify the types of the input parameters to make the code more readable.

If your method doesn't have any input parameters, you write a pair of empty parentheses, like this:

```
() => {Console.WriteLine("No parameters here."}};
```

If you have only one input parameter, you can skip the parentheses:

```
n => {n * n};
```

Finally, if your method has only one statement, you can skip the braces as well:

```
n => n * n
```

So, what's the difference between lambda expressions and anonymous methods? Anonymous methods were introduced in C# 2.0 specifically to deal with situations where you didn't want to define a method for a delegate; that's why anonymous methods use the `delegate` keyword, and can be used only in the context of delegates. Lambda expressions were introduced in C# 3.0 to take that idea further. Specifically, lambda expressions were introduced to work with LINQ, the Language Integrated Query, which has to do with handling data. You'll see more about LINQ in Chapter 21. For now, you can use lambda expressions anywhere you'd want to use an anonymous method.

Summary

- Modern GUIs rely on events generated by the user or by the system to know what action to take.
- A delegate is a reference to a method of a particular signature and return type.
- Delegates allow polymorphism by encapsulating a method that matches the delegate signature. The method encapsulated by the delegate is decided at runtime.
- An object can publish a series of events to which other classes can subscribe. The publishing class defines a delegate and an event based on that delegate. The subscribing class creates a method that matches the signature of the delegate, and registers that method with an instance of the delegate.
- In .NET, all event handlers return `void`, and take two parameters. The first parameter is of type `object` and is the object that raises the event; the second argument is an object of type `EventArgs` or of a type derived from `EventArgs`, which may contain useful information about the event.
- Event handlers subscribe to delegates using the `+=` operator and unsubscribe using the `-=` operator.
- The keyword `event` ensures that event handlers can only subscribe or unsubscribe to the event. Handlers can't call the delegate event directly, nor can they access its internal members.
- Instead of passing a method name to a delegate, you can pass a block of code, using the keyword `delegate`. This creates an anonymous method.
- A lambda expression is an expression using the operator `=>` that returns an unnamed method. Lambda expressions are similar to anonymous methods, but aren't restricted to being used as delegates.

This chapter introduced a lot of new ideas, and possibly made you think differently about how methods work. A lot of what delegates do can also be done with interfaces, but as you've seen, delegates really come into their own as event handlers. Throughout this chapter, we've emphasized that one of the main functions of event handlers is to work with a GUI interface, like Windows, but we haven't shown you how to do that yet. In the next chapter, you're finally going to break out of the console window and see how to make some Windows applications. This is the one you've been waiting for.

Test Your Knowledge: Quiz

Question 17-1. What is the purpose of a delegate?

Question 17-2. Are delegates value types or reference types?

Question 17-3. Suppose a Phone class has defined an OnPhoneRings delegate. How would you instantiate a delegate called myDelegate to refer to the myMethod method?

Question 17-4. Define the OnPhoneRings delegate from the preceding question as an event to signal that the phone has rung.

Question 17-5. Give an example of how you might call the delegated method from the previous question through the delegate.

Question 17-6. What does the event keyword do?

Question 17-7. How do you pass information into the method that is called through the event?

Question 17-8. What properties or methods does System.EventArgs have?

Question 17-9. How can you create delegated methods anonymously?

Question 17-10. What is returned by a lambda expression?

Test Your Knowledge: Exercises

Exercise 17-1. Write a countdown alarm program that uses delegates to notify anyone who is interested that the designated amount of time has passed. You'll need a class to simulate the countdown clock that accepts a message and a number of seconds to wait (supplied by the user). After waiting the appropriate amount of time, the countdown clock should call the delegate and pass the message to any registered observers. (When you're calculating the time to wait, remember that Thread.Sleep( ) takes an argument in milliseconds, and requires a using System.Threading statement.) Create an observer class as well that echoes the received message to the console.

Exercise 17-2. Change the program you wrote in Exercise 17-1 to ensure that the event can be published to multiple handlers safely.

Exercise 17-3. Rewrite the observer class in Exercise 17-2 to use an anonymous method.

Exercise 17-4. Rewrite the observer class in Exercise 17-3 to use a lambda expression instead of an anonymous method.

CHAPTER 18

Creating Windows Applications

All of the previous chapters have used console applications to demonstrate the C# language. This allowed us to focus on the language itself, without being distracted by more complicated issues such as windows, mice, and controls.

That being said, for many people the only reason to learn C# is to create Windows applications or web applications, or both. On the following pages, you will learn how to create Windows applications using the tools provided by Visual Studio. Chapter 19 will show you how to create visually rich applications using the Windows Presentation Foundation (WPF), which was introduced in .NET 3.0.

Windows application programming is a complicated topic that can occupy an entire book in itself—in fact, *Programming .NET Windows Applications*, by Jesse Liberty and Dan Hurwitz (O'Reilly), is one of those books. Windows programming is one of the most advanced topics we'll cover in this book. Therefore, this will be something of a whirlwind tour. This chapter is also something of a culminating project, however, as you're going to see a number of techniques that you've learned in recent chapters, such as event handlers, generics, collections, and of course, the more basic elements of the language that we've been using throughout the book.

In this chapter, you'll be creating the most complex application you've written so far. It's a Windows application that will allow you to copy files from one location on your computer to another. It works, and once you're done, you can use it for yourself.

Creating a Simple Windows Form

The first difference you'll notice between the applications in this chapter and the ones you've written up to this point is that Windows applications have a visual component, called a *form*. The interface you see is the form, and the buttons, text boxes, and other widgets that make up the form are called *controls*. You build simply by dragging and dropping controls onto a work area. Some code goes into creating the appearance and default behavior of the controls, but all of that is created for you by Visual Studio, and you never have to see it.

And that's the second thing you'll notice: up until now, just about every bit of code that you worked with was written exclusively by you. You saw back in Chapter 2, though, that Visual Studio is capable of inserting prefabricated code snippets to save you time. This is a larger extension of the same idea. In fact, you won't see `Main( )` anymore, because Windows takes care of that part. Your functional code will be contained in event handlers, and the objects you create will be called from those event handlers.

In effect, moving from the command line to Windows programming entails an entirely different metaphor of programming—a *visual* metaphor, hence the name of Visual Studio.

Using the Visual Studio Designer

Although you *can* build a Windows application using any text editor, there's really no point. As you've already seen, Visual Studio increases your productivity, and integrates an editor, compiler, test environment, and debugger into a single work environment. Few serious .NET developers build commercial applications outside Visual Studio.

We'll get to the full-blown example for this chapter very shortly, but first you'll start off with a simple Windows application. Open Visual Studio and choose File → New Project, or select the Create: Project link on the Start page. In the New Project window, select Windows Forms Application (instead of the console application you've been using up until now). Create a new C# Windows application and name it Learning CSharp Windows Forms, as shown in Figure 18-1. You may name the project anything you like, and the name can include spaces, as shown, but no special characters other than the hyphen and underscore, which is why we've spelled out the # symbol.

> We created the project in this chapter using Visual C# 2008 Express. If you're using the full version of Visual Studio 2008, your screens will look different. Everything will still work, but Visual Studio has more options, so you may need to look around a bit to find the ones we use here.

Visual Studio responds by creating a Windows Forms application and, best of all, putting you into a design environment. This is the visual environment we were talking about earlier, and this is where you'll create your application.

The Design window displays a blank Windows form (`Form1`). Select View → Toolbox or press the keyboard shortcut Ctrl-W, then X to display the Toolbox, because you'll need it in a minute. Then select View → Properties Window (or press Ctrl-W, P) to bring up the Properties window as well. You may need to drag the Properties window to its traditional place on the lower right, docking it there as we showed you in Chapter 2.

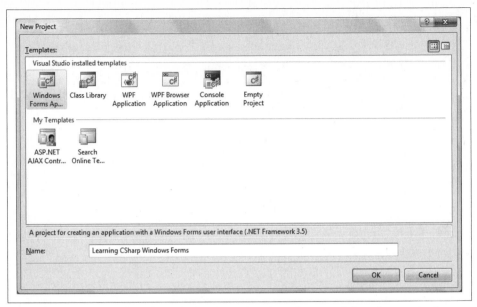

Figure 18-1. You create a Windows Application project from the same dialog where you've been creating console applications.

 Visual Studio allows a great deal of personalization. If you're using a fresh installation of Visual Studio or Visual C#, you should find that all the default settings and keyboard shortcuts work as we're describing them here. If your copy of Visual Studio has been customized, though, you may encounter different settings.

Before proceeding, take a look around your environment, as shown in Figure 18-2. The Toolbox, on the left side of the screen, is filled with controls that you can add to your Windows Forms application, simply by dragging and dropping them onto the form. In the upper-right corner, you should see the Solution Explorer, a window that displays all the files in your projects (if not, click View → Solution Explorer). From this point on, your applications will consist of multiple files. Already you can see the familiar *Program.cs* in the Solution Explorer, but you're looking at *Form1.cs* right now. The Solution Explorer helps you switch from one file to another. In the lower-right corner is the Properties window. Each of your controls is actually a class, and like any class, there are a number of internal members, called *properties*. Instead of reading the code in an editor window, as you're used to, you can view and set the properties straight from the Properties window.

Time to check that part out. Click on a label in the Toolbox, and then drag it onto the form. You'll see some guide lines that indicate where on the form the label will go, but it doesn't really matter where you put it for this example. Also notice that the label gives itself a name, label1. The purpose of this name is to distinguish this label

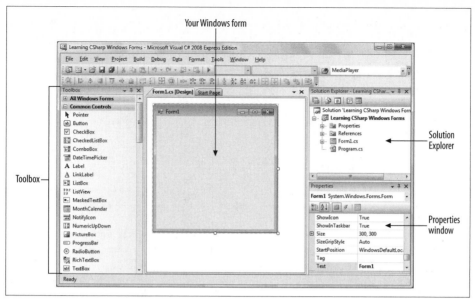

Figure 18-2. The design environment has a lot of helpful tools that you'll be using as you create your form.

from any other labels you add to the page, although you're free to change it to a more meaningful name. In fact, meaningful names are good practice, and we'll use them in the file-copier example later in the chapter, but label1 will do for this example. Click on the label, and its properties will appear in the Properties window, as shown in Figure 18-3.

You'll notice that there are a lot of properties, most having to do with format and appearance. That makes sense; this is a label, after all. To add text to label1, you edit its Text property. Scroll up or down until you can see the Text property for label1. Then click in the space next to the word *Text*, and type in "Hello World". As soon as you finish typing and click somewhere else, the text of label1 on the form changes to "Hello World".

Now change the font for the lettering in the HelloWorld label. Scroll up or down until you find the Font property, then click the + sign next to the property to expand it. Then click on the ellipsis next to the Font property to open the Font editor, as shown in Figure 18-4. Play around with the formatting as much as you like, then click OK to accept your changes, or else Cancel.

A label is nice and visual, but it doesn't do much by itself. From the Toolbox, drag a button control onto the form, somewhere near your label. Click on the button to access its properties in the Properties window, and change its Text property to Cancel. You can always tell which control's properties you're looking at by checking the drop-down box at the top of the Properties window.

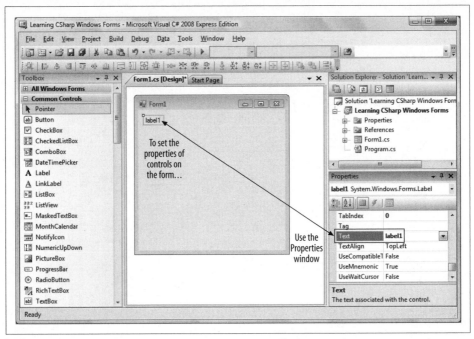

Figure 18-3. You can edit the properties for a control visually, by using the Properties window.

Now run the application by clicking the Start Debugging button, or by pressing F5. Notice that with most console applications, you had to press Ctrl-F5 so that the console window wouldn't vanish on you; that's not the case here. That's your new Windows application, running in a window by itself, separate from Visual Studio, as shown in Figure 18-5. You can see that it even has its own button on the Windows taskbar. You did all of that without writing any code at all; Visual Studio took care of all of it. You can drag the window around by its title bar, maximize or minimize it, or even close it…but don't do that just yet.

Now click the Cancel button. Oops, nothing happens. The button highlights like a regular Windows button, and its appearance changes when you click it, but that's it. That's because when you click the button, the button raises the `Click` event, but that event doesn't have a handler yet, so nothing happens. Click on the X to close your application and return to the Design view.

Click on the Cancel button so that its properties are shown in the Properties window. Notice at the top of the window a series of buttons, as shown in Figure 18-6. The first two simply reorder the properties in the window, either by category or alphabetically. The third button displays the properties for the control, which is the default. The lightning bolt button, however, displays the possible events for the control. As you hover the cursor over each button, a tool tip tells you what it is for.

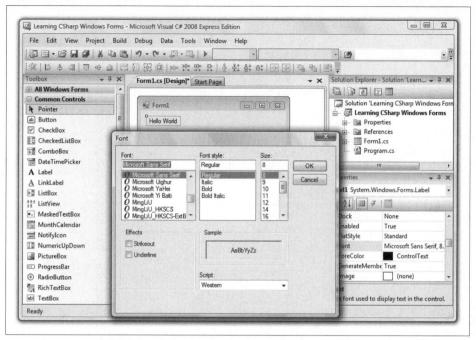

Figure 18-4. The Properties window provides access to lots of visual properties of your controls, such as editing the font.

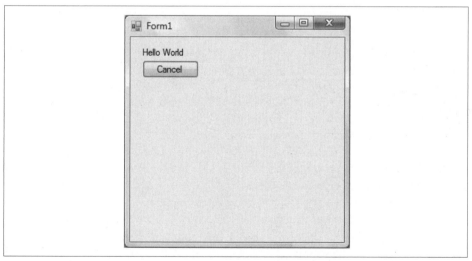

Figure 18-5. Your first Windows application is running. It may not look like much, but all the window features you'd expect are present automatically.

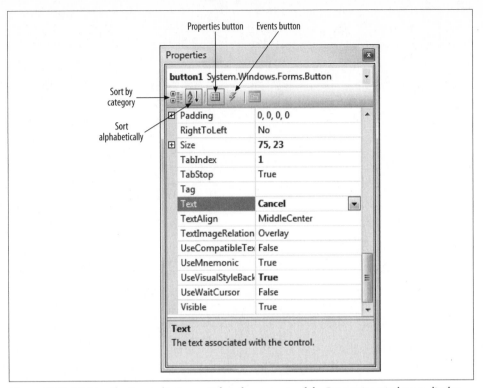

Figure 18-6. Clicking the Events button switches the contents of the Properties window to display the events for a control.

Click on the lightning bolt to change the Properties window to show all the events for the button. To have the Cancel button do something, you'll need to create a handler for the Click event. You can type a name for your handler into the space next to Click in the Properties window, but it's easier to just double-click in the space and Visual Studio will create an event handler name for you. In either case, Visual Studio then places you in the editor for the event handler so that you can add the logic. Take a look at the tabs at the top of the code window. You'll see that the page you're currently looking at is *Form1.cs*, and there's also a tab for Form1.cs [Design]. The Design view that you've seen so far is where you do the visual design of your form. The code page, which you're looking at now, is where you keep the event handler code for your form. Notice, though, that this isn't the complete code for your program; the line public partial class Form1 : Form indicates that this is a *partial class*, which means pretty much what it sounds like—Visual Studio is showing you only part of the class definition for Form1, and is taking care of the rest of the code out of your sight.

You also won't find Main( ) here, which makes sense, because this is only the class file for Form1. If you look in the Solution Explorer in the upper-right corner of Visual

Studio, you'll see all the files in this project, including *Program.cs*. If you double-click that file to open it, you'll see that it's very brief. In fact, all it does is a bit of setup, and then it calls `Application.Run(new Form1( ));`, which runs the form.

Click the tab to get back to *Form1.cs*, if you're not already there. When you double-clicked in the Properties window for the button on `Form1`, Visual Studio added the method for the event handler, but it's empty at the moment. Visual Studio created the name for the method by concatenating the control name (`button1`) with the event (`Click`), separated by an underscore. When you add the event from Design mode, Visual Studio places the cursor inside the method body, so if it's not there, click there now. Add a line to the event so that it looks like this:

```
private void button1_Click( object sender, EventArgs e )
{
    Application.Exit( );
}
```

This logic just says to exit the application when the button is clicked. Notice that as you try to enter the method call `Application.Exit( )`, IntelliSense tries to help you.

 Every control has a *default* event—the event most commonly handled by that control. In the case of the `Button` control, the default event is `Click`. You can save time by double-clicking on the control (in the Design view) if you want Visual Studio to create and name an event handler for you. That is, rather than the steps mentioned previously (click on the button, click on the lightning bolt button, double-click on the space next to Click), you could have just double-clicked on the button; the effect would be the same because you are implementing the default event.

Now run your program again (by clicking the Start Debugging icon or by pressing F5). Your form shows up in its own window, the same as before. Now click the Cancel button. This time, the event handler you just wrote is called, and the application closes. Well done—you've written a simple Windows application with a functioning event handler. Now it's time to move on to a more challenging application.

Creating a Real-World Application

Now you have a general idea of how Windows applications work, and it's time to get more ambitious and employ what you've learned in the previous 17 chapters. You'll build a utility named `FileCopier` that copies all the files from a group of directories selected by the user to a single target directory or device, such as a floppy, or a backup hard drive on the company network. Although you won't implement every possible feature for this application, this example will provide a good introduction to what it is like to build meaningful Windows applications.

The example you're about to create is much more complex than anything you've done in this book so far. However, if you walk through the code slowly, you'll find that you've already learned everything you need in the previous chapters. The goal of creating Windows applications is to mix drag-and-drop design with rather straightforward C# blocks to handle the logic.

For the purposes of this example and to keep the code simple, you'll focus on the user interface and the steps needed to *wire up* its various controls. The final application UI is shown in Figure 18-7.

The user interface for FileCopier consists of the following controls:

- Labels (Source Files, Target Files, and Status).
- Buttons (Clear, Copy, Delete, and Cancel).
- An "Overwrite if exists" checkbox.
- A text box displaying the path of the selected target directory.
- TreeView controls (source and target directories). You may not be familiar with the term *TreeView*, but you've almost certainly seen them before. Windows uses them to indicate hierarchical structures, such as the arrangement of files and directories in Windows Explorer.

All of these controls are available in the General section of the Toolbox, and you can simply drag them onto the form, as you'll see in a minute.

The goal is to allow the user to check files (or entire directories) in the left TreeView (the source). If the user clicks the Copy button, the files checked on the left side will be copied to the target directory specified on the right-side TreeView control. If the user clicks Delete the checked files will be deleted.

Creating the Basic UI Form

The first task is to create a new project, by selecting File → New Project. In the New Project dialog box, select Windows Forms Application, and name the project "File-Copier".

The IDE puts you into the designer, with Form1 showing, as before. This is where you'll create the UI for your application. This form will need to be a bit bigger than the last one, so expand the form a bit by dragging one of the little boxes in the corners of the form until it's somewhat larger (the exact size doesn't really matter; you can always adjust it later). With the form itself selected, you can see the form properties in the Properties window. Change the (Name) property to FrmFileCopier and the Text property to File Copier.

Drag-and-drop a couple of Label controls onto the top of the form—these will go above the two TreeView controls. Set the Name property of the left Label to lblSource,

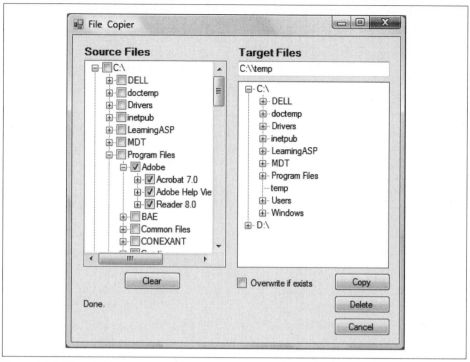

Figure 18-7. *The FileCopier user interface has a range of different controls, but they all use a similar event handler mechanism.*

and the `Name` property of the `Label` on the right to `lblTarget`. Set the `Text` properties of the two labels to "Source Files" and "Target files", respectively. Adjust the font settings a bit so that the labels are easier to read—10pt bold should work fine.

> You'll notice that when we name the controls in this example, we're giv-ing each control a prefix that indicates what kind of control it is—txt for `TextBox` controls, `lbl` for `Label` controls, and so on. This practice is called *Hungarian notation*. Microsoft's official naming guidelines prohibit using Hungarian notation for public identifiers. The controls on a form, though, are private, so the issue is a bit muddier. We think that naming a control `lblSource`, rather than just `Source`, makes it easier to identify later when you're editing the code. Therefore, we'll use Hungarian nota-tion for the control names in this example.

Next, add a `TextBox` control immediately under the "Target Files" label, and set its `Name` property to `txtTargetDir`. You'll use this `TextBox` to display the full path of the directory where the user wants to copy the files. The Source side of the application doesn't need such a `Textbox`, because the file location will be obvious from the `TreeView`, and because there may be multiple source directories.

Next, add the two TreeView controls that take up most of the space on the form. Select a TreeView and drag its corners to make it a bit larger, as shown in Figure 18-8. Notice that Visual Studio helps you line up the controls on the form neatly with each other. Name the TreeView on the left tvwSource, and the one on the right tvwTargetDir.

There's another property you need to set on the TreeView controls. On the source TreeView, you want to display checkboxes next to the directories and files that will show in the window so that the user can select multiple directories. To accomplish that, set the CheckBoxes property on tvwSource to True—just click in the box next to CheckBoxes, and you'll see a drop-down list from which you can select True or False. In the destination TreeView control, you want users to be able to select only a single destination directory, which means you don't want the checkboxes. The default for the CheckBoxes property is False, so you shouldn't need to make any changes to tvwTargetDir, but select it anyway and make sure it's set properly. That takes care of the TreeView controls.

On the left side of the form, underneath tvwSource, add a button. Name it btnClear, and set its Text property to "Clear". You'll use this button to clear the left TreeView. Underneath that button, add another Label control. Name it lblStatus, and set its Text property to "Status". You'll use this label to report any status messages to the user. Don't worry about its font properties.

On the right side of the form, underneath and aligned with the left edge of tvwTargetDir, add a Checkbox control. Name it chkOverwrite, and set its Text property to "Overwrite if exists". If the user tries to copy a file to a target directory that already has a file with the same name, you want to give the user the option of overwriting the target file, or leaving it alone. This checkbox is where the user will make that choice.

Finally, add three buttons in a column, underneath and aligned with the right edge of tvwTargetDir. Name these buttons btnCopy, btnDelete, and btnCancel, in that order, and set their Text properties to Copy, Delete, and Cancel, respectively. These buttons will do pretty much what they say they will.

That's it for the design of the form. Your form should look something like Figure 18-8 right now, although your dimensions may be slightly different. You can run your application now, if you want, to see what the form looks like on its own, although the controls won't do anything yet, of course.

So much for the easy part. Visual Studio generates code to set up the form and initializes all the controls, but it doesn't fill the TreeView controls, or provide event handlers for any of the buttons. That you must do by hand, starting with the TreeView controls in the next section. It's some complicated code, but we'll walk you through it.

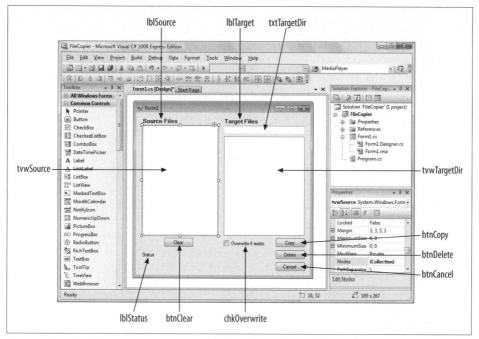

Figure 18-8. The FileCopier form is more complex than HelloWorld, but each of these controls has a purpose, as you'll see.

Populating the TreeView Controls

The two `TreeView` controls work nearly identically, except that the left control, `tvwSource`, lists the directories and files, and the right control, `tvwTargetDir`, lists only directories. The `CheckBoxes` property on `tvwSource` is set to `true`, and on `tvwTargetDir`, it is set to `false`. Also, although `tvwSource` will allow the user to select multiple files, which is the default for `TreeView` controls, you will enforce single selection for `tvwTargetDir`.

Although there are differences, most of the code for these two controls is held in common. Instead of writing out all the code twice, you'll use a technique called *factoring*— putting the common code in one convenient place for objects to access. In this case, you'll factor the common code for both `TreeView` controls into a shared method, `FillDirectoryTree`. When you call this method, you'll pass in the `TreeView` control (so the method knows which `TreeView` to fill) with a Boolean (also called a *flag*) indicating whether to get the files that are currently present (you'll see how this works in a bit). You'll call this method from the constructor for the `Form` itself, once for each of the two controls. Click on the Form1.cs tab at the top of the main window in Visual Studio to switch to the code for the form. If that tab isn't there, click the View Code button at the top of the Solution Explorer to open *Form1.cs*. Locate the constructor for the form (`public FrmFileCopier()`), and add these two method calls:

```
FillDirectoryTree(tvwSource, true);
FillDirectoryTree(tvwTargetDir, false);
```

The `FillDirectoryTree` implementation names the `TreeView` parameter tvw. This will represent the source `TreeView` and the destination `TreeView` in turn. You'll need some classes from `System.IO`, so add a using `System.IO` statement at the top of *Form1.cs*.

Next, add the method declaration to *Form1.cs*:

```
private void FillDirectoryTree(TreeView tvw, bool isSource)
{
}
```

Right now, the code for *Form1.cs* should look like this:

```
using System;
using System.Collections.Generic;
using System.ComponentModel;
using System.Data;
using System.Drawing;
using System.Linq;
using System.Text;
using System.Windows.Forms;
using System.IO;

namespace FileCopier
{
    public partial class FrmFileCopier : Form
    {
        public FrmFileCopier()
        {
            InitializeComponent();
            FillDirectoryTree(tvwSource, true);
            FillDirectoryTree(tvwTargetDir, false);
        }
        private void FillDirectoryTree(TreeView tvw, bool isSource)
        {
        }
    }
}
```

You haven't done anything with the `TreeView` controls, but you've set things up so that you'll have a place to put your code.

TreeNode objects

You're now going to fill in the code for the `FillDirectoryTree()` method you just created. The `TreeView` control has a property, `Nodes`, which gets a `TreeNodeCollection` object. (We discussed collections in Chapter 14.) The `TreeNodeCollection` is a collection of `TreeNode` objects, each of which represents a node in the tree. The first thing you need to do is empty that collection, so add this code to the method:

```
tvw.Nodes.Clear();
```

The TreeView, the TreeNodeCollection, and the TreeNode class are all defined by the Framework Class Library (FCL). In fact, nearly all the classes used in this example are defined by the framework (as opposed to being defined by you) and can be fully explored in the help files.

There is, unfortunately, no accepted convention to distinguish between individually user-defined classes (such as FrmFileCopier) and framework-defined classes (such as Environment). On the other hand, if you come across a class that you haven't defined explicitly, it is a safe bet that it is part of the framework, and you can confirm that with the help files documentation.

Next you need to fill the TreeView's Nodes collection, but first you need to know about a programming concept called *recursion*. In a nutshell, recursion occurs when a method calls itself, or when method A calls method B, which calls method A, repeating until some condition is met. In this case, you want to get a list of all the directories on your drive. You'd start at the root—say, C:—and read in all the directories. Then you take the first directory, which might be *C:\Applications*, and you get all the subdirectories there. If there are subdirectories in *C:\Applications*—say, *C:\Applications\Adobe*—you make that your new root and start over again. This process continues until you reach a directory that has no subdirectories, only files (which are called *leaves* in node terminology). Then the recursion backs up one level and gets the next directory in line, and starts the process again, until there are no more directories left to check. It's complicated to explain, but it's quite simple, even elegant, in code. Because you don't know how many levels deep your file structure goes, you tell the method to keep calling itself until it runs out of directories. You'll see how this works in a minute.

So, you'll fill the Nodes collection by recursing through the directories of all the drives. First, you need to get all the logical drives on the local system. To do so, call a static method of the Environment object, GetLogicalDrives(). The Environment class provides information about and access to the current platform environment—that's your machine, and the operating system running on it; almost certainly Windows in this case. You can use the Environment object to get the machine name, OS version, system directory, and so forth from the computer on which you are running your program. Add the following line to your method:

```
string[] strDrives = Environment.GetLogicalDrives();
```

GetLogicalDrives() returns an array of strings, each of which represents the root directory of one of the logical drives. You will iterate over that collection, adding nodes to the TreeView control as you go. Start the loop like this:

```
foreach (string rootDirectoryName in strDrives)
{
```

You process each drive within the foreach loop.

The very first thing you need to determine is whether the drive is available (that is, it is not a floppy drive without a floppy in it). Our hack for that is to get the list of top-level directories from the drive by calling GetDirectories() on a DirectoryInfo object created for the root directory:

```
DirectoryInfo dir = new DirectoryInfo(rootDirectoryName);
dir.GetDirectories();
```

The DirectoryInfo class has instance methods for creating, moving, and enumerating through directories, their files, and their subdirectories.

The GetDirectories() method returns a list of directories, but you don't actually need this list for anything. The only reason you're calling it here is because it will generate an exception if the drive is not ready (if there's no disk in the drive, or if a network drive is unavailable).

Wrap the call in a try block, and leave the catch block empty. The effect is that if an exception is thrown, the drive is skipped. You could catch more specific exceptions, but for the moment, you'll just catch any exception. At this point, your foreach loop looks like this:

```
foreach (string rootDirectoryName in strDrives)
{
    try
    {
        DirectoryInfo dir = new DirectoryInfo(rootDirectoryName);
        dir.GetDirectories();  // forces an exception if the drive isn't ready
    }
    catch
    {
    }
}
```

Once you know that the drive is ready, you'll need to create a TreeNode to hold the root directory of the drive, and then add that node to the Nodes collection of the TreeView control (which is named tvw in this method). Add the following code inside the try block, after the check of GetDirectories():

```
TreeNode ndRoot = new TreeNode(rootDirectoryName);
tvw.Nodes.Add(ndRoot);
```

The TreeView control displays a + sign next to directories that have subdirectories within them, as you've seen in Windows Explorer. To get the + signs right in the TreeView, you must find at least two levels of directories. You don't want to recurse through all the subdirectories on your machine, however, because that would be too slow. For now, you'll get the first two levels, and later you'll see how to get additional subdirectories only when the user asks for them.

The job of the GetSubDirectoryNodes() method is to recurse two levels deep, passing in the root node, the name of the root directory, a flag indicating whether you want files, and the current level (you always start at level 1):

```
if ( isSource )
{
    GetSubDirectoryNodes(ndRoot, ndRoot.Text, true, 1 );
}
else
{
    GetSubDirectoryNodes(ndRoot, ndRoot.Text, false, 1 );
}
```

This if/else looks a bit confusing, we admit. You may be wondering why you would want the files, and why you need to pass in ndRoot.Text if you're already passing in ndRoot. You will see why these steps are needed when you recurse back into GetSubDirectoryNodes.

After the empty catch block, add the following line:

```
Application.DoEvents( );
```

This instructs your application to release its hold on the processor long enough to update the user interface. This keeps the user informed and happy, and avoids the problem of looking like your program has hung while performing a long procedure.

You are now finished with FillDirectoryTree( ), but you still need to write the method GetSubDirectoryNodes( ). Save your project now, but don't bother trying to run it; you'll just get an error.

Recursing through the subdirectories

Next, you need to create the method that gets the subdirectory nodes. Create a new method called GetSubDirectoryNodes( ) immediately following the method you just finished. The parameters passed to GetSubDirectoryNodes( ) include the node where the method was called, the full pathname of that node, the Boolean for retrieving the filenames, and the level, all of which you saw in FillDirectoryTree( ). Notice that the node passed in is named parentNode. The current level of nodes will be considered children to the node passed in. This is how you map the directory structure to the hierarchy of the tree view.

GetSubDirectoryNodes( ) begins by once again calling GetDirectories( ), this time stashing away the resulting array of DirectoryInfo objects in an array called dirSubs. Add this code to *Form1.cs*:

```
private void GetSubDirectoryNodes(
    TreeNode parentNode, string fullName, bool getFileNames, int level)
{
    DirectoryInfo dir = new DirectoryInfo(fullName);
    DirectoryInfo[] dirSubs = dir.GetDirectories();
```

Now you've got your arrays, so you're going to iterate over each one, and add each subdirectory as a subnode. You want to skip any subdirectories that are marked Hidden, though, because those are probably system directories, and you don't want to mess with those. So, open the foreach loop and add the following if:

```
foreach (DirectoryInfo dirSub in dirSubs)
{
    if ( (dirSub.Attributes & FileAttributes.Hidden) != 0 )
    {
        continue;
    }
}
```

FileAttributes is an enum; other possible values include Archive, Compressed, Directory, Encrypted, Normal, ReadOnly, and a few others, but they are rarely used. The property dirSub.Attributes is what's called a *bit pattern*—a series of zeros and ones; in this case, it's a bit pattern of the current attributes of the directory. FileAttributes.Hidden is another bit pattern. You can combine these two patterns with the & operator, which is called a *bitwise AND* (notice that's not the same as the logical AND operator, &&). You don't need to know exactly how it works, but for a nonhidden directory, the result of the bitwise AND will be zero. If the result isn't zero, the directory is hidden, and you want to skip it with the continue statement.

 Although you can use the bitwise AND in this example without knowing anything more about it you may want to look up the details in another source, such as MSDN.

If you reach the next line of your foreach loop, you can be sure you're looking at a nonhidden directory, so you want to create a new TreeNode object for it. Add the following code to create a TreeNode with the subdirectory name, and add it to the Nodes collection of the node passed in to the method (parentNode):

```
TreeNode subNode = new TreeNode(dirSub.Name);
parentNode.Nodes.Add(subNode);
```

Remember that 1 you passed into GetDirectorySubNodes( )? You passed a 1 because you want your recursion to go only two levels deep, and the 1 indicates that you're at the top level of recursion. You need to check that value against a limit so that you'll know when to stop recursing. You could just hardcode the 2, but it's best to define it as a constant. By convention, member constants and variables are declared at the top of the class declaration, so add the following highlighted line just inside the class definition:

```
partial class FrmFileCopier : Form
{
    private const int MaxLevel = 2;
```

Later on, if you're on an especially powerful machine, or if you're willing to wait while the recursion happens, you can increase the value of that constant. There's no need to do that, though, because you'll see a little later that you'll retrieve subdirectories only when the user selects them, which saves processor power.

Now move back to the foreach loop within GetSubDirectoryNodes. The next bit of code is where the recursion takes place. If the current level is less than the constant you just defined, you want to have the GetSubDirectoryNodes( ) method call itself, but with different parameters. You pass in the node you just added to the `TreeView`, along with its full path, the Boolean for the filenames, and the level, increased by 1. Add this code to `GetSubDirectoryNodes( )`:

```
if ( level < MaxLevel )
{
    GetSubDirectoryNodes(subNode, dirSub.FullName, getFileNames, level+1 );
}
```

The call to the `TreeNode` constructor uses the `Name` property of the `DirectoryInfo` object, and the call to `GetSubDirectoryNodes( )` uses the `FullName` property. If your directory is *C:\Windows\Media\Sounds*, the `FullName` property returns the full path and the `Name` property returns just *Sounds*. You pass in just the name to the node constructor, because you want just the directory name displayed in the tree view. You pass in the full name with the path to the `GetSubDirectoryNodes( )` method so that the method can locate all the subdirectories on the disk. This answers the question asked earlier as to why you need to pass in the root node's name the first time you call this method. What is passed in isn't the name of the node; it is the full path to the directory represented by the node!

Go ahead and run the program now. You should see that the `TreeView` controls populate themselves properly with the drives on your machine. You can expand those directories to two levels deep by clicking the + signs. Nothing else works yet, but this is a good start. If the application doesn't run properly, check the error messages to see where you might be going wrong. Use the debugging techniques from Chapter 9 if you need to.

Getting the files in the directory

Once you've recursed through the subdirectories, it is time to get the files for the directory if the `getFileNames` flag is `true`. To do so, call the `GetFiles( )` method on the `DirectoryInfo` object. An array of `FileInfo` objects is returned. Be sure to add a closing bracket to the `foreach` loop, and then add this code below it:

```
if (getFileNames)
{
    // Get any files for this node.
    FileInfo[] files = dir.GetFiles( );
```

The `FileInfo` class provides instance methods for manipulating files.

You can now iterate over this collection, accessing the `Name` property of the `FileInfo` object and passing that name to the constructor of a `TreeNode`, which you then add to the parent node's `Nodes` collection (thus creating a child node). This whole process is similar to what you did with the directories, but there is no recursion this time because files don't have subdirectories. Put the following code inside the `if` statement you just created, and remember to close the `if` afterward:

```
foreach (FileInfo file in files)
{
```

```
        TreeNode fileNode = new TreeNode(file.Name);
        parentNode.Nodes.Add(fileNode);
    }
```

That's all it takes to fill the two tree views. Run the application now, and you'll see that the TreeView controls are populated with subdirectories and files.

If you're confused about how this recursion works, try stepping through the code in the Visual Studio debugger. Pay particular attention to the recursion, watching as the TreeView builds its nodes.

Handling the TreeView Events

You have the TreeView controls loaded now, but there are still a lot of events to handle in this example. First, the user might click Cancel, Copy, Clear, or Delete. Second, the user might fire events in either TreeView. We'll consider the TreeView events first, as they are the more interesting, and potentially the more challenging.

Clicking the source TreeView

There are two TreeView objects, each with its own event handler. Consider the source TreeView object first. The user checks the files and directories she wants to copy from. Each time the user clicks the checkbox indicating a file or directory, a number of events are raised, most of which you can safely ignore. The event you must handle, though, is called AfterCheck.

That means you'll need to implement a custom event handler method, named tvwSource_AfterCheck( ). The implementation of AfterCheck( ) delegates the work to a recursive method named SetCheck( ) that you'll also write. The SetCheck( ) method will recursively set the checkmark for all the contained folders.

To add the AfterCheck( ) event, select the tvwSource control, click the Events icon in the Properties window, and then double-click AfterCheck. This will add the event and place you in the code editor. All you're doing here is adding a method call to the event handler, so add the highlighted code here:

```
private void tvwSource_AfterCheck (object sender, TreeViewEventArgs e)
{
    SetCheck(e.Node,e.Node.Checked);
}
```

If this event was raised, that means the user checked (or cleared) a checkbox somewhere in the TreeView, and what you need to do is find out which node just got checked, and check (or clear) the checkboxes of all of that node's subdirectories and files. The event handler passes in the sender object and an object of type TreeViewEventArgs. You can get the node that raised the event from this TreeViewEventArgs object (e). The Node itself has a property called Checked, which indicates whether the checkbox for that node is checked or cleared. You then call

SetCheck( ), passing in the node that raised the event, and of the Boolean indicating whether the node has been checked.

Each node has a `Nodes` property, which gets a `TreeNodeCollection` containing all the subnodes. SetCheck( ) recurses through the current node's `Nodes` collection, setting each subnode's checkmark to match that of the node that was checked.

For each `TreeNode` in the `Nodes` collection, you first want to set its `Checked` property to whatever was passed in as a parameter. Then you want to check to see whether the current node is a leaf (has no subdirectories). A node is a leaf if its own `Nodes` collection has a count of 0. If it is a leaf, you do nothing. If it is not a leaf, you call SetCheck( ) again, recursively, passing in the current node and the `Checked` property. To do all of this, add the following method to your code after the event handler:

```
private void SetCheck( TreeNode node, bool check )
{
    foreach ( TreeNode n in node.Nodes )
    {
        n.Checked = check;   // check the node
        if ( n.Nodes.Count != 0 )
        {
            SetCheck( n, check );
        }
    }
}
```

This propagates the checkmark (or clears the checkmark) down through the entire structure. Run your application again now and check it out. When you check a directory, all its files and child directories should be checked automatically. If it's not working, put a breakpoint in SetCheck( ), and step through the method.

Expanding a directory

Each time you click a + sign next to a directory in the source `TreeView` (or in the target), you want to expand that directory. The `TreeView` control does that automatically, but as you've seen, it gets subdirectories only two levels deep, to save on processing. What you want, though, is to check for subdirectories *only* in the subdirectory the user selects, and only when he selects it. To do that, you'll need an event handler for the `TreeView` control's `BeforeExpand` event—as you might expect, this code runs after the user has clicked the + sign, but before the `TreeView` expands that directory. Because the event handlers will be identical for both the source and the target tree views, you'll create a shared event handler (assigning the same event handler to both). Go back to the Design view, select the tvwSource control, double-click the `BeforeExpand` event, and add this code:

```
private void tvwSource_BeforeExpand(object sender, TreeViewCancelEventArgs e)
{
    tvwExpand(sender, e.Node);

}
```

The EventArgs object for the BeforeExpand event is TreeViewCancelEventArgs, which isn't very intuitive, but that doesn't really matter, because all you need from it is the node that the user clicked, which TreeViewCancelEventArgs does have. Pass the sender (you'll see why in a minute) and the Node to the tvwExpand( ) method.

Now you need to add the tvwExpand( ) method. Add this code immediately after the event handler:

```
private void tvwExpand(object sender, TreeNode currentNode)
{
    TreeView tvw = (TreeView)sender;
    bool getFiles = (tvw == tvwSource);
    string fullName = currentNode.FullPath;
    currentNode.Nodes.Clear( );
    GetSubDirectoryNodes(currentNode, fullName, getFiles, 1);
}
```

You have the current node, passed in from the event arguments; you get its full pathname (which you will need as a parameter to GetSubDirectoryNodes), and then you must clear its collection of subnodes, because you are going to refill that collection by calling in to GetSubDirectoryNodes:

```
currentNode.Nodes.Clear( );
```

Why do you clear the subnodes and then refill them? Take a look at the call to GetSubDirectoryNodes( ):

```
GetSubDirectoryNodes( currentNode, fullName, getFiles, 1 );
```

When you make the call this time, the level parameter is 1, so when the user clicks a node, this code will get two levels of subnodes for the node the user clicked, and *only* that node. That saves processor power, because you're digging deep into the directory structure only at the node the user selected. If the user continues to click the + for deeper directories, the code will continue to retrieve subdirectories, but only when they're needed.

There's an extra bit of code here, though. If this event came from the source TreeView, you want to display the files in the current node. If the event came from the destination TreeView, though, you don't want to display the files (because a file isn't a valid destination for a file-copy process). GetSubDirectoryNodes( ) knows how to account for that, with the getFiles Boolean parameter. Therefore, you cast the sender object to a TreeView called tvw, and check to see whether tvw is the source TreeView. If it is, you set getFiles to true; otherwise, it's set to false:

```
TreeView tvw = (TreeView)sender;
bool getFiles = (tvw == tvwSource);
```

Then you can pass getFiles to GetSubDirectoryNodes( ), and expect it to retrieve the files or not, whichever is appropriate.

Now go back to the Design view, select the target TreeView, create its BeforeExpand event, and add the call to twvExpand( ):

```
private void tvwTargetDir_BeforeExpand(object sender, TreeViewCancelEventArgs e)
{
    tvwExpand(sender, e.Node);
}
```

Clicking the target TreeView

The second event handler for the target TreeView (in addition to BeforeExpand) is
somewhat trickier. The event itself is AfterSelect. (Remember that the target
TreeView doesn't have checkboxes, so you need to handle AfterSelect, not
AfterCheck.) The user can select only one directory at a time, and you want to take
that one directory chosen and put its full path into the text box above the target
TreeView. Click the Design View tab, select tvwTargetDir, and double-click next to its
AfterSelect property to create the event hander. Add the following code to the event
handler:

```
private void tvwTargetDir_AfterSelect(object sender, TreeViewEventArgs e)
{
    string theFullPath = e.Node.FullPath;

    if (theFullPath.EndsWith("\\"))
    {
        theFullPath = theFullPath.Substring(0, theFullPath.Length - 1);
    }

    txtTargetDir.Text = theFullPath;
}
```

This is pretty simple code, but you need to adjust the string a bit. You can get the full
pathname from the selected node easily:

```
string theFullPath = e.Node.FullPath;
```

However, if the selected node is a directory, the pathname will end with a backslash,
and you don't want to display that in the text box. Therefore, if the string ends in a
backslash, you need to remove it (subtract 1 from the Length property):

```
if (theFullPath.EndsWith("\\"))
{
    theFullPath = theFullPath.Substring(0, theFullPath.Length - 1);
}
```

Notice that you need to use EndsWith("\\") for your test, not simply EndsWith("\").
That's because the \ is the escape character, so if you want to check for it, you need
to escape it. (See Chapter 15 if you need a refresher on strings.)

Once you have the string the way you want it, you simply assign it to the Text property of the TextBox control:

```
txtTargetDir.Text = theFullPath;
```

That takes care of the events associated with the TreeView controls. Run the application now to make sure the two TreeView controls and the TextBox behave as you'd

expect them to. This is all good stuff, but your file-copy application still doesn't copy any files yet. That's because you haven't created the event handlers for the buttons.

Handling the Button Events

The four buttons on the page (Clear, Copy, Delete, and Cancel) are the controls that will do the actual work of the application. In fact, only the Copy button is particularly challenging, but we'll take each one in turn.

Handling the Clear button event

The purpose of the Clear button is to clear any checked boxes in the source TreeView. Given the SetCheck( ) method that you developed earlier, handling the Clear button's Click event is trivial. In the Design tab, double-click on the Clear button to create its default event handler (Click). Then add this bit of code to the handler:

```
private void btnClear_Click( object sender, System.EventArgs e )
{
    foreach ( TreeNode node in tvwSource.Nodes )
    {
        SetCheck( node, false );
    }
}
```

All you're doing here is calling the SetCheck( ) method on the root nodes and telling them to recursively uncheck all their contained nodes.

Implementing the Copy button event

Now that you can check the files and pick the target directory, you're ready to handle the Copy click event. The very first thing you need to do is to get a list of which files were selected. What you want is an array of FileInfo objects, but you have no idea how many objects will be in the list. This is a perfect job for a generic List. Double-click the Copy button to create the event handler. Then add the following code to call a method called GetFileList( ), which will take responsibility for filling the list:

```
private void btnCopy_Click( object sender, System.EventArgs e )
{
    List<FileInfo> fileList = GetFileList();
```

Let's pick that method apart before returning to the event handler. Create the new method below the btnCopy_Click handler.

Start by instantiating a new List object to hold the strings representing the names of all the files selected:

```
private List<FileInfo> GetFileList()
{
    List<string> fileNames = new List<string>();
```

To get the selected filenames, you can iterate through the source TreeView control:

```
foreach ( TreeNode theNode in tvwSource.Nodes )
{
    GetCheckedFiles( theNode, fileNames );
}
```

To see how this works, you'll create the GetCheckedFiles() method before you go any further with GetFileList(). Create this method now below GetFileList(). This method is pretty simple: it examines the node it was handed. If that node has no children (node.Nodes.Count == 0), it is a leaf. If that leaf is checked, you get the full path and add it to the ArrayList passed in as a parameter. Add the following code to your new method:

```
private void GetCheckedFiles( TreeNode node,List<string> fileNames )
{
    // if this is a leaf...
    if ( node.Nodes.Count == 0 )
    {
        // if the node was checked...
        if ( node.Checked )
        {
            // add the full path to the arrayList
            fileNames.Add(node.FullPath);
        }
    }
}
```

If the node is *not* a leaf, you recurse down the tree, finding the child nodes. Add the following code to complete the method:

```
else
{
    foreach (TreeNode n in node.Nodes)
    {
        GetCheckedFiles(n,fileNames);
    }
}
}
```

This returns the List filled with all the filenames. Back in GetFileList(), you'll use this List of filenames to create a second List, this time to hold the actual FileInfo objects—this will give you the actual files to copy, not just their names. You start by creating the new List<FileInfo>. Add this code to GetFileList():

```
List<FileInfo> fileList = new List<FileInfo>();
```

You're using type-safe List objects here so that the compiler will flag any objects added to the collection that aren't of type FileInfo.

You can now iterate through the filenames in fileNames, picking out each name and instantiating a FileInfo object with it. You can detect whether a given name is a file or a directory by calling the Exists property, which will return false if the File object you created is actually a directory. If it is a File, you can add it to the fileList that you just created. Add the following code to GetFileList():

```
foreach ( string fileName in fileNames )
{
   FileInfo file = new FileInfo( fileName );
   if ( file.Exists )
   {
      fileList.Add( file );
   }
}
```

It would be a good idea to work your way through the list of selected files in order from largest to smallest so that you can pack the target disk as tightly as possible. You must therefore sort the List. You can call the Sort( ) method of the List, but how will it know how to sort FileInfo objects?

To solve this, you must pass in an IComparer<T> interface. You learned about using interfaces back in Chapter 13, and generics in Chapter 14. You'll create a class called FileComparer that will implement this generic interface for FileInfo objects. Add the following code as a nested class inside the FrmFileCopier class, but outside any existing methods:

```
public class FileComparer : IComparer<FileInfo>
{
```

This class has only one method, Compare( ), which takes two FileInfo objects as arguments. Add the following method to the class:

```
public int Compare(FileInfo file1, FileInfo file2)
{
```

The normal approach is to return 1 if the first object (file1) is larger than the second (file2), to return –1 if the opposite is true, and to return 0 if they are equal. In this case, however, you want the list sorted from big to small, so you should reverse the return values.

 Because this is the only use of the Compare method, it is reasonable to put this special knowledge (that the sort is from big to small) right into the Compare method itself. The alternative is to sort small to big, and have the *calling* method reverse the results.

The Length property of the FileInfo class makes it easy to compare the size of the two files. Add the following code to the Compare( ) method:

```
public int Compare(FileInfo file1, FileInfo file2)
{
   if ( file1.Length > file2.Length )
   {
      return -1;
   }
   if ( file1.Length < file2.Length )
   {
      return 1;
   }
```

```
        return 0;
    }
```

Now you can use the `IComparer` interface. Return to `GetFileList()`, and add the following code to instantiate the `IComparer` reference and pass it to the `Sort()` method of `fileList`:

```
    IComparer<FileInfo> comparer = ( IComparer<FileInfo> ) new FileComparer();
    fileList.Sort( comparer );
```

With that done, you can return `fileList` to the calling method by adding this line:

```
    return fileList;
```

The calling method was `btnCopy_Click`. Remember, you went off to `GetFileList()` in the first line of the event handler:

```
    protected void btnCopy_Click (object sender, System.EventArgs e)
    {
        List<FileInfo> fileList = GetFileList();
```

At this point, you've returned with a sorted list of `File` objects, each representing a file selected in the source `TreeView`.

You can now iterate through the list, copying the files and updating the UI. Add the following `foreach` loop to `btnCopy_Click` to accomplish that:

```
    foreach ( FileInfo file in fileList )
    {
        try
        {
            lblStatus.Text = "Copying " + txtTargetDir.Text +
                "\\" + file.Name + "...";
            Application.DoEvents();
            // copy the file to its destination location
            file.CopyTo( txtTargetDir.Text + "\\" +
                file.Name, chkOverwrite.Checked );
        }
        catch ( Exception ex )
        {
            MessageBox.Show( ex.Message );
        }
    }
    lblStatus.Text = "Done.";
```

The first thing this loop does is write the progress to the `lblStatus` label. You output a message, "Copying", followed by whatever is currently showing in `txtTargetDir`, which must be the target directory the user selected. Then you add a backslash and the filename being copied. Next, the loop calls `Application.DoEvents()` to give the UI an opportunity to redraw; if you didn't, your status message would never show up.

Then the loop calls `CopyTo()` on the file, passing in the target directory (again, obtained from the `txtTargetDir`), and a Boolean flag indicating whether the file should be overwritten if it already exists. `CopyTo()` is a method of the `FileInfo` class that takes a `FileInfo` object and a Boolean.

The copy is wrapped in a try block because you can anticipate any number of things going wrong when copying files—the file might be in use, the target directory might become unavailable, the target disk could be full, or many other things. In a commercial-grade application, you'd create custom exceptions to handle all of these possibilities. For now, though, if any exception is thrown, you'll pop up a dialog box showing the error.

That's it; you've implemented file copying! Not so hard, was it? The CopyTo( ) method does most of the work. You're not done yet, though; there are still two more buttons to handle.

Handling the Delete button event

The code to handle the Delete event is simple, but it will give us an opportunity to show you how message boxes work. Double-click the Delete button to create the handler. The very first thing you do is ask the user whether she is sure she wants to delete the files. Copy this code to the btnDelete_Click handler:

```
private void btnDelete_Click( object sender, System.EventArgs e )
{
    // ask them if they are sure
    System.Windows.Forms.DialogResult result =
        MessageBox.Show(
        "Are you quite sure?",              // msg
        "Delete Files",                     // caption
        MessageBoxButtons.OKCancel,         // buttons
        MessageBoxIcon.Exclamation,         // icons
        MessageBoxDefaultButton.Button2 );  // default button
```

You can use the MessageBox class's static Show( ) method, passing in five parameters: first, the message you want to display, as a string; second, the title for the message box as a string, which will be "Delete Files" in this case. The rest of the parameters are flags, as follows: MessageBox.OKCancel indicates that you want the message box to have two buttons: OK and Cancel. You don't need to write any code for these buttons; they work automatically. The MessageBox.IconExclamation flag specifies the icon that you want to appear in the message box: an exclamation mark in this case. Finally, the MessageBox.DefaultButton.Button2 flag sets which of the buttons you asked for should be the default choice. In this case, you're choosing the second button (Cancel).

Notice that you're not just displaying the dialog box here; you're capturing the user's choice in a variable called result. When the user chooses OK or Cancel, the result is passed back as a System.Windows.Forms.DialogResult enumerated value. You can test this value to see whether the user selected OK; add this line to the event handler:

```
if ( result == System.Windows.Forms.DialogResult.OK )
{
```

If the condition is true, you can get the list of filenames with the `GetFileList()` method you created before. Then you iterate through the list, deleting each file as you go. The `FileInfo` class also has a `Delete()` method that you can use here. Add this code to your handler:

```
List<FileInfo> fileNames = GetFileList();
foreach ( FileInfo file in fileNames )
{
    try
    {
        // update the label to show progress
        lblStatus.Text = "Deleting " +
            txtTargetDir.Text + "\\" +
            file.Name + "...";
        Application.DoEvents();
        file.Delete();
    }
    catch ( Exception ex )
    {
        // you may want to do more than
        // just show the message
        MessageBox.Show( ex.Message );
    }
}
lblStatus.Text = "Done.";
Application.DoEvents();
```

This code is very similar to the copy code, except that the method that is called on the file is `Delete()`. Everything is enclosed in a `try` block, for the same reason as before, and the status label is updated accordingly.

Handling the Cancel button event

The final button to handle is the Cancel button, which is quite trivial. Double-click the Cancel button to create its `Click` event handler, and add the following code:

```
protected void btnCancel_Click (object sender, System.EventArgs e)
{
    Application.Exit();
}
```

Source Code

There you go—one complete, functional Windows application. Go ahead and test it out, but be careful what files you delete, because you won't get them back. You may also run into permission issues, if you're trying to access sensitive files or directories. Example 18-1 provides the full commented source code for this example.

ASP.NET

One of the goals of Microsoft's .NET initiative is to make it just as easy to create web applications as it is to create Windows applications. ASP.NET fulfills that goal for the Web. With ASP.NET, you can create applications using controls that are very similar to the ones you saw in this chapter, in a visual design environment that's nearly identical to the form designer you used here. The difference between creating a Windows application and a web page is that in ASP.NET, you can either place the controls visually, or view the HTML source for the page and add controls as though you were writing HTML. You store the code for the web page in a separate file, just as you did in this chapter, but in ASP.NET, that code can be written in either C# or Visual Basic; it makes no difference to the web page.

If you're using the full version of Visual Studio 2008, you can already create ASP.NET web pages; you just need to select ASP.NET Web Page in the New Project dialog box. However, we've written this book for the most part using C# Express, which doesn't support ASP.NET, so we won't go any further into the topic here.

If you want to learn ASP.NET, you should find it quite easy. Your C# skills will be very useful, and you'll already be accustomed to the IDE from this book. Microsoft offers a free IDE called Visual Web Developer, which is the ASP.NET equivalent to C# Express. You may also want to pick up a copy of *Learning ASP.NET 3.5*, by Jesse Liberty et al. (O'Reilly), which applies the "learning" style of this book to the topic of ASP.NET.

Example 18-1. FileCopier source code

```csharp
using System;
using System.Collections.Generic;
using System.ComponentModel;
using System.Data;
using System.Drawing;
using System.Linq;
using System.Text;
using System.Windows.Forms;
using System.IO;

namespace FileCopier
{
    public partial class FrmFileCopier : Form
    {
        private const int MaxLevel = 2;

        public FrmFileCopier()
        {
            InitializeComponent();
            FillDirectoryTree(tvwSource, true);
            FillDirectoryTree(tvwTargetDir, false);
        }
```

Example 18-1. FileCopier source code (continued)

```csharp
        // the nested FileComparer class implements
        // IComparer, and allows you to compare two
        // FileInfo objects by file size. Note that
        // you're comparing large to small, so the
        // expected results are reversed.
        public class FileComparer : IComparer<FileInfo>
        {
            public int Compare(FileInfo file1, FileInfo file2)
            {
                if (file1.Length > file2.Length)
                {
                    return -1;
                }
                if (file1.Length < file2.Length)
                {
                    return 1;
                }
                return 0;
            }
        }

        // method for both TreeView controls that fills the TreeViews
        // with the contents of the local drives.
        private void FillDirectoryTree(TreeView tvw, bool isSource)
        {
            // clear the tree first
            tvw.Nodes.Clear();

            // find the root drives for root nodes
            string[] strDrives = Environment.GetLogicalDrives();

            // Iterate through the drives, adding them to the tree
            foreach (string rootDirectoryName in strDrives)
            {
                try
                {
                    // If a drive is not ready, it will be skipped
                    DirectoryInfo dir = new DirectoryInfo(rootDirectoryName);
                    dir.GetDirectories();
                        // forces an exception if the drive isn't ready

                    // create a new TreeNode object
                    TreeNode ndRoot = new TreeNode(rootDirectoryName);

                    // add the TreeNode to the TreeView's collection
                    // for each root directory
                    tvw.Nodes.Add(ndRoot);

                    //  Add subdirectory nodes.
                    //  If the Treeview is the source,
                    //  then also get the filenames.
```

Example 18-1. FileCopier source code (continued)

```
            if (isSource)
            {
                GetSubDirectoryNodes(ndRoot, ndRoot.Text, true, 1);
            }
            else
            {
                GetSubDirectoryNodes(ndRoot, ndRoot.Text, false, 1);
            }
        }
        // The catch block does nothing in this example, but you
        // could add custom exception code here.
        catch
        {
        }
        Application.DoEvents();
    }
}


// Gets all the subdirectories below the directory node
// that was passed in, and adds them to the directory tree.
// The parameters passed in are the parent node
// for this subdirectory,
// the full pathname of this subdirectory,
// and a Boolean to indicate
// whether or not to get the files in the subdirectory.
private void GetSubDirectoryNodes(TreeNode parentNode, string fullName,
                                  bool getFileNames, int level)
{
    DirectoryInfo dir = new DirectoryInfo(fullName);
    DirectoryInfo[] dirSubs = dir.GetDirectories();

    // add a child node for each subdirectory
    foreach (DirectoryInfo dirSub in dirSubs)
    {
        // Skip hidden folders
        if ((dirSub.Attributes & FileAttributes.Hidden) != 0)
        {
            continue;
        }

        // Create a new node and add it to the tree
        TreeNode subNode = new TreeNode(dirSub.Name);
        parentNode.Nodes.Add(subNode);

        // If this is the first level of recursion,
        // call the method again recursively.
        if (level < MaxLevel)
        {
            GetSubDirectoryNodes(subNode, dirSub.FullName,
                                 getFileNames, level + 1);
        }
    }
```

Example 18-1. FileCopier source code (continued)

```
            if (getFileNames)
            {
                // Get any files for this node.
                FileInfo[] files = dir.GetFiles( );

                // Create a node for each file, if any
                foreach (FileInfo file in files)
                {
                    TreeNode fileNode = new TreeNode(file.Name);
                    parentNode.Nodes.Add(fileNode);
                }
            }
        }
    }


    private void Form1_Load(object sender, EventArgs e)
    {

    }

    private void tvwSource_AfterCheck(object sender, TreeViewEventArgs e)
    {
        SetCheck(e.Node, e.Node.Checked);
    }

    // Recursively checks all subdirectories
    // when the parent directory is checked
    private void SetCheck(TreeNode node, bool check)
    {
        foreach (TreeNode n in node.Nodes)
        {
            n.Checked = check;   // check the node
            if (n.Nodes.Count != 0)
            {
                SetCheck(n, check);
            }
        }
    }

    private void tvwSource_BeforeExpand(object sender,
                                TreeViewCancelEventArgs e)
    {
        tvwExpand(sender, e.Node);
    }
    private void tvwTargetDir_BeforeExpand(object sender,
                                TreeViewCancelEventArgs e)
    {
        tvwExpand(sender, e.Node);
    }

    // recursively gets the subdirectories
    // when a directory is expanded
```

Example 18-1. FileCopier source code (continued)

```csharp
        private void tvwExpand(object sender, TreeNode currentNode)
        {
            TreeView tvw = (TreeView)sender;
            bool getFiles = (tvw == tvwSource);
            string fullName = currentNode.FullPath;
            currentNode.Nodes.Clear( );
            GetSubDirectoryNodes(currentNode, fullName, getFiles, 1);
        }

        private void tvwTargetDir_AfterSelect(object sender,
                                             TreeViewEventArgs e)
        {
            // get the full path for the selected directory
            string theFullPath = e.Node.FullPath;

            // if it is not a leaf, it will end with a backslash
            // remove the backslash
            if (theFullPath.EndsWith("\\"))
            {
                theFullPath = theFullPath.Substring(0,
                                            theFullPath.Length - 1);
            }
            // insert the path in the text box
            txtTargetDir.Text = theFullPath;

        }


        private void btnClear_Click(object sender, EventArgs e)
        {
            // clears all the checked directories
            // in the source TreeView
            foreach (TreeNode node in tvwSource.Nodes)
            {
                SetCheck(node, false);
            }
        }

        private void btnCopy_Click(object sender, EventArgs e)
        {
            // get the sorted list of files
            List<FileInfo> fileList = GetFileList( );

            // copy the files
            foreach (FileInfo file in fileList)
            {
                try
                {
                    lblStatus.Text = "Copying " + txtTargetDir.Text +
                                "\\" + file.Name + "...";
                    Application.DoEvents( );
                    // copy the file to its destination location
```

Example 18-1. FileCopier source code (continued)

```
                file.CopyTo(txtTargetDir.Text + "\\" + file.Name,
                        chkOverwrite.Checked);
            }
            catch (Exception ex)
            {
                MessageBox.Show(ex.Message);
            }
        }
        lblStatus.Text = "Done.";

    }

    private List<FileInfo> GetFileList()
    {
        // create an unsorted array list of the full filenames
        List<string> fileNames = new List<string>();
        foreach (TreeNode theNode in tvwSource.Nodes)
        {
            GetCheckedFiles(theNode, fileNames);
        }

        // Create a list to hold the FileInfo objects
        List<FileInfo> fileList = new List<FileInfo>();

        // for each of the filenames in the unsorted list
        // if the name corresponds to a file (and not a directory),
        // add it to the file list
        foreach (string fileName in fileNames)
        {
            // create a file with the name
            FileInfo file = new FileInfo(fileName);
            // see if the file exists on the disk
            // this fails if it is a directory
            if (file.Exists)
            {
                fileList.Add(file);
            }
        }

        // Create an instance of the IComparer interface
        IComparer<FileInfo> comparer =
                (IComparer<FileInfo>)new FileComparer();

        // pass the comparer to the sort method so that the list
        // is sorted by the compare method of comparer.
        fileList.Sort(comparer);
        return fileList;
    }

    private void GetCheckedFiles(TreeNode node, List<string> fileNames)
    {
        // if this is a leaf...
```

Example 18-1. FileCopier source code (continued)

```
            if (node.Nodes.Count == 0)
            {
                // if the node was checked...
                if (node.Checked)
                {
                    // add the full path to the arrayList
                    fileNames.Add(node.FullPath);
                }
            }
            else
            {
                foreach (TreeNode n in node.Nodes)
                {
                    GetCheckedFiles(n, fileNames);
                }
            }
        }

        private void btnDelete_Click(object sender, EventArgs e)
        {
            // ask them if they are sure
            System.Windows.Forms.DialogResult result = MessageBox.Show(
                "Are you quite sure?",              // msg
                "Delete Files",                     // caption
                MessageBoxButtons.OKCancel,         // buttons
                MessageBoxIcon.Exclamation,         // icons
                MessageBoxDefaultButton.Button2);   // default button
            if (result == System.Windows.Forms.DialogResult.OK)
            {
                List<FileInfo> fileNames = GetFileList();
                foreach (FileInfo file in fileNames)
                {
                    try
                    {
                        // update the label to show progress
                        lblStatus.Text = "Deleting " + txtTargetDir.Text +
                                        "\\" + file.Name + "...";
                        Application.DoEvents();
                        file.Delete();
                    }
                    catch (Exception ex)
                    {
                        // you may want to do more than
                        // just show the message
                        MessageBox.Show(ex.Message);
                    }
                }
                lblStatus.Text = "Done.";
                Application.DoEvents();

            }
        }
```

Example 18-1. FileCopier source code (continued)

```
        private void btnCancel_Click(object sender, EventArgs e)
        {
            Application.Exit();
        }
    }
}
```

Summary

- C# and Visual Studio are designed to create Windows applications with visual design tools that enable you to drag-and-drop controls onto a form.

- The application window itself is called a *form*, and the items that you drag onto the form are known as *controls*.

- Windows applications use an event-driven design, meaning that the application responds to events raised by the user or the system, and most of your code will reside in event handlers.

- Windows automatically provides the code to initialize the form and the controls; you don't need to write any of it.

- The Properties window allows you to change the properties of a control without having to edit the code by hand.

- The Events window (available from a button in the Properties window) helps you to create event handlers for all the possible events for your control. Simply double-click the event, and Visual Studio will create a skeleton event handler and then take you to the appropriate point in the code, so you can enter your logic.

- You can double-click a control itself to have Visual Studio create the default event handler for that control.

- Visual Studio divides the Design view of the form from the code page, where the code for the event handlers is kept.

- The partial keyword in the class definition indicates that Visual Studio is hiding the initialization code for the form and the controls. The partial class file is where you keep your event handler code.

- Windows has a number of built-in classes and methods that you can use to control aspects of the form, including the Application class and the Form class.

- Factoring is a technique where you place common code, used by several different methods or handlers, in a single dedicated method for easier access.

Now you've taken C# beyond the console window and into the realm of creating Windows applications. As you've seen, it's not that hard, and Visual Studio takes care of a lot of the Windows fundamentals for you, leaving you free to concentrate on your code. There's a lot more to learn about Windows programming than we can cover in this chapter, and we hope that if you're interested, you'll seek out other sources to learn more, and of course, experiment on your own.

The Windows Forms system has been around for a while, though. The newest version of the Windows programming framework is the Windows Presentation Foundation (WPF), which ships with Windows Vista and is also available for Windows XP SP2 and Windows Server 2003. Although you can be sure that Windows Forms will be available for a long while yet, the next chapter will bring you up-to-date with the latest in Windows presentation.

Test Your Knowledge: Quiz

Question 18-1. What is the name for the buttons, text boxes, and other items on a Windows form?

Question 18-2. How do you add a Button control to a Windows form in Visual Studio?

Question 18-3. How do you set the properties of a control?

Question 18-4. What does it mean that Windows is an event-driven environment?

Question 18-5. What sort of code do you need to make a button respond to being clicked?

Question 18-6. Name two ways to create an event handler in Visual Studio.

Question 18-7. Where does Visual Studio keep the event handlers you create for your form's controls?

Question 18-8. What is the meaning of the partial class keyword?

Question 18-9. What method would you call to close the application?

Question 18-10. What is recursion?

Test Your Knowledge: Exercises

Exercise 18-1. Create a Windows application that displays the word "Hello" in a label, and has a button that changes the display to "Goodbye".

Exercise 18-2. Modify the first exercise by dragging a timer (found in the Components section of the Toolbox) onto the form and having the timer change the message from "Hello" to "Goodbye" and back once per second. Change the button to turn this behavior on and off. Use the Microsoft Help files to figure out how to use the timer to accomplish this exercise.

Exercise 18-3. Create a Windows application that calculates sales tax for a given amount. The user can enter an amount in a text box, and then can enter a sales tax between 0 and 25%, in increments of 0.25%. When the user clicks the Submit button, the tax is calculated, and both the tax and the total are output in a label. The application should look something like Figure 18-9 when it runs.

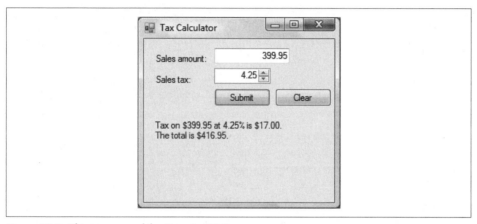

Figure 18-9. This is your goal for Exercise 18-3.

The amount is entered in a Textbox control, but for the tax, you want to restrict the values the user can enter, so you should use a numericUpDown control—use the Help files or IntelliSense to examine the properties for that control and figure out how to use them to your advantage. There's a Clear button that clears the "Amount" TextBox when clicked.

To output a double with two decimal places, use ToString("F"). The F applies the two-decimal-place formatting. You may also want to implement some exception handling to ensure that the user enters a number in the TextBox.

CHAPTER 19

Windows Presentation Foundation

The Windows Forms techniques you learning in Chapter 18 are great, and they represent a major improvement in user experience over the console applications you've used for most of this book. Time and familiarity have a way of changing expectations, though, and Windows Forms have been around for a very long time in programming years. As rival operating environments grow and mature, and people become accustomed to sophisticated interface design on the Web, users' expectations for interfaces have changed. Although Windows Forms are powerful, they don't leave a whole lot of flexibility for designers to show off, and those designers who do try need to be programmers as well if they want to get the most out of Windows Forms. Microsoft has responded to those concerns with the Windows Presentation Foundation (WPF).

The purpose of WPF is to provide a solution that's similar to the Windows Forms techniques you just learned, but provides greater flexibility of design. In Windows Forms, you used the visual designer to create the layout of the form, but you kept the code in a separate part of the file. WPF keeps the idea of separating the *presentation* (the look of the form) from the *implementation* (the event handler code), but it gives you direct control over the presentation. Instead of allowing access to only the Design view of your form in a visual interface, WPF represents the design in a form of XML, specifically created for WPF. This form of XML is called the XAML (pronounced "ZAM-el"), which stands for eXtensible Application Markup Language.

 If you're familiar with ASP.NET, this XAML idea will sound familiar to you. WPF borrows the ASP.NET idea of having a markup file and a code-behind file, except the markup is in XAML instead of HTML. Using XAML gives the markup greater flexibility over HTML, but you lose the familiarity that many web developers have with HTML. If you're not familiar with ASP.NET, don't worry about it. You don't need to know ASP.NET to understand WPF; just know that the idea is similar.

Using XAML to define the presentation of your application opens up all sorts of design possibilities that Windows Forms just aren't capable of. You may have already seen some of the possibilities in the Aero interface that Windows Vista uses, with its animated menus and transitions, and semitransparent "Glass" appearance. The WPF elements, though, go beyond the standard Windows controls.

Even more significant than *what* you can do with WPF is *how* you can do it. XAML is robust enough that you can define some event handlers (called *triggers*) entirely within the XAML, without writing formal handlers for them at all. In this chapter, you'll start out very simply with a Hello World application to get the hang of using XAML. We'll also show you how to use animations and some of the other elements, and finish up with a more elaborate application that displays data interactively.

 To complete the examples and exercises in this chapter, you'll need to have WPF on your machine. WPF is already installed on Windows Vista, and it's available for Windows XP Service Pack 2 by download-ing the .NET Framework 3.5.

Your First WPF Application

The best way to learn WPF is to start off with a traditional Hello World application. From within C# Express or Visual Studio, create a new project. When the New Project dialog box appears, select WPF Application as the project type, and name the project "Hello WPF".

Visual Studio will create the project and open a WPF editing window for you, as you can see in Figure 19-1.

Notice the split window in the middle of the IDE. It shows a visual representation of your form on the top, called the Design view, and the XAML markup on the bottom.

Before you do anything else, take a look at the code that's automatically created for you in the XAML window. It looks something like this:

```
<Window x:Class="Hello_WPF.Window1"
    xmlns="http://schemas.microsoft.com/winfx/2006/xaml/presentation"
    xmlns:x="http://schemas.microsoft.com/winfx/2006/xaml"
    Title="Window1" Height="300" Width="300">
    <Grid>

    </Grid>
</Window>
```

The first thing you see is the opening tag for the Window element itself. That element contains a reference to the Class for the application, created by default. The x refers to the default namespace for this application. (You can change the namespace if you like, but x is the default.) The xmlns properties define the namespace for the applica-tion, by referring to the XML schema for WPF, as defined by Microsoft. In short, this is where you'll find the specification of the elements that you can use in this file. You don't really need to worry much about this for the moment, although later, you'll see how to add your own elements to the namespace.

XML Crash Course

XAML is a form of XML (eXtensible Markup Language), which is similar in appearance to HTML, the markup language used to create web pages. The difference is that HTML tags define not only the type of content (paragraph, image, text box, and so on), but also the appearance, or presentation, of that content (bold, italic, blinking, and so on). XML takes the presentation elements out of the language, and also extends its usefulness beyond just defining web pages. XML documents can define any sort of data, as long as the document adheres to the defined *schema* for that document—the set of valid elements.

Although you certainly can define web pages or text documents with XML, you can also define other relationships, like this:

```
<schedule>
  <shifts>
    <shift name="morning" startTime="8:00" endTime="4:00">
      <managers>
        <manager>Johnson</manager>
        <manager>Singh</manager>
      </managers>
    </shift>
    <shift name="evening" startTime="4:00" endTime="12:00">
      <managers>
        <manager>Bradley</manager>
      </managers>
    </shift>
  </shifts>
</schedule>
```

In this example, you can see several XML syntax rules at work:

- All element names are enclosed in angle brackets: <>.
- Each opening tag has a corresponding closing tag; closing tags start with a forward slash: /.
- Hierarchical order must be maintained; elements can't overlap. In other words, you can't close the <schedule> element before you close the <shifts> element.
- Element attributes can be defined within the opening tag, such as the name attribute on the <shift> element.

Some elements are self-closing; they don't have content, but they can have attributes:

```
<book title="Dubliners" author="Joyce" />
```

There's a lot more to XML than that, but you don't need to know the details to understand the XAML in this chapter. If you'd like to learn more, you can pick up *XML in a Nutshell* by Elliotte Rusty Harold and W. Scott Means (O'Reilly).

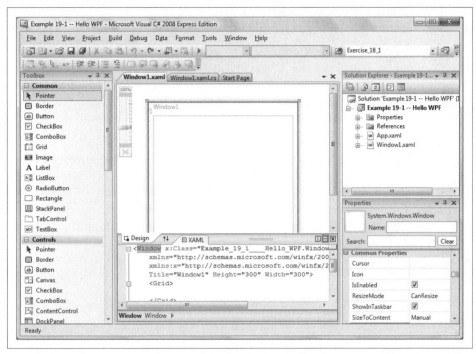

Figure 19-1. When you create a WPF project, the IDE opens with the XAML window in two views: the Design view on top, and the XAML markup below.

Next, you'll find three attributes for the Window itself: Title, Height, and Width. All three of these attributes are pretty self-explanatory, and they're reflected in the Design view as shown in Figure 19-1. Go ahead and change the Width property from 300 to 100 and you'll see the window immediately shrink in the Design view. Change it back when you're done. You can also click on the window in the Design view, and all those properties will be available for you to change in the Properties window, just as you did with Windows Forms.

The final thing to notice in this XAML is the Grid element. The Grid is a subelement of the Window element, used for laying out the controls. For now, you'll just put the controls inside the Grid; we'll worry about positioning later.

Next, find the Label control in the Common section of the Toolbox. Drag the Label onto the window, anywhere you like. Notice that the guide lines don't appear when you're placing the control, like they did in Windows Forms. Instead, they appear after you've placed the Label. Once you've dropped the Label, the guide lines appear, and you can drag the Label around to an aesthetically pleasing spot.

As with the Window element, you can change the properties of the Label element in the Properties window, but it is easier to change them in the XAML window.

When you added the Label, a line appeared in the XAML that looks something like this, depending on where you placed the Label:

```
<Label Height="28" Margin="77,28,81,0" Name="label1" VerticalAlignment="Top">Label</
Label>
```

You can see the Name attribute in the middle of the line there. You won't find it in the Properties window, though. Edit the XAML window, and change the Name to lblHello. The other elements are for positioning; leave them the way they are for right now.

Now drag a Button control from the Toolbox onto the window, underneath the Label. In the XAML, change the Name to btnHello. Instead of having a Text property, as buttons did in Windows Forms, there's a Content property for the Button. You won't see the Content property directly in the XAML window; that's because the content of the button is between the <Button> and </Button> tags, where it currently says "Button". Change that text to "Say Hello", either in the XAML window or in the Properties window. Your IDE should look something like Figure 19-2 at this point.

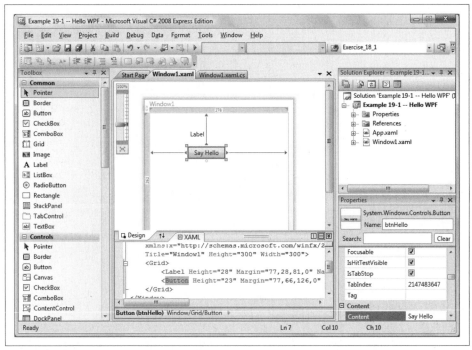

Figure 19-2. When you place controls onto the Window element in the Design view, the appropriate XAML is automatically added to the XAML window. Changes you make to the XAML are also reflected in the Design view.

So far, so good. Double-click btnHello, and you'll be taken to the code file, just as you were in Windows Forms, except this is called the code-behind file. The event handler is created for you, just like before. Add the following highlighted code to change the text of the label when the button is clicked:

```
private void btnHello_Click(object sender, RoutedEventArgs e)
{
    lblHello.Content = "Hello WPF!";
}
```

Notice here that instead of setting the value of lblHello.Text, as you would have done in Windows Forms, you're changing the Content property of lblHello. That's all you need to do. Now run the application, and click the button. The content of the Label changes, just as you'd expect, as shown in Figure 19-3.

Figure 19-3. In this simple application, WPF behaves much like Windows Forms.

WPF Differences from Windows Forms

What you did in Hello WPF isn't much different from what you could have done in Windows Forms. There are a few differences, however, even in this simple application, which aren't readily apparent. For example, run the program again, and try stretching out the borders of the window, as shown in Figure 19-4.

Notice how the "Say Hello" button stretches as you stretch the window. That wouldn't happen in Windows Forms without some extra tweaking on your part (you can load one of the examples from Chapter 18 if you want to check that). In fact, the label stretches too, but you can't see that because the Label control has no border, and it's the same color as the background.

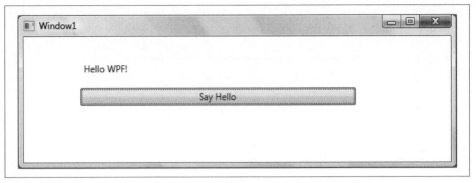

Figure 19-4. When you stretch the window in WPF, the controls stretch with it.

If the button doesn't stretch for you, you probably have the button placed too far to one side of the window, so the margin is set to zero. Go back to the Design view and move the button until you see the arrows connecting the left and right sides of the button to the sides of the window.

Close the application and go back to the *Window1.xaml* window to see how that happened. Expand the XAML part of the window so that you can see it better. You'll find that it looks something like Example 19-1, although the actual values will probably be different in your case.

Example 19-1. The XAML for your Hello WPF application is simple, but there's a lot going on here

```
<Window x:Class="Example_19_1____Hello_WPF.Window1"
    xmlns="http://schemas.microsoft.com/winfx/2006/xaml/presentation"
    xmlns:x="http://schemas.microsoft.com/winfx/2006/xaml"
    Title="Window1" Height="300" Width="300">
    <Grid>
        <Label Height="28" Margin="77,28,81,0" Name="lblHello"
            VerticalAlignment="Top">Label</Label>
        <Button Height="23" Margin="77,66,126,0" Name="btnHello"
            VerticalAlignment="Top" Click="btnHello_Click">
            Say Hello</Button>
    </Grid>
</Window>
```

We talked about the Window and Grid elements earlier. Within the Grid, you can see two elements: the Button and the Label that you added. The label has a handful of properties: the Name property that you changed earlier; a Height property that defines the height of the window, in units; a VerticalAlignment property that indicates which side of the window the control is aligned with; and finally, the Margin property.

The Margin property requires a bit of explanation; its value is set with four integers, separated by commas. Those integers indicate the distance between the control and each of the four sides, in a strict order: left, top, right, and bottom. If any of the values are zero, as is the case with the bottom values in this example, the distance doesn't matter. If you use a single integer, all four sides use that value as the margin. You can also use two integers, in which case the first integer sets the left and right margins and the second sets the top and bottom margins.

In our example, the button is always 77 units from the left side of the window, and 126 units from the right. It's 66 units from the top, but the bottom doesn't matter. So, if you resize the window horizontally, the button stretches to keep the distances constant (unless you make the window too small). If you resize the bottom edge, though, the button doesn't move.

 Units in WPF are always 1/96 of an inch. The standard Windows resolution is 96 pixels to an inch, so at normal resolution, one unit is one pixel. These units are absolute, though, so if you're using a different resolution, 96 pixels might be more or less than an inch, but 96 units is always 1 inch.

Now you're going to alter the properties of the controls in the XAML window, just to see what it can do. First, select the Grid element. You can do this either by clicking in the window, anywhere that's not one of the controls, or by simply clicking on the <Grid> element in the XAML window. Either way, you'll see the properties of the Grid element in the Properties window. In the Brushes section, click the Background property and set it to whatever you like (we chose IndianRed for this example). You can also simply type in the XAML window: type a space after the word *Grid*, and IntelliSense will provide a list of all the available properties and methods. Once you select Background, IntelliSense will provide a list of all the available background colors. You could do this with a Windows form as well, but your color choices would be somewhat more limited.

Now that you've changed the background color of the Grid, your Label control may be a bit harder to read. Click on the Label and scroll to the Brushes section in the Properties window. Set the Background property to whatever you like (we used Slate-Gray), and set the Foreground to White. Now scroll up to the Appearance section, and set the Opacity property to 0.5. This is a property that's not available in Windows Forms. Click the Button control and set its Opacity to 0.5 as well. Run your application now, and you'll see that the two controls have a translucent property to them, which is something similar to the Aero interface in Windows Vista. Example 19-2 shows the XAML for this application, simple as it is.

Example 19-2. You can easily edit the properties of controls in the XAML file to create effects that aren't possible in Windows Forms

```
<Window x:Class="Example_19_2____Properties_in_WPF.Window1"
    xmlns="http://schemas.microsoft.com/winfx/2006/xaml/presentation"
    xmlns:x="http://schemas.microsoft.com/winfx/2006/xaml"
    Title="Window1" Height="300" Width="300">
    <Grid Background="IndianRed">
        <Label Height="28" Margin="77,28,81,0" Name="lblHello"
                VerticalAlignment="Top" Opacity="0.5"
                Background="SlateGray" Foreground="White">
                Label</Label>
        <Button Height="23" Margin="77,66,126,0" Name="btnHello"
                VerticalAlignment="Top" Click="btnHello_Click"
                Opacity="0.5">Say Hello</Button>
    </Grid>
</Window>
```

Using Resources

You've seen how you can affect the properties of a single control, but in an application with more than one control, you wouldn't want to have to set each control's properties individually. That's where *resources* come in. You define a resource for an entire WPF application, where it can be used by any appropriate control.

To see how this works, you'll add another Label and Button to your Hello WPF example. Drag a Label control to somewhere near the upper-left corner of the window. Drag a Button control next to the Say Hello button. You can see in the Design window that the new controls have the Windows standard appearance, not the custom appearance that you gave the two older controls. In some cases, that's fine, but most of the time, you'll want all the controls in your application to have a consistent appearance.

For the Label, change its name to lblTop, and set its Content property to "WPF Test". You won't do anything programmatically with this label; it's just for demonstration purposes. You might as well give the button something to do, though. Change its Name to btnCancel, and its Content property to "Cancel". Double-click the button to create its event handler, and add the following code:

```
this.Close();
```

In a WPF application, you use the Close() method to end the application, rather than Application.Exit(), as you would in Windows Forms.

To get the controls of each type to have the same appearance, you'll define a Style element as a resource. Resources are generally scoped to particular elements. You could create a resource for each individual control, but it's easier to do it at the scope of the Window element.

In the XAML window, after the opening `Window` tag, enter the following code:

```xml
<Window.Resources>
    <Style x:Key="btnStyle" TargetType="Button">
        <Setter Property="Opacity" Value="0.5" />
    </Style>
    <Style x:Key="lblStyle" TargetType="Label">
        <Setter Property="Opacity" Value="0.5" />
        <Setter Property="Background" Value="SlateGray" />
        <Setter Property="Foreground" Value="White" />
    </Style>
</Window.Resources>
```

You start off with the `Window.Resources` element; that's clear enough. The next line defines the `Style` element. As we mentioned before, the `x` is used to indicate the namespace for this application. Here, you're defining a `Key` as part of the namespace so that other elements can refer to it elsewhere in the form. We've given the `Key` a value of btnStyle, to make it obvious what it's referring to, but just as you saw with dictionaries back in Chapter 14, a `Key` can be anything you like, as long as you can find it later. The `TargetType` property restricts the style to being applied to `Button` controls only; it's not strictly necessary, but if you defined a style specifically for `Button` controls, without using the `TargetType` property, and later tried to apply that style to a `TextBox`, you could cause an error, depending on the specific styles you defined.

Once you've opened the `Style` element, you can define some `Setter` elements. These, as the name implies, set properties of the target. In this case, the only change you're making to the `Button` control is to set the `Opacity` property to 0.5, so you provide the `Property`, and then the `Value`.

You then close the `Style` element for the `Button`, and open one for the `Label` control, cleverly named lblStyle. This style has a few more properties than btnStyle does, but they're all pretty simple.

The next step is to apply those styles to the individual controls. You do that within the element for each control, with the `Style` attribute:

```xml
<Label Style="{StaticResource lblStyle}" Height="28"
    Margin="77,83,81,0" Name="lblHello" VerticalAlignment="Top">
    Label</Label>
```

In this case, you define the `Style` property with a static resource, which means that the control element will look for the style definition with the appropriate name elsewhere in the XAML file, within the scope that it can access. You defined lblStyle as a resource for the entire `Window`, so the `Label` can find and use that resource. Note that the curly braces are required.

Now apply the lblStyle to the other `Label`, and the btnStyle to the two `Button` controls. You should find that the styles are applied immediately in the Design window, and of course they stay if you run the application. The entire XAML file for this example is shown in Example 19-3.

Example 19-3. When you define a resource for the Window element, that resource is available to all the elements in the window

```
<Window x:Class="Example_19_3____Classes_and_Styles.Window1"
    xmlns="http://schemas.microsoft.com/winfx/2006/xaml/presentation"
    xmlns:x="http://schemas.microsoft.com/winfx/2006/xaml"
    Title="Window1" Height="300" Width="300">
    <Window.Resources>
        <Style x:Key="btnStyle" TargetType="Button">
            <Setter Property="Opacity" Value="0.5" />
        </Style>
        <Style x:Key="lblStyle" TargetType="Label">
            <Setter Property="Opacity" Value="0.5" />
            <Setter Property="Background" Value="SlateGray" />
            <Setter Property="Foreground" Value="White" />
        </Style>
    </Window.Resources>
    <Grid Background="IndianRed">
        <Label Style="{StaticResource lblStyle}" Height="28"
               Margin="77,83,81,0" Name="lblHello"
               VerticalAlignment="Top">Label</Label>
        <Button Style="{StaticResource btnStyle}" Height="23"
               Margin="77,0,126,105" Name="btnHello"
               VerticalAlignment="Bottom" Click="btnHello_Click">
               Say Hello</Button>
        <Label Style="{StaticResource lblStyle}" Height="28"
               HorizontalAlignment="Left" Margin="15,18,0,0"
               Name="lblTop" VerticalAlignment="Top" Width="120">
               WPF Test</Label>
        <Button Style="{StaticResource btnStyle}" Height="23"
               HorizontalAlignment="Right" Margin="0,0,26,105"
               Name="btnCancel" VerticalAlignment="Bottom"
               Width="75" Click="btnCancel_Click">Cancel</Button>
    </Grid>
</Window>
```

Animations

This control and resource stuff is great, but it's not exactly exciting, we know. We promised you animations, and animations you shall have. The best way to make animations in WPF is with a tool called Expression Blend (available at *http://www.microsoft.com/expression*), but in this case, we'll show you how to do it the hard way so that you'll know what's going on in the XAML. In this example, you're going to start with a simple square, and perform some of the more basic animations on it. The square is in fact an instance of the built-in Rectangle control, which is part of the WPF schema. However, you can apply these animations to many other controls.

The first thing to do is define the Rectangle control. Create a new WPF project to start with. You could drag a Rectangle control out of the toolbar onto the window, but in this case, it's easier to just define the rectangle in the XAML. Add the following element inside the <Grid> element:

```
<Rectangle Name="myRectangle" Width="100" Height="100">
</Rectangle>
```

Now you should see a square in the Design window, 100 units on a side. You didn't define the `Margin` property, so the square will be centered in the window, which is fine. The first thing you're going to do is animate the color of the square, and to do that, you'll need the square to have some color first. If you click on the `Rectangle` element, you'll see it has a `Fill` property, which is the interior color of the square (as opposed to the outside border, which we'll leave blank). You could simply set the `Fill` property to a color, but you can't manipulate the `Fill` property directly from an event, which is what you'll want to do later. That means you have to define a `Brush`, which is a property of `Fill` that you use for applying color, and other drawing properties. Inside the `Rectangle` element, add this new subelement:

```
<Rectangle.Fill>
    <SolidColorBrush x:Name="rectangleBrush" Color="Blue" />
</Rectangle.Fill>
```

What you've done here is define a `Brush`, specifically a `SolidColorBrush`—there are more complicated `Brush` types, used for gradients and other fancy drawing tools, but we'll stick with a solid color here. Notice specifically that you've used the x element to give this brush a name that can be referred to elsewhere in the code—that's critical to the animation, as you'll see in a moment.

Triggers and Storyboards

So far, you haven't animated anything. To start the animation, you'll need a *trigger*. Triggers are attached to WPF elements, and they're similar to event handlers in that they react to events within the application, but they don't necessarily require you to write any code. This trigger will be attached to the `Rectangle` element, so below your new `<Rectangle.Fill>` element, add another element, `<Rectangle.Triggers>`:

```
<Rectangle.Fill>
    <SolidColorBrush x:Name="rectangleBrush" Color="Blue" />
</Rectangle.Fill>
<Rectangle.Triggers>

</Rectangle.Triggers>
```

Notice that IntelliSense provides the closing tag for you. This subelement will hold any triggers you define for `Rectangle`, and you'll add one in a moment.

Much like event handlers, triggers need events to react to. WPF defines two different kinds of events, routed events and attached events. Routed events are events raised normally by a single control; attached events are more complicated, so we won't worry about them here. You're going to use a routed event for this trigger, the `Loaded` event on the `Rectangle` element. As the name implies, this event is fired when the `Rectangle` element is loaded, which happens as soon as the application starts. Add that trigger element now, and then we'll define the animation to go inside it:

```
<Rectangle.Triggers>
    <EventTrigger RoutedEvent="Rectangle.Loaded">

    </EventTrigger>
</Rectangle.Triggers>
```

Animations live inside special elements called *storyboards*, so that's what you need to define next. The trigger element can't contain just a storyboard by itself; it has to contain a storyboard action. Therefore, you first need to add a `<BeginStoryboard>` element inside the `EventTrigger` element. Inside the `BeginStoryboard` element, you define the `Storyboard`:

```
<Rectangle.Triggers>
    <EventTrigger RoutedEvent="Rectangle.Loaded">
        <BeginStoryboard>
            <Storyboard>

            </Storyboard>
        </BeginStoryboard>
    </EventTrigger>
</Rectangle.Triggers>
```

You can also define a storyboard elsewhere in your code, as a resource. You'll see how that works in the next example, but we won't do that here.

After all these nested elements, it's finally time to get to the animation. WPF defines several different kinds of animations, depending on what you're animating. You can think of an animation as changing a property of an element over time. For example, if you define an animation to make a rectangle increase in width, you're changing its `Width` property, which is defined as a `double` data type, so you'd use the `DoubleAnimation` for the animation type. In this case, you're going to change the color of the square, so you'll use the `ColorAnimation` type. Add the following code inside the `Storyboard` element:

```
<EventTrigger RoutedEvent="Rectangle.Loaded">
    <BeginStoryboard>
        <Storyboard>
            <ColorAnimation
                Storyboard.TargetName="rectangleBrush"
                Storyboard.TargetProperty="Color"
                From="Blue" To="Red" Duration="0:0:10"
                AutoReverse="True" RepeatBehavior="Forever" />
        </Storyboard>
    </BeginStoryboard>
</EventTrigger>
```

This all breaks down pretty easily. First, you open the `<ColorAnimation>` tag. Then you define the `TargetName` of the storyboard; that's the `rectangleBrush` you defined earlier, and now you know why you gave it a name, so you could refer to it down here. You also have a `TargetProperty` to indicate what property of the target `Brush` you're going to change, which in this case is `Color`. So far, so good.

The next few elements define how the animation works. The From property indicates the starting value of the animation; in this case, the starting color. The To property indicates the value where you want to end up; in this case, Red. The Duration indicates how long it takes for the value to change from the starting value to the final value. The duration is measured in hours, minutes, and seconds, so 0:0:10 means the color change will take 10 seconds to happen. The last line just adds a bit of class to the animation: the AutoReverse property indicates that the animation will turn the square blue, then back to red, automatically. The RepeatBehavior is used to limit how many times the animation will repeat; the value of Forever means that it'll repeat until the user closes the application.

Run your application now. You'll see your square, centered in the window, slowly changing from blue through purple to red, and back again, every 10 seconds. Feel free to stop the application and play with the values to get different effects.

 If you wanted to shift colors between more than two values—say, down the spectrum from red to yellow to green to blue—you'd use a different type of animation called ColorAnimationUsingKeyFrames. That's a little complex for this example, though.

The result looks like Figure 19-5, and the full XAML is shown in Example 19-4.

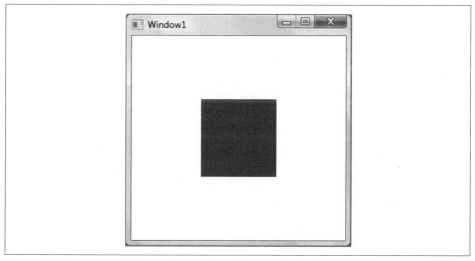

Figure 19-5. You can't tell this on the page, but this square is slowly changing color.

Example 19-4. You can create animation effects entirely in XAML, without having to write any C# code

```
<Window x:Class="Example_19_4____Animations.Window1"
    xmlns="http://schemas.microsoft.com/winfx/2006/xaml/presentation"
    xmlns:x="http://schemas.microsoft.com/winfx/2006/xaml"
```

Example 19-4. You can create animation effects entirely in XAML, without having to write any C# code (continued)

```
      Title="Window1" Height="300" Width="300">
      <Grid>
          <Rectangle Name="myRectangle" Width="100" Height="100">
              <Rectangle.Fill>
                  <SolidColorBrush x:Name="rectangleBrush"
                                   Color="Blue" />
              </Rectangle.Fill>
              <Rectangle.Triggers>
                  <EventTrigger RoutedEvent="Rectangle.Loaded">
                      <BeginStoryboard>
                          <Storyboard>
                              <ColorAnimation
                                  Storyboard.TargetName=
                                      "rectangleBrush"
                                  Storyboard.TargetProperty="Color"
                                  From="Blue" To="Red"
                                  Duration="0:0:10"
                                  AutoReverse="True"
                                  RepeatBehavior="Forever" />
                          </Storyboard>
                      </BeginStoryboard>
                  </EventTrigger>
              </Rectangle.Triggers>
          </Rectangle>
      </Grid>
</Window>
```

It's important to note here that you haven't written a single line of C# code for this example. This entire animation happened declaratively, in the XAML file. WPF contains the code to automate all of this for you.

Animations As Resources

We mentioned earlier that you can define an animation as a resource; in this next example, we'll show you how. You'll rotate the square in the window, and you'll see how it can respond to user events.

Rotating elements in WPF is pretty easy. You'll need to add a RenderTransform property to the Rectangle, just like you added the Fill element to hold the Brush. Add the following element after the Rectangle.Fill element from earlier:

```
<Rectangle.RenderTransform>
    <RotateTransform x:Name="rectangleRotate" Angle="0.0" />
</Rectangle.RenderTransform>
```

You've defined a RenderTransform element, with two properties. As with the Brush, you've given the RotateTransform a name, so you can refer to it from elsewhere in your code. You've also given it a starting angle, in this case, 0.

If you're going to rotate an element, you need to define the point on which the rotation will center; the hinge, if you want to imagine it that way. The default for a Rectangle is the upper-left corner, but we'd rather use the center point of the square instead. So, go back up to the definition of the Rectangle element, and add the following property:

```
<Rectangle Name="myRectangle" Width="100" Height="100"
           RenderTransformOrigin="0.5,0.5">
```

The RenderTransformOrigin property is a nice shortcut for defining rotation points. Instead of requiring you to count pixels from the edge of the element, or the window, you can provide two coordinates between 0 and 1 that define the point in relation to the edges of the element. In this case, 0.5,0.5 indicates halfway through each dimension, or the exact center of the square.

Now that you have the necessary properties set on the rectangle, you can define the animation in a storyboard. This time, you'll define the storyboard as a resource for the window itself so that other elements in the window can use this rotate animation. Go up to the Window definition, and define a subelement, <Window.Resources>, before the <Grid> element, like this:

```
<Window x:Class="Example_19_5____More_animation.Window1"
    xmlns="http://schemas.microsoft.com/winfx/2006/xaml/presentation"
    xmlns:x="http://schemas.microsoft.com/winfx/2006/xaml"
    Title="Window1" Height="300" Width="300">
    <Window.Resources>

    </Window.Resources>
    <Grid>
```

Within the Resources element, you'll define the storyboard. You don't need the <BeginStoryboard> element this time, because you're not defining an action, you're just defining the storyboard itself. Add the following code for the storyboard:

```
<Window.Resources>
    <Storyboard x:Key="Rotate">
        <DoubleAnimation
            Storyboard.TargetName="rectangleRotate"
            Storyboard.TargetProperty="Angle"
            From="0.0" To="360.0" Duration="0:0:10"
            RepeatBehavior="Forever"/>
    </Storyboard>
</Window.Resources>
```

Notice first that you're providing the storyboard itself with a name that can be referenced elsewhere in the code; that's necessary because this is a resource for the entire window.

As before, the storyboard contains an animation. This time, you're changing the angle of the Rectangle, which is expressed as a double, so you're using a DoubleAnimation. You provide the TargetName and TargetProperty, just as you did in the previous example, but this time you're targeting the RotateTransform property instead of the Brush. The From and To elements go from zero to 360, or a full rotation, and the Duration indicates that it'll take 10 seconds to accomplish. The RepeatBehavior property indicates that the square will keep rotating until something stops it.

Now you've defined the animation, but it's not associated with any triggers. Instead of having the animation start when the Rectangle loads, you'll have it start when the user moves the mouse over the square. To do that, you'll need a new EventTrigger element, associated with a different event. Add the following code inside the <Rectangle.Triggers> element, but after the closing tag of the trigger that's already there:

```
<EventTrigger RoutedEvent="Rectangle.MouseEnter">
    <BeginStoryboard Storyboard="{StaticResource Rotate}"
                     x:Name="BeginRotateStoryboard"/>
</EventTrigger>
```

The RoutedEvent that you're using this time is called MouseEnter, and it's raised by the Rectangle itself. Within the trigger is the BeginStoryboard element that you saw in the previous example, but instead of defining the storyboard here, you have a reference to the resource you defined earlier for the Window. You've also given the BeginStoryboard a name, so you can refer to that later; you'll see why in a minute.

For now, run the application, move the mouse over the square, and you'll see that the square rotates as it continues to change colors, as you'd see in Figure 19-6 if this book weren't black-and-white and static. You can experiment with the values in the storyboard, and with the angle and rotation origin defined in the Rectangle as well.

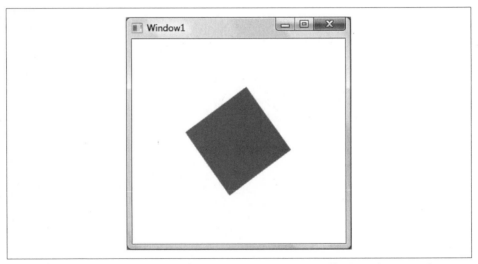

Figure 19-6. You still can't see it, but now the square is rotating in addition to changing color.

Let's take this animation one step further, and have the animation pause when the user moves the mouse off the square. To do that, you simply need to add another `EventTrigger`, after the one you just added, to handle a different event:

```
<EventTrigger RoutedEvent="Rectangle.MouseLeave">
    <PauseStoryboard BeginStoryboardName="BeginRotateStoryboard" />
</EventTrigger>
```

Here, you're handling the `MouseLeave` event, which is raised when the cursor exits the element. Instead of the `BeginStoryboard`, you're using a `PauseStoryboard` action here, which halts the execution of the `BeginStoryboard` in the previous trigger—that's why you gave it a name, so you could refer to it here.

Run your application again, and you'll see that the animation stops when the mouse leaves the square. If you bring the mouse back inside the square the animation starts again, but the angle starts over from zero. Fixing that would be somewhat more complicated, and beyond the scope of this chapter. Once again, notice that you still haven't written any C# code to accomplish these animations, even with the event triggers. The full XAML file for this example is shown in Example 19-5.

Example 19-5. This time you're creating the animation as a resource at the window level, but you still don't need to write any C# code

```
<Window x:Class="Example_19_5____More_animation.Window1"
    xmlns="http://schemas.microsoft.com/winfx/2006/xaml/presentation"
    xmlns:x="http://schemas.microsoft.com/winfx/2006/xaml"
    Title="Window1" Height="300" Width="300">
    <Window.Resources>
        <Storyboard x:Key="Rotate">
            <DoubleAnimation
                Storyboard.TargetName="rectangleRotate"
                Storyboard.TargetProperty="Angle"
                From="0.0" To="360.0" Duration="0:0:10"
                RepeatBehavior="Forever"/>
        </Storyboard>
    </Window.Resources>
    <Grid>
        <Rectangle Name="myRectangle" Width="100" Height="100"
                RenderTransformOrigin="0.5,0.5">
            <Rectangle.Fill>
                <SolidColorBrush x:Name="rectangleBrush"
                                 Color="Blue" />
            </Rectangle.Fill>
            <Rectangle.RenderTransform>
                <RotateTransform x:Name="rectangleRotate"
                                 Angle="0.0" />
            </Rectangle.RenderTransform>
            <Rectangle.Triggers>
                <EventTrigger RoutedEvent="Rectangle.Loaded">
                    <BeginStoryboard>
                        <Storyboard>
                            <ColorAnimation
```

Example 19-5. This time you're creating the animation as a resource at the window level, but you still don't need to write any C# code (continued)

```
                    Storyboard.TargetName=
                              "rectangleBrush"
                    Storyboard.TargetProperty="Color"
                    From="Blue" To="Red"
                    Duration="0:0:10"
                    AutoReverse="True"
                    RepeatBehavior="Forever" />
              </Storyboard>
          </BeginStoryboard>
        </EventTrigger>
        <EventTrigger RoutedEvent="Rectangle.MouseEnter">
            <BeginStoryboard
                Storyboard="{StaticResource Rotate}"
                x:Name="BeginRotateStoryboard"/>
        </EventTrigger>
        <EventTrigger RoutedEvent="Rectangle.MouseLeave">
            <PauseStoryboard
                BeginStoryboardName="BeginRotateStoryboard" />
        </EventTrigger>
      </Rectangle.Triggers>
    </Rectangle>
  </Grid>
</Window>
```

C# and WPF

So far, just about everything you've done with WPF has been *declarative*; that is, all the functionality has taken place in the XAML file. WPF is specifically designed that way, to be useful to designers as well as to developers. The only C# you've had to write so far has been some very rudimentary event handlers. In this section you're going to create an example that more closely resembles a production application, and that's going to involve a supporting class, and some event handlers.

In this example, you're going to grab the images of the first 20 presidents of the United States from the White House's website, and present them in a custom WPF control, a modified ListBox control. The control will not be wide enough to show all 20 images, so you'll provide a horizontal scroll bar, and as the user moves the mouse over an image, you'll provide feedback by enlarging that image (from 75 to 85) and increasing its opacity from 75% to 100%. As the user moves the mouse off the image, you'll return the image to its smaller, dimmer starting point.

This application will use some declarative animation, as you've already seen, although slightly subtler than the rotating square. In addition, when the user clicks on an image, you'll handle the click and display the name of the president using a C# event handler, and then you'll reach into the control and place the president's name into the title bar of the control.

Figure 19-7 shows the result of scrolling to the 16th president and clicking on the image. Note that the name of the president is displayed in the title bar and that the image of President Lincoln is both larger and brighter than the surrounding images.

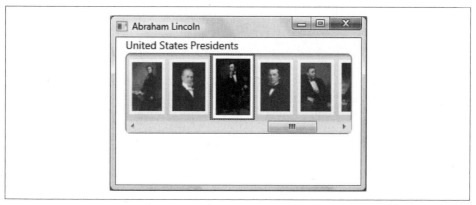

Figure 19-7. The Presidential Browser application makes use of some slightly subtler animations, but most of it still takes place in the XAML.

Grids and Stack Panels

Create a new WPF application called Presidential Browser. Up until now, you've placed all your elements in the default Grid control that WPF provides. This time, though, you want two items in the grid—the text block that says "United States Presidents" and the sideways ListBox of photographs, so you can make use of WPF's layout elements.

In addition to the grid element, WPF provides a layout object called a *stack panel*. A stack panel lets you stack a set of objects one on top of (or next to) another set of objects. That turns out to be very useful for laying out your page. If you want a stack that is horizontal and vertical (essentially a table), that's what the grid element is for. A grid has columns and rows, both counting from zero.

You'll create a simple grid of two rows and one column, and inside each row you'll place a stack panel. The top stack panel will hold the text, and the bottom stack panel will hold the ListBox that will, in turn, hold the photos. We'll break this down for you and take it one step at a time.

To begin, set the width of the Window element to 330 and the height to 230. Next, give the grid some dimensions, by adding properties to the grid element. A width of 300 and a height of 190 should do it. Add the properties like this:

```
<Grid Width="300" Height="190" >
```

Next, you'll need to define the rows in the grid element. That's easy enough to do with the `RowDefinition` element, but you'll need to put that within a `<Grid.RowDefinitions>` element, like this:

```
<Grid Width="300" Height="190">
    <Grid.RowDefinitions>
        <RowDefinition Height="20" />
        <RowDefinition Height="*" />
    </Grid.RowDefinitions>
```

You know that you want the first row to be a fixed 20 units high, so that number's hardcoded. The second row, though, should be whatever space is left in the grid. You could do the math yourself (and come up with 170), but the * element lets WPF do it for you.

The next things you need to add to the `Grid` are the two `StackPanel` elements. These are relatively easy: you just add the `StackPanel` elements inside the `<Grid>` tags. Inside each `StackPanel`, you'll add a `TextBlock` element, which does what it sounds like—it holds text. The `TextBlock` is a flexible control for displaying text, but here we're just using it to align the text in the panel. Add the following code to the XAML:

```
<StackPanel Grid.Row="0">
    <TextBlock FontSize="14">United States Presidents
    </TextBlock>
</StackPanel>
<StackPanel Grid.Row="1">
    <TextBlock Text="Bottom Stack Panel" VerticalAlignment="Center"/>
</StackPanel>
```

The first thing you need to notice here is that the rows in the grid are numbered from zero, the same as with arrays. The `TextBlock` element has a property for `FontSize`; it also has font weight and font family and the other features you might expect in a text element.

Your XAML code should now look like Example 19-6.

Example 19-6. This is the starting XAML for the Presidential Browser application, with the layout elements in place

```
<Window x:Class="Presidential_Browser.Window1"
    xmlns="http://schemas.microsoft.com/winfx/2006/xaml/presentation"
    xmlns:x="http://schemas.microsoft.com/winfx/2006/xaml"
    Title="Window1" Height="300" Width="300">
    <Grid Width="300" Height="190">
        <Grid.RowDefinitions>
            <RowDefinition Height="20" />
            <RowDefinition Height="*" />
        </Grid.RowDefinitions>
        <StackPanel Grid.Row="0">
            <TextBlock Text="Top Stack Panel" VerticalAlignment="Center"/>
        </StackPanel>
        <StackPanel Grid.Row="1">
            <TextBlock Text="Bottom Stack Panel" VerticalAlignment="Center"/>
```

Example 19-6. This is the starting XAML for the Presidential Browser application, with the layout elements in place (continued)

```
        </StackPanel>
    </Grid>
</Window>
```

Defining ListBox styles

Your next goal is to get the pictures into a ListBox and to turn the ListBox sideways so that the pictures scroll along, as shown previously in Figure 19-7.

To accomplish that, we need to do two things: we need to work with the style of the ListBox, and we need to work with its data. We'll take these one at a time to make it clear.

You've created a Brush as a resource before; now you'll make one for the entire Window element, in a Window.Resources section. This brush will be a LinearGradientBrush, which is a bit fancier than the Fill brush you used before. The gradient brush uses a nice shading effect that changes gradually through the colors identified in the GradientStop elements. The exact details aren't important, but you should note that we're giving this resource a name, as all resources have, so we can use it on the ListBox later. Create a Window.Resources section at the top of your XAML file, and add this code:

```
<Window.Resources>
    <LinearGradientBrush x:Key="ListBoxGradient"
            StartPoint="0,0" EndPoint="0,1">
        <GradientStop Color="#90000000" Offset="0" />
        <GradientStop Color="#40000000" Offset="0.005" />
        <GradientStop Color="#10000000" Offset="0.04" />
        <GradientStop Color="#20000000" Offset="0.945" />
        <GradientStop Color="#60FFFFFF" Offset="1" />
    </LinearGradientBrush>
</Window.Resources>
```

Briefly, all linear gradients are considered as occurring on a line ranging from 0 to 1. You can set the start points and endpoints (traditionally, the start point 0,0 is the upper-left corner and the endpoint 1,1 is the lower-right corner, making the linear gradient run on an angle). We've set the linear gradient to end at 0,1, making the gradient run from top to bottom, giving a horizontal gradient, moving through five colors, unevenly spaced.

The next resource you need to define is a Style object. We haven't specifically applied a style as a resource yet, but Style objects work like any other resource: they manage the properties of their targets, in this case, their style properties.

A difference in this case is that instead of defining a TargetName for the resource, you'll define a TargetType. That means that the style will be applied to all objects of a specific type (in this case, ListBox). Within the Style, you define a Template, which means that the style definition can be applied to objects, or modified by them.

Within that, there's a set of properties defined for the Border element, most of which are pretty self-explanatory. Notice that for a background, the Border element uses the ListBoxGradient brush that you defined a moment ago.

Within the Border element is a ScrollViewer element. This element is what gives the ListBox a horizontal scroll bar, but not a vertical one. Within the ScrollViewer is another StackPanel element—this is where you'll keep the images of the presidents. The IsItemsHost property indicates that this StackPanel will hold other objects (you'll see how this works in a bit), and the Orientation and HorizontalAlignment properties simply orient the StackPanel inside the ScrollViewer.

Add the following Style within the Window.Resources element, right after the LinearGradientBrush:

```
<Style x:Key="SpecialListStyle" TargetType="{x:Type ListBox}">
    <Setter Property="Template">
        <Setter.Value>
            <ControlTemplate TargetType="{x:Type ListBox}" >
                <Border BorderBrush="Gray"
                        BorderThickness="1"
                        CornerRadius="6"
                        Background="{DynamicResource ListBoxGradient}" >
                    <ScrollViewer
                        VerticalScrollBarVisibility="Disabled"
                        HorizontalScrollBarVisibility="Visible">
                        <StackPanel IsItemsHost="True"
                        Orientation="Horizontal"
                        HorizontalAlignment="Left" />
                    </ScrollViewer>
                </Border>
            </ControlTemplate>
        </Setter.Value>
    </Setter>
</Style>
```

Triggers and animations

The style for the ListBox that you just created contains a StackPanel that contains items. The next thing you'll do is define the style for these items. The items, you'll recall, are the images of the presidents that you're displaying. We mentioned that these images will change appearance when the user moves the mouse over them. You saw earlier in the chapter how to interact with the user's mouse movements—you'll need to define some triggers. The Triggers will reside in the Style, rather than being attached to a specific instance of a control.

This style begins by setting its target type, as the last style did (ListBoxItems), and three properties: MaxHeight, MinHeight, and Opacity. The MaxHeight and MinHeight properties have the same value, which means that the size of the items is fixed, but you'll be able to change that dynamically, as you'll see shortly. The Opacity of a control is defined as a value between 0 and 1:

```
<Style x:Key="SpecialListItem"
    TargetType="{x:Type ListBoxItem}">
        <Setter Property="MaxHeight"  Value="75" />
        <Setter Property="MinHeight"  Value="75" />
        <Setter Property="Opacity"    Value=".75" />
```

The style then sets a couple of triggers. As with the triggers you saw earlier in the chapter, these triggers associate an `EventTrigger` with a `RoutedEvent`. Specifically, the first trigger uses the `MouseEnter` event that you saw in an earlier example:

```
<EventTrigger RoutedEvent="Mouse.MouseEnter">
```

In this case, the event will be kicked off when the mouse enters the object that is associated with this `EventTrigger` (that object will be the `ListBox` item), as opposed to targeting a specific control as you did earlier in the chapter. Within that `EventTrigger` you defined an `EventTrigger.Actions` element. In this case, the action is `BeginStoryBoard`, and there is a single, unnamed `Storyboard`:

```
<EventTrigger RoutedEvent="Mouse.MouseEnter">
    <EventTrigger.Actions>
        <BeginStoryboard>
            <Storyboard>
                <DoubleAnimation Duration="0:0:0.2"
                    Storyboard.TargetProperty="MaxHeight"  To="85" />
                <DoubleAnimation Duration="0:0:0.2"
                    Storyboard.TargetProperty="Opacity" To="1.0" />
            </Storyboard>
        </BeginStoryboard>
    </EventTrigger.Actions>
</EventTrigger>
```

The action is inside the storyboard, where you'll find two animations. These are `DoubleAnimation` elements, because you're changing two properties with double values. These two animations are defined to have a duration of 2/10 of a second. The `TargetProperty` refers to the property of the object to be animated (that is, the `ListBox` item)—in the first case, the height of the `ListBox` item, which will be animated to a height of 85 (from a starting point of 75). The second animation will change the opacity from its starting point of .75 to 1 (making it appear to brighten). The other trigger is for the `MouseLeave` event, and just reverses the effects.

Here's the XAML for the entire style; add this to the `Windows.Resources` section:

```
<Style x:Key="SpecialListItem"
    TargetType="{x:Type ListBoxItem}">
        <Setter Property="MaxHeight"  Value="75" />
        <Setter Property="MinHeight"  Value="75" />
        <Setter Property="Opacity"    Value=".75" />
    <Style.Triggers>
        <EventTrigger RoutedEvent="Mouse.MouseEnter">
            <EventTrigger.Actions>
                <BeginStoryboard>
                    <Storyboard>
                        <DoubleAnimation Duration="0:0:0.2"
```

```
                    Storyboard.TargetProperty="MaxHeight"
                        To="85" />
                <DoubleAnimation Duration="0:0:0.2"
                    Storyboard.TargetProperty="Opacity"
                        To="1.0" />
            </Storyboard>
        </BeginStoryboard>
    </EventTrigger.Actions>
</EventTrigger>

<EventTrigger RoutedEvent="Mouse.MouseLeave">
    <EventTrigger.Actions>
        <BeginStoryboard>
            <Storyboard>
                <DoubleAnimation Duration="0:0:0.2"
                    Storyboard.TargetProperty="MaxHeight" />
                <DoubleAnimation Duration="0:0:0.2"
                    Storyboard.TargetProperty="Opacity" />
            </Storyboard>
        </BeginStoryboard>
    </EventTrigger.Actions>
</EventTrigger>
        </Style.Triggers>
    </Style>
```

Adding Data

We're now going to cheat somewhat, and rather than getting our data from a web service or from a database, we're going to put it right into our resources. The data will consist of a generic list of ImageURL objects. You haven't heard of these types of objects before, because you're going to create the class right now. Right-click on the project file in the Solution Explorer and choose Add → Class. When the Add New Item dialog box appears, the Class item will be selected automatically. Leave it selected, and give the class file a name of *PhotoCatalog.cs*. Visual Studio will automatically open a new class file for you. Add the code in Example 19-7, and be sure to add the using System.Windows.Media.Imaging statement, because you'll need it, and also be sure to add the public modifier to the class name.

Example 19-7. The ImageURL class defines a new class that you'll be able to use in the XAML application namespace

```
using System;
using System.Collections.Generic;
using System.Windows.Media.Imaging;

namespace PhotoCatalog
{
    public class ImageURL
    {
        public string Path { get; private set; }
        public Uri ImageURI { get; set; }
```

```
        public BitmapFrame Image { get; private set; }
        public string Name { get;  set; }

        public ImageURL() { }

        public ImageURL(string path, string name)
        {
            Path = path;
            ImageURI = new Uri(Path);
            Image = BitmapFrame.Create(ImageURI);
            Name = name;
        }
        public override string ToString()
        {
            return Path;
        }
    }

    public class Images : List<ImageURL> { }

}
```

You've actually created two classes here. The first class, ImageURL, is designed to act as a *wrapper*—that is, it'll hold the properties for an image that you retrieve given the path to an image, or a URI from which we can create an image. Note that you override ToString() to return the Path property, even though we haven't explicitly created the backing variable.

The second class is at the very bottom: Images derives from a generic list of ImageURL objects. The implementation is empty—all you're really doing with this class is providing an alias for List<ImageURL>.

Instantiating objects declaratively

Now that you've declared these classes, you can create instances of them in the Resources section of the XAML file—you're not limited to the types defined by the XAML namespace. However, before you can use your new type, you must first include the class in your XAML file by creating a namespace for this project. At the top of the XAML file, you'll find the other namespace declarations for this project; they all start with xmlns:. Add your own xmlns statement, and call the new namespace local, like this:

```
    xmlns:local="clr-namespace:Presidential_Browser"
```

As soon as you type **local=**, IntelliSense will help you out with the rest of the namespace. You'll probably notice an error message in the Design window at that point, and you'll need to reload the designer. Go ahead and do that, and everything will be fine.

Now that you have the local namespace, you can create an instance of the Images class in the Window.Resources section, like this:

```
<local:Images x:Key="Presidents"></local:Images>
```

This is the XAML equivalent of writing:

```
List<ImageURL> Presidents = new List<ImageURL>( );
```

You then add to that list by creating instances of ImageURL between the opening and closing tags of the Images declaration:

```
<local:ImageURL ImageURI="http://www.whitehouse.gov/history/presidents/images/
gw1.gif" Name="George Washington" />
```

Again, this is the XAML equivalent of writing:

```
ImageURL newImage = new ImageURL(
    "http://www.whitehouse.gov/history/presidents/images/gw1.gif,"
    "George Washington");
Presidents.Add(newImage);
```

You'll need to do that 20 times, once for each of the first 20 presidents. The URL is somewhat long, so you might want to cut and paste it, or you can download the code listing for this chapter from *http://www.oreilly.com* and cut and paste that part. Now you have a static data resource you can refer to in the rest of your XAML file; and that completes the Resources section.

Using the Data in the XAML

Now that you've defined the resource, the next step is to provide a way for the Grid element to access the data in that resource. To do that, provide a DataContext for the Grid:

```
<Grid Width="300" Height="190"
    DataContext="{StaticResource Presidents}">
```

Every Framework object has a DataContext object, usually null. If you don't instruct the object otherwise, it will look up the object hierarchy from where it is defined until it finds an object that does have a DataContext defined, and then it will use that DataContext as its data source. You can use virtually anything as a DataContext—a database, an XML file, or, as in this case, a static resource.

Defining the ListBox

Now that you've got all the resources in place, you're finally ready to define the ListBox and the template for its contents in the second StackPanel. The first thing you need to do is set some of the properties for the ListBox element:

```
<StackPanel Grid.Row="1" Grid.ColumnSpan="3" >
  <ListBox Style="{StaticResource SpecialListStyle}"
```

```
Name="PresPhotoListBox" Margin="0,0,0,20"
SelectionChanged="PresPhotoListBox_SelectionChanged"
ItemsSource="{Binding }"
IsSynchronizedWithCurrentItem="True" SelectedIndex="0"
ItemContainerStyle="{StaticResource SpecialListItem}" >
```

The first line shown here places the stack panel into the grid at row offset 1 (the second row). The `ListBox` itself has its style set to a `StaticResource` (the `SpecialListStyle` resource you defined earlier in the Resources section). The `ListBox` is named:

```
Name="PresPhotoListBox"
```

And an event handler is defined for anytime an image is clicked:

```
SelectionChanged="PresPhotoListBox_SelectionChanged"
```

The source for each item is set to `Binding`, indicating that you're binding to the source in the parent element (which you just defined in the `Grid` element's `DataContext` property). Finally, the `ItemContainerStyle` is set, again, to the style defined earlier in the Resources section.

Each item in the `ListBox` will be drawn from the (unknown) number of items in the data (which in this case happens to be statically placed in the Resources, but could well be dynamically drawn from a web service). To do this, we'll need a template for how to draw each item. Add the following code as a subelement of the `ListBox` element:

```
<ListBox.ItemTemplate>
    <DataTemplate>
        <Border VerticalAlignment="Center"
            HorizontalAlignment="Center" Padding="4"
            Margin="2" Background="White">
            <Image Source="{Binding Path=ImageURI}" />
        </Border>
    </DataTemplate>
</ListBox.ItemTemplate>
```

Within the `ListBox.ItemTemplate`, you place a `DataTemplate`; this is necessary if you want to show anything more than simple text derived from the data retrieved. In this case, you place a `Border` object within the `DataTemplate`, and within the `Border` object you place the `Image` object. It is the `Image` object you really care about (though the `Border` object helps with placement). The `Image` requires a source; here, you add `Binding` (indicating that you are binding to the current source), and you state that you'll be using the `ImageURI` property to set the `Path`. Because the source you're binding to is a list of `ImageURL` objects, and each `ImageURL` has four public properties (`Path`, `ImageURI`, `Image`, and `Name`), this is the critical piece of data required to tell the `DataTemplate` how to get the information necessary to create the image in the `ListBox`.

Event Handling

Except for defining the `ImageURL` class, everything you've done so far in this example has been done declaratively, in the XAML file. Now it's finally time to write some C# in this example. You may have noticed that you did create an event handler for when the user changes the selected item in the `ListBox`:

```
SelectionChanged="PresPhotoListBox_SelectionChanged"
```

This is typically done by clicking on an image (though you can accomplish this with the arrow keys as well). This event will fire the event handler in the code-behind file, which is, finally, C#.

The event handler is, as you would expect, in the code-behind file, *Window1.xaml.cs*. Switch to that file now, and add the following event handler:

```
private void PresPhotoListBox_SelectionChanged(
        object sender, SelectionChangedEventArgs e)
{
    ListBox lb = sender as ListBox;
    if (lb != null)
    {

        if (lb.SelectedItem != null)
        {

            string chosenName =
                (lb.SelectedItem as ImageURL).Name.ToString( );
            Title = chosenName;

        }
    }
    else
    {
        throw new ArgumentException(
            "Expected ListBox to call selection changed in
            PresPhotoListBox_SelectionChanged");
    }
}
```

Like all event handlers in .NET, this handler receives two parameters: the sender (in this case, the `ListBox`) and an object derived from `EventArgs`.

In the code shown, you cast the sender to the `ListBox` type (and consider it an exception if the sender is not a `ListBox`, as that is the only type of object that should be sending to this event handler).

You then check to make sure that the `selectedItem` is not null (during startup it is possible that it can be null). Assuming it is not null, you cast the `selectedItem` to an `ImageURL`, extract the `Name` property, and assign it to a temporary variable, `chosenName`, which we then in turn assign to the title of the window.

The interim variable is useful only for debugging; there is no other reason not to write:

```
Title = (lb.SelectedItem as ImageURL).Name.ToString( );
```

 You can also get at both the currently selected president's ImageURL and the previously selected ImageURL through the SelectionChangedEventArgs parameter.

The Complete XAML File

If you're not sitting in front of your computer right now, Example 19-8 has the complete XAML listing. Please replace the ellipses (...) in the URLs in this listing with:

```
http://www.whitehouse.gov/history/presidents/images
```

We omitted this long URL from the listing to save space.

Example 19-8. Here is the complete XAML listing for the Presidential Browser application

```
<Window x:Class="Presidential_Browser.Window1"
    xmlns="http://schemas.microsoft.com/winfx/2006/xaml/presentation"
    xmlns:x="http://schemas.microsoft.com/winfx/2006/xaml"
    xmlns:local="clr-namespace:Presidential_Browser"
    Title="Window1" Height="300" Width="300">
    <Window.Resources>
        <LinearGradientBrush x:Key="ListBoxGradient"
            StartPoint="0,0" EndPoint="0,1">
            <GradientStop Color="#90000000" Offset="0" />
            <GradientStop Color="#40000000" Offset="0.005" />
            <GradientStop Color="#10000000" Offset="0.04" />
            <GradientStop Color="#20000000" Offset="0.945" />
            <GradientStop Color="#60FFFFFF" Offset="1" />
        </LinearGradientBrush>
        <Style x:Key="SpecialListStyle" TargetType="{x:Type ListBox}">
            <Setter Property="Template">
                <Setter.Value>
                    <ControlTemplate TargetType="{x:Type ListBox}" >
                        <Border BorderBrush="Gray"
                                BorderThickness="1"
                                CornerRadius="6"
                                Background=
                                   "{DynamicResource ListBoxGradient}" >
                            <ScrollViewer
                                VerticalScrollBarVisibility="Disabled"
                                HorizontalScrollBarVisibility="Visible">
                                <StackPanel IsItemsHost="True"
                                            Orientation="Horizontal"
                                            HorizontalAlignment="Left" />
                            </ScrollViewer>
                        </Border>
                    </ControlTemplate>
```

```xml
                </Setter.Value>
            </Setter>
        </Style>
        <Style x:Key="SpecialListItem"
               TargetType="{x:Type ListBoxItem}">
            <Setter Property="MaxHeight"  Value="75" />
            <Setter Property="MinHeight"  Value="75" />
            <Setter Property="Opacity"    Value=".75" />
            <Style.Triggers>
                <EventTrigger RoutedEvent="Mouse.MouseEnter">
                    <EventTrigger.Actions>
                        <BeginStoryboard>
                            <Storyboard>
                                <DoubleAnimation Duration="0:0:0.2"
                                    Storyboard.TargetProperty="MaxHeight"
                                    To="85" />
                                <DoubleAnimation Duration="0:0:0.2"
                                    Storyboard.TargetProperty="Opacity"
                                    To="1.0" />
                            </Storyboard>
                        </BeginStoryboard>
                    </EventTrigger.Actions>
                </EventTrigger>

                <EventTrigger RoutedEvent="Mouse.MouseLeave">
                    <EventTrigger.Actions>
                        <BeginStoryboard>
                            <Storyboard>
                                <DoubleAnimation Duration="0:0:0.2"
                                    Storyboard.TargetProperty="MaxHeight" />
                                <DoubleAnimation Duration="0:0:0.2"
                                    Storyboard.TargetProperty="Opacity" />
                            </Storyboard>
                        </BeginStoryboard>
                    </EventTrigger.Actions>
                </EventTrigger>
            </Style.Triggers>
        </Style>
        <local:Images x:Key="Presidents">
            <local:ImageURL ImageURI=".../gw1.gif" Name="George Washington" />
            <local:ImageURL ImageURI=".../ja2.gif" Name="John Adams" />
            <local:ImageURL ImageURI=".../tj3.gif" Name="Thomas Jefferson" />
            <local:ImageURL ImageURI=".../jm4.gif" Name="James Madison" />
            <local:ImageURL ImageURI=".../jm5.gif" Name="James Monroe" />
            <local:ImageURL ImageURI=".../ja6.gif" Name="John Quincy Adams" />
            <local:ImageURL ImageURI=".../aj7.gif" Name="Andrew Jackson" />
            <local:ImageURL ImageURI=".../mb8.gif" Name="Martin Van Buren" />
            <local:ImageURL ImageURI=".../wh9.gif" Name="William H. Harrison" />
            <local:ImageURL ImageURI=".../jt10_1.gif" Name="John Tyler" />
            <local:ImageURL ImageURI=".../jp11.gif" Name="James K. Polk" />
            <local:ImageURL ImageURI=".../zt12.gif" Name="Zachary Taylor" />
```

```xaml
        <local:ImageURL ImageURI=".../mf13.gif" Name="Millard Fillmore" />
        <local:ImageURL ImageURI=".../fp14.gif" Name="Franklin Pierce" />
        <local:ImageURL ImageURI=".../jb15.gif" Name="James Buchanan" />
        <local:ImageURL ImageURI=".../al16.gif" Name="Abraham Lincoln" />
        <local:ImageURL ImageURI=".../aj17.gif" Name="Andrew Johnson" />
        <local:ImageURL ImageURI=".../ug18.gif" Name="Ulysses S. Grant" />
        <local:ImageURL ImageURI=".../rh19.gif" Name="Rutherford B. Hayes" />
        <local:ImageURL ImageURI=".../jg20.gif" Name="James Garfield" />
    </local:Images>

</Window.Resources>
<Grid Width="300" Height="190"
      DataContext="{StaticResource Presidents}">
    <Grid.RowDefinitions>
        <RowDefinition Height="20" />
        <RowDefinition Height="*" />
    </Grid.RowDefinitions>
    <StackPanel Grid.Row="0">
        <TextBlock FontSize="14" Grid.Row="0" >
            United States Presidents</TextBlock>
    </StackPanel>
    <StackPanel Grid.Row="1" Grid.ColumnSpan="3" >
        <ListBox Style="{StaticResource SpecialListStyle}"
                Name="PresPhotoListBox" Margin="0,0,0,20"
                SelectionChanged="PresPhotoListBox_SelectionChanged"
                ItemsSource="{Binding }"
                IsSynchronizedWithCurrentItem="True"
                SelectedIndex="0"
                ItemContainerStyle=
                    "{StaticResource SpecialListItem}" >
        <ListBox.ItemTemplate>
            <DataTemplate>
                <Border VerticalAlignment="Center"
                        HorizontalAlignment="Center"
                        Padding="4" Margin="2" Background="White">
                    <Image Source="{Binding Path=ImageURI}" />
                </Border>
            </DataTemplate>
        </ListBox.ItemTemplate>
        </ListBox>
    </StackPanel>
  </Grid>
</Window>
```

Run the application now, and you should see that it looks like Figure 19-7 (shown previously). The individual images animate when you mouse over them, and clicking one changes the title bar of the window to show the president's name.

Silverlight

As you've seen with WPF, the flexibility of defining the design of your interface in XML lets you include features that you wouldn't have thought possible before. In fact, you can make Windows applications that don't look like Windows applications at all, but more like web applications. The idea of separating the design of the application from the underlying functionality opens up interesting possibilities.

In Windows and WPF applications, both the interface and the functional code reside on your local machine; the separation is entirely in the design stage. On the Web, though, the application usually resides on a remote server, with the client using only a browser. ASP.NET with AJAX brings the two a bit closer together, where some of the controls are created in code that runs in the browser, reducing the number of times the browser needs to get data from the server, which makes for a faster, smoother user experience.

Silverlight narrows the gap even more, by bringing the WPF tools to run in browsers over the Web. Silverlight requires a browser plug-in that the remote user has to accept. That plug-in contains a carefully chosen subset of the Common Language Runtime (CLR), allowing Silverlight applications to use managed code languages like VB.NET or C# and to implement applications built on a subset of XAML.

The net result is that Silverlight applications are *much* faster, are richer, and have capabilities that are simply not possible with AJAX, but they are limited to running on IE, Firefox, and Safari on Windows, the Mac, and Linux, for now. Silverlight is in version 2.0 at the time of this writing, and a lot of development remains to be done, but the possibilities are very exciting.

Learning Silverlight is not hard, and what you've learned about XAML in this chapter gives you a significant head start, but there is quite a bit to it. A full discussion would require a book in itself. See *Programming Silverlight* by Jesse Liberty and Tim Heuer (O'Reilly) to learn more.

Summary

- Windows Presentation Foundation (WPF) is a system intended to combine the functionality of Windows Forms with greater flexibility in interface design.

- In WPF, the presentation of the application is kept in a separate file, written in XAML, which is a dialect of XML.

- When you start a new WPF project, Visual Studio opens both the Design window and the XAML window. Changes made in one window are immediately reflected in the other.

- The XAML file uses a Window element as its root element.

- Each WPF application uses a distinct namespace, defined by the Microsoft XAML schema, and you can add your own objects to that namespace.

- XAML contains several elements for positioning other elements within the application, including the Grid and Stackpanel elements.

- You can set the properties of XAML elements in the Properties window, or by editing the XAML directly.

- Event handlers for WPF elements are kept in a code file, written in C# or another .NET language.

- Resources allow you to define properties for use by any appropriate element in the application.

- Resources require you to define a key in the current namespace so that you can refer to them later in the application.

- A Style element, which can be defined on an element or as a resource, can contain a number of Setter elements that define specific properties of the target element.

- Routed events in WPF can be associated with triggers, which can change the properties of elements in response to events. Triggers can be defined on individual elements, or as resources.

- Animation elements are contained within Storyboard elements. There are different animation elements depending on the type of the value that the animation is changing.

- A trigger can contain a storyboard action, which can contain a storyboard element, but a trigger cannot contain a storyboard by itself.

- Many triggers can be declared completely declaratively, without needing to write any C# code.

- The DataContext property allows an element to access a data source.

Your skills have come a long way from where they were at the beginning of the book, through the various pieces of the C# language, and now into Windows applications in a couple of different ways. There's still one major piece of the development puzzle that we've left untouched, though: handling data. You saw in the Presidential Browser application in this chapter that you had to handcode the URLs for 20 images into the Resources section of your application; that's a real pain. It would have been much easier if you could have read the information directly from a repository of some kind. Fortunately, many such repositories are available, from simple XML files to full-fledged SQL databases, and C# can access many of them. We'll spend the final two chapters of this book looking at how to access data from C#, first with ADO.NET and then with the newer Language Integrated Query (LINQ) methods.

Test Your Knowledge: Quiz

Question 19-1. What is XAML?

Question 19-2. What are two ways to edit the properties of a XAML element?

Question 19-3. What does the x: refer to in element definitions?

Question 19-4. What's the syntax for the Margin property?

Question 19-5. If you had an application with 32 buttons, what's the easiest way to ensure that all the buttons are colored blue?

Question 19-6. What property should you use to ensure that your style will be applied to controls of only a certain type?

Question 19-7. What element allows you to handle certain WPF events within the XAML file?

Question 19-8. What kind of control contains an animation?

Question 19-9. What is the purpose of the BeginStoryboard element?

Question 19-10. What property do you use to enable an element to access a data source?

Test Your Knowledge: Exercises

Exercise 19-1. We'll start things off simply. Create a WPF application with several Button and TextBox controls. Set the TextBox controls to have white text on a blue background, and the Button controls to have green text on a gray background.

Exercise 19-2. Now you'll create your own animation. Create a WPF application with a single Button control (it doesn't have to do anything). Add an animation that increases the size of the button from the standard size to 300 units wide by 200 units high, and then reverses itself.

Exercise 19-3. Create a rectangle, 100 by 200. Add three buttons to the application: one to rotate the rectangle clockwise, the second to rotate it counterclockwise, and the third to stop the rotation.

CHAPTER 20

ADO.NET and Relational Databases

Most of the applications that you've written so far in this book have been short-lived things. They do their thing and end, and any information they need is either hard-coded or supplied by the user. That's to be expected when you're learning a language, but in the real world, many applications deal with large quantities of data, derived from somewhere else. That data could be in a database, or a text document, or an XML file, or one of tons of other storage methods. Dealing with data is another complex topic that can fill whole books on its own, but we're going to give you a taste of it in this chapter and the next, starting with the traditional ADO.NET, and then introducing you to the brand-new Language Integrated Query (LINQ).

ADO.NET was designed to provide a *disconnected* data architecture, though it does have a connected alternative. In a disconnected architecture, data is retrieved from a database and cached (stored) on your local machine. You manipulate the data on your local computer and connect to the database only when you wish to alter records or acquire new data.

There are significant advantages to disconnecting your data architecture from your database. The biggest advantage is that your application, whether running on the Web or on a local machine, will create a reduced burden on the database server, which may help your application to scale well; that is, it doesn't impose a substantially greater burden as the number of users increases. Database connections are resource-intensive, and it is difficult to have thousands (or hundreds of thousands) of simultaneous continuous connections. A disconnected architecture is resource-frugal, though there are times that all you want to do is connect to the database, suck out a stream of data, and disconnect; and ADO.NET has a Reader class that allows for that as well.

ADO.NET typically connects to the database to retrieve data, and connects again to update data when you've made changes. Most applications spend most of their time simply reading through data and displaying it; ADO.NET provides a disconnected subset of the data for your use while reading and displaying, but it is up to you as the developer to keep in mind that the data in the database may change while you are disconnected, and to plan accordingly.

Relational Databases and SQL

Although one can certainly write an entire book on relational databases, and another on SQL, the essentials of these technologies aren't hard to understand, and you'll understand the chapter better if we spend a little time on the basics. A *database* is a repository of data. A *relational database* organizes your data into tables. In this chapter, we'll use the Northwind database, which is available as a free download from Microsoft. It was originally intended for a much older version of SQL Server, but it works well for our examples in this chapter without requiring too much installation work on your part.

Installing the Northwind Database

The Northwind database is a database file that's intended for testing and practice purposes. To use the database, you'll need to make sure that you have SQL Server Express edition. If you're using Visual Studio, it was installed by default. If you're using C# Express, installing SQL Server was optional, and if you followed the instructions in Chapter 1, you already have it installed. If not, head back to Chapter 1 and check out the installation instructions there.

If you're using Windows Vista, you're going to need to do a bit of extra work (if not, you can skip the next few paragraphs). Vista requires that only an administrator can install and access databases, but your default user isn't automatically added to the SQL Server Administrators group. Fortunately, there's an easy fix for this problem:

1. Go to *C:\Program Files\Microsoft SQL Server\90\Shared* (assuming you installed SQL Server to its default location).

2. Run the *SqlProv.exe* application.

3. You'll see the usual Windows Vista confirmation window. Click Confirm.

4. This starts the User Provisioning Tool, shown in Figure 20-1. In the "User to provision" box, make sure the computer name and the username of the user you want to grant permissions to are entered; they should be there automatically. The "Available permissions" box looks like it should have a long list, but there's really only one permission available, and it should be selected already.

5. Click the >> button to grant permission to that user, and then click OK to close the tool.

Next, download the Northwind database from this location:

> *http://www.microsoft.com/downloads/details.aspx?FamilyID=06616212-0356-46A0-8DA2-EEBC53A68034*

You'll download an *.msi* file, which you can then run to install the databases on your hard drive. By default, they install to *c:\SQL Server 2000 Sample Databases*.

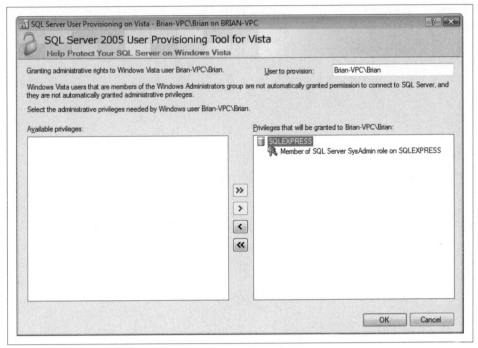

Figure 20-1. The User Provisioning Tool allows you to grant SQL Server administrative permissions to a Vista user account, which will save you a lot of headaches.

If you're using Windows Vista Home Edition, use Windows Explorer to navigate to the folder where the files are installed. Right-click anywhere in the folder and select Properties. The Properties window will likely show you that this folder is read-only. Clear that checkbox, and when you're asked, apply the setting to files and subfolders as well. If you don't do this, you won't be able to access the database.

Next, open a command-line window: on Windows XP and older versions, select Start → Run, and type "cmd" in the Run dialog box. On Vista, simply click Start, then type "cmd" and press Enter. A command window will open. Change to the directory where the databases are stored:

```
cd c:\SQL Server 2000 Sample Databases
```

Then enter this command (all on one line):

```
sqlcmd -E -S.\sqlexpress -i instnwnd.sql
```

If you've done it correctly, you should see the following messages:

```
Changed database context to 'master'.
Changed database context to 'northwind'.
```

If you see that, you've succeeded. If not, go back and check the permissions in the folder, or try typing the sqlcmd command again.

Once you have Northwind installed, you should check to make sure that you can make a data connection to it from your applications.

1. Start Visual Studio and create a new project; it doesn't matter what kind.

2. There's a special window in the IDE that shows your database connections, but it goes by two different names. In C# Express, it's called Database Explorer; in Visual Studio, it's Server Explorer. If the window isn't open already, select View → Other Windows → Database Explorer (or Server Explorer in Visual Studio) to open it.

3. The Database Explorer will probably contain a single item, Data Connections. To add a connection to the Northwind database, right-click Data Connections and select Add Connection.

4. The Choose Data Source box opens, looking like Figure 20-2. Select Microsoft SQL Server Database File, and click Continue.

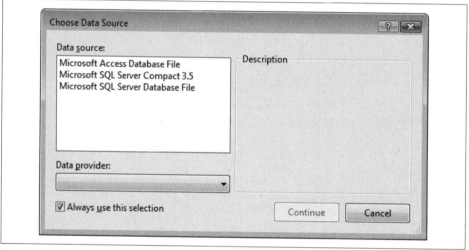

Figure 20-2. You'll be using a SQL Server database, so select Microsoft SQL Server Database File.

5. The Add Connection dialog box opens next, shown in Figure 20-3. Click the Browse button and navigate to the *Northwind.mdf* file. If you installed Northwind to the default directory, the file should be in *C:\SQL Server 2000 Sample Databases*.

6. After you've selected the *.mdf* file, it should be listed in the "Database file name (new or existing)" field. If it isn't, you may need to reinstall Northwind. Click the Test Connection button to make sure everything worked (this may take awhile to respond, so be patient).

7. Click OK. The *Northwind.mdf* database now appears in the Database Explorer, and you're ready to go.

Figure 20-3. Use the Add Connection dialog box to select the Northwind database and test the connection.

Tables, Records, and Columns

The Northwind database describes a fictional company buying and selling food products. The data for Northwind is divided into 13 *tables*, or broad sets of data, including Customers, Employees, Orders, Order Details, Products, and so forth.

Every table in a relational database is organized into *rows*, where each row represents a single record—say, the data for a single product order. The rows are organized into *columns*, which represent categories of data. All the rows in a table have the same column structure. For example, the Orders table has these columns: OrderID, CustomerID, EmployeeID, OrderDate, and so on.

For any given order, you need to know the customer's name, address, contact name, and so forth. You could store that information with each order, but that would be very inefficient. Instead, you use a second table called Customers, in which each row represents a single customer. In the Customers table is a column for the CustomerID. Each customer has a unique ID, and that field is marked as the *primary key* for that table. A primary key is the column or combination of columns that uniquely identifies a record in a given table.

The Orders table uses the CustomerID as a *foreign key*. A foreign key is a column (or combination of columns) that is a primary (or otherwise unique) key from a different table. The Orders table uses the CustomerID (the primary key used in the Customers table) to identify which customer has placed the order. To determine the address for the order, you can use the CustomerID to look up the customer record in the Customers table.

This use of foreign keys is particularly helpful in representing one-to-many or many-to-one relationships among tables. By separating information into tables that are linked by foreign keys, you avoid having to repeat information in records. A single customer, for example, can have multiple orders, but it is inefficient to place the same customer information (name, phone number, credit limit, and so on) in every order record. The process of removing redundant information from your records and shifting it to separate tables is called *normalization*.

Normalization

Normalization not only makes your use of the database more efficient, but it also reduces the likelihood of data corruption. If you kept the customer's name in both the Customers table and the Orders table, you would run the risk that a change in one table might not be reflected in the other. Thus, if you changed the customer's address in the Customers table, that change might not be reflected in every row in the Orders table (and a lot of work would be necessary to make sure that it was reflected). By keeping only the CustomerID in Orders, you are free to change the address in Customers, and the change is automatically reflected for each order.

Just as C# programmers want the compiler to catch bugs at compile time rather than at runtime, database programmers want the database to help them avoid data corruption. The compiler helps avoid bugs in C# by enforcing the rules of the language (for example, you can't use a variable you haven't defined yet). SQL Server and other modern relational databases avoid bugs by enforcing *constraints* that you define. For example, the Customers database marks the CustomerID as a primary key. This creates a primary key constraint in the database, which ensures that each CustomerID is unique. If you were to enter a customer named Liberty Associates, Inc., with the CustomerID of LIBE, and then tried to add Liberty Mutual Funds with a CustomerID of LIBE, the database would reject the second record because of the primary key constraint.

Declarative Referential Integrity

Relational databases use *declarative referential integrity* (DRI) to establish constraints on the relationships among the various tables. For example, you might declare a constraint on the Orders table that dictates that no order can have a CustomerID unless that CustomerID represents a valid record in Customers. This helps avoid two types of mistakes. First, you can't enter a record with an invalid CustomerID. Second, you can't delete a customer record if that CustomerID is used in any order. The integrity of your data and its relationships is thus protected.

SQL

The most popular language for querying and manipulating databases is Structured Query Language (SQL), usually pronounced "sequel." SQL is a declarative language, as opposed to a procedural language, and it can take awhile to get used to working with a declarative language when you are used to languages such as C#.

The heart of SQL is the *query*. A query is a statement that returns a set of records from the database. The queries in Transact-SQL (the version used by SQL Server) are very similar to the queries used in LINQ (as you'll see in the next chapter), though the actual syntax is slightly different.

For example, you might like to see all the CompanyNames and CustomerIDs of every record in the Customers table in which the customer's address is in London. To do so, you'd write this query:

```
Select CustomerID, CompanyName from Customers where city = 'London'
```

This returns the following six records as output:

```
CustomerID CompanyName
---------- -----------------------------------------
AROUT      Around the Horn
BSBEV      B's Beverages
CONSH      Consolidated Holdings
EASTC      Eastern Connection
NORTS      North/South
SEVES      Seven Seas Imports
```

You can also sort the results based on a field:

```
Select CustomerID, CompanyName from Customers where city = 'London'
order by CompanyName
```

SQL is capable of much more powerful queries. For example, suppose the Northwind manager would like to know what products were purchased in July 1996 by the customer "Vins et alcools Chevalier." This turns out to be somewhat complicated. The Order Details table knows the ProductID for all the products in any given order. The Orders table knows which CustomerIDs are associated with an order. The Customers table knows the CustomerID for a customer, and the Products table knows the product name for the ProductID. How do you tie all this together? Here's the query:

```
select o.OrderID, productName
from [Order Details] od
join orders o on o.OrderID = od.OrderID
join products p on p.ProductID = od.ProductID
join customers c on o.CustomerID = c.CustomerID
where c.CompanyName = 'Vins et alcools Chevalier'
and orderDate >= '7/1/1996' and orderDate < '8/1/1996'
```

This asks the database to get the OrderID and the product name from the relevant tables. This line:

```
from [Order Details] od
```

creates an *alias* od for the Order Details table. The rest of the statement says that the database should look at od, and then join that with the Orders table (aliased to o) for every record in which the OrderID in the Order Details table (od.OrderID) is the same as the OrderID in the Orders table (o.OrderID).

When you join two tables, you can say, "Get every matching record that exists in either table" (this is called an *outer join*), or, as we've done here, "Get only those matching records that exist in both tables" (called an *inner join*). That is, an inner join states to get only the records in Orders that match the records in Order Details by having the same value in the OrderID field (on o.Orderid = od.Orderid).

 SQL joins are inner joins by default. Writing join statements is the same as writing inner join statements.

The SQL statement then goes on to ask the database to create an inner join with Products (aliased to p), getting every row in which the ProductID in the Products table is the same as the ProductID in the Order Details table.

Then, create an inner join with customers for those rows where the CustomerID is the same in both the Orders table and the Customers table.

Finally, tell the database to constrain the results to only those rows in which the CompanyName is the one you want, and the dates are in July:

```
where c.CompanyName = 'Vins et alcools Chevalier'
and orderDate >= '7/1/1996' and orderDate <= '7/31/1996'
```

The collection of constraints finds only three records that match:

```
OrderID      ProductName
-----------  ----------------------------------------
10248        Queso Cabrales
10248        Singaporean Hokkien Fried Mee
10248        Mozzarella di Giovanni
```

This output shows that there was only one order (10248) in which the customer had the right ID and in which the date of the order was July 1996. That order produced three records in the Order Details table, and using the product IDs in these three records, you got the product names from the Products table.

You can use SQL not only for searching for and retrieving data, but also for creating, updating, and deleting tables, and generally for managing and manipulating both the content and the structure of the database.

The ADO.NET Object Model

The ADO.NET object model is rich, but at its heart it is a fairly straightforward set of classes. The most important of these is the DataSet. The DataSet represents a subset of the entire database, cached on your machine without a continuous connection to the database.

Periodically, you'll reconnect the DataSet to its parent database, update the database with changes you've made to the DataSet, and update the DataSet with changes in the database made by other users or processes. That's how ADO.NET maintains its disconnected nature that we mentioned at the start of the chapter.

This is highly efficient, but to be effective, the DataSet must be a robust subset of the database, capturing not just a few rows from a single table, but also a set of tables with all the metadata necessary to represent the relationships and constraints of the original database. This is, not surprisingly, what ADO.NET provides.

The DataSet is composed of DataTable objects as well as DataRelation objects. These are accessed as properties of the DataSet object. The Tables property returns a DataTableCollection, which in turn contains all the DataTable objects.

DataTables and DataColumns

You can create a DataTable programmatically or as a result of a query against the database. The DataTable has a number of public properties, including the Columns collection, which returns the DataColumnCollection object, which in turn consists of DataColumn objects. Each DataColumn object represents a column in a table.

DataRelations

In addition to the Tables collection, the DataSet has a Relations property, which returns a DataRelationCollection consisting of DataRelation objects. Each DataRelation represents a relationship between two tables through DataColumn objects. For example, in the Northwind database, the Customers table is in a relationship with the Orders table through the CustomerID column.

The nature of this relationship is one-to-many, or parent-to-child. For any given order, there will be exactly one customer, but any given customer might be represented in any number of orders.

Rows

The Rows collection of the DataTable returns a set of rows for that table. You use this collection to examine the results of queries against the database, iterating through the rows to examine each record in turn, typically with a foreach loop. You'll see this in the example in this chapter.

DataAdapter

The DataSet is an abstraction of a relational database. ADO.NET uses a DataAdapter as a bridge between the DataSet and the data source, which is the underlying database. DataAdapter provides the Fill( ) method to retrieve data from the database and populate the DataSet.

Instead of tying the DataSet object too closely to your database architecture, ADO.NET uses a DataAdapter object to mediate between the DataSet object and the database. This decouples the DataSet from the database and allows a single DataSet to represent more than one database or other data source.

DbCommand and DbConnection

The DbConnection object represents a connection to a data source. This connection can be shared among different command objects. The DbCommand object allows you to send a command (typically, a SQL statement or a stored procedure) to the database. Often, these objects are implicitly created when you create a DataAdapter, but you can explicitly access these objects; for example, you can declare a connection string as follows:

```
string connectionString = "server=.\\sqlexpress;" +
"Trusted_Connection=yes; database=Northwind";
```

You can then use this connection string to create a connection object or to create a DataAdapter object.

DataReader

An alternative to creating a DataSet (and a DataAdapter) is to create a DataReader. The DataReader provides connected, forward-only, read-only access to a collection of tables by executing either a SQL statement or stored procedures. DataReaders are lightweight objects that are ideally suited for filling controls with data and then breaking the connection to the backend database.

Getting Started with ADO.NET

Enough theory! Let's write some code and see how this works. Working with ADO.NET can be complex, but for many queries, the model is surprisingly simple. In this example, you'll create a console application and list out bits of information from the Customers table in the Northwind database.

Create a new console application (we'll go back to console applications to keep things simple here). When the application opens, add the following two using statements to the top:

```
using System.Data;
using System.Data.SqlClient;
```

The first thing you're going to need in the program itself is a way to identify the location of the SQL Server instance to your program. This is commonly called the *connection string*. It's a simple enough string format, and once you've defined it, you can use the same string anytime you want to access Northwind. If you're using SQL Server Express, as installed with C# Express in Chapter 1, the access path is simple: `.\sqlexpress`. However, because you're defining a string, you need to escape the slash character, as we discussed in Chapter 15 (or you could also use a literal string). Create the connection string like this (all on one line):

```
string connectionString = "server=.\\sqlexpress;
        Trusted_Connection=yes;database=Northwind";
```

The next thing you need is a string to hold the SQL command itself. SQL Server can't understand C# directly, so you can't treat the entries in the database as though they were C# objects. (It'd be nice if you could, though, and that's why LINQ was created, as you'll see in the next chapter.) So, you need to create a string object to hold the SQL statement that will retrieve the data you want. This is called the command string. In this case, you want to retrieve (Select) the company name and the contact name columns from the Customers table. To do that, you'll use this simple SQL statement in the commandString variable (again, on one line):

```
string commandString = "Select CompanyName,
        ContactName from Customers";
```

Now that you have the connection string and the command string, you need to contact the database, and for that, you need a DataAdapter object, as we mentioned earlier. There are several kinds of DataAdapter objects, each for a different kind of database. In this case, you're using a SQL Server database, so you need a SqlDataAdapter object. The constructor takes two parameters, not surprisingly, the command string and the connection string. So, now create the DataAdapter (inside Main()), like this:

```
SqlDataAdapter myDataAdapter =
    new SqlDataAdapter(commandString, connectionString);
```

You have the DataAdapter in hand now, but you need a DataSet object before you can do anything with the data. So, create a new DataSet object:

```
DataSet myDataSet = new DataSet();
```

Then you call the Fill() method of the myDataAdapter, passing in your new DataSet. This fills the DataSet with the data that you obtain from the SQL select statement:

```
myDataAdapter.Fill(myDataSet);
```

That's it. You now have a DataSet, and you can query, manipulate, and otherwise manage the data. To display the data you retrieved, you'll need a DataTable object. The DataSet object has a collection of tables, but your select statement retrieved only a single table, so you need to access only the first one, like this:

```
DataTable myDataTable = myDataSet.Tables[0];
```

Each DataTable contains a set of DataRow objects, as we mentioned, and each of those rows contains keys for each data field in the row. The two column names in the table you retrieved are CompanyName and ContactName, so you can access their values and output each company and contact name using a foreach loop, like this:

```
foreach (DataRow dataRow in myDataTable.Rows)
{
    Console.WriteLine("CompanyName: {0}. Contact: {1}",
        dataRow["CompanyName"], dataRow["ContactName"]);
}
```

Example 20-1 contains the complete source code for this example.

Example 20-1. This very simple example just retrieves information from a table

```
using System;
using System.Collections.Generic;
using System.Linq;
using System.Text;
using System.Data;
using System.Data.SqlClient;

namespace Example_20_1____ADO.NET
{
    class Program
    {
        static void Main(string[] args)
        {
            // create the data connection
            string connectionString = "server=.\\sqlexpress;
                Trusted_Connection=yes;database=Northwind";

            // create the string to hold the SQL command
            // to get records from the Customers table
            string commandString = "Select CompanyName,
                            ContactName from Customers";

            // create the data adapter with the
            // connection string and command
            SqlDataAdapter myDataAdapter =
                new SqlDataAdapter(commandString, connectionString);

            // Create and fill the DataSet object
            DataSet myDataSet = new DataSet();
            myDataAdapter.Fill(myDataSet);

            // Retrieve the Customers table
            DataTable myDataTable = myDataSet.Tables[0];

            // iterate over the rows collection and output the fields
            foreach (DataRow dataRow in myDataTable.Rows)
```

Example 20-1. This very simple example just retrieves information from a table (continued)

```
        {
            Console.WriteLine("CompanyName: {0}. Contact: {1}",
                dataRow["CompanyName"], dataRow["ContactName"]);
        }


    }
  }
}
```

The output is quite lengthy (it's a long table), but the first part of it looks like this:

```
CompanyName: Alfreds Futterkiste. Contact: Maria Anders
CompanyName: Ana Trujillo Emparedados y helados. Contact: Ana Trujillo
CompanyName: Antonio Moreno Taquería. Contact: Antonio Moreno
CompanyName: Around the Horn. Contact: Thomas Hardy
CompanyName: Berglunds snabbköp. Contact: Christina Berglund
CompanyName: Blauer See Delikatessen. Contact: Hanna Moos
CompanyName: Blondesddsl père et fils. Contact: Frédérique Citeaux
CompanyName: Bólido Comidas preparadas. Contact: Martín Sommer
CompanyName: Bon app'. Contact: Laurence Lebihan
CompanyName: Bottom-Dollar Markets. Contact: Elizabeth Lincoln
CompanyName: B's Beverages. Contact: Victoria Ashworth
CompanyName: Cactus Comidas para llevar. Contact: Patricio Simpson
CompanyName: Centro comercial Moctezuma. Contact: Francisco Chang
CompanyName: Chop-suey Chinese. Contact: Yang Wang
CompanyName: Comércio Mineiro. Contact: Pedro Afonso
```

Summary

- ADO.NET provides classes that allow you to retrieve and manipulate data from databases for use in your code.
- ADO.NET was designed to use a disconnected data architecture, meaning that information is retrieved and stored locally, to diminish use of resource-intensive database connections.
- A database is a structured repository of information, and a relational database is a database that organizes the data into tables.
- The tables in relational databases are further divided into rows, where each row represents a single record, and columns, which represent categories of data.
- The primary key in a table is a column containing values that are unique for each record in that table.
- A foreign key is a column that serves as the primary key for a different table, and helps to create one-to-many relationships among data in separate tables.
- Normalization is the process of removing redundant information from records into separate tables, which reduces complexity and speeds up the retrieval process.

- Constraints set limitations on data to avoid data conflicts and errors.
- SQL is a language commonly used to access and manipulate databases. The fundamental operation in SQL is the query.
- Defining filters with a query allows you to retrieve specific subsets of information.
- Using a join in a query allows you to retrieve data based on membership in more than one table.
- In C#, the DataSet object represents a subset of data retrieved from the database.
- The DataSet object contains a collection called Tables, which in turn contains DataTable objects.
- The DataTable object contains a collection called Columns, which contains DataColumn objects, and a collection called Rows, which contains DataRow objects.
- The Rows collection allows you to examine the results of your query, usually by iterating over the collection with a loop.
- The DataAdapter is a class that forms a bridge between the database and the DataSet class, using a connection string and a query string. The DataAdapter can then be used to populate the DataSet object using the Fill( ) method.

As we said at the beginning of this chapter, data access is a complex topic, and this chapter just scratches the surface of it. There's plenty more to explore, beyond the simple SQL commands we showed you here. The remarkable thing about the SQL you learned in this chapter is that it opens up a different way of thinking about data access—using a query to extract and filter just the data you want. Once you get the hang of thinking in queries, it's pretty simple. It's a methodology that could be applied outside the database, to other kinds of data objects. In fact, it has been—it's called LINQ, it's new to C# 3.0, and it's the subject of the final chapter.

Test Your Knowledge: Quiz

Question 20-1. What makes a relational database different from any other kind of database?

Question 20-2. What's a primary key?

Question 20-3. What's a foreign key?

Question 20-4. Imagine a fictitious database for a bookseller. What query would you use to retrieve the contents of the Title column in the Books table?

Question 20-5. In the same fictitious database, what query would you use to retrieve the contents of the Author column where the value in the Publisher column is "OReilly"?

Question 20-6. Why would you want to use a join?

Question 20-7. What .NET class represents a set of data retrieved from the database?

Question 20-8. What's the most common way to view the rows in a DataTable object?

Question 20-9. What's the purpose of the DataAdapter class?

Question 20-10. What method of the DataAdapter class do you use to provide the DataSet with the retrieved data?

Test Your Knowledge: Exercises

Exercise 20-1. Let's start with a simple exercise. The Northwind database contains a table named Orders. Write a program to retrieve the order date and shipped date of all the records in the Orders table.

Exercise 20-2. We'll try something slightly more complicated now. Write a program to display the name and ID of products with fewer than 10 units in stock.

Exercise 20-3. Now for an exercise that involves multiple tables. Write a program to display the first and last names of the employees in region 1.

CHAPTER 21

LINQ

As you saw in Chapter 20, SQL is a powerful tool for retrieving and filtering information from a database. Once you become accustomed to the syntax, with its `selects` and `froms` and `joins`, it's somewhat intuitive as well. However, SQL commands don't integrate well with C#, as you saw. You need the bridge of `DataAdapter` and `DataSet` objects to connect the database query with your application. The Language Integrated Query (LINQ) is the solution to that problem. LINQ is a new feature of .NET that C# 3.0 takes advantage of, which makes it easier to work with data, as you'll see in the second part of the chapter.

Another useful feature of LINQ is that you can address a number of different data sources using similar syntax. In this chapter we'll show you how to use LINQ with SQL, but you don't need to use LINQ with a traditional database—it can retrieve data from XML files and other data sources equally well.

Perhaps the most interesting feature of LINQ is that you can query more than just data stored in other files. You can use LINQ to query collections that are held in-memory, that is, collection classes within your own code. So, for example, if you have a collection of `Book` objects, you can use LINQ to query for all the books by a single author, or published after a certain date. You could certainly write C# code to accomplish that, but the query syntax is arguably more natural and certainly briefer. Because this use of LINQ is easy to understand and is potentially useful, we'll start with that, and then move on to using it with a SQL database.

Querying In-Memory Data

As you've seen elsewhere in this book, C# allows you to create classes that are complex, with many different properties, which sometimes are objects of other classes as well. You've also seen how to create collections of objects that you can manipulate in different ways. Sometimes that complexity works against you, though. Suppose you have a class that represents shipping orders for a warehouse. You could keep a ton of data in such an object, which would make it very versatile, but what if you just wanted to extract a list of the zip codes where your customers live, for demographic purposes? You could write some code to go through the entire collection of objects and pull out just the zip codes. It wouldn't be terribly difficult, but it might be time-consuming. If that information were in a database, you could issue a simple SQL query, like you learned about in Chapter 20, but collections can't be queried like a database...until now. Using LINQ, you can issue a SQL-like query against a collection in your code to get another collection containing just the data you want. An example will help make this clear.

Before you can start, you'll need a collection to work with, so we'll define a quick and simple Book class, like so:

```
public class Book
{
    public string Title { get; set; }
    public string Author { get; set; }
    public string Publisher { get; set; }
    public int PublicationYear { get; set; }
}
```

This is a very basic class, with three string fields and one int field.

Next, we'll define a generic List<Book>, and fill it with a handful of Book objects. This is a relatively short list, and it wouldn't be that hard to sort through by hand, if you needed to. That's because we're keeping the List short for demonstration purposes; in other cases, it might be a list of hundreds of items read in from a file or someplace else:

```
List<Book> bookList = new List<Book>
{
    new Book { Title = "Learning C# 3.0",
               Author = "Jesse Liberty",
               Publisher = "O'Reilly",
               PublicationYear = 2008 },
    new Book { Title = "Programming C# 3.0",
               Author = "Jesse Liberty",
               Publisher = "O'Reilly",
               PublicationYear = 2008 },
    new Book { Title = "C# 3.0 Cookbook",
               Author = "Jay Hilyard",
               Publisher = "O'Reilly",
               PublicationYear = 2007 },
    new Book { Title = "C# 3.0 in a Nutshell",
               Author = "Ben Albahari",
               Publisher = "O'Reilly",
               PublicationYear = 2007 },
    new Book { Title = "Head First C#",
               Author = "Andrew Stellman",
               Publisher = "O'Reilly",
               PublicationYear = 2007 },
```

```
    new Book { Title = "Programming C#, fourth edition",
              Author = "Jesse Liberty",
              Publisher = "O'Reilly",
              PublicationYear = 2005 }
};
```

Now you need to issue a query. Suppose you want to find all the books in the list that were authored by Jesse Liberty. You'd use a query like this:

```
IEnumerable<Book> resultsAuthor =
    from testBook in bookList
    where testBook.Author == "Jesse Liberty"
    select testBook;
```

Let's take this apart. The query returns an enumerable collection of Book objects, or to put it another way, it'll return an instance of IEnumerable<Book>. A LINQ data source must implement IEnumerable, and the result of the query must as well.

The rest of the query resembles a SQL query. You use a *range variable*, in this case, testBook, in the same way you would the iteration variable in a foreach loop. Because your query is operating on bookList, which was previously defined as a List<Book>, the compiler automatically defines testBook as a Book type.

As with the SQL query you saw in the previous chapter, the from clause defines the range variable, and the in clause identifies the source. The where clause is used to filter the data. In this case, you're testing a condition with a Boolean expression, as you would with any C# object.

The select clause returns the results of the query, as an enumerable collection. This is called *projection* in database terminology. In this example, we returned the entire Book object, but you can return just some of the fields instead, like this:

```
select testBook.Title;
```

Now that you have a collection of Book objects, you can use a foreach loop to process them; in this case, outputting them to the console:

```
foreach (Book testBook in resultsAuthor)
{
    Console.WriteLine("{0}, by {1}", testBook.Title, testBook.Author);
}
```

You can use any legal Boolean expression in your where clause; for example, you could return all the books published before 2008, like this:

```
IEnumerable<Book> resultsDate =
    from testBook in bookList
    where testBook.PublicationYear < 2008
    select testBook;
```

This simple example, with both queries, is shown in Example 21-1.

Example 21-1. You can use LINQ to query the contents of collections; this collection is very simple, but for large collections, this technique is powerful

```csharp
using System;
using System.Collections.Generic;
using System.Linq;
using System.Text;

namespace Example_21_1____Querying_Collections
{
    // simple book class
    public class Book
    {
        public string Title { get; set; }
        public string Author { get; set; }
        public string Publisher { get; set; }
        public int PublicationYear { get; set; }
    }

    class Program
    {
        static void Main(string[] args)
        {
            List<Book> bookList = new List<Book>
            {
                new Book { Title = "Learning C# 3.0",
                           Author = "Jesse Liberty",
                           Publisher = "O'Reilly",
                           PublicationYear = 2008 },
                new Book { Title = "Programming C# 3.0",
                           Author = "Jesse Liberty",
                           Publisher = "O'Reilly",
                           PublicationYear = 2008 },
                new Book { Title = "C# 3.0 Cookbook",
                           Author = "Jay Hilyard",
                           Publisher = "O'Reilly",
                           PublicationYear = 2007 },
                new Book { Title = "C# 3.0 in a Nutshell",
                           Author = "Ben Albahari",
                           Publisher = "O'Reilly",
                           PublicationYear = 2007 },
                new Book { Title = "Head First C#",
                           Author = "Andrew Stellman",
                           Publisher = "O'Reilly",
                           PublicationYear = 2007 },
                new Book { Title = "Programming C#, fourth edition",
                           Author = "Jesse Liberty",
                           Publisher = "O'Reilly",
                           PublicationYear = 2005 }
            };

            // find books by Jesse Liberty
```

Example 21-1. You can use LINQ to query the contents of collections; this collection is very simple, but for large collections, this technique is powerful (continued)

```
        IEnumerable<Book> resultsAuthor =
            from testBook in bookList
            where testBook.Author == "Jesse Liberty"
            select testBook;

        Console.WriteLine("Books by Jesse Liberty:");
        foreach (Book testBook in resultsAuthor)
        {
            Console.WriteLine("{0}, by {1}", testBook.Title,
                testBook.Author);
        }

        // find books published before 2008
        IEnumerable<Book> resultsDate =
            from testBook in bookList
            where testBook.PublicationYear < 2008
            select testBook;

        Console.WriteLine("\nBooks published before 2008:");
        foreach (Book testBook in resultsDate)
        {
            Console.WriteLine("{0}, by {1}, {2}", testBook.Title,
                testBook.Author, testBook.PublicationYear);
        }

    }
  }
}
```

The output looks like this:

```
Books by Jesse Liberty:
Learning C# 3.0, by Jesse Liberty
Programming C# 3.0, by Jesse Liberty
Programming C#, fourth edition, by Jesse Liberty

Books published before 2008:
C# 3.0 Cookbook, by Jay Hilyard, 2007
C# 3.0 in a Nutshell, by Ben Albahari, 2007
Head First C#, by Andrew Stellman, 2007
Programming C#, fourth edition, by Jesse Liberty, 2005
```

 You might expect that the data would be retrieved from the data source when you create the IEnumerable<T> instance to hold the results. In fact, the data isn't retrieved until you try to do something with the data in the IEnumerable<T>. In this case, that's when you output the contents in the foreach statement. This behavior is helpful because databases with many connections may be changing all the time; LINQ doesn't retrieve the data until the last possible moment, right before you're going to use it.

Anonymous Types and Implicitly Typed Variables

In Example 21-1, when you retrieve the information from the collection, you retrieve the entire Book object, but you output only the title and author. That's somewhat wasteful, because you're retrieving more information than you actually need. Since you need just the title and author, it would be preferable to be able to say something like this:

```
IEnumerable<Book> resultsAuthor =
    from testBook in bookList
    where testBook.Author == "Jesse Liberty"
    select testBook.Title, testBook.Author;
```

That construction will cause an error, though, because your query can return only one type of object. You could define a new class—say, bookTitleAuthor—to hold just the two bits of information you need, but that would also be wasteful, because the class would get used in only one spot in your program, right here when you retrieve and then output the data. Instead, you can just define a new class on the fly, like this:

```
IEnumerable<Book> resultsAuthor =
    from testBook in bookList
    where testBook.Author == "Jesse Liberty"
    select new { testBook.Title, testBook.Author };
```

Notice that this class doesn't have a name; it doesn't really need one, because you're using it only in this one spot. Therefore, this feature is called an *anonymous type*. Based on the select statement, the compiler determines the number and types of the properties for the class (two strings, in this case), and creates the class accordingly.

This code won't work yet, though. You're assigning the results of the query (now a collection of anonymous objects) to a collection of type <Book>. Obviously, that's a type mismatch, and you'll need to change the type. But what do you change it to, if you don't know the name of the anonymous type? That's where implicitly typed variables come in. As we mentioned way back in Chapter 3, C# has the ability to *infer* the type of a variable based on the value you're assigning to it. Even though you don't know the name of the anonymous type, the compiler has assigned it as an identifier, and can recognize that type when it's used. Therefore, your new query looks like this:

```
var resultsAuthor =
    from testBook in bookList
    where testBook.Author == "Jesse Liberty"
    select new { testBook.Title, testBook.Author };
```

Now resultsAuthor is a collection of anonymous objects, and the compiler is perfectly fine with that. All you need to know is that resultsAuthor is a collection that implements IEnumerable, and you can go ahead and use it to output the results:

```
Console.WriteLine("Books by Jesse Liberty:");
foreach (var testBook in resultsAuthor)
```

```
        {
            Console.WriteLine("{0}, by {1}", testBook.Title, testBook.Author);
        }
```

We've replaced the Book type in the foreach loop with var, but the compiler still knows what type testBook is, because it's a member of the collection resultsAuthor, and the compiler knows what type that is, even if you don't.

These changes are shown in Example 21-2, although we've omitted the Book class definition and the creation of the List for space, because those haven't changed.

Example 21-2. With anonymous types and implicitly typed variables, you can use the results of a query even when they're a complex type

```
using System;
using System.Collections.Generic;
using System.Linq;
using System.Text;

namespace Example_21_2____Anonymous_Types
{
    // simple book class
    public class Book
    {
        ...
    }

    class Program
    {
        static void Main(string[] args)
        {
            List<Book> bookList = new List<Book>
            {
                ...
            };

            // find books by Jesse Liberty
            var resultsAuthor =
                from testBook in bookList
                where testBook.Author == "Jesse Liberty"
                select new { testBook.Title, testBook.Author };

            Console.WriteLine("Books by Jesse Liberty:");
            foreach (var testBook in resultsAuthor)
            {
                Console.WriteLine("{0}, by {1}", testBook.Title,
                                    testBook.Author);
            }
        }
    }
}
```

Lambda Expressions

Back in Chapter 17 we mentioned that lambda expressions were created for use with LINQ, to create expressions that return a method instead of a single return value. The same query we've been using all along could be written like this with lambda expressions:

```
var resultsAuthor =
    bookList.Where(bookEval => bookEval.Author == "Jesse Liberty");
```

As we mentioned in the previous section, the keyword var lets the compiler infer that resultsAuthor is an IEnumerable collection. You can interpret this whole statement as "fill the IEnumerable collection resultsAuthor from the collection bookList with each member such that the Author property is equal to the string 'Jesse Liberty'."

The variable bookEval isn't declared anywhere; it can be any valid name. The Boolean expression on the righthand side is *projected* onto the variable, which is passed to the Where method to use to evaluate the collection. This method syntax takes some getting used to, and it can be easier to use LINQ's query syntax, but you should know how to use the alternative. This example is shown in Example 21-3.

Example 21-3. The LINQ method syntax uses lambda expressions to evaluate the data retrieved from the data source

```
using System;
using System.Collections.Generic;
using System.Linq;
using System.Text;

namespace Example_21_3____Lambda_Expressions
{
    // simple book class
    public class Book
    {
        ...
    }

    class Program
    {
        static void Main(string[] args)
        {
            List<Book> bookList = new List<Book>
            {
                ...
            };

            // find books by Jesse Liberty
            var resultsAuthor =
                bookList.Where(bookEval =>
                    bookEval.Author == "Jesse Liberty");
```

```
            Console.WriteLine("Books by Jesse Liberty:");
            foreach (var testBook in resultsAuthor)
            {
                Console.WriteLine("{0}, by {1}",
                    testBook.Title, testBook.Author);
            }

        }
    }
}
```

Ordering and Joining

As you saw in Chapter 20, you can also order the results of your queries, and join data from two different tables in your query. You have this same ability in your LINQ queries. For example, to retrieve the Book objects in your collection, ordered by author name (author's first name, since the author's full name is a single string), you'd use this query:

```
var resultList =
    from myBook in bookList
    orderby myBook.Author
    select myBook;
```

That output will look like this:

```
Books by author:
Head First C#, by Andrew Stellman
C# 3.0 in a Nutshell, by Ben Albahari
C# 3.0 Cookbook, by Jay Hilyard
Learning C# 3.0, by Jesse Liberty
Programming C# 3.0, by Jesse Liberty
Programming C#, fourth edition, by Jesse Liberty
```

The full code for this example is shown in Example 21-4.

Example 21-4. Ordering the results of a query is simple; just use the OrderBy keyword

```
using System;
using System.Collections.Generic;
using System.Linq;
using System.Text;

namespace Example_21_4_____Ordering_Results
{
    // simple book class
    public class Book
    {
        public string Title { get; set; }
        public string Author { get; set; }
```

```
        public string Publisher { get; set; }
        public int PublicationYear { get; set; }
    }

    class Program
    {
        static void Main(string[] args)
        {
            List<Book> bookList = new List<Book>
            {
                new Book { Title = "Learning C# 3.0",
                           Author = "Jesse Liberty",
                           Publisher = "O'Reilly",
                           PublicationYear = 2008 },
                new Book { Title = "Programming C# 3.0",
                           Author = "Jesse Liberty",
                           Publisher = "O'Reilly",
                           PublicationYear = 2008 },
                new Book { Title = "C# 3.0 Cookbook",
                           Author = "Jay Hilyard",
                           Publisher = "O'Reilly",
                           PublicationYear = 2007 },
                new Book { Title = "C# 3.0 in a Nutshell",
                           Author = "Ben Albahari",
                           Publisher = "O'Reilly",
                           PublicationYear = 2007 },
                new Book { Title = "Head First C#",
                           Author = "Andrew Stellman",
                           Publisher = "O'Reilly",
                           PublicationYear = 2007 },
                new Book { Title = "Programming C#, fourth edition",
                           Author = "Jesse Liberty",
                           Publisher = "O'Reilly",
                           PublicationYear = 2005 }
            };

            var resultList =
                from myBook in bookList
                orderby myBook.Author
                select myBook;

            Console.WriteLine("Books by author:");
            foreach (var testBook in resultList)
            {
                Console.WriteLine("{0}, by {1}", testBook.Title,
                                  testBook.Author);
            }
        }
    }
}
```

When you join two tables in SQL, as you did in Chapter 20, you retrieve fields from two or more tables based on their common columns (their foreign keys). To do the same for in-memory collections, you need to join two separate collections. For example, here's a class that represents a book purchase order:

```
public class PurchaseOrder
{
    public int OrderNumber { get; set; }
    public string Title { get; set; }
    public int Quantity { get; set; }
}
```

You can imagine another collection using a List of these PurchaseOrder objects. Here's a partial list:

```
List<PurchaseOrder> orderList = new List<PurchaseOrder>
{
    new PurchaseOrder { OrderNumber = 23483,
                        Title = "C# 3.0 Cookbook",
                        Quantity = 57 },
```

If you wanted to return the title, author, and quantity for a particular book or books, you'd need to join the information from the two collections. The Title property is the common field here. It's the primary key in the bookList collection, and a foreign key in the orderList collection. The query you'd use looks like this:

```
var resultList =
    from myBook in bookList
    join myOrder in orderList on myBook.Title equals myOrder.Title
    where myOrder.Quantity >= 50
    select new {myBook.Title, myBook.Author, myOrder.Quantity};
```

The from and select clauses aren't any different from what you've seen so far; you're defining an anonymous type here to hold the date you want. The join clause is a bit different, though. You're joining the bookList collection with the orderList collection to create a new data set to search on. The first part of the join just looks like a from; you're specifying the second collection to use:

```
join myOrder in orderList
```

You have to specify some way to correlate the information in the two collections, though—how can you tell which orders go with which book records? They have the Title property in common. If the Title property of the book is the same as the Title property of the order, that's a match. The on part of the join clause indicates that you're defining the condition:

```
join myOrder in orderList on myBook.Title equals myOrder.Title
```

Note that you have to use the keyword equals to define the join condition, rather than the == operator.

The where clause specifies that you want the records of orders with more than 50 copies sold. A full example using this query is shown in Example 21-5.

Example 21-5. The Join keyword allows you to combine the data from two different collections into a single result set

```
using System;
using System.Collections.Generic;
using System.Linq;
using System.Text;

namespace Example_21_5____Joining_results
{
    using System;
using System.Collections.Generic;
using System.Linq;
using System.Text;

    // simple book class
    public class Book
    {
        public string Title { get; set; }
        public string Author { get; set; }
        public string Publisher { get; set; }
        public int PublicationYear { get; set; }
    }

    public class PurchaseOrder
    {
        public int OrderNumber { get; set; }
        public string Title { get; set; }
        public int Quantity { get; set; }
    }

    class Program
    {
        static void Main(string[] args)
        {
            List<Book> bookList = new List<Book>
            {
                new Book { Title = "Learning C# 3.0",
                           Author = "Jesse Liberty",
                           Publisher = "O'Reilly",
                           PublicationYear = 2008 },
                new Book { Title = "Programming C# 3.0",
                           Author = "Jesse Liberty",
                           Publisher = "O'Reilly",
                           PublicationYear = 2008 },
                new Book { Title = "C# 3.0 Cookbook",
                           Author = "Jay Hilyard",
                           Publisher = "O'Reilly",
                           PublicationYear = 2007 },
                new Book { Title = "C# 3.0 in a Nutshell",
                           Author = "Ben Albahari",
                           Publisher = "O'Reilly",
                           PublicationYear = 2007 },
```

Example 21-5. The Join keyword allows you to combine the data from two different collections into a single result set (continued)

```
                    new Book { Title = "Head First C#",
                               Author = "Andrew Stellman",
                               Publisher = "O'Reilly",
                               PublicationYear = 2007 },
                    new Book { Title = "Programming C#, fourth edition",
                               Author = "Jesse Liberty",
                               Publisher = "O'Reilly",
                               PublicationYear = 2005 }
            };

            List<PurchaseOrder> orderList = new List<PurchaseOrder>
            {
                new PurchaseOrder { OrderNumber = 23483,
                                    Title = "C# 3.0 Cookbook",
                                    Quantity = 57 },
                new PurchaseOrder { OrderNumber = 57284,
                                    Title = "Head First C#",
                                    Quantity = 42 },
                new PurchaseOrder { OrderNumber = 56389,
                                    Title = "Programming C# 3.0",
                                    Quantity = 12 },
                new PurchaseOrder { OrderNumber = 95639,
                                    Title = "C# 3.0 Cookbook",
                                    Quantity = 122 },
                new PurchaseOrder { OrderNumber = 57493,
                                    Title = "C# 3.0 in a Nutshell",
                                    Quantity = 43 },
                new PurchaseOrder { OrderNumber = 73558,
                                    Title = "Programming C# 3.0",
                                    Quantity = 99 },
                new PurchaseOrder { OrderNumber = 45385,
                                    Title = "C# 3.0 Cookbook",
                                    Quantity = 35 },
            };

            var resultList =
                from myBook in bookList
                join myOrder in orderList on myBook.Title equals myOrder.Title
                where myOrder.Quantity >= 50
                select new {myBook.Title, myBook.Author, myOrder.Quantity};

            Console.WriteLine("Book orders with quantities
                              greater than 50:");
            foreach (var testBook in resultList)
            {
                Console.WriteLine("Title: {0}\tAuthor: {1}
                                  \tQuantity: {2}", testBook.Title,
                                  testBook.Author, testBook.Quantity);
            }
        }
    }
}
```

The results of the query look like this:

```
Book orders with quantities greater than 50:
Title: Programming C# 3.0      Author: Jesse Liberty    Quantity: 99
Title: C# 3.0 Cookbook   Author: Jay Hilyard      Quantity: 57
Title: C# 3.0 Cookbook   Author: Jay Hilyard      Quantity: 122
```

Using LINQ with SQL

Although using SQL-like syntax with your in-memory collections is the more inter-esting and unusual use of LINQ, it's natural to use the SQL-like syntax with SQL databases. With LINQ, instead of using the DataAdapter and DataSet classes you learned about in Chapter 20, you can treat the tables in a SQL database as classes, and work with the data directly, as though the tables were objects created in your code.

Create a new console application to see how this works. To use the LINQ data fea-tures, you'll need to add a *reference* to the System.Data.Linq namespace, which is something you haven't done before, but it's simple. Right-click on the *References* folder of your project in the Solution Explorer. You'll see the Add Reference dialog shown in Figure 21-1.

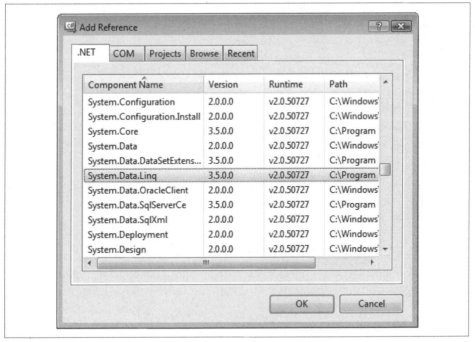

Figure 21-1. You'll need to add a reference to the System.Data.Linq namespace before you can use LINQ with a SQL database.

Now that you have the reference, you need to add some using statements to take advantage of them in your program:

```
using System.Data;
using System.Data.Linq;
using System.Data.Linq.Mapping;
```

As we mentioned earlier, when you're using LINQ and SQL, you can treat the database tables as classes, and the columns as members. It just requires a bit of extra work on your part. You'll retrieve some simple information from Northwind's Employees table in this example.

 If you did the examples in Chapter 20, you should already have the Northwind database installed and attached on your machine. If not, turn back to Chapter 20 for detailed instructions.

Create the following class in your application:

```
[Table(Name = "Employees")]
public class Employee
{
    [Column]
    public int EmployeeID { get; set; }
    [Column]
    public string FirstName { get; set; }
    [Column]
    public string LastName { get; set; }
}
```

You've probably noticed the extra code in square brackets that's unfamiliar to you. These are called *attributes*, and they're used in a lot of different places in C# to provide extra modifiers to your classes. In this case, you're using the Table attribute to indicate that this class is drawn from a table, specifically the Employees table in the associated database. Each of the public properties in the class has a Column attribute to indicate that the property is associated with a column in the table.

As you probably remember from Chapter 20, you always need a data context before you can work with a database. With LINQ, creating the data context is much easier. Add the following line to Main( ):

```
DataContext db = new DataContext("Data Source = .\\SQLExpress;" +
    "Initial Catalog=Northwind;Integrated Security=True");
```

Notice that the DataContext object's constructor takes a string as its parameter—the same connection string that you used to connect to the database in Chapter 20.

The DataContext object has an important method, GetTable( ), which is how you retrieve the data table from the database and assign it to a generic Table collection. The collection holds the type of objects that you defined earlier in the application. So, add this Table<Employee> declaration to your application (after the DataContext line):

```
Table<Employee> employees = db.GetTable<Employee>( );
```

That's all you need to retrieve the data. Now, though, you'll need a query. For this example, you'll simply retrieve all the employee rows in the table. That's where the LINQ syntax you saw earlier in this chapter comes in. You don't need to create a query string; just use the LINQ syntax directly:

```
var dbQuery = from emp in employees select emp;
```

Although dbQuery is declared using the var keyword, it returns an IEnumerable collection, which means that you can iterate over it with a foreach loop, just like you would any other collection. Add this code to output some of the data:

```
foreach (var employee in dbQuery)
{
    Console.WriteLine("{0}\t{1} {2}", employee.EmployeeID,
        employee.FirstName, employee.LastName);
}
```

Simple, right? No more worrying about DataSet or DataRow objects. Example 21-6 shows the complete code for this example.

Example 21-6. You can access a SQL database with LINQ by simply treating the tables and columns in the database as though they were objects in your code

```
using System;
using System.Collections.Generic;
using System.Linq;
using System.Text;
using System.Data;
using System.Data.Linq;
using System.Data.Linq.Mapping;

namespace Example_21_6____LINQ_and_SQL
{
    [Table(Name = "Employees")]
    public class Employee
    {
        [Column] public int EmployeeID { get; set; }
        [Column] public string FirstName { get; set; }
        [Column] public string LastName { get; set; }
    }

    class Program
    {
        static void Main()
        {
            DataContext db = new DataContext("Data Source = .\\SQLExpress;
                Initial Catalog=Northwind;Integrated Security=True");

            Table<Employee> employees = db.GetTable<Employee>();
            var dbQuery = from emp in employees select emp;

            foreach (var employee in dbQuery)
            {
```

Example 21-6. You can access a SQL database with LINQ by simply treating the tables and columns in the database as though they were objects in your code (continued)

```
          Console.WriteLine("{0}\t{1} {2}", employee.EmployeeID,
              employee.FirstName, employee.LastName);
        }
      }
    }
  }
}
```

The results look like this:

```
1       Nancy Davolio
2       Andrew Fuller
3       Janet Leverling
4       Margaret Peacock
5       Steven Buchanan
6       Michael Suyama
7       Robert King
8       Laura Callahan
9       Anne Dodsworth
```

 LINQ can also be used to access data sources that aren't traditional database structures, such as XML files. Although we're not covering LINQ to XML specifically in this book, you can use the same LINQ syntax with XML that you've used elsewhere in this chapter.

Using the Object Relational Designer

As you can see, using LINQ to SQL is a lot easier than the ADO.NET syntax you used in Chapter 20. That's still not the easiest way of going about it, though. This is Visual Studio, isn't it? So, why not put a little visual in your database access? That's where the Object Relational Designer comes in. As with many visual components, it's easier to show this than to explain it.

Create a new console application to start. Check the Database Explorer to make sure you still have access to the Northwind database. (If not, see Chapter 20 for instructions on how to connect to Northwind.) Switch back to the Solution Explorer, right-click the project name, and select Add → New Item. When the Add New Item dialog box opens, select LINQ to SQL Classes. The dialog will suggest a default name of *DataClasses1.dbml*; that's fine for this exercise. Click Add.

Two things happen right away, which you can see in Figure 21-2. First, the IDE changes to show the Object Relational Designer (O/R Designer), which is empty at the moment. The second thing is that several files are added to your project: *DataClasses1.dbml*, and two associated files named *DataClasses1.dbml.layout* and *DataClasses1.designer.cs*. The *.dbml* part, as you may have guessed, indicates that this is a Database Markup Language file, which is really just in XML.

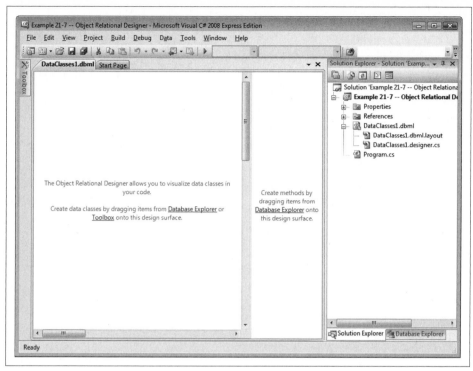

Figure 21-2. When you add the LINQ to SQL classes, the Object Relational Designer opens automatically.

To see how this works, you'll have to add some tables to the O/R Designer. Switch to the Database Explorer, expand Northwind, and expand the *Tables* folder. Now drag the Orders table directly onto the O/R Designer. If you get a message asking whether you want to copy the data to this project, click Yes. It may take a minute, but you'll see the Orders table represented visually, with icons for each of the columns in the table, and a key icon indicating the primary key for this table. Now drag on the Order Details and Products tables as well. These tables are also represented visually, and the connections between them are shown as well. You can drag them around to see them better if you like, but your IDE should look something like Figure 21-3 now.

Notice in Figure 21-3 that the arrows from both the Order and Product tables point toward the Order Details table. That's because the primary key from each of those two tables is used as a foreign key in Order Details.

Switch back to the Solution Explorer and take a look at what's happened here. Double-click *DataClasses1.dbml.layout*. You'll be told the file is already open, and you'll be asked whether you want to close it. Click Yes. When the file opens, you'll see a lot of XML. This is the markup representation of what you just created visually. For the most part, you'll never need to look at this file, but we wanted you to see what the O/R Designer does for you.

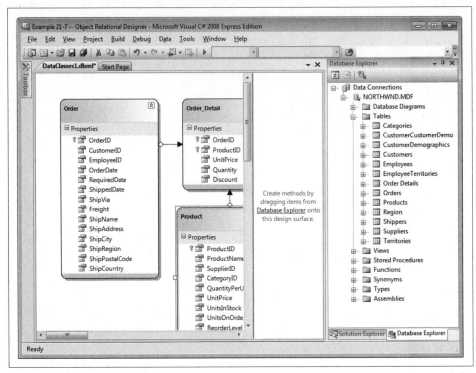

Figure 21-3. The Object Relational Designer gives you a visual representation of your data, and the connections between the tables.

Next open the *DataClasses1.designer.cs* file. This is a huge file, all automatically generated from the contents of the tables, and if you scroll through it, you'll find properties for every column so that you can retrieve and set them. You shouldn't ever need to edit this file either.

So, what does all this autogenerated code do for you? Perhaps not quite as much as you think, but it will save you from some of the larger headaches of dealing with databases. Switch to the *Program.cs* file now, and add the code shown in Example 21-7.

Example 21-7. When you use the Object Relational Designer, a lot of the database code is generated for you, letting you focus on your classes

```
using System;
using System.Collections.Generic;
using System.Linq;
using System.Text;

namespace Example_21_7____Object_Relational_Designer
{
    class Program
    {
```

```
static void Main( )
{
    DataClasses1DataContext myContext =
        new DataClasses1DataContext( );

    // find a single product record
    Product foundProduct = myContext.Products.Single(
                            p => p.ProductID == 1);
    Console.WriteLine("Found product #{0}, {1}",
        foundProduct.ProductID, foundProduct.ProductName);

    // return a list of order records
    var orderList =
        from order in myContext.Order_Details
        where order.OrderID >= 10250 && order.OrderID <= 10255
        select order;

    Console.WriteLine("\nProduct Orders between 10250 and 10255");
    foreach (Order_Detail order in orderList)
    {
        Console.WriteLine("ID: {0}\tQty: {1}\tProduct: {2}",
                order.OrderID, order.Quantity,
                order.Product.ProductName);
    }
}
```

The output looks like this:

```
Found product #1, Chai

Product Orders between 10250 and 10255
ID: 10250       Qty: 10 Product: Jack's New England Clam Chowder
ID: 10250       Qty: 35 Product: Manjimup Dried Apples
ID: 10250       Qty: 15 Product: Louisiana Fiery Hot Pepper Sauce
ID: 10251       Qty: 6  Product: Gustaf's Knäckebröd
ID: 10251       Qty: 15 Product: Ravioli Angelo
ID: 10251       Qty: 20 Product: Louisiana Fiery Hot Pepper Sauce
ID: 10252       Qty: 40 Product: Sir Rodney's Marmalade
ID: 10252       Qty: 25 Product: Geitost
ID: 10252       Qty: 40 Product: Camembert Pierrot
ID: 10253       Qty: 20 Product: Gorgonzola Telino
ID: 10253       Qty: 42 Product: Chartreuse verte
ID: 10253       Qty: 40 Product: Maxilaku
ID: 10254       Qty: 15 Product: Guaraná Fantástica
ID: 10254       Qty: 21 Product: Pâté chinois
ID: 10254       Qty: 21 Product: Longlife Tofu
ID: 10255       Qty: 20 Product: Chang
ID: 10255       Qty: 35 Product: Pavlova
ID: 10255       Qty: 25 Product: Inlagd Sill
ID: 10255       Qty: 30 Product: Raclette Courdavault
```

There are several differences to notice between this code and Example 21-6.

First, you didn't need to add any using statements; those are taken care of for you, in the other classes. Next, DataClasses1DataContext is a pregenerated class that knows how to access Northwind already. All you had to do was call the default constructor—no more messing around with connection strings. That by itself is worth the trouble.

Also notice that you didn't define any classes here. You don't need to define a Table class, or classes to represent the fields in the database. All of that already exists in the *DataClasses1.designer.cs* file. That means you can treat the columns in the database as regular types:

```
Product foundProduct = myContext.Products.Single(
                          p => p.ProductID == 1);
```

You didn't define Product anywhere; the O/R Designer did it for you, but you can use a Product object just like any other object. These classes even have their own methods defined for them, such as the Single() method, which is used to retrieve a single record. You can retrieve a collection using the same LINQ syntax you're now used to:

```
var orderList =
    from order in myContext.Order_Details
    where order.OrderID >= 10250 && order.OrderID <= 10255
    select order;
```

orderList is an IEnumerable collection of anonymous types, based on the return value of the select statement.

Finally, notice one interesting thing in the WriteLine() statement:

```
Console.WriteLine("ID: {0}\tQty: {1}\tProduct: {2}",
        order.OrderID, order.Quantity,
        order.Product.ProductName);
```

You've retrieved the OrderID and Quantity values from the Order Details table, treating Order_Details as though it were an ordinary object. ProductName isn't in the Order Details table, though. The Order Details table is related to the Product table by the foreign key (ProductID). That means you can access the Product class, and its ProductID field, from Order_Details. And that's exactly how this works: order.Product.ProductName gets you the field you want.

 The name of the table is "Order Details" with a space, but C# class names can't include spaces, so the Object Relational Designer changes it to an underscore for you. You may also have noticed that when the O/R Designer displays the class name graphically, it's singular. IntelliSense always provides the correct class name for you.

Now you've reached a point where interacting with the database is nearly invisible. The LINQ syntax made the querying easier, and the Object Relational Designer makes accessing the database easier yet.

Summary

- Language Integrated Query (LINQ) is a new technology that allows you to query data sources from within your code, without needing to rely on specific data translation classes.

- LINQ uses the same syntax with traditional databases, but also other data sources such as XML files, and even with collections in your application.

- LINQ allows you to issue queries against collections in your code, returning a subset that's easier to work with.

- A LINQ data source collection must implement IEnumerable, and the collection the query returns must as well.

- The range variable is used to define the parameters of the query. It can be any valid C# name, and C# will automatically infer its type based on the returned values.

- Once you have the enumerable collection of returned results, you can manipulate them as you would any generic collection.

- You can use anonymous types and the var keyword in your queries to have the compiler infer the types in the query, whether simple or complex.

- You can use lambda expressions in your queries to define a method for evaluating the stored data, and then project the results onto a variable.

- The join clause can unite the data from two different collections, but it has a special syntax, requiring the name of the collection to join with, the field you're joining on in each collection, and the fields that should be in the return set.

- LINQ to SQL classes allows you to use the LINQ syntax to query a SQL database.

- You need to include a reference to the System.Data.Linq namespace to use LINQ to SQL.

- LINQ to SQL allows you to use attributes on classes so that they behave like tables, and on properties so that they behave like columns.

- LINQ to SQL also features a DataContext class that can take a connection string in the constructor.

- The Object Relational Designer adds a visual component to LINQ to SQL classes. You can drag-and-drop database tables directly onto the design surface, and the O/R Designer will supply appropriate backing code for the classes that represent the data.

- You can use the automatically created classes as though they were ordinary classes in your code, simplifying database access.

LINQ is a remarkable new technology that has the potential to partially bridge the gap that's existed between software development and database administration.

Beyond that, you've seen how useful the LINQ syntax can be even without a database in play. With that said, however, LINQ is a very new technology, and it's still evolving. It remains to be seen how well developers and database professionals will embrace it, or whether something else will come along. In that sense, unlike most of the rest of the book, this chapter represents something you're not likely to see right away as you practice with C#, but we anticipate that LINQ will grow in popularity, and may become as much a part of the language as any of the other features you've seen so far.

That brings you to the end of the book, but not the end of learning C#. As we promised at the beginning, you started with the very fundamentals of the language and moved into intermediate topics like interfaces and delegates, and we presented a broad introduction to some more advanced topics in the last few chapters. As you've guessed, there's a lot more to the language that we haven't covered in this book, but now you have a foundation to build upon. There are many excellent books out there for going more deeply into C#, one of which is this book's companion volume, *Programming C# 3.0*, by Jesse Liberty and Donald Xie (O'Reilly), where you'll find additional detail and deeper discussion of the topics in this book. The best thing you can do to continue learning C#, however, is to practice writing code. The exercises you've done throughout this book are just a beginning; you can rewrite and extend them as much as you like. If you're not sure about some syntax, or a language feature, try it out! If you're wrong, most of the time the compiler will throw an exception, which can teach you as much as getting it right the first time.

Test Your Knowledge: Quiz

Question 21-1. What sorts of data sources can you query with LINQ?

Question 21-2. What is the return type of a LINQ query?

Question 21-3. Which LINQ keyword returns the result of a query?

Question 21-4. If you're trying to return a complex type from a LINQ query, what language feature do you need to use?

Question 21-5. What data type is needed for the range variable in a LINQ query?

Question 21-6. What does a lambda expression return, when used in a LINQ query?

Question 21-7. What reference do you need to add to your project to use LINQ to SQL?

Question 21-8. What attribute do you use to define a class as representing a SQL table?

Question 21-9. How do you add table classes to your application using the Object Relational Designer?

Question 21-10. What parameters do you need to pass to the constructor of the data context class when you're using the Object Relational Designer?

Test Your Knowledge: Exercises

Exercise 21-1. For the first exercise in this chapter, we're going to bring back the good old Box class from earlier in the book. It's a quick and easy class, with Length, Width, and Height properties, and a quick method to display a box. Here's the code for the class:

```
public class Box
{
    public int Length { get; set; }
    public int Width { get; set; }
    public int Height { get; set; }

    public void DisplayBox()
    {
        Console.WriteLine("{0}x{1}x{2}", Length, Width, Height);
    }
}
```

Create a List of Box objects, at least five, with dimensions of whatever you like, and then use a LINQ query to extract all those boxes with a Length and Width greater than 3.

Exercise 21-2. Use LINQ to SQL, but not the Object Relational Designer, to retrieve all the orders from the Order Details table where the quantity ordered is greater than 100. (You'll have to use a short type for the quantity, or else you'll get an error.)

Exercise 21-3. Using the Object Relational Designer, find out which employees (first and last names) have serviced orders placed by the customer named Ernst Handel.

Answers to Quizzes and Exercises

Chapter 1: C# and .NET Programming

Quiz Solutions

Solution to Question 1-1. The Common Language Runtime (CLR) is the component of the .NET Framework that allows you to compile and execute applications written in either C# or Visual Basic .NET.

Solution to Question 1-2. The .NET Framework specifies how .NET constructs intrinsic types, classes, interfaces, and so forth.

Solution to Question 1-3. Calling C# a "safe" language refers to "type safety"—the ability of the compiler to ensure that the objects you create are of the expected type.

Solution to Question 1-4. Keywords are reserved for use by the language and cannot be used to identify objects or methods you create.

Solution to Question 1-5. The job of the compiler is to turn your source code into Microsoft Intermediate Language (MSIL).

Solution to Question 1-6. The Microsoft Intermediate Language is the native language for .NET and is compiled into an executable application by the Just In Time (JIT) compiler.

Solution to Question 1-7. The Just In Time compiler turns your MSIL code into an application in memory.

Solution to Question 1-8. Namespaces are used to ensure that identifiers are unique across libraries of classes. In other words, they ensure that a name that you use in your code doesn't conflict with a name used by Microsoft, or anybody else.

Solution to Question 1-9. A string is a class with many abilities and uses, but in its simplest form, a string is text enclosed in double quotation marks.

Solution to Question 1-10. The four kinds of applications you can build with Visual Studio 2008 are Console, Windows, Web, and Web Services applications.

Exercise Solution

Solution to Exercise 1-1. Write an application that emits the words "What a great book!" to the console window.

Hint: open Visual Studio, create a console application, and, if you get stuck, consider copying or modifying the code shown in the chapter. Remember, these exercises are for your own edification, no one is grading them, and making mistakes is an opportunity to explore and learn more—this is true in just about everything except nuclear physics.

So, *Don't Panic*!

To accomplish this exercise, you simply need to follow the same steps that you did to create Hello World in the chapter. Create a new console application from the Start Page, and give it whatever name you like, although "Exercise 1-1" is a reasonable name. When Visual Studio creates a code skeleton for you, click inside the Main( ) method and insert the following line:

```
Console.WriteLine("What a great book!");
```

Notice that we didn't use the System namespace in this line, because the using statement takes care of that. The exact code you use may vary somewhat, depending on what you chose to name your namespace and your class, and how you phrased your string, but one solution appears in Example A-1.

Example A-1. One solution to Exercise 1-1

```
using System;
using System.Collections.Generic;
using System.Linq;
using System.Text;

namespace Exercise_1_1
{
    class Program
    {
        static void Main(string[] args)
        {
```

Example A-1. One solution to Exercise 1-1 (continued)

```
        Console.WriteLine("What a great book!");
    }
  }
}
```

Chapter 2: Visual Studio 2008 and C# Express 2008

Quiz Solutions

Solution to Question 2-1. A project results in the production of an executable or a library. Most solutions consist of a single project, but many consist of two or more projects.

Solution to Question 2-2. To move windows in the IDE, click and drag on the title bar; use the indicators for placement.

Solution to Question 2-3. The pushpin button toggles between locking the window in place and hiding it as a tab.

Solution to Question 2-4. F5 runs the program with debugging; Ctrl-F5 runs without debugging. For console applications that do not require any input, Ctrl-F5 is more useful, so you can see the output.

Solution to Question 2-5. The Clipboard Ring allows you to store more than one item on the clipboard.

Solution to Question 2-6. Press Ctrl-Shift-V to cycle through all the selections in the Clipboard Ring.

Solution to Question 2-7. Find Symbol allows you to search for symbols (namespaces, classes, and interfaces) and their members (properties, methods, events, and variables).

Solution to Question 2-8. A bookmark is a tool for returning to a specific place in your code.

Solution to Question 2-9. IntelliSense is an editing tool that supplies suggestions for completing keywords, based on what you've typed. It's a useful tool for saving keystrokes.

Solution to Question 2-10. A code snippet is a complete outline of a commonly used programming structure with replaceable items to speed development.

Exercise Solutions

Solution to Exercise 2-1. Insert a bookmark before the `Console.Writeline()` statement in Hello World. Navigate away from it and then use the Bookmarks menu item to return to it.

Placing a bookmark in code is simple. Simply click on the line containing the `WriteLine()` statement, and then select Edit → Bookmarks → Toggle Bookmark to set the bookmark. You'll see a light blue square in the left margin, next to the line. Your Visual Studio window should look something like Figure A-1. Navigate away from that line by clicking anywhere else in the program. Now select Edit → Bookmarks → Next Bookmark (or Previous Bookmark; either will work, because there's only one bookmark in the file), and your cursor will be returned to the line with the `WriteLine()`. That's not terribly useful in a program as short as this one, but if your program is 50 pages long, you'll be glad for bookmarks.

You may want to select Edit → Bookmarks → Clear Bookmarks when you're done, to remove the bookmark.

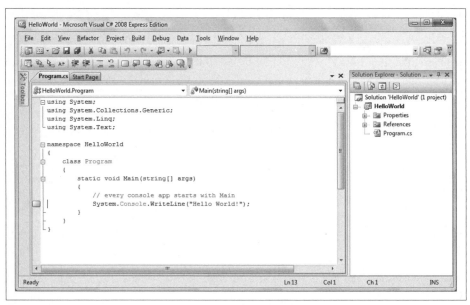

Figure A-1. Exercise 2-1.

Solution to Exercise 2-2. Undock the Solution Explorer window from the right side of the IDE and move it to the left. Leave it there if you like or move it back.

This task is relatively easy. Simply click on the title bar of the Solution Explorer and drag it away from the right side to undock it, drag it to the arrow pointing left, and release it. Your Visual Studio window should look something like Figure A-2.

Simply reverse the process to move the window back to the right, unless you prefer the Solution Explorer on the left, of course.

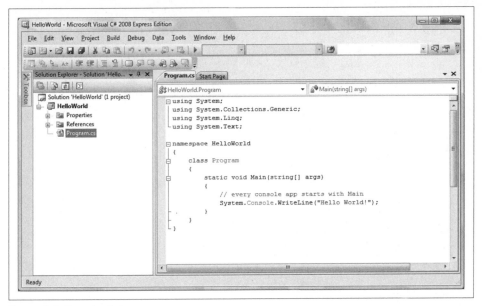

Figure A-2. Exercise 2-2.

Solution to Exercise 2-3.   Insert a code snippet for a for loop from the Edit → IntelliSense menu into your Hello World program. (It won't do anything for now; you'll learn about for loops in Chapter 5.)

First, click after the semicolon at the end of the WriteLine( ) statement and press Enter once to clear some space. Now select Edit → IntelliSense → Insert Snippet. You'll see a small drop-down asking you to choose between NetFX30 and Visual C#. Select Visual C# and the drop-down will change to a list of possible snippets. Click for, and the for loop will be inserted for you. Your Visual Studio window should look something like Figure A-3.

Chapter 3: C# Language Fundamentals

Quiz Solutions

Solution to Question 3-1.   A statement is a complete C# instruction, and must end in a semicolon (;).

Solution to Question 3-2.   A variable of type bool can have one of two values: true or false.

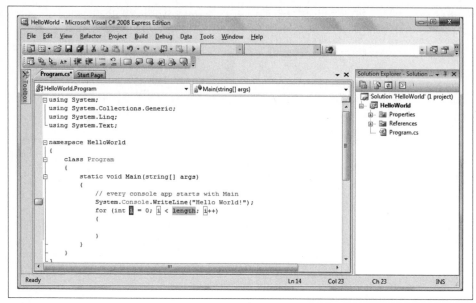

Figure A-3. Exercise 2-3.

Solution to Question 3-3. C# contains both intrinsic types and user-defined types. *Intrinsic* types are built-in, and don't do much other than hold values. *User-defined* types are much more flexible, and have abilities determined by code you write, as you'll see later in the book.

Solution to Question 3-4. A `float` requires four bytes of memory and a `double` takes eight bytes, and thus a `double` can represent much larger values with greater precision. The compiler assumes that any number with a decimal component is a `double` by default. If you want to specify a `float`, you need to add the suffix `f` to the value.

Solution to Question 3-5. A variable is a placeholder for a value. A variable must have an identifier (or a name) and a type.

Solution to Question 3-6. In C, if you wish to use a variable of any type (such as passing it as a parameter to a method) you must first assign it a value. You can initialize a variable without assigning it a value, but you can't use it in any way until it is assigned.

Solution to Question 3-7. The first two statements are fine. The first is just a simple assignment with no conversion. The second line is an implicit conversion—the `int` is implicitly converted to a `long` without any trouble. The third statement is a problem, though—you can't convert a `long` to an `int`, and the compiler will say so. To fix this, you need to cast the `long` to an `int`, like this:

```
int newInt = (int) myLong;
```

Solution to Question 3-8. In a nutshell, you should use a constant for any information that you know won't change; everything else should be a variable. Specifically:

Your age in years
> This should be a variable, because it changes. Unless you're in kindergarten, age is normally stated as a whole number, and it's unlikely to be much more than 100, so a `short` is appropriate here. But in practice, you'd probably use an `int`, to avoid unnecessary confusion.

The speed of light in meters per second
> The speed of light never changes (or so says Einstein, anyway, and we believe him), so you should use a constant. Its speed is about 3×10^8 meters per second, so a `float` would do nicely here. However, the compiler defaults to a `double`, which is also fine.

The number of widgets in your warehouse
> This number can change (or so you hope), so a constant isn't appropriate. Depending on the size of a widget, an `int` is probably your best choice here. Because the number can't possibly be negative, you could also use a `uint`, which would give you some breathing room if you happen to have more than 2 billion widgets, but that's a bit picky.

The amount of money in your bank account
> Again, you would hope that this value can change, so you wouldn't want to use a constant. A `float` or `double` would certainly work here, but the best choice is `decimal`, which .NET provides specifically for monetary transactions where a high degree of precision is required.

The text of the U.S. Declaration of Independence
> Because you're using text, a `string` is the best choice here. And because you're talking about a document that cannot change, a constant would be appropriate. If you wanted to parse or manipulate the text in any way, you'd have to create a new string, but that's a topic for later.

Solution to Question 3-9. You would refer to the constant that represents the wavelength of green light like this:

```
WavelengthsOfLight.Green
```

Its value is 5300.

Solution to Question 3-10. A string literal consists of characters enclosed in double quotes.

Exercise Solutions

Solution to Exercise 3-1. We'll start easy for this project. Write a short program that creates five variables, one of each of the following types: int, float, double, char, and string. Name the variables whatever you like. Initialize the variables with the following values:

- int: 42
- float: 98.6
- double: 12345.6789
- char: Z
- string: The quick brown fox jumped over the lazy dogs.

Then output the values to the console.

This exercise isn't too much different from the examples in the chapter, particularly Example 3-3. The only difference is that here, you're using a variety of different data types instead of just int, and that the different types have slightly different syntax. Remember to append an f after the value for the float, to put the value for the char in single quotes, and to put the string in double quotes, and you'll be fine. If you should happen to get any of those wrong, don't worry; the compiler will provide an error message to let you know where you went wrong.

One solution is shown in Example A-2.

Example A-2. One solution to Exercise 3-1

```
using System;
using System.Collections.Generic;
using System.Linq;
using System.Text;

namespace Exercise_3_1
{
  class Exercise
  {
    static void Main( )
    {
      int myInt = 42;
      float myFloat = 98.6f;
      double myDouble = 12345.6789;
      char myChar = 'Z';
      string myString = "The quick brown fox jumped over the
                         lazy dogs.";
      Console.WriteLine("myInt: {0}, myFloat: {1}, myDouble: {2},
                         myChar: {3}, myString: {4}", myInt, myFloat,
                         myDouble, myChar, myString);
    }
  }
}
```

The output should look like this (although where the line breaks on your screen depends on the size of your console window):

```
myInt: 42, myFloat: 98.6, myDouble: 12345.6789, myChar: Z, myString:
The quick brown fox jumped over the lazy dogs.
```

Solution to Exercise 3-2. As you gain more experience with programming, you'll frequently find yourself adapting some code that you wrote before, instead of writing a new program from scratch—and there's no time like the present to start. Modify the program in Exercise 3-1 so that after you've output the values of the variables the first time, you change them to the following:

- int: 25
- float: 100.3
- double: 98765.4321
- char: M
- string: A quick movement of the enemy will jeopardize six gun boats

Then output the values to the console a second time.

This exercise is only marginally more difficult than the last. The only trick here is to remember that when you change the value of an existing variable, you don't need to declare the type again. If you do, you'll get an error. So, the reassignment of the int shouldn't look like this:

```
int myInt = 42;
```

If you do that, the compiler will think you're trying to create a new variable with the same name as one that already exists, and you'll get an error. Instead, you just write this:

```
myInt = 42;
```

And there you go. Example A-3 shows what the code should look like.

Example A-3. One solution to Exercise 3-2

```
using System;
using System.Collections.Generic;
using System.Linq;
using System.Text;

namespace Exercise_3_2
{
  class Exercise
  {
    static void Main( )
    {
      int myInt = 42;
      float myFloat = 98.6f;
      double myDouble = 12345.6789;
```

Example A-3. One solution to Exercise 3-2 (continued)

```
        char myChar = 'Z';
        string myString = "The quick brown fox jumped over the
                        lazy dogs.";
        Console.WriteLine("myInt: {0}, myFloat: {1}, myDouble: {2},
                        myChar: {3}, myString: {4}", myInt, myFloat,
                        myDouble, myChar, myString);


        myInt = 25;
        myFloat = 100.3f;
        myDouble = 98765.4321;
        myChar = 'M';
        myString = "A quick movement of the enemy will jeopardize
                    six gun boats.";
        Console.WriteLine("myInt: {0}, myFloat: {1}, myDouble: {2},
                        myChar: {3}, myString: {4}", myInt, myFloat,
                        myDouble, myChar, myString);
    }
  }
}
```

The output should look like this (again, the line breaks on your screen depend on the size of your console window):

```
myInt: 42, myFloat: 98.6, myDouble: 12345.6789, myChar: Z, myString:
The quick brown fox jumped over the lazy dogs.
myInt: 25, myFloat: 100.3, myDouble: 98765.4321, myChar: M, myString:
A quick movement of the enemy will jeopardize six gun boats.
```

By the way, you can thank Brian's ninth-grade typing teacher for that second string; it's another sentence that uses every letter in the alphabet.

Solution to Exercise 3-3. Write a new program to declare a constant double. Call the constant Pi, set its value to 3.14159, and output its value to the screen. Then change the value of Pi to 3.1 and output its value again. What happens when you try to compile this program?

This program is even simpler than the previous one. All you have to do is remember to use the keyword const when you declare the constant. Example A-4 shows the code.

Example A-4. One solution to Exercise 3-3

```
using System;
using System.Collections.Generic;
using System.Linq;
using System.Text;

namespace Exercise_3_3
{
    class Exercise
    {
```

Example A-4. One solution to Exercise 3-3 (continued)

```csharp
    static void Main()
    {
        const double Pi = 3.14159;
        Console.WriteLine("The value of pi is: {0}", Pi);
        Pi = 3.1;
        Console.WriteLine("The value of pi is: {0}", Pi);
    }
  }
}
```

This program won't compile, as you probably found out, because you're trying to assign a value to a constant. Instead, you receive a compiler error that reads, "The left-hand side of an assignment must be a variable, property or indexer."

You can "fix" the program by commenting out the reassignment line, but that just gives you two identical lines of output. If you really want to change the value of Pi, you'll either have to edit your code by hand, or not use a constant. So, when you use a constant in your code, you need to be certain that you'll never want to change it at runtime.

Solution to Exercise 3-4. Write a new program and create a constant enumeration with constants for each month of the year. Give each month the value equal to its numeric place in the calendar, so January is 1, February is 2, and so on. Then output the value for June, with an appropriate message.

For this exercise, you declare an enumeration just as you saw in Example 3-5. This time, though, you fill in the months of the year appropriately. When you write your Writeline() statement in Main(), be sure to use the proper notation to refer to the constant you want (Months.June in this case), and remember to cast Months.June to an int.

Example A-5 shows what the code should look like.

Example A-5. One solution to Exercise 3-4

```csharp
using System;
using System.Collections.Generic;
using System.Linq;
using System.Text;

namespace Exercise_3_4
{
    class Exercise
    {
        // declare the enumeration
        enum Months : int
        {
            January = 1,
            February = 2,
```

Example A-5. One solution to Exercise 3-4 (continued)

```
            March = 3,
            April = 4,
            May = 5,
            June = 6,
            July = 7,
            August = 8,
            September = 9,
            October = 10,
            November = 11,
            December = 12
        }

    static void Main(string[] args)
    {
        Console.WriteLine("June is month number {0}.",
                        (int) Months.June);
    }
  }
}
```

And the output should look something like this, depending on what message you inserted:

```
June is month number 6.
```

Chapter 4: Operators

Quiz Solutions

Solution to Question 4-1. The = operator is the assignment operator, used to assign a value to a variable. The == operator is the equality operator, which tests the equality of two values and returns a Boolean. Confusing the two is a very common mistake, and a common source of errors.

Solution to Question 4-2. To assign the same value to multiple variables, simply chain the assignments, like this:

```
int a = b = c = d = 36;
```

Solution to Question 4-3. When you divide two doubles, the solution has a fractional portion, expressed as a decimal, as you would expect. When you divide two ints, the compiler discards any fractional remainder.

Solution to Question 4-4. The purpose of the % operator is to return the remainder from an integer division. It's very useful in controlling loops, as you'll see later.

Solution to Question 4-5. The output of the operations is:

- 32
- 6
- 4 (Be careful of the order of operations here; the division (8 / 4) takes place before the addition and the subtraction)

Be sure to take note of the parentheses and the order of operator precedence, as discussed in Table 4-3.

Solution to Question 4-6. Because the self-assignment operators are used here, the value of myInt changes with each step, forming a new input for the next step.

```
myInt += 5;
myInt = 30
myInt -= 15;
myInt = 15
myInt *= 4;
myInt = 60
myInt /= 3;
myInt = 20
```

Solution to Question 4-7. The prefix operator increments (or decrements) the original value, and then assigns the new value to the result. The postfix operator assigns the original value to the result, and then increments (or decrements) the original value.

Solution to Question 4-8. The expressions evaluate to:

1. True
2. True
3. False
4. 5 (This expression evaluates to 5, not to true; remember that assignment returns the value assigned)

Solution to Question 4-9. The expressions evaluate to:

1. True. x > y is true, and y < x is also true, so the entire expression is true.
2. False. x > y is true, so !(x > y) is false.
3. True. x < y is false, so !(x < y) is true. !(x < y) is true, and (x > y) is also true, so the entire expression together is true. Note that the ! is evaluated before the &&.
4. True. This one is tricky, because of the nested parentheses, but if you take it one step at a time, you can work it out. (x > y) is true, and !(x < y) is also true, so ((x > y) || !(x < y)) all evaluates to true. The other side of the &&, (x > y), is also true, so you end up with true && true, which evaluates to true. As you can see, you need to be very careful how you nest your parentheses.

5. False. The parentheses in this expression could drive you mad, but you don't actually need to bother with them. Take a look at the second half of the expression, on the right side of the &&. You'll see (x == y). You know that (x == y) is false. Because anything && false evaluates to false, you don't need to bother with that nest of parentheses on the left. No matter what the left side evaluates to, the whole expression will be false. This is called *short-circuit evaluation*.

Solution to Question 4-10. The correct order of operations is:

```
++
%
!=
&&
?:
```

Exercise Solutions

Solution to Exercise 4-1. Write a program that assigns the value 25 to variable x, and 5 to variable y. Output the sum, difference, product, quotient, and modulus of x and y.

As always, there are a variety of ways to accomplish this task. However you do it, though, you must start by assigning two variables, x and y. From there, you could use temporary variables to hold each of the values you calculate, and output them all in a WriteLine() statement. Or you could just do the math in the WriteLine(), as shown in Example A-6.

Example A-6. One solution to Exercise 4-1

```
using System;
using System.Collections.Generic;
using System.Linq;
using System.Text;

namespace Exercise_4_1
{
    class Program
    {
        static void Main()
        {
            int x = 25;
            int y = 5;
            Console.WriteLine("sum: {0}, difference: {1}, product: {2},
                        quotient: {3}, modulus: {4}.", x + y, x - y,
                        x * y, x / y, x % y);
        }
    }
}
```

The output looks like this:

```
sum: 30, difference: 20, product: 125, quotient: 5, modulus: 0.
```

Solution to Exercise 4-2. What will be the output of the following method? Why?

```
static void Main( )
{
    int varA = 5;
    int varB = ++varA;
    int varC = varB++;
    Console.WriteLine( "A: {0}, B: {1}, C: {2}", varA, varB, varC );
}
```

Of course, you could simply type in this code and see what the output is, but that won't tell you *why* the output is what it is. Let's start with the output:

```
A: 6, B: 7, C: 6
```

Now let's take this apart one line at a time. The first line is simple enough:

```
int varA = 5;
```

You've set varA to 5. No problem:

```
int varB = ++varA;
```

The trick now is that actually two things are going on in this line. First, varA is incremented, from 5 to 6. Because you're using the prefix operator, the increment happens before the assignment. Second, varB is set to the new value of varA, which is 6. So, at the moment, both varA and varB are 6:

```
int varC = varB++;
```

Again, two things are happening here. This time, because you're using the postfix operator, the assignment happens first—varC is set equal to the current value of varB, which is 6. Then varB is incremented to 7, but the value of varC has already been assigned, so it doesn't change. Therefore, when you get to the output, varA is 6, varB is 7, and varC is 6.

The lesson here is that if you want to set varB to be one more than varA, just use this:

```
varB = varA + 1;
```

instead of trying to save keystrokes with the increment operators. No matter how many keystrokes it saves, code is useful only if you can understand what it does.

Solution to Exercise 4-3. Imagine an amusement park ride that holds two passengers. Because of safety restrictions, the combined weight of the two passengers must be more than 100 pounds, but no more than 300 pounds. Now imagine a family of four who want to ride this ride. Abby weighs 135 pounds, Bob weighs 175 pounds, their son Charlie weighs 55 pounds, and their daughter Dawn weighs 45 pounds.

Write a program that calculates whether the weight of the two combined passengers falls within the accepted range. Use constants for the maximum and minimum weights, and for the weight of each family member. The output should look something like this, for Abby and Dawn:

```
Abby and Dawn can ride? True
```

Calculate three separate cases: whether the two parents can ride together, just Bob and Charlie, and just the kids.

As always, there are several ways to solve this problem. No matter what you choose, though, you need to determine whether the combined weight of the two passengers is between the maximum and minimum weights. The obvious choice for this is to use a logical and, like this:

```
bool canRide = ((weight1 + weight2) > minWeight) &&
((weight1 + weight2) <= maxWeight);
```

The `bool` `canRide` will be true only if the combined weight is both greater than the minimum weight and less than the maximum weight.

If you had access to user input and looping statements, you could make this application much fancier, but you'll learn about those in the next chapter. Example A-7 shows one solution that fits the requirements.

Example A-7. One solution to Exercise 4-3

```
using System;
using System.Collections.Generic;
using System.Linq;
using System.Text;

namespace Exercise_4_3
{
    class Program
    {
        static void Main(string[] args)
        {
            const int weightAbby = 135;
            const int weightBob = 175;
            const int weightCharlie = 55;
            const int weightDawn = 45;
            const int minWeight = 100;
            const int maxWeight = 300;

            bool canRide;
            int weight1, weight2;

            // Abby + Bob
            weight1 = weightAbby;
            weight2 = weightBob;
            canRide = ((weight1 + weight2) > minWeight) &&
                        ((weight1 + weight2) <= maxWeight);
```

Example A-7. One solution to Exercise 4-3 (continued)

```
        Console.WriteLine("Abby and Bob can ride? {0}", canRide);

        // Bob + Charlie
        weight1 = weightBob;
        weight2 = weightCharlie;
        canRide = ((weight1 + weight2) > minWeight) &&
                ((weight1 + weight2) <= maxWeight);
        Console.WriteLine("Bob and Charlie can ride? {0}", canRide);

        // Charlie + Dawn
        weight1 = weightCharlie;
        weight2 = weightDawn;
        canRide = ((weight1 + weight2) > minWeight) &&
                ((weight1 + weight2) <= maxWeight);
        Console.WriteLine("Charlie and Dawn can ride? {0}", canRide);

    }
  }
}
```

Solution to Exercise 4-4. Now it's time for a little high school math. Take a sphere of radius 5. Calculate and output the surface area, and the volume of the sphere. Then use the ternary operator to indicate which of the two is greater. Make Pi a constant float, and use a value of 3.14159 for precision. You should probably also make the radius a constant.

This application isn't too difficult, but it does require that you remember some math formulas (or know where to look them up online). The formula for the surface area of a sphere is $4\pi r^2$, and the formula for the volume is $4/3\pi r^3$. C# doesn't have a built-in operator for raising to a power, so you can simply multiply the radius by itself two or three times, as needed.

To calculate the radius, you'd need something like this:

```
    float surfaceArea = 4f * Pi * (radius * radius);
```

To calculate the surface area, you'd need something like this:

```
    float volume = (4f / 3f) * Pi * (radius * radius * radius);
```

Note that you need to use the f suffix on the float values. It's not strictly necessary on the 4 in the surface area calculation, but it's crucial in the volume calculation. Remember that (4/3) is 1.33333 in floating-point division, but it's just 1 in integer division.

The ternary operator isn't difficult; just compare the two values and assign the larger one to a variable, which you can then output. (We do know that the surface area is in square units, and the volume is in cubic units, so you can't really compare the two numbers, but we'll overlook that for the purpose of this exercise.)

One solution is shown in Example A-8.

Example A-8. One solution to Exercise 4-4

```
using System;
using System.Collections.Generic;
using System.Linq;
using System.Text;

namespace Exercise_4_4
{
   class Program
   {
      static void Main( )
      {
         const float Pi = 3.14159f;
         const float radius = 5f;
         float surfaceArea = 4f * Pi * (radius * radius);
         Console.WriteLine("Surface area is: {0}", surfaceArea);
         float volume = (4f / 3f) * Pi * (radius * radius * radius);
         Console.WriteLine("Volume is: {0}", volume);
         float greater = surfaceArea > volume ? surfaceArea : volume;
         Console.WriteLine("The greater of these is: {0}", greater);

      }
   }
}
```

Chapter 5: Branching

Quiz Solutions

Solution to Question 5-1. The if, if...else, and switch statements are used for conditional branching.

Solution to Question 5-2. False. In C#, an if statement's condition must evaluate to a *Boolean* expression.

Solution to Question 5-3. The braces make maintenance easier. If you add a second statement later, you are less likely to create a logic error because it is obvious what "block" of statements the if refers to.

Solution to Question 5-4. Either a numeric value or a string can be placed in a switch statement.

Solution to Question 5-5. False. If the statement has no body, you can fall through. For example:

```
case morning:
case afternoon:
```

```
    someAction( );
    break;
```

Solution to Question 5-6. Two uses of goto are:

- To go to a label in your code
- To go to a different case statement in a switch statement

Solution to Question 5-7. do...while evaluates its condition at the end of the loop rather than at the beginning, and thus is guaranteed to run at least once.

Solution to Question 5-8. The header of a for loop includes the *initializer*, in which you create and initialize the counter variable; the *expression*, in which you test the value of the counter variable; and the *iterator*, in which you update the value of the counter variable. All three parts are optional.

Solution to Question 5-9. In a loop, the continue keyword causes the remainder of the body of the loop to be skipped and the next iteration of the loop to begin immediately.

Solution to Question 5-10. Two ways of creating an infinite loop are:

```
for (;;)
while(true)
```

Exercise Solutions

Solution to Exercise 5-1. Create a program that counts from 1 to 10 three times, using the while, do...while, and for statements, and outputs the results to the screen.

There's nothing tricky about this exercise; you're simply using each of the three loop types to count to 10. Remember to initialize your counter at 1 for each loop, and to set the condition to be counter <= 10, rather than counter < 10, or you'll find your loop stopping at 9. If you want to be fancy, you can output on one line, using Write( ), and include an if statement to add a comma after each number except the last, as we've done here. Example A-9 shows the code.

Example A-9. One solution to Exercise 5-1

```
using System;
using System.Collections.Generic;
using System.Linq;
using System.Text;

namespace Exercise_5_1
{
    class Program
    {
```

Example A-9. One solution to Exercise 5-1 (continued)

```
static void Main( )
{
    Console.WriteLine( "while" );
    int counter = 1;
    while ( counter <= 10 )
    {
        Console.Write( counter );
        if ( counter < 10 )
        {
            Console.Write( ", " );
        }
        counter++;
    }
    Console.WriteLine( "\ndo..while" );
    counter = 1;
    do
    {
        Console.Write( counter );
        if ( counter < 10 )
        {
            Console.Write( ", " );
        }
        counter++;
    } while ( counter <= 10 );
    Console.WriteLine( "\nfor" );
    for ( int ctr = 1; ctr <= 10; ctr++ )
    {
        Console.Write( ctr );
        if ( ctr < 10 )
        {
            Console.Write( ", " );
        }
    }
    Console.WriteLine( "\nDone" );
}
}
}
```

Solution to Exercise 5-2. Create a program that accepts an integer from the user as input, then evaluates whether that input is zero, odd or even, a multiple of 10, or too large (more than 100) by using multiple levels of if statements.

The solution to this exercise is going to be a rat's nest of if statements, no matter what you do. However, the order in which you make the tests is critical. First, you need to test whether the number is too large (more than 100), because if it is, you stop right there. Inside that if, you check whether it's odd or even, because if it's odd, you stop there too. Inside the second if, you check whether it's zero. Inside that, you check whether it's a multiple of 10. That's how you get four levels of if, and some very nasty code. Example A-10 shows one way to do it.

Example A-10. One solution to Exercise 5-2

```csharp
using System;
using System.Collections.Generic;
using System.Linq;
using System.Text;

namespace Exercise_5_2
{
    class Program
    {
        static void Main( )
        {
            while (true)
            {
                Console.Write("Enter a number please: ");
                string theEntry = Console.ReadLine( );
                int theNumber = Convert.ToInt32(theEntry);

                // Logic: if the number is greater than 100, say it is too big
                // if it is even but not a multiple of 10 say it is even
                // if it is a multiple of 10, say so
                // if it is not even, say it is odd
                if (theNumber <= 100)
                {
                    if (theNumber % 2 == 0)
                    {
                        if (theNumber == 0)
                        {
                            Console.WriteLine("Zero is not even or odd or a
                                               multiple of 10");
                        }
                        else
                        {
                            if (theNumber % 10 == 0)
                            {
                                Console.WriteLine("You have picked a multiple
                                                   of 10");
                            }
                            else
                            {
                                Console.WriteLine("Your number is even");
                            } // end else not a multiple of 10
                        } // end else not zero
                    } // end if even
                    else
                    {
                        Console.WriteLine("What an odd number to enter");
                    }
                } // end if not too big
                else
                {
                    Console.WriteLine("Your number is too big for me.");
                }
```

Example A-10. One solution to Exercise 5-2 (continued)

```
            } // end while
        }
    }
}
```

Solution to Exercise 5-3. Rewrite the program from Exercise 5-2 to do the same work with a switch statement.

The switch statement makes a nice alternative to programs that have lots of nested if statements. To rewrite the program using a switch, you first have to define an enum that outlines the various possibilities. Then you'll need a series of (nonnested) if statements to determine which of the enum options applies. Once you've done that, you can use a switch to output the appropriate statement, and even include a default that accounts for unexpected input. One solution is shown in Example A-11.

Example A-11. One solution to Exercise 5-3

```
using System;
using System.Collections.Generic;
using System.Linq;
using System.Text;

namespace Exercise_5_3
{
    class Program
    {
        enum numericCondition
        {
            even,
            multiple,
            odd,
            tooBig,
            unknown,
            zero
        }
        static void Main( )
        {
            while (true)
            {
                Console.Write("Enter a number, please: ");
                string theEntry = Console.ReadLine( );
                int theNumber = Convert.ToInt32(theEntry);

                numericCondition condition = numericCondition.unknown;  // initialize
                condition = (theNumber % 2 == 0) ?
                            numericCondition.even : numericCondition.odd;
                if (theNumber % 10 == 0) condition = numericCondition.multiple;
                if (theNumber == 0) condition = numericCondition.zero;
                if (theNumber > 100) condition = numericCondition.tooBig;
```

Example A-11. One solution to Exercise 5-3 (continued)

```
            // switch on the condition and display the correct message
            switch (condition)
            {
                case numericCondition.even:
                    Console.WriteLine("Your number is even");
                    break;
                case numericCondition.multiple:
                    Console.WriteLine("You have picked a multiple of 10");
                    break;
                case numericCondition.odd:
                    Console.WriteLine("What an odd number to enter");
                    break;
                case numericCondition.tooBig:
                    Console.WriteLine("Your number is too big for me.");
                    break;
                case numericCondition.zero:
                    Console.WriteLine("zero is not even or odd
                                       or a multiple of 10");
                    break;
                default:
                    Console.WriteLine("I'm sorry, I didn't understand that.");
                    break;
            }
        }
      }
    }
  }
}
```

You could make the case that this solution is more complicated than Example A-10. After all, you still have a bunch of if statements to set the value of the enum, even if they're not nested. And the solution here is obviously longer than Example A-10. However, we believe that the switch statement used here is easier to read and maintain, which may take a bit longer to write now, but will save you time in the future.

Solution to Exercise 5-4.   Create a program that initializes a variable i at 0 and counts up, and initializes a second variable j at 25 and counts down. Use a for loop to increment i and decrement j simultaneously. When i is greater than j, end the loop and print out the message "Crossed over!"

This exercise is tricky. It's possible to use two counter variables in the header of a for loop, although it's not commonly done. In this case, you need to declare i and j before starting the loop. Then, in the header, you initialize i to 0 and j to 25. You want the loop to end when i has become less than j, so your condition is simple: i < j. You want i to count up and j to count down, so for your iterator, you use i++ and j--. As soon as i becomes less than j, the loop ends, so you output the final message outside the loop. Example A-12 shows one possible solution.

Example A-12. One solution to Exercise 5-4

```
namespace Exercise_5_4
{
   class Program
   {
      static void Main( )
      {
         int i;
         int j;
         for (i = 0, j = 25; i < j; ++i, --j )
         {
            Console.WriteLine("i: {0}; j: {1}", i, j);
         }
         Console.WriteLine( "Crossed over! i: {0}; j: {1}", i, j );
      }
   }
}
```

The output looks like this:

```
i: 0; j: 25
i: 1; j: 24
i: 2; j: 23
i: 3; j: 22
i: 4; j: 21
i: 5; j: 20
i: 6; j: 19
i: 7; j: 18
i: 8; j: 17
i: 9; j: 16
i: 10; j: 15
i: 11; j: 14
i: 12; j: 13
Crossed over! i: 13; j: 12
```

Chapter 6: Object-Oriented Programming

Quiz Solutions

Solution to Question 6-1. New (user-defined) types are most often created in C# with the keyword class.

Solution to Question 6-2. A class defines a new type; an object is an instance of that type.

Solution to Question 6-3. Making your member fields private allows you to change how you store that data (as a member variable, or in a database) without breaking your client's code.

Solution to Question 6-4. Encapsulation is the principle of keeping each class discrete and self-contained, so you can change the implementation of one class without affecting any other class.

Solution to Question 6-5. Specialization allows a new class to "inherit" many of the characteristics of an existing class, and to be used polymorphically with that class. Specialization is implemented in C# through inheritance.

Solution to Question 6-6. Polymorphism is the ability to treat derived classes as though they were all instances of their base class, yet have each derived class specialize its own implementation of the base class's methods.

Solution to Question 6-7. The *is-a* relationship is established through inheritance. The *has-a* relationship is implemented through aggregation (making one type a member variable of another type).

Solution to Question 6-8. Access modifiers indicate which class's methods have access to a given field, property, or method of a class. Public members are available to methods of any class; private members are available only to methods of instances of the same class.

Solution to Question 6-9. State is the current conditions and values of an object, and is implemented with properties and member variables. Capabilities are what the object can do, exposed through public methods. Responsibilities are the promises a well-designed class makes to the clients of that class.

Solution to Question 6-10. A use-case scenario is a tool for the analysis of a problem. In a use-case scenario, you walk through the details of how your product will be used by one user to accomplish one task, noting which classes interact and what their responsibilities are.

Exercise Solutions

Solution to Exercise 6-1. A visual representation of a class, its member fields and methods, and its place in the hierarchy is called a *class diagram*. There are several accepted methods for drawing a class diagram, but we won't hold you to any of those right now. For this example, simply draw a class diagram for a class named vehicle, listing some properties and methods that you think that class should have. Then add to your diagram the derived classes car, boat, and plane, and list their properties and methods (remember that all derived classes inherit the properties and methods of their parent class).

The rule of thumb when you're designing a parent class is to keep it as simple as it needs to be—include those properties and methods you need, but nothing extraneous. Leave the specialization to the derived classes; that's what they're there for. There are lots of ways to define these classes, but Figure A-4 shows one example.

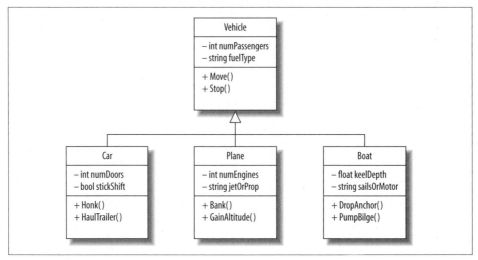

Figure A-4. One solution to Exercise 6-1.

We're using a common drawing convention that shows each class as a box with three sections. The top section shows the class name, the middle section shows its member fields, and the bottom section shows its member methods. The arrow leading from the lower three boxes to the upper one indicates that the lower three classes are all inherited from the upper one.

We've decided that all vehicles have a number of passengers, and a type of fuel (even if it's human-powered pedaling). Those are the member fields, and you'll notice we've assigned a type to each of them. We've also decided that all vehicles can move and stop; those are the methods.

We've gone on to derive three child classes, `Car`, `Plane`, and `Boat`. Each class inherits the properties and methods of the parent, so `Car` has a number of passengers, for example. However, cars have to specify the number of doors, and whether they're stick-shift or automatic. Cars can also honk, and haul a trailer, which neither of the other two classes can do. Both `Plane` and `Boat` have their own specialized properties and methods, which are probably different from the ones you thought of.

Solution to Exercise 6-2. You've defined a class as a diagram; now try defining one in code. Define a class `Book`, in which a book has a title, author, and ISBN, and the book can be read or shelved. You don't need to fill in the code for any methods you include; simply include a comment in the body, like we did for the `Dog` class earlier in the chapter.

This definition is relatively simple. We've given you the requirements for the class; you just need to decide which ones are methods and which are properties. Example A-13 shows what we had in mind.

Example A-13. Our solution to Exercise 6-2

```
class Book
{
    private String title;
    private String author;
    private String ISBN;

    public void Read( )     // member method
    {
        // code here to read book
    }
    public void Shelve( )  // member method
    {
        // code here to shelve book
    }
}
```

This isn't real code, and it won't compile without Main( ). In Chapter 7, you'll see how to create a class definition.

Chapter 7: Classes and Objects

Quiz Solutions

Solution to Question 7-1. A class defines a new type; an object is a single instance of that type.

Solution to Question 7-2. The keyword private indicates that access is limited to methods of the defining class.

Solution to Question 7-3. The keyword public indicates that access is available to methods in any class.

Solution to Question 7-4. When you create an instance of an object, the class's constructor is called.

Solution to Question 7-5. A default constructor is a constructor that takes no parameters. If you do not create any constructor at all for your class, a default constructor is implicitly created.

Solution to Question 7-6. None. A constructor is not defined to return a type, and is not marked void.

Solution to Question 7-7. You can initialize the value of a member variable either in the constructor, using assignment, or when the member variable is created:

```
private int myVariable = 88;
```

Technically, only the latter is truly initialization; assigning it in the constructor is not as efficient.

Solution to Question 7-8. this refers to the object itself—the current instance of the class.

Solution to Question 7-9. A static method has no this reference. It does not belong to an instance; it belongs to the class and can call only other static methods.

You access a static method through the name of the class:

```
Dog myDog = new Dog( );
myDog.InstanceMethod( );
Dog.StaticMethod( );
```

Of course, from within any method (including static methods), you can instantiate a class, and then call methods on that instance.

You can even instantiate an instance of your own class, and then call *any* nonstatic method of that object, as we did with (static) Main( ) calling (nonstatic) Test( ).

Solution to Question 7-10. Instances of classes are reference types and are created on the heap. Intrinsic types (such as integers) and structs are value types and are created on the stack.

Exercise Solutions

Solution to Exercise 7-1. Write a program with a Math class that has four methods: Add, Subtract, Multiply, and Divide, each of which takes two parameters. Call each method from Main( ) and provide an appropriate output statement to demonstrate that each method works. You don't need to have the user provide input; just provide the two integers to the methods within Main( ).

This is a reasonably simple exercise; all you need to do is remember how to define a new class, and then write the various methods for it. The code for the methods is simple enough; you just have to make sure to choose parameters that you can understand. left and right make good parameter names for mathematical methods like these.

Then you have to write a brief Main( ) that declares an instance of the Math class, and then calls each method in turn, providing the appropriate parameters. You store the returned values in variables, and then output them to the console. We chose to use the numbers 3 and 5 for the operands, but you can use whatever you like. Example A-14 shows our solution to this exercise.

Example A-14. Our solution to Exercise 7-1

```
using System;
using System.Collections.Generic;
using System.Linq;
using System.Text;

namespace Exercise_7_1
{
    class Math
    {
        public int Add( int left, int right )
        {
          return left + right;
        }
        public int Subtract( int left, int right )
        {
            return left - right;
        }
        public int Multiply( int left, int right )
        {
            return left * right;
        }
        public float Divide( float left, float right )
        {
            return left / right;
        }
    }    // end class Math
    class Program
    {
        static void Main( )
        {
            Math m = new Math( );
            int sum =        m.Add(3,5);
            int difference = m.Subtract(3,5);
            int product =    m.Multiply(3,5);
            float quotient = m.Divide(3.0f, 5.0f);
            Console.WriteLine("sum: {0}, difference: {1}, product: {2},
                    quotient: {3}", sum, difference, product, quotient);
        }
    }
}
```

Solution to Exercise 7-2. Modify the program from Exercise 7-1 so that you do not have to create an instance of Math to call the four methods. Call the four methods again from Main( ) to demonstrate that they work.

The difference here is that you don't want to create an instance of the Math class to do the work, which makes logical sense, since "math" isn't a real-world object that you would normally model an instance of. That means you'll need to use static methods to avoid creating an instance. The class stays mostly the same, except that you add the static keyword to each method name.

Now, in Main( ), instead of declaring an instance of Math, you can simply call the methods directly on the class, and do not create an instance first. In fact, the .NET Framework has a static Math class with methods for things like logarithms and trigonometric functions that you use in exactly this way. Example A-15 shows one solution.

Example A-15. One solution to Exercise 7-2

```
using System;
using System.Collections.Generic;
using System.Linq;
using System.Text;

namespace Exercise_7_2
{
    class Math
    {
        static public int Add( int left, int right )
        {
            return left + right;
        }
        static public int Subtract( int left, int right )
        {
            return left - right;
        }
        static public int Multiply( int left, int right )
        {
            return left * right;
        }
        static public float Divide( float left, float right )
        {
            return left / right;
        }
    }    // end class Math
    class Program
    {
        static void Main( string[] args )
        {
            int sum =       Math.Add( 3, 5 );
            int difference = Math.Subtract(3,5);
            int product =   Math.Multiply(3,5);
            float quotient = Math.Divide(3.0f, 5.0f);
            Console.WriteLine("sum: {0}, difference: {1}, product: {2},
                    quotient: {3}", sum, difference, product, quotient);
        }
    }
}
```

Solution to Exercise 7-3. Create a class Book that you could use to keep track of book objects. Each Book object should have a title, author, publisher, and ISBN (which should be a string, rather than a numeric type, so that the ISBN can start with a 0 or include an *X*). The class should have a DisplayBook( ) method to output that information to the console. In Main( ), create three Book objects with this data:

Programming C# 3.0	Jesse Liberty and Donald Xie	O'Reilly	9780596527433
C# 3.0 In a Nutshell	Joseph Albahari and Ben Albahari	O'Reilly	9780596527570
C# 3.0 Cookbook	Jay Hilyard and Stephen Teilhet	O'Reilly	9780596516109

Because all three books have the same publisher, you should initialize that field in your class.

The Book class is simple enough to create. The only difference in this exercise is that you have to initialize the publisher member to the string "O'Reilly" when you declare it, and then adjust your constructor accordingly. One solution is shown in Example A-16.

Example A-16. One solution to Exercise 7-3

```
using System;
using System.Collections.Generic;
using System.Linq;
using System.Text;

namespace Exercise_7_3
{
    class Book
    {
        private string title;
        private string author;
        private string publisher = "O'Reilly";
        private string isbn;

        public void OutputBook( )
        {
            Console.WriteLine("Title: {0}, Author: {1}, Publisher: {2},
                        ISBN: {3}", title, author, publisher, isbn);
        }

        //constructor
        public Book(string myTitle, string myAuthor, string myIsbn)
        {
            title = myTitle;
            author = myAuthor;
            isbn = myIsbn;
        }
    }

    class Program
```

Example A-16. One solution to Exercise 7-3 (continued)

```
{
    static void Main( )
    {
        Book firstBook = new Book("Programming C# 3.0",
                        "Jesse Liberty and Donald Xie", "9780596527433");
        Book secondBook = new Book("C# 3.0 In a Nutshell",
                        "Joseph Albahari and Ben Albahari", "9780596527570");
        Book thirdBook = new Book("C# 3.0 Cookbook",
                        "Jay Hilyard and Stephen Teilhet", "9780596516109");

        Console.WriteLine("First book:");
        firstBook.OutputBook( );
        Console.WriteLine("Second book:");
        secondBook.OutputBook( );
        Console.WriteLine("Third book:");
        thirdBook.OutputBook( );
    }
}
}
```

Solution to Exercise 7-4. You might think it isn't possible to draw geometric shapes using the console output, and you'd be mostly right. We can simulate drawing shapes, though, by imagining a graph and displaying, say, the coordinates of the four corners of a square. Start with a class called Point. This is a simple enough class; it should have members for an *x* coordinate and a *y* coordinate, a constructor, and a method for displaying the coordinates in the form (*x*,*y*). For now, make the x and y members public, to keep things simple.

Now create a class Square. Internally, the class should keep track of all four points of the square, but in the constructor, you should accept just a single Point and a length (make it an integer, to keep it simple). You should also have a method to output the coordinates of all four points. In Main( ), create the initial Point, then create a Square and output its corners.

The difference in this exercise is that you'll be using objects of one class (Point) as internal members of another class (Square). That's not tricky, but the first time you do it, it may be unexpected. The Point class is simple enough to create; you just need two internal members; call them whatever you like. We suggested that you make the members public because the Square class will need to access them as well. There's a better way to access the members of another class; you'll learn that in Chapter 8.

```
public class Point
{
    public int xCoord;
    public int yCoord;
```

```csharp
    public void DisplayPoint()
    {
        Console.WriteLine("({0}, {1})", xCoord, yCoord);
    }

    //constructor
    public Point(int x, int y)
    {
        xCoord = x;
        yCoord = y;
    }
}
```

Now that you have the `Point` class, you need four of them to make up the `Square` class. We specified that the constructor for the `Square` should take just one `Point` and a length. Therefore, the class needs to work out the other points and assign them to the internal members. We've done that in the constructor. You can access the *x* and *y* coordinates of the point you passed in to the constructor, add the length as appropriate, and generate the other three points:

```csharp
public class Square
{
    private Point topLeft;
    private Point topRight;
    private Point bottomRight;
    private Point bottomLeft;
    private int sideLength;

    public void displaySquare()
    {
        Console.WriteLine("The four corners are:");
        topLeft.DisplayPoint();
        topRight.DisplayPoint();
        bottomLeft.DisplayPoint();
        bottomRight.DisplayPoint();
    }

    //constructor
    public Square(Point myPoint, int myLength)
    {
        sideLength = myLength;
        topLeft = myPoint;
        topRight = new Point(topLeft.xCoord + sideLength, topLeft.yCoord);
        bottomLeft = new Point(topLeft.xCoord, topLeft.yCoord + sideLength);
        bottomRight = new Point(topLeft.xCoord + sideLength, topLeft.yCoord +
                               sideLength);
    }
}
```

As always, there are many possible solutions, but one of them is shown in full in Example A-17.

Example A-17. One solution to Exercise 7-4

```csharp
using System;
using System.Collections.Generic;
using System.Linq;
using System.Text;

namespace Exercise_7_4
{
    public class Point
    {
        public int xCoord;
        public int yCoord;

        public void DisplayPoint()
        {
            Console.WriteLine("({0}, {1})", xCoord, yCoord);
        }

        //constructor
        public Point(int x, int y)
        {
            xCoord = x;
            yCoord = y;
        }
    }

    public class Square
    {
        private Point topLeft;
        private Point topRight;
        private Point bottomRight;
        private Point bottomLeft;
        private int sideLength;

        public void displaySquare()
        {
            Console.WriteLine("The four corners are:");
            topLeft.DisplayPoint();
            topRight.DisplayPoint();
            bottomLeft.DisplayPoint();
            bottomRight.DisplayPoint();
        }

        //constructor
        public Square(Point myPoint, int myLength)
        {
            sideLength = myLength;
            topLeft = myPoint;
            topRight = new Point(topLeft.xCoord + sideLength, topLeft.yCoord);
            bottomLeft = new Point(topLeft.xCoord, topLeft.yCoord + sideLength);
            bottomRight = new Point(topLeft.xCoord + sideLength,
                                    topLeft.yCoord + sideLength);
        }
```

Example A-17. One solution to Exercise 7-4 (continued)

```
    }
    class Program
    {
        static void Main(string[] args)
        {
            Point startPoint = new Point(3, 3);
            int length = 5;
            Square mySquare = new Square(startPoint, length);
            mySquare.displaySquare( );
        }
    }
}
```

Chapter 8: Inside Methods

Quiz Solutions

Solution to Question 8-1.   Method overloading allows the author of the class to create a method with varying input parameters, rather than having to have many methods with different names that serve similar purposes.

Solution to Question 8-2.   Overloaded methods must differ in the number of parameters, the parameter types, or both. Simply differing in return type is not an overload.

Solution to Question 8-3.   The signature of a method is its name and the types on its parameter list.

Solution to Question 8-4.   Properties are public accessors to your encapsulated data. Properties appear to the class creator as methods, but to the class's clients as fields.

Solution to Question 8-5.   Properties enforce encapsulation through data hiding. They isolate the internal members of the class from the client. If you change how the internal values are generated, the property will seem to be unchanged, to outside callers.

Solution to Question 8-6.   To create a read-only property, do not implement the set part of the property. No special notation is required.

Solution to Question 8-7.   Automatic properties provide a shorter way for you to create a property, if all you need to do is set or retrieve a value.

Solution to Question 8-8.   You retrieve multiple return values from a method by passing in parameters by reference and getting the results back in those parameters.

Solution to Question 8-9. If you want to pass a value object (variable) by reference, you use the keyword ref in the call to the method and in the declaration of the method.

Solution to Question 8-10. If you want to pass a value object by reference, but do not want to initialize it before making the method call, you must use the keyword out in the call to the method and in the declaration of the method.

Exercise Solutions

Solution to Exercise 8-1. Write a program with an overloaded method for tripling the value of the argument. You don't need to create a separate class for this; just use static methods right in Tester. One version of the method should triple an int value, and the other version should triple a float value. Call both methods to demonstrate that they work.

You don't need to do much to accomplish this exercise. Simply create two static methods named Tripler( ), or whatever you choose to call them. Because they're overloaded methods, they must have the same name, but one should take an int and the other a float. The implementation of the methods themselves is simple; just remember to multiply the parameter by 3.0f for the float, rather than just 3. Example A-18 shows one solution.

Example A-18. One solution to Exercise 8-1

```
using System;
using System.Collections.Generic;
using System.Linq;
using System.Text;

namespace Exercise_8_1
{
    class Tester
    {
        public void Run( )
        {
            int x = 5;
            float y = 5.2f;
            Console.WriteLine("Triple {0} = {1}", x, Tripler(x));
            Console.WriteLine("Triple {0} = {1}", y, Tripler(y));
        }
        static int Tripler(int theVal)
        {
            return theVal * 3;
        }
        static float Tripler(float theVal)
        {
            return theVal * 3.0f;
        }
        static void Main( )
```

Example A-18. One solution to Exercise 8-1 (continued)

```
        {
            Tester t = new Tester();
            t.Run();
        }
    }
}
```

Solution to Exercise 8-2. Create a Dog class, where the Dog objects have both a weight and a color, hidden from the client. Create a Dog object, then retrieve its color and display it to the user. Ask the user for a weight, and use that input to set the Dog's weight.

This exercise also isn't particularly difficult, but properties are supposed to make things easy. The key to this exercise is to create the weight and color members as private member fields, and then provide two properties with get and set accessors. Technically, the exercise asked you to create only a getter for color and a setter for weight, but it doesn't hurt to have both. One solution is shown in Example A-19.

Example A-19. One solution to Exercise 8-2

```
using System;
using System.Collections.Generic;
using System.Linq;
using System.Text;

namespace Exercise_8_2
{
    public class Dog
    {
        private int weight;
        private string color;

        public int Weight
        {
            get
            {
                return weight;
            }
            set
            {
                weight = value;
            }
        }

        public string Color
        {
            get
            {
                return color;
            }
            set
```

Example A-19. One solution to Exercise 8-2 (continued)

```
            {
                color = value;
            }
        }

        public void DisplayDog( )
        {
            Console.WriteLine("The dog weighs {0} pounds and is {1}.",
                               weight, color);
        }

        public Dog(int myWeight, string myColor)
        {
            weight = myWeight;
            color = myColor;
        }
    }

    class Tester
    {
        public void Run( )
        {
            Dog fluffy = new Dog(25, "brown");
            fluffy.DisplayDog( );
            Console.WriteLine("The dog is still {0}.", fluffy.Color);
            Console.Write("What is the dog's new weight? ");
            int newWeight = Convert.ToInt32(Console.ReadLine( ));
            fluffy.Weight = newWeight;
            fluffy.DisplayDog( );

        }
        static void Main( )
        {
            Tester t = new Tester( );
            t.Run( );
        }
    }
}
```

If you really want to be fancy, you could use automatic properties instead of spelling out the properties the long way:

```
public int Weight { get; set; }
public string Color { get; set; }
```

However, you'd have to be sure to remove the private members shown in Example A-19, and change the references to weight and color in DisplayDog( ) and to Weight and Color in the constructor.

Solution to Exercise 8-3. Write a program with just one method that takes an int value, supplied by the user, and returns both double and triple that value. You don't need a separate class; just put the method in Tester. In Run( ), output the results to the console to make sure it worked.

Since the exercise is asking you to return two values from a single method, that means you'll have to use reference parameters. The method itself is simple. Just remember to create and initialize some variables in Run( ) to hold the values you'll return. Example A-20 shows how it's done.

Example A-20. One solution to Exercise 8-3

```
using System;
using System.Collections.Generic;
using System.Linq;
using System.Text;

namespace Exercise_8_3
{
    class Tester
    {
        public void Run()
        {
            Console.Write("Input an integer: ");
            int x = Convert.ToInt32(Console.ReadLine());
            int doubleX = 0;
            int tripleX = 0;
            DoublerAndTripler(x, ref doubleX, ref tripleX);
            Console.WriteLine("Double {0} = {1}; triple {2} = {3}",
                             x, doubleX, x, tripleX);
        }
        static void DoublerAndTripler(int theVal, ref int doubleValue,
                                      ref int tripleValue)
        {
            doubleValue = theVal * 2;
            tripleValue = theVal * 3;
        }
        static void Main()
        {
            Tester t = new Tester();
            t.Run();
        }
    }
}
```

Solution to Exercise 8-4. Modify the program from Exercise 8-3 so that you don't need to initialize the variables that will hold the doubled and tripled values before calling the method.

This time, you'll use out parameters instead of ref parameters. In this case, all you have to do is not initialize doubleX and tripleX when they're created, and change ref to out in the method call. One solution is shown in Example A-21.

Example A-21. One solution to Exercise 8-4

```
using System;
using System.Collections.Generic;
using System.Linq;
using System.Text;

namespace Exercise_8_4
{
    class Tester
    {
        public void Run()
        {
            Console.Write("Input an integer: ");
            int x = Convert.ToInt32(Console.ReadLine());
            int doubleX;      // uninitialized
            int tripleX;      // uninitialized
            DoublerAndTripler(x, out doubleX, out tripleX);
            Console.WriteLine("Double {0} = {1}; triple {2} = {3}",
                              x, doubleX, x, tripleX);
        }
        static void DoublerAndTripler(int theVal, out int doubleValue,
                                      out int tripleValue)
        {
            doubleValue = theVal * 2;
            tripleValue = theVal * 3;
        }
        static void Main()
        {
            Tester t = new Tester();
            t.Run();
        }
    }
}
```

Chapter 9: Basic Debugging

Quiz Solutions

Solution to Question 9-1. The simplest way to set a breakpoint is to go to the line where you want execution to stop, and click in the left margin. A red dot will appear on the line.

Solution to Question 9-2. When the execution stops, the breakpoint will have a yellow arrow pointing to the highlighted line of code.

Solution to Question 9-3. Pressing F10 steps over a method; pressing F11 steps into the method.

Solution to Question 9-4. Right-clicking on the line where the breakpoint is set opens a context menu that allows you to disable the breakpoint, or to set conditions on the breakpoint (in Visual Studio only).

Solution to Question 9-5. The Locals window shows all the variables that are in scope at the breakpoint. The Autos window shows variables used in the current and previous statement.

Solution to Question 9-6. In the Locals window (and the Autos window as well), objects that have internal state appear with a + sign next to them. Clicking the plus sign expands the object so that you can view its internal state.

Solution to Question 9-7. The easiest way to set a watch on a variable is by either right-clicking on the variable and choosing "Add to Watch window," or by clicking and dragging the variable directly onto the Watch window.

Solution to Question 9-8. To open a QuickWatch window, you right-click on the variable and choose QuickWatch, or select Debug → QuickWatch (in Visual Studio only).

Solution to Question 9-9. The call stack shows which method called the current method, and which method called that method, and so forth. This allows you to determine the exact path your code followed to bring you to the current method.

Solution to Question 9-10. In the Call Stack window, simply click on a method call and you'll be taken to that point in your code.

Exercise Solutions

Solution to Exercise 9-1. You'll use the following program for this exercise. Either type it into Visual Studio, or copy it from this book's website. Note that this is spaghetti code—you'd never write method calls like this, but that's why this is the debugging chapter:

```
using System;
using System.Collections.Generic;
using System.Linq;
using System.Text;

namespace Exercise_9_1
{
    class Tester
```

```
{
    public void Run( )
    {
        int myInt = 42;
        float myFloat = 9.685f;
        Console.WriteLine("Before starting: \n value of myInt:
                {0} \n value of myFloat: {1}", myInt, myFloat);
        // pass the variables by reference
        Multiply( ref myInt, ref myFloat );
        Console.WriteLine("After finishing: \n value of myInt:
                {0} \n value of myFloat: {1}", myInt, myFloat);
    }
    private static void Multiply (ref int theInt,
                                    ref float theFloat)
    {
        theInt = theInt * 2;
        theFloat = theFloat *2;
        Divide( ref theInt, ref theFloat);
    }
    private static void Divide (ref int theInt,
                                    ref float theFloat)
    {
        theInt = theInt / 3;
        theFloat = theFloat / 3;
        Add(ref theInt, ref theFloat);
    }
    public static void Add(ref int theInt,
                                ref float theFloat)
    {
        theInt = theInt + theInt;
        theFloat = theFloat + theFloat;
    }
    static void Main( )
    {
        Tester t = new Tester( );
        t.Run( );
    }
}
}
```

1. Place a breakpoint in Run( ) on the following line, and then run the program:

```
Console.WriteLine("Before starting: \n value of myInt:
                {0} \n value of myFloat: {1}", myInt, myFloat);
```

What are the values of myInt and myFloat at the breakpoint?

2. Step into the Multiply( ) method, up to the call to Divide( ). What are the values of theInt and theFloat at this point?

3. Stop debugging, run the program again, and when it reaches the breakpoint in Run( ), set a watch on myInt. Step through the methods. When does the value of myInt change?

4. Set another breakpoint in Add( ) at this line:

```
theInt = theInt + theInt;
```

Run the program. How many calls are in the call stack when the program reaches this breakpoint?

The solutions to these tasks are as follows:

1. As shown in the Locals window, myInt is 42 and myFloat is 9.685, because both have just been set.

2. theInt is 84 and theFloat is 19.37.

3. The value of myInt doesn't change until control returns to Run( ), after the Multiply( ) method has finished.

4. There are five calls in the call stack at this point: Main( ), Run( ), Multiply( ), Divide( ), and Add( ).

Solution to Exercise 9-2.   The program in this exercise is similar to the first, but it has a logic error. Type this program into Visual Studio, or download it from this book's website:

```
using System;
using System.Collections.Generic;
using System.Linq;
using System.Text;

namespace Exercise_9_2
{
    class Tester
    {
        public void Run()
        {
            int myInt = 42;
            float myFloat = 9.685f;
            Console.WriteLine("Before starting: \n value of myInt:
                    {0} \n value of myFloat: {1}", myInt, myFloat);
            // pass the variables by reference
            Multiply( ref myInt, ref myFloat );
            Console.WriteLine("After finishing: \n value of myInt:
                    {0} \n value of myFloat: {1}", myInt, myFloat);
        }
        private static void Multiply (ref int theInt,
                                        ref float theFloat)
        {
            theInt = theInt * 2;
            theFloat = theFloat *2;
            Divide( ref theInt, ref theFloat);
        }
        private static void Divide (ref int theInt,
                                      ref float theFloat)
```

```
        {
            theInt = theInt * 3;
            theFloat = theFloat * 3;
            Add(ref theInt, ref theFloat);
        }
        public static void Add(ref int theInt,
                                  ref float theFloat)
        {
            theInt = theInt - theInt;
            theFloat = theFloat - theFloat;
        }
        static void Main( )
        {
            Tester t = new Tester( );
            t.Run( );
        }
    }
}
```

If you run this program, you will not get the same results as you did in the previous example. Use the debugging tools you just learned about to find the error. Correct the error, and then run the program again to see whether the results are correct.

You could find this error by setting a breakpoint on the call to Run( ), and stepping through the code from there, watching the values of theInt and theFloat. You could also find it by setting breakpoints on each of the method calls and examining the values of theInt and theFloat each time.

The first errors you'll probably find are these in Divide( ):

```
theInt = theInt * 3;
theFloat = theFloat * 3;
```

theInt and theFloat are multiplied by 3, not divided. However, if you fix these errors and run the program, the result is still 0 for both variables. That's because there are two more errors in Add( ):

```
theInt = theInt - theInt;
theFloat = theFloat - theFloat;
```

As you can see, the programmer isn't a very good typist—the variables are subtracted instead of added. If you fix these errors, the program will run as expected.

Solution to Exercise 9-3. Type the following program into Visual Studio, or download it from the book's website:

```
using System;
using System.Collections.Generic;
using System.Linq;
using System.Text;

namespace Exercise_9_3
{
```

```
class Program
{
    public static int Factorial(int myInt)
    {
        int result = 1;
        for (int i = 1; i < myInt; i++)
        {
            result = result * i;
        }
        return result;
    }

    static void Main()
    {
        int input = 5;
        Console.WriteLine("{0} factorial is {1}",
                            input, Factorial(input) );
    }
}
```

This program is supposed to take the factorial of the value of input, except it's not working properly. (The factorial of n is the product of all the positive integers less than or equal to n. So, the factorial of 5 is $5 \times 4 \times 3 \times 2 \times 1 = 120$.) Find the error and resolve it.

When you run the program, you'll see that instead of calculating the factorial of 5 as 120, this program calculates it as 24. If you set a breakpoint on the line where Factorial() is called and step through the method, you'll see that in the loop, i never reaches the value of 5, so the loop ends and the result is wrong. There are a few ways to fix this, but the easiest is to change the condition in the for loop from i < myInt to i <= myInt.

Chapter 10: Arrays

Quiz Solutions

Solution to Question 10-1. Arrays always begin with index (or offset) zero, so the seventh member of an array has index 6.

Solution to Question 10-2. No. Every array declares the type of objects it will hold. You can undermine this type safety by creating an array of Objects (which will hold anything, because everything derives from Object), but that is not advised.

Solution to Question 10-3. When you instantiate an array, you specify the number of elements in square brackets.

Solution to Question 10-4. Arrays are reference types and are created on the heap.

Solution to Question 10-5. The highest index in any array is always represented by Length - 1.

Solution to Question 10-6. You can explicitly call new or just imply the size of the array. For example, if you have three Employee objects named moe, larry, and curly:

```
Employee[] myEmpArray = new Employee[3] = { moe, larry, curly };
```

or:

```
Employee[] myEmpArray = { moe, larry, curly };
```

Solution to Question 10-7. There are a number of ways to iterate through the items in an array, but one of the most common is to use a for loop, using the loop's control variable as the indexer in the array. An even simpler method is to use the foreach statement.

Solution to Question 10-8. The params keyword allows you to pass in an indefinite number of parameters, all of the same type, which will be treated as an array. You can, if you wish, also pass in an array.

Solution to Question 10-9. A rectangular array is a multidimensional array where each row has the same length. A jagged array is an array of arrays; the rows can be of unequal length.

Solution to Question 10-10. To arrange a random array of float values from greatest to least, you first call the Sort( ) method, and then the Reverse( ) method.

Exercise Solutions

Solution to Exercise 10-1. Declare a Dog class with two private members: weight (an int) and name (a string). Be sure to add properties to access the members. Then create an array that holds three Dog objects (Milo, 26 pounds; Frisky, 10 pounds; and Laika, 50 pounds). Output each dog's name and weight.

The purpose of this exercise is simply to get you comfortable with using objects in arrays. The Dog class is quite simple to create, with its private members and getters and setters for each. All you have to do then is instantiate three Dog objects, instantiate the array, and assign the objects to the array (which you can do using the quick element initialization method, instead of using a loop). You'll need a loop, either for or foreach, to output the values. Example A-22 shows one possible solution.

Example A-22. One solution to Exercise 10-1

```csharp
using System;
using System.Collections.Generic;
using System.Linq;
using System.Text;

namespace Exercise_10_1
{
    public class Dog
    {
        public Dog(int theWeight, string theName)
        {
            this.weight = theWeight;
            this.name = theName;
        }
        public int Weight
        {
            get
            {
                return weight;
            }
            set
            {
                weight = value;
            }
        }
        public string Name
        {
            get
            {
                return name;
            }
            set
            {
                name = value;
            }
        }
        private int weight;
        private string name;
    }
    public class Tester
    {
        public void Run()
        {
            Dog milo = new Dog(26, "Milo");
            Dog frisky = new Dog(10, "Frisky");
            Dog laika = new Dog(50, "Laika");
            Dog[] dogArray = { milo, frisky, laika };
            // output array values
            foreach (Dog d in dogArray)
            {
                Console.WriteLine("Dog {0} weighs {1} pounds.",
                                    d.Name, d.Weight);
```

Example A-22. One solution to Exercise 10-1 (continued)

```
        }
    }
    static void Main( )
    {
        Tester t = new Tester( );
        t.Run( );
    }
    }
}
```

Solution to Exercise 10-2.   Create an array of 10 integers. Populate the array by having the user enter integers at the console (use Console.Readline). Don't worry about error checking for this exercise. Output the integers sorted from greatest to least.

Creating an array to hold 10 integers should be easy for you at this point. You'll need to use a for loop to get the values of the 10 integers from the user. Once you have the array loaded, you have to call Sort( ) and then Reverse( ) on the array to sort the integers from greatest to least. Example A-23 shows one way of doing it.

Example A-23. One solution to Exercise 10-2

```
using System;
using System.Collections.Generic;
using System.Linq;
using System.Text;

namespace Exercise_10_2
{
    public class Tester
    {
        public void Run( )
        {
            int[] intArray = new int[10];
            Console.WriteLine("You'll be asked to enter 10 integers");
            // enter data into the array
            for (int i = 0; i < intArray.Length; i++)
            {
                Console.Write("Enter an integer: ");
                string theEntry = Console.ReadLine( );
                intArray[i] = Convert.ToInt32(theEntry);
            }
            // sort and reverse the array
            Array.Sort(intArray);
            Array.Reverse(intArray);
            Console.WriteLine("\nValues:");
            foreach (int j in intArray)
            {
                Console.WriteLine("{0}", j);
            }
        }
        static void Main( )
```

Example A-23. One solution to Exercise 10-2 (continued)

```
        {
            Tester t = new Tester();
            t.Run();
        }
    }
}
```

Solution to Exercise 10-3. Extend Exercise 10-1 by creating a two-dimensional array that represents a collection of strings that indicate the awards each dog has won at dog shows. Each dog may have a different number of awards won. Output the contents of the array to check its validity.

You're obviously going to need a two-dimensional array for this exercise. Since we told you that each dog may have won a different number of awards, you can tell it's going to be a jagged two-dimensional array. The Dog class hasn't changed any from the previous exercise, so there's nothing to do there. You'll have to create the new jagged array and populate it by hand. To output the contents of the array, you'll need a pair of nested for loops. Example A-24 shows a possible solution.

Example A-24. One solution to Exercise 10-3

```
using System;
using System.Collections.Generic;
using System.Linq;
using System.Text;

namespace Exercise_10_3
{
    public class Dog
    {
        public Dog(int theWeight, string theName)
        {
            this.weight = theWeight;
            this.name = theName;
        }
        public int Weight
        {
            get
            {
                return weight;
            }
            set
            {
                weight = value;
            }
        }
        public string Name
        {
            get
            {
                return name;
```

Example A-24. One solution to Exercise 10-3 (continued)

```csharp
            }
            set
            {
                name = value;
            }
        }
        private int weight;
        private string name;
    }
    public class Tester
    {
        public void Run()
        {
            const int rows = 3;
            // declare and populate the dogs array
            Dog milo = new Dog(26, "Milo");
            Dog frisky = new Dog(10, "Frisky");
            Dog laika = new Dog(50, "Laika");
            Dog[] dogArray = { milo, frisky, laika };

            // declare the dogAwards array as 3 rows high
            string[][] dogAwardsArray = new string[rows][];

            // declare the rows
            dogAwardsArray[0] = new string[3];
            dogAwardsArray[1] = new string[1];
            dogAwardsArray[2] = new string[2];

            // Populate the rows
            dogAwardsArray[0][0] = "Best in Show";
            dogAwardsArray[0][1] = "Best of Breed";
            dogAwardsArray[0][2] = "Judge's Cup";
            dogAwardsArray[1][0] = "Best Toy Tog";
            dogAwardsArray[2][0] = "Best Working Dog";
            dogAwardsArray[2][1] = "Best Large Dog";

            // Output the contents
            for (int i = 0; i < dogAwardsArray.Length; i++)
            {
                Console.WriteLine("{0}'s awards: ", dogArray[i].Name);
                for (int j = 0; j < dogAwardsArray[i].Length; j++)
                {
                    Console.WriteLine("\t{0}", dogAwardsArray[i][j]);
                }
            }
        }
        static void Main()
        {
            Tester t = new Tester();
            t.Run();
        }
    }
}
```

Solution to Exercise 10-4. Create a two-dimensional array that represents a chessboard (an 8-by-8 array). Each element in the array should contain the string "black" or the string "white," depending on where it is on the board. Create a method that initializes the array with the strings. Then create a method that asks the reader to enter two integers for the coordinates of a square, and returns whether that square is black or white.

The interesting part of this exercise isn't in returning the answer to the reader, it's in setting up the board as a two-dimensional array. It's pretty easy to imagine a chessboard as a two-dimensional array, where each element is either the string "white" or the string "black." You also know that there will be only eight rows and eight columns (so you might as well make those constants). Let's take one row at a time. If it's an even-numbered row (if the row index % 2 is equal to zero), it starts with a black square. So, you assign every even-numbered square in that row the value of "black". Every square that isn't assigned "black" is assigned "white". The next row has to start with a white square, so you'll need an if/else to assign the opposite values to the next row. In the end, you'll end up with an if/else inside a for loop, inside an if/else, inside a for loop, as shown in Example A-25.

Once you have the entire two-dimensional array created, it's easy to take the user input and simply output the value of the string at those coordinates. Remember, though, that the user is entering a coordinate between 1 and 8, but the dimensions of the array range from 0 to 7, so when the user asks for the coordinates at (row, column), you'll need to actually retrieve the value at chessboard[(row - 1), (column - 1)].

Example A-25. One solution to Exercise 10-4

```
using System;
using System.Collections.Generic;
using System.Linq;
using System.Text;

namespace Exercise_10_4
{
    public class Tester
    {
        public void Run()
        {
            const int rows = 8;
            const int columns = 8;

            // create an 8x8 array
            string[,] chessboardArray = new string[rows, columns];

            // populate the chessboard array
            for (int i = 0; i < rows; i++)
            {
                // if row starts with a black square
                if ((i % 2) == 0)
```

Example A-25. One solution to Exercise 10-4 (continued)

```
                {
                    for (int j = 0; j < columns; j++)
                    {
                        if ((j % 2) == 0)
                        {
                            chessboardArray[i, j] = "black";
                        }
                        else
                        {
                            chessboardArray[i, j] = "white";
                        }
                    }
                }
                // else row starts with a white square
                else
                {
                    for (int j = 0; j < columns; j++)
                    {
                        if ((j % 2) == 0)
                        {
                            chessboardArray[i, j] = "white";
                        }
                        else
                        {
                            chessboardArray[i, j] = "black";
                        }
                    }
                }
            }

            // ask the user for coordinates to test
            Console.Write("Enter the row to test (1 through 8): ");
            string rowEntry = Console.ReadLine();
            int testRow = Convert.ToInt32(rowEntry);
            Console.Write("Enter the column to test (1 through 8): ");
            string colEntry = Console.ReadLine();
            int testCol = Convert.ToInt32(colEntry);

            // output the value at those coordinates
            Console.WriteLine("The square at {0}, {1} is {2}.", testRow,
            testCol, chessboardArray[(testRow - 1), (testCol - 1)]);
        }
        static void Main()
        {
            Tester t = new Tester();
            t.Run();
        }
    }
}
```

Chapter 11: Inheritance and Polymorphism

Quiz Solutions

Solution to Question 11-1. This relationship between specialization and generalization is reciprocal: if you have three types with similar functionality, you can factor that similarity out of the three types into a generalized type. At the same time, the three types are now specialized forms of the more generalized type.

Inheritance is also implicitly hierarchical: you can imagine a tree with the most generalized type at the top and each level of specialization descending from levels above. A generalized type may have many specializations, but each specialized type may have only one generalization.

Solution to Question 11-2. In C#, the principle of specialization is implemented through inheritance.

Solution to Question 11-3. The syntax for inheritance is:

```
class <identifier> : <base class>
```

Solution to Question 11-4. To implement polymorphism, you create a virtual method in the base class, and then override it in the derived class.

Solution to Question 11-5. The more usual meaning of new is to allocate memory on the heap. The special meaning in inheritance is that you are not overriding a base method; you are creating a new method that intentionally hides and replaces the base class method.

Solution to Question 11-6. To call a base class constructor from a derived class, after the parameter list but before the opening brace put a colon followed by the keyword base and two parentheses. Pass the parameters for the base class constructor within the parentheses.

Solution to Question 11-7. An abstract method has no implementation in the base class, but must be overridden and implemented in any derived class that does not itself want to be abstract. Any class with an abstract method (even if inherited) is itself abstract and may not be instantiated.

Solution to Question 11-8. A sealed class is one that the compiler will not let you derive from. Classes are marked sealed when the designer of the class does not want anyone to create a derived version.

Solution to Question 11-9. The base class of `Int32`, and all types in C#, is `Object`.

Solution to Question 11-10. If you don't specifically define a base class for your user-defined class, the default base class is `Object`.

Exercise Solutions

Solution to Exercise 11-1. Create a base class, `Telephone`, and derive a class `ElectronicPhone` from it. In `Telephone`, create a protected string member `phonetype` and a public method `Ring()` which outputs a text message such as this: "Ringing the <phonetype>." In `ElectronicPhone`, the constructor should set the phonetype to "Digital." In the `Run()` method, call `Ring()` on the `ElectronicPhone` to test the inheritance.

This exercise isn't too tricky; you simply need to define the base class (`Telephone`) with a constructor, a single member variable (`phonetype`), and a single method (`Ring()`). Then derive the new class `ElectronicPhone` using the appropriate syntax, and create a constructor that sets phonetype accordingly. You don't need to override the `Ring()` method, because there's no functionality to add to the base class method. Example A-26 shows one solution.

Example A-26. One solution to Exercise 11-1

```
using System;
using System.Collections.Generic;
using System.Linq;
using System.Text;

namespace Exercise_11_1
{
    public class Telephone
    {
        protected string phonetype;
        public void Ring()
        {
            Console.WriteLine("Ringing the {0} phone...", phonetype);
        }
    }
    public class ElectronicPhone : Telephone
    {
        public ElectronicPhone()
        {
            this.phonetype = "Digital";   // access protected member
        }
    }

    public class Tester
    {

        public void Run()
```

Example A-26. One solution to Exercise 11-1 (continued)

```
        {
            ElectronicPhone phone = new ElectronicPhone( );
            phone.Ring( ); // accessing the base method
        }
        static void Main( )
        {
            Tester t = new Tester( );
            t.Run( );
        }
    }
}
```

Solution to Exercise 11-2. Extend Exercise 11-1 to illustrate a polymorphic method. Have the derived class override the Ring( ) method to display a different message.

The only trick here is that you have to make sure to mark the Ring( ) method in the base class as virtual, and be sure to use the override keyword on the Ring( ) method in the derived class. Example A-27 shows how to do that.

Example A-27. One solution to Exercise 11-2

```
using System;
using System.Collections.Generic;
using System.Linq;
using System.Text;

namespace Exercise_11_2
{
    public class Telephone
    {
        protected string phonetype;
        public virtual void Ring( )  // now virtual
        {
            Console.WriteLine("Ringing the {0} phone. Ring Ring.", phonetype);
        }
    }
    public class ElectronicPhone : Telephone
    {
        public ElectronicPhone( )
        {
            this.phonetype = "Digital";   // access protected member
        }
        public override void Ring( )       // override
        {
            Console.WriteLine("Ringing the {0} phone. Beep Beep.", phonetype);
        }
    }
    public class Tester
    {
        public void Run( )
        {
```

Example A-27. One solution to Exercise 11-2 (continued)

```
            // assign derived instance to base reference
            Telephone phone = new ElectronicPhone( );
            phone.Ring( ); // accessing the polymorphic method
        }
        static void Main( )
        {
            Tester t = new Tester( );
            t.Run( );
        }
    }
}
```

Solution to Exercise 11-3. Change the Telephone class to abstract, and make Ring( ) an abstract method. Derive two new classes from Telephone: DigitalPhone and Talking-Phone. Each derived class should set the phonetype, and override the Ring( ) method.

This time around, the Telephone has become abstract (there may be some social commentary there, but this is just a programming book, so we'll leave it alone). Be sure to mark both the Ring( ) method and the class itself as abstract. Now the derived classes are obligated to override the Ring( ) method appropriately. Example A-28 shows the code.

Example A-28. One solution to Exercise 11-3. Exercise 11-3

```
using System;
using System.Collections.Generic;
using System.Linq;
using System.Text;

namespace Exercise_11_3
{
    public abstract class Telephone
    {
        protected string phonetype;
        public abstract void Ring( ); // now abstract
    }
    public class DigitalPhone : Telephone
    {
        public DigitalPhone( )
        {
            this.phonetype = "Digital";   // access protected member
        }
        public override void Ring( )      // implement
        {
            Console.WriteLine("Ringing the {0} phone. Beep Beep.", phonetype);
        }
    }
    public class TalkingPhone : Telephone
    {
```

Example A-28. One solution to Exercise 11-3. Exercise 11-3 (continued)

```
        public TalkingPhone()
        {
            this.phonetype = "Talking";    // access protected member
        }
        public override void Ring()        // implement
        {
            Console.WriteLine("Ringing the {0} phone. You have a call.",
                            phonetype);
        }
    }
    public class Tester
    {
        public void Run()
        {
            // assign derived instance to base reference
            Telephone phone1 = new DigitalPhone();
            Telephone phone2 = new TalkingPhone();
            phone1.Ring(); // accessing the polymorphic method
            phone2.Ring(); // accessing the polymorphic method
        }
        static void Main()
        {
            Tester t = new Tester();
            t.Run();
        }
    }
}
```

Solution to Exercise 11-4. Phones these days do a lot more than ring, as you know. Add a method to DigitalPhone called VoiceMail() that outputs the message "You have a message. Press Play to retrieve." Now add a new class, DigitalCellPhone, that derives from DigitalPhone and implements a version of VoiceMail() that outputs the message "You have a message. Call to retrieve."

For this exercise, you'll need to derive DigitalCellPhone from DigitalPhone, which is a perfectly normal thing to do. As you'll see, you can even treat DigitalCellPhone polymorphically as a Telephone. For the VoiceMail() method, you'll need to add that method to DigitalPhone, and declare it virtual so that DigitalCellPhone can override it. You'll also need a DigitalCellPhone class that inherits from DigitalPhone. Note that DigitalCellPhone doesn't need its own Ring() method; it can just use the inherited method from DigitalPhone.

When you test the classes down in Run(), you'll find that if you declare DigitalCellPhone as a Telephone, you can use its Ring() method, but not VoiceMail(). That's because Telephone doesn't have a VoiceMail() method. To use VoiceMail() polymorphically, you'll need to declare your DigitalCellPhone as a type DigitalPhone. One way to do it is shown in Example A-29.

Example A-29. One solution to Exercise 11-4

```csharp
using System;
using System.Collections.Generic;
using System.Linq;
using System.Text;

namespace Exercise_11_4
{
    public abstract class Telephone
    {
        protected string phonetype;
        public abstract void Ring(); // now abstract
    } // end abstract class Telephone

    public class DigitalPhone : Telephone
    {
        public DigitalPhone()
        {
            this.phonetype = "Digital";    // access protected member
        }
        public override void Ring()        // implement abstract method
        {
            Console.WriteLine("Ringing the {0} phone. Beep Beep.", phonetype);
        }
        public virtual void VoiceMail()
        {
            Console.WriteLine("You have a message. Press Play to retrieve.");
        }
    } //end class DigitalPhone

    public class TalkingPhone : Telephone
    {
        public TalkingPhone()
        {
            this.phonetype = "Talking";    // access protected member
        }
        public override void Ring()        // implement abstract method
        {
            Console.WriteLine("Ringing the {0} phone. You have a call.",
                            phonetype);
        }
    } //end class TalkingPhone

    public class DigitalCellPhone : DigitalPhone
    {
        public DigitalCellPhone()
        {
            this.phonetype = "Digital Cell"; // access protected member
        }

        // no need to implement Ring(); it uses its parent class ring.
```

```
    public override void VoiceMail()
    {
        Console.WriteLine("You have a message. Call to retrieve.");
    }
} // end class DigitalCellPhone

public class Tester
{
    public void Run()
    {
        // assign derived instance to base reference
        Telephone phone1 = new DigitalPhone();
        Telephone phone2 = new TalkingPhone();
        Telephone phone3 = new DigitalCellPhone();
        phone1.Ring(); // accessing the polymorphic method
        phone2.Ring(); // accessing the polymorphic method
        phone3.Ring(); // accessing the polymorphic method

        DigitalPhone phone4 = new DigitalPhone();
        DigitalPhone phone5 = new DigitalCellPhone();
        phone4.VoiceMail();
        phone5.VoiceMail();
    }
    static void Main()
    {
        Tester t = new Tester();
        t.Run();
    }
}
}
```

Chapter 12: Operator Overloading

Quiz Solutions

Solution to Question 12-1. Operator overloading is the process of writing methods for your class that allow clients of your class to interact with your class using standard operators (such as + and ==).

Solution to Question 12-2. Operators are implemented as static methods.

Solution to Question 12-3. To overload an operator, you use the keyword operator along with the operator you're overloading. For example, to overload the addition operator, you would use the keyword operator+.

Solution to Question 12-4. The compiler interprets the statement as a call to the method:

```
public static Fraction operator+(f2, f1)
```

Solution to Question 12-5. This answer is subjective, but it seems likely that choices A and D are the most reasonable. Choices B and C are not completely unreasonable, but aren't intuitive, and would be difficult for later developers to maintain.

Solution to Question 12-6. The < and > operators are paired, as are the <= and >= operators. If you overload one of the operators in a pair, you must overload the other.

Solution to Question 12-7. If you overload the == operator, you must also overload the != operator, and the Equals( ) method.

Solution to Question 12-8. The Equals( ) method is used to ensure that your class is compatible with other .NET languages that do not allow operator overloading, but do allow method overloading.

Solution to Question 12-9. To overload the conversion operators, you use either the keyword implicit or the keyword explicit, along with the keyword operator, and the name of the type you're converting to.

Solution to Question 12-10. Use implicit conversion when you know the conversion will succeed without the risk of losing information. Use explicit conversion if information might be lost.

Exercise Solutions

Solution to Exercise 12-1. Create a class Invoice, which has a string property vendor and a double property amount, as well as a method to output the two properties of the invoice. Overload the addition operator so that if the vendor properties match, the amount properties of the two invoices are added together in a new invoice. If the vendor properties do not match, the new invoice is blank. Include some test code to test the addition operator.

This exercise is fairly straightforward. The Invoice class is simple enough to create; you just need to write the two private members, a constructor, and an output method. Then you need to create an overloaded addition operator for your class. The operator should first make sure the vendor fields match, and if they do, should create a new Invoice (using the constructor) with the greater amount. Example A-30 shows one solution.

Example A-30. One solution to Exercise 12-1

```csharp
using System;
using System.Collections.Generic;
using System.Linq;
using System.Text;

namespace Exercise_12_1
{
    public class Invoice
    {
        private string vendor;
        private double amount;
        // constructor

        public Invoice(string vendor, double amount)
        {
            this.vendor = vendor;
            this.amount = amount;
        }
        // Overloaded operator + takes two invoices.
        // If the vendors are the same, the two amounts are added.
        // If not, the operation fails, and a blank invoice is returned.
        public static Invoice operator+ (Invoice lhs, Invoice rhs)
        {
            if (lhs.vendor == rhs.vendor)
            {
                return new Invoice(lhs.vendor, lhs.amount + rhs.amount);
            }
            Console.WriteLine("Vendors don't match; operation failed.");
            return new Invoice("", 0);
        }
        public void PrintInvoice()
        {
            Console.WriteLine("Invoice from {0} for ${1}.", vendor, amount);
        }
    }

    public class Tester
    {
        public void Run()
        {
            Invoice firstInvoice = new Invoice("TinyCorp", 345);
            Invoice secondInvoice = new Invoice("SuperMegaCo", 56389.53);
            Invoice thirdInvoice = new Invoice("SuperMegaCo", 399.65);
            Console.WriteLine("Adding first and second invoices.");
            Invoice addedInvoice = firstInvoice + secondInvoice;
            addedInvoice.PrintInvoice();
            Console.WriteLine("Adding second and third invoices.");
            Invoice otherAddedInvoice = secondInvoice + thirdInvoice;
            otherAddedInvoice.PrintInvoice();
        }
        static void Main()
        {
```

Example A-30. One solution to Exercise 12-1 (continued)

```
            Tester t = new Tester();
            t.Run();
        }
    }
}
```

Solution to Exercise 12-2.   Modify the Invoice class so that two invoices are considered equal if the vendor and amount properties match. Test your methods.

Starting with the previous code is easy enough. The first change you need to make is to override the == operator, exactly as we showed you in the chapter. Once you've done that, you also need to override the != operator and the Equals( ) method. Add some test cases in Run( ) to make sure this works. Example A-31 has our solution.

Example A-31. Our solution to Exercise 12-2

```
using System;
using System.Collections.Generic;
using System.Linq;
using System.Text;

namespace Exercise_12_2
{
    using System;

    public class Invoice
    {
        private string vendor;
        private double amount;

        // constructor
        public Invoice(string vendor, double amount)
        {
            this.vendor = vendor;
            this.amount = amount;
        }

        // Overloaded operator + takes two invoices.
        // If the vendors are the same, the two amounts are added.
        // If not, the operation fails, and a blank invoice is returned.
        public static Invoice operator +(Invoice lhs, Invoice rhs)
        {
            if (lhs.vendor == rhs.vendor)
            {
                return new Invoice(lhs.vendor, lhs.amount + rhs.amount);
            }
            Console.WriteLine("Vendors don't match; operation failed.");
            return new Invoice("", 0);
        }

        // overloaded equality operator
```

Example A-31. Our solution to Exercise 12-2 (continued)

```
    public static bool operator ==(Invoice lhs, Invoice rhs)
    {
        if (lhs.vendor == rhs.vendor && lhs.amount == rhs.amount)
        {
            return true;
        }
        return false;
    }

    // overloaded inequality operator, delegates to ==
    public static bool operator !=(Invoice lhs, Invoice rhs)
    {
        return !(lhs == rhs);
    }

    // method for determining equality; tests for same type,
    // then delegates to ==
    public override bool Equals(object o)
    {
        if (!(o is Invoice))
        {
            return false;
        }
        return this == (Invoice)o;
    }

    public void PrintInvoice()
    {
        Console.WriteLine("Invoice from {0} for ${1}.", this.vendor,
                        this.amount);
    }
}

public class Tester
{
    public void Run()
    {
        Invoice firstInvoice = new Invoice("TinyCorp", 399.65);
        Invoice secondInvoice = new Invoice("SuperMegaCo", 56389.53);
        Invoice thirdInvoice = new Invoice("SuperMegaCo", 399.65);
        Invoice testInvoice = new Invoice("SuperMegaCo", 399.65);
        if (testInvoice == firstInvoice)
        {
            Console.WriteLine("First invoice matches.");
        }
        else if (testInvoice == secondInvoice)
        {
            Console.WriteLine("Second invoice matches.");
        }
        else if (testInvoice == thirdInvoice)
        {
            Console.WriteLine("Third invoice matches.");
```

Example A-31. Our solution to Exercise 12-2 (continued)

```
                }
                else
                {
                    Console.WriteLine("No matching invoices.");
                }
            }
            static void Main()
            {
                Tester t = new Tester();
                t.Run();
            }
        }
    }
}
```

Try changing the values of testInvoice to make sure all the cases work.

Solution to Exercise 12-3. Modify the Invoice class once more so that you can determine whether one invoice is greater than or less than another. Test your methods.

In this exercise, you'll need to overload a couple of methods that you haven't seen in the chapter: the greater-than and less-than operators. Fortunately, overloading those methods isn't much more difficult than overloading the equality operator. However, you need to be sure you override both operators. Remember that you can't simply define the less-than operator as the opposite of the greater-than operator, the way you can with == and !=, because if the operands are equal, both less-than and greater-than should return false. Example A-32 shows a possible solution.

Example A-32. One solution to Exercise 12-3

```
using System;
using System.Collections.Generic;
using System.Linq;
using System.Text;

namespace Exercise_12_3
{
    public class Invoice
    {
        private string vendor;
        private double amount;

        // constructor
        public Invoice(string vendor, double amount)
        {
            this.vendor = vendor;
            this.amount = amount;
        }

        // Overloaded operator + takes two invoices.
        // If the vendors are the same, the two amounts are added.
```

Example A-32. One solution to Exercise 12-3 (continued)

```
    // If not, the operation fails, and a blank invoice is returned.
    public static Invoice operator +(Invoice lhs, Invoice rhs)
    {
        if (lhs.vendor == rhs.vendor)
        {
            return new Invoice(lhs.vendor, lhs.amount + rhs.amount);
        }
        Console.WriteLine("Vendors don't match; operation failed.");
        return new Invoice("", 0);
    }

    // overloaded equality operator
    public static bool operator ==(Invoice lhs, Invoice rhs)
    {
        if (lhs.vendor == rhs.vendor && lhs.amount == rhs.amount)
        {
            return true;
        }
        return false;
    }

    // overloaded inequality operator, delegates to ==
    public static bool operator !=(Invoice lhs, Invoice rhs)
    {
        return !(lhs == rhs);
    }

    // method for determining equality; tests for same type,
    // then delegates to ==
    public override bool Equals(object o)
    {
        if (!(o is Invoice))
        {
            return false;
        }
        return this == (Invoice)o;
    }

    public static bool operator< (Invoice lhs, Invoice rhs)
    {
        if (lhs.amount < rhs.amount)
        {
            return true;
        }
        return false;
    }

    public static bool operator> (Invoice lhs, Invoice rhs)
    {
        if (lhs.amount > rhs.amount)
        {
            return true;
```

Example A-32. One solution to Exercise 12-3 (continued)

```
        }
        return false;
    }

    public void PrintInvoice()
    {
        Console.WriteLine("Invoice from {0} for ${1}.", this.vendor,
                          this.amount);
    }
}


public class Tester
{

    public Invoice WhichIsGreater(Invoice invoice1, Invoice invoice2)
    {
        if (invoice1 > invoice2)
        {
            return invoice1;
        }
        else
        {
            return invoice2;
        }
    }

    public void Run()
    {
        Invoice firstInvoice = new Invoice("TinyCorp", 399.65);
        Invoice secondInvoice = new Invoice("SuperMegaCo", 56389.53);
        Invoice thirdInvoice = new Invoice("SuperMegaCo", 399.65);
        Invoice tempInvoice;

        if (!(firstInvoice == secondInvoice))
        {
            Console.WriteLine("Greater Invoice:");
            tempInvoice = WhichIsGreater(firstInvoice, secondInvoice);
            tempInvoice.PrintInvoice();
        }
        else
        {
            Console.WriteLine("firstInvoice and secondInvoice are equal");
        }

        if (!(secondInvoice == thirdInvoice))
        {
            Console.WriteLine("Greater Invoice:");
            tempInvoice = WhichIsGreater(secondInvoice, thirdInvoice);
            tempInvoice.PrintInvoice();
        }
        else
```

Example A-32. One solution to Exercise 12-3 (continued)

```
            {
                    Console.WriteLine("secondInvoice and thirdInvoice are equal");
            }

        }

        static void Main( )
        {
            Tester t = new Tester( );
            t.Run( );
        }
    }
}
```

We didn't implement the <= or >= methods in this example, but you should go ahead and try it on your own.

Solution to Exercise 12-4.   Create a class Foot and a class Meter. Each should have a single parameter that stores the length of the object, and a simple method to output that length. Create a casting operator for each class: one that converts a Foot object to a Meter object, and one that converts a Meter object to a Foot object. Test these operators to make sure they work.

First, it should be said that the Foot and Meter classes don't make a lot of sense in the real world. It would most likely be better to create a class Measurement, or something similar, that could output the length in either feet or meters. Still, you've got two classes, so you should be able to convert between them. Since you're using two user-defined classes here, you won't be able to write an implicit conversion. Therefore, Foot needs an explicit conversion to Meter, and Meter needs an explicit conversion to Foot. For example, here's the declaration for the Foot class's conversion to Meter:

```
    public static explicit operator Meter(Foot theFoot)
```

Note that this operator is public, static, and explicit. The body of the operator method isn't really challenging, but remember that it should return an object of class Meter. The Meter class operator is similar. Example A-33 shows one way to do it.

Example A-33. One solution to Exercise 12-4

```
using System;
using System.Collections.Generic;
using System.Linq;
using System.Text;

namespace Exercise_12_4
{
    public class Foot
    {
        private double length;

        public static explicit operator Meter(Foot theFoot)
```

Example A-33. One solution to Exercise 12-4 (continued)

```
        {
            return new Meter(theFoot.length * 0.3048);
        }

        public void OutputFoot()
        {
            Console.Write("{0} feet", length);
        }

        // constructor
        public Foot(double length)
        {
            this.length = length;
        }
    }

    public class Meter
    {
        private double length;

        public static explicit operator Foot (Meter theMeter)
        {
            return new Foot(theMeter.length * 3.28);
        }

        public void OutputMeter()
        {
            Console.Write("{0} meters", length);
        }

        // constructor
        public Meter(double length)
        {
            this.length = length;
        }
    }

    class Tester
    {
        public void Run()
        {
            Foot myFoot = new Foot(5);
            Meter myMeter = new Meter(3);

            Console.Write("Length of myFoot = ");
            myFoot.OutputFoot();
            Console.Write(", ");
            ((Meter)myFoot).OutputMeter();
            Console.WriteLine();

            Console.Write("Length of myMeter = ");
            myMeter.OutputMeter();
```

```
            Console.Write(", ");
            ((Foot)myMeter).OutputFoot();
            Console.WriteLine();

        }

        static void Main(string[] args)
        {
            Tester t = new Tester();
            t.Run();
        }
    }
}
```

Chapter 13: Interfaces

Quiz Solutions

Solution to Question 13-1. The interface defines the methods, properties, and so forth that the implementing class must provide. The implementing class provides these members and, optionally, additional members.

Solution to Question 13-2. Every class has exactly one base class (either explicit, or the object class by default), but may implement zero, one, or more interfaces. An abstract base class serves as the base to a derived class that must implement all of its abstract methods; otherwise, that derived class is also abstract.

Solution to Question 13-3. You can't create an instance of an interface. To access the interface methods, you must create an instance of a class that implements the interface.

Solution to Question 13-4. You'd use the following syntax to create a class that inherits from a parent and implements two interfaces:

```
class MyClass : MyBase, ISuppose, IDo {...}
```

Note that the base class must come first after the colon.

Solution to Question 13-5. The is and as operators are used to test whether a class implements an interface.

Solution to Question 13-6. is returns a Boolean, which is false if the interface is not implemented. as attempts to make the cast, unlike is, and returns null if the cast fails. Using the as operator can be more efficient.

Solution to Question 13-7. Extending an interface is very much like deriving a class. The new interface inherits all the members of the parent interface, and can also include additional methods.

Solution to Question 13-8. The syntax for extending an interface is:

```
ExtendedInterface : OriginalInterface
```

For example, you would read:

```
ILoggedCompressible : ICompressible
```

as "`ILoggedCompressible` extends `ICompressible`."

Solution to Question 13-9. The class implementing a method of the interface can mark that method `virtual`, and the implementation of the method can then be overridden in derived classes.

Solution to Question 13-10. Explicit interface implementation identifies the member of the interface by naming the interface itself (e.g., `IStorable.Write( )`). This is done to differentiate implementation methods when there might otherwise be an ambiguity, such as when implementing multiple interfaces that have methods with the same signature.

Exercise Solutions

Solution to Exercise 13-1. Define an interface `IConvertible` that indicates that the class can convert a string to C# or VB. The interface should have two methods: `ConvertToCSharp` and `ConvertToVB`. Each method should take a string and return a string.

In this exercise, you're not actually creating code that will run; you're just defining the interface. As you learned, the methods of the interface don't have any implementation, they just have signatures. Example A-34 shows this simple interface.

Example A-34. One solution to Exercise 13-1

```
using System;
using System.Collections.Generic;
using System.Linq;
using System.Text;

namespace Exercise_13_1
{
    interface IConvertible
    {
        string ConvertToCSharp(string stringToConvert);
        string ConvertToVB(string stringToConvert);
    }
}
```

Solution to Exercise 13-2. Implement that interface and test it by creating a class ProgramHelper that implements IConvertible. You don't have to write methods to convert the string; just use simple string messages to simulate the conversion. Test your new class with a string of fake code to make sure it works.

In this exercise, you'll actually implement the interface that you derived earlier, although your code doesn't need to do anything more than say that it's converting the string. The string we used in Run( ) is just dummy text representing a string of VB code. In Run( ), we pass the string to the ConvertToVB( ) method, and then pass it back to the ConvertToCSharp( ) method. Example A-35 shows the way we did it.

Example A-35. Our solution to Exercise 13-2

```
using System;
using System.Collections.Generic;
using System.Linq;
using System.Text;

namespace Exercise_13_2
{
    interface IConvertible
    {
        string ConvertToCSharp(string stringToConvert);
        string ConvertToVB(string stringToConvert);
    }
    public class ProgramHelper : IConvertible
    {
        public ProgramHelper( ) // constructor
        {
            Console.WriteLine("Creating ProgramHelper");
        }
        public string ConvertToCSharp(string stringToConvert)
        {
            Console.WriteLine("Converting the string you passed
                            in to CSharp syntax");
            return "This is a C# String.";
        }
        public string ConvertToVB(string stringToConvert)
        {
            Console.WriteLine("Converting the string you passed
                            in to VB syntax");
            return "This is a VB String.";
        }
    }

    class Tester
    {
        public void Run( )
        {
            // Create a ProgramHelper object
            ProgramHelper theProgramHelper = new ProgramHelper( );
```

Example A-35. Our solution to Exercise 13-2 (continued)

```
        // convert a line of CSharp to vb
        string vbString = theProgramHelper.ConvertToVB("This is
                                    a VB String to convert.");
        Console.WriteLine(vbString);

        // convert the converted line back to CSharp
        string cSharpString = theProgramHelper.ConvertToCSharp(vbString);
        Console.WriteLine(cSharpString);
    }
    static void Main()
    {
        Tester t = new Tester();
        t.Run();
    }
}
}
```

Solution to Exercise 13-3. Extend the IConvertible interface by creating a new interface, ICodeChecker. The new interface should implement one new method, CodeCheckSyntax, which takes two strings: the string to check and the language to use. The method should return a bool. Revise the ProgramHelper class from Question 13-2. to use the new interface.

The first thing you need to do in this exercise is to add the ICodeChecker interface with its bool, making sure to use the proper syntax to extend IConvertible. Change ProgramHelper to implement ICodeChecker, which also means that it implements IConvertible. We've added some code in Run( ) to convert the string, then check the syntax, convert it back again, and check the syntax again. Example A-36 shows how we did it.

Example A-36. One solution to Exercise 13-3

```
using System;
using System.Collections.Generic;
using System.Linq;
using System.Text;

namespace Exercise_13_3
{
    interface IConvertible
    {
        string ConvertToCSharp(string stringToConvert);
        string ConvertToVB(string stringToConvert);
    }

    interface ICodeChecker : IConvertible
    {
        bool CheckCodeSyntax(string stringToCheck, string whichLang);
    }
```

Example A-36. One solution to Exercise 13-3 (continued)

```csharp
public class ProgramHelper : ICodeChecker
{
    public ProgramHelper( ) // constructor
    {
        Console.WriteLine("Creating ProgramHelper");
    }

    public string ConvertToCSharp(string stringToConvert)
    {
        Console.WriteLine("Converting the string you passed in
                          to CSharp syntax");
        return "This is a C# String.";
    }

    public string ConvertToVB(string stringToConvert)
    {
        Console.WriteLine("Converting the string you passed in
                          to VB syntax");
        return "This is a VB String.";
    }

    public bool CheckCodeSyntax(string stringToCheck,
                               string whichLang)
    {
        switch (whichLang)
        {
            case "CSharp":
                Console.WriteLine("Checking the string for
                                  C# Syntax: {0}", stringToCheck);
                return true;
            case "VB":
                Console.WriteLine("Checking the string for
                                  VB Syntax: {0}", stringToCheck);
                return true;
            default:
                return false;
        }
    }
} // end class ProgramHelper

class Tester
{
    public void Run( )
    {
        // Create a ProgramHelper object
        ProgramHelper theProgramHelper = new ProgramHelper( );

        // convert a line of CSharp to VB
        string cSharpString = theProgramHelper.ConvertToCSharp(
                              "This is a VB string to convert.");
        Console.WriteLine(cSharpString);
```

Example A-36. One solution to Exercise 13-3 (continued)

```
                Console.WriteLine("Checking the string for syntax... Result {0}",
                                theProgramHelper.CheckCodeSyntax(
                                                cSharpString, "CSharp"));

                // convert the converted line back to VB
                string vbString = theProgramHelper.ConvertToVB(cSharpString);
                Console.WriteLine(vbString);
                Console.WriteLine("Checking the string for syntax... Result {0}",
                                theProgramHelper.CheckCodeSyntax(
                                                vbString, "VB"));
        }

        static void Main()
        {
            Tester t = new Tester();
            t.Run();
        }
    }
}
```

Solution to Exercise 13-4. Demonstrate the use of is and as. Create a new class, ProgramConverter, which implements IConvertible. ProgramConverter should implement the ConvertToCSharp() and ConvertToVB() methods. Revise ProgramHelper so that it derives from ProgramConverter and implements ICodeChecker. Test your class by creating an array of ProgramConverter objects, some of which are ProgramConverters and some of which are ProgramHelpers. Then call the conversion methods and the code check methods on each item in the array to test which ones implement ICodeChecker and which ones do not.

For this exercise, you need to first define the new class ProgramConverter, and give it the ConvertToCSharp() and ConvertToVB() methods. Then derive ProgramHelper from ProgramConverter, You can remove the ConvertToCSharp() and ConvertToVB() methods from ProgramHelper, because they'll be inherited from ProgramConverter. In Run(), you'll need to create the array of ProgramConverter objects, either manually, or randomly as we did in the chapter. Then use the is or as operator to test each element of the array to see which interfaces they implement. Example A-37 shows how we did it.

Example A-37. Our solution to Exercise 13-4

```
using System;
using System.Collections.Generic;
using System.Linq;
using System.Text;

namespace Exercise_13_4
{
    interface IConvertible
```

```
{
    string ConvertToCSharp( string stringToConvert );
    string ConvertToVB( string stringToConvert );
}

interface ICodeChecker : IConvertible
{
    bool CheckCodeSyntax( string stringToCheck, string whichLang );
}

public class ProgramConverter : IConvertible
{
    public ProgramConverter( ) // constructor
    {
        Console.WriteLine( "Creating ProgramConverter" );
    }

    public string ConvertToCSharp( string stringToConvert )
    {
        Console.WriteLine( "Converting the string you passed in
                            to CSharp syntax" );
        return "This is a C# string.";
    }

    public string ConvertToVB( string stringToConvert )
    {
        Console.WriteLine( "Converting the string you passed in
                            to VB syntax" );
        return "This is a VB string.";
    }
}

public class ProgramHelper : ProgramConverter, ICodeChecker
{
    public ProgramHelper( ) // constructor
    {
        Console.WriteLine( "Creating ProgramHelper" );
    }

    public bool CheckCodeSyntax( string stringToCheck, string whichLang )
    {
        switch ( whichLang )
        {
            case "CSharp":
                Console.WriteLine("Checking the string {0}
                                   for C# Syntax", stringToCheck );
                return true;
            case "VB":
                Console.WriteLine("Checking the string {0}
                                   for VB Syntax", stringToCheck );
                return true;
            default:
```

Example A-37. Our solution to Exercise 13-4 (continued)

```
                    return false;
            }
        }
    }

    class Tester
    {
        static void Main( )
        {
            Tester t = new Tester( );
            t.Run( );
        }
        public void Run( )
        {
            ProgramConverter[] converters = new ProgramConverter[4];
            converters[0] = new ProgramConverter( );
            converters[1] = new ProgramHelper( );
            converters[2] = new ProgramHelper( );
            converters[3] = new ProgramConverter( );
            foreach ( ProgramConverter pc in converters )
            {
                string vbString =  pc.ConvertToCSharp( "This is a VB
                                            string to convert.");
                Console.WriteLine( vbString );
                ProgramHelper ph = pc as ProgramHelper;
                if ( ph != null )
                {
                    ph.CheckCodeSyntax( vbString, "VB" );
                }
                else
                {
                    Console.WriteLine( "No vb syntax check -
                                    not a Program helper" );
                }
                string cSharpString = pc.ConvertToCSharp( vbString );
                Console.WriteLine( cSharpString );
                if ( ph != null )
                {
                    ph.CheckCodeSyntax( vbString, "CSharp" );
                }
                else
                {
                    Console.WriteLine( "No csharp syntax check -
                                    not a Program helper" );
                }
            }
        }
    }
}
```

Chapter 14: Generics and Collections

Quiz Solutions

Solution to Question 14-1. Indexers are unnamed. You use the this keyword to create an indexer:

```
public string this[int index]
```

Solution to Question 14-2. Any type can be used, although it's most common to use integers.

Solution to Question 14-3. The elements of the collection that you want to sort must implement IComparable.

Solution to Question 14-4. Generics allow you to create type-safe collections without specifying the type the collection will hold when you create the collection.

Solution to Question 14-5. The IEnumerable<T> interface allows your collection to support a foreach loop.

Solution to Question 14-6. The purpose of the yield keyword is to return a value to the IEnumerator object, within the GetEnumerator( ) method.

Solution to Question 14-7. The size of an array is fixed when you create it. A List<T> expands dynamically when you add more elements.

Solution to Question 14-8. The Capacity property of a List indicates the number of elements that the List has room for. The Capacity is increased automatically when more elements are added.

Solution to Question 14-9. A Stack is a "last-in, first-out" collection, and a Queue is a "first-in, first-out" collection. In a Queue, elements are removed in the same order they were inserted. In a Stack, elements are removed in the opposite order.

Solution to Question 14-10. The key in a Dictionary takes the place of an indexer, and allows you to retrieve the associated value. The key can be any type, but it's usually short. The value is usually a much larger or more complex object associated with the key.

Exercise Solutions

Solution to Exercise 14-1. Create an abstract Animal class that has private members weight and name, and abstract methods Speak( ), Move( ), and ToString( ). Derive from Animal a Cat class and a Dog class that override the methods appropriately. Create an Animal array, populate it with Dogs and Cats, and then call each member's overridden virtual methods.

The purpose of this exercise is to set up the rest of the exercises in this chapter, and to remind you of how to use arrays and indexers polymorphically. The Animal, Dog, and Cat classes are simple enough to create, although you should remember to make the appropriate methods of Animal abstract. You then need to override those abstract methods in Dog and Cat. In Run( ), you need to allocate enough space for the array of animals, to use a loop (a foreach works well), and to call the overridden virtual methods on each element as an Animal. In our case, we also added a method that only Cat objects have (Purr( )). Within the foreach loop, we cast each Animal to Cat, and if the cast succeeds, call the Purr( ) method. Example A-38 shows how we did it.

Example A-38. One solution to Exercise 14-1

```
using System;
using System.Collections.Generic;
using System.Linq;
using System.Text;

namespace Exercise_14_1
{
    abstract public class Animal
    {
        protected int weight;
        protected string name;
        public Animal(int weight, string name)
        {
            this.weight = weight;
            this.name = name;
        }
        abstract public void Speak();
        abstract public void Move();
        abstract public override string ToString()
    }

    public class Dog : Animal
    {
        public string Breed { get; set; }
        public Dog(int weight, string name, string breed)
            : base(weight, name)
        {
            this.Breed = breed;
        }
        public override void Speak()
```

Example A-38. One solution to Exercise 14-1 (continued)

```
        {
            Console.WriteLine("Woof");
        }
        public override void Move()
        {
            Console.WriteLine("Run, run, run, drool.");
        }
        public override string ToString()
        {
            return "My name is " + this.name + ", I weigh " +
             this.weight + ", and I am a " + this.Breed + "\n";
        }
    }

    public class Cat : Animal
    {
        public Cat(int weight, string name) : base(weight, name)
        {
        }
        public override void Speak()
        {
            Console.WriteLine("Meow");
        }
        public override void Move()
        {
            Console.WriteLine("Run, tumble, nap.");
        }
        public override string ToString()
        {
            return "My name is " + this.name + ", I weigh " +
                    this.weight + ", and I know how to purr!\n";
        }
        public void Purr()
        {
            Console.WriteLine("Purrrrrrrrrrrrrrrrrrrrrrrrrrrrrr\n");
        }
    }

    public class Tester
    {
        public void Run()
        {
            Animal[] myAnimals = new Animal[5];
            myAnimals[0] = new Dog(72, "Milo", "Golden");
            myAnimals[1] = new Cat(12, "Shakespeare");
            myAnimals[2] = new Cat(10, "Allegra");
            myAnimals[3] = new Dog(50, "Dingo", "mixed breed");
            myAnimals[4] = new Dog(20, "Brandy", "Beagle");
            foreach (Animal a in myAnimals)
            {
                a.Speak();
                a.Move();
```

Example A-38. One solution to Exercise 14-1 (continued)

```
                Console.WriteLine(a);
                Cat c = a as Cat;  // cast to cat
                if (c != null)     // if it is a cat
                {
                    c.Purr();      // only cats purr
                }
            }
        }
        static void Main()
        {
            Tester t = new Tester();
            t.Run();
        }
    }
}
```

Solution to Exercise 14-2.   Replace the array in Exercise 14-1 with a List. Sort the animals by size. You can simplify by just calling ToString() before and after the sort. Remember that you'll need to implement IComparable.

The first thing you need to do here is replace the array in Run() with a List, specifically a List<Animal>. You don't need to worry about the size of the List; you can just call Add() to add each element to the List. Output the values of the list (using a foreach) once, then call Sort() on the List, and output the values again.

For the Sort() to work, you'll need to make sure Animal implements IComparable. To sort on the animal's weight, you'll need a CompareTo() method that delegates responsibility for the comparison to the int version of CompareTo(), using Animal.weight. Example A-39 shows one way.

Example A-39. One solution to Exercise 14-2

```
using System;
using System.Collections.Generic;
using System.Linq;
using System.Text;

namespace Exercise_14_2
{
    abstract public class Animal : IComparable
    {
        protected int weight;
        protected string name;
        public Animal(int weight, string name)
        {
            this.weight = weight;
            this.name = name;
        }
        abstract public void Speak();
        abstract public void Move();
        abstract public override string ToString();
```

```csharp
        public int CompareTo(Object rhs)
        {
            Animal otherAnimal = rhs as Animal;
            if (otherAnimal != null)
            {
                return this.weight.CompareTo(otherAnimal.weight);
            }
            else
            {
                throw new ApplicationException("Expected to compare animals");
            }
        }
    }

    public class Dog : Animal
    {
        public string Breed { get; set; }

        public Dog(int weight, string name, string breed)
            : base(weight, name)
        {
            this.Breed = breed;
        }
        public override void Speak()
        {
            Console.WriteLine("Woof");
        }
        public override void Move()
        {
            Console.WriteLine("Run, run, run, drool.");
        }
        public override string ToString()
        {
            return "My name is " + this.name + ", I weigh " +
                    this.weight + ", and I am a " + this.Breed;
        }
    }

    public class Cat : Animal
    {
        public Cat(int weight, string name) : base(weight, name)
        {
        }

        public override void Speak()
        {
            Console.WriteLine("Meow");
        }
        public override void Move()
        {
            Console.WriteLine("Run, tumble, nap.");
        }
```

Example A-39. One solution to Exercise 14-2 (continued)

```
        }
        public override string ToString()
        {
            return "My name is " + this.name + ", I weigh "
                    + this.weight + ", and I know how to purr!";
        }
        public void Purr()
        {
            Console.WriteLine("Purrrrrrrrrrrrrrrrrrrrrrrrrrrrrrr\n");
        }
    }

    public class Tester
    {
        public void Run()
        {
            List<Animal> myAnimals = new List<Animal>();
            myAnimals.Add(new Dog(72, "Milo", "Golden"));
            myAnimals.Add(new Cat(12, "Shakespeare"));
            myAnimals.Add(new Cat(10, "Allegra"));
            myAnimals.Add(new Dog(50, "Dingo", "mixed breed"));
            myAnimals.Add(new Dog(20, "Brandy", "Beagle"));
            foreach (Animal a in myAnimals)
            {
                Console.WriteLine(a);
            }
            Console.WriteLine("\nAfter sorting by size...");
            myAnimals.Sort();
            foreach (Animal a in myAnimals)
            {
                Console.WriteLine(a);
            }
        }
        static void Main()
        {
            Tester t = new Tester();
            t.Run();
        }
    }
}
```

Solution to Exercise 14-3. Replace the list from Exercise 14-2 with both a Stack and a Queue. Remove the sort function. Output the contents of each collection and see the difference in the order in which the animals are returned.

There's not a whole lot of challenge to this particular exercise. The goal is to give you some experience using both a stack and a queue. The definitions of the classes don't change in this exercise; the only difference is in Run(). As you would expect, if you add the Animal objects to the stack and the queue in the same order, when you output the contents the stack is reversed; the queue isn't. One solution is shown in Example A-40.

Example A-40. One solution to Exercise 14-3

```csharp
using System;
using System.Collections.Generic;
using System.Linq;
using System.Text;

namespace Exercise_14_3
{
    abstract public class Animal : IComparable
    {
        protected int weight;
        protected string name;
        public Animal(int weight, string name)
        {
            this.weight = weight;
            this.name = name;
        }
        abstract public void Speak();
        abstract public void Move();
        abstract public override string ToString();

        public int CompareTo(Object rhs)
        {
            Animal otherAnimal = rhs as Animal;
            if (otherAnimal != null)
            {
                return this.weight.CompareTo(otherAnimal.weight);
            }
            else
            {
                throw new ApplicationException("Expected to compare animals");
            }
        }
    }

    public class Dog : Animal
    {
        public string Breed { get; set; }

        public Dog(int weight, string name, string breed)
            : base(weight, name)
        {
            this.Breed = breed;
        }
        public override void Speak()
        {
            Console.WriteLine("Woof");
        }
        public override void Move()
        {
            Console.WriteLine("Run, run, run, drool.");
        }
        public override string ToString()
```

Example A-40. One solution to Exercise 14-3 (continued)

```
        {
            return "My name is " + this.name + ", I weigh "
                    + this.weight + ", and I am a " + this.Breed;
        }
    }

    public class Cat : Animal
    {
        public Cat(int weight, string name)
            : base(weight, name)
        {
        }

        public override void Speak()
        {
            Console.WriteLine("Meow");
        }
        public override void Move()
        {
            Console.WriteLine("Run, tumble, nap.");
        }
        public override string ToString()
        {
            return "My name is " + this.name + ", I weigh "
                    + this.weight + ", and I know how to purr!";
        }
        public void Purr()
        {
            Console.WriteLine("Purrrrrrrrrrrrrrrrrrrrrrrrrrrrr\n");
        }
    }

    public class Tester
    {
        public void Run()
        {
            Console.WriteLine("Adding in the order: Milo,
                        Shakespeare, Allegra, Dingo, Brandy");
            Stack<Animal> myStackOfAnimals = new Stack<Animal>();
            myStackOfAnimals.Push(new Dog(72, "Milo", "Golden"));
            myStackOfAnimals.Push(new Cat(12, "Shakespeare"));
            myStackOfAnimals.Push(new Cat(10, "Allegra"));
            myStackOfAnimals.Push(new Dog(50, "Dingo", "mixed breed"));
            myStackOfAnimals.Push(new Dog(20, "Brandy", "Beagle"));

            Queue<Animal> myQueueOfAnimals = new Queue<Animal>();
            myQueueOfAnimals.Enqueue(new Dog(72, "Milo", "Golden"));
            myQueueOfAnimals.Enqueue(new Cat(12, "Shakespeare"));
            myQueueOfAnimals.Enqueue(new Cat(10, "Allegra"));
            myQueueOfAnimals.Enqueue(new Dog(50, "Dingo", "mixed breed"));
            myQueueOfAnimals.Enqueue(new Dog(20, "Brandy", "Beagle"));
```

Example A-40. One solution to Exercise 14-3 (continued)

```
            Console.WriteLine("The stack...");
            foreach (Animal a in myStackOfAnimals)
            {
                Console.WriteLine(a);
            }

            Console.WriteLine("The queue...");
            foreach (Animal a in myQueueOfAnimals)
            {
                Console.WriteLine(a);
            }
        }
        static void Main( )
        {
            Tester t = new Tester( );
            t.Run( );
        }
    }
}
```

Solution to Exercise 14-4. Rewrite Exercise 14-2 to allow Animals to be sorted either by weight or alphabetically by name.

This exercise is similar to Example 14-6 in the chapter. You've already implemented IComparable for Animal, but now you need to add an overloaded CompareTo( ) method that can compare based on either weight or name. For that, you'll need to create an AnimalComparer class with a ComparisonType enumeration. Then you'll need to add a case statement to the overloaded CompareTo( ) method to delegate to either the CompareTo( ) for int, or the one for string. Example A-41 shows our solution. Note that we removed many of the extra methods of Animal, Cat, and Dog for this example, because they're not needed to sort the animals.

Example A-41. One solution to Exercise 14-4

```
using System;
using System.Collections.Generic;
using System.Linq;
using System.Text;

namespace Exercise_14_4
{
    abstract public class Animal : IComparable<Animal>
    {
        protected int weight;
        protected string name;
        public Animal(int weight, string name)
        {
            this.weight = weight;
            this.name = name;
        }
```

Example A-41. One solution to Exercise 14-4 (continued)

```csharp
    // ** new **
    public static AnimalComparer GetComparer( )
    {
        return new Animal.AnimalComparer( );
    }
    public int CompareTo(Animal rhs)
    {
        return this.weight.CompareTo(rhs.weight);
    }
    // ** new **
    public int CompareTo(Animal rhs,
        Animal.AnimalComparer.ComparisonType whichComparison)
    {
        switch (whichComparison)
        {
            case AnimalComparer.ComparisonType.Name:
                return this.name.CompareTo(rhs.name);
            case AnimalComparer.ComparisonType.Size:
                return this.weight.CompareTo(rhs.weight);
        }
        return -1;  // all paths must return a value
    }

    // nested class   ** new **
    public class AnimalComparer : IComparer<Animal>
    {
        // how do you want to compare?
        public enum ComparisonType
        {
            Size,
            Name
        };
        private Animal.AnimalComparer.ComparisonType whichComparison;
        public Animal.AnimalComparer.ComparisonType WhichComparison
        {
            get { return whichComparison; }
            set { whichComparison = value; }
        }

        // compare two Animals using the previously set
        // whichComparison value
        public int Compare(Animal lhs, Animal rhs)
        {
            return lhs.CompareTo(rhs, whichComparison);
        }
    }    // end nested class
}        // end class Animal


public class Dog : Animal
{
    public Dog(int weight, string name, string breed) :
```

Example A-41. One solution to Exercise 14-4 (continued)

```
            base(weight, name)
        { }
        public override string ToString( )
        {
            return "My name is " + this.name + ", and I weigh " + this.weight;
        }
    }

    public class Cat : Animal
    {
        public Cat(int weight, string name) :
            base(weight, name)
        { }
        public override string ToString( )
        {
            return "My name is " + this.name + ", and I weigh " + this.weight;
        }
    }

    public class Tester
    {
        public void Run( )
        {
            List<Animal> myAnimals = new List<Animal>( );
            myAnimals.Add(new Dog(70, "Milo", "Golden"));
            myAnimals.Add(new Cat(10, "Shakespeare"));
            myAnimals.Add(new Cat(15, "Allegra"));
            myAnimals.Add(new Dog(50, "Dingo", "mixed breed"));
            myAnimals.Add(new Dog(20, "Brandy", "Beagle"));
            Console.WriteLine("Before sorting...");
            foreach (Animal a in myAnimals)
            {
                Console.WriteLine(a);
            }
            Console.WriteLine("\nAfter sorting by default (weight)...");
            myAnimals.Sort( );
            foreach (Animal a in myAnimals)
            {
                Console.WriteLine(a);
            }
            Console.WriteLine("\nAfter sorting by name...");
            Animal.AnimalComparer animalComparer = Animal.GetComparer( );
            animalComparer.WhichComparison =
                    Animal.AnimalComparer.ComparisonType.Name;
            myAnimals.Sort(animalComparer);
            foreach (Animal a in myAnimals)
            {
                Console.WriteLine(a);
            }
            Console.WriteLine("\nAfter sorting explicitly by size...");
            animalComparer.WhichComparison =
                    Animal.AnimalComparer.ComparisonType.Size;
```

Example A-41. One solution to Exercise 14-4 (continued)

```
            myAnimals.Sort(animalComparer);
            foreach (Animal a in myAnimals)
            {
                Console.WriteLine(a);
            }
        }
        static void Main()
        {
            Tester t = new Tester();
            t.Run();
        }
    }
}
```

Chapter 15: Strings

Quiz Solutions

Solution to Question 15-1. string (lowercase) is the C# keyword that maps to the .NET Framework String class. They may be used interchangeably.

Solution to Question 15-2. IComparable guarantees that strings can be sorted. ICloneable guarantees that you can call the Clone method on a string object and get back a new duplicate string. IConvertible allows strings to be converted to other types (such as integers). And IEnumerable guarantees that strings can be iterated over in foreach loops.

Solution to Question 15-3. A string literal is a quoted string, provided by the programmer, such as "Hello".

Solution to Question 15-4. An escape character embedded in a string indicates that the character or punctuation that follows is to be treated as an instruction rather than as part of the string. \n indicates a new line. \" indicates that the quote symbol is part of the string, not terminating it.

Solution to Question 15-5. Verbatim strings are taken "as is" and thus do not require escape characters. Where \\ would indicate a single backslash in a normal string, in a verbatim string it indicates two backslashes. Verbatim strings must include an @ character before the first double quote.

Solution to Question 15-6. The fact that strings are immutable means they cannot be changed. When you appear to change a string, what actually happens is that a new string is created and the old string is destroyed by the garbage collector if it is no longer referenced.

Solution to Question 15-7. You can call the Concat method of the String class to join two strings, but it is more common to use the overloaded + operator.

Solution to Question 15-8. Given an array of delimiters, Split( ) returns the substrings of the original string, as broken up by the specified delimiters.

Solution to Question 15-9. StringBuilder objects are mutable. When the StringBuilder has the complete set of characters you want, you call ToString( ) to get back a string object, which is then immutable.

Solution to Question 15-10. Regular expressions constitute a language for identifying and manipulating strings using both literals and metacharacters.

Exercise Solutions

Solution to Exercise 15-1. Create the following six strings:

- String 1: "Hello "
- String 2: "World"
- String 3 (a verbatim string): "Come visit us at *http://www.LibertyAssociates.com*"
- String 4: a concatenation of strings 1 and 2
- String 5: "world"
- String 6: a copy of string 3

Once you have the strings created, do the following:

1. Output the length of each string.
2. Output the third character in each string.
3. Output whether the character *H* appears in each string.
4. Output which strings are the same as string 2.
5. Output which strings are the same as string 2, ignoring case.

Creating the strings is relatively easy: you need to remember to keep the space in String 1 and to use a verbatim string (with an @ symbol) for String 3. You can concatenate Strings 1 and 2 using Concat( ) or the + operator, and you can use Copy( ) to create String 6.

For the other parts of the exercise, you can just put all the code directly in Test( ). You could put all the strings into an array, and iterate over the array for each test, but with only six elements it's fine to test them each individually.

For part 1, you just need to output the Length of each string:

```
Console.WriteLine( "s1: {0} [{1}]", s1.Length, s1 );
```

Part 2 is also simple. To get the third character in each string, use the index operator, but remember that indexes start at zero, so the third character is at index [2]:

```
Console.WriteLine( "s1: {0} [{1}]", s1[2], s1 );
```

For part 3, to determine whether there's a specific character in the string, you can use IndexOf( ) to test for that character. If the character isn't in the string, IndexOf( ) returns –1. Therefore, if the returned index is greater than or equal to zero, the character is in the string. To be completely accurate about it, you can use ToUpper( ) or ToLower( ) on each string first so that you're testing for both uppercase and lowercase instances of the character. We're using the ternary operator here (from Chapter 4) to return "yes" or "nope":

```
Console.WriteLine( "s1: {0} [{1}]",
    s1.ToUpper( ).IndexOf( 'H' ) >= 0 ? "yes" : "nope", s1 );
```

In part 4, you need to test whether a string is the same as String 2. That's what the String.Compare( ) method is for. Again, we're using the ternary operator for the output:

```
Console.WriteLine( "s1: {0} [{1}]",
    String.Compare( s1, s2 ) == 0 ? "Same!" : "Different", s1 );
```

Part 5 is very similar to part 4, but this time, you use the overloaded version of Compare( ) and set the third parameter to "true" so that Compare( ) will ignore case:

```
Console.WriteLine( "s1: {0} [{1}]",
    String.Compare( s1, s2, true ) == 0 ? "Same!" : "Different", s1 );
```

Example A-42 shows our code for conducting all the tests in one program.

Example A-42. Our solution to Exercise 15-1

```
using System;
using System.Collections.Generic;
using System.Linq;
using System.Text;

namespace Exercise_15_1
{
    class Tester
    {
        public void Run( )
        {
            // creating the six strings
            string s1 = "Hello ";
            string s2 = "World";
            string s3 = @"Come visit us at http://www.LibertyAssociates.com";
            string s4 = s1 + s2;
            string s5 = "world";
            string s6 = string.Copy(s3);

            // returning the length of each string
            Console.WriteLine("Here's how long our strings are...");
            Console.WriteLine("s1: {0} [{1}]", s1.Length, s1);
```

Example A-42. Our solution to Exercise 15-1 (continued)

```
Console.WriteLine("s2: {0} [{1}]", s2.Length, s2);
Console.WriteLine("s3: {0} [{1}]", s3.Length, s3);
Console.WriteLine("s4: {0} [{1}]", s4.Length, s4);
Console.WriteLine("s5: {0} [{1}]", s5.Length, s5);
Console.WriteLine("s6: {0} [{1}]", s6.Length, s6);

// returning the third character in each string
Console.WriteLine("\nHere's the third character
                    in each string...");
Console.WriteLine("s1: {0} [{1}]", s1[2], s1);
Console.WriteLine("s2: {0} [{1}]", s2[2], s2);
Console.WriteLine("s3: {0} [{1}]", s3[2], s3);
Console.WriteLine("s4: {0} [{1}]", s4[2], s4);
Console.WriteLine("s5: {0} [{1}]", s5[2], s5);
Console.WriteLine("s6: {0} [{1}]", s6[2], s6);

// testing for the character H in each string
Console.WriteLine("\nIs there an h in the string?");
Console.WriteLine("s1: {0} [{1}]",
        s1.ToUpper().IndexOf('H') >= 0 ? "yes" : "nope", s1);
Console.WriteLine("s2: {0} [{1}]",
        s2.ToUpper().IndexOf('H') >= 0 ? "yes" : "nope", s2);
Console.WriteLine("s3: {0} [{1}]",
        s3.ToUpper().IndexOf('H') >= 0 ? "yes" : "nope", s3);
Console.WriteLine("s4: {0} [{1}]",
        s4.ToUpper().IndexOf('H') >= 0 ? "yes" : "nope", s4);
Console.WriteLine("s5: {0} [{1}]",
        s5.ToUpper().IndexOf('H') >= 0 ? "yes" : "nope", s5);
Console.WriteLine("s6: {0} [{1}]",
        s6.ToUpper().IndexOf('H') >= 0 ? "yes" : "nope", s6);

// testing for strings the same as String 2
Console.WriteLine("\nWhich strings are the same as s2 [{0}]?", s2);
Console.WriteLine("s1: {0} [{1}]",
        String.Compare(s1, s2) == 0 ? "Same!" : "Different", s1);
Console.WriteLine("s2: {0} [{1}]",
        String.Compare(s2, s2) == 0 ? "Same!" : "Different", s2);
Console.WriteLine("s3: {0} [{1}]",
        String.Compare(s3, s2) == 0 ? "Same!" : "Different", s3);
Console.WriteLine("s4: {0} [{1}]",
        String.Compare(s4, s2) == 0 ? "Same!" : "Different", s4);
Console.WriteLine("s5: {0} [{1}]",
        String.Compare(s5, s2) == 0 ? "Same!" : "Different", s5);
Console.WriteLine("s6: {0} [{1}]",
        String.Compare(s6, s2) == 0 ? "Same!" : "Different", s6);

// testing for strings the same as String 2, ignoring case
Console.WriteLine("\nWhich strings are the same as s2 [{0}]
                    ignoring case?", s2);
Console.WriteLine("s1: {0} [{1}]",
    String.Compare(s1, s2, true) == 0 ? "Same!" : "Different", s1);
```

Example A-42. Our solution to Exercise 15-1 (continued)

```
        Console.WriteLine("s2: {0} [{1}]",
            String.Compare(s2, s2, true) == 0 ? "Same!" : "Different", s2);
        Console.WriteLine("s3: {0} [{1}]",
            String.Compare(s3, s2, true) == 0 ? "Same!" : "Different", s3);
        Console.WriteLine("s4: {0} [{1}]",
            String.Compare(s4, s2, true) == 0 ? "Same!" : "Different", s4);
        Console.WriteLine("s5: {0} [{1}]",
            String.Compare(s5, s2, true) == 0 ? "Same!" : "Different", s5);
        Console.WriteLine("s6: {0} [{1}]",
            String.Compare(s6, s2, true) == 0 ? "Same!" : "Different", s6);
    }
    static void Main()
    {
        Tester t = new Tester();
        t.Run();
    }
  }
}
```

Solution to Exercise 15-2.   Take the following famous string:

> To be, or not to be: That is the question: Whether 'tis nobler in the mind to suffer the
> slings and arrows of outrageous fortune, or to take arms against a sea of troubles, and
> by opposing end them?

Reverse the order of the words in the string, and output the reversed string to the
console.

The trick to reversing the order of words in a string is that you have to break the
string apart into its component words, and then put the words back together into a
new string. Taking a string apart is easy; that's what Split() is for. In this case, the
string contains spaces, commas, and colons, so you can use all three of those as
delimiters.

Split() returns an array, and conveniently, the array class has the Reverse() static
method, so you can quite easily get the words into reverse order. Once you have your
reversed array, you just need a StringBuilder with a foreach loop to create the new,
reversed string. Example A-43 shows one way to do it.

Example A-43. One solution to Exercise 15-2

```
using System;
using System.Collections.Generic;
using System.Linq;
using System.Text;

namespace Exercise_15_2
{
    class Tester
    {
        public void Run()
```

Example A-43. One solution to Exercise 15-2 (continued)

```
        {
            string myString = "To be, or not to be: That is the " +
                              "question: Whether 'tis nobler in " +
                              "the mind to suffer the slings and " +
                              "arrows of outrageous fortune, or to " +
                              "take arms against a sea of troubles, " +
                              "and by opposing end them?";

            char[] delimiters = {',', ':', ' '};

            String[] theStringArray = myString.Split(delimiters);
            Array.Reverse(theStringArray);

            StringBuilder sBuilder = new StringBuilder();
            foreach (String subString in theStringArray)
            {
                sBuilder.AppendFormat("{0} ",subString);
            }

            Console.WriteLine(sBuilder);

        }
        static void Main()
        {
            Tester t = new Tester();
            t.Run();
        }
    }
}
```

Solution to Exercise 15-3.   Take the following famous string:

> We choose to go to the moon. We choose to go to the moon in this decade and do the
> other things, not because they are easy, but because they are hard, because that goal
> will serve to organize and measure the best of our energies and skills, because that
> challenge is one that we are willing to accept, one we are unwilling to postpone, and
> one which we intend to win, and the others, too.

Write a program to determine and output to the screen the number of times the
word *the* occurs in this string.

There are a number of ways to address this exercise. One valid way is to use the
IndexOf( ) method to determine the index of the first instance of the string "the".
That works fine, but IndexOf( )finds only the first instance of the string. To find the
next instance, you'll need to use Substring( ) to cut off the beginning of the string
you're searching, from the first character up to the first character after the word *the*.

That's not actually too hard, because IndexOf( ) returns the index of the letter *t* in
the, so IndexOf("the ") + 4 gives you the index of the first word after *the*. It's +4
instead of +3 because the search string includes a space—that way, you'll find only
instances of the word *the*, as opposed to the word *these* or *thesaurus*. Every time you

find an instance of *the*, you take a substring and increment a counter. If you do it all in a while loop, you can chop down the string until there's no instances of *the* remaining—when IndexOf("the ") returns –1. Example A-44 shows how we did it.

Example A-44. One solution to Exercise 15-3

```
using System;
using System.Collections.Generic;
using System.Linq;
using System.Text;

namespace Exercise_15_3
{
    class Tester
    {
        public void Run()
        {
            int theCount = 0;
            string theString = "We choose to go to the moon. " +
                               "We choose to go to the moon in " +
                               "this decade and do the other " +
                               "things, not because they are easy, " +
                               "but because they are hard, " +
                               "because that goal will serve to " +
                               "organize and measure the best of " +
                               "our energies and skills, because " +
                               "that challenge is one that we are " +
                               "willing to accept, one we are " +
                               "unwilling to postpone, and one which " +
                               "we intend to win, and the others, too. ";

            while (theString.IndexOf("the ") != -1)
            {
                theString = theString.Substring(theString.IndexOf("the ")
                                        + 4);
                theCount++;
            }
            Console.WriteLine("The word \"the\" occurs {0} times
                        in the string.", theCount);
        }
    }
    class Program
    {
        static void Main()
        {
            Tester t = new Tester();
            t.Run();
        }
    }
}
```

Another way to solve this exercise would be to split the string into an array of substrings, and then compare each element in the array to the string "the". That way is equally valid, but it creates a lot of strings in the array.

Solution to Exercise 15-4.   Take the following string:

> We hold these truths to be self-evident, that all men are created equal, that they are endowed by their Creator with certain unalienable Rights, that among these are Life, Liberty and the pursuit of Happiness.

and use a regular expression to split the string into words. Then create a new string that lists each word, one to a line, each prefaced with a line number.

There are a number of ways to accomplish splitting up a string into words. As you saw in the chapter, splitting a string with a Regex is more efficient than using the string's Split( ) method. To do that, you'll need to define a Regex with delimiters that match a comma, a space, or a comma followed by a space (you need that third one so that the Regex doesn't separate commas from spaces). You then need to use the Split( ) method of the Regex class, as we showed you in Example 15-9, to split the string into its component words. Then you use a foreach loop, with a StringBuilder object to create the new string. Each time through the loop, you increment your counter to create the line number, and append a substring and a newline (\n) to the StringBuilder. Example A-45 shows one way to do it.

Be sure to add the using System.Text.RegularExpressions statement to the top of your program, or the Regex won't work.

Example A-45. One solution to Exercise 15-4

```
using System;
using System.Collections.Generic;
using System.Linq;
using System.Text;
using System.Text.RegularExpressions;

namespace Exercise_15_4
{
    class Tester
    {
        public void Run( )
        {
            string importantString = "We hold these truths to be self-evident, " +
                                      "that all men are created equal, that " +
                                      "they are endowed by their Creator with " +
                                      "certain unalienable Rights, that among " +
                                      "these are Life, Liberty and the pursuit " +
                                      "of Happiness.";

            Regex theRegex = new Regex(" |, |,");
            StringBuilder sBuilder = new StringBuilder( );
            int id = 1;
```

Example A-45. One solution to Exercise 15-4 (continued)

```
        foreach (string subString in theRegex.Split(importantString))
        {
            sBuilder.AppendFormat("{0}: {1}\n", id++, subString);
        }
        Console.WriteLine("{0}", sBuilder);
    }
    static void Main()
    {
        Tester t = new Tester();
        t.Run();
    }
  }
}
```

Chapter 16: Throwing and Catching Exceptions

Quiz Solutions

Solution to Question 16-1. An exception is an object (derived from System.Exception) that contains information about a problematic event. The framework supports throwing exceptions to stop processing and catching events to handle the problem and resume processing.

Solution to Question 16-2. The difference between a bug and an exception is that a bug is an error in programming, one that should be caught either by the compiler or in testing before you turn the program over to users. An exception is code that accounts for a situation that can't be avoided during coding, but can be predicted, such as a lost database connection.

Solution to Question 16-3. To generate an exception, you use the throw keyword, although the system will generate some exceptions on its own.

Solution to Question 16-4. To handle an exception, you wrap the code you think might generate the exception in a try block. The code to handle the exception goes in an associated catch block.

Solution to Question 16-5. If no exception handler is found in the method that throws an event, the stack is unwound until a handler is found, or else the exception is handled by the CLR, which terminates the program.

Solution to Question 16-6. After the handler's code is run, the program execution resumes with the code immediately following the handler (that is, after the catch block). Depending on where the handler is located in your code, and where the exception is thrown, you may be unable to return to the method where the exception was generated.

Solution to Question 16-7. The syntax for throwing a new `ArgumentNull` exception is:

```
throw new Sytem.ArgumentNullException();
```

Solution to Question 16-8. You can write multiple exception handlers to handle different types of exceptions; the first handler that catches the thrown exception will prevent further handling. Beware of inheritance complications in the ordering of your handlers.

Solution to Question 16-9. If you have code that must run whether or not an exception is thrown (to close a file, for example), place that code in the `finally` block. You must have a `try` before the `finally`, but a `catch` is optional.

Solution to Question 16-10. You often won't need a custom exception class; C# provides many exception types for your needs. However, you may want to create a custom exception to define a situation that's unique to the design of your program, and would not be an error outside it.

Exercise Solutions

Solution to Exercise 16-1. Create a simple array of three integers. Ask the user which array element she wants to see. Output the integer that the user asked for (remember that the user probably won't ask for a zero-based index). Provide a way for the user to indicate whether she wants another integer, or to end the program. Provide a handler that deals with invalid input.

This is a simple exercise, but the point is to create the error handler. Setting up the array is easy, as is asking the user for input. If you're keeping the user's requested index in a variable called `theEntry`, for example, remember to return `theIntArray[theEntry - 1]` to account for the fact that the user probably won't be thinking in terms of zero-based indexes.

To allow the user to keep asking for integers until she gets bored, wrap the whole thing in a `while` loop with a simple Boolean for a control variable. Initialize the Boolean to `true` before you start the loop. Then, inside the loop, ask the user whether she wants to try again, and use another `ReadLine()` to get the response. If the response is `"Y"` (or `"y"` for safety), you leave the Boolean set to `true` and go around the loop again. If it's anything else, change the Boolean to `false` and terminate the program.

None of that is the interesting part, though. Enclose the input line and the output for the selected index in a `try` block. Immediately after the `try` block, insert a generic `catch` block to output a message that the error is invalid. This `catch` block will handle whatever exception is raised, regardless of what kind of exception it is. The user can enter a number that's out of range, a string, or anything else. Then execution continues with the test for the loop, allowing the user to try again if she gave bad input. Example A-46 shows one solution.

Example A-46. One solution to Exercise 16-1

```
using System;
using System.Collections.Generic;
using System.Linq;
using System.Text;

namespace Exercise_16_1
{
    class Tester
    {
        public void Run()
        {
            bool tryAgain = true;
            while (tryAgain)
            {
                int[] theIntArray = new int[] { 15, 27, 34 };
                Console.Write("Which array member would you like? ");

                try
                {
                    int theEntry = Convert.ToInt32(Console.ReadLine());
                    Console.WriteLine("The entry you asked for is {0}",
                                      theIntArray[theEntry - 1]);
                }

                catch
                {
                    Console.WriteLine("That isn't a valid entry.");
                }

                Console.Write("Try again (y/n)? ");
                string theReply = Console.ReadLine();
                tryAgain = (theReply == "y" || theReply == "Y");
            }
        }

        static void Main(string[] args)
        {
            Tester t = new Tester();
            t.Run();
        }
    }
}
```

Solution to Exercise 16-2. Modify the example in Exercise 16-1 to handle two specific errors: the IndexOutOfRangeException, which is used when the user enters a number that's not valid for the array, and the FormatException, which is used when the entered value doesn't match the expected format—in this case, if the user enters something that isn't a number. Leave the existing handler as a default.

You already have most of the program to start with. In this case you simply need to add two exception handlers with appropriate code. It doesn't matter whether you catch the IndexOutOfRangeException or the FormatException first, but you must make sure that both handlers appear *before* the generic catch block, or the generic block will catch all the exceptions. Example A-47 shows one way to do it.

Example A-47. One solution to Exercise 16-2

```
using System;
using System.Collections.Generic;
using System.Linq;
using System.Text;

namespace Exercise_16_2
{
    class Tester
    {
        public void Run( )
        {
            bool tryAgain = true;
            while (tryAgain)
            {
                int[] theIntArray = new int[] { 15, 27, 34 };
                Console.Write("Which array member would you like? ");

                try
                {
                    int theEntry = Convert.ToInt32(Console.ReadLine( ));
                    Console.WriteLine("The entry you asked for is {0}",
                                theIntArray[theEntry - 1]);
                }

                catch (IndexOutOfRangeException)
                {
                    Console.WriteLine("Please enter a number from 1 to
                                {0}.", theIntArray.Length);
                }

                catch (FormatException)
                {
                    Console.WriteLine("Please enter a number.");
                }
```

```
            catch
            {
                Console.WriteLine("That isn't a valid entry.");
            }

            Console.Write("Try again (y/n)? ");
            string theReply = Console.ReadLine();
            tryAgain = (theReply == "y" || theReply == "Y");
        }
    }

    static void Main(string[] args)
    {
        Tester t = new Tester();
        t.Run();
    }
  }
}
```

Solution to Exercise 16-3. Create a Cat class with one int property: Age. Write a program that creates a List of Cat objects in a try block. Create multiple catch statements to handle an ArgumentOutOfRangeException and an unknown exception, and a finally block to simulate deallocating the Cat objects. Write test code to throw an exception that you will catch and handle.

Refer back to Chapter 14 if you don't remember how to create a generic List<T>, in this case a List<Cat>. This exercise isn't too different from the last one, in that you're still trying to allocate an invalid index inside the try block, and creating a catch block to handle two different types of exceptions. The difference in this case is the inclusion of a finally block, to take care of cleaning up the mystery resource you allocated. Example A-48 shows how we did it.

Example A-48. Our solution to Exercise 16-3

```
using System;
using System.Collections.Generic;
using System.Linq;
using System.Text;

namespace Exercise_16_3
{
    class Cat
    {
        public int Age { get; set; }
        public Cat(int age)
        {
            this.Age = age;
        }
    }
    class Tester
```

Example A-48. Our solution to Exercise 16-3 (continued)

```
{
    private void CatManager(Cat kitty)
    {
        Console.WriteLine("Managing a cat who is " + kitty.Age +
                            " years old");
    }
    public void Run( )
    {
        try
        {
            Console.WriteLine("Allocate resource that must
                                be deallocated here");
            List<Cat> cats = new List<Cat>( );
            cats.Add(new Cat(5));
            cats.Add(new Cat(7));
            CatManager(cats[1]); // pass in the second cat
            CatManager(cats[2]); // pass in the nonexistent third cat
        }

        catch (System.ArgumentOutOfRangeException)
        {
            Console.WriteLine("We're sorry; your cat does not exist.");
        }
        catch (Exception e)
        {
            Console.WriteLine("Unknown exception caught" + e.Message);
        }
        finally
        {
            Console.WriteLine("Deallocation of resource here.");
        }
    }
    static void Main( )
    {
        Console.WriteLine("Enter Main...");
        Tester t = new Tester( );
        t.Run( );
        Console.WriteLine("Exit Main...");
    }
}
}
```

The output from this example would look like this:

```
Enter Main...
Allocate resource that must be deallocated here
Managing a cat who is 7 years old
We're sorry; your cat does not exist.
Deallocation of resource here.
Exit Main...
```

Your output may vary, depending on how you wrote your test code.

Solution to Exercise 16-4. Modify the test code you wrote in Exercise 16-3 so that it does not throw an error. Create a custom error type CustomCatError that derives from System.ApplicationException, and create a handler for it. Add a method to CatManager that checks the cat's age and throws a new error of type CustomCatError if the age is less than or equal to 0, with an appropriate message. Write some test code to test your new exception.

This exercise is similar to Exercise 16-3, but this time you'll need to create a custom error class. Fortunately, the custom error class is empty and simply passes the exception message to its base class, so that's not too hard. Because the system can't throw your custom exception automatically, you'll need to add a TestCat( ) method to test the cat's age and, if appropriate, throw a new CustomCatError object with an appropriate message. Our solution is in Example A-49.

Example A-49. Our solution to Exercise 16-4

```
using System;
using System.Collections.Generic;
using System.Linq;
using System.Text;

namespace Exercise_16_4
{
    class Cat
    {
        public int Age { get; set;}
        public Cat(int age)
        {
            this.Age = age;
        }
    }

    // custom exception class
    public class CustomCatException : System.ApplicationException
    {
        public CustomCatException(string message) : base(message)
            // pass the message up to the base class
        {
        }
    }

    class Tester
    {
        private void CheckCat(Cat testCat)
        {
            if (testCat.Age <= 0)
            {
                // create a custom exception instance
                CustomCatException e = new CustomCatException("Your cat
                                       is too young.");
```

Example A-49. Our solution to Exercise 16-4 (continued)

```
                e.HelpLink = "http://www.libertyassociates.com";
                throw e;
            }
        }
    private void CatManager(Cat kitty)
    {
        CheckCat(kitty);
        Console.WriteLine("Managing a cat who is " + kitty.Age + " years old");
    }
    public void Run( )
    {
        try
        {
            Console.WriteLine("Allocate resource that must
                              be deallocated here");
            List<Cat> cats = new List<Cat>( );
            cats.Add(new Cat(7));
            cats.Add(new Cat(-2));
            CatManager(cats[0]); // pass in the first cat
            CatManager(cats[1]); // pass in the second cat
        }
        // catch custom exception
        catch (CustomCatException e)
        {
            Console.WriteLine("\nCustomCatException! Msg: {0}", e.Message);
            Console.WriteLine("\nHelpLink: {0}\n", e.HelpLink);
        }
        catch (System.ArgumentOutOfRangeException)
        {
            Console.WriteLine("We're sorry; your cat does not exist.");
        }
        catch (Exception e)
        {
            Console.WriteLine("Unknown exception caught" + e.Message);
        }
        finally
        {
            Console.WriteLine("Deallocation of resource here.");
        }
    }
    static void Main( )
    {
        Console.WriteLine("Enter Main...");
        Tester t = new Tester( );
        t.Run( );
        Console.WriteLine("Exit Main...");
    }
}
}
```

Chapter 17: Delegates and Events

Quiz Solutions

Solution to Question 17-1. The purpose of a delegate is to decouple the method(s) called from the calling code. It allows the designer of an object to define the delegate, and the user of the object to define which method will be called when the delegate is invoked.

Solution to Question 17-2. Delegates are reference types, but instead of referring to an object, they refer to a method.

Solution to Question 17-3. You instantiate a previously defined delegate named OnPhoneRings like this:

```
OnPhoneRings myDelegate = new OnPhoneRings(myMethod);
```

Solution to Question 17-4. The following is the standard way to define a delegate for an event handler:

```
public delegate void PhoneRangHandler
( object sender, EventArgs e );
```

You then use the event keyword to restrict the delegate such that it can be invoked only by the defining class:

```
public event PhoneRangHandler PhoneHasRung;
```

Solution to Question 17-5. Here is how to call a delegated method:

```
PhoneHasRung(this, new EventArgs());
```

Solution to Question 17-6. The event keyword limits the use of the delegate in the following ways:

- You can only add a method using +=.
- You can only remove a method using -=.
- The delegate can be invoked only by the class that defines it.

Solution to Question 17-7. To pass information to the method called through the event, define the delegate to take as its second parameter an object of a type derived from EventArgs. Pass the information through properties of that object.

Solution to Question 17-8. System.EventArgs has no methods or properties other than those it inherits from Object, and a public, static field named Empty. The point of System.EventArgs is that it allows you to derive a class that contains whatever properties you need to pass to the event handlers.

Solution to Question 17-9. Rather than creating a method that matches the delegate's signature and then assigning the name of that method to the delegate, anonymous methods allow you to directly assign an unnamed delegate method by providing the implementation in line with the assignment.

Solution to Question 17-10. A lambda expression doesn't return a type, but rather a reference to a method. Lambda expressions are similar to anonymous methods, but they have applications outside of event handlers.

Exercise Solutions

Solution to Exercise 17-1. Write a countdown alarm program that uses delegates to notify anyone who is interested that the designated amount of time has passed. You'll need a class to simulate the countdown clock that accepts a message and a number of seconds to wait (supplied by the user). After waiting the appropriate amount of time, the countdown clock should fire off an event and pass the message to any registered observers. (When you're calculating the time to wait, remember that Thread.Sleep( ) takes an argument in milliseconds, and requires a using System. Threading statement.) Create an observer class as well that echoes the received message to the console.

The CountDownClock example isn't that much different from the Clock example you saw in the chapter, although it behaves a bit differently. In Tester.Run( ), you ask the user for a string message, and a number of seconds to wait, which you then pass to the instance of CountDownClock. To wait the appropriate number of seconds, you simply use Thread.Sleep(seconds * 1000) so that you're waiting for seconds instead of milliseconds. Once the appropriate amount of time has passed, you check to see whether the event has any subscribers, and then call the delegate. You'll need to create a class that derives from EventArgs to hold the message, and pass that to the delegate.

The observer class is relatively simple. It needs to create an event handler that echoes the message to the console, and register that event handler with the delegate. We haven't used the event keyword in this exercise, so this handler is still "dangerous."

 When you're testing this program, be sure to use a relatively small amount of time to wait, or you could be staring at an inactive console for some time.

There are, as always, many ways to solve this exercise. One way is shown in Example A-50.

Example A-50. One solution to Exercise 17-1

```csharp
using System;
using System.Collections.Generic;
using System.Linq;
using System.Text;
using System.Threading;

namespace Exercise_17_1
{
    // a class to hold the message to display
    public class CountDownClockEventArgs : EventArgs
    {
        public string message;
        public CountDownClockEventArgs(string message)
        {
            this.message = message;
        }
    }
    // The publisher; the class to which other
    // classes will subscribe. Provides the delegate TimeExpired
    // that fires when the requested amount of time has passed
    public class CountDownClock
    {
        private int seconds;
        private string message;

        // tell me the message to display, and how many seconds to wait

        public CountDownClock(string message, int seconds)
        {
            this.message = message;
            this.seconds = seconds;
        }

        // the delegate
        public delegate void TimesUpEventHandler
        (
            object countDownClock,
            CountDownClockEventArgs alarmInformation
        );

        // an instance of the delegate
        public TimesUpEventHandler TimeExpired;
        // Wait until time has elapsed, then check to see
        // if anyone is listening, and send the message
        public void Run()
        {
            // sleep until time has elapsed
            Thread.Sleep(seconds * 1000);
            if (TimeExpired != null)
            {
                // Create the CountDownClockEventArgs to hold the message
```

Example A-50. One solution to Exercise 17-1 (continued)

```
            CountDownClockEventArgs e =
                    new CountDownClockEventArgs(this.message);
            // fire the event
            TimeExpired(this, e);
        }
    }
}


// an observer
public class CountDownTimerDisplay
{
    CountDownClock.TimesUpEventHandler myHandler;
    public CountDownTimerDisplay(CountDownClock cdc)
    {
        myHandler = new CountDownClock.TimesUpEventHandler(TimeExpired);
        // register the event handler and start the timer
        cdc.TimeExpired += myHandler;
    }
    // Alert the user that the time has expired
    public void TimeExpired(object theClock, CountDownClockEventArgs e)
    {
        Console.WriteLine("You requested to receive this message: {0}",
                        e.message);
    }
}
// an observer.
public class Tester
{
    public void Run( )
    {
        Console.Write("Enter your alert message: ");
        string message = Console.ReadLine( );

        // Ask for how many seconds to wait
        Console.Write("How many seconds to wait? ");
        int seconds = Convert.ToInt32(Console.ReadLine( ));

        // Create the clock class
        CountDownClock cdc = new CountDownClock(message, seconds);

        // Create the observer class
        CountDownTimerDisplay display = new CountDownTimerDisplay(cdc);
        cdc.Run( );
    }
}
public class Program
{
    public static void Main( )
    {
        Tester t = new Tester( );
        t.Run( );
    }
```

Example A-50. One solution to Exercise 17-1 (continued)

```
    }
}
```

Solution to Exercise 17-2. Change the program you wrote in Exercise 17-1 to ensure that the event can be published to multiple handlers safely.

The event keyword guarantees that the event the CountDownClock is publishing can only be subscribed to or unsubscribed from. This change is easy, so we won't show the whole code here. The relevant portion is shown in Example A-51.

Example A-51. The solution to Exercise 17-2

```
// the delegate
public delegate void TimesUpEventHandler
(
    object countDownClock,
    CountDownClockEventArgs alarmInformation
);

// an instance of the delegate
public event TimesUpEventHandler TimeExpired;
```

Solution to Exercise 17-3. Rewrite the observer class in Exercise 17-2 to use an anonymous method.

You may have noticed that the event handler method in Exercises 17-1 and 17-2 is pretty simple; all it does is output the message to the console. This is a perfect candidate for an anonymous method. To make the method anonymous, you need to delete the code that instantiates the handler, and instead move the call to Console. WriteLine to the line that registers the handler. The only changes here are to the observer class, so that's all that Example A-52 shows.

Example A-52. The solution to Exercise 17-3

```
public class CountDownTimerDisplay
{
    public CountDownTimerDisplay(CountDownClock cdc)
    {
        // register the event handler and start the timer
        cdc.TimeExpired += delegate(object theClock, CountDownClockEventArgs e)
        {
            Console.WriteLine("You requested to receive this message: {0}",
                            e.message);
        };
    }
}
```

Solution to Exercise 17-4.   Rewrite the observer class in Exercise 17-3 to use a lambda expression instead of an anonymous method.

Again, the only change you have to make is to the event registration code in the observer class. You need to remove the keyword delegate and insert the lambda operator =>. You don't actually need the braces, since the method is only one statement, but it doesn't hurt to leave them in, either. Example A-53 shows the solution.

Example A-53. The solution to Exercise 17-4

```
public class CountDownTimerDisplay
{
    public CountDownTimerDisplay(CountDownClock cdc)
    {
        // register the event handler and start the timer
        cdc.TimeExpired += (object theClock, CountDownClockEventArgs e) =>
        {
            Console.WriteLine("You requested to receive this message: {0}",
                            e.message);
        };
    }
}
```

Chapter 18: Creating Windows Applications

Quiz Solutions

Solution to Question 18-1.   The various widgets on a Windows form are all known as *controls*.

Solution to Question 18-2.   To add a `Button` control to a Windows form in Visual Studio, simply drag the `Button` from the Toolbox onto the form wherever you want it. Visual Studio takes care of the code to initialize the control.

Solution to Question 18-3.   To set the properties of a control, click on the control on the form. This causes the control's properties to appear in the Properties window. From the Properties window, you can set a number of available properties for each control.

Solution to Question 18-4.   Windows is an event-driven environment in that the code initializes forms that wait to respond to user or system actions—events—rather than running procedurally from start to finish.

Solution to Question 18-5.   To make a button respond to being clicked, you need to create an event handler to handle the `Click` event for the button.

Solution to Question 18-6. The two ways to create an event handler in Visual Studio are as follows:

- Go to the Properties window, click on the lightning bolt button to open the events, and then fill in a name or double-click next to the event to let Visual Studio create the name.
- Double-click on the control to create the default handler with a name provided by Visual Studio.

Solution to Question 18-7. When you create an event handler for a control on your form, Visual Studio automatically takes you to the code page of your form.

Solution to Question 18-8. The partial keyword indicates that the code page you see in Visual Studio is not the complete class for the form. Visual Studio hides the initialization code for the controls, so you don't need to worry about it.

Solution to Question 18-9. Call the Application.Exit( ) method to close the application.

Solution to Question 18-10. Recursion is a method that is calling itself (such as calling MethodA( ) from within the body of MethodA( )).

Exercise Solutions

Solution to Exercise 18-1. Create a Windows application that displays the word "Hello" in a label, and has a button that changes the display to "Goodbye".

This exercise is similar to the Hello World exercise from earlier in the chapter. You've seen how to add a Label control and a Button control, and how to change their Text and font properties accordingly, so setting up that much is simple.

What you need now is an event handler to change the text of the label when the button is clicked. You've seen how to set the Text property elsewhere in this chapter, so that's not too hard. Here is the event handler for the button:

```
private void button1_Click( object sender, EventArgs e )
{
    label1.Text = "Goodbye";
}
```

Of course, once the text of the label has changed, you can't change it back. You could add an if statement that changes the text from "Hello" to "Goodbye", or vice versa, every time the button is clicked. You can see the full source code solution to Exercise 18-1 on the website for this book, although there isn't much to it. Figure A-5 is a picture of the form.

Figure A-5. Exercise 18-1: The form.

Solution to Exercise 18-2. Modify the first exercise by dragging a timer (found in the Components section of the Toolbox) onto the form and having the timer change the message from "Hello" to "Goodbye" and back once per second. Change the button to turn this behavior on and off. Use the Microsoft Help files to figure out how to use the timer to accomplish this exercise.

Here are the steps you need to follow:

1. Create a new project named Exercise 18-2.

2. Set the form to the size of the form in Exercise 18-1 (213, 119).

3. Optionally copy the two controls (label and button) from the first exercise (or drag on new ones).

4. Set the form's text to "Hello Goodbye". Set the Text of the button to "Start".

5. Drag a Timer control from the Components section of the Toolbox onto the form. It won't show up on the form itself; it will appear in a special section at the bottom of the window called the *tray*, as shown in Figure A-6.

6. Set the timer's Interval property to 1,000 and its Enabled property to false. This ensures that the timer won't start until the button is clicked at least once.

7. Double-click on the timer to create the timer1_Tick event handler, which will fire every 1,000 milliseconds (every 1 second).

8. Add a Boolean property (which we've called isHello) to the class, outside the methods, and initialize it to true.

9. Add the following code to the timer1_Tick handler. This code will alternate the text in the label by checking (and changing) the Boolean value isHello:

```
private void timer1_Tick(object sender, EventArgs e)
{
    isHello = !isHello;
    if (isHello)
    {
        label1.Text = "Hello";
    }
    else
```

```
            {
                label1.Text = "Goodbye";
            }
        }
    }
```

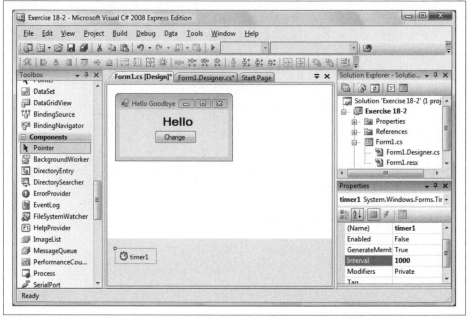

Figure A-6. Adding the timer.

10. Change the button1_Click event handler, adding the following code. This code will test whether the timer is running (if so, its IsEnabled property is true) to start the timer and set the button's text to "Stop", or to stop the timer and set the button's text to "Start":

```
private void button1_Click(object sender, EventArgs e)
{
    if (!timer1.Enabled)
    {
        timer1.Start( );
        this.button1.Text = "Stop";
    }
    else
    {
        timer1.Stop( );
        this.button1.Text = "Start";
    }
}
```

The source code for this example is presented in Example A-54.

Example A-54. Using a timer to switch the message every second

```csharp
using System;
using System.Collections.Generic;
using System.ComponentModel;
using System.Data;
using System.Drawing;
using System.Linq;
using System.Text;
using System.Windows.Forms;

namespace Exercise_18_2
{
    public partial class frmHelloGoodbye : Form
    {
        bool isHello = true;
        public frmHelloGoodbye()
        {
            InitializeComponent();
        }

        private void button1_Click(object sender, EventArgs e)
        {
            if (!timer1.Enabled)
            {
                timer1.Start();
                this.button1.Text = "Stop";
            }
            else
            {
                timer1.Stop();
                this.button1.Text = "Start";
            }
        }

        private void timer1_Tick(object sender, EventArgs e)
        {
            isHello = !isHello;
            if (isHello)
            {
                label1.Text = "Hello";
            }
            else
            {
                label1.Text = "Goodbye";
            }
        }
    }
}
```

Solution to Exercise 18-3. Create a Windows application that calculates sales tax for a given amount. The user can enter an amount in a text box, and then can enter a sales tax between 0 and 25%, in increments of 0.25%. When the user clicks the Submit button, the tax is calculated, and both the tax and the total are output in a label. The application should look something like Figure A-7 when it runs.

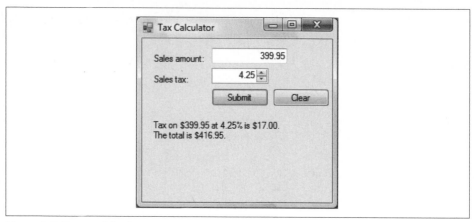

Figure A-7. Your goal for Exercise 18-3.

The amount is entered in a Textbox control, but for the tax, you want to restrict the values the user can enter, so you should use a numericUpDown control—use the Help files or IntelliSense to examine the properties for that control and figure out how to use them to your advantage. There's a Clear button that clears the "Amount" TextBox when clicked.

To output a double with two decimal places, use ToString("F"). The F applies the two-decimal-place formatting. You may also want to implement some exception handling to ensure that the user enters a number in the TextBox.

The C# code in this exercise is mostly trivial, but the point is to extract the values from the controls, use them, and then output them to the user. As always, the exact names and layout of the controls are up to you, but we'll show you how we did it. Start by setting up your form. Set the Text property of the form itself to "Tax Calculator". Then add two label controls (lblAmount and lblTax); these don't do anything except provide label text for the controls, so set their Text properties as you see in the figure. Then add a TextBox control (txtAmount). Set the TextAlign property to Right, to make it a bit neater. You can't really restrict what a user enters in a TextBox, so you'll need some exception handling later.

The control in this exercise that you're probably not familiar with is the numericUpDown control. Although the amount can be any numeric value, the tax is strictly defined—between 0 and 25, in increments of 0.25. The numericUpDown control has properties that allow those restrictions. Call your control nudTax, set its Maximum property to 25, leave the Minimum property at 0 (the default), and set the Increment property to 0.25. That takes care of the numeric requirements. Set the TextAlign property to Right, so it'll line up with the TextBox.

Now you'll need two buttons: btnSubmit, and btnClear. Set the Text properties for each of these as you see in the figure. We'll come back to the event handlers in a minute.

The last control you need is a Label to show the output. Place it below the buttons, call it lblResult, and delete its Text property for the moment.

Now you need event handlers for the two buttons. The handler for btnClear is simple. You just want to clear the TextBox, so simply call txtAmount.Clear( ).

The handler for btnSubmit is where you'll do the work. The only tricky bit here is that the text entered in txtAmount is a string, so you'll need to convert it to a double if you want to work with it. Fortunately, Convert.ToDouble( ) works just fine there. The numericUpDown control doesn't have a Text property—because it can hold only numeric values, it has a Value property instead. The first thing to do is calculate the amount of the tax:

```
double tax = Convert.ToDouble(txtAmount.Text) *
    (Convert.ToDouble(nudTax.Value) * 0.01);
```

Then add the tax to the amount:

```
double total = Convert.ToDouble(txtAmount.Text) + tax;
```

The tax and total variables are doubles, so you'll need to convert them back to strings before you can add them to the result string. That's where the ToString("F") method comes in:

```
string resultString = "Tax on $"
                    + txtAmount.Text
                    + " at "
                    + nudTax.Value
                    + "% is $"
                    + tax.ToString("F")
                    + ".\nThe total is $"
                    + total.ToString("F")
                    + ".";
```

Now just assign the result string to the Text property of lblResult:

```
lblResult.Text = resultString;
```

This application will work fine, assuming the user enters only a numeric value in the TextBox. Users can't always be trusted that way, though, so you should wrap the code you've written so far in a try block, and add a catch block for a FormatException, which is the kind of exception that will be raised if the user enters letters in the TextBox. There are lots of different ways to deal with the exception; we chose to pop up a MessageBox that explains the problem, and then we clear the TextBox as well:

```
catch (FormatException)
{
    DialogResult error = MessageBox.Show(
```

```
            "Please enter a number",
            "Format Error",
            MessageBoxButtons.OK,
            MessageBoxIcon.Error);
        txtAmount.Clear();
    }
```

The code for the *Form1.cs* file is shown in Example A-55.

Example A-55. One solution to Exercise 18-3

```
using System;
using System.Collections.Generic;
using System.ComponentModel;
using System.Data;
using System.Drawing;
using System.Linq;
using System.Text;
using System.Windows.Forms;

namespace Exercise_18_3
{
    public partial class Form1 : Form
    {
        public Form1()
        {
            InitializeComponent();
        }

        private void btnSubmit_Click(object sender, EventArgs e)
        {
            try
            {
                double tax = Convert.ToDouble(txtAmount.Text) *
                        (Convert.ToDouble(nudTax.Value) * 0.01);
                double total = Convert.ToDouble(txtAmount.Text)
                            + tax;
                string resultString = "Tax on $"
                                    + txtAmount.Text
                                    + " at "
                                    + nudTax.Value
                                    + "% is $"
                                    + tax.ToString("F")
                                    + ".\nThe total is $"
                                    + total.ToString("F")
                                    + ".";

                lblResult.Text = resultString;
            }
            catch (FormatException)
            {
                DialogResult error = MessageBox.Show(
                    "Please enter a number",
                    "Format Error",
```

```
                MessageBoxButtons.OK,
                MessageBoxIcon.Error);
            txtAmount.Clear();
        }
    }

    private void btnClear_Click(object sender, EventArgs e)
    {
        txtAmount.Clear();
    }

  }
}
```

Chapter 19: Windows Presentation Foundation

Quiz Solutions

Solution to Question 19-1.   XAML is a subset of XML intended for use with WPF. It has a schema created by Microsoft with elements for Windows applications.

Solution to Question 19-2.   You can edit the properties of a XAML element in the Properties window, or directly in the XAML window. Either way, any changes you make will immediately be reflected in the Design window.

Solution to Question 19-3.   The x: refers to the current namespace for the application. You need to use it to define properties that will be used elsewhere in the application.

Solution to Question 19-4.   The Margin property takes four comma-separated values, representing the distance, in units, from the left, top, right, and bottom of the window. A zero for any of the values indicates that the distance is not fixed.

Solution to Question 19-5.   When you have a number of controls of the same type, you could style each control individually, but it would be easier to define a Style element as a resource.

Solution to Question 19-6.   The TargetType property, applied to a Style, restricts the style to a certain type of control.

Solution to Question 19-7.   The Trigger element is used for handling events within the XAML file.

Solution to Question 19-8.   Animations are contained in Storyboard controls.

Solution to Question 19-9. A `Trigger` element can contain a storyboard action, but not a `Storyboard` element directly. The `BeginStoryboard` element provides that action, and can contain a storyboard.

Solution to Question 19-10. The `DataContext` property allows an element to access a data source.

Exercise Solutions

Solution to Exercise 19-1. We'll start things off simply. Create a WPF application with several `Button` and `TextBox` controls. Set the `TextBox` controls to have white text on a blue background, and the `Button` controls to have green text on a gray background.

This exercise isn't particularly challenging, but it does enable you to practice the use of styles. You first create a new WPF project. Then drag several `Button` and `TextBox` controls onto the form; it doesn't matter where. You could certainly copy the same `Style` attributes to each control, but that's a pain. Instead, you should define a style resource for each control in the `Windows.Resources` section. Remember to give each style an `x:Key` property so that you can reference it later from within the controls, and remember to have each control reference the style as a `StaticResource`. Example A-56 shows the full XAML file for this exercise.

Example A-56. One solution to Exercise 19-1

```
<Window x:Class="Exercise_19_1.Window1"
    xmlns="http://schemas.microsoft.com/winfx/2006/xaml/presentation"
    xmlns:x="http://schemas.microsoft.com/winfx/2006/xaml"
    Title="Window1" Height="300" Width="300">
    <Window.Resources>
        <Style x:Key="buttonStyle" TargetType="Button">
            <Setter Property="Foreground" Value="White" />
            <Setter Property="Background" Value="Blue" />
        </Style>
        <Style x:Key="textboxStyle" TargetType="TextBox">
            <Setter Property="Foreground" Value="Green" />
            <Setter Property="Background" Value="Gray" />
        </Style>
    </Window.Resources>
    <Grid>
        <TextBox Style="{StaticResource textboxStyle}" Height="23" Margin="19,56,139,0"
Name="textBox1" VerticalAlignment="Top">TextBox1</TextBox>
        <Button Style="{StaticResource buttonStyle}" Height="23"
HorizontalAlignment="Right" Margin="0,38,51,0" Name="button1" VerticalAlignment="Top"
Width="75">Buttton1</Button>
        <Button Style="{StaticResource buttonStyle}" HorizontalAlignment="Left"
Margin="34,115,0,124" Name="button2" Width="75">Button2</Button>
        <TextBox Style="{StaticResource textboxStyle}" HorizontalAlignment="Right"
Margin="0,109,3,130" Name="textBox2" Width="120">TextBox2</TextBox>
```

```
        <Button Style="{StaticResource buttonStyle}" Height="23"
HorizontalAlignment="Right" Margin="0,0,37,56" Name="button3" VerticalAlignment="Bottom"
Width="75">Button3</Button>
        <TextBox Style="{StaticResource textboxStyle}" Height="23" Margin="19,0,139,55.48"
Name="textBox3" VerticalAlignment="Bottom">TextBox3</TextBox>
    </Grid>
</Window>
```

Solution to Exercise 19-2. Now you'll create your own animation. Create a WPF application with a single Button control (it doesn't have to do anything). Add an animation that increases the size of the button from the standard size to 300 units wide by 200 units high, and then reverses itself.

All you're doing in this exercise is creating a simple animation. Start by placing a standard Button control on the form; it doesn't matter where. Within the Button element, place a Triggers element. Remember that triggers require an action, so within the Triggers section, place a BeginStoryboard element. Inside that, place a Storyboard element, and inside the storyboard, a DoubleAnimation—the Height and Width properties are of type double. From there, it's easy to define an animation that targets the Button control and changes the Height.

You'll need to define a second DoubleAnimation element to change the Width property of the Button, but this animation is easy; it's nearly identical to the first. You can place both in the same storyboard.

The standard size of a default Button control is 23 high × 75 wide, which you could find out from the Properties window for the Button, but you don't actually need to know that. If you omit the From attribute in the animation, WPF will use the existing values as the default.

The full XAML for this exercise is shown in Example A-57.

Example A-57. The XAML for Exercise 19-2

```
<Window x:Class="Exercise_19_2.Window1"
    xmlns="http://schemas.microsoft.com/winfx/2006/xaml/presentation"
    xmlns:x="http://schemas.microsoft.com/winfx/2006/xaml"
    Title="Window1" Height="300" Width="300">
    <Grid>
        <Button Height="23" Margin="55,44,0,0" Name="button1"
                VerticalAlignment="Top" HorizontalAlignment="Left"
                Width="75" Content="Button">
            <Button.Triggers>
                <EventTrigger RoutedEvent="Button.Loaded">
                    <BeginStoryboard>
                        <Storyboard>
                            <DoubleAnimation
                                Storyboard.TargetName="button1"
                                Storyboard.TargetProperty="Height"
                                To="200" Duration="0:0:5"
```

Example A-57. The XAML for Exercise 19-2 (continued)

```
                                AutoReverse="True"
                                RepeatBehavior="Forever" />
                    <DoubleAnimation
                        Storyboard.TargetName="button1"
                        Storyboard.TargetProperty="Width"
                        To="300" Duration="0:0:5"
                        AutoReverse="True"
                        RepeatBehavior="Forever" />
                </Storyboard>
            </BeginStoryboard>
        </EventTrigger>
    </Button.Triggers>

    </Button>
</Grid>
</Window>
```

Solution to Exercise 19-3.   Create a rectangle, 100×200. Add three buttons to the application: one to rotate the rectangle clockwise, the second to rotate it counterclockwise, and the third to stop the rotation.

The point to this exercise is to connect two separate triggers to the same property, specifically, the RotateTransform property of the rectangle. This isn't actually too difficult; you simply have two triggers with the same target. The Stop button also needs to stop both storyboards, but that's not difficult either.

The XAML for this exercise is shown in Example A-58.

Example A-58. One solution to Exercise 19-3

```
<Window x:Class="Exercise_19_3.Window1"
    xmlns="http://schemas.microsoft.com/winfx/2006/xaml/presentation"
    xmlns:x="http://schemas.microsoft.com/winfx/2006/xaml"
    Title="Window1" Height="311" Width="295">
    <Window.Triggers>
        <EventTrigger RoutedEvent="ButtonBase.Click"
                    SourceName="btnClockwise">
            <BeginStoryboard Name="rotateClockwise">
                <Storyboard>
                    <DoubleAnimation Storyboard.TargetName="rectRotate"
                                    Storyboard.TargetProperty="Angle"
                                    From="0.0" To="360.0" Duration="0:0:10"
                                    RepeatBehavior="Forever"/>
                </Storyboard>
            </BeginStoryboard>
        </EventTrigger>
        <EventTrigger RoutedEvent="ButtonBase.Click"
                    SourceName="btnCounterclockwise">
            <BeginStoryboard  Name="rotateCounterclockwise">
                <Storyboard>
                    <DoubleAnimation Storyboard.TargetName="rectRotate"
```

```
                               Storyboard.TargetProperty="Angle"
                               From="360.0" To="0.0" Duration="0:0:10"
                               RepeatBehavior="Forever"/>
                       </Storyboard>
                   </BeginStoryboard>
               </EventTrigger>
               <EventTrigger RoutedEvent="ButtonBase.Click" SourceName="btnStop">
                   <PauseStoryboard BeginStoryboardName="rotateClockwise" />
                   <PauseStoryboard BeginStoryboardName="rotateCounterclockwise" />
               </EventTrigger>
           </Window.Triggers>

       <Grid>
           <Rectangle Margin="110,21,113,0" Name="myRectangle" Stroke="Black"
                     Height="100" VerticalAlignment="Top"
                     RenderTransformOrigin="0.5,0.5" Fill="Cyan">
               <Rectangle.RenderTransform>
                   <RotateTransform x:Name="rectRotate" Angle="0.0" />
               </Rectangle.RenderTransform>
           </Rectangle>
           <Button Height="23" HorizontalAlignment="Left" Margin="20,0,0,106"
                   Name="btnClockwise" VerticalAlignment="Bottom"
                   Width="75">Clockwise</Button>
           <Button Height="23" HorizontalAlignment="Right" Margin="0,0,26,106"
                   Name="btnCounterclockwise" VerticalAlignment="Bottom"
                   Width="109">Counterclockwise</Button>
           <Button Height="23" Margin="100,0,103,58" Name="btnStop"
                   VerticalAlignment="Bottom">Stop</Button>
       </Grid>
   </Window>
```

Chapter 20: ADO.NET and Relational Databases

Quiz Solutions

Solution to Question 20-1. In a relational database, the data is organized into tables, and the queries are defined by the relationships among the tables.

Solution to Question 20-2. A primary key is a column that contains values that are unique to the table in which it resides, which allows you to uniquely identify each row.

Solution to Question 20-3. A foreign key is a column in a table that is also the primary key in a different table. This allows you to identify the relationship among the tables.

Solution to Question 20-4. To retrieve the contents of the Title column in the Books table the appropriate query would be:

```
Select Title from Books
```

Solution to Question 20-5. To retrieve the contents of the Author column where the value in the Publisher column is "OReilly", the appropriate query would be:

```
Select Author from Books where Publisher = 'OReilly'
```

Solution to Question 20-6. You would want to use a join when you want to filter the information retrieved from one table based on the contents of a different table.

Solution to Question 20-7. The DataSet object represents a subset of retrieved data, and can be used to view or manipulate the data.

Solution to Question 20-8. One good way to view the rows in a DataTable object is to iterate over the Rows collection with a foreach loop.

Solution to Question 20-9. The DataAdapter class provides the bridge between your application and the database. The DataAdapter can take a connection string and a query string, and can then be used to provide that data to a DataSet object.

Solution to Question 20-10. Use the DataAdapter.Fill( ) method to transfer the data to a DataSet for manipulation.

Exercise Solutions

Solution to Exercise 20-1. Let's start with a simple exercise. The Northwind database contains a table named Orders. Write a program to retrieve the order date and shipped date of all the records in the Orders table.

This exercise is, as we said, rather simple. The code from Example 20-1 serves nicely as a template. However, Example 20-1 uses the Customers table, and we specified the Orders table. You can expand the *Tables* folder in the Database Explorer to see the various tables available in Northwind, and then expand the Orders table to see the various columns, which include OrderDate and ShippedDate. From there, it's just a matter of rewriting the command string, like this:

```
string commandString = "Select OrderDate, ShippedDate from Orders";
```

Example A-59 has the full code for this exercise.

Example A-59. One solution to Exercise 20-1

```
using System;
using System.Collections.Generic;
using System.Linq;
using System.Text;
using System.Data;
using System.Data.SqlClient;
```

Example A-59. One solution to Exercise 20-1 (continued)

```csharp
namespace Exercise_20_1
{
    class Program
    {
        static void Main(string[] args)
        {
            // create the data connection
            string connectionString = "server=.\\sqlexpress; " +
                    "Trusted_Connection=yes;database=Northwind";

            // create the string to hold the SQL command
            // to get records from the Customers table
            string commandString =
                "Select OrderDate, ShippedDate from Orders";

            // create the data adapter with the
            // connection string and command
            SqlDataAdapter myDataAdapter =
                new SqlDataAdapter(commandString, connectionString);

            // Create and fill the DataSet object
            DataSet myDataSet = new DataSet();
            myDataAdapter.Fill(myDataSet);

            // Retrieve the Orders table
            DataTable myDataTable = myDataSet.Tables[0];

            // iterate over the rows collection and output the fields
            foreach (DataRow dataRow in myDataTable.Rows)
            {
                Console.WriteLine("Order Date: {0}. Shipped Date: {1}",
                        dataRow["OrderDate"], dataRow["ShippedDate"]);
            }

        }
    }
}
```

Solution to Exercise 20-2. We'll try something slightly more complicated now. Write a program to display the name and ID of products with fewer than 10 units in stock.

This is another rather simple exercise, again focusing on the command string. This time, you need to include a where clause in your string. From the Products table, you want to retrieve the ProductID and ProductName columns, if the UnitsInStock column is less than 10. Note that you don't actually retrieve the UnitsInStock column; you only use it to determine which records to retrieve. The command string looks like this:

```csharp
string commandString = "Select ProductID, ProductName
                        from Products where UnitsInStock < 10";
```

The full listing for this exercise is shown in Example A-60.

Example A-60. One solution to Exercise 20-2

```csharp
using System;
using System.Collections.Generic;
using System.Linq;
using System.Text;
using System.Data;
using System.Data.SqlClient;

namespace Exercise_20_2
{
    class Program
    {
        static void Main(string[] args)
        {
            // create the data connection
            string connectionString = "server=.\\sqlexpress; " +
                    "Trusted_Connection=yes;database=Northwind";

            // create the string to hold the SQL command
            // to get records from the Customers table
            string commandString = "Select ProductID, " +
                    "ProductName from Products " +
                    "where UnitsInStock < 10";

            // create the data adapter with the
            // connection string and command
            SqlDataAdapter myDataAdapter =
                new SqlDataAdapter(commandString, connectionString);

            // Create and fill the DataSet object
            DataSet myDataSet = new DataSet();
            myDataAdapter.Fill(myDataSet);

            // Retrieve the Orders table
            DataTable myDataTable = myDataSet.Tables[0];

            // iterate over the rows collection
            // and output the fields
            Console.WriteLine(
                    "Products with less than 10 units in stock:");
            foreach (DataRow dataRow in myDataTable.Rows)
            {
                Console.WriteLine("ProductID: {0} \tProduct Name: {1}",
                    dataRow["ProductID"], dataRow["ProductName"]);
            }

        }
    }
}
```

The output looks like this, if you want to check your results:

```
Products with less than 10 units in stock:
ProductID: 5    Product Name: Chef Anton's Gumbo Mix
ProductID: 8    Product Name: Northwoods Cranberry Sauce
ProductID: 17   Product Name: Alice Mutton
ProductID: 21   Product Name: Sir Rodney's Scones
ProductID: 29   Product Name: Thüringer Rostbratwurst
ProductID: 31   Product Name: Gorgonzola Telino
ProductID: 32   Product Name: Mascarpone Fabioli
ProductID: 45   Product Name: Rogede sild
ProductID: 53   Product Name: Perth Pasties
ProductID: 66   Product Name: Louisiana Hot Spiced Okra
ProductID: 68   Product Name: Scottish Longbreads
ProductID: 74   Product Name: Longlife Tofu
```

(Somebody needs to order more of Chef Anton's Gumbo Mix.) If you want to check your results against what's in the database itself, right-click on the Products table in Database Explorer and select Show Table Data.

Solution to Exercise 20-3. Now for an exercise that involves multiple tables. Write a program to display the first and last names of the employees in region 1.

This exercise involves the join keyword, and requires you to look around in the tables a bit. If you open the Region table, you'll find the RegionID column, which is the value you want to compare. But the Region table doesn't mention EmployeeIDs. The Employees table has a column EmployeeID, which is a good start, and a column Region, but the values there don't match up with any columns in the Region table. Instead, you need to look at the EmployeeTerritories table. You can join Employees to EmployeeTerritories on the EmployeeID column. The only other column in the EmployeeTerritories table is the TerritoryID column, which is the foreign key for the Territories table. In the Territories table, you'll find the TerritoryID column, and—aha!—the RegionID column. So, you can craft a query like this:

```
string commandString = "select e.FirstName, e.LastName "+
                    "from Employees e "+
                    "join EmployeeTerritories et on e.EmployeeID =
                            et.EmployeeID "+
                    "join Territories t on et.TerritoryID =
                            t.TerritoryID "+
                    "join Region r on t.RegionID = r.RegionID "+
                    "where r.RegionID = 1";
```

The where clause checks for the employees in region 1, and the three join clauses chain back up to the Employees table, where you select the first and last name fields. The full code for this exercise is found in Example A-61.

Example A-61. The solution to Exercise 20-3

```csharp
using System;
using System.Collections.Generic;
using System.Linq;
using System.Text;
using System.Data;
using System.Data.SqlClient;

namespace Exercise_20_3
{
    class Program
    {
        static void Main(string[] args)
        {
            // create the data connection
            string connectionString = "server=.\\sqlexpress; " +
                    "Trusted_Connection=yes;database=Northwind";

            // create the string to hold the SQL command
            // to get records from the Customers table
            string commandString = "select e.FirstName, e.LastName " +
                                "from Employees e "+
                                "join EmployeeTerritories et on " +
                                "e.EmployeeID = et.EmployeeID " +
                                "join Territories t on et.TerritoryID = " +
                                "t.TerritoryID "+
                                "join Region r on t.RegionID = " +
                                "r.RegionID " +
                                "where r.RegionID = 1";

            // create the data adapter with the
            // connection string and command
            SqlDataAdapter myDataAdapter =
                new SqlDataAdapter(commandString, connectionString);

            // Create and fill the DataSet object
            DataSet myDataSet = new DataSet();
            myDataAdapter.Fill(myDataSet);

            // Retrieve the Orders table
            DataTable myDataTable = myDataSet.Tables[0];

            // iterate over the rows collection
            // and output the fields
            Console.WriteLine("Employees in Region 1:");
            foreach (DataRow dataRow in myDataTable.Rows)
            {
                Console.WriteLine("{0} {1}",
                    dataRow["FirstName"], dataRow["LastName"]);
            }

        }
```

Example A-61. The solution to Exercise 20-3 (continued)

```
    }
}
```

Chapter 21: LINQ

Quiz Solutions

Solution to Question 21-1. LINQ allows you to query several different types of data sources, including SQL Server databases, XML files, and in-memory collections.

Solution to Question 21-2. A LINQ query returns a collection that implements IEnumerable. The type of the objects in the collection is irrelevant.

Solution to Question 21-3. The select keyword returns the result of a LINQ query.

Solution to Question 21-4. You don't need to use any special syntax to return a complex type from a LINQ query. The compiler can infer the type, even if it's unnamed.

Solution to Question 21-5. The range variable in a LINQ query doesn't have to be any type; it just has to be a valid C# name. The compiler will infer its type.

Solution to Question 21-6. The lambda expression in a LINQ query returns a method used to evaluate the data set. That data is projected onto the range variable.

Solution to Question 21-7. When you use LINQ to SQL, you need to add a reference to the System.Data.Linq namespace, not the System.Linq namespace that's added by default and supports all the basic LINQ functions.

Solution to Question 21-8. Use the [Table] attribute, with the Name of the table to define a class as representing a SQL table.

Solution to Question 21-9. To add table classes in the Object Relational Designer, you must establish a connection to the database, and then simply drag the tables onto the design surface. The classes will be generated for you automatically.

Solution to Question 21-10. The constructor of the data context class using the Object Relational Designer doesn't require any parameters; it's generated automatically.

Exercise Solutions

Solution to Exercise 21-1. For the first exercise in this chapter, we're going to bring back the good old Box class from earlier in the book. It's a quick and easy class, with Length, Width, and Height properties, and a quick method to display a box. Here's the code for the class:

```
public class Box
{
    public int Length { get; set; }
    public int Width { get; set; }
    public int Height { get; set; }

    public void DisplayBox()
    {
        Console.WriteLine("{0}x{1}x{2}",
                Length, Width, Height);
    }
}
```

Create a List of Box objects, at least five, with dimensions and colors of whatever you like, and then use a LINQ query to extract all those boxes with a Length and Width greater than 3.

The challenge here isn't in creating the List; that's simple enough. Once you have that created, you need to issue the correct query. Here's one that works:

```
IEnumerable<Box> resultList =
    from myBox in boxList
    where myBox.Length > 3 && myBox.Width > 3
    select myBox;
```

You know you're dealing with a collection of Box objects, so you don't need to use an anonymous type here. Example A-62 shows the solution to this exercise.

Example A-62. The solution to Exercise 21-1

```
using System;
using System.Collections.Generic;
using System.Linq;
using System.Text;

namespace Exercise_21_1
{
    public class Box
    {
        public int Length { get; set; }
        public int Width { get; set; }
        public int Height { get; set; }

        public void DisplayBox()
        {
```

Example A-62. The solution to Exercise 21-1 (continued)

```
        Console.WriteLine("{0}x{1}x{2}", Length, Width, Height);
    }
}

class Program
{
    static void Main(string[] args)
    {
        List<Box> boxList = new List<Box>
        {
            new Box { Length = 4,
                      Width = 6,
                      Height = 2 },
            new Box { Length = 3,
                      Width = 1,
                      Height = 4 },
            new Box { Length = 5,
                      Width = 12,
                      Height = 3 },
            new Box { Length = 4,
                      Width = 7,
                      Height = 5 },
            new Box { Length = 3,
                      Width = 7,
                      Height = 1 }
        };

        IEnumerable<Box> resultList =
            from myBox in boxList
            where myBox.Length > 3 && myBox.Width > 3
            select myBox;

        Console.WriteLine("Boxes greater than 3 units in
                          length or width:");
        foreach (Box b in resultList)
        {
            b.DisplayBox();
        }
    }
}
}
```

Solution to Exercise 21-2. Use LINQ to SQL, but not the Object Relational Designer, to retrieve all the orders from the Order Details table where the quantity ordered is greater than 100. (You'll have to use a short type for the quantity, or else you'll get an error.)

You're using LINQ to SQL here, but without the O/R Designer, there are some extra steps you'll need to take. First, be sure to add a reference to the System.Data.Linq namespace, and add the appropriate using statements.

Then you'll need to define the `OrderDetails` class, and give it the correct attributes:

```
[Table(Name = "Order Details")]
public class OrderDetails
{
    [Column] public int OrderID { get; set; }
    [Column] public int ProductID { get; set; }
    [Column] public short Quantity { get; set; }
}
```

Define the data context (on one line):

```
DataContext db = new DataContext("Data Source = .\\SQLExpress;
Initial Catalog=Northwind;Integrated Security=True");
```

And get the table data:

```
Table<OrderDetails> orderDetails = db.GetTable<OrderDetails>();
```

Finally, you need to create the query, which isn't too difficult:

```
var dbQuery = from od in orderDetails
              where od.Quantity > 100
              select od;
```

Example A-63 shows the full code for this exercise.

Example A-63. The full code for Exercise 21-2

```
using System;
using System.Collections.Generic;
using System.Linq;
using System.Text;
using System.Data.Linq;
using System.Data.Linq.Mapping;

namespace Exercise_21_2
{
    [Table(Name = "Order Details")]
    public class OrderDetails
    {
        [Column] public int OrderID { get; set; }
        [Column] public int ProductID { get; set; }
        [Column] public short Quantity { get; set; }
    }

    class Program
    {
        static void Main()
        {
            DataContext db = new DataContext("Data Source = .\\SQLExpress;
                    Initial Catalog=Northwind;Integrated Security=True");

            Table<OrderDetails> orderDetails = db.GetTable<OrderDetails>();
            var dbQuery = from od in orderDetails
                          where od.Quantity > 100
                          select od;
```

Example A-63. The full code for Exercise 21-2 (continued)

```
            Console.WriteLine("Products ordered in quantities of more than 100:");
            foreach (OrderDetails od in dbQuery)
            {
                Console.WriteLine("Order #{0}\tQty: {1}\tProduct:{2}",
                        od.OrderID, od.Quantity, od.ProductID);
            }
        }
    }
}
```

Solution to Exercise 21-3. Using the Object Relational Designer, find out which employees (first and last names) have serviced orders placed by the customer named Ernst Handel.

The first thing you need to do in this exercise is right-click the project, select Add → New Item, and add the LINQ to SQL classes. In the O/R Designer, the Customer name is in the Customers table, the Employee name is in the Employees table, and they're joined by the Orders table, so add all three of those tables to the designer.

The first thing you need to is to add the default constructor for the data context in Main( ):

```
    DataClasses1DataContext myContext = new DataClasses1DataContext( );
```

Now it's just a matter of crafting the right query. You want to work with the Orders table, so start there. Remember that from the Orders table (call it o), you can access the fields of the related tables, so o.Customer.CompanyName will let you check for all orders placed by Ernst Handel. From there, o.Employee.FirstName and o.Employee. LastName give you the names you want. The query looks like this:

```
    var orderList =
        from o in db.Orders
        where o.Customer.CompanyName == "Ernst Handel"
        select new { o.Employee.FirstName, o.Employee.LastName };
```

You need to use an anonymous type for the collection because you're returning two strings. The full code for this example is shown in Example A-64.

Example A-64. The full code for Exercise 21-3

```
using System;
using System.Collections.Generic;
using System.Linq;
using System.Text;

namespace Exercise_21_3
{
    class Program
    {
        static void Main( )
        {
```

Example A-64. The full code for Exercise 21-3 (continued)

```
            DataClasses1DataContext db = new DataClasses1DataContext( );

        var orderList =
            from o in db.Orders
            where o.Customer.CompanyName == "Ernst Handel"
            select new { o.Employee.FirstName, o.Employee.LastName };

        Console.WriteLine("Employees who've contacted Ernst Handel:");
        foreach(var order in orderList)
        {
            Console.WriteLine("{0} {1}", order.FirstName, order.LastName );
        }
    }
  }
}
```

Index

Symbols

+ (addition operator), 70
+= (addition self-assignment operator), 73
&& (and operator), 77
<...> (angle brackets), enclosing XML
  elements, 444
= (assignment operator), 53, 68, 69, 80, 337
@ (at symbol), preceding verbatim string
  literals, 333
\ (backslash), preceding escaped
  characters, 52, 332
& (bitwise AND operator), 420
{...} (braces), 12
 enclosing class body, 135
 enclosing initial array values, 204
 enclosing single-statement if blocks, 90
 enclosing substitution parameters, 52
 styles of, 93
: (colon)
 preceding base class, 222, 263
 preceding base constructor, 225
 preceding interface, 263
+ (concatenation operator), 336
? : (conditional operator), 78
— (decrement by 1 operator), 73–75
/ (division operator), 70
/= (division self-assignment operator), 73
. (dot operator), 12
"..." (double quotes), enclosing strings, 63,
  332

== (equals operator), 76, 339
> (greater than operator), 76
>= (greater than or equal operator), 76
++ (increment by 1 operator), 73–75
=> (lambda operator), 400
< (less than operator), 76
<= (less than or equal operator), 76
% (modulus operator), 71, 110
%= (modulus self-assignment operator), 73
* (multiplication operator), 70
*= (multiplication self-assignment
  operator), 73
\n (newline), 52
!= (not equals operator), 76
! (not operator), 77
|| (or operator), 77
(...) (parentheses), enclosing type for explicit
  conversion, 57
; (semicolon), ending statements with, 46
'...' (single quotes), enclosing chars, 49
/ (slash), preceding closing XML tags, 444
/*...*/ (slash asterisk), enclosing
  comments, 13
// (slash, double), preceding comments, 13
[...] (square brackets)
 enclosing attributes, 506
 index operator, 198, 199
 indexer property, 294
– (subtraction operator), 70
–= (subtraction self-assignment operator), 73
\t (tab), 52

We'd like to hear your suggestions for improving our indexes. Send email to *index@oreilly.com*.

A

L

Label control, 412
Label element, XAML, 445, 448
lambda expressions, 400, 499
lambda operator (=>), 400
Language Integrated Query (see LINQ)
last-in, first-out (LIFO) collection (see stacks)
LastIndexOf( ) method
    arrays, 214
    lists, 308
    strings, 344
Learning ASP.NET 3.5 (Liberty et al.), 17,
    432
left angle bracket (<), less than operator, 76
left angle bracket, equals sign (<=), less than
    or equal operator, 76
Length property
    arrays, 200, 214
    StringBuilder, 349
    strings, 334, 342
less than operator (<), 76
less than or equal operator (<=), 76
Liberty, Jesse
    Learning ASP.NET 3.5, 17, 432
    Programming .NET Windows
        Applications, 404
    Programming ASP.NET, 43
    Programming C# 3.0, xvii, 1
LIFO (last-in, first-out) collection (see stacks)
lightbulb joke, 134
line number, moving to, 32
LINQ (Language Integrated Query), 492
    accessing databases using, 505–508
    queries using (see queries (LINQ))
Linq namespace, System.Data, 505
List Members command, IntelliSense, 35
ListBox control example, 294–298, 299–302,
    303–307
ListBox element, XAML
    defining, 468
    style of, 463–464
lists (List<T> class), 307–310
    methods of, 308
    properties of, 307
    sorting, 310–319
literal constants, 58
Loaded event, Rectangle element, 453
local variables, 141, 155
Locals window, 184–188
location of projects, 9

logical operators, 77–78
    precedence of, 80
    short-circuit evaluation of, 92–94
long type (C#), 47, 48
loops, 85, 104
    arrays using, 200–203, 207–210
    do...while loops, 108
    for loops, 109–117
    foreach loops, 203, 303, 306
    forever loops, 116
    goto statement for, 105
    while loops, 106

M

MacDonald, Brian (Learning ASP.NET
    3.5), 17, 432
Macro Explorer window, 40
Main( ) method, 13, 136
Margin property, Label element, 448
Mastering Regular Expressions, Third
    Edition (Friedl), 30, 351
Match( ) method, Regex, 352
Matches( ) method, Regex, 352
mathematical operators, 69–72, 80
MaxCapacity property, StringBuilder, 349
.mdb file extension, 24
MDI (Multiple Document Interface), 26
Means, W. Scott (XML in a Nutshell), 444
MediaStorage class example, 381–385
members, 148–153
    (see also fields; methods; properties)
memory allocation, 155–159
menus, 29
    (see also specific menus)
Message property, Exception class, 371
metaphors, objects as, 122
methods, 13, 124, 134
    abstract, 234
    access to (see access modifiers)
    accessors, 170–173, 297
    anonymous, 399
    calling, 86, 138
    constructors, 142–144, 225
    encapsulating (see delegates)
    hiding base class methods, 223, 225
    in interfaces
        defining, 265
        overriding, 280–285
    lambda expressions returning, 400
    naming conventions for, 60

About the Authors

Jesse Liberty, Silverlight geek, is a developer community program manager for Microsoft's Silverlight.net. His areas of interest include control development, Live Mesh, Linq and data-services, cross-platform programming, hyper-video, and most of all, building strong communication between Microsoft and the developer community.

Liberty is a monthly guest on the *Sparkling Client* podcast, his blog is a required resource for Silverlight programmers, and he is the author of two dozen books, including O'Reilly's *Programming .NET 3.5*, *Learning ASP.NET with AJAX*, and *Programming Silverlight*. His 20 years of programming experience include stints as a distinguished software engineer at AT&T, software architect/lead programmer for PBS, and vice president of Information Technology at Citibank. Jesse can be reached at *http://silverlight.net/blogs/JesseLiberty*.

Brian MacDonald is a technical editor specializing in Microsoft .NET programming topics. He has edited *Programming C#*, *Programming ASP.NET 3.5*, and *Programming WCF* (all from O'Reilly). He is also the coauthor of O'Reilly's *Learning C# 2005*, *Learning ASP.NET 2.0 with AJAX*, and *Learning ASP.NET 3.5*. He lives with his wife and son in southeastern Pennsylvania.

Colophon

The animal on the cover of *Learning C# 3.0* is a butterflyfish, which is a tropical marine fish from the family *Chaetodontidae*. Butterflyfish live mainly among the reefs of the Atlantic, Pacific, and Indian oceans. Occasionally mistaken for angelfish (the angelfish is larger), butterflyfish can be recognized by their contrasting color patterns of black, orange, blue, red, or yellow. Their vibrant colors also make them a popular aquarium attraction.

Although the fish are striking in appearance, many species of butterflyfish do have the ability to fool their predators. In addition to swimming nimbly through coral reefs, the four-eyed butterflyfish is so named because of a large dark spot surrounded by a white ring on each side of the back of its body; predators often mistake these prominent dark spots for the butterflyfish's eyes, which are smaller and partly obscured by a dark, vertical stripe.

While some butterflyfish never mate, others in the species will find a partner and remain monogamous for the rest of their lives. Once partnered, the two butterflyfish will find an area of coral reef that is suitable for them and will defend their home from others of its kind by changing the colors on their bodies, an act that is interpreted by intruders as an aggressive maneuver.

For food, the butterfly fish will peck at coral and rock formations and eat polyps, worms, and various small invertebrates. The fish's particular eating habits may ultimately drive it to extinction, some scientists say, as coral reefs are deteriorating because of overexploitation by humans, pollution, and climate change.

The cover image is from *Johnson's Natural History*. The cover font is Adobe ITC Garamond. The text font is Linotype Birka; the heading font is Adobe Myriad Condensed; and the code font is LucasFont's TheSansMonoCondensed.

Related Titles from O'Reilly

.NET and C#

ADO.NET Cookbook

ADO.NET 3.5 Cookbook, *2nd Edition*

ASP.NET 2.0 Cookbook, *2nd Edition*

ASP.NET 2.0: A Developer's Notebook

Building an ASP.NET Web 2.0 Portal

C# 3.0 in a Nutshell, *3rd Edition*

C# Cookbook, *2nd Edition*

C# Design Patterns

C# in a Nutshell, *2nd Edition*

C# Language Pocket Reference

Exchange Server 2007 Administration: The Definitive Guide

Head First C#

Learning ASP.NET 2.0 with AJAX

Learning C# 2005, *2nd Edition*

Learning WCF

MCSE Core Elective Exams in a Nutshell

.NET and XML

.NET Gotchas

Programming Atlas

Programming ASP.NET, *3rd Edition*

Programming ASP.NET AJAX

Programming C#, *4th Edition*

Programming MapPoint in .NET

Programming .NET 3.5

Programming .NET Components, *2nd Edition*

Programming .NET Security

Programming .NET Web Services

Programming Visual Basic 2005

Programming WCF Services

Programming WPF, *2nd Edition*

Programming Windows Presentation Foundation

Programming the .NET Compact Framework

Visual Basic 2005: A Developer's Notebook

Visual Basic 2005 Cookbook

Visual Basic 2005 in a Nutshell, *3rd Edition*

Visual Basic 2005 Jumpstart

Visual C# 2005: A Developer's Notebook

Visual Studio Hacks

Windows Developer Power Tools

XAML in a Nutshell

The O'Reilly Advantage

Stay Current and Save Money

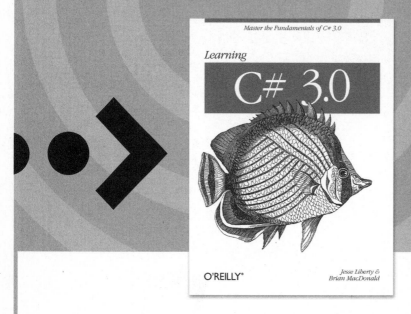